William Shakespeare

FOUR COMEDIES

The Taming of the Shrew
A Midsummer Night's Dream
The Merchant of Venice
Twelfth Night

Edited by
David Bevington

David Scott Kastan,
James Hammersmith,
and Robert Kean Turner,
Associate Editors

With a Foreword by
Joseph Papp

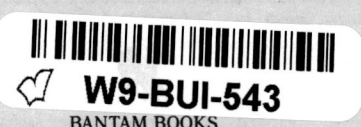

W9-BUI-543

BANTAM BOOKS
TORONTO / NEW YORK / LONDON / SYDNEY / AUCKLAND

FOUR COMEDIES

*A Bantam Book / published by arrangement
with Scott, Foresman and Company*

PUBLISHING HISTORY

*Scott, Foresman edition published / January 1980
Bantam edition, with newly edited text and substantially revised,
edited, and amplified notes, introductions, and other
materials, published / February 1988
Valuable advice on staging matters has been
provided by Richard Hosley.
Collations checked by Eric Rasmussen.
Additional editorial assistance by Claire McEachern.*

ISBN 0-553-21281-8

Published simultaneously in the United States and Canada

*Bantam Books are published by Bantam Books, a division of Bantam Doubleday
Dell Publishing Group, Inc. Its trademark, consisting of the words "Bantam
Books" and the portrayal of a rooster, is Registered in U.S. Patent and Trademark
Office and in other countries. Marca Registrada. Bantam Books, 1540 Broadway,
New York, New York 10036.*

PRINTED IN THE UNITED STATES OF AMERICA

OPM   18   17   16   15

Contents

Foreword

It's hard to imagine, but Shakespeare wrote all of his plays with a quill pen, a goose feather whose hard end had to be sharpened frequently. How many times did he scrape the dull end to a point with his knife, dip it into the inkwell, and bring up, dripping wet, those wonderful words and ideas that are known all over the world?

In the age of word processors, typewriters, and ballpoint pens, we have almost forgotten the meaning of the word "blot." Yet when I went to school, in the 1930s, my classmates and I knew all too well what an inkblot from the metal-tipped pens we used would do to a nice clean page of a test paper, and we groaned whenever a splotch fell across the sheet. Most of us finished the school day with ink-stained fingers; those who were less careful also went home with ink-stained shirts, which were almost impossible to get clean.

When I think about how long it took me to write the simplest composition with a metal-tipped pen and ink, I can only marvel at how many plays Shakespeare scratched out with his goose-feather quill pen, year after year. Imagine him walking down one of the narrow cobblestoned streets of London, or perhaps drinking a pint of beer in his local alehouse. Suddenly his mind catches fire with an idea, or a sentence, or a previously elusive phrase. He is burning with impatience to write it down—but because he doesn't have a ballpoint pen or even a pencil in his pocket, he has to keep the idea in his head until he can get to his quill and parchment.

He rushes back to his lodgings on Silver Street, ignoring the vendors hawking brooms, the coaches clattering by, the piteous wails of beggars and prisoners. Bounding up the stairs, he snatches his quill and starts to write furiously, not even bothering to light a candle against the dusk. "To be, or not to be," he scrawls, "that is the—." But the quill point has gone dull, the letters have fattened out illegibly, and in the middle of writing one of the most famous passages in the history of dramatic literature, Shakespeare has to stop to sharpen his pen.

Taking a deep breath, he lights a candle now that it's dark, sits down, and begins again. By the time the candle has burned out and the noisy apprentices of his French Huguenot landlord have quieted down, Shakespeare has finished Act 3 of *Hamlet* with scarcely a blot.

Early the next morning, he hurries through the fog of a London summer morning to the rooms of his colleague Richard Burbage, the actor for whom the role of Hamlet is being written. He finds Burbage asleep and snoring loudly, sprawled across his straw mattress. Not only had the actor performed in *Henry V* the previous afternoon, but he had then gone out carousing all night with some friends who had come to the performance.

Shakespeare shakes his friend awake, until, bleary-eyed, Burbage sits up in his bed. "Dammit, Will," he grumbles, "can't you let an honest man sleep?" But the playwright, his eyes shining and the words tumbling out of his mouth, says, "Shut up and listen—tell me what you think of *this*!"

He begins to read to the still half-asleep Burbage, pacing around the room as he speaks. ". . . Whether 'tis nobler in the mind to suffer the slings and arrows of outrageous fortune—"

Burbage interrupts, suddenly wide awake, "That's excellent, very good, 'the slings and arrows of outrageous fortune,' yes, I think it will work quite well. . . ." He takes the parchment from Shakespeare and murmurs the lines to himself, slowly at first but with growing excitement.

The sun is just coming up, and the words of one of Shakespeare's most famous soliloquies are being uttered for the first time by the first actor ever to bring Hamlet to life. It must have been an exhilarating moment.

Shakespeare wrote most of his plays to be performed live by the actor Richard Burbage and the rest of the Lord Chamberlain's men (later the King's men). Today, however, our first encounter with the plays is usually in the form of the printed word. And there is no question that reading Shakespeare for the first time isn't easy. His plays aren't comic books or magazines or the dime-store detective novels I read when I was young. A lot of his sentences are complex. Many of his words are no longer used in our everyday speech. His profound thoughts are often condensed into poetry, which is not as straightforward as prose.

Yet when you hear the words spoken aloud, a lot of the language may strike you as unexpectedly modern. For Shakespeare's plays, like any dramatic work, weren't really meant to be read; they were meant to be spoken, seen, and performed. It's amazing how lines that are so troublesome in print can flow so naturally and easily when spoken.

I think it was precisely this music that first fascinated me. When I was growing up, Shakespeare was a stranger to me. I had no particular interest in him, for I was from a different cultural tradition. It never occurred to me that his plays might be more than just something to "get through" in school, like science or math or the physical education requirement we had to fulfill. My passions then were movies, radio, and vaudeville—certainly not Elizabethan drama.

I was, however, fascinated by words and language. Because I grew up in a home where Yiddish was spoken, and English was only a second language, I was acutely sensitive to the musical sounds of different languages and had an ear for lilt and cadence and rhythm in the spoken word. And so I loved reciting poems and speeches even as a very young child. In first grade I learned lots of short nature verses—"Who has seen the wind?," one of them began. My first foray into drama was playing the role of Scrooge in Charles Dickens's *A Christmas Carol* when I was eight years old. I liked summoning all the scorn and coldness I possessed and putting them into the words, "Bah, humbug!"

From there I moved on to longer and more famous poems and other works by writers of the 1930s. Then, in junior high school, I made my first acquaintance with Shakespeare through his play *Julius Caesar*. Our teacher, Miss McKay, assigned the class a passage to memorize from the opening scene of the play, the one that begins "Wherefore rejoice? What conquest brings he home?" The passage seemed so wonderfully theatrical and alive to me, and the experience of memorizing and reciting it was so much fun, that I went on to memorize another speech from the play on my own.

I chose Mark Antony's address to the crowd in Act 3,

scene 2, which struck me then as incredibly high drama.
Even today, when I speak the words, I feel the same thrill I
did that first time. There is the strong and athletic Antony
descending from the raised pulpit where he has been speaking, right into the midst of a crowded Roman square. Holding the torn and bloody cloak of the murdered Julius
Caesar in his hand, he begins to speak to the people of
Rome:

> If you have tears, prepare to shed them now.
> You all do know this mantle. I remember
> The first time ever Caesar put it on;
> 'Twas on a summer's evening in his tent,
> That day he overcame the Nervii.
> Look, in this place ran Cassius' dagger through.
> See what a rent the envious Casca made.
> Through this the well-belovèd Brutus stabbed,
> And as he plucked his cursèd steel away,
> Mark how the blood of Caesar followed it,
> As rushing out of doors to be resolved
> If Brutus so unkindly knocked or no;
> For Brutus, as you know, was Caesar's angel.
> Judge, O you gods, how dearly Caesar loved him!
> This was the most unkindest cut of all . . .

I'm not sure now that I even knew Shakespeare had written a lot of other plays, or that he was considered "timeless," "universal," or "classic"—but I knew a good speech
when I heard one, and I found the splendid rhythms of
Antony's rhetoric as exciting as anything I'd ever come
across.

Fifty years later, I still feel that way. Hearing good actors
speak Shakespeare gracefully and naturally is a wonderful
experience, unlike any other I know. There's a satisfying
fullness to the spoken word that the printed page just can't
convey. This is why seeing the plays of Shakespeare performed live in a theater is the best way to appreciate them.
If you can't do that, listening to sound recordings or watching film versions of the plays is the next best thing.

But if you do start with the printed word, use the play as a
script. Be an actor yourself and say the lines out loud. Don't
worry too much at first about words you don't immediately
understand. Look them up in the footnotes or a dictionary,

but don't spend too much time on this. It is more profitable (and fun) to get the sense of a passage and sing it out. Speak naturally, almost as if you were talking to a friend, but be sure to enunciate the words properly. You'll be surprised at how much you understand simply by speaking the speech "trippingly on the tongue," as Hamlet advises the Players.

You might start, as I once did, with a speech from *Julius Caesar*, in which the tribune (city official) Marullus scolds the commoners for transferring their loyalties so quickly from the defeated and murdered general Pompey to the newly victorious Julius Caesar:

> Wherefore rejoice? What conquest brings he home?
> What tributaries follow him to Rome
> To grace in captive bonds his chariot wheels?
> You blocks, you stones, you worse than senseless
>   things!
> O you hard hearts, you cruel men of Rome,
> Knew you not Pompey? Many a time and oft
> Have you climbed up to walls and battlements,
> To towers and windows, yea, to chimney tops,
> Your infants in your arms, and there have sat
> The livelong day, with patient expectation,
> To see great Pompey pass the streets of Rome.

With the exception of one or two words like "wherefore" (which means "why," not "where"), "tributaries" (which means "captives"), and "patient expectation" (which means patient waiting), the meaning and emotions of this speech can be easily understood.

From here you can go on to dialogues or other more challenging scenes. Although you may stumble over unaccustomed phrases or unfamiliar words at first, and even fall flat when you're crossing some particularly rocky passages, pick yourself up and stay with it. Remember that it takes time to feel at home with anything new. Soon you'll come to recognize Shakespeare's unique sense of humor and way of saying things as easily as you recognize a friend's laughter.

And then it will just be a matter of choosing which one of Shakespeare's plays you want to tackle next. As a true fan of his, you'll find that you're constantly learning from his plays. It's a journey of discovery that you can continue for the rest of your life. For no matter how many times you read or see a particular play, there will always be something new there that you won't have noticed before.

Why do so many thousands of people get hooked on Shakespeare and develop a habit that lasts a lifetime? What can he really say to us today, in a world filled with inventions and problems he never could have imagined? And how do you get past his special language and difficult sentence structure to understand him?

The best way to answer these questions is to go see a live production. You might not know much about Shakespeare, or much about the theater, but when you watch actors performing one of his plays on the stage, it will soon become clear to you why people get so excited about a playwright who lived hundreds of years ago.

For the story—what's happening in the play—is the most accessible part of Shakespeare. In *A Midsummer Night's Dream*, for example, you can immediately understand the situation: a girl is chasing a guy who's chasing a girl who's chasing another guy. No wonder *A Midsummer Night's Dream* is one of the most popular of Shakespeare's plays: it's about one of the world's most popular pastimes—falling in love.

But the course of true love never did run smooth, as the young suitor Lysander says. Often in Shakespeare's comedies the girl whom the guy loves doesn't love him back, or she loves him but he loves someone else. In *The Two Gentlemen of Verona*, Julia loves Proteus, Proteus loves Sylvia, and Sylvia loves Valentine, who is Proteus's best friend. In the end, of course, true love prevails, but not without lots of complications along the way.

For in all of his plays—comedies, histories, and tragedies—Shakespeare is showing you human nature. His characters act and react in the most extraordinary ways—and sometimes in the most incomprehensible ways. People are always trying to find motivations for what a character does. They ask, "Why does Iago want to destroy Othello?"

The answer, to me, is very simple—because that's the way Iago is. That's just his nature. Shakespeare doesn't explain his characters; he sets them in motion—and away they go. He doesn't worry about whether they're likable or not. He's interested in interesting people, and his most fascinating characters are those who are unpredictable. If you lean back in your chair early on in one of his plays, thinking you've figured out what Iago or Shylock (in *The Merchant of Venice*) is up to, don't be too sure—because that great judge of human nature, Shakespeare, will surprise you every time.

He is just as wily in the way he structures a play. In *Macbeth,* a comic scene is suddenly introduced just after the bloodiest and most treacherous slaughter imaginable, of a guest and king by his host and subject, when in comes a drunk porter who has to go to the bathroom. Shakespeare is tickling your emotions by bringing a stand-up comic on-stage right on the heels of a savage murder.

It has taken me thirty years to understand even some of these things, and so I'm not suggesting that Shakespeare is immediately understandable. I've gotten to know him not through theory but through practice, the practice of the *living* Shakespeare—the playwright of the theater.

Of course the plays are a great achievement of dramatic literature, and they should be studied and analyzed in schools and universities. But you must always remember, when reading all the words *about* the playwright and his plays, that *Shakespeare's* words came first and that in the end there is nothing greater than a single actor on the stage speaking the lines of Shakespeare.

Everything important that I know about Shakespeare comes from the practical business of producing and directing his plays in the theater. The task of classifying, criticizing, and editing Shakespeare's printed works I happily leave to others. For me, his plays really do live on the stage, not on the page. That is what he wrote them for and that is how they are best appreciated.

Although Shakespeare lived and wrote hundreds of years ago, his name rolls off my tongue as if he were my brother. As a producer and director, I feel that there is a professional relationship between us that spans the centuries. As a human being, I feel that Shakespeare has enriched my understanding of life immeasurably. I hope you'll let him do the same for you.

❖

Does *The Taming of the Shrew* have anything to say to us today, or is it hopelessly outdated by its male chauvinism? After all, here's a guy, Petruchio, who starves his wife, Kate, half to death, mocks and embarrasses her publicly, calls her "my goods, my chattels . . . my house, My household stuff, my field, my barn, My horse, my ox, my ass, my anything," and hurls verbal abuse at her—all in the name of taming her, the shrew. After a play full of this kind of treatment from her husband, Kate does indeed seem chastened: in her last speech she advises the other "froward wives" to honor and obey their men and acknowledges her own submission by putting her hand beneath Petruchio's foot. "Such duty as the subject owes the prince," she says, "Even such a woman oweth to her husband."

This is certainly bound to raise the hackles of many women, and even some men, who feel that Kate has betrayed the principles of the women's movement. But if we approach the play unburdened by present-day politics, we will find that the last speech is the culmination of a hard-fought and hard-won love between Kate and Petruchio, and that the notion of one-upmanship isn't part of the picture.

Shakespeare says quite plainly that if two people are really in love, the issue of who does what for whom does not exist. It's taken for granted in *The Taming of the Shrew* that Kate's last speech is certainly not the basis for their relationship, but will serve to bring out the best in Petruchio. Remember—Kate isn't the only one who has learned a lesson. The teacher Petruchio has also been a student and beneficiary of the painful lessons both have undergone.

On the stage, the playing is the thing. For example, when Meryl Streep and Raul Julia played Kate and Petruchio at the Delacorte Theater in Central Park, it was quite clear that the two characters cared for each other intensely. These wonderful actors entered the spirit of the play so wholeheartedly that they brought the characters to life and made what happens in the play totally believable.

Kate is one of Shakespeare's intelligent women who will not be pushed around. She is dumbfounded when Petruchio attempts to do just that. But his intention, as she discovers, is not to dominate but to rid her of an intractable manner she herself dislikes; he alone has the chutzpah to tackle her.

Petruchio deserves a medal for understanding Kate so well; instead, Shakespeare gave him a play!

❖

You may be a corporate executive or a plain everyday wage slave, a brilliant student or a high-school dropout, eight years old or eighty-plus—but dollars to doughnuts you'll laugh your head off at the antics of Nick Bottom and company in *A Midsummer Night's Dream.*

A group of workingmen meet in a wood (that is also, unbeknownst to them, an enchanted fairyland) and set out to rehearse a play. All of them are shy and modest, with one large exception: Nick Bottom. He is an arrogant, pushy, pompous bully, an egotistical know-it-all—in plain words, a big ass.

But he gets his comeuppance. First we see him actually transformed into an ass through a spell cast by a mischievous wood sprite called Puck; then we see him adored by the beautiful and sexy Queen of the Fairies, Titania, who has been bewitched by her jealous lover, Oberon; and finally we see him awakened from his midsummer night's dream. Typically, in calling it "Bottom's Dream," he takes the credit away from his creator, William Shakespeare.

Two sets of desperate lovers chase each other through the forest, while two magical monarchs, Titania and Oberon, contend for supremacy of the leafy kingdom. To add to the magic, tiny wood creatures abound, with such names as Peaseblossom, Cobweb, Moth, and Mustardseed. Along the way we light upon some of Shakespeare's loveliest poetry—such as Oberon's description of a white blossom turning "purple with love's wound."

And, in the midst of all this enchantment of love and passion, Nick Bottom and his "hempen homespuns"—Quince, Snug, Flute, and Starveling—press on with their hilarious efforts to make a play. The mingling of all these is what makes *A Midsummer Night's Dream* Shakespeare's most captivating comedy.

❖

The Merchant of Venice has been one of Shakespeare's most popular—and controversial—plays wherever it has been performed. The controversy usually centers around the way Shylock the Jew is portrayed and treated. Many people think that Shakespeare himself was being anti-Semitic here. I personally don't believe this, judging from the humanity in all the works of this great writer, especially this one. It's difficult for me to label *The Merchant of Venice* as anti-Semitic when it has one of the most eloquent pleas to our sense of common humanity ever uttered on the stage:

> Hath not a Jew eyes? Hath not a Jew hands, organs, dimensions, senses, affections, passions? Fed with the same food, hurt with the same weapons, subject to the same diseases, healed by the same means, warmed and cooled by the same winter and summer, as a Christian is? If you prick us, do we not bleed? If you tickle us, do we not laugh? If you poison us, do we not die? And if you wrong us, shall we not revenge?

There is no indication that the romantic lead, Bassanio, and the woman he marries, Portia, are prejudiced against Shylock because he's a Jew. Portia's goal is to save Antonio's life in order to free her new husband from his obligations to the merchant. Bassanio wants to rescue a friend to whom he's heavily indebted. It would be difficult to prove that anything either of them says has an unusually anti-Semitic prejudice.

And yet there is anti-Semitism *within* the play. We find it most virulently in Antonio, the merchant of Venice, and his henchmen Salerio and Solanio, very strongly in Gratiano, somewhat in Lorenzo, and especially in the comedian Launcelot Gobbo, Shylock's former servant.

The Merchant of Venice was the first play we at the New York Shakespeare Festival produced at the Delacorte Theater in Central Park, with George C. Scott as Shylock. I can remember telling George not to play for sympathy, not to be nice, not to turn the other cheek, but to feel the righteous anger that belongs to him. After all, Shylock has been so kicked around and spat on just for trying to make a living that it would be unnatural for him *not* to want vengeance. He's taunted in the streets; his daughter runs away with a

Christian, taking his money and jewels with her; the ruling elite in Venice, personified by Antonio, are arrayed against him—who wouldn't press for his pound of flesh in those circumstances?

Shakespeare provides Shylock with a rationale—but not an excuse—for his behavior. But Antonio, unlike Shylock, has no real reason for his hatred and cruelty toward the Jewish man; nor can there ever be a rational explanation for anti-Semitism. Antonio treats Shylock abominably. In the early scenes of the play we learn that he has spurned and spat upon him, calling him a dog, and Antonio goes on to say, "I am as like to call thee so again, To spit on thee again, to spurn thee too." In the trial scene, Shylock is threatened with the confiscation of all of his remaining money and property. The compromise suggested by Antonio requires, among other things, that Shylock change his religion—the cruelest punishment that could be devised.

One of the most poignant moments Shakespeare gives Shylock occurs when Tubal tells him that Jessica, Shylock's daughter, who has run off with Lorenzo, has traded a family ring for a monkey. "It was my turquoise," says Shylock, "I had it of Leah when I was a bachelor. I would not have given it for a wilderness of monkeys." What makes me sad here is that Jessica seems to have completely disregarded the emotional value of the ring. There seems to be very little triumph in her act; instead, Jessica must suffer the consequences of her actions, as we perceive in the last scenes of the play, where she is unaccountably melancholic.

Because of Shylock, *The Merchant of Venice* can easily be called a tragedy. He will always remain a complex, fascinating character. No wonder so many actors want to play him, to understand him, and to enter into his tragedy—he is one of the greatest dramatic figures of all time.

❖

I've always loved the scene in *Twelfth Night* where the steward Malvolio discovers the love letter addressed to him that he imagines was written by the Lady Olivia. In having Malvolio read it out loud, Shakespeare gives us a glimpse of a man whose fantastic ambitions and exaggerated sense of his own worth make him an obvious target for those in the play—Sir Toby Belch, Sir Andrew Aguecheek, Maria, and Fabian—who cannot tolerate his pomposity.

There's no question that Malvolio is the character of greatest interest to Shakespeare, because he subjects him to the cruellest kind of treatment at the hands of Olivia's alcoholic uncle and his cohorts. While the audience is led to enjoy the antics and mischief perpetrated on this puritanical figure, Shakespeare (as usual), is not content with a simplistic attitude toward this important character. Instead, the playwright encourages us to feel sympathetic toward Malvolio for his tribulations in the later scene, tribulations that seem overly severe.

At the end of the play, Feste, the Fool, echoes the very words that Malvolio himself uttered in reading the planted letter: "Some are born great, some achieve greatness, and some have greatness thrust upon them." These words linger in our minds as we apply them to the world outside the play. We think of people who *are* born great and seem to have a natural genius; others who achieve greatness through hard work in the arts, in the sciences, in sports, in politics; and still others who unexpectedly have greatness thrust upon them, such as a vice president who may suddenly become the president of the United States after an assassination or a resignation.

JOSEPH PAPP

JOSEPH PAPP GRATEFULLY ACKNOWLEDGES THE HELP OF ELIZABETH KIRKLAND IN PREPARING THIS FOREWORD.

Four Comedies

In the 1590s, during the first decade of his career as dramatist and actor, Shakespeare concentrated mainly on English history plays and romantic comedies. His only tragedies at that time (apart from his history plays, in which tragic events often occur) were an early revenge play, *Titus Andronicus* (c. 1589–1591), and *Romeo and Juliet* (c. 1594–1596); the great tragedies came later. Shakespeare meantime achieved considerable fame as a historical dramatist with his *Henry VI* plays and *Richard III* (c. 1589–1594), with *King John* (c. 1594–1595), and with the four-play sequence from *Richard II* through the two parts of *Henry IV* to *Henry V* (c. 1595–1599). And at the same time he was experimenting with and perfecting his own special kind of romantic comedy, probably beginning with *The Comedy of Errors* (c. 1589–1593), an imitation of the Latin dramatist Plautus; *Love's Labor's Lost* (c. 1588–1589, perhaps later revised), a love comedy in the mannered style of John Lyly; and *The Two Gentlemen of Verona* (c. 1590–1594), an apprenticeship to the romantic fiction of Italy. He achieved major successes with *The Taming of the Shrew* (c. 1592–1594) and *A Midsummer Night's Dream* (c. 1594–1595) and went on in the second half of the decade to produce immortal comedies at the rate of approximately one a year: *The Merchant of Venice* and *Much Ado about Nothing* by 1599, *The Merry Wives of Windsor* in 1597 or possibly 1600, *As You Like It* by 1600, and *Twelfth Night* by 1602. Shakespeare then turned to tragedy and away from historical drama and romantic comedy, as though he had said what he had to say in these genres. His subsequent comedies tend to be dark problem plays, such as *Measure for Measure, All's Well That Ends Well,* and *Troilus and Cressida* (c. 1601–1604), or, toward the end of his career, tragicomic romances, such as *Pericles, Cymbeline, The Winter's Tale,* and *The Tempest* (c. 1607–1611).

The present collection offers four of Shakespeare's most enduring romantic comedies from the period of the 1590s. In these plays we can see Shakespeare developing the form of comedy we associate with his name. They are all romantic comedies in at least two senses: their main action is about love, and they contain elements of the improbable and the miraculous. Courtship is a staple of Shakespearean comic plotting; these comedies regularly end with a parade of couples to the altar and a festive gathering of those who long to celebrate the joys of love. Some of these plays, because of their comic emphasis on mating rituals and the battle of the sexes, as in *The Taming of the Shrew,* are also called love-game comedies (see David Stevenson's *The Love-Game Comedy* [New York: Columbia University Press, 1946]). Elements of the improbable are no less prominent and help define the way in which Shakespearean comedy is so different from the drawing-room social comedy of dramatists such as William Congreve and George Bernard Shaw. Fairies complicate the love relationships of the four lovers in *A Midsummer Night's Dream* and have their own quarrels as well; a beggar turns lord for a day in *The Taming of the Shrew* and beholds a play presented in his honor; Portia's wooers in *The Merchant of Venice* must venture across the seas to a mountaintop retreat and choose among three caskets in order to gain the hand of the fair lady; Illyria in *Twelfth Night* is (as its name suggests) a place of illusion and delirium, where Viola disguises herself as a young man and is mistaken for her supposedly dead brother.

Shakespearean comedy achieves a festive and celebratory mood that is all the more theatrically effective because of the perils with which the comedy must deal. The term "festive" comedy emphasizes this sense in which the joyous holiday impulse of carnival must do unremitting battle with the Lenten spirit. Antonio in *The Merchant of Venice* is inexplicably sad when the play begins; something is amiss or incomplete in his mercantile world. His Venice is a place of conflict and hatred as well as laughter, and indeed his very life is soon threatened by Shylock's vengeful demand for a pound of Antonio's flesh. The play's comic ending must not only unite the lovers in marriage but rescue Antonio from a terrible death. *A Midsummer Night's Dream,* for all its hilarity, gives us ample glimpses of the dark side of love, embodied in the forest of Athens. There the lovers must learn what it is to be lost, rejected, and misunderstood before they can find their true selves in marriage. The opposing worlds of revelry and sobriety, carnival and Lent, are contained within Olivia's household in *Twelfth Night*, as the merriment of Sir Toby, Sir Andrew, and Feste the Clown is officiously interrupted by the killjoy apostle of decorum, Malvolio. In *The Taming of the Shrew*, Kate must endure a purgative vision of illusion until she is finally brought to submission by Petruchio. For Shakespeare, comic resolution is something precariously achieved in the face of a very real threat.

The related theme of something precious that is lost and rediscovered adds a recurring note of somberness, even sadness, to the festive gaiety of these comedies, thereby deepening our sense of the worth of the eventual comic triumph. The motif of loss at sea appears in Antonio's wrecked vessels in *The Merchant of Venice*, as well as in Viola's shipwreck on the coast of Illyria and the supposed loss of her brother at sea in *Twelfth Night*. Disguise and mistaken identity, central to all the plays in this present collection, not only propel the comic plot toward resolution and the removal of disguise, but hint at deeper meaning of confused identity and eventual discovery of self. The feast is a recurring dramatic image of reconciliation and harmony, as in the wedding banquet of *The Taming of the Shrew*, the marriage festivities and after-dinner entertainments of *A Midsummer Night's Dream*, the gathering of friends at Belmont in *The Merchant of Venice*, and the below-stairs camaraderie of *Twelfth Night*. Shakespeare often uses song, as well, to express these harmonies, while again reminding us of the darker side of comedy. Feste's first song in *Twelfth Night* celebrates a "present mirth" that enjoys "present laughter," but the song also acknowledges that "what's to come is still unsure," and Feste's final plaintive ditty about the rain that "raineth every day" points the audience toward the everyday reality to which we must all return.

The devices of illusion in these comedies say much about theatrical illusion, even the illusoriness of life itself. Most of *The Taming of the Shrew* takes the form of an entertainment devised to hoodwink a drunken peddler; the play is a part of his confused after-dinner sleep. The characters in *Twelfth Night* awaken, as from a dream of mistaken identities, to the reality of adulthood and marriage. Portia and Nerissa use their wedding rings to tease their new husbands with a seeming nightmare of betrayed vows and cuckoldry in *The Merchant of Venice*, though, as always in Shakespearean romantic comedy, the experience provides release and clarification. Puck in *A Midsummer Night's Dream* sees dramatic art as illusion to which the audience surrenders itself and from which it awakens to consider that it has "but slumbered here / While these visions did appear." Shakespeare the comic artist is a creator of illusion that is at once unsubstantial and immortal, like the fairies themselves, and his comedies celebrate this magic of his art.

The Playhouse

This early copy of a drawing by Johannes de Witt of the Swan Theatre in London (c. 1596), made by his friend Arend van Buchell, is the only surviving contemporary sketch of the interior of a public theater in the 1590s.

From other contemporary evidence, including the stage directions and dialogue of Elizabethan plays, we can surmise that the various public theaters where Shakespeare's plays were produced (the Theatre, the Curtain, the Globe) resembled the Swan in many important particulars, though there must have been some variations as well. The public playhouses were essentially round, or polygonal, and open to the sky, forming an acting arena approximately 70 feet in diameter; they did not have a large curtain with which to open and close a scene, such as we see today in opera and some traditional theater. A platform measuring approximately 43 feet across and 27 feet deep, referred to in the de Witt drawing as the *proscaenium*, projected into the yard, *planities sive arena*. The roof, *tectum*, above the stage and supported by two pillars, could contain machinery for ascents and descents, as were required in several of Shakespeare's late plays. Above this roof was a hut, shown in the drawing with a flag flying atop it and a trumpeter at its door announcing the performance of a play. The underside of the stage roof, called the heavens, was usually richly decorated with symbolic figures of the sun, the moon, and the constellations. The platform stage stood at a height of 5½ feet or so above the yard, providing room under the stage for underworldly effects. A trapdoor, which is not visible in this drawing, gave access to the space below.

The structure at the back of the platform (labeled *mimorum aedes*), known as the tiring-house because it was the actors' attiring (dressing) space, featured at least two doors, as shown here. Some theaters seem to have also had a discovery space, or curtained recessed alcove, perhaps between the two doors—in which Falstaff could have hidden from the sheriff (*1 Henry IV*, 2.4) or Polonius could have eavesdropped on Hamlet and his mother (*Hamlet*, 3.4). This discovery space probably gave the actors a means of access to and from the tiring-house. Curtains may also have been hung in front of the stage doors on occasion. The de Witt drawing shows a gallery above the doors that extends across the back and evidently contains spectators. On occasions when action "above" demanded the use of this space, as when Juliet appears at her "window" (*Romeo and Juliet*, 2.2 and 3.5), the gallery seems to have been used by the actors, but large scenes there were impractical.

The three-tiered auditorium is perhaps best described by Thomas Platter, a visitor to London in 1599 who saw on that occasion Shakespeare's *Julius Caesar* performed at the Globe:

The playhouses are so constructed that they play on a raised platform, so that everyone has a good view. There are different galleries and places [*orchestra, sedilia, porticus*], however, where the seating is better and more comfortable and therefore more expensive. For whoever cares to stand below only pays one English penny, but if he wishes to sit, he enters by another door [*ingressus*] and pays another penny, while if he desires to sit in the most comfortable seats, which are cushioned, where he not only sees everything well but can also be seen, then he pays yet another English penny at another door. And during the performance food and drink are carried round the audience, so that for what one cares to pay one may also have refreshment.

Scenery was not used, though the theater building itself was handsome enough to invoke a feeling of order and hierarchy that lent itself to the splendor and pageantry onstage. Portable properties, such as thrones, stools, tables, and beds, could be carried or thrust on as needed. In the scene pictured here by de Witt, a lady on a bench, attended perhaps by her waiting-gentlewoman, receives the address of a male figure. If Shakespeare had written *Twelfth Night* by 1596 for performance at the Swan, we could imagine Malvolio appearing like this as he bows before the Countess Olivia and her gentlewoman, Maria.

THE TAMING OF
THE SHREW

THE TAMING OF
THE SHREW

Introduction

Like his other early comedies, *The Taming of the Shrew* (c. 1592–1594) looks forward to Shakespeare's mature comic drama in several ways. By skillfully juxtaposing two plots and an induction, or framing plot, it offers contrasting views on the battle of the sexes. This debate on the nature of the love relationship will continue through many later comedies. The play also adroitly manipulates the device of mistaken identity, as in *The Comedy of Errors*, inverting appearance and reality, dream and waking, and the master-servant relationship in order to create a transformed Saturnalian world anticipating that of *A Midsummer Night's Dream* and *Twelfth Night*.

The Induction sets up the theme of illusion, using an old motif known as "The Sleeper Awakened" (as found for example in *The Arabian Nights*). This device frames the main action of the play, giving to it an added perspective. *The Taming of the Shrew* purports in fact to be a play within a play, an entertainment devised by a witty nobleman as a practical joke on a drunken tinker, Christopher Sly. The jest is to convince Sly that he is not Sly at all, but an aristocrat suffering delusions. Outlandishly dressed in new finery, Sly is invited to witness a play from the gallery over the stage. In a rendition called *The Taming of a Shrew* (printed in 1594 and now generally thought to be taken from an earlier version of Shakespeare's play, employing a good deal of conscious originality along with some literary borrowing and even plagiarism), the framing plot concludes by actually putting Sly back out on the street in front of the alehouse where he was found. He awakes, recalls the play as a dream, and proposes to put the vision to good use by taming his own wife. Whether this ending reflects an epilogue now lost from the text of Shakespeare's play cannot be said, but it does reinforce the idea of the play as Sly's fantasy. Like Puck at the end of *A Midsummer Night's Dream*, urging us to dismiss what we have seen as the product of our own slumbering, Sly continually reminds us that the play is only an illusion or shadow.

With repeated daring, Shakespeare calls attention to the

contrived nature of his artifact, the play. When, for example, Sly is finally convinced that he is in fact a noble lord recovering from madness and lustily proposes to hasten off to bed with his long-neglected wife, we are comically aware that the "wife" is an impostor, a young page in disguise. Yet this counterfeiting of roles is no more unreal than the employment of Elizabethan boy-actors for the parts of Katharina and Bianca in the "real" play. As we watch Sly watching a play, levels of meaning interplay in this evocative fashion. Again, the paintings offered to Sly by his new attendants call attention to art's ability to confound illusion and reality. In one painting, Cytherea is hidden by reeds "Which seem to move and wanton with her breath / Even as the waving sedges play wi' th' wind," and in another painting Io appears "As lively painted as the deed was done" (Induction. 2.50–56). Sly's function, then, is that of the naive observer who inverts illusion and reality in his mind, concluding that his whole previous life of tinkers and alehouses and Cicely Hackets has been unreal. As his attendants explain to him, "These fifteen years you have been in a dream, / Or when you waked, so waked as if you slept" (79–80). We as audience laugh at Sly's naiveté, and yet we too are moved and even transformed by an artistic vision that we know to be illusory.

Like Sly, many characters in the main action of the play are persuaded, or nearly persuaded, to be what they are not. Lucentio and Tranio exchange roles of master and servant. Bianca's supposed tutors are in fact her wooers, using their lessons to disguise messages of love. Katharina is prevailed upon by her husband, Petruchio, to declare that the sun is the moon and that an old gentleman (Vincentio) is a fair young maiden. Vincentio is publicly informed that he is an impostor, and that the "real" Vincentio (the Pedant) is at that very moment looking at him out of the window of his son Lucentio's house. This last ruse does not fool the real Vincentio, but it nearly succeeds in fooling everyone else. Baptista Minola is about to commit Vincentio to jail for the infamous slander of asserting that the supposed Lucentio is only a servant in disguise. Vincentio, as the newly arrived stranger, is able to see matters as they really are; but the dwellers of Padua have grown so accustomed to the mad and improbable fictions of their life that they are not easily awakened to reality.

Shakespeare multiplies these devices of illusion by combining two entirely distinct plots, each concerned at least in part with the comic inversion of appearance and reality: the shrew-taming plot involving Petruchio and Kate, and the more conventional romantic plot involving Lucentio and Bianca. The latter plot is derived from the *Supposes* of George Gascoigne, a play first presented at Gray's Inn in 1566 as translated from Ariosto's neoclassical comedy *I Suppositi*, 1509. (Ariosto's work in turn was based upon Terence's *Eunuchus* and Plautus' *Captivi*.) The "Supposes" are mistaken identities or misunderstandings, the kind of hilarious farcical mix-ups Shakespeare had already experimented with in *The Comedy of Errors*. Shakespeare has, as usual, both romanticized his source and moralized it in a characteristically English way. The heroine, who in the Roman comedy of Plautus and Terence would have been a courtesan, and who in *Supposes* is made pregnant by her clandestine lover, remains thoroughly chaste in Shakespeare's comedy. Consequently she has no need for a pander, or go-between, such as the bawdy duenna, or nurse, of *Supposes*. The satire directed at the heroine's unwelcome old wooer is far less savage than in *Supposes*, where the "pantaloon," Dr. Cleander, is a villainously corrupt lawyer epitomizing the depravity of "respectable" society. Despite Shakespeare's modifications, however, the basic plot remains an effort to foil parental authority. The young lovers, choosing each other for romantic reasons, must fend off the materialistic calculations of their parents.

In a stock situation of this sort, the character types are also conventional. Gremio, the aged wealthy wooer, is actually labeled a "pantaloon" in the text (3.1.36–37) to stress his neoclassical ancestry. (Lean and foolish old wooers of this sort were customarily dressed in pantaloons, slippers, and spectacles on the Italian stage.) Gremio is typically "the graybeard," and Baptista Minola is "the narrow-prying father" (3.2.145–146). Even though Shakespeare renders these characters far less unattractive than in *Supposes*, their worldly behavior still invites reprisal from the young. Since Baptista Minola insists on selling his daughter Bianca to the highest bidder, it is fitting that her wealthiest suitor (the supposed Lucentio) should turn out in the end to be a penniless servant (Tranio) disguised as a man of affluence and position. In his traditional role as the clever servant of neoclassical comedy, Tranio skillfully apes the mannerisms of respectable society. He can deal in the mere surfaces, clothes or reputation, out of which a man's social importance is created, and can even furnish himself with a rich father. Gremio and Baptista deserve to be foiled because they accept the illusion of respectability as real.

Even the romantic lovers of this borrowed plot are largely conventional. To be sure, Shakespeare emphasizes their virtuous qualities and their sincerity. He adds Hortensio (not in *Supposes*) to provide Lucentio with a genuine, if foolish, rival and Bianca with two wooers closer to her age than old Gremio. Lucentio and Bianca deserve their romantic triumph; they are self-possessed, witty, and steadfast to each other. Yet we know very little about them, nor have they seen deeply into each other. Lucentio's love talk is laden with conventional images in praise of Bianca's dark eyes and scarlet lips. At the play's end, he discovers, to his surprise, that she can be willful, even disobedient. Has her appearance of virtue concealed something from him and from us? Because the relationship between these lovers is superficial, they are appropriately destined to a superficial marriage as well. The passive Bianca becomes the proud and defiant wife.

By contrast, Petruchio and Kate are the more interesting lovers, whose courtship involves mutual self-discovery. Admittedly, we must not overstate the case. Especially at first, these lovers are also stock types: the shrew tamer and his proverbially shrewish wife. Although Shakespeare seems not to have used any single source for this plot, he was well acquainted with crude misogynistic stories demonstrating the need for putting women in their place. In a ballad called *A Merry Jest of a Shrewd and Curst Wife Lapped in Morel's Skin* (printed c. 1550), for example, the husband tames his shrewish spouse by flaying her bloody with birch rods and then wrapping her in the freshly salted skin of a plow horse named Morel. (This shrewish wife, like Kate, has an obedient and gentle younger sister who is their father's favorite.)

Other features of Shakespeare's plot can be found in similar tales: the tailor scolded for devising a gown of outlandish fashion (Gerard Legh's *Accidence of Armory*, 1562), the wife obliged to agree with her husband's assertion of some patent falsehood (Don Juan Manuel's *El Conde Lucanor*, 1335), and the three husbands' wager on their wives' obedience (*The Book of the Knight of La Tour-Landry*, printed 1484). In the raw spirit of this sexist tradition, so unlike the refined Italianate sentiment of his other plot, Shakespeare introduces Petruchio as a man of reckless bravado who is ready to marry the ugliest or sharpest-tongued woman alive so long as she is rich. However much he may later be attracted by Kate's fiery spirit, his first attraction to her is crassly financial. Kate is, moreover, a thoroughly disagreeable young woman at first, described by those who know her as "intolerable curst / And shrewd, and froward" (1.2.88–89) and aggressive in her bullying of Bianca. She and Petruchio meet as grotesque comic counterparts. At the play's end, the traditional pattern of male dominance and female acquiescence is still prominent. Kate achieves peace only by yielding to a socially ordained patriarchal framework in which a husband is the princely ruler of his wife.

Within this male-oriented frame of reference, however, Petruchio and Kate are surprisingly like Benedick and Beatrice of *Much Ado about Nothing*. Petruchio, for all his rant, is increasingly drawn to Kate by her spirit. As wit-combatants they are worthy of each other's enmity—or love. No one else in the play is a fit match for either of them. Kate too is attracted to Petruchio, despite her war of words. Her guise of hostility is part defensive protection, part testing of his sincerity. If she is contemptuous of the wooers she has seen till now, she has good reason to be. We share her condescension toward the aged Gremio or the laughably inept Hortensio. She rightly fears that her father wishes to dispose of her so that he may auction off Bianca to the wealthiest competitor. Kate's jaded view of such marriage brokering is entirely defensible. Not surprisingly she first views Petruchio, whose professed intentions are far from reassuring, as another mere adventurer in love. She is impressed by his "line" in wooing her, but needs to test his constancy and sincerity. Possibly she is prepared to accept

the prevailing Elizabethan view of marriage, with its domi-
nant role for the husband, but only if she can choose a man
deserving of her respect. She puts down most men with a
shrewish manner that challenges their very masculinity;
Petruchio is the first to be man enough to "board" her.
Kate's rejection of men does not leave her very happy, however genuine her disdain is for most of those who come to
woo. Petruchio's "schooling" is therefore curative. Having
wooed and partly won her, he tests her with his late arrival
at the marriage, his unconventional dress, and his crossing
all her desires. In this display of willfulness, he shows her
an ugly picture of what she herself is like. Most of all, however, he succeeds because he insists on what she too desires: a well-defined relationship tempered by mutual
respect and love. Kate is visibly a more contented person at
the play's end. Her closing speech, with its fine blend of
irony and self-conscious hyperbole, together with its seriousness of concern, expresses beautifully the way in which
Kate's independence of spirit and her newfound acceptance of a domestic role are successfully fused.

The Taming of the Shrew
in Performance

It is an odd kind of tribute to *The Taming of the Shrew* that it has inspired over the centuries so many adaptations and offshoots. Although Shakespeare's original play was popular in its own day and was kept in repertory seemingly through much of Shakespeare's lifetime, only in greatly altered forms did it enjoy stage success through much of the seventeenth, eighteenth, and early nineteenth centuries. These transformations were probably a response to the play's uncanny ability to make audiences of any era uncomfortable with its presentation of the war of the sexes.

Most adaptations seem to have had a twofold objective: to reinterpret the problematic taming and submission of Kate, and to do something with the unfinished Induction, or frame, of Christopher Sly. From the first, adapters of the play have felt a need to exaggerate, on both sides, the aggression between male and female. The anonymous *The Taming of a Shrew* (derived, sometime before 1594, from a now-lost early version of Shakespeare's play) specifies at one point that Ferando, the renamed Petruchio, is to enter *"with a piece of meat upon his dagger's point"*—presumably to terrorize Kate. Conversely, *The Woman's Prize, or The Tamer Tamed*, written by John Fletcher (Shakespeare's successor as chief dramatist to the acting company, the King's men) in 1611, provides a comic counterpart to the male victory in Shakespeare's play. In Fletcher's version Petruchio, remarried after Kate's death, meets his match in a woman who has nothing but scorn for tameness in wives. Petruchio has to learn to pacify his wife with gifts and is locked up and deceived by her, until a happy ending of sorts is worked out. Fletcher's premise, it would seem, is that the story of a husband's triumph in marriage ought to be answered by one in which the wife triumphs in her turn.

In subsequent adaptations, Shakespeare's portrayal of sexual warfare is pushed both toward further brutalizing the misogynistic elements (already present in Shakespeare's source, the ballad called *A Shrewd and Curst Wife*

Lapped in Morel's Skin) and toward giving the woman a chance to get back at her male tormentor. In *Sauny the Scot* by John Lacy, produced at the Drury Lane Theatre in 1667, Petruchio is indeed a brute. He threatens to whip Kate if she refuses him in marriage, insists she is suffering from a toothache so that he can summon a surgeon to pull one of her teeth, proclaims her dead and actually lashes her to her bier, and then complacently commends his wife when at last she submits to him. She is allowed only two lines to explain her views on the subject of obedience. The title of this adaptation comes from the name of Petruchio's comic servant (Grumio in Shakespeare), who speaks in such a broad Scottish dialect that Samuel Pepys, in 1667, had trouble understanding what was said. James Worsdale's *A Cure for a Scold* (Theatre Royal, Drury Lane, 1735, with Charles Macklin as Petruchio) retained much of Lacy's misogynistic humor, including the tooth-drawing episode. Lacy and Worsdale both provide their shrews with hints of reprisal: the women vow to tame their husbands if given a chance, and Worsdale's Peg Worthy (the renamed Kate, played by Kitty Clive) submits to her husband only after she has feigned death and thereby tricked him into demonstrating his affection for her. These versions by Lacy and Worsdale were immensely popular throughout the Restoration and the first half of the eighteenth century, eclipsing Shakespeare's original in the repertory.

Their popular successor, David Garrick's *Catharine and Petruchio*, held the stage without serious rival for nearly a century after its first performance in 1754 at Drury Lane. Like its predecessors, it at once brutalizes and intensifies the encounters of Kate and Petruchio. In order to focus on the warring lovers, Garrick eliminated both the Induction and the whole Bianca-Lucentio plot, and Kate's father, in this version, is unrelenting in his insistence that she marry or be disowned. It may have been Garrick who first gave Petruchio a whip; in any event, for decades afterward it was an obligatory prop. Yet Kate's speech after her wooing, in Act 1, includes a promise (or threat) of independence of spirit: "Sister Bianca now shall see / The poor abandoned Catharine, as she calls me, / Can hold her head as high, and be as proud, / And make her husband stoop unto her lure, / As she or e'er a wife in Padua." Garrick's instincts were sound in appraising the tastes of his day, for his shortened version (often part of a double bill) remained successful in England and America throughout the nineteenth century. In 1867, Henry Irving performed it with Ellen Terry at the Queen's Theatre, and in 1897 Herbert Beerbohm Tree presented Garrick's shortened version as an afterpiece for the opening night of Her Majesty's Theatre.

English audiences did not see a version close to Shakespeare's until 1844, when the play was produced by Benjamin Webster at the Haymarket Theatre with the Induction intact and with an attempt at Elizabethan costuming as conceived by J. R. Planché. The mise-en-scène was laid in a nobleman's hall as though for the entertainment of Christopher Sly, with no more scenery than could be supplied by two screens and a pair of curtains. Players in the Induction were made up to resemble playwrights Shakespeare and Ben Jonson and the actor Richard Tarlton. The dialogue of the play as a whole kept reasonably close to the original. In 1856 Samuel Phelps produced a slightly cut version of Shakespeare's text at the Sadler's Wells Theatre. He preserved the Induction (playing Sly himself), excised most of the play's bawdy, and softened Kate's character. The United States was provided with its first view of Shakespeare's play in 1887 by Augustin Daly at his theater in New York. The production featured handsome sets inspired by the painter Veronese and a commanding performance of Kate by Ada Rehan. In 1913 at the Prince of Wales Theatre, John Martin-Harvey, advised by William Poel, presented a robust, good-natured *Taming of the Shrew* that attempted to recreate the staging conventions of the Elizabethan theater.

Ever since being reestablished in its own right, *The Taming of the Shrew* has challenged actors and audiences alike to come to terms with its delicate balancing of misogyny and forbearance in marriage. Inevitably the critical point in a performance is the moment of Kate's final speech. How are we to take her gesture of submission? As early as 1908 in Melbourne, Australia, and then in 1914 in New York, Margaret Anglin delivered Kate's long speech on obedience with a mocking suggestion of a private understanding between her and her husband. Conversely, more conventional productions have succeeded with audiences that were still willing to enjoy a comedy of male triumph in the battle of the sexes. Oscillating between these poles of interpretation, the play has become something of a problem play. At the Shakespeare Festival performance in Ashland, Oregon, in 1977, when Petruchio refused to accept Kate's gesture of placing her hand beneath his foot and instead returned her cap to her, audiences were divided as to whether the belated gesture made up for all that Kate had undergone or was simply an attempt on the part of the acting company to be up-to-date.

The Royal Shakespeare Company, at Stratford-upon-Avon in 1978, confronted the potential offensiveness of Kate's submission by refusing to underplay the difficulty: Kate and the other women smouldered in resentment, while the men basked in complacency. One reviewer congratulated the director, Michael Bogdanov, on the honesty with which he tackled this "barbaric and disgusting" play. In 1975, at the Open Space Theatre in London, Charles Marowitz's adaptation called *The Shrew* had already taken this line of interpretation to its logical but frightening conclusion by playing the schooling of Kate as an illustration of the techniques of brainwashing. The ordeal ended in madness and rape for Katharina, and her final speech of submission was delivered as though by rote.

More temperately responsive to Shakespeare's text was the encounter of Meryl Streep and Raul Julia in Wilford Leach's production at the Delacorte Theatre in New York in 1978; Julia unabashedly called upon his own Latin American heritage of machismo to motivate Petruchio's way with women, while Streep, herself a modern woman, approached the role of Kate with the kind of ironic distance made possible by a self-aware and historical perspective. An ironic point of view gave to both actors a chance to enjoy role-playing and yet to preserve an essential part of their own integrity. In a 1960 production by the Royal Shakespeare Company, John Barton's direction of Peter O'Toole and Peggy Ashcroft, as Petruchio and Kate, stressed a good-natured playfulness between a man and a woman who obviously love each other from the start. Elizabeth Taylor and Richard Burton, in a very uneven film version by Franco Zeffirelli (1967), found in their best moments a modern idiom through which to explore the emotional nuances of an aggressive courtship; Taylor played Kate as a hot-tempered tomboy, understandably wary of male claims of prerogative, who has to decide how to respond to an attractive and virile man who seems to want her as a woman but whose motives are otherwise far from clear.

An entirely different strategy sometimes employed in modern productions is to downplay the complexities of the husband-wife issue and to focus instead on hilarity, as in the boisterous production at the Broadway Theatre in New York in 1935 starring Alfred Lunt and Lynn Fontaine, Clifford Williams's 1973 farce for the Royal Shakespeare Company, and a zany *commedia dell'arte* performance by the American Conservatory Theatre of San Francisco in 1976.

The Induction has required solutions as varied and ingenious as those for the wife-taming plot. The anonymous adaptation *The Taming of a Shrew* completed the framing plot of the Induction with an epilogue in which Sly awakens to find himself a beggar once again, ready to apply the lessons he has learned from the play to his own private life. In *Sauny the Scot* the Induction was simply left out. In 1716 Charles Johnson and Christopher Bullock went in the other direction in their nearly contemporaneous adaptations (both called *The Cobbler of Preston*) by making a whole short play out of the Induction. *A Cure for a Scold* and Garrick's *Catharine and Petruchio* also did without, so that the Induction was not often seen in conjunction with the rest of the play before Webster's revival of 1844. But even thereafter, Frank Benson omitted it in 1901 at the Comedy Theatre, as did William Bridges-Adams at Stratford-upon-Avon in 1919 and Dennis Carey, after opening night, at the Old Vic in 1954. Sir Barry Jackson, on the other hand, kept Sly and the Lord in view until the very end of the play, in one of the boxes, dressed in modern dress (Court Theatre, 1928). Ben Iden Payne at Stratford-upon-Avon in 1935 and Tyrone Guthrie at the Old Vic in 1939 similarly kept Sly onstage throughout.

The epilogue from *A Shrew* has been revived at times, as at the Old Vic in 1931 and at Stratford-upon-Avon in 1953. The Stratford Festival in Canada in the 1960s ended the play by having its performers, a band of strolling players, pack up and go off in search of another audience. The so-called Young Vic Company, on tour in the 1970s, conceived of Sly as a frustrated actor who eventually turns up in the play proper in the role of the Pedant, thus recalling a doubling effect used earlier at the New Theatre in 1937. Cole Porter's musical of 1948, *Kiss Me Kate*, converted the idea of a framing plot and a play-within-the-play into a story of actors whose tempestuous love life offstage reflects the difficulties of the wooers they portray.

Shakespeare's text calls for the second scene of the Induction to be played "aloft," that is, in the gallery at the back of the main stage, though the scene is longer, more elaborate, and more peopled with actors than is normal for action "above" in Shakespearean drama, and there is no interaction with persons below on the main stage as in most such scenes. If Sly were to continue to sit in the gallery throughout the play, his presence would complicate the staging of Act 5, scene 1, in which the gallery seems to be needed for a window in the house of Lucentio. In the anonymous *A Shrew*, where Sly does remain throughout, he appears to be situated at one side of the stage, not aloft. Shakespeare may have had to deal with varying theatrical conditions if the play was acted first in one theatre and then in another. We are not likely ever to know for certain how the Induction was staged in its original performances. In its own way, Shakespeare's Induction has remained as much a challenge to directors and actors of *The Taming of the Shrew* as has the battle for mastery between Petruchio and Kate.

THE TAMING OF
THE SHREW

[*Dramatis Personae*

CHRISTOPHER SLY, *a tinker and beggar,*
HOSTESS *of an alehouse,*
A LORD,
A PAGE, SERVANTS, HUNTSMEN,
PLAYERS,

} *Persons in the Induction*

BAPTISTA, *a rich gentleman of Padua*
KATHARINA, *the shrew, also called Katharine and Kate,*
  Baptista's elder daughter
BIANCA, *Baptista's younger daughter*

PETRUCHIO, *a gentleman of Verona, suitor to Katharina*
GRUMIO, *Petruchio's servant*
CURTIS, NATHANIEL, PHILIP, JOSEPH, NICHOLAS, PETER, *and other*
  servants of Petruchio

GREMIO, *elderly suitor to Bianca*
HORTENSIO, *suitor to Bianca*
LUCENTIO, *son of Vincentio, in love with Bianca*
TRANIO, *Lucentio's servant*
BIONDELLO, *Lucentio's servant*
VINCENTIO, *a gentleman of Pisa*
A PEDANT (*or Merchant*) *of Mantua*
A WIDOW, *courted by Hortensio*

A TAILOR
A HABERDASHER
AN OFFICER
Other Servants of Baptista and Lucentio

SCENE: *Padua, and Petruchio's country house in Italy; the*
  Induction is located in the countryside and at a Lord's house
  in England]

Induction 1
Enter beggar (Christopher Sly) and Hostess.

SLY I'll feeze you, in faith. 1

HOSTESS A pair of stocks, you rogue! 2

SLY You're a baggage. The Slys are no rogues. Look in 3
the chronicles; we came in with Richard Conqueror. 4
Therefore *paucas pallabris*, let the world slide. Sessa! 5

HOSTESS You will not pay for the glasses you have
burst?

SLY No, not a denier. Go by, Saint Jeronimy, go to thy 8
cold bed and warm thee. 9

HOSTESS I know my remedy; I must go fetch the third- 10
borough. [*Exit.*] 11

SLY Third, or fourth, or fifth borough, I'll answer him 12
by law. I'll not budge an inch, boy. Let him come, and
kindly. *Falls asleep.* 14

*Wind horns [within]. Enter a Lord from hunting,
with his train.*

LORD
Huntsman, I charge thee, tender well my hounds. 15
Breathe Merriman—the poor cur is embossed— 16
And couple Clowder with the deep-mouthed brach. 17
Sawst thou not, boy, how Silver made it good
At the hedge corner, in the coldest fault? 19
I would not lose the dog for twenty pound.

FIRST HUNTSMAN
Why, Bellman is as good as he, my lord.

**Induction 1. Location: Before an alehouse, and subsequently before the
Lord's house nearby. (See ll. 75, 135.)**
1 feeze you i.e., fix you, get even with you   **2 A . . . stocks** i.e., I'll have
you put in the stocks   **3 baggage** contemptible woman or prostitute
4 Richard (Sly's mistake for "William.")   **5 paucas pallabris** i.e., *pocas
palabras*, "few words." (Spanish.)   **Sessa** (Of doubtful meaning; perhaps
"be quiet," "cease," or "let it go.")   **8 denier** French copper coin of
little value.   **Go . . . Jeronimy** (Sly's variation of an often-quoted line
from Kyd's *The Spanish Tragedy*, expressing impatience.)   **8–9 go . . .
thee** (Perhaps a proverb; see *King Lear* 3.4.46–47.)   **10–11 thirdborough**
constable   **12 Third** (Sly shows his ignorance; the *third* in "thirdborough" derives from the Old English word *frith*, peace.)   **14 kindly**
welcome   **s.d. Wind** blow   **15 tender** care for   **16 embossed** foaming at
the mouth from exhaustion   **17 brach** bitch hound   **19 fault** loss of scent

He cried upon it at the merest loss,   22
And twice today picked out the dullest scent.
Trust me, I take him for the better dog.

LORD
Thou art a fool. If Echo were as fleet,
I would esteem him worth a dozen such.
But sup them well and look unto them all.
Tomorrow I intend to hunt again.

FIRST HUNTSMAN   I will, my lord.

LORD [*Seeing Sly*]
What's here? One dead, or drunk? See, doth he breathe?

SECOND HUNTSMAN [*Examining Sly*]
He breathes, my lord. Were he not warmed with ale,
This were a bed but cold to sleep so soundly.

LORD
O monstrous beast, how like a swine he lies!
Grim death, how foul and loathsome is thine image!   34
Sirs, I will practice on this drunken man.   35
What think you, if he were conveyed to bed,
Wrapped in sweet clothes, rings put upon his fingers,   37
A most delicious banquet by his bed,   38
And brave attendants near him when he wakes,   39
Would not the beggar then forget himself?

FIRST HUNTSMAN
Believe me, lord, I think he cannot choose.

SECOND HUNTSMAN
It would seem strange unto him when he waked.

LORD
Even as a flattering dream or worthless fancy.   43
Then take him up, and manage well the jest.
Carry him gently to my fairest chamber,
And hang it round with all my wanton pictures.
Balm his foul head in warm distillèd waters,
And burn sweet wood to make the lodging sweet.
Procure me music ready when he wakes
To make a dulcet and a heavenly sound.
And if he chance to speak, be ready straight,   51

---

22 cried . . . loss bayed to signal recovery of the scent after it had been
completely lost **34 image** likeness (since sleep was regarded as a
likeness of death) **35 practice on** play a joke on **37 sweet** perfumed
38 banquet light repast **39 brave** finely arrayed **43 fancy** flight of
imagination **51 straight** at once

And with a low submissive reverence
Say, "What is it your honor will command?"
Let one attend him with a silver basin
Full of rosewater and bestrewed with flowers;
Another bear the ewer, the third a diaper,   56
And say, "Will 't please your lordship cool your hands?"
Someone be ready with a costly suit
And ask him what apparel he will wear;
Another tell him of his hounds and horse,
And that his lady mourns at his disease.
Persuade him that he hath been lunatic,
And when he says he is, say that he dreams,
For he is nothing but a mighty lord.
This do, and do it kindly, gentle sirs.   65
It will be pastime passing excellent,   66
If it be husbanded with modesty.   67

FIRST HUNTSMAN
My lord, I warrant you we will play our part
As he shall think by our true diligence   69
He is no less than what we say he is.

LORD
Take him up gently and to bed with him,
And each one to his office when he wakes.   72
          [*Some bear out Sly.*] *Sound trumpets* [*within*].
Sirrah, go see what trumpet 'tis that sounds.   73
                              [*Exit Servingman.*]
Belike some noble gentleman that means,   74
Traveling some journey, to repose him here.

          Enter Servingman.

How now? Who is it?
SERVINGMAN   An 't please your honor, players
That offer service to your lordship.

          Enter Players.

LORD
Bid them come near.—Now, fellows, you are welcome.

---

56 ewer jug, pitcher.   **diaper** towel   **65 kindly** naturally (and thus
persuasively)   **66 passing** surpassingly   **67 husbanded with modesty**
managed with decorum   **69 As** so that   **72 office** duty   **73 Sirrah**
(Usual form of address to inferiors.)   **74 Belike** perhaps

PLAYERS   We thank your honor.

LORD
  Do you intend to stay with me tonight?

FIRST PLAYER
  So please your lordship to accept our duty.   81

LORD
  With all my heart. This fellow I remember
  Since once he played a farmer's eldest son.—
  'Twas where you wooed the gentlewoman so well.
  I have forgot your name, but sure that part
  Was aptly fitted and naturally performed.

SECOND PLAYER
  I think 'twas Soto that your honor means.

LORD
  'Tis very true. Thou didst it excellent.
  Well, you are come to me in happy time,   89
  The rather for I have some sport in hand   90
  Wherein your cunning can assist me much.
  There is a lord will hear you play tonight.
  But I am doubtful of your modesties,   93
  Lest, overeyeing of his odd behavior—   94
  For yet his honor never heard a play—
  You break into some merry passion   96
  And so offend him; for I tell you, sirs,
  If you should smile he grows impatient.

FIRST PLAYER
  Fear not, my lord, we can contain ourselves
  Were he the veriest antic in the world.   100

LORD [To a Servingman]
  Go, sirrah, take them to the buttery,   101
  And give them friendly welcome every one.
  Let them want nothing that my house affords.   103
                         Exit one with the Players.
  Sirrah, go you to Barthol'mew my page,   104
  And see him dressed in all suits like a lady.   105

81 duty expression of respect   **89 happy** opportune   **90 The rather for**
the more so since   **93 doubtful** apprehensive.   **modesties** discretion,
self-control   **94 overeyeing of** witnessing   **96 merry passion** outburst of
laughter   **100 antic** buffoon or eccentric   **101 buttery** pantry, or a room
for storing liquor (in butts) and other provisions   **103 want** lack
104 Barthol'mew (Pronounced "Bartlemy.")   **105 in all suits** in every
detail

That done, conduct him to the drunkard's chamber,
And call him "madam," do him obeisance.
Tell him from me, as he will win my love,   108
He bear himself with honorable action,
Such as he hath observed in noble ladies
Unto their lords, by them accomplishèd.
Such duty to the drunkard let him do
With soft low tongue and lowly courtesy,
And say, "What is 't your honor will command,
Wherein your lady and your humble wife
May show her duty and make known her love?"
And then with kind embracements, tempting kisses,
And with declining head into his bosom,
Bid him shed tears, as being overjoyed
To see her noble lord restored to health,
Who for this seven years hath esteemèd him   121
No better than a poor and loathsome beggar.
And if the boy have not a woman's gift
To rain a shower of commanded tears,
An onion will do well for such a shift,   125
Which in a napkin being close conveyed   126
Shall in despite enforce a watery eye.
See this dispatched with all the haste thou canst.
Anon I'll give thee more instructions.   129

Exit a Servingman.

I know the boy will well usurp the grace,   130
Voice, gait, and action of a gentlewoman.
I long to hear him call the drunkard husband,
And how my men will stay themselves from laughter
When they do homage to this simple peasant.
I'll in to counsel them. Haply my presence
May well abate the overmerry spleen   136
Which otherwise would grow into extremes.

[Exeunt.]

♣

108 him i.e., the page Bartholomew   **121 him** himself   **125 shift** purpose   **126 napkin** handkerchief.   **close** secretly   **129 Anon** soon
130 usurp assume   **136 spleen** mood. (The spleen was the supposed
seat of laughter and anger.)

Induction 2   *Enter aloft the drunkard [Sly],*
with Attendants; some with
apparel, basin, and ewer and other
appurtenances; and Lord.

SLY   For God's sake, a pot of small ale.   1

FIRST SERVANT
   Will 't please your lordship drink a cup of sack?   2

SECOND SERVANT
   Will 't please your honor taste of these conserves?   3

THIRD SERVANT
   What raiment will your honor wear today?

SLY   I am Christophero Sly, call not me "honor" nor
   "lordship." I ne'er drank sack in my life; and if you
   give me any conserves, give me conserves of beef.   7
   Ne'er ask me what raiment I'll wear, for I have no
   more doublets than backs, no more stockings than   9
   legs, nor no more shoes than feet—nay, sometimes
   more feet than shoes, or such shoes as my toes look
   through the overleather.

LORD
   Heaven cease this idle humor in your honor!   13
   O, that a mighty man of such descent,
   Of such possessions and so high esteem,
   Should be infusèd with so foul a spirit!

SLY   What, would you make me mad? Am not I Christopher Sly, old Sly's son of Burton-heath, by birth a   18
   peddler, by education a cardmaker, by transmutation   19
   a bearherd, and now by present profession a tinker?   20
   Ask Marian Hacket, the fat alewife of Wincot, if she   21

Induction 2. Location: A bedchamber in the Lord's house.
s.d. aloft i.e., in the gallery over the rear facade of the stage   **1 small**
weak (and therefore cheap)   **2 sack** sweet Spanish wine (suited for a
gentleman to drink)   **3 conserves** candied fruit   **7 conserves of beef**
preserved (salted) beef   **9 doublets** men's jackets   **13 idle** vain, foolish.
humor whim, fancy   **18 Burton-heath** (Perhaps Barton-on-the-Heath,
about sixteen miles from Stratford, the home of Shakespeare's aunt.)
19 cardmaker maker of cards or combs used to prepare wool for spinning   **20 bearherd** keeper of a performing bear.   **tinker** pot-mender
21 Wincot small village about four miles from Stratford. (The parish
register shows that there were Hackets living there in 1591.)

know me not. If she say I am not fourteen pence on 22
the score for sheer ale, score me up for the lyingest 23
knave in Christendom. What, I am not bestraught: 24
here's—

THIRD SERVANT
O, this it is that makes your lady mourn!

SECOND SERVANT
O, this is it that makes your servants droop!

LORD
Hence comes it that your kindred shuns your house,
As beaten hence by your strange lunacy.   29
O noble lord, bethink thee of thy birth,
Call home thy ancient thoughts from banishment,   31
And banish hence these abject lowly dreams.
Look how thy servants do attend on thee,
Each in his office ready at thy beck.
Wilt thou have music? Hark, Apollo plays,   *Music.* 35
And twenty cagèd nightingales do sing.
Or wilt thou sleep? We'll have thee to a couch,
Softer and sweeter than the lustful bed
On purpose trimmed up for Semiramis.   39
Say thou wilt walk; we will bestrew the ground.
Or wilt thou ride? Thy horses shall be trapped,   41
Their harness studded all with gold and pearl.
Dost thou love hawking? Thou hast hawks will soar
Above the morning lark. Or wilt thou hunt?
Thy hounds shall make the welkin answer them   45
And fetch shrill echoes from the hollow earth.

FIRST SERVANT
Say thou wilt course, thy greyhounds are as swift   47
As breathèd stags, ay, fleeter than the roe.   48

SECOND SERVANT
Dost thou love pictures? We will fetch thee straight
Adonis painted by a running brook,   50

22–23 **on the score** in debt (since such reckonings were originally
notched or scored on a stick) 23 **sheer** nothing but. **score me up for**
reckon me to be 24 **bestraught** distracted 29 **As** as if 31 **ancient**
former 35 **Apollo** i.e., as god of music 39 **Semiramis** legendary queen
of Assyria famous for her voluptuousness 41 **trapped** adorned
45 **welkin** sky, heavens 47 **course** hunt the hare 48 **breathèd** in good
physical condition, with good wind. **roe** small, swift deer 50 **Adonis** a
young huntsman with whom Venus is vainly in love. (See Shakespeare's
poem *Venus and Adonis*.)

And Cytherea all in sedges hid,   51
Which seem to move and wanton with her breath,   52
Even as the waving sedges play wi' th' wind.

LORD
We'll show thee Io as she was a maid,   54
And how she was beguilèd and surprised,
As lively painted as the deed was done.

THIRD SERVANT
Or Daphne roaming through a thorny wood,   57
Scratching her legs that one shall swear she bleeds,
And at that sight shall sad Apollo weep,
So workmanly the blood and tears are drawn.   60

LORD
Thou art a lord and nothing but a lord.
Thou hast a lady far more beautiful
Than any woman in this waning age.   63

FIRST SERVANT
And till the tears that she hath shed for thee
Like envious floods o'errun her lovely face,   65
She was the fairest creature in the world;
And yet she is inferior to none.   67

SLY
Am I a lord? And have I such a lady?
Or do I dream? Or have I dreamed till now?
I do not sleep: I see, I hear, I speak,
I smell sweet savors, and I feel soft things.
Upon my life, I am a lord indeed,
And not a tinker nor Christopher Sly.
Well, bring our lady hither to our sight,
And once again a pot o' the smallest ale.

SECOND SERVANT
Will 't please your mightiness to wash your hands?
O, how we joy to see your wit restored!   77
O, that once more you knew but what you are!

51 **Cytherea** one of the names for Venus (because of her association
with the island of Cythera). **sedges** grassy marsh plants   52 **wanton**
play seductively   54 **Io** one of Jupiter's lovers, transformed by him into
a heifer to conceal her from the envious Juno   57 **Daphne** a wood
nymph beloved by Apollo, changed by Diana into a laurel tree to preserve her from Apollo's assault   60 **workmanly** skillfully   63 **waning**
degenerate   65 **envious** spiteful   67 **yet** even today   77 **wit** mental
faculties, senses

These fifteen years you have been in a dream,
Or when you waked, so waked as if you slept.

SLY

These fifteen years! By my fay, a goodly nap.   81
But did I never speak of all that time?   82

FIRST SERVANT

O, yes, my lord, but very idle words;
For though you lay here in this goodly chamber,
Yet would you say ye were beaten out of door,
And rail upon the hostess of the house,   86
And say you would present her at the leet,   87
Because she brought stone jugs and no sealed quarts.   88
Sometimes you would call out for Cicely Hacket.

SLY   Ay, the woman's maid of the house.

THIRD SERVANT

Why, sir, you know no house nor no such maid,
Nor no such men as you have reckoned up,
As Stephen Sly, and old John Naps of Greece,   93
And Peter Turf, and Henry Pimpernel,
And twenty more such names and men as these,
Which never were nor no man ever saw.

SLY

Now Lord be thankèd for my good amends!   97

ALL

Amen.

Enter [the Page as a] lady, with Attendants.

SLY   I thank thee. Thou shalt not lose by it.

PAGE

How fares my noble lord?

SLY   Marry, I fare well,   99
For here is cheer enough. Where is my wife?

PAGE

Here, noble lord. What is thy will with her?

---

81 fay faith   **82 of** during   **86 house** tavern   **87 present** bring accusa-
tion against.   **leet** manorial court   **88 sealed quarts** quart containers
officially stamped as a guarantee of that capacity   **93 Stephen . . .
Greece** (A Stephen Sly lived in Stratford during Shakespeare's day.
Greece is an apparent error for *Greet*, a Gloucestershire hamlet not far
from Stratford.)   **97 amends** recovery   **99 Marry** A mild oath, derived
from "by Mary."

SLY
  Are you my wife and will not call me husband?
  My men should call me "lord"; I am your goodman.   103
PAGE
  My husband and my lord, my lord and husband,
  I am your wife in all obedience.
SLY
  I know it well.—What must I call her?
LORD   Madam.
SLY Al'ce madam, or Joan madam?
LORD
  Madam, and nothing else. So lords call ladies.
SLY
  Madam wife, they say that I have dreamed
  And slept above some fifteen year or more.
PAGE
  Ay, and the time seems thirty unto me,
  Being all this time abandoned from your bed.   112
SLY
  'Tis much. Servants, leave me and her alone.
  Madam, undress you and come now to bed.
PAGE
  Thrice-noble lord, let me entreat of you
  To pardon me yet for a night or two,
  Or, if not so, until the sun be set.
  For your physicians have expressly charged,
  In peril to incur your former malady,
  That I should yet absent me from your bed.
  I hope this reason stands for my excuse.
SLY Ay, it stands so that I may hardly tarry so long. But 122
  I would be loath to fall into my dreams again. I will
  therefore tarry in despite of the flesh and the blood.

     Enter a [Servant as] messenger.

SERVANT
  Your honor's players, hearing your amendment,
  Are come to play a pleasant comedy;
  For so your doctors hold it very meet,   127
  Seeing too much sadness hath congealed your blood,

---

103 goodman (A homely term for "husband.") **112 abandoned** banished **122 stands** is the case (with bawdy pun) **127 meet** suitable

And melancholy is the nurse of frenzy.
Therefore they thought it good you hear a play
And frame your mind to mirth and merriment,
Which bars a thousand harms and lengthens life.

SLY Marry, I will, let them play it. Is not a comonty a   133
    Christmas gambold or a tumbling-trick?   134

PAGE
No, my good lord, it is more pleasing stuff.

SLY What, household stuff?

PAGE It is a kind of history.   137

SLY Well, we'll see 't. Come, madam wife, sit by my
    side and let the world slip; we shall ne'er be younger.
                              [*They sit over the stage.*] *Flourish.*

133, 134 comonty, gambold (Sly's words for *comedy* and *gambol*.)
137 history story

1.1   *Enter Lucentio and his man Tranio.*

LUCENTIO
Tranio, since for the great desire I had
To see fair Padua, nursery of arts,   2
I am arrived for fruitful Lombardy,   3
The pleasant garden of great Italy,
And by my father's love and leave am armed
With his good will and thy good company,
My trusty servant, well approved in all,   7
Here let us breathe and haply institute   8
A course of learning and ingenious studies.   9
Pisa, renownèd for grave citizens,
Gave me my being, and my father first,   11
A merchant of great traffic through the world,   12
Vincentio, come of the Bentivolii.
Vincentio's son, brought up in Florence,
It shall become to serve all hopes conceived   15
To deck his fortune with his virtuous deeds.   16
And therefore, Tranio, for the time I study,
Virtue and that part of philosophy
Will I apply that treats of happiness   19
By virtue specially to be achieved.
Tell me thy mind, for I have Pisa left
And am to Padua come, as he that leaves
A shallow plash to plunge him in the deep   23
And with satiety seeks to quench his thirst.

TRANIO
Mi perdonate, gentle master mine.   25
I am in all affected as yourself,   26
Glad that you thus continue your resolve

1.1. **Location: Padua. A street before Baptista's house.**
2 Padua . . . arts (Padua's was one of the most renowned of universities
during Shakespeare's time.)   **3 am arrived for** have arrived at. (Padua is
not in Lombardy, but imprecise maps may have allowed Shakespeare to
think of Lombardy as comprising all of northern Italy.)   **7 approved**
tested and proved trustworthy   **8 breathe** pause, remain.   **institute**
begin   **9 ingenious** i.e., "ingenuous," liberal, befitting a well-born
person   **11 first** i.e., before me   **12 of great traffic** involved in extensive
trade   **15 It . . . conceived** i.e., it will befit me, Lucentio, to fulfill all the
hopes entertained for me by my friends and relatives   **16 deck** adorn
19 apply study.   **treats of** discusses, concerns   **23 plash** pool   **25 Mi
perdonate** pardon me   **26 affected** disposed

To suck the sweets of sweet philosophy.
Only, good master, while we do admire
This virtue and this moral discipline,
Let's be no stoics nor no stocks, I pray,   31
Or so devote to Aristotle's checks   32
As Ovid be an outcast quite abjured.   33
Balk logic with acquaintance that you have,   34
And practice rhetoric in your common talk;
Music and poesy use to quicken you;   36
The mathematics and the metaphysics,
Fall to them as you find your stomach serves you.   38
No profit grows where is no pleasure ta'en.
In brief, sir, study what you most affect.   40

LUCENTIO
Gramercies, Tranio, well dost thou advise.   41
If, Biondello, thou wert come ashore,   42
We could at once put us in readiness,
And take a lodging fit to entertain
Such friends as time in Padua shall beget.
But stay awhile, what company is this?

TRANIO
Master, some show to welcome us to town.   47

*Enter Baptista with his two daughters Katharina
and Bianca, Gremio a pantaloon, [and] Hortensio
suitor to Bianca. Lucentio [and] Tranio stand by.*

BAPTISTA
Gentlemen, importune me no farther,
For how I firmly am resolved you know:
That is, not to bestow my youngest daughter
Before I have a husband for the elder.
If either of you both love Katharina,

---

31 stocks wooden posts, devoid of feeling (with a play on *stoics*)
32 devote devoted.   **checks** restraints   **33 As** so that.   **Ovid** Latin love
poet (used here to typify amorous light entertainment as contrasted
with the serious philosophic study of Aristotle)   **34 Balk logic** argue,
bandy words   **36 quicken** refresh   **38 stomach** inclination, appetite
40 affect find pleasant   **41 Gramercies** many thanks   **42 Biondello**
(Lucentio apostrophizes his absent servant.)   **come ashore** (Padua,
though inland, is given a harbor by Shakespeare, unless he is thinking
of the canals that crossed northern Italy in the sixteenth century.)
47 s.d. pantaloon foolish old man, a stock character in Italian comedy

Because I know you well and love you well,
Leave shall you have to court her at your pleasure.

GREMIO
To cart her rather; she's too rough for me.   55
There, there, Hortensio, will you any wife?

KATHARINA [*To Baptista*]
I pray you, sir, is it your will
To make a stale of me amongst these mates?   58

HORTENSIO
"Mates," maid? How mean you that? No mates for you,
Unless you were of gentler, milder mold.

KATHARINA
I' faith, sir, you shall never need to fear:
Iwis it is not halfway to her heart.   62
But if it were, doubt not her care should be
To comb your noddle with a three-legged stool,
And paint your face, and use you like a fool.   65

HORTENSIO
From all such devils, good Lord deliver us!

GREMIO   And me too, good Lord!

TRANIO [*Aside to Lucentio*]
Husht, master, here's some good pastime toward.   68
That wench is stark mad or wonderful froward.   69

LUCENTIO [*Aside to Tranio*]
But in the other's silence do I see
Maid's mild behavior and sobriety.
Peace, Tranio!

TRANIO [*Aside to Lucentio*]
Well said, master; mum, and gaze your fill.

BAPTISTA
Gentlemen, that I may soon make good
What I have said—Bianca, get you in,
And let it not displease thee, good Bianca,
For I will love thee ne'er the less, my girl.

---

55 cart carry in a cart through the streets by way of punishment or public exposure (with a play on *court*) **58 stale** laughingstock (with a play on the meaning "harlot," since a harlot might well be carted). **mates** rude fellows. (But Hortensio takes the word in the sense of "husband.") **62 Iwis** indeed. **it** i.e., marriage. **her** i.e., my, Kate's **65 paint** i.e., make red with scratches **68 toward** in prospect **69 froward** perverse

KATHARINA   A pretty peat! It is best   78
  Put finger in the eye, an she knew why.   79

BIANCA
  Sister, content you in my discontent.—
  Sir, to your pleasure humbly I subscribe.
  My books and instruments shall be my company,
  On them to look and practice by myself.

LUCENTIO [*Aside to Tranio*]
  Hark, Tranio, thou mayst hear Minerva speak.   84

HORTENSIO
  Signor Baptista, will you be so strange?   85
  Sorry am I that our good will effects
  Bianca's grief.

GREMIO   Why will you mew her up,   87
  Signor Baptista, for this fiend of hell,
  And make her bear the penance of her tongue?   89

BAPTISTA
  Gentlemen, content ye; I am resolved.
  Go in, Bianca.   [*Exit Bianca.*]
  And for I know she taketh most delight   92
  In music, instruments, and poetry,
  Schoolmasters will I keep within my house
  Fit to instruct her youth. If you, Hortensio,
  Or Signor Gremio, you, know any such,
  Prefer them hither; for to cunning men   97
  I will be very kind, and liberal
  To mine own children in good bringing up.
  And so farewell.—Katharina, you may stay,
  For I have more to commune with Bianca.   *Exit.* 101

KATHARINA
  Why, and I trust I may go too, may I not?
  What, shall I be appointed hours,
  As though, belike, I knew not what to take,
  And what to leave? Ha!   *Exit.*

GREMIO   You may go to the devil's dam. Your gifts are 106
so good, here's none will hold you:—Their love is not 107

---

78 peat darling, pet **79 Put . . . eye** i.e., weep. **an** if **84 Minerva**
goddess of wisdom **85 strange** distant, estranged **87 mew** coop (as
one would a falcon) **89 her . . . her** i.e., Bianca . . . Katharina's **92 for**
because **97 Prefer** recommend. **cunning** skillful, learned **101 commune** discuss **106 dam** mother **107 Their love** i.e., men's love of
women

so great, Hortensio, but we may blow our nails to- 108
gether, and fast it fairly out. Our cake's dough on both 109
sides. Farewell. Yet, for the love I bear my sweet
Bianca, if I can by any means light on a fit man to
teach her that wherein she delights, I will wish him to 112
her father.

HORTENSIO So will I, Signor Gremio. But a word, I
pray. Though the nature of our quarrel yet never
brooked parle, know now, upon advice, it toucheth us 116
both—that we may yet again have access to our fair
mistress and be happy rivals in Bianca's love—to labor
and effect one thing specially.

GREMIO What's that, I pray?

HORTENSIO Marry, sir, to get a husband for her sister.

GREMIO A husband? A devil.

HORTENSIO I say a husband.

GREMIO I say a devil. Think'st thou, Hortensio, though
her father be very rich, any man is so very a fool to be 125
married to hell?

HORTENSIO Tush, Gremio, though it pass your patience
and mine to endure her loud alarums, why, man, 128
there be good fellows in the world, an a man could
light on them, would take her with all faults, and
money enough.

GREMIO I cannot tell; but I had as lief take her dowry 132
with this condition, to be whipped at the high cross 133
every morning.

HORTENSIO Faith, as you say, there's small choice in
rotten apples. But come, since this bar in law makes 136
us friends, it shall be so far forth friendly maintained
till by helping Baptista's eldest daughter to a husband
we set his youngest free for a husband, and then have
to 't afresh. Sweet Bianca! Happy man be his dole! He 140

108–109 blow . . . together i.e., twiddle our thumbs, wait patiently
109 fast . . . out abstain as best we can. **Our cake's dough** i.e., we're
out of luck, getting nowhere **112 wish** commend **116 brooked parle**
tolerated conference. **advice** reflection. **toucheth** concerns **125 very**
utterly **128 alarums** i.e., loud, startling noises. (A military metaphor.)
132 had as lief would as willingly **133 high cross** cross set on a pedes-
tal in a marketplace or center of a town **136 bar in law** obstruction to
our (legal) cause **140 Happy . . . dole** i.e., may happiness be the reward
of him who wins. (Proverbial.)

that runs fastest gets the ring. How say you, Signor 141
Gremio?

GREMIO I am agreed, and would I had given him the
best horse in Padua to begin his wooing that would
thoroughly woo her, wed her, and bed her and rid the
house of her! Come on.   *Exeunt ambo.* 146
                        Manent Tranio and Lucentio.

TRANIO
I pray, sir, tell me, is it possible
That love should of a sudden take such hold?

LUCENTIO
O Tranio, till I found it to be true,
I never thought it possible or likely.
But see, while idly I stood looking on,
I found the effect of love in idleness,   152
And now in plainness do confess to thee,
That art to me as secret and as dear   154
As Anna to the Queen of Carthage was,   155
Tranio, I burn, I pine, I perish, Tranio,
If I achieve not this young modest girl.
Counsel me, Tranio, for I know thou canst;
Assist me, Tranio, for I know thou wilt.

TRANIO
Master, it is no time to chide you now.
Affection is not rated from the heart.   161
If love have touched you, naught remains but so,
"Redime te captum quam queas minimo."   163

LUCENTIO
Gramercies, lad. Go forward. This contents;
The rest will comfort, for thy counsel's sound.

TRANIO
Master, you looked so longly on the maid,   166
Perhaps you marked not what's the pith of all.   167

141 the ring (An allusion to the sport of riding at the ring, with quibble
on "wedding ring.")   **146 s.d. ambo** both.   **Manent** they remain onstage   **152 love in idleness** the flower heartsease or pansy, to which was
attributed magical power in love. (See *A Midsummer Night's Dream,*
2.1.168.)   **154 secret** trusted, intimate   **155 Anna** confidante of her
sister Dido, Queen of Carthage, beloved of Aeneas   **161 rated** driven
away by chiding   **163 Redime . . . minimo** buy yourself out of bondage
for as little as you can. (From Terence's *Eunuchus* as quoted in Lily's
Latin Grammar.)   **166 so longly** for such a long time; perhaps, also, so
longingly   **167 pith** core, essence

LUCENTIO

O, yes, I saw sweet beauty in her face,
Such as the daughter of Agenor had,   169
That made great Jove to humble him to her hand,   170
When with his knees he kissed the Cretan strand.   171

TRANIO

Saw you no more? Marked you not how her sister
Began to scold and raise up such a storm
That mortal ears might hardly endure the din?

LUCENTIO

Tranio, I saw her coral lips to move,
And with her breath she did perfume the air.
Sacred and sweet was all I saw in her.

TRANIO [*Aside*]

Nay, then, 'tis time to stir him from his trance.—
I pray, awake, sir. If you love the maid,
Bend thoughts and wits to achieve her. Thus it stands:
Her elder sister is so curst and shrewd   181
That till the father rid his hands of her,
Master, your love must live a maid at home,
And therefore has he closely mewed her up,
Because she will not be annoyed with suitors.   185

LUCENTIO

Ah, Tranio, what a cruel father's he!
But art thou not advised he took some care   187
To get her cunning schoolmasters to instruct her?

TRANIO

Ay, marry, am I, sir; and now 'tis plotted.

LUCENTIO

I have it, Tranio.

TRANIO   Master, for my hand,   190
Both our inventions meet and jump in one.   191

LUCENTIO

Tell me thine first.

TRANIO   You will be schoolmaster,
And undertake the teaching of the maid:
That's your device.

169 daughter of Agenor Europa, beloved of Jupiter, who took the form
of a bull in order to abduct her   **170 him** himself   **171 kissed** i.e., knelt
on   **181 curst** shrewish.   **shrewd** ill-natured   **185 Because** so that
187 advised aware   **190 for my hand** for my part, i.e., it's my guess
191 inventions plans.   **jump** tally, agree

LUCENTIO   It is. May it be done?
TRANIO
  Not possible; for who shall bear your part,
  And be in Padua here Vincentio's son,
  Keep house and ply his book, welcome his friends,
  Visit his countrymen, and banquet them?
LUCENTIO
  Basta, content thee, for I have it full.   199
  We have not yet been seen in any house,
  Nor can we be distinguished by our faces
  For man or master. Then it follows thus:
  Thou shalt be master, Tranio, in my stead,
  Keep house, and port, and servants, as I should.   204
  I will some other be, some Florentine,
  Some Neapolitan, or meaner man of Pisa.   206
  'Tis hatched and shall be so. Tranio, at once
  Uncase thee. Take my colored hat and cloak.   208
  When Biondello comes, he waits on thee,
  But I will charm him first to keep his tongue.   210
TRANIO   So had you need.
  In brief, sir, sith it your pleasure is,   212
  And I am tied to be obedient—
  For so your father charged me at our parting,
  "Be serviceable to my son," quoth he,
  Although I think 'twas in another sense—
  I am content to be Lucentio,
  Because so well I love Lucentio.
                              [*They exchange clothes.*]
LUCENTIO
  Tranio, be so, because Lucentio loves.
  And let me be a slave, t' achieve that maid
  Whose sudden sight hath thralled my wounded eye.   221

      Enter Biondello.

  Here comes the rogue.—Sirrah, where have you been?
BIONDELLO
  Where have I been? Nay, how now, where are you?

199 Basta enough. **full** i.e., fully thought out **204 port** state, style of
living **206 meaner** of a lower social class **208 Uncase** i.e., remove hat
and cloak. **colored** (as opposed to blue generally worn by servants; see
4.1.81) **210 charm** i.e., persuade **212 sith** since **221 Whose sudden
sight** i.e., the sudden sight of whom

Master, has my fellow Tranio stol'n your clothes?
Or you stol'n his? Or both? Pray, what's the news?

LUCENTIO

Sirrah, come hither. 'Tis no time to jest,
And therefore frame your manners to the time.
Your fellow Tranio here, to save my life,
Puts my apparel and my countenance on,   229
And I for my escape have put on his;
For in a quarrel since I came ashore
I killed a man, and fear I was descried.   232
Wait you on him, I charge you, as becomes,   233
While I make way from hence to save my life.
You understand me?

BIONDELLO   I, sir?—Ne'er a whit.   235

LUCENTIO

And not a jot of Tranio in your mouth.
Tranio is changed into Lucentio.

BIONDELLO

The better for him. Would I were so too!

TRANIO

So could I, faith, boy, to have the next wish after,
That Lucentio indeed had Baptista's youngest daughter.
But, sirrah, not for my sake, but your master's, I advise
You use your manners discreetly in all kind of compa-
    nies.
When I am alone, why, then I am Tranio,
But in all places else your master Lucentio.

LUCENTIO   Tranio, let's go.

One thing more rests, that thyself execute: 246
To make one among these wooers. If thou ask me why,
Sufficeth my reasons are both good and weighty.   248

                                                            Exeunt.

    The presenters above speak.

FIRST SERVANT

My lord, you nod. You do not mind the play.   249

---

229 countenance bearing, manner   **232 descried** observèd   **233 as
becomes** as is suitable   **235 I, sir** (Lucentio may hear this as "Ay,
sir.")   **246 rests** remains to be done   **248 Sufficeth** it suffices that
s.d. presenters characters of the Induction, whose role it is to "present"
the play proper   **249 mind** attend to

SLY   Yes, by Saint Anne, do I. A good matter, surely.
   Comes there any more of it?
PAGE [*As Lady*]   My lord, 'tis but begun.
SLY   'Tis a very excellent piece of work, madam lady;
   would 'twere done!   *They sit and mark.* 254

1.2   *Enter Petruchio and his man Grumio.*

PETRUCHIO
   Verona, for a while I take my leave
   To see my friends in Padua, but of all
   My best belovèd and approvèd friend,
   Hortensio; and I trow this is his house.   4
   Here, sirrah Grumio, knock, I say.
GRUMIO   Knock, sir? Whom should I knock? Is there any
   man has rebused your worship?   7
PETRUCHIO   Villain, I say, knock me here soundly.   8
GRUMIO   Knock you here, sir? Why, sir, what am I, sir,
   that I should knock you here, sir?
PETRUCHIO
   Villain, I say, knock me at this gate,   11
   And rap me well, or I'll knock your knave's pate.
GRUMIO
   My master is grown quarrelsome. I should knock you
      first,
   And then I know after who comes by the worst.
PETRUCHIO   Will it not be?
   Faith, sirrah, an you'll not knock, I'll ring it.   16
   I'll try how you can *sol fa*, and sing it.   17
                         He wrings him by the ears.
GRUMIO
   Help, masters, help! My master is mad.
PETRUCHIO
   Now knock when I bid you, sirrah villain.

254 s.d. mark observe

1.2. Location: Padua. Before Hortensio's house.
4 trow believe   **7 rebused** (A blunder for *abused*.)   **8 me** i.e., for me.
(But Grumio, perhaps intentionally, misunderstands.)   **11 gate** door
16 ring sound loudly, using a circular knocker (with a pun on *wring*)
17 I'll . . . sing it i.e., I'll make you cry out, howl

Enter Hortensio.

HORTENSIO   How now, what's the matter? My old friend
   Grumio, and my good friend Petruchio? How do you
   all at Verona?

PETRUCHIO
   Signor Hortensio, come you to part the fray?
   Con tutto il cuore, ben trovato, may I say.   24

HORTENSIO
   Alla nostra casa ben venuto,   25
   Molto onorato signor mio Petruchio.—   26
   Rise, Grumio, rise. We will compound this quarrel.   27

GRUMIO   Nay, 'tis no matter, sir, what he 'leges in Latin.   28
   If this be not a lawful cause for me to leave his service!
   Look you, sir: he bid me knock him and rap him
   soundly, sir. Well, was it fit for a servant to use his
   master so, being perhaps, for aught I see, two-and-   32
   thirty, a pip out?   33
   Whom would to God I had well knocked at first,
   Then had not Grumio come by the worst.

PETRUCHIO
   A senseless villain! Good Hortensio,
   I bade the rascal knock upon your gate,
   And could not get him for my heart to do it.

GRUMIO   Knock at the gate? O heavens! Spake you not
   these words plain, "Sirrah, knock me here, rap me
   here, knock me well, and knock me soundly"? And
   come you now with "knocking at the gate"?

PETRUCHIO
   Sirrah, begone, or talk not, I advise you.

HORTENSIO
   Petruchio, patience, I am Grumio's pledge.   44
   Why, this's a heavy chance twixt him and you,   45
   Your ancient, trusty, pleasant servant Grumio.   46
   And tell me now, sweet friend, what happy gale
   Blows you to Padua here from old Verona?

24 Con . . . trovato with all my heart, well met   **25–26 Alla . . . Petruchio** welcome to our house, my much honored Petruchio. (Italian.)
27 compound settle   **28 'leges** alleges   **32–33 two . . . out** i.e., drunk.
(Derived from the card game called *one-and-thirty*.)   **33 pip** a spot on a
playing card. (Hence *a pip out* means "off by one," or "one in excess of
thirty-one.")   **44 pledge** surety   **45 heavy chance** sad occurrence
46 ancient long-standing

PETRUCHIO
Such wind as scatters young men through the world
To seek their fortunes farther than at home,
Where small experience grows. But in a few,   51
Signor Hortensio, thus it stands with me:
Antonio, my father, is deceased,
And I have thrust myself into this maze,
Haply to wive and thrive as best I may.
Crowns in my purse I have, and goods at home,
And so am come abroad to see the world.

HORTENSIO
Petruchio, shall I then come roundly to thee   58
And wish thee to a shrewd ill-favored wife?
Thou'dst thank me but a little for my counsel.
And yet I'll promise thee she shall be rich,
And very rich. But thou'rt too much my friend,
And I'll not wish thee to her.

PETRUCHIO
Signor Hortensio, twixt such friends as we
Few words suffice. And therefore, if thou know
One rich enough to be Petruchio's wife—
As wealth is burden of my wooing dance—   67
Be she as foul as was Florentius' love,   68
As old as Sibyl, and as curst and shrewd   69
As Socrates' Xanthippe, or a worse,   70
She moves me not, or not removes, at least,
Affection's edge in me, were she as rough
As are the swelling Adriatic seas.
I come to wive it wealthily in Padua;
If wealthily, then happily in Padua.

GRUMIO   Nay, look you, sir, he tells you flatly what his
mind is. Why, give him gold enough and marry him   77

---

51 in a few in short   **58 come roundly** speak plainly   **67 burden** undersong, i.e., basis   **68 foul** ugly.   **Florentius' love** (An allusion to Gower's
version in *Confessio Amantis* of the fairy tale of the knight who promised to marry an ugly old woman if she solved the riddle he must
answer. After the fulfillment of all promises, she became young and
beautiful. Another version of this story is Chaucer's "Tale of the Wife of
Bath," from *The Canterbury Tales*.)   **69 Sibyl** prophetess of Cumae to
whom Apollo gave as many years of life as she held grains of sand in
her hand   **70 Xanthippe** the philosopher's notoriously shrewish wife
77 mind intention

to a puppet or an aglet-baby, or an old trot with ne'er 78
a tooth in her head, though she have as many diseases
as two-and-fifty horses. Why, nothing comes amiss, so
money comes withal. 81

HORTENSIO
Petruchio, since we are stepped thus far in,
I will continue that I broached in jest. 83
I can, Petruchio, help thee to a wife
With wealth enough, and young and beauteous,
Brought up as best becomes a gentlewoman.
Her only fault, and that is faults enough,
Is that she is intolerable curst
And shrewd, and froward, so beyond all measure
That, were my state far worser than it is, 90
I would not wed her for a mine of gold.

PETRUCHIO
Hortensio, peace! Thou know'st not gold's effect.
Tell me her father's name and 'tis enough;
For I will board her though she chide as loud 94
As thunder when the clouds in autumn crack.

HORTENSIO
Her father is Baptista Minola,
An affable and courteous gentleman.
Her name is Katharina Minola,
Renowned in Padua for her scolding tongue.

PETRUCHIO
I know her father, though I know not her,
And he knew my deceasèd father well.
I will not sleep, Hortensio, till I see her;
And therefore let me be thus bold with you
To give you over at this first encounter, 104
Unless you will accompany me thither.

GRUMIO [To Hortensio] I pray you, sir, let him go while
the humor lasts. O' my word, an she knew him as well 107
as I do, she would think scolding would do little good
upon him. She may perhaps call him half a score

---

78 **aglet-baby** small figure carved on the tag of a lace.   **trot** old hag;
also, prostitute   81 **withal** with it   83 **that** what   90 **state** estate
94 **board** accost. (A metaphor from naval warfare.)   104 **give you over**
leave you   107 **humor** whim

knaves or so. Why, that's nothing; an he begin once,
he'll rail in his rope tricks. I'll tell you what, sir, an   111
she stand him but a little, he will throw a figure in her   112
face and so disfigure her with it that she shall have
no more eyes to see withal than a cat. You know him
not, sir.

HORTENSIO
Tarry, Petruchio, I must go with thee,
For in Baptista's keep my treasure is.   117
He hath the jewel of my life in hold,   118
His youngest daughter, beautiful Bianca,
And her withholds from me and other more,   120
Suitors to her and rivals in my love,
Supposing it a thing impossible,
For those defects I have before rehearsed,
That ever Katharina will be wooed.
Therefore this order hath Baptista ta'en,
That none shall have access unto Bianca
Till Katharine the curst have got a husband.

GRUMIO   Katharine the curst!
A title for a maid of all titles the worst.

HORTENSIO
Now shall my friend Petruchio do me grace,   130
And offer me disguised in sober robes
To old Baptista as a schoolmaster
Well seen in music, to instruct Bianca,   133
That so I may by this device at least
Have leave and leisure to make love to her,   135
And unsuspected court her by herself.

*Enter Gremio [with a paper], and Lucentio
disguised [as a schoolmaster].*

GRUMIO   Here's no knavery! See, to beguile the old
folks, how the young folks lay their heads together!
Master, master, look about you. Who goes there, ha?

---

111 rope tricks i.e., a blunder for "rhetricks," i.e., rhetoric (?) or tricks
worthy of hanging (?)   **112 stand** withstand. **figure** figure of speech
117 keep keeping (with suggestion of "fortified place" where one would
store a treasure)   **118 hold** confinement (with a similar pun on "strong-
hold")   **120 other** others   **130 grace** a favor   **133 seen** skilled
135 make love to woo

HORTENSIO
  Peace, Grumio, it is the rival of my love.
  Petruchio, stand by awhile.   [*They stand aside.*]
GRUMIO [*Aside*]
  A proper stripling and an amorous!   142
GREMIO [*To Lucentio*]
  O, very well, I have perused the note.   143
  Hark you, sir, I'll have them very fairly bound—
  All books of love, see that at any hand—   145
  And see you read no other lectures to her.   146
  You understand me. Over and besides
  Signor Baptista's liberality,
  I'll mend it with a largess. Take your paper too,   149
                   [*Giving Lucentio the note*]
  And let me have them very well perfumed,   150
  For she is sweeter than perfume itself
  To whom they go to. What will you read to her?
LUCENTIO
  Whate'er I read to her, I'll plead for you
  As for my patron, stand you so assured,
  As firmly as yourself were still in place—   155
  Yea, and perhaps with more successful words
  Than you, unless you were a scholar, sir.
GREMIO
  O this learning, what a thing it is!
GRUMIO [*Aside*]
  O this woodcock, what an ass it is!   159
PETRUCHIO Peace, sirrah!
HORTENSIO [*Coming forward*]
  Grumio, mum!—God save you, Signor Gremio.
GREMIO
  And you are well met, Signor Hortensio.
  Trow you whither I am going? To Baptista Minola.   163
  I promised to inquire carefully
  About a schoolmaster for the fair Bianca,
  And by good fortune I have lighted well

142 proper stripling handsome young fellow. (Said ironically, in reference to Gremio.) **143 note** (Evidently, a list of books for Bianca's tutoring.) **145 at any hand** in any case **146 read . . . lectures** teach no other lessons **149 mend** improve, increase. **largess** gift of money **150 them** i.e., the books **155 as** as if. **in place** present **159 woodcock** (A bird easily caught; proverbially stupid.) **163 Trow** know

On this young man—for learning and behavior
Fit for her turn, well read in poetry
And other books, good ones, I warrant ye.

HORTENSIO
'Tis well. And I have met a gentleman
Hath promised me to help me to another,   171
A fine musician to instruct our mistress.
So shall I no whit be behind in duty
To fair Bianca, so beloved of me.

GREMIO
Beloved of me, and that my deeds shall prove.

GRUMIO [*Aside*]   And that his bags shall prove.   176

HORTENSIO
Gremio, 'tis now no time to vent our love.   177
Listen to me, and if you speak me fair,   178
I'll tell you news indifferent good for either.   179
Here is a gentleman whom by chance I met,
Upon agreement from us to his liking,   181
Will undertake to woo curst Katharine,
Yea, and to marry her, if her dowry please.

GREMIO   So said, so done, is well.
Hortensio, have you told him all her faults?

PETRUCHIO
I know she is an irksome brawling scold.
If that be all, masters, I hear no harm.

GREMIO
No, sayst me so, friend? What countryman?

PETRUCHIO
Born in Verona, old Antonio's son.
My father dead, my fortune lives for me,
And I do hope good days and long to see.

GREMIO
O sir, such a life with such a wife were strange.
But if you have a stomach, to 't i' God's name.
You shall have me assisting you in all.
But will you woo this wildcat?

PETRUCHIO   Will I live?

---

171 **Hath** who has   176 **bags** moneybags   177 **vent** express   178 **fair**
civilly, courteously   179 **indifferent** equally   181 **Upon . . . liking** who,
on terms agreeable to him. (In ll. 213–214 we learn that Bianca's suitors
will *bear his charge of wooing*.)

GRUMIO [*Aside*]
   Will he woo her? Ay, or I'll hang her.
PETRUCHIO
   Why came I hither but to that intent?
   Think you a little din can daunt mine ears?
   Have I not in my time heard lions roar?
   Have I not heard the sea, puffed up with winds,
   Rage like an angry boar chafèd with sweat?
   Have I not heard great ordnance in the field,   202
   And heaven's artillery thunder in the skies?
   Have I not in a pitchèd battle heard
   Loud 'larums, neighing steeds, and trumpets' clang?   205
   And do you tell me of a woman's tongue,
   That gives not half so great a blow to hear
   As will a chestnut in a farmer's fire?
   Tush, tush! Fear boys with bugs.
GRUMIO [*Aside*]   For he fears none.   209
GREMIO   Hortensio, hark.
   This gentleman is happily arrived,   211
   My mind presumes, for his own good and ours.
HORTENSIO
   I promised we would be contributors
   And bear his charge of wooing whatsoe'er.   214
GREMIO
   And so we will, provided that he win her.
GRUMIO [*Aside*]
   I would I were as sure of a good dinner.   216

      Enter Tranio brave [as Lucentio], and Biondello.

TRANIO
   Gentlemen, God save you. If I may be bold,
   Tell me, I beseech you, which is the readiest way
   To the house of Signor Baptista Minola?
BIONDELLO   He that has the two fair daughters, is 't he
   you mean?
TRANIO   Even he, Biondello.
GREMIO
   Hark you, sir, you mean not her to—

---

202 ordnance artillery   **205 'larums** calls to arms   **209 Fear . . . bugs**
frighten children with bugbears, bogeymen   **211 happily** fortunately,
just when needed   **214 charge** expense   **216 s.d. brave** elegantly
dressed

TRANIO
  Perhaps him and her, sir. What have you to do?   224
PETRUCHIO
  Not her that chides, sir, at any hand, I pray.
TRANIO
  I love no chiders, sir. Biondello, let's away.
LUCENTIO [*Aside*]
  Well begun, Tranio.
HORTENSIO   Sir, a word ere you go.
  Are you a suitor to the maid you talk of, yea or no?
TRANIO
  An if I be, sir, is it any offense?
GREMIO
  No, if without more words you will get you hence.
TRANIO
  Why, sir, I pray, are not the streets as free
  For me as for you?
GREMIO   But so is not she.
TRANIO
  For what reason, I beseech you?
GREMIO   For this reason, if you'll know,
  That she's the choice love of Signor Gremio.
HORTENSIO
  That she's the chosen of Signor Hortensio.
TRANIO
  Softly, my masters! If you be gentlemen,
  Do me this right: hear me with patience.
  Baptista is a noble gentleman,
  To whom my father is not all unknown;
  And were his daughter fairer than she is,
  She may more suitors have, and me for one.
  Fair Leda's daughter had a thousand wooers;   242
  Then well one more may fair Bianca have,
  And so she shall. Lucentio shall make one,
  Though Paris came in hope to speed alone.   245
GREMIO
  What, this gentleman will outtalk us all.

---

224 him and her i.e., both Baptista Minola and his daughter. **What . . . do** what's that to you **242 Leda's daughter** Helen of Troy **245 Though** even if. **Paris** Trojan prince who abducted Helen from her husband, Menelaus. **speed** succeed

LUCENTIO
  Sir, give him head. I know he'll prove a jade.   247
PETRUCHIO
  Hortensio, to what end are all these words?
HORTENSIO [*To Tranio*]
  Sir, let me be so bold as ask you,
  Did you yet ever see Baptista's daughter?
TRANIO
  No, sir, but hear I do that he hath two,
  The one as famous for a scolding tongue
  As is the other for beauteous modesty.
PETRUCHIO
  Sir, sir, the first's for me. Let her go by.
GREMIO
  Yea, leave that labor to great Hercules,
  And let it be more than Alcides' twelve.   256
PETRUCHIO
  Sir, understand you this of me, in sooth: 257
  The youngest daughter, whom you hearken for,   258
  Her father keeps from all access of suitors,
  And will not promise her to any man
  Until the elder sister first be wed.
  The younger then is free, and not before.
TRANIO
  If it be so, sir, that you are the man
  Must stead us all, and me amongst the rest;   264
  And if you break the ice and do this feat,
  Achieve the elder, set the younger free
  For our access, whose hap shall be to have her   267
  Will not so graceless be to be ingrate.
HORTENSIO
  Sir, you say well, and well you do conceive.   269
  And since you do profess to be a suitor,
  You must, as we do, gratify this gentleman,   271
  To whom we all rest generally beholding.   272

247 prove a jade tire like an ill-conditioned horse   **256 Alcides'** descendant of Alcaeus (i.e., Hercules, who, noted for the achievement of the twelve great labors, is the only one capable of conquering Katharina)   **257 sooth** truth   **258 hearken for** lie in wait for, seek to win   **264 Must stead** who must help   **267 whose hap** he whose good fortune   **269 conceive** understand   **271 gratify** reward, requite   **272 beholding** beholden, indebted

TRANIO
   Sir, I shall not be slack, in sign whereof,
   Please ye we may contrive this afternoon   274
   And quaff carouses to our mistress' health,   275
   And do as adversaries do in law,   276
   Strive mightily, but eat and drink as friends.

GRUMIO, BIONDELLO
   O excellent motion! Fellows, let's be gone.   278

HORTENSIO
   The motion's good indeed, and be it so.
   Petruchio, I shall be your *ben venuto*.   *Exeunt.* 280

❖

---

274 contrive spend, pass (time) **275 quaff carouses** drink toasts
276 adversaries opposing lawyers **278 motion** suggestion **280 ben
venuto** welcome, i.e., host

2.1 *Enter Katharina and Bianca [with her hands tied].*

BIANCA
Good sister, wrong me not, nor wrong yourself,
To make a bondmaid and a slave of me.
That I disdain. But for these other goods,   3
Unbind my hands, I'll pull them off myself,
Yea, all my raiment, to my petticoat,
Or what you will command me will I do,
So well I know my duty to my elders.

KATHARINA
Of all thy suitors, here I charge thee, tell
Whom thou lov'st best. See thou dissemble not.

BIANCA
Believe me, sister, of all the men alive
I never yet beheld that special face
Which I could fancy more than any other.

KATHARINA
Minion, thou liest. Is 't not Hortensio?   13

BIANCA
If you affect him, sister, here I swear   14
I'll plead for you myself but you shall have him.

KATHARINA
O, then belike you fancy riches more:
You will have Gremio to keep you fair.   17

BIANCA
Is it for him you do envy me so?
Nay, then, you jest, and now I well perceive
You have but jested with me all this while.
I prithee, sister Kate, untie my hands.

KATHARINA
If that be jest, then all the rest was so.

                                        Strikes her.

        Enter Baptista.

BAPTISTA
Why, how now, dame, whence grows this insolence?—

2.1. Location: Padua. Baptista's house.
3 goods possessions   **13 Minion** hussy   **14 affect** love   **17 fair** resplendent with finery

Bianca, stand aside. Poor girl, she weeps.
Go ply thy needle, meddle not with her.—
For shame, thou hilding of a devilish spirit,   26
Why dost thou wrong her that did ne'er wrong thee?
When did she cross thee with a bitter word?

KATHARINA
Her silence flouts me, and I'll be revenged.
                                   Flies after Bianca.

BAPTISTA
What, in my sight? Bianca, get thee in.
                                   Exit [Bianca].

KATHARINA
What, will you not suffer me? Nay, now I see
She is your treasure, she must have a husband;
I must dance barefoot on her wedding day,   33
And for your love to her lead apes in hell.   34
Talk not to me. I will go sit and weep
Till I can find occasion of revenge.   [*Exit.*]

BAPTISTA
Was ever gentleman thus grieved as I?
But who comes here?   38

> *Enter Gremio, Lucentio [as a schoolmaster] in the
> habit of a mean man, Petruchio, with [Hortensio
> as a musician, and] Tranio [as Lucentio] with his
> boy [Biondello] bearing a lute and books.*

GREMIO   Good morrow, neighbor Baptista.
BAPTISTA   Good morrow, neighbor Gremio. God save
you, gentlemen.

PETRUCHIO
And you, good sir. Pray, have you not a daughter
Called Katharina, fair and virtuous?

BAPTISTA
I have a daughter, sir, called Katharina.

GREMIO
You are too blunt. Go to it orderly.

PETRUCHIO
You wrong me, Signor Gremio; give me leave.—

---

26 hilding vicious (hence worthless) beast   **33, 34 dance . . . day, lead
. . . hell** (Popularly supposed to be the fate of old maids.)   **38 s.d. mean**
of low social station. (Said here of a schoolmaster.)

I am a gentleman of Verona, sir,
That, hearing of her beauty and her wit,
Her affability and bashful modesty,
Her wondrous qualities and mild behavior,
Am bold to show myself a forward guest
Within your house, to make mine eye the witness
Of that report which I so oft have heard.
And, for an entrance to my entertainment,   54
I do present you with a man of mine,
                        [*Presenting Hortensio*]
Cunning in music and the mathematics,
To instruct her fully in those sciences,   57
Whereof I know she is not ignorant.
Accept of him, or else you do me wrong.
His name is Litio, born in Mantua.

BAPTISTA
You're welcome, sir, and he, for your good sake.
But for my daughter Katharine, this I know,
She is not for your turn, the more my grief.

PETRUCHIO
I see you do not mean to part with her,
Or else you like not of my company.

BAPTISTA
Mistake me not, I speak but as I find.
Whence are you, sir? What may I call your name?

PETRUCHIO
Petruchio is my name, Antonio's son,
A man well known throughout all Italy.

BAPTISTA
I know him well. You are welcome for his sake.   70

GREMIO
Saving your tale, Petruchio, I pray,   71
Let us that are poor petitioners speak too.
Bacare! You are marvelous forward.   73

PETRUCHIO
O, pardon me, Signor Gremio, I would fain be doing.   74

---

54 entrance entrance fee.   **entertainment** reception   **57 sciences** subjects, branches of knowledge   **70 know** know of (see also l. 105)
71 Saving with all due respect for   **73 Bacare** stand back   **74 fain**
gladly.   **doing** getting on with the business (with sexual suggestion)

GREMIO
  I doubt it not, sir, but you will curse your wooing.—
  Neighbors, this is a gift very grateful, I am sure of it. [*To* 76
  Baptista.] To express the like kindness, myself, that have
  been more kindly beholding to you than any, freely give
  unto you this young scholar [*Presenting Lucentio*],
  that hath been long studying at Rheims, as cunning
  in Greek, Latin, and other languages as the other in
  music and mathematics. His name is Cambio. Pray, 82
  accept his service.
BAPTISTA A thousand thanks, Signor Gremio. Wel-
  come, good Cambio. [*To Tranio.*] But, gentle sir,
  methinks you walk like a stranger. May I be so bold to 86
  know the cause of your coming?
TRANIO
  Pardon me, sir, the boldness is mine own,
  That, being a stranger in this city here,
  Do make myself a suitor to your daughter,
  Unto Bianca, fair and virtuous.
  Nor is your firm resolve unknown to me,
  In the preferment of the eldest sister.
  This liberty is all that I request,
  That upon knowledge of my parentage
  I may have welcome 'mongst the rest that woo,
  And free access and favor as the rest.   97
  And toward the education of your daughters
  I here bestow a simple instrument,
  And this small packet of Greek and Latin books.
  If you accept them, then their worth is great.
       [*Biondello brings forward the lute and books.*]
BAPTISTA
  Lucentio is your name? Of whence, I pray?   102
TRANIO
  Of Pisa, sir, son to Vincentio.
BAPTISTA
  A mighty man of Pisa. By report   104

76 grateful pleasing   **82 Cambio** (In Italian, appropriately, the word
means "change" or "exchange.")   **86 walk like a stranger** keep your
distance, stand apart   **97 favor** leave, permission   **102 Lucentio . . .
name** (Baptista may have learned this information from a note accom-
panying the books and lute.)   **104 report** reputation

I know him well. You are very welcome, sir.
[*To Hortensio.*] Take you the lute, [*To Lucentio*] and you
   the set of books;
You shall go see your pupils presently.   107
Holla, within!
      Enter a Servant.

                  Sirrah, lead these gentlemen
To my daughters, and tell them both
These are their tutors. Bid them use them well.
      [*Exit Servant, with Lucentio and Hortensio.*]
We will go walk a little in the orchard,   111
And then to dinner. You are passing welcome,   112
And so I pray you all to think yourselves.

PETRUCHIO
Signor Baptista, my business asketh haste,
And every day I cannot come to woo.
You knew my father well, and in him me,
Left solely heir to all his lands and goods,
Which I have bettered rather than decreased.
Then tell me, if I get your daughter's love,
What dowry shall I have with her to wife?

BAPTISTA
After my death the one half of my lands,
And in possession twenty thousand crowns.   122

PETRUCHIO
And, for that dowry, I'll assure her of
Her widowhood, be it that she survive me,   124
In all my lands and leases whatsoever.
Let specialties be therefore drawn between us,   126
That covenants may be kept on either hand.

BAPTISTA
Ay, when the special thing is well obtained,
That is, her love; for that is all in all.

PETRUCHIO
Why, that is nothing, for I tell you, Father,
I am as peremptory as she proud-minded;
And where two raging fires meet together,

107 **presently** immediately   111 **orchard** garden   112 **passing** exceedingly   122 **in possession** i.e., in immediate possession   124 **widowhood**
i.e., widow's share of the estate   126 **specialties** terms of contract

They do consume the thing that feeds their fury.
Though little fire grows great with little wind,
Yet extreme gusts will blow out fire and all.
So I to her, and so she yields to me,
For I am rough and woo not like a babe.

BAPTISTA
Well mayst thou woo, and happy be thy speed!
But be thou armed for some unhappy words.

PETRUCHIO
Ay, to the proof, as mountains are for winds,   140
That shakes not, though they blow perpetually.   141

Enter Hortensio [as Litio], with his head broke.

BAPTISTA
How now, my friend, why dost thou look so pale?

HORTENSIO
For fear, I promise you, if I look pale.

BAPTISTA
What, will my daughter prove a good musician?

HORTENSIO
I think she'll sooner prove a soldier.
Iron may hold with her, but never lutes.   146

BAPTISTA
Why, then thou canst not break her to the lute?   147

HORTENSIO
Why, no, for she hath broke the lute to me.
I did but tell her she mistook her frets,   149
And bowed her hand to teach her fingering,
When, with a most impatient devilish spirit,
"Frets, call you these?" quoth she, "I'll fume with them."
And with that word she struck me on the head,
And through the instrument my pate made way;
And there I stood amazèd for a while,
As on a pillory, looking through the lute,   156

---

140 to the proof i.e., in armor, proof against her shrewishness
141 shakes shake.   **s.d. broke** i.e., with a bleeding cut. (Hortensio
usually appears on stage with his head emerging through a broken
lute.)   **146 hold with** hold out against   **147 break** train (with pun in the
next line)   **149 frets** ridges or bars on the fingerboard of the lute. (But
Kate puns on the sense of "fume," "be indignant.")   **156 pillory**
wooden collar used as punishment

While she did call me rascal fiddler
And twangling Jack, with twenty such vile terms,   158
As had she studied to misuse me so.

PETRUCHIO
Now, by the world, it is a lusty wench!   160
I love her ten times more than e'er I did.
O, how I long to have some chat with her!

BAPTISTA [*To Hortensio*]
Well, go with me and be not so discomfited.
Proceed in practice with my younger daughter;   164
She's apt to learn and thankful for good turns.—
Signor Petruchio, will you go with us,
Or shall I send my daughter Kate to you?

PETRUCHIO
I pray you, do.   *Exeunt. Manet Petruchio.*
            I'll attend her here,   168
And woo her with some spirit when she comes.
Say that she rail, why then I'll tell her plain
She sings as sweetly as a nightingale.
Say that she frown, I'll say she looks as clear
As morning roses newly washed with dew.
Say she be mute and will not speak a word,
Then I'll commend her volubility
And say she uttereth piercing eloquence.
If she do bid me pack, I'll give her thanks,   177
As though she bid me stay by her a week.
If she deny to wed, I'll crave the day   179
When I shall ask the banns and when be married.   180
But here she comes; and now, Petruchio, speak.

            Enter Katharina.

Good morrow, Kate, for that's your name, I hear.

KATHARINA
Well have you heard, but something hard of hearing.   183
They call me Katharine that do talk of me.

PETRUCHIO
You lie, in faith, for you are called plain Kate,

---

158 Jack knave   **160 lusty** lively   **164 practice** instruction   **168 s.d.
Manet** he remains onstage   **177 pack** begone   **179 deny** refuse   **180 ask
the banns** have a reading of the required announcement in church of a
forthcoming marriage   **183 heard, hard** (Pronounced nearly alike.)

And bonny Kate and sometimes Kate the curst;
But Kate, the prettiest Kate in Christendom,
Kate of Kate Hall, my superdainty Kate,
For dainties are all Kates, and therefore, Kate,   189
Take this of me, Kate of my consolation: 190
Hearing thy mildness praised in every town,
Thy virtues spoke of, and thy beauty sounded,   192
Yet not so deeply as to thee belongs,
Myself am moved to woo thee for my wife.

KATHARINA
Moved? In good time! Let him that moved you hither   195
Remove you hence. I knew you at the first
You were a movable.

PETRUCHIO   Why, what's a movable?   197

KATHARINA
A joint stool.

PETRUCHIO   Thou hast hit it. Come, sit on me.   198

KATHARINA
Asses are made to bear, and so are you.   199

PETRUCHIO
Women are made to bear, and so are you.

KATHARINA
No such jade as you, if me you mean.   201

PETRUCHIO
Alas, good Kate, I will not burden thee,
For knowing thee to be but young and light.   203

KATHARINA
Too light for such a swain as you to catch,   204
And yet as heavy as my weight should be.

PETRUCHIO
Should be? Should—buzz!   206

189 all Kates (with a quibble on *cates*, confections, delicacies) **190 of me** from me **192 sounded** proclaimed (with a quibble on "plumbed," as indicated by *deeply* in the next line) **195 In good time** forsooth, indeed **197 movable** (1) one easily changed or dissuaded (2) an article of furniture **198 joint stool** a well-fitted stool made by an expert craftsman **199 bear** carry (with puns in the following lines suggesting "bear children" and "support a man during sexual intercourse") **201 jade** an ill-conditioned horse **203 light** (1) of delicate stature (2) lascivious (3) lacking a *burden* (see previous line) in the musical sense of lacking a bass undersong or accompaniment (4) elusive (in the following line) **204 swain** young rustic in love **206 buzz** i.e., a bee (punning on *be*) should make a buzzing sound; also, an interjection expressing impatience or contempt.

KATHARINA   Well ta'en, and like a buzzard. 206

PETRUCHIO
O slow-winged turtle, shall a buzzard take thee?

KATHARINA
Ay, for a turtle, as he takes a buzzard.

PETRUCHIO
Come, come, you wasp, i' faith, you are too angry. 209

KATHARINA
If I be waspish, best beware my sting.

PETRUCHIO
My remedy is then to pluck it out.

KATHARINA
Ay, if the fool could find it where it lies.

PETRUCHIO
Who knows not where a wasp does wear his sting?
In his tail.

KATHARINA   In his tongue.

PETRUCHIO   Whose tongue?

KATHARINA
Yours, if you talk of tails, and so farewell. 217

PETRUCHIO
What, with my tongue in your tail? Nay, come again.
Good Kate, I am a gentleman—

KATHARINA   That I'll try. *She strikes him.*

PETRUCHIO
I swear I'll cuff you, if you strike again.

KATHARINA   So may you lose your arms.
If you strike me, you are no gentleman,
And if no gentleman, why then no arms. 223

PETRUCHIO
A herald, Kate? O, put me in thy books! 224

KATHARINA   What is your crest, a coxcomb? 225

---

206 buzzard (1) figuratively, a fool (2) in the next line, an inferior kind of
hawk, fit only to overtake a slow-winged *turtle* or turtledove, as Petruchio might overtake Kate (3) a buzzing insect, caught by a turtle
209 wasp i.e., waspish, scolding woman (but suggested by *buzzard*,
buzzing insect)   **217 talk of tails** i.e., idly tells stories (with pun on *tale,
tail*)   **223 no arms** no coat of arms (with pun on *arms* as limbs of the
body)   **224 books** (1) books of heraldry, heraldic registers (2) grace,
favor   **225 crest** (1) armorial device (2) a rooster's comb, setting up the
joke on *coxcomb*, the cap of the court fool

PETRUCHIO
A combless cock, so Kate will be my hen.
KATHARINA
No cock of mine; you crow too like a craven.   227
PETRUCHIO
Nay, come, Kate, come, you must not look so sour.
KATHARINA
It is my fashion when I see a crab.   229
PETRUCHIO
Why, here's no crab, and therefore look not sour.
KATHARINA   There is, there is.
PETRUCHIO
Then show it me.
KATHARINA   Had I a glass, I would.
PETRUCHIO   What, you mean my face?
KATHARINA   Well aimed of such a young one.   234
PETRUCHIO
Now, by Saint George, I am too young for you.
KATHARINA
Yet you are withered.
PETRUCHIO   'Tis with cares.
KATHARINA   I care not.
PETRUCHIO
Nay, hear you, Kate. In sooth, you scape not so.
KATHARINA
I chafe you if I tarry. Let me go.
PETRUCHIO
No, not a whit. I find you passing gentle.
'Twas told me you were rough and coy and sullen,   240
And now I find report a very liar,
For thou art pleasant, gamesome, passing courteous,   242
But slow in speech, yet sweet as springtime flowers.   243
Thou canst not frown, thou canst not look askance,   244
Nor bite the lip, as angry wenches will,
Nor hast thou pleasure to be cross in talk;
But thou with mildness entertain'st thy wooers,
With gentle conference, soft and affable.

227 craven a cock that is not "game" or willing to fight   **229 crab** crab apple   **234 aimed of** guessed for.   **young** i.e., inexperienced. (But Petruchio picks up the word in the sense of "strong.")   **240 coy** disdainful   **242 gamesome** playful, spirited   **243 But slow** never anything but slow   **244 askance** scornfully

Why does the world report that Kate doth limp?
O slanderous world! Kate like the hazel twig
Is straight and slender, and as brown in hue
As hazelnuts, and sweeter than the kernels.
O, let me see thee walk. Thou dost not halt.   253

KATHARINA
Go, fool, and whom thou keep'st command.   254

PETRUCHIO
Did ever Dian so become a grove   255
As Kate this chamber with her princely gait?
O, be thou Dian, and let her be Kate,
And then let Kate be chaste and Dian sportful!   258

KATHARINA
Where did you study all this goodly speech?

PETRUCHIO
It is extempore, from my mother wit.   260

KATHARINA
A witty mother! Witless else her son.   261

PETRUCHIO   Am I not wise?   262

KATHARINA   Yes, keep you warm.   263

PETRUCHIO
Marry, so I mean, sweet Katharine, in thy bed.
And therefore, setting all this chat aside,
Thus in plain terms: your father hath consented
That you shall be my wife; your dowry 'greed on;
And, will you, nill you, I will marry you.   268
Now, Kate, I am a husband for your turn,   269
For by this light, whereby I see thy beauty—
Thy beauty that doth make me like thee well—
Thou must be married to no man but me;

> *Enter Baptista, Gremio, [and] Tranio [as*
> *Lucentio].*

For I am he am born to tame you, Kate,

---

253 halt limp   **254 whom thou keep'st** i.e., those whom you employ,
your servants   **255 Dian** Diana, goddess of the hunt and of chastity.
become adorn   **258 sportful** amorous   **260 mother wit** native intelligence   **261 Witless . . . son** i.e., without the intelligence inherited from
her, he would have none at all   **262–263 wise . . . warm** (An allusion to
the proverbial phrase "enough wit to keep oneself warm.")   **268 nill
you** will you not   **269 for your turn** to suit you

And bring you from a wild Kate to a Kate   274
Conformable as other household Kates.
Here comes your father. Never make denial;
I must and will have Katharine to my wife.

BAPTISTA
Now, Signor Petruchio, how speed you with my
    daughter?

PETRUCHIO
How but well, sir, how but well?
It were impossible I should speed amiss.   280

BAPTISTA
Why, how now, daughter Katharine, in your dumps?

KATHARINA
Call you me daughter? Now, I promise you,   282
You have showed a tender fatherly regard,
To wish me wed to one half lunatic,
A madcap ruffian and a swearing Jack,
That thinks with oaths to face the matter out.   286

PETRUCHIO
Father, 'tis thus: yourself and all the world,
That talked of her, have talked amiss of her.
If she be curst, it is for policy,   289
For she's not froward, but modest as the dove.   290
She is not hot, but temperate as the morn.
For patience she will prove a second Grissel,   292
And Roman Lucrece for her chastity.   293
And to conclude, we have 'greed so well together
That upon Sunday is the wedding day.

KATHARINA
I'll see thee hanged on Sunday first.

GREMIO   Hark, Petruchio, she says she'll see thee hanged
first.

TRANIO
Is this your speeding? Nay then, good night our part!

274 **wild Kate** (with a quibble on *wildcat*)   280 **speed** fare, get on
282 **promise** assure   286 **face** brazen   289 **policy** cunning, ulterior
motive   290 **froward** willful, perverse   292 **Grissel** patient Griselda, the
epitome of wifely patience and devotion (whose story was told by
Chaucer in "The Clerk's Tale" of *The Canterbury Tales* and earlier by
Boccaccio and Petrarch)   293 **Roman Lucrece** Lucretia, a Roman lady
who took her own life after her chastity had been violated by the Tarquin prince, Sextus. (Shakespeare told the story in *The Rape of Lucrece*.)

PETRUCHIO
Be patient, gentlemen, I choose her for myself.
If she and I be pleased, what's that to you?
'Tis bargained twixt us twain, being alone,
That she shall still be curst in company.
I tell you, 'tis incredible to believe
How much she loves me. O, the kindest Kate!
She hung about my neck, and kiss on kiss
She vied so fast, protesting oath on oath,   307
That in a twink she won me to her love.
O, you are novices! 'Tis a world to see   309
How tame, when men and women are alone,
A meacock wretch can make the curstest shrew.—   311
Give me thy hand, Kate. I will unto Venice
To buy apparel 'gainst the wedding day.—   313
Provide the feast, Father, and bid the guests;
I will be sure my Katharine shall be fine.   315

BAPTISTA
I know not what to say. But give me your hands.
God send you joy, Petruchio! 'Tis a match.

GREMIO, TRANIO
Amen, say we. We will be witnesses.

PETRUCHIO
Father, and wife, and gentlemen, adieu.
I will to Venice. Sunday comes apace.
We will have rings and things, and fine array;
And kiss me, Kate, we will be married o' Sunday.   322
          Exeunt Petruchio and Katharine [separately].

GREMIO
Was ever match clapped up so suddenly?   323

BAPTISTA
Faith, gentlemen, now I play a merchant's part,
And venture madly on a desperate mart.   325

TRANIO
'Twas a commodity lay fretting by you;   326
'Twill bring you gain, or perish on the seas.

---

307 vied went me one better, kiss for kiss   **309 a world** worth a whole
world   **311 meacock** cowardly   **313 'gainst** in anticipation of   **315 fine**
elegantly dressed   **322 kiss me** (Petruchio probably kisses her.)
323 clapped up settled (by a shaking of hands)   **325 desperate mart**
risky venture   **326 lay fretting** i.e., which lay in storage being destroyed
by moths, weevils, or spoilage (with a pun on "chafing")

BAPTISTA
  The gain I seek is quiet in the match.
GREMIO
  No doubt but he hath got a quiet catch.   329
  But now, Baptista, to your younger daughter.
  Now is the day we long have lookèd for.
  I am your neighbor, and was suitor first.
TRANIO
  And I am one that love Bianca more
  Than words can witness or your thoughts can guess.
GREMIO
  Youngling, thou canst not love so dear as I.
TRANIO
  Graybeard, thy love doth freeze.
GREMIO   But thine doth fry.
  Skipper, stand back. 'Tis age that nourisheth.   337
TRANIO
  But youth in ladies' eyes that flourisheth.
BAPTISTA
  Content you, gentlemen. I will compound this strife.   339
  'Tis deeds must win the prize, and he of both   340
  That can assure my daughter greatest dower
  Shall have my Bianca's love.
  Say, Signor Gremio, what can you assure her?
GREMIO
  First, as you know, my house within the city
  Is richly furnishèd with plate and gold,
  Basins and ewers to lave her dainty hands;   346
  My hangings all of Tyrian tapestry;   347
  In ivory coffers I have stuffed my crowns;
  In cypress chests my arras counterpoints,   349
  Costly apparel, tents, and canopies,   350
  Fine linen, Turkey cushions bossed with pearl,   351
  Valance of Venice gold in needlework,   352
  Pewter and brass, and all things that belongs
  To house or housekeeping. Then at my farm

---

329 quiet catch (Said ironically; Gremio is sure that Kate will be anything but quiet.)   **337 Skipper** flighty fellow   **339 compound** settle
340 he of both i.e., the one of you two   **346 lave** wash   **347 Tyrian** dark
red or purple   **349 arras counterpoints** counterpanes of tapestry
350 tents bed-curtains   **351 Turkey** Turkish.   **bossed** embossed
352 Valance drapery around the canopy or bed frame

I have a hundred milch kine to the pail,   355
Sixscore fat oxen standing in my stalls,
And all things answerable to this portion.   357
Myself am struck in years, I must confess,   358
And if I die tomorrow, this is hers,
If whilst I live she will be only mine.

TRANIO
That "only" came well in. Sir, list to me:
I am my father's heir and only son.
If I may have your daughter to my wife,
I'll leave her houses three or four as good,
Within rich Pisa walls, as any one
Old Signor Gremio has in Padua,
Besides two thousand ducats by the year   367
Of fruitful land, all which shall be her jointure.   368
What, have I pinched you, Signor Gremio?

GREMIO
Two thousand ducats by the year of land!
[*Aside.*] My land amounts not to so much in all.—
That she shall have, besides an argosy   372
That now is lying in Marseilles' road.   373
[*To Tranio.*] What, have I choked you with an argosy?

TRANIO
Gremio, 'tis known my father hath no less
Than three great argosies, besides two galliases   376
And twelve tight galleys. These I will assure her,   377
And twice as much, whate'er thou offerest next.

GREMIO
Nay, I have offered all. I have no more,
And she can have no more than all I have.
[*To Baptista.*] If you like me, she shall have me and mine.

TRANIO
Why, then the maid is mine from all the world,
By your firm promise. Gremio is outvied.

BAPTISTA
I must confess your offer is the best;

355 milch kine to the pail dairy cattle   **357 answerable to** on the same
scale as   **358 struck** advanced   **367 ducats** gold coins   **368 Of** from.
jointure marriage settlement   **372 argosy** merchant vessel of the largest
size   **373 road** roadstead, harbor   **376 galliases** heavy, low-built vessels   **377 tight** watertight

And, let your father make her the assurance,   385
She is your own; else, you must pardon me.
If you should die before him, where's her dower?

TRANIO
That's but a cavil. He is old, I young.

GREMIO
And may not young men die as well as old?

BAPTISTA
Well, gentlemen, I am thus resolved:
On Sunday next, you know
My daughter Katharine is to be married.
Now on the Sunday following shall Bianca
Be bride [*To Tranio*] to you, if you make this assurance;
If not, to Signor Gremio.
And so I take my leave, and thank you both.   *Exit.*

GREMIO
Adieu, good neighbor.—Now I fear thee not.
Sirrah young gamester, your father were a fool
To give thee all, and in his waning age
Set foot under thy table. Tut, a toy!   400
An old Italian fox is not so kind, my boy.   *Exit.*

TRANIO
A vengeance on your crafty withered hide!
Yet I have faced it with a card of ten.   403
'Tis in my head to do my master good.
I see no reason but supposed Lucentio
Must get a father, called supposed Vincentio,
And that's a wonder. Fathers commonly
Do get their children; but in this case of wooing,   408
A child shall get a sire, if I fail not of my cunning.
                                             Exit.

❖

385 let provided   **400 Set . . . table** i.e., become a dependent in your
household.   **a toy** nonsense   **403 faced . . . ten** brazened it out with only
a ten-spot of cards   **408 get** beget (with a play on *get*, obtain, in l. 406)

3.1 *Enter Lucentio [as Cambio], Hortensio [as Litio], and Bianca.*

LUCENTIO
Fiddler, forbear. You grow too forward, sir.
Have you so soon forgot the entertainment
Her sister Katharine welcomed you withal?

HORTENSIO
But, wrangling pedant, this is
The patroness of heavenly harmony.
Then give me leave to have prerogative,   6
And when in music we have spent an hour
Your lecture shall have leisure for as much.   8

LUCENTIO
Preposterous ass, that never read so far   9
To know the cause why music was ordained!
Was it not to refresh the mind of mån
After his studies or his usual pain?   12
Then give me leave to read philosophy,
And, while I pause, serve in your harmony.   14

HORTENSIO
Sirrah, I will not bear these braves of thine.   15

BIANCA
Why, gentlemen, you do me double wrong
To strive for that which resteth in my choice.
I am no breeching scholar in the schools;   18
I'll not be tied to hours nor 'pointed times,
But learn my lessons as I please myself.
And, to cut off all strife, here sit we down.
[*To Hortensio.*] Take you your instrument, play you the
    whiles;
His lecture will be done ere you have tuned.

HORTENSIO
You'll leave his lecture when I am in tune?

LUCENTIO
That will be never. Tune your instrument.
                    [*Hortensio moves aside and tunes.*]

3.1. Location: The same.
6 prerogative precedence   **8 lecture** lesson   **9 Preposterous** inverting
the natural order of things, unreasonable   **12 pain** labor   **14 serve in**
present, serve up   **15 braves** insults   **18 breeching scholar** i.e., schoolboy liable to be whipped

BIANCA   Where left we last?
LUCENTIO   Here, madam. [*Reads.*]
  "Hic ibat Simois; hic est Sigeia tellus;   28
  Hic steterat Priami regia celsa senis."   29
BIANCA   Conster them.   30
LUCENTIO   *"Hic ibat,"* as I told you before, *"Simois,"* I
  am Lucentio, *"hic est,"* son unto Vincentio of Pisa,
  "Sigeia tellus," disguised thus to get your love; *"Hic
  steterat,"* and that Lucentio that comes a-wooing,
  "Priami," is my man Tranio, *"regia,"* bearing my port,   35
  "celsa senis," that we might beguile the old panta-   36
  loon.   37
HORTENSIO   Madam, my instrument's in tune.
BIANCA   Let's hear. [*He plays.*] O fie! The treble jars.
LUCENTIO   Spit in the hole, man, and tune again.   40
                              [*Hortensio moves aside.*]
BIANCA   Now let me see if I can conster it: *"Hic ibat Si-
  mois,"* I know you not, *"hic est Sigeia tellus,"* I trust
  you not; *"Hic steterat Priami,"* take heed he hear us
  not, *"regia,"* presume not, *"celsa senis,"* despair not.
HORTENSIO
  Madam, 'tis now in tune.   [*He plays again.*]
LUCENTIO   All but the bass.
HORTENSIO
  The bass is right; 'tis the base knave that jars.
  [*Aside.*] How fiery and forward our pedant is!
  Now, for my life, the knave doth court my love.
  Pedascule, I'll watch you better yet.   49
BIANCA [*To Lucentio*]
  In time I may believe, yet I mistrust.
LUCENTIO
  Mistrust it not, for, sure, Aeacides   51
  Was Ajax, called so from his grandfather.

28–29 Hic . . . senis here flowed the river Simois; here is the Sigeian
land; here stood the lofty palace of old Priam. (Ovid, *Heroides*,
1.33–34.)   **30 Conster** construe   **35 port** social position, style of
living   **36–37 pantaloon** foolish old man, i.e., Gremio   **40 Spit in the
hole** i.e., to make the peg stick   **49 Pedascule** (A word contemptuously
coined by Hortensio, the vocative of *pedasculus*, little pedant.)
51 Aeacides descendant of Aeacus, King of Aegina, father of Telamon
and grandfather of Ajax. (Lucentio is pretending to go on with his
lesson.)

BIANCA
　I must believe my master; else, I promise you,
　I should be arguing still upon that doubt.
　But let it rest.—Now, Litio, to you:
　Good master, take it not unkindly, pray,
　That I have been thus pleasant with you both.   57
HORTENSIO [*To Lucentio*]
　You may go walk, and give me leave awhile.
　My lessons make no music in three parts.
LUCENTIO
　Are you so formal, sir? Well, I must wait,   60
　[*Aside*] And watch withal; for, but I be deceived,   61
　Our fine musician groweth amorous.
　　　　　　　　　　　　　　[*He moves aside.*]
HORTENSIO
　Madam, before you touch the instrument,
　To learn the order of my fingering,   64
　I must begin with rudiments of art,
　To teach you gamut in a briefer sort,   66
　More pleasant, pithy, and effectual
　Than hath been taught by any of my trade.
　And there it is in writing, fairly drawn.   69
　　　　　　　　　　　　　　[*He gives her a paper.*]
BIANCA
　Why, I am past my gamut long ago.
HORTENSIO
　Yet read the gamut of Hortensio.
BIANCA [*Reads*]
　"*Gamut* I am, the ground of all accord,   72
　A re, to plead Hortensio's passion;
　B mi, Bianca, take him for thy lord,
　C fa ut, that loves with all affection.   75
　D sol re, one clef, two notes have I;
　E la mi, show pity, or I die."

57 pleasant merry **60 formal** precise **61 but** unless **64 order**
method **66 gamut** the scale, from the alphabet name (*gamma*) of the
first note plus *ut*, its syllable name, now commonly called *do*. (The
gamut of Hortensio begins on G instead of on C.) **69 drawn** set out,
copied **72 ground** bass note, foundation. **accord** harmony **75 fa ut**
(The note C is the fourth note, or *fa*, of a scale based on G, but is the
first note, *ut*, or *do*, of the more universal major scale based on C.
Similarly, Đ is fifth note or *sol* in the G scale but second or *re* in the C
scale; similarly with E as sixth and third.)

Call you this gamut? Tut, I like it not.
Old fashions please me best; I am not so nice   79
To change true rules for odd inventions.

> *Enter a [Servant as] messenger.*

SERVANT
Mistress, your father prays you leave your books
And help to dress your sister's chamber up.
You know tomorrow is the wedding day.

BIANCA
Farewell, sweet masters both, I must be gone.
> [*Exeunt Bianca and Servant.*]

LUCENTIO
Faith, mistress, then I have no cause to stay.   [*Exit.*]

HORTENSIO
But I have cause to pry into this pedant.
Methinks he looks as though he were in love.
Yet if thy thoughts, Bianca, be so humble
To cast thy wandering eyes on every stale,   89
Seize thee that list. If once I find thee ranging,   90
Hortensio will be quit with thee by changing.   *Exit.* 91

❖

3.2   *Enter Baptista, Gremio, Tranio [as Lucentio],*
Katharine, Bianca, [Lucentio as Cambio], and
others, attendants.

BAPTISTA [*To Tranio*]
Signor Lucentio, this is the 'pointed day
That Katharine and Petruchio should be married,
And yet we hear not of our son-in-law.
What will be said? What mockery will it be,
To want the bridegroom when the priest attends   5
To speak the ceremonial rites of marriage?
What says Lucentio to this shame of ours?

---

79 nice capricious   **89 stale** decoy, bait   **90 Seize . . . list** let him who
wants you have you.   **ranging** inconstant   **91 be quit** get even.   **chang-**
ing i.e., loving another

3.2. Location: Padua. Before Baptista's house.
5 want lack

KATHARINA
  No shame but mine. I must, forsooth, be forced
  To give my hand opposed against my heart
  Unto a mad-brain rudesby full of spleen,   10
  Who wooed in haste and means to wed at leisure.
  I told you, I, he was a frantic fool,
  Hiding his bitter jests in blunt behavior.
  And, to be noted for a merry man,
  He'll woo a thousand, 'point the day of marriage,
  Make friends, invite, and proclaim the banns,
  Yet never means to wed where he hath wooed.
  Now must the world point at poor Katharine
  And say, "Lo, there is mad Petruchio's wife,
  If it would please him come and marry her!"

TRANIO
  Patience, good Katharine, and Baptista too.
  Upon my life, Petruchio means but well,
  Whatever fortune stays him from his word.
  Though he be blunt, I know him passing wise;
  Though he be merry, yet withal he's honest.

KATHARINA
  Would Katharine had never seen him though!
                                    Exit weeping.

BAPTISTA
  Go, girl, I cannot blame thee now to weep,
  For such an injury would vex a very saint,
  Much more a shrew of thy impatient humor.

    Enter Biondello.

BIONDELLO Master, master! News, and such old news 30
as you never heard of!
BAPTISTA Is it new and old too? How may that be?
BIONDELLO Why, is it not news to hear of Petruchio's
coming?
BAPTISTA Is he come?
BIONDELLO Why, no, sir.
BAPTISTA What, then?
BIONDELLO He is coming.
BAPTISTA When will he be here?

---

10 rudesby unmannerly fellow. **spleen** i.e., changeable temper **30 old**
rare; or perhaps referring to Petruchio's old clothes

BIONDELLO When he stands where I am and sees you
there.

TRANIO But say, what to thine old news?   42

BIONDELLO Why, Petruchio is coming in a new hat and
an old jerkin; a pair of old breeches thrice turned; a   44
pair of boots that have been candle-cases, one buck-   45
led, another laced; an old rusty sword ta'en out of the
town armory, with a broken hilt, and chapeless; with   47
two broken points; his horse hipped, with an old   48
mothy saddle and stirrups of no kindred; besides,
possessed with the glanders and like to mose in the   50
chine, troubled with the lampass, infected with the   51
fashions, full of windgalls, sped with spavins, rayed   52
with the yellows, past cure of the fives, stark spoiled   53
with the staggers, begnawn with the bots, swayed in   54
the back and shoulder-shotten; near-legged before,   55
and with a half-cheeked bit and a headstall of sheep's   56
leather which, being restrained to keep him from   57
stumbling, hath been often burst and now repaired
with knots; one girth six times pieced, and a woman's   59

42 to about **44 jerkin** man's jacket. **turned** i.e., with the material
reversed to get more wear **45 candle-cases** i.e., discarded boots, used
only as a receptacle for candle ends **47 chapeless** without the chape,
the metal plate or mounting of a scabbard, especially that which covers
the point **48 points** tagged laces for attaching hose to doublet. **hipped**
lamed in the hip. (Almost all the diseases here named are described in
Gervase Markham's *How to Choose, Ride, Train, and Diet both Hunting
Horses and Running Horses . . . Also a Discourse of Horsemanship*,
probably first published in 1593.) **50 glanders** contagious disease in
horses causing swelling the jaw and mucous discharge from
the nostrils **50–51 mose in the chine** suffer from glanders **51 lampass**
a thick spongy flesh growing over a horse's upper teeth and hindering
his eating **52 fashions** i.e., farcins, or farcy, a disease like glanders.
windgalls soft tumors or swellings generally found on the fetlock joint,
so called from having been supposed to contain air. **sped** far gone.
spavins a disease of the hock, marked by a small bony enlargement
inside the leg. **rayed** defiled **53 yellows** jaundice. **fives** avives, a
glandular disease causing swelling behind the ear **54 staggers** a
disease causing palsylike staggering. **bots** parasitic worms
55 shoulder-shotten with sprained or dislocated shoulder. **near-legged
before** with knock-kneed forelegs **56 half-cheeked bit** one to which the
bridle is attached halfway up the cheek or sidepiece and thus not giving
sufficient control over the horse. **headstall** part of the bridle over the
head **56–57 sheep's leather** (i.e., of inferior quality; pigskin was used
for strongest harness) **57 restrained** drawn back **59 pieced** mended

crupper of velour, which hath two letters for her name 60
fairly set down in studs, and here and there pieced
with packthread.

BAPTISTA Who comes with him?

BIONDELLO O, sir, his lackey, for all the world capari- 64
soned like the horse; with a linen stock on one leg and 65
a kersey boot-hose on the other, gartered with a red 66
and blue list; an old hat, and the humor of forty fancies 67
pricked in 't for a feather—a monster, a very monster 68
in apparel, and not like a Christian footboy or a gentleman's lackey.

TRANIO

'Tis some odd humor pricks him to this fashion;   71
Yet oftentimes he goes but mean-appareled.

BAPTISTA I am glad he's come, howsoe'er he comes.

BIONDELLO Why, sir, he comes not.

BAPTISTA Didst thou not say he comes?

BIONDELLO Who? That Petruchio came?

BAPTISTA Ay, that Petruchio came.

BIONDELLO No, sir, I say his horse comes, with him on
his back.

BAPTISTA Why, that's all one.   80

BIONDELLO

Nay, by Saint Jamy,
I hold you a penny,   82
A horse and a man
Is more than one,
And yet not many.

Enter Petruchio and Grumio.

PETRUCHIO

Come, where be these gallants? Who's at home?

BAPTISTA You are welcome, sir.

PETRUCHIO And yet I come not well.

BAPTISTA And yet you halt not.   89

---

60 crupper leather loop passing under the horse's tail and fastened to
the saddle. **velour** velvet **64–65 caparisoned** outfitted **65 stock**
stocking **66 kersey boot-hose** overstocking of coarse material for
wearing under boots **67 list** strip of cloth. **the humor . . . fancies** i.e.,
with a caprice equal to some forty imaginings (?) **68 pricked** pinned
71 humor pricks whim that spurs **80 all one** the same thing **82 hold**
wager **89 halt** limp, move slowly

TRANIO
   Not so well appareled as I wish you were.
PETRUCHIO
   Were it better, I should rush in thus.   91
   But where is Kate? Where is my lovely bride?
   How does my father? Gentles, methinks you frown.
   And wherefore gaze this goodly company
   As if they saw some wondrous monument,   95
   Some comet, or unusual prodigy?   96
BAPTISTA
   Why, sir, you know this is your wedding day.
   First were we sad, fearing you would not come,
   Now sadder that you come so unprovided.   99
   Fie, doff this habit, shame to your estate,   100
   An eyesore to our solemn festival!
TRANIO
   And tell us what occasion of import
   Hath all so long detained you from your wife
   And sent you hither so unlike yourself?
PETRUCHIO
   Tedious it were to tell, and harsh to hear.
   Sufficeth I am come to keep my word,
   Though in some part enforcèd to digress,   107
   Which at more leisure I will so excuse
   As you shall well be satisfied withal.
   But where is Kate? I stay too long from her.
   The morning wears; 'tis time we were at church.
TRANIO
   See not your bride in these unreverent robes.
   Go to my chamber; put on clothes of mine.
PETRUCHIO
   Not I, believe me. Thus I'll visit her.
BAPTISTA
   But thus, I trust, you will not marry her.
PETRUCHIO
   Good sooth, even thus. Therefore ha' done with words.
   To me she's married, not unto my clothes.

---

91 Were it even if it (my apparel) were.   **rush** come quickly (referring to
halt not in l. 89)   **95 monument** portent   **96 prodigy** omen   **99 unprovided** ill equipped   **100 estate** position, station   **107 digress** i.e., deviate
from my promise

Could I repair what she will wear in me   118
As I can change these poor accoutrements,
'Twere well for Kate and better for myself.
But what a fool am I to chat with you,
When I should bid good morrow to my bride
And seal the title with a lovely kiss!   *Exit.* 123

TRANIO
He hath some meaning in his mad attire.
We will persuade him, be it possible,
To put on better ere he go to church.

BAPTISTA
I'll after him and see the event of this.   127
          Exit [with all but Tranio and Lucentio].

TRANIO
But, sir, love concerneth us to add   128
Her father's liking, which to bring to pass,   129
As I before imparted to your worship,
I am to get a man—whate'er he be
It skills not much, we'll fit him to our turn—   132
And he shall be Vincentio of Pisa,
And make assurance here in Padua
Of greater sums than I have promisèd.
So shall you quietly enjoy your hope
And marry sweet Bianca with consent.

LUCENTIO
Were it not that my fellow schoolmaster
Doth watch Bianca's steps so narrowly,
'Twere good, methinks, to steal our marriage,   140
Which once performed, let all the world say no,
I'll keep mine own, despite of all the world.

TRANIO
That by degrees we mean to look into,
And watch our vantage in this business.   144
We'll overreach the graybeard, Gremio,
The narrow-prying father, Minola,   146

---

118 Could . . . me if I could amend in my character what she'll have to
put up with   **123 lovely** loving   **127 event** outcome   **128–129 love . . .
liking** i.e., our love plot to secure Bianca makes it our business to
secure Baptista's approval of the feigned "Lucentio" as wooer
132 skills matters   **140 steal our marriage** i.e., elope   **144 vantage**
opportunity, advantage   **146 narrow-prying** suspicious, watchful

The quaint musician, amorous Litio,   147
All for my master's sake, Lucentio.

    Enter Gremio.

Signor Gremio, came you from the church?

GREMIO
As willingly as e'er I came from school.

TRANIO
And is the bride and bridegroom coming home?

GREMIO
A bridegroom, say you? 'Tis a groom indeed,   152
A grumbling groom, and that the girl shall find.

TRANIO
Curster than she? Why, 'tis impossible.

GREMIO
Why, he's a devil, a devil, a very fiend.

TRANIO
Why, she's a devil, a devil, the devil's dam.   156

GREMIO
Tut, she's a lamb, a dove, a fool to him.   157
I'll tell you, Sir Lucentio. When the priest
Should ask if Katharine should be his wife,
"Ay, by gogs wouns," quoth he, and swore so loud   160
That all amazed the priest let fall the book,
And as he stooped again to take it up
This mad-brained bridegroom took him such a cuff   163
That down fell priest and book, and book and priest.
"Now take them up," quoth he, "if any list."   165

TRANIO
What said the wench when he rose again?

GREMIO
Trembled and shook, forwhy he stamped and swore   167
As if the vicar meant to cozen him.   168
But after many ceremonies done,
He calls for wine. "A health!" quoth he, as if
He had been aboard, carousing to his mates   171

---

147 quaint skillful   **152 a groom indeed** i.e., a fine bridegroom he is.
(Said ironically, with pun on the sense of "servant," "rough fellow.")
156 dam mother   **157 a fool to** i.e., a pitiable weak creature compared
with   **160 gogs wouns** God's (Christ's) wounds   **163 took** gave, struck
165 list choose   **167 forwhy** because   **168 cozen** cheat   **171 aboard**
aboard ship

After a storm; quaffed off the muscatel
And threw the sops all in the sexton's face,   173
Having no other reason
But that his beard grew thin and hungerly   175
And seemed to ask him sops as he was drinking.
This done, he took the bride about the neck
And kissed her lips with such a clamorous smack
That at the parting all the church did echo.
And I seeing this came thence for very shame,
And after me, I know, the rout is coming.   181
Such a mad marriage never was before.
Hark, hark! I hear the minstrels play.   *Music plays.*

*Enter Petruchio, Kate, Bianca, Hortensio [as
Litio], Baptista [with Grumio, and train].*

PETRUCHIO
Gentlemen and friends, I thank you for your pains.
I know you think to dine with me today,
And have prepared great store of wedding cheer,
But so it is my haste doth call me hence,
And therefore here I mean to take my leave.

BAPTISTA
Is 't possible you will away tonight?

PETRUCHIO
I must away today, before night come.
Make it no wonder. If you knew my business,   191
You would entreat me rather go than stay.
And, honest company, I thank you all   193
That have beheld me give away myself
To this most patient, sweet, and virtuous wife.
Dine with my father, drink a health to me,
For I must hence; and farewell to you all.

TRANIO
Let us entreat you stay till after dinner.

PETRUCHIO
It may not be.

GREMIO   Let me entreat you.

PETRUCHIO
It cannot be.

173 **sops** cakes or bread soaked in the wine   175 **hungerly** hungry
looking, having a starved or famished look   181 **rout** crowd, wedding
party   191 **Make** consider   193 **honest** worthy, kind

KATHARINA   Let me entreat you.

PETRUCHIO
I am content.

KATHARINA   Are you content to stay?

PETRUCHIO
I am content you shall entreat me stay;
But yet not stay, entreat me how you can.

KATHARINA
Now, if you love me, stay.

PETRUCHIO   Grumio, my horse.   204

GRUMIO   Ay, sir, they be ready; the oats have eaten the   205
horses.   206

KATHARINA   Nay, then,
Do what thou canst, I will not go today,
No, nor tomorrow, not till I please myself.
The door is open, sir, there lies your way;
You may be jogging whiles your boots are green.   211
For me, I'll not be gone till I please myself.
'Tis like you'll prove a jolly surly groom,   213
That take it on you at the first so roundly.   214

PETRUCHIO
O Kate, content thee; prithee, be not angry.

KATHARINA
I will be angry. What hast thou to do?—   216
Father, be quiet. He shall stay my leisure.   217

GREMIO
Ay, marry, sir, now it begins to work.   218

KATHARINA
Gentlemen, forward to the bridal dinner.
I see a woman may be made a fool
If she had not a spirit to resist.

PETRUCHIO
They shall go forward, Kate, at thy command.—
Obey the bride, you that attend on her.
Go to the feast, revel and domineer,   224

---

204 horse horses   **205–206 oats . . . horses** (A comic inversion.)   **211 be
. . . green** (Proverbial for "getting an early start," with a sarcastic
allusion to his unseemly attire.)   **green** fresh, new   **213 like** likely.
jolly arrogant, overbearing   **214 take it on you** i.e., throw your weight
around.   **roundly** unceremoniously   **216 What . . . do** i.e., what business is it of yours   **217 stay my leisure** wait until I am ready   **218 it . . .
work** things are starting to happen   **224 domineer** feast riotously

Carouse full measure to her maidenhead,
Be mad and merry, or go hang yourselves.
But for my bonny Kate, she must with me.   227
Nay, look not big, nor stamp, nor stare, nor fret;   228
I will be master of what is mine own.
She is my goods, my chattels; she is my house,
My household stuff, my field, my barn,
My horse, my ox, my ass, my anything;   232
And here she stands, touch her whoever dare.
I'll bring mine action on the proudest he   234
That stops my way in Padua.—Grumio,
Draw forth thy weapon; we are beset with thieves.   236
Rescue thy mistress, if thou be a man.—
Fear not, sweet wench, they shall not touch thee, Kate!
I'll buckler thee against a million.   239

       Exeunt Petruchio, Katharina, [and Grumio].

BAPTISTA
Nay, let them go, a couple of quiet ones.

GREMIO
Went they not quickly, I should die with laughing.

TRANIO
Of all mad matches never was the like.

LUCENTIO
Mistress, what's your opinion of your sister?

BIANCA
That, being mad herself, she's madly mated.

GREMIO
I warrant him, Petruchio is Kated.   245

BAPTISTA
Neighbors and friends, though bride and bridegroom
   wants   246
For to supply the places at the table,   247
You know there wants no junkets at the feast.   248
Lucentio, you shall supply the bridegroom's place,
And let Bianca take her sister's room.

---

227 for as for **228 big** threatening **232 ox . . . anything** (This catalogue
of a man's possessions is from the Tenth Commandment.) **234 action**
(1) lawsuit (2) attack **236 Draw** (Perhaps Petruchio and Grumio actually
draw their swords.) **239 buckler** shield, defend **245 Kated** Gremio's
invention for "mated (and matched) with Kate" **246 wants** are lacking **246–247 wants For to supply** are not present to fill **248 junkets**
sweetmeats

TRANIO
  Shall sweet Bianca practice how to bride it?   251
BAPTISTA
  She shall, Lucentio. Come, gentlemen, let's go.
                            Exeunt.

❖

251 bride it play the bride

4.1 *Enter Grumio.*

GRUMIO Fie, fie on all tired jades, on all mad masters, 1
and all foul ways! Was ever man so beaten? Was ever 2
man so rayed? Was ever man so weary? I am sent be- 3
fore to make a fire, and they are coming after to warm
them. Now, were not I a little pot and soon hot, my 5
very lips might freeze to my teeth, my tongue to the
roof of my mouth, my heart in my belly, ere I should
come by a fire to thaw me. But I, with blowing the
fire, shall warm myself; for, considering the weather,
a taller man than I will take cold. Holla, ho! Curtis! 10

Enter Curtis.

CURTIS Who is that calls so coldly?
GRUMIO A piece of ice. If thou doubt it, thou mayst
slide from my shoulder to my heel with no greater a
run but my head and my neck. A fire, good Curtis.
CURTIS Is my master and his wife coming, Grumio?
GRUMIO O, ay, Curtis, ay, and therefore fire, fire; cast 16
on no water. 17
CURTIS Is she so hot a shrew as she's reported?
GRUMIO She was, good Curtis, before this frost. But,
thou know'st, winter tames man, woman, and beast;
for it hath tamed my old master and my new mistress
and myself, fellow Curtis.
CURTIS Away, you three-inch fool! I am no beast. 23
GRUMIO Am I but three inches? Why, thy horn is a foot, 24
and so long am I at the least. But wilt thou make a fire,
or shall I complain on thee to our mistress, whose
hand, she being now at hand, thou shalt soon feel, to
thy cold comfort, for being slow in thy hot office? 28

4.1. Location: Petruchio's country house. A table is set out, with seats.
1 jades ill-conditioned horses **2 ways** roads **3 rayed** dirtied **5 a little
. . . hot** (Proverbial expression for a person of small stature soon an-
gered.) **10 taller** (with play on the meaning "better," "finer")
16–17 cast . . . water (Alludes to the round "Scotland's burning," in
which the phrase "Fire, fire!" is followed by "Pour on water, pour on
water.") **23 three-inch fool** (Another reference to Grumio's size.) **I am
no beast** (Curtis protests being called *fellow* by Grumio, since Grumio in
his previous speech has paralleled himself with *beast*.) **24 horn** i.e.,
cuckold's horn **28 hot office** i.e., duty of providing a fire

CURTIS   I prithee, good Grumio, tell me, how goes the
    world?

GRUMIO   A cold world, Curtis, in every office but thine,
    and therefore fire. Do thy duty, and have thy duty, for 32
    my master and mistress are almost frozen to death.

CURTIS   There's fire ready, and therefore, good Grumio,
    the news.

GRUMIO   Why, "Jack boy, ho, boy!" and as much news 36
    as wilt thou.

CURTIS   Come, you are so full of coney-catching!   38

GRUMIO   Why, therefore fire, for I have caught extreme
    cold. Where's the cook? Is supper ready, the house
    trimmed, rushes strewed, cobwebs swept, the serving- 41
    men in their new fustian, their white stockings, and 42
    every officer his wedding garment on? Be the jacks fair 43
    within, the jills fair without, the carpets laid, and 44
    everything in order?

CURTIS   All ready; and therefore, I pray thee, news.

GRUMIO   First know my horse is tired, my master and
    mistress fallen out.

CURTIS   How?

GRUMIO   Out of their saddles into the dirt—and thereby
    hangs a tale.

CURTIS   Let's ha 't, good Grumio.

GRUMIO   Lend thine ear.

CURTIS   Here.

GRUMIO   There.   [*He cuffs Curtis.*]

CURTIS   This 'tis to feel a tale, not to hear a tale.

GRUMIO   And therefore 'tis called a sensible tale, and this 57
    cuff was but to knock at your ear and beseech
    listening. Now I begin: Imprimis, we came down a foul 59
    hill, my master riding behind my mistress—

CURTIS   Both of one horse?   61

GRUMIO   What's that to thee?

32 have thy duty receive your reward   **36 Jack . . . boy** (The first
line of another round or catch.)   **38 coney-catching** cheating,
trickery (with a play on *catch*, round, in the previous line)   **41 rushes**
(Used to cover the floor.)   **42 fustian** coarse cloth of cotton and flax
43 officer household servant   **43, 44 jacks, jills** drinking measures
of one-half and one-fourth pints (with quibble on "servingmen" and
"maidservants")   **44 carpets** table covers   **57 sensible** (1) capable of
being felt (2) showing good sense   **59 Imprimis** in the first place.
foul muddy   **61 of** on

CURTIS Why, a horse.

GRUMIO Tell thou the tale. But hadst thou not crossed 64
me, thou shouldst have heard how her horse fell and
she under her horse; thou shouldst have heard in how
miry a place, how she was bemoiled, how he left her 67
with the horse upon her, how he beat me because her
horse stumbled, how she waded through the dirt to
pluck him off me, how he swore, how she prayed that
never prayed before, how I cried, how the horses ran
away, how her bridle was burst, how I lost my crupper, with many things of worthy memory, which now
shall die in oblivion and thou return unexperienced to
thy grave.

CURTIS By this reckoning he is more shrew than she.

GRUMIO Ay, and that thou and the proudest of you all
shall find when he comes home. But what talk I of 78
this? Call forth Nathaniel, Joseph, Nicholas, Philip,
Walter, Sugarsop, and the rest. Let their heads be
sleekly combed, their blue coats brushed, and their 81
garters of an indifferent knit; let them curtsy with their 82
left legs, and not presume to touch a hair of my master's horsetail till they kiss their hands. Are they all
ready?

CURTIS They are.

GRUMIO Call them forth.

CURTIS Do you hear, ho? You must meet my master to
countenance my mistress.   89

GRUMIO Why, she hath a face of her own.

CURTIS Who knows not that?

GRUMIO Thou, it seems, that calls for company to countenance her.

CURTIS I call them forth to credit her.   94

Enter four or five Servingmen.

GRUMIO Why, she comes to borrow nothing of them.

NATHANIEL Welcome home, Grumio!

64 crossed thwarted, interrupted   **67 bemoiled** befouled with mire
78 what why   **81 blue coats** (Usual dress for servingmen.)   **82 indifferent** i.e., well matched and not flamboyant   **89 countenance** pay
respects to (with a following pun on the meaning "face")   **94 credit**
pay respects to (with another pun following, on "extending financial
credit")

PHILIP How now, Grumio!

JOSEPH What, Grumio!

NICHOLAS Fellow Grumio!

NATHANIEL How now, old lad?

GRUMIO Welcome, you; how now, you; what, you; fellow, you—and thus much for greeting. Now, my spruce companions, is all ready and all things neat? 103

NATHANIEL All things is ready. How near is our master?

GRUMIO E'en at hand, alighted by this; and therefore be not—Cock's passion, silence! I hear my master. 107

Enter Petruchio and Kate.

PETRUCHIO
Where be these knaves? What, no man at door
To hold my stirrup, nor to take my horse? 109
Where is Nathaniel, Gregory, Philip?

ALL SERVANTS Here, here, sir, here, sir.

PETRUCHIO
Here, sir! Here, sir! Here, sir! Here, sir!
You loggerheaded and unpolished grooms!
What, no attendance? No regard? No duty?
Where is the foolish knave I sent before? 115

GRUMIO
Here, sir, as foolish as I was before.

PETRUCHIO
You peasant swain, you whoreson malt-horse drudge! 117
Did I not bid thee meet me in the park
And bring along these rascal knaves with thee?

GRUMIO
Nathaniel's coat, sir, was not fully made,
And Gabriel's pumps were all unpinked i' the heel. 121
There was no link to color Peter's hat, 122
And Walter's dagger was not come from sheathing. 123

103 **spruce** lively 107 **Cock's passion** by God's (Christ's) suffering
109 **hold my stirrup** i.e., help me dismount 115 **before** ahead (with pun
in next line on "previously") 117 **swain** rustic. **whoreson . . . drudge**
worthless plodding work animal, such as would be used on a treadmill
to grind malt 121 **pumps** lowcut shoes. **unpinked** lacking in eyelets
or in ornamental tracing in the leather 122 **link** torch, the smoke or
soot of which was used as blackening 123 **sheathing** being fitted with
a sheath

There were none fine but Adam, Ralph, and Gregory;   124
The rest were ragged, old, and beggarly.
Yet, as they are, here are they come to meet you.

PETRUCHIO
Go, rascals, go, and fetch my supper in.
                              Exeunt Servants.
[*Sings.*] "Where is the life that late I led?
Where are those—" Sit down, Kate, and welcome.—
                              [*They sit at table.*]
Soud, soud, soud, soud!   130

        Enter Servants with supper.

Why, when, I say?—Nay, good sweet Kate, be merry.—
Off with my boots, you rogues! You villains, when?
            [*A Servant takes off Petruchio's boots.*]
[*Sings.*] "It was the friar of orders gray,   133
        As he forth walkèd on his way—"   134
Out, you rogue! You pluck my foot awry.   135
                              [*He kicks the Servant.*]
Take that, and mend the plucking off the other.
Be merry, Kate.—Some water, here; what, ho!

        Enter one with water.

Where's my spaniel Troilus? Sirrah, get you hence,
And bid my cousin Ferdinand come hither—
                              [*Exit Servant.*]
One, Kate, that you must kiss and be acquainted with.
Where are my slippers? Shall I have some water?
Come, Kate, and wash, and welcome heartily.
            [*Servant offers water, but spills some.*]
You whoreson villain, will you let it fall?
                              [*He strikes the Servant.*]

KATHARINA
Patience, I pray you, 'twas a fault unwilling.   144

PETRUCHIO
A whoreson, beetle-headed, flap-eared knave!—   145

124 fine well clothed   **130 Soud** (A nonsense song, or expression of
impatience, or perhaps "food!")   **133–134 "It . . . way"** (A fragment of a
bawdy ballad.)   **135 Out** (Exclamation of anger or reproach.)   **144 unwilling** accidental   **145 beetle-headed** i.e., blockheaded (since a *beetle* is
a pounding tool)

Come, Kate, sit down. I know you have a stomach.   146
Will you give thanks, sweet Kate, or else shall I?—   147
What's this? Mutton?

FIRST SERVANT   Ay.

PETRUCHIO   Who brought it?

PETER   I.

PETRUCHIO
'Tis burnt, and so is all the meat.
What dogs are these? Where is the rascal cook?
How durst you, villains, bring it from the dresser   151
And serve it thus to me that love it not?
There, take it to you, trenchers, cups, and all.   153
                [*He throws the meat, etc., at them.*]
You heedless joltheads and unmannered slaves!   154
What, do you grumble? I'll be with you straight.   155
                         [*They run out.*]

KATHARINA
I pray you, husband, be not so disquiet.
The meat was well, if you were so contented.

PETRUCHIO
I tell thee, Kate, 'twas burnt and dried away,
And I expressly am forbid to touch it;
For it engenders choler, planteth anger,   160
And better 'twere that both of us did fast,
Since, of ourselves, ourselves are choleric,
Than feed it with such overroasted flesh.
Be patient. Tomorrow 't shall be mended,
And for this night we'll fast for company.
Come, I will bring thee to thy bridal chamber.
                                   Exeunt.

    Enter Servants severally.

NATHANIEL   Peter, didst ever see the like?
PETER   He kills her in her own humor.   168

---

146 stomach appetite (with a suggestion also of "temper")   **147 give thanks** say grace   **151 dresser** sideboard   **153 trenchers** wooden dishes or plates   **154 joltheads** blockheads   **155 with you straight** after you at once (to get even for this)   **160 choler** the humor or bodily fluid, hot and dry in character, that supposedly produced ill temper and was thought to be aggravated by the eating of roast meat   **168 kills . . . humor** i.e., uses anger to subdue anger in her

Enter Curtis.

GRUMIO Where is he?
CURTIS In her chamber, making a sermon of continency   170
   to her,
   And rails, and swears, and rates, that she, poor soul,   172
   Knows not which way to stand, to look, to speak,
   And sits as one new risen from a dream.
   Away, away! For he is coming hither.   [*Exeunt.*]

   Enter Petruchio.

PETRUCHIO
   Thus have I politicly begun my reign,
   And 'tis my hope to end successfully.
   My falcon now is sharp and passing empty,   178
   And till she stoop she must not be full-gorged,   179
   For then she never looks upon her lure.
   Another way I have to man my haggard,   181
   To make her come and know her keeper's call:
   That is, to watch her, as we watch these kites   183
   That bate and beat and will not be obedient.   184
   She ate no meat today, nor none shall eat.
   Last night she slept not, nor tonight she shall not.
   As with the meat, some undeservèd fault
   I'll find about the making of the bed,
   And here I'll fling the pillow, there the bolster,
   This way the coverlet, another way the sheets.
   Ay, and amid this hurly I intend   191
   That all is done in reverent care of her.
   And in conclusion she shall watch all night,
   And if she chance to nod I'll rail and brawl,
   And with the clamor keep her still awake.
   This is a way to kill a wife with kindness;
   And thus I'll curb her mad and headstrong humor.   197

---

170 **sermon of continency** lecture on self-restraint   172 **rates** scolds
178 **sharp** hungry   179 **stoop** fly down to the lure   181 **man** tame (with
a pun on the sense of "assert masculine authority").   **haggard** wild
female hawk; hence, an intractable woman   183 **watch her** keep her
watching, i.e., awake.   **kites** a kind of hawk (with a pun on *Kate*)
184 **bate and beat** beat the wings impatiently and flutter away from the
hand or perch   191 **intend** pretend   197 **humor** disposition

He that knows better how to tame a shrew,
Now let him speak; 'tis charity to show.   *Exit.* 199

❧

4.2   *Enter Tranio [as Lucentio] and Hortensio [as*
       Litio].

TRANIO
   Is 't possible, friend Litio, that Mistress Bianca
   Doth fancy any other but Lucentio?
   I tell you, sir, she bears me fair in hand.   3
HORTENSIO
   Sir, to satisfy you in what I have said,
   Stand by and mark the manner of his teaching.
                              [*They stand aside.*]

   Enter Bianca [and Lucentio as Cambio].

LUCENTIO
   Now, mistress, profit you in what you read?   6
BIANCA
   What, master, read you? First resolve me that.   7
LUCENTIO
   I read that I profess, the Art to Love.   8
BIANCA
   And may you prove, sir, master of your art!
LUCENTIO
   While you, sweet dear, prove mistress of my heart!
             [*They move aside and court each other.*]
HORTENSIO [*To Tranio, coming forward*]
   Quick proceeders, marry! Now tell me, I pray,   11
   You that durst swear that your mistress Bianca
   Loved none in the world so well as Lucentio.

199 'tis charity to show it's benevolent to share such wisdom. (On the
rhyme with *shrew*, see also the play's final lines.)

4.2. Location: Padua. Before Baptista's house.
3 bears . . . hand gives me encouragement, leads me on   **6 read** (Evidently, both Bianca and "Cambio" carry books.)   **7 resolve** answer
8 that I profess what I practice.   **Art to Love** Ovid's *Ars Amandi*
11 proceeders (1) workers, doers (2) candidates for academic degrees (as
suggested by the phrase *master of your art* in l. 9)

TRANIO

  O despiteful love! Unconstant womankind!   14

  I tell thee, Litio, this is wonderful.   15

HORTENSIO

  Mistake no more. I am not Litio,

  Nor a musician, as I seem to be,

  But one that scorn to live in this disguise   18

  For such a one as leaves a gentleman   19

  And makes a god of such a cullion.   20

  Know, sir, that I am called Hortensio.

TRANIO

  Signor Hortensio, I have often heard

  Of your entire affection to Bianca;   23

  And since mine eyes are witness of her lightness,   24

  I will with you, if you be so contented,

  Forswear Bianca and her love forever.

HORTENSIO

  See how they kiss and court! Signor Lucentio,

  Here is my hand, and here I firmly vow

                      [*Giving his hand*]

  Never to woo her more, but do forswear her

  As one unworthy all the former favors

  That I have fondly flattered her withal.   31

TRANIO

  And here I take the like unfeignèd oath,

  Never to marry with her though she would entreat.

  Fie on her, see how beastly she doth court him!

HORTENSIO

  Would all the world but he had quite forsworn!   35

  For me, that I may surely keep mine oath,

  I will be married to a wealthy widow,

  Ere three days pass, which hath as long loved me

  As I have loved this proud disdainful haggard.   39

  And so farewell, Signor Lucentio.

  Kindness in women, not their beauteous looks,

---

14 despiteful cruel **15 wonderful** cause for wonder **18 scorn** scorns
19 such a one i.e., Bianca **20 cullion** base fellow (referring to "Cambio"; literally the word means "testicle") **23 entire** sincere **24 lightness** wantonness **31 fondly** foolishly **35 Would . . . forsworn** i.e., may everyone in the world forsake her except the penniless "Cambio," and may she thus get what she deserves **39 haggard** wild hawk

Shall win my love. And so I take my leave,
In resolution as I swore before.   [*Exit.*] 43
TRANIO   [*As Lucentio and Bianca come forward again*]
Mistress Bianca, bless you with such grace
As 'longeth to a lover's blessèd case!   45
Nay, I have ta'en you napping, gentle love,   46
And have forsworn you with Hortensio.
BIANCA
Tranio, you jest. But have you both forsworn me?
TRANIO
Mistress, we have.
LUCENTIO   Then we are rid of Litio.
TRANIO
I' faith, he'll have a lusty widow now,   50
That shall be wooed and wedded in a day.
BIANCA   God give him joy!
TRANIO   Ay, and he'll tame her.
BIANCA   He says so, Tranio?
TRANIO
Faith, he is gone unto the taming school.
BIANCA
The taming school! What, is there such a place?
TRANIO
Ay, mistress, and Petruchio is the master,
That teacheth tricks eleven-and-twenty long,   58
To tame a shrew and charm her chattering tongue.

     Enter Biondello.

BIONDELLO
O master, master, I have watched so long
That I am dog-weary, but at last I spied
An ancient angel coming down the hill   62
Will serve the turn.
TRANIO   What is he, Biondello?   63

43 **In resolution** determined   45 **'longeth** belongs   46 **ta'en you napping** i.e., surprised you   50 **lusty** merry, lively   58 **eleven . . . long** i.e.,
in sufficient number (alluding to the card game called "one-and-thirty"
referred to at 1.2.32–33)   62 **ancient angel** i.e., fellow of the good old
stamp. (Literally, an "angel" or gold coin bearing the stamp of the
archangel Michael and thus distinguishable from more recent debased
coinage.)   63 **Will . . . turn** who will serve our purposes

BIONDELLO
  Master, a marcantant, or a pedant,   64
  I know not what, but formal in apparel,
  In gait and countenance surely like a father.
LUCENTIO And what of him, Tranio?
TRANIO
  If he be credulous and trust my tale,
  I'll make him glad to seem Vincentio
  And give assurance to Baptista Minola
  As if he were the right Vincentio.
  Take in your love, and then let me alone.   72
               [*Exeunt Lucentio and Bianca.*]

    Enter a Pedant.

PEDANT
  God save you, sir!
TRANIO   And you sir! You are welcome.
  Travel you far on, or are you at the farthest?
PEDANT
  Sir, at the farthest for a week or two,
  But then up farther, and as far as Rome,
  And so to Tripoli, if God lend me life.
TRANIO
  What countryman, I pray?
PEDANT   Of Mantua.
TRANIO
  Of Mantua, sir? Marry, God forbid!
  And come to Padua, careless of your life?
PEDANT
  My life, sir! How, I pray? For that goes hard.   81
TRANIO
  'Tis death for anyone in Mantua
  To come to Padua. Know you not the cause?
  Your ships are stayed at Venice, and the Duke,   84
  For private quarrel twixt your duke and him,
  Hath published and proclaimed it openly.
  'Tis marvel, but that you are but newly come,
  You might have heard it else proclaimed about.

---

64 marcantant merchant. **pedant** schoolmaster (though at ll. 90–91 he
speaks more like a merchant) **72 let me alone** i.e., count on me
81 goes hard is serious indeed **84 stayed** detained

PEDANT
  Alas, sir, it is worse for me than so,
  For I have bills for money by exchange   90
  From Florence, and must here deliver them.
TRANIO
  Well, sir, to do you courtesy,
  This will I do, and this I will advise you—
  First, tell me, have you ever been at Pisa?
PEDANT
  Ay, sir, in Pisa have I often been,
  Pisa renownèd for grave citizens.
TRANIO
  Among them know you one Vincentio?
PEDANT
  I know him not, but I have heard of him;
  A merchant of incomparable wealth.
TRANIO
  He is my father, sir, and, sooth to say,
  In count'nance somewhat doth resemble you.
BIONDELLO [*Aside*]   As much as an apple doth an oyster,
  and all one.   103
TRANIO
  To save your life in this extremity,
  This favor will I do you for his sake;
  And think it not the worst of all your fortunes
  That you are like to Sir Vincentio.
  His name and credit shall you undertake,   108
  And in my house you shall be friendly lodged.
  Look that you take upon you as you should.   110
  You understand me, sir. So shall you stay
  Till you have done your business in the city.
  If this be courtesy, sir, accept of it.
PEDANT
  O sir, I do, and will repute you ever
  The patron of my life and liberty.
TRANIO
  Then go with me to make the matter good.   116
  This, by the way, I let you understand:

90 **bills . . . exchange** promissory notes   103 **all one** no matter
108 **credit** reputation   110 **take upon you** play your part   116 **make . . .
good** carry out the plan

My father is here looked for every day,
To pass assurance of a dower in marriage   119
Twixt me and one Baptista's daughter here.
In all these circumstances I'll instruct you.
Go with me to clothe you as becomes you.

Exeunt.

❖

4.3   *Enter Katharina and Grumio.*

GRUMIO
No, no, forsooth, I dare not for my life.

KATHARINA
The more my wrong, the more his spite appears.   2
What, did he marry me to famish me?
Beggars that come unto my father's door
Upon entreaty have a present alms;   5
If not, elsewhere they meet with charity.
But I, who never knew how to entreat,
Nor never needed that I should entreat,
Am starved for meat, giddy for lack of sleep,   9
With oaths kept waking, and with brawling fed.
And that which spites me more than all these wants,
He does it under name of perfect love,
As who should say, if I should sleep or eat,   13
'Twere deadly sickness or else present death.
I prithee, go and get me some repast,
I care not what, so it be wholesome food.

GRUMIO   What say you to a neat's foot?   17

KATHARINA
'Tis passing good; I prithee, let me have it.

GRUMIO
I fear it is too choleric a meat.
How say you to a fat tripe finely broiled?

KATHARINA
I like it well, good Grumio, fetch it me.

---

119 pass assurance convey a legal guarantee

4.3. Location: Petruchio's house. A table is set out, with seats.
2 my wrong the wrong done to me   **5 present** immediate (as in l. 14)
9 meat food   **13 As who** as if one   **17 neat's** ox's

GRUMIO
    I cannot tell. I fear 'tis choleric.
    What say you to a piece of beef and mustard?
KATHARINA
    A dish that I do love to feed upon.
GRUMIO
    Ay, but the mustard is too hot a little.
KATHARINA
    Why then, the beef, and let the mustard rest.
GRUMIO
    Nay then, I will not; you shall have the mustard
    Or else you get no beef of Grumio.
KATHARINA
    Then both, or one, or anything thou wilt.
GRUMIO
    Why then, the mustard without the beef.
KATHARINA
    Go, get thee gone, thou false deluding slave,
                                        Beats him.
    That feed'st me with the very name of meat!
    Sorrow on thee and all the pack of you,
    That triumph thus upon my misery!
    Go, get thee gone, I say.

        Enter Petruchio and Hortensio with meat.

PETRUCHIO
    How fares my Kate? What, sweeting, all amort?   36
HORTENSIO
    Mistress, what cheer?
KATHARINA   Faith, as cold as can be.
PETRUCHIO
    Pluck up thy spirits; look cheerfully upon me.
    Here, love, thou see'st how diligent I am
    To dress thy meat myself and bring it thee.   40
    I am sure, sweet Kate, this kindness merits thanks.
    What, not a word? Nay, then thou lov'st it not,
    And all my pains is sorted to no proof.   43
    Here, take away this dish.
KATHARINA   I pray you, let it stand.

36 all amort dejected, dispirited   **40 dress** prepare   **43 sorted to no proof** proved to be to no purpose

PETRUCHIO
    The poorest service is repaid with thanks,
    And so shall mine before you touch the meat.
KATHARINA   I thank you, sir.
HORTENSIO
    Signor Petruchio, fie, you are to blame.
    Come, Mistress Kate, I'll bear you company.
                                    [*They sit at table.*]
PETRUCHIO [*Aside to Hortensio*]
    Eat it up all, Hortensio, if thou lovest me.—
    Much good do it unto thy gentle heart!
    Kate, eat apace. And now, my honey love,
    Will we return unto thy father's house
    And revel it as bravely as the best,   54
    With silken coats and caps and golden rings,
    With ruffs and cuffs and farthingales and things,   56
    With scarves and fans and double change of bravery,   57
    With amber bracelets, beads, and all this knavery.
    What, hast thou dined? The tailor stays thy leisure,
    To deck thy body with his ruffling treasure.   60

        Enter Tailor [*with a gown*].

    Come, tailor, let us see these ornaments.
    Lay forth the gown.

        Enter Haberdasher [*with a cap*].
                        What news with you, sir?
HABERDASHER
    Here is the cap your worship did bespeak.
PETRUCHIO
    Why, this was molded on a porringer—   64
    A velvet dish. Fie, fie, 'tis lewd and filthy.   65
    Why, 'tis a cockle or a walnut shell,   66
    A knack, a toy, a trick, a baby's cap.   67
    Away with it! Come, let me have a bigger.
KATHARINA
    I'll have no bigger. This doth fit the time,   69
    And gentlewomen wear such caps as these.

54 **bravely** splendidly dressed   56 **farthingales** hooped petticoats
57 **bravery** finery   60 **ruffling treasure** finery trimmed with ruffles
64 **porringer** porridge bowl   65 **lewd** vile   66 **cockle** cockleshell
67 **trick** trifle   69 **fit the time** suit the current fashion

PETRUCHIO
  When you are gentle, you shall have one too,
  And not till then.
HORTENSIO [*Aside*] That will not be in haste.
KATHARINA
  Why, sir, I trust I may have leave to speak,
  And speak I will. I am no child, no babe.
  Your betters have endured me say my mind,
  And if you cannot, best you stop your ears.
  My tongue will tell the anger of my heart,
  Or else my heart, concealing it, will break,
  And rather than it shall, I will be free
  Even to the uttermost, as I please, in words.
PETRUCHIO
  Why, thou sayst true. It is a paltry cap,
  A custard-coffin, a bauble, a silken pie.   82
  I love thee well in that thou lik'st it not.
KATHARINA
  Love me or love me not, I like the cap,
  And it I will have, or I will have none.
                    [*Exit Haberdasher.*]
PETRUCHIO
  Thy gown? Why, ay. Come, tailor, let us see 't.
  O, mercy, God, what masquing stuff is here?   87
  What's this, a sleeve? 'Tis like a demi-cannon.   88
  What, up and down carved like an apple tart?   89
  Here's snip and nip and cut and slish and slash,
  Like to a censer in a barber's shop.   91
  Why, what i' devil's name, tailor, call'st thou this?   92
HORTENSIO [*Aside*]
  I see she's like to have neither cap nor gown.
TAILOR
  You bid me make it orderly and well,
  According to the fashion and the time.
PETRUCHIO
  Marry, and did. But if you be remembered,   96

---

82 custard-coffin pastry crust for a custard   **87 masquing** i.e., suited only for a masque   **88 demi-cannon** large cannon   **89 up and down** all over, exactly.   **like an apple tart** i.e., with slashing or slits like the slits on the crust of fruit tarts, here revealing the brighter fabric underneath   **91 censer** perfuming pan having an ornamental lid   **92 i'** in (the)   **96 be remembered** recollect

I did not bid you mar it to the time.
Go, hop me over every kennel home, 98
For you shall hop without my custom, sir.
I'll none of it. Hence, make your best of it.

KATHARINA
I never saw a better-fashioned gown,
More quaint, more pleasing, nor more commendable. 102
Belike you mean to make a puppet of me.

PETRUCHIO
Why, true, he means to make a puppet of thee.

TAILOR
She says your worship means to make a puppet of her.

PETRUCHIO
O, monstrous arrogance! Thou liest, thou thread, thou
thimble,
Thou yard, three-quarters, half-yard, quarter, nail! 107
Thou flea, thou nit, thou winter cricket thou! 108
Braved in mine own house with a skein of thread? 109
Away, thou rag, thou quantity, thou remnant, 110
Or I shall so be-mete thee with thy yard 111
As thou shalt think on prating whilst thou liv'st! 112
I tell thee, I, that thou hast marred her gown.

TAILOR
Your worship is deceived. The gown is made
Just as my master had direction.
Grumio gave order how it should be done.

GRUMIO   I gave him no order. I gave him the stuff.

TAILOR
But how did you desire it should be made?

GRUMIO   Marry, sir, with needle and thread.

TAILOR
But did you not request to have it cut?

GRUMIO   Thou hast faced many things. 121

TAILOR   I have.

GRUMIO   Face not me. Thou hast braved many men; 123

---

98 hop . . . home hop on home over every street gutter   **102 quaint**
elegant   **107 nail** a measure of length for cloth: 2¼ inches   **108 nit**
louse egg   **109 Braved** defied.   **with** by   **110 quantity** fragment
111 be-mete measure, i.e., thrash.   **yard** yardstick   **112 think on prating**
i.e., remember this thrashing and think twice before talking so again
121 faced trimmed. (But Grumio puns on the meaning "bullied.")
123 Face bully.   **braved** dressed finely

brave not me. I will neither be faced nor braved. I say 124
unto thee, I bid thy master cut out the gown, but I did
not bid him cut it to pieces. Ergo, thou liest. 126

TAILOR   Why, here is the note of the fashion to testify.
[He displays his bill.]

PETRUCHIO   Read it.

GRUMIO   The note lies in 's throat if he say I said so.

TAILOR *[Reads]*   "Imprimis, a loose-bodied gown—"

GRUMIO   Master, if ever I said loose-bodied gown, 131
sew me in the skirts of it and beat me to death with
a bottom of brown thread. I said a gown. 133

PETRUCHIO   Proceed.

TAILOR *[Reads]*   "With a small compassed cape—" 135

GRUMIO   I confess the cape.

TAILOR *[Reads]*   "With a trunk sleeve—" 137

GRUMIO   I confess two sleeves.

TAILOR *[Reads]*   "The sleeves curiously cut." 139

PETRUCHIO   Ay, there's the villainy.

GRUMIO   Error i' the bill, sir, error i' the bill. I commanded the sleeves should be cut out and sewed up
again, and that I'll prove upon thee, though thy little 143
finger be armed in a thimble.

TAILOR   This is true that I say. An I had thee in place 145
where, thou shouldst know it. 146

GRUMIO   I am for thee straight. Take thou the bill, give 147
me thy mete-yard, and spare not me. 148

HORTENSIO   God-a-mercy, Grumio, then he shall have
no odds.

PETRUCHIO   Well, sir, in brief, the gown is not for me.

GRUMIO   You are i' the right, sir, 'tis for my mistress.

PETRUCHIO   Go, take it up unto thy master's use. 153

GRUMIO   Villain, not for thy life! Take up my mistress'
gown for thy master's use!

PETRUCHIO   Why, sir, what's your conceit in that? 156

---

124 **brave** defy   126 **Ergo** therefore   131 **loose-bodied gown** (Grumio
plays on *loose*, wanton; a gown fit for a prostitute.)   133 **bottom** ball
wound from a skein. (A weaver's term.)   135 **compassed** with the edges
forming a semicircle   137 **trunk** full, wide   139 **curiously** elaborately
143 **prove upon thee** prove by fighting you   145–146 **in place where** in a
suitable place   147 **bill** (1) the note ordering the gown (2) a weapon, a
halberd   148 **mete-yard** measuring stick   153 **use** i.e., whatever use he
can make of it. (But Grumio deliberately misinterprets in a bawdy
sense.)   156 **conceit** idea

GRUMIO
   O, sir, the conceit is deeper than you think for:
   Take up my mistress' gown to his master's use!
   O, fie, fie, fie!
PETRUCHIO [*Aside to Hortensio*]
   Hortensio, say thou wilt see the tailor paid.—
   [*To Tailor.*] Go take it hence, begone, and say no more.
HORTENSIO [*Aside to Tailor*]
   Tailor, I'll pay thee for thy gown tomorrow.
   Take no unkindness of his hasty words.
   Away, I say. Commend me to thy master.

                                      Exit Tailor.
PETRUCHIO
   Well, come, my Kate. We will unto your father's
   Even in these honest mean habiliments.   166
   Our purses shall be proud, our garments poor,
   For 'tis the mind that makes the body rich;
   And as the sun breaks through the darkest clouds,
   So honor peereth in the meanest habit.   170
   What, is the jay more precious than the lark
   Because his feathers are more beautiful?
   Or is the adder better than the eel
   Because his painted skin contents the eye?   174
   O, no, good Kate; neither art thou the worse
   For this poor furniture and mean array.   176
   If thou account'st it shame, lay it on me.
   And therefore frolic; we will hence forthwith,
   To feast and sport us at thy father's house.
   [*To Grumio.*] Go call my men, and let us straight to him;
   And bring our horses unto Long Lane end.
   There will we mount, and thither walk on foot.
   Let's see, I think 'tis now some seven o'clock,
   And well we may come there by dinnertime.   184
KATHARINA
   I dare assure you, sir, 'tis almost two,
   And 'twill be suppertime ere you come there.
PETRUCHIO
   It shall be seven ere I go to horse.

166 honest mean habiliments respectable, plain clothes **170 peereth** is
seen. **habit** attire **174 painted** patterned **176 furniture** furnishings
of attire **184 dinnertime** i.e., about noon

Look what I speak, or do, or think to do,   188
You are still crossing it.—Sirs, let 't alone.   189
I will not go today, and ere I do
It shall be what o'clock I say it is.

HORTENSIO [*Aside*]
Why, so this gallant will command the sun.

                              [*Exeunt.*]

❖

4.4   *Enter Tranio [as Lucentio], and the Pedant*
        dressed like Vincentio [booted].

TRANIO
Sir, this is the house. Please it you that I call?

PEDANT
Ay, what else? And but I be deceived,   2
Signor Baptista may remember me,   3
Near twenty years ago, in Genoa,
Where we were lodgers at the Pegasus.   5

TRANIO
'Tis well; and hold your own in any case   6
With such austerity as 'longeth to a father.

    Enter Biondello.

PEDANT
I warrant you. But, sir, here comes your boy;
'Twere good he were schooled.   9

TRANIO
Fear you not him.—Sirrah Biondello,
Now do your duty throughly, I advise you.   11
Imagine 'twere the right Vincentio.

BIONDELLO   Tut, fear not me.

---

188 Look what whatever **189 still crossing** always contradicting or defying

4.4. Location: Padua. Before Baptista's house.
s.d. booted (signifying travel) **2 but** unless **3 may remember** (The Pedant is rehearsing what he is to say.) **5 the Pegasus** i.e., an inn, so named after the famous winged horse of classical myth **6 hold your own** play your part **9 schooled** i.e., rehearsed in his part **11 throughly** thoroughly

TRANIO
But hast thou done thy errand to Baptista?
BIONDELLO
I told him that your father was at Venice,
And that you looked for him this day in Padua.
TRANIO
Thou'rt a tall fellow. Hold thee that to drink.   17
                                    [*He gives money.*]
Here comes Baptista. Set your countenance, sir.

   Enter Baptista and Lucentio [as Cambio]. [The]
   Pedant [stands] bareheaded.

Signor Baptista, you are happily met.
[*To the Pedant.*] Sir, this is the gentleman I told you of.
I pray you, stand good father to me now;
Give me Bianca for my patrimony.
PEDANT   Soft, son!
Sir, by your leave, having come to Padua
To gather in some debts, my son Lucentio
Made me acquainted with a weighty cause
Of love between your daughter and himself;
And, for the good report I hear of you
And for the love he beareth to your daughter
And she to him, to stay him not too long,
I am content, in a good father's care,
To have him matched. And if you please to like
No worse than I, upon some agreement
Me shall you find ready and willing
With one consent to have her so bestowed;
For curious I cannot be with you,   36
Signor Baptista, of whom I hear so well.
BAPTISTA
Sir, pardon me in what I have to say;
Your plainness and your shortness please me well.
Right true it is your son Lucentio here
Doth love my daughter, and she loveth him,
Or both dissemble deeply their affections.
And therefore, if you say no more than this,
That like a father you will deal with him

17 **tall** fine. **Hold . . . drink** take that and buy a drink   **36 curious**
overly particular

And pass my daughter a sufficient dower,   45
The match is made and all is done.
Your son shall have my daughter with consent.

TRANIO

I thank you, sir. Where then do you know best
We be affied and such assurance ta'en   49
As shall with either part's agreement stand?

BAPTISTA

Not in my house, Lucentio, for you know
Pitchers have ears, and I have many servants.
Besides, old Gremio is hearkening still,   53
And happily we might be interrupted.   54

TRANIO

Then at my lodging, an it like you.   55
There doth my father lie, and there this night   56
We'll pass the business privately and well.   57
Send for your daughter by your servant here.
          [*He indicates Lucentio, and winks at him.*]
My boy shall fetch the scrivener presently.   59
The worst is this, that at so slender warning
You are like to have a thin and slender pittance.   61

BAPTISTA

It likes me well. Cambio, hie you home,
And bid Bianca make her ready straight.
And if you will, tell what hath happened:
Lucentio's father is arrived in Padua,
And how she's like to be Lucentio's wife.
                              [*Exit Lucentio.*]

BIONDELLO

I pray the gods she may, with all my heart!

TRANIO

Dally not with the gods, but get thee gone.
                              Exit [*Biondello*].
Signor Baptista, shall I lead the way?
Welcome! One mess is like to be your cheer.   70
Come, sir, we will better it in Pisa.

---

45 pass settle on, give   **49 affied** betrothed   **53 hearkening still** continually listening   **54 happily** haply, perhaps   **55 an it like** if it please   **56 lie** lodge   **57 pass** transact   **59 scrivener** notary, one to draw up contracts   **61 like** likely.   **slender pittance** i.e., scanty banquet   **70 mess** dish.   **cheer** entertainment

BAPTISTA   I follow you.

               Exeunt [Tranio, Pedant, and Baptista].

    Enter Lucentio [as Cambio] and Biondello.

BIONDELLO   Cambio!

LUCENTIO   What sayst thou, Biondello?

BIONDELLO   You saw my master wink and laugh upon
you?

LUCENTIO   Biondello, what of that?

BIONDELLO   Faith, nothing; but he's left me here behind
to expound the meaning or moral of his signs and   79
tokens.

LUCENTIO   I pray thee, moralize them.   81

BIONDELLO   Then thus. Baptista is safe, talking with the   82
deceiving father of a deceitful son.

LUCENTIO   And what of him?

BIONDELLO   His daughter is to be brought by you to the
supper.

LUCENTIO   And then?

BIONDELLO   The old priest at Saint Luke's church is at
your command at all hours.

LUCENTIO   And what of all this?

BIONDELLO   I cannot tell, except they are busied about a   91
counterfeit assurance. Take you assurance of her,   92
cum privilegio ad imprimendum solum. To the   93
church take the priest, clerk, and some sufficient hon-   94
est witnesses.

If this be not that you look for, I have no more to say,

But bid Bianca farewell forever and a day.

               [Biondello starts to leave.]

LUCENTIO   Hear'st thou, Biondello?

BIONDELLO   I cannot tarry. I knew a wench married in
an afternoon as she went to the garden for parsley to
stuff a rabbit, and so may you, sir. And so, adieu, sir.
My master hath appointed me to go to Saint Luke's, to

---

79 moral hidden meaning   **81 moralize** elucidate   **82 safe** i.e., safely
deceived   **91 except** unless   **92 counterfeit assurance** pretended betrothal agreement.   **Take . . . of her** legalize your claim to her (by
marriage)   **93 cum . . . solum** with exclusive printing rights. (A copy-
right formula often appearing on the title pages of books, here jokingly
applied to the marriage.)   **94 sufficient** financially competent, well-to-do

bid the priest be ready to come against you come with 103
your appendix.   *Exit.* 104

LUCENTIO
I may, and will, if she be so contented.
She will be pleased; then wherefore should I doubt?
Hap what hap may, I'll roundly go about her.   107
It shall go hard if Cambio go without her.   *Exit.* 108

❖

4.5 *Enter Petruchio, Kate, and Hortensio.*

PETRUCHIO
Come on, i' God's name, once more toward our father's. 1
Good Lord, how bright and goodly shines the moon!

KATHARINA
The moon? The sun. It is not moonlight now.

PETRUCHIO
I say it is the moon that shines so bright.

KATHARINA
I know it is the sun that shines so bright.

PETRUCHIO
Now, by my mother's son, and that's myself,
It shall be moon, or star, or what I list,   7
Or ere I journey to your father's house.—   8
Go on, and fetch our horses back again—
Evermore crossed and crossed, nothing but crossed!

HORTENSIO [*To Katharina*]
Say as he says, or we shall never go.

KATHARINA
Forward, I pray, since we have come so far,
And be it moon, or sun, or what you please;
An if you please to call it a rush candle,   14
Henceforth I vow it shall be so for me.

---

103 against you come in anticipation of your arrival   **104 appendix**
something appended, i.e., the bride (continuing the metaphor of printing)   **107 roundly . . . her** set about marrying her in no uncertain
terms   **108 go hard** be unfortunate (with bawdy pun)

4.5. Location: A road on the way to Padua.
1 our father's our father's house   **7 list** please   **8 Or ere** before
14 rush candle a rush dipped into tallow; hence a very feeble light

PETRUCHIO
I say it is the moon.
KATHARINA   I know it is the moon.
PETRUCHIO
Nay, then you lie. It is the blessèd sun.
KATHARINA
Then, God be blest, it is the blessèd sun.
But sun it is not when you say it is not,
And the moon changes even as your mind.
What you will have it named, even that it is,
And so it shall be so for Katharine.
HORTENSIO
Petruchio, go thy ways, the field is won.
PETRUCHIO
Well, forward, forward, thus the bowl should run,
And not unluckily against the bias.   25
But, soft! Company is coming here.

          Enter Vincentio.

[*To Vincentio.*] Good morrow, gentle mistress. Where
     away?—   27
Tell me, sweet Kate, and tell me truly too,
Hast thou beheld a fresher gentlewoman?
Such war of white and red within her cheeks!
What stars do spangle heaven with such beauty
As those two eyes become that heavenly face?—
Fair lovely maid, once more good day to thee.—
Sweet Kate, embrace her for her beauty's sake.
HORTENSIO [*Aside*]
'A will make the man mad, to make a woman of him.   35
KATHARINA [*Embracing Vincentio*]
Young budding virgin, fair and fresh and sweet,
Whither away, or where is thy abode?
Happy the parents of so fair a child!
Happier the man whom favorable stars
Allots thee for his lovely bedfellow!

---

25 against the bias off its proper course. (The *bias* is an off-center
weight in a bowling ball enabling the bowler to roll the ball in an
oblique or curving path; it runs *unluckily*, that is, unsuccessfully,
against the bias when it encounters an obstacle.)   **27 Where away**
where are you going   **35 'A** he

PETRUCHIO
Why, how now, Kate? I hope thou art not mad.
This is a man, old, wrinkled, faded, withered,
And not a maiden, as thou sayst he is.

KATHARINA
Pardon, old father, my mistaking eyes,
That have been so bedazzled with the sun
That everything I look on seemeth green.   46
Now I perceive thou art a reverend father.
Pardon, I pray thee, for my mad mistaking.

PETRUCHIO
Do, good old grandsire, and withal make known
Which way thou travelest—if along with us,
We shall be joyful of thy company.

VINCENTIO
Fair sir, and you my merry mistress,
That with your strange encounter much amazed me,
My name is called Vincentio; my dwelling Pisa,
And bound I am to Padua, there to visit
A son of mine, which long I have not seen.

PETRUCHIO
What is his name?

VINCENTIO   Lucentio, gentle sir.

PETRUCHIO
Happily met, the happier for thy son.
And now by law, as well as reverend age,
I may entitle thee my loving father.
The sister to my wife, this gentlewoman,
Thy son by this hath married. Wonder not,   62
Nor be not grieved. She is of good esteem,   63
Her dowry wealthy, and of worthy birth;
Besides, so qualified as may beseem   65
The spouse of any noble gentleman.
Let me embrace with old Vincentio,
And wander we to see thy honest son,
Who will of thy arrival be full joyous.

                              [*He embraces Vincentio.*]

VINCENTIO
But is this true? Or is it else your pleasure,

---

46 green young and fresh   **62 by this** by this time   **63 esteem** reputation   **65 beseem** befit

Like pleasant travelers, to break a jest
Upon the company you overtake?

HORTENSIO
I do assure thee, father, so it is.

PETRUCHIO
Come, go along, and see the truth hereof,
For our first merriment hath made thee jealous.   75

Exeunt [all but Hortensio].

HORTENSIO
Well, Petruchio, this has put me in heart.
Have to my widow! And if she be froward,   77
Then hast thou taught Hortensio to be untoward.   78

Exit.

❖

---

75 jealous suspicious **77 Have to** i.e., now for. **froward** perverse
78 untoward unmannerly

5.1   *Enter Biondello, Lucentio [no longer*
disguised], and Bianca. Gremio is out before
[and stands aside].

BIONDELLO   Softly and swiftly, sir, for the priest is
ready.
LUCENTIO   I fly, Biondello. But they may chance to need
thee at home; therefore leave us.
BIONDELLO   Nay, faith, I'll see the church a' your back,   5
and then come back to my master's as soon as I can.
               [Exeunt Lucentio, Bianca, and Biondello.]
GREMIO
I marvel Cambio comes not all this while.

       Enter Petruchio, Kate, Vincentio, Grumio, with
       attendants.

PETRUCHIO
Sir, here's the door; this is Lucentio's house.
My father's bears more toward the marketplace;   9
Thither must I, and here I leave you, sir.
VINCENTIO
You shall not choose but drink before you go.
I think I shall command your welcome here,
And, by all likelihood, some cheer is toward.   13
                                        Knock.
GREMIO [*Advancing*]   They're busy within. You were
best knock louder.   15

       Pedant looks out of the window.

PEDANT   What's he that knocks as he would beat down
the gate?
VINCENTIO   Is Signor Lucentio within, sir?
PEDANT   He's within, sir, but not to be spoken withal.

5.1. Location: Padua. Before Lucentio's house.
s.d. out before i.e., onstage first. (Gremio does not see Biondello, Lucentio, and Bianca as they steal to church, or else does not recognize
Lucentio in his own person.)   **5 a' your back** at your back, behind you
(i.e., I'll see you in church and safely married)   **9 father's** i.e., father-in-
law's, Baptista's.   **bears** lies. (A nautical term.)   **13 toward** in prospect   **15 s.d. window** i.e., probably the gallery to the rear, over the
stage

VINCENTIO What if a man bring him a hundred pound
or two, to make merry withal?

PEDANT Keep your hundred pounds to yourself. He
shall need none, so long as I live.

PETRUCHIO [*To Vincentio*] Nay, I told you your son was
well beloved in Padua.—Do you hear, sir? To leave
frivolous circumstances, I pray you, tell Signor 26
Lucentio that his father is come from Pisa and is here
at the door to speak with him.

PEDANT Thou liest. His father is come from Padua and
here looking out at the window.

VINCENTIO Art thou his father?

PEDANT Ay, sir, so his mother says, if I may believe
her.

PETRUCHIO [*To Vincentio*] Why, how now, gentleman!
Why, this is flat knavery, to take upon you another 35
man's name.

PEDANT Lay hands on the villain. I believe 'a means to
cozen somebody in this city under my countenance.   38

Enter Biondello.

BIONDELLO [*To himself*] I have seen them in the church
together, God send 'em good shipping! But who is 40
here? Mine old master Vincentio! Now we are undone
and brought to nothing.

VINCENTIO [*Seeing Biondello*] Come hither, crack-hemp. 43

BIONDELLO I hope I may choose, sir.   44

VINCENTIO Come hither, you rogue. What, have you
forgot me?

BIONDELLO Forgot you? No, sir. I could not forget you,
for I never saw you before in all my life.

VINCENTIO What, you notorious villain, didst thou
never see thy master's father, Vincentio?

BIONDELLO What, my old worshipful old master? Yes,
. marry, sir, see where he looks out of the window.

VINCENTIO Is 't so, indeed?   *He beats Biondello.*

---

26 circumstances matters **35 flat** downright **38 cozen** cheat. **under
my countenance** by pretending to be me **40 good shipping** bon voyage,
good fortune **43 crack-hemp** i.e., rogue likely to end up being hanged
44 choose do as I choose

BIONDELLO Help, help, help! Here's a madman will
  murder me.   [*Exit.*]
PEDANT Help, son! Help, Signor Baptista!
                          [*Exit from the window.*]
PETRUCHIO Prithee, Kate, let's stand aside and see the
  end of this controversy.   [*They stand aside.*]

    Enter [*below*] *Pedant with servants, Baptista,*
    [*and*] *Tranio* [*as Lucentio*].

TRANIO Sir, what are you that offer to beat my servant? 59
VINCENTIO What am I, sir? Nay, what are you, sir? O
  immortal gods! O fine villain! A silken doublet, a vel-
  vet hose, a scarlet cloak, and a copatain hat! O, I am 62
  undone, I am undone! While I play the good husband 63
  at home, my son and my servant spend all at the uni-
  versity.
TRANIO How now, what's the matter?
BAPTISTA What, is the man lunatic?
TRANIO Sir, you seem a sober ancient gentleman by
  your habit, but your words show you a madman. 69
  Why, sir, what 'cerns it you if I wear pearl and gold? 70
  I thank my good father, I am able to maintain it. 71
VINCENTIO Thy father! O villain, he is a sailmaker in
  Bergamo.
BAPTISTA You mistake, sir, you mistake, sir. Pray, what
  do you think is his name?
VINCENTIO His name! As if I knew not his name! I have
  brought him up ever since he was three years old, and
  his name is Tranio.
PEDANT Away, away, mad ass! His name is Lucentio,
  and he is mine only son, and heir to the lands of me,
  Signor Vincentio.
VINCENTIO Lucentio! O, he hath murdered his master!
  Lay hold on him, I charge you, in the Duke's name.
  O, my son, my son! Tell me, thou villain, where is my
  son Lucentio?
TRANIO Call forth an officer.

---

59 **offer** dare, presume   62 **copatain** high-crowned, sugar-loaf shape
63 **good husband** careful provider, manager   69 **habit** clothing
70 **'cerns** concerns   71 **maintain** afford

[*Enter an Officer.*]

Carry this mad knave to the jail. Father Baptista, I
charge you see that he be forthcoming.   88
VINCENTIO   Carry me to the jail?
GREMIO   Stay, officer, he shall not go to prison.
BAPTISTA   Talk not, Signor Gremio, I say he shall go to
prison.
GREMIO   Take heed, Signor Baptista, lest you be coney-   93
catched in this business. I dare swear this is the right   94
Vincentio.
PEDANT   Swear, if thou dar'st.
GREMIO   Nay, I dare not swear it.
TRANIO   Then thou wert best say that I am not Lucentio.   98
GREMIO   Yes, I know thee to be Signor Lucentio.
BAPTISTA   Away with the dotard! To the jail with him!

Enter Biondello, Lucentio, and Bianca.

VINCENTIO   Thus strangers may be haled and abused.   101
   —O monstrous villain!
BIONDELLO   O! We are spoiled and—yonder he is. Deny   103
him, forswear him, or else we are all undone.
                    *Exeunt Biondello, Tranio, and Pedant, as fast
                    as may be. [Lucentio and Bianca] kneel.*

LUCENTIO
Pardon, sweet Father.
VINCENTIO   Lives my sweet son?
BIANCA
Pardon, dear Father.
BAPTISTA   How hast thou offended?
Where is Lucentio?
LUCENTIO   Here's Lucentio,
Right son to the right Vincentio,
That have by marriage made thy daughter mine,
While counterfeit supposes bleared thine eyne.   110

88 forthcoming ready to stand trial when required   **93–94 coney-
catched** tricked   **98 wert best** might as well   **101 haled** hauled about,
maltreated   **103 spoiled** ruined   **110 supposes** suppositions, false
appearances (with an allusion to Gascoigne's *Supposes,* an adaptation of
I Suppositi by Ariosto, from which Shakespeare took the Lucentio-
Bianca plot of intrigue).   **eyne** eyes

GREMIO
  Here's packing, with a witness, to deceive us all!   111
VINCENTIO
  Where is that damnèd villain Tranio,
  That faced and braved me in this matter so?   113
BAPTISTA
  Why, tell me, is not this my Cambio?
BIANCA
  Cambio is changed into Lucentio.   115
LUCENTIO
  Love wrought these miracles. Bianca's love
  Made me exchange my state with Tranio,   117
  While he did bear my countenance in the town,   118
  And happily I have arrivèd at the last
  Unto the wishèd haven of my bliss.
  What Tranio did, myself enforced him to;
  Then pardon him, sweet Father, for my sake.
VINCENTIO I'll slit the villain's nose, that would have
  sent me to the jail.
BAPTISTA [*To Lucentio*] But do you hear, sir? Have you
  married my daughter without asking my good will?
VINCENTIO Fear not, Baptista, we will content you, go
  to. But I will in, to be revenged for this villainy. *Exit.*
BAPTISTA And I, to sound the depth of this knavery.
                                        Exit.
LUCENTIO Look not pale, Bianca; thy father will not
  frown.   *Exeunt [Lucentio and Bianca].*
GREMIO
  My cake is dough, but I'll in among the rest,   132
  Out of hope of all but my share of the feast.   [*Exit.*]   133
KATHARINA Husband, let's follow, to see the end of
  this ado.
PETRUCHIO First kiss me, Kate, and we will.
KATHARINA What, in the midst of the street?
PETRUCHIO What, art thou ashamed of me?
KATHARINA No, sir, God forbid, but ashamed to kiss.

---

111 packing conspiracy **113 faced and braved** bullied and defied
115 Cambio is changed (A pun; *Cambio* in Italian means "change" or
"exchange.") **117 state** social station **118 countenance** appearance
132 My . . . dough i.e., I'm out of luck **133 Out . . . but** having hope for
nothing other than

PETRUCHIO
   Why, then let's home again. [*To Grumio.*] Come, sirrah,
      let's away.
KATHARINA
   Nay, I will give thee a kiss. [*She kisses him.*] Now pray
      thee, love, stay.
PETRUCHIO
   Is not this well? Come, my sweet Kate.
   Better once than never, for never too late.   *Exeunt.* 143

✤

5.2   *Enter Baptista, Vincentio, Gremio, the Pedant,
         Lucentio, and Bianca; [Petruchio, Kate,
         Hortensio,] Tranio, Biondello, Grumio, and
         Widow; the servingmen with Tranio bringing in
         a banquet.*

LUCENTIO
   At last, though long, our jarring notes agree,
   And time it is, when raging war is done,
   To smile at scapes and perils overblown.   3
   My fair Bianca, bid my father welcome,
   While I with selfsame kindness welcome thine.
   Brother Petruchio, sister Katharina,
   And thou, Hortensio, with thy loving widow,
   Feast with the best, and welcome to my house.
   My banquet is to close our stomachs up   9
   After our great good cheer. Pray you, sit down,   10
   For now we sit to chat as well as eat.   [*They sit.*]
PETRUCHIO
   Nothing but sit and sit, and eat and eat!
BAPTISTA
   Padua affords this kindness, son Petruchio.
PETRUCHIO
   Padua affords nothing but what is kind.

---

143 once at some time. (Cf. "better late than never.")

5.2. Location: Padua. Lucentio's house.
s.d. banquet i.e., dessert   **3 scapes** escapes, close calls   **9 stomachs**
appetites (with pun on "quarrels")   **10 our . . . cheer** i.e., the wedding
feast at Baptista's

HORTENSIO
  For both our sakes, I would that word were true.

PETRUCHIO
  Now, for my life, Hortensio fears his widow.   16

WIDOW
  Then never trust me if I be afeard.

PETRUCHIO
  You are very sensible, and yet you miss my sense:
  I mean Hortensio is afeard of you.   19

WIDOW
  He that is giddy thinks the world turns round.

PETRUCHIO
  Roundly replied.

KATHARINA   Mistress, how mean you that?   21

WIDOW   Thus I conceive by him.   22

PETRUCHIO
  Conceives by me! How likes Hortensio that?

HORTENSIO
  My widow says, thus she conceives her tale.   24

PETRUCHIO
  Very well mended. Kiss him for that, good widow.

KATHARINA
  "He that is giddy thinks the world turns round":
  I pray you, tell me what you meant by that.

WIDOW
  Your husband, being troubled with a shrew,
  Measures my husband's sorrow by his woe—   29
  And now you know my meaning.

KATHARINA
  A very mean meaning.

WIDOW   Right, I mean you.   31

---

16 fears is afraid of. (But the Widow takes the word in the sense of
"frightens"; she protests she is not at all *afeard*, frightened by Hortensio.) **19 afeard** (Petruchio takes up the Widow's word and uses it in the
sense of "suspicious," fearful she will be untrue.) **21 Roundly** boldly
22 Thus . . . him i.e., that's what I think of him, Petruchio. (But Petruchio takes up *conceives* in the sense of "is made pregnant.") **24 conceives** devises (with a possible pun on *tale, tail*) **29 Measures** judges
31 very mean contemptible. (But the Widow takes up *mean* in the sense
of "have in mind," and Kate replies in the sense of "moderate in shrewishness.")

KATHARINA

  And I am mean indeed, respecting you.   32

PETRUCHIO   To her, Kate!

HORTENSIO   To her, widow!

PETRUCHIO

  A hundred marks, my Kate does put her down.   35

HORTENSIO   That's my office.

PETRUCHIO

  Spoke like an officer. Ha' to thee, lad!   37

                             Drinks to Hortensio.

BAPTISTA

  How likes Gremio these quick-witted folks?

GREMIO

  Believe me, sir, they butt together well.   39

BIANCA

  Head, and butt! An hasty-witted body   40

  Would say your head and butt were head and horn.   41

VINCENTIO

  Ay, mistress bride, hath that awakened you?

BIANCA

  Ay, but not frighted me. Therefore I'll sleep again.

PETRUCHIO

  Nay, that you shall not; since you have begun,

  Have at you for a bitter jest or two!   45

BIANCA

  Am I your bird? I mean to shift my bush;   46

  And then pursue me as you draw your bow.

  You are welcome all.

                 Exit Bianca [with Kate and Widow].

PETRUCHIO

  She hath prevented me. Here, Signor Tranio,   49

  This bird you aimed at, though you hit her not.   50

---

32 respecting compared to   **35 marks** coins worth 13 shillings 4 pence.
put her down overcome her. (But Hortensio takes up the phrase
in a bawdy sense.)   **37 officer** (playing on Hortensio's speaking of his
office or function).   **Ha'** have, i.e., here's   **39 butt** butt heads   **40 butt**
tail, bottom   **41 head and horn** (alluding to the familiar joke about
cuckold's horns)   **45 Have at** I shall come at.   **bitter** sharp   **46 Am . . .
bush** i.e., if you mean to shoot your barbs at me, I intend to move out of
the way, as a bird would fly to another bush (with a possible bawdy
double meaning)   **49 prevented** forestalled   **50 This bird** i.e., Bianca,
whom Tranio courted (*aimed at*) in his disguise as Lucentio

Therefore a health to all that shot and missed.   51
                            [He offers a toast.]

TRANIO
  O, sir, Lucentio slipped me like his greyhound,   52
  Which runs himself and catches for his master.

PETRUCHIO
  A good swift simile, but something currish.   54

TRANIO
  'Tis well, sir, that you hunted for yourself;
  'Tis thought your deer does hold you at a bay.   56

BAPTISTA
  O ho, Petruchio! Tranio hits you now.

LUCENTIO
  I thank thee for that gird, good Tranio.   58

HORTENSIO
  Confess, confess, hath he not hit you here?

PETRUCHIO
  'A has a little galled me, I confess;
  And as the jest did glance away from me,   61
  'Tis ten to one it maimed you two outright.

BAPTISTA
  Now, in good sadness, son Petruchio,   63
  I think thou hast the veriest shrew of all.

PETRUCHIO
  Well, I say no. And therefore for assurance   65
  Let's each one send unto his wife;
  And he whose wife is most obedient
  To come at first when he doth send for her
  Shall win the wager which we will propose.

HORTENSIO
  Content. What's the wager?

LUCENTIO   Twenty crowns.

PETRUCHIO   Twenty crowns!
  I'll venture so much of my hawk or hound,   72
  But twenty times so much upon my wife.

LUCENTIO   A hundred, then.

---

51 a health a toast   **52 slipped** unleashed   **54 swift** (1) quick-witted
(2) concerning swiftness. **currish** (1) ignoble (2) concerning dogs **56 deer**
(punning on *dear*). **does . . . bay** turns on you like a cornered animal
and holds you at a distance **58 gird** sharp, biting jest **61 glance away**
ricochet off **63 sadness** seriousness **65 assurance** proof **72 of** on

HORTENSIO Content.
PETRUCHIO A match. 'Tis done.
HORTENSIO Who shall begin?
LUCENTIO That will I.
  Go, Biondello, bid your mistress come to me.
BIONDELLO I go.   *Exit.*
BAPTISTA
  Son, I'll be your half Bianca comes.   81
LUCENTIO
  I'll have no halves; I'll bear it all myself.

        Enter Biondello.

  How now, what news?
BIONDELLO
  Sir, my mistress sends you word
  That she is busy and she cannot come.
PETRUCHIO
  How? She's busy and she cannot come!
  Is that an answer?
GREMIO   Ay, and a kind one too.
  Pray God, sir, your wife send you not a worse.
PETRUCHIO I hope better.
HORTENSIO
  Sirrah Biondello, go and entreat my wife
  To come to me forthwith.   *Exit Biondello.*
PETRUCHIO   O ho, entreat her!
  Nay, then she must needs come.
HORTENSIO   )   I am afraid, sir,
  Do what you can, yours will not be entreated.

        Enter Biondello.

  Now, where's my wife?
BIONDELLO
  She says you have some goodly jest in hand.
  She will not come. She bids you come to her.
PETRUCHIO
  Worse and worse. She will not come!
  O, vile, intolerable, not to be endured!
  Sirrah Grumio, go to your mistress.
  Say I command her come to me.   *Exit [Grumio].*

81 be your half take half your bet

HORTENSIO
  I know her answer.
PETRUCHIO   What?
HORTENSIO   She will not.
PETRUCHIO
  The fouler fortune mine, and there an end.

    Enter Katharina.

BAPTISTA
  Now, by my halidom, here comes Katharina!   103
KATHARINA
  What is your will, sir, that you send for me?
PETRUCHIO
. Where is your sister, and Hortensio's wife?
KATHARINA
  They sit conferring by the parlor fire.
PETRUCHIO
  Go fetch them hither. If they deny to come,
  Swinge me them soundly forth unto their husbands.   108
  Away, I say, and bring them hither straight.
                         [Exit Katharina.]
LUCENTIO
  Here is a wonder, if you talk of a wonder.
HORTENSIO
  And so it is. I wonder what it bodes.
PETRUCHIO
  Marry, peace it bodes, and love, and quiet life,
  An awful rule, and right supremacy,   113
  And, to be short, what not that's sweet and happy.
BAPTISTA
  Now, fair befall thee, good Petruchio!
  The wager thou hast won, and I will add
  Unto their losses twenty thousand crowns,
  Another dowry to another daughter,
  For she is changed as she had never been.   119
PETRUCHIO
  Nay, I will win my wager better yet,

---

103 by my halidom (Originally an oath by the holy relics, but confused
with an oath to the Virgin Mary.) **108 Swinge** thrash. **me** i.e., at my
behest. (*Me* is used colloquially.) **113 awful rule** authority commanding
awe or respect **119 as . . . been** as if she had never existed, i.e., she is
totally changed

And show more sign of her obedience,
Her new-built virtue and obedience.

 Enter Kate, Bianca, and Widow.

See where she comes, and brings your froward wives
As prisoners to her womanly persuasion.—
Katharine, that cap of yours becomes you not.
Off with that bauble. Throw it underfoot.

          [She obeys.]

WIDOW
 Lord, let me never have a cause to sigh
 Till I be brought to such a silly pass!   128

BIANCA
 Fie, what a foolish duty call you this?

LUCENTIO
 I would your duty were as foolish too.
 The wisdom of your duty, fair Bianca,
 Hath cost me an hundred crowns since suppertime.

BIANCA
 The more fool you, for laying on my duty.   133

PETRUCHIO
 Katharine, I charge thee tell these headstrong women
 What duty they do owe their lords and husbands.

WIDOW
 Come, come, you're mocking; we will have no telling.

PETRUCHIO
 Come on, I say, and first begin with her.

WIDOW She shall not.

PETRUCHIO
 I say she shall—and first begin with her.

KATHARINA
 Fie, fie! Unknit that threatening unkind brow,
 And dart not scornful glances from those eyes,
 To wound thy lord, thy king, thy governor.
 It blots thy beauty as frosts do bite the meads,
 Confounds thy fame as whirlwinds shake fair buds, 144
 And in no sense is meet or amiable.
 A woman moved is like a fountain troubled,   146

---

128 pass state of affairs **133 laying** wagering **144 Confounds thy
fame** ruins your reputation **146 moved** angry

Muddy, ill-seeming, thick, bereft of beauty;
And while it is so, none so dry or thirsty
Will deign to sip or touch one drop of it.
Thy husband is thy lord, thy life, thy keeper,
Thy head, thy sovereign; one that cares for thee,
And for thy maintenance commits his body
To painful labor both by sea and land,
To watch the night in storms, the day in cold,
Whilst thou liest warm at home, secure and safe;
And craves no other tribute at thy hands
But love, fair looks, and true obedience—
Too little payment for so great a debt.
Such duty as the subject owes the prince,
Even such a woman oweth to her husband;
And when she is froward, peevish, sullen, sour,   161
And not obedient to his honest will,
What is she but a foul contending rebel
And graceless traitor to her loving lord?
I am ashamed that women are so simple   165
To offer war where they should kneel for peace,
Or seek for rule, supremacy, and sway
When they are bound to serve, love, and obey.
Why are our bodies soft and weak and smooth,
Unapt to toil and trouble in the world,   170
But that our soft conditions and our hearts   171
Should well agree with our external parts?
Come, come, you froward and unable worms!   173
My mind hath been as big as one of yours,   174
My heart as great, my reason haply more,
To bandy word for word and frown for frown;
But now I see our lances are but straws,
Our strength as weak, our weakness past compare,
That seeming to be most which we indeed least are.
Then vail your stomachs, for it is no boot,   180
And place your hands below your husband's foot,
In token of which duty, if he please,
My hand is ready; may it do him ease.   183

161 peevish obstinate   **165 simple** foolish   **170 Unapt** unfit   **171 condi-**
tions qualities   **173 unable worms** i.e., poor feeble creatures   **174 big**
haughty   **180 vail your stomachs** lower your pride.   **boot** profit, use
183 do him ease give him pleasure

PETRUCHIO
Why, there's a wench! Come on, and kiss me, Kate.
                                        [*They kiss.*]
LUCENTIO
Well, go thy ways, old lad, for thou shalt ha 't.
VINCENTIO
'Tis a good hearing when children are toward.   186
LUCENTIO
But a harsh hearing when women are froward.
PETRUCHIO   Come, Kate, we'll to bed.
We three are married, but you two are sped.   189
[*To Lucentio.*] 'Twas I won the wager, though you hit the
     white,   190
And, being a winner, God give you good night!
                              Exit Petruchio [*and Kate*].
HORTENSIO
Now, go thy ways, thou hast tamed a curst shrew.   192
LUCENTIO
'Tis a wonder, by your leave, she will be tamed so.
                                        [*Exeunt.*]

---

186 'Tis . . . toward i.e., one likes to hear when children are obedient
189 We . . . sped i.e., all we three men have taken wives, but you two are
done for (*sped*) through disobedient wives   **190 the white** the center of
the target (with quibble on the name of Bianca, which in Italian means
"white")   **192 shrew** pronounced "shrow" (and thus spelled in the
Folio). See also 4.1.198 and 5.2.28.

Date and Text

The Taming of the Shrew was not printed until the First Folio of 1623. Francis Meres does not mention the play in 1598 in his *Palladis Tamia: Wit's Treasury* (a slender volume on contemporary literature and art; valuable because it lists most of Shakespeare's plays that existed at that time), unless it is the mysterious *"Loue labours wonne"* on his list. (Meres is not totally accurate, for he omits *Henry VI* from the history plays.) The play must have existed prior to 1598, however, for its style is comparable with that of *The Two Gentlemen of Verona* and other early comedies. Moreover, a play called *The Taming of A Shrew* appeared in print in 1594 (Stationers' Register, May 1594). The relationship of that text to Shakespeare's play is problematic, and several theories prevail. One is that *A Shrew* represents a source for Shakespeare's play, or even an early version by Shakespeare. If, as seems more likely, *A Shrew* is later, then it may be an imitation by some rival dramatist, who relied chiefly on his memory and who changed characters' names and the location to make the play seem his. More probably, it is a somewhat uncharacteristic kind of reported or "bad" quarto, reconstructed and "improved" upon by a writer who also borrowed admiringly from Christopher Marlowe and other Elizabethan dramatists. In either case, Shakespeare's play would have to be dated earlier than May 1594.

The title page of *A Shrew* proclaims that "it was sundry times acted by the *Right honorable the Earle of* Pembrook his seruants." Quite possibly this derivative version was merely trying to capitalize on the original's stage success and was in fact describing performances of Shakespeare's play. Theater owner and manager Philip Henslowe's record of a performance of *"the Tamynge of A Shrowe"* in 1594 at Newington Butts, a mile south of London Bridge, may also refer to Shakespeare's play; certainly the minute distinction between "A Shrew" and "The Shrew" is one that the official records of the time would overlook. The Admiral's men and the Lord Chamberlain's men, acting companies, were playing at Newington Butts at the time, either jointly or alternatingly. Since Shakespeare's company, the Chamberlain's, later owned *The Shrew*, they may well have owned and acted it on this occasion in 1594, having obtained it from the Earl of Pembroke's men when that company disbanded in 1593. Many of Pembroke's leading players joined the Chamberlain's, Shakespeare quite possibly among them. (The possibility that he came to the Chamberlain's from Lord Strange's men seems less certain today than it once did.) It is entirely possible, then, that *The Shrew* was acted by Pembroke's men in 1592–1593 and subsequently passed along to the Chamberlain's.

The Folio text of this play is now generally thought to have been printed from Shakespeare's working manuscript or possibly from a transcript incorporating some minor theatrical changes.

Textual Notes

These textual notes are not a historical collation, either of the early folios or of more recent editions; they are simply a record of departures in this edition from the copy text. The reading adopted in this edition appears in boldface, followed by the rejected reading from the copy text, i.e., the First Folio. Only major alterations in punctuation are noted. Changes in lineation are not indicated, nor are some minor and obvious typographical errors.

Abbreviations used:
F the First Folio
s.d. stage direction
s.p. speech prefix

Copy Text: The First Folio.

Ind.1. s.d. Christopher Sly [printed at the end of the s.d. in F]   **1 s.p. [and elsewhere] Sly** Begger   **10–11 thirdborough** Headborough   **16 Breathe** Brach   **21 s.p. [and elsewhere] First Huntsman** Hunts   **81 s.p. First Player** 2. Player   **87 s.p. Second Player** Sinckto   **99 s.p. First Player** Plai   **134 peasant.** peasant,

Ind.2. 2 lordship Lord   **18 Sly's** Sies   **26 s.p. [and elsewhere] Third Servant** 3 Man   **27 s.p. [and elsewhere] Second Servant** 2 Man   **47 s.p. [and elsewhere] First Servant** 1 Man   **53 wi' th'** with   **99 s.p. [and elsewhere] Page** Lady   **125 s.p. Servant** Mes   **133 it. Is** it is

1.1. 13 Vincentio Vincentio's   **14 brought** brough   **24 satiety** sacietie   **25 Mi perdonate** Me Pardonato   **47 s.d. suitor** sister   **57 s.p. [and elsewhere] Katharina** Kate   **146 s.d. Manent** Manet   **163 captum** captam   **208 colored** Conlord   **227 time.** time   **244 your** you   **248 s.d. speak** speakes

1.2. 17 s.d. wrings rings   **18 masters** mistris   **24 Con . . . trovato** Contutti le core bene trobatto   **25 ben** bene   **26 Molto** multo   **onorato** honorata   **33 pip** peepe   **45 this's** this   **51 grows. But** growes but   **72 she is** she is   **120 me and other** me. Other   **171 help me** helpe one   **189 Antonio's** Butonios   **212 ours** yours   **265 feat** seeke   **280 ben** Been

2.1. 8 thee, tell tel   **79 unto you** vnto   **104 Pisa. By** Pisa by   **153 struck** stroke   **157 rascal fiddler** Rascall, fidler   **168 s.d. Exeunt** Exit   **186 bonny** bony   **244 askance** a sconce   **322 s.d. Exeunt** Exit   **328 in me** me   **352 Valance** Vallens   **355 pail** pale   **373 Marseilles'** Marcellus

3.1. 28 Sigeia sigeria [also at ll. 33 and 42]   **43 steterat** staterat   **47 [Aside]** Luc   **50 s.p. Bianca** [not in F]   **51 s.p. Lucentio** Bian   **53 s.p. Bianca** Hort   **76 clef** Cliffe   **80 change** charge   **odd** old   **81 s.p. Servant** Nicke

3.2. 29 of thy of   **30 old news** newes   **33 hear** heard   **54 swayed** Waid   **56 cheeked** chekt   **130 As I** As   **150 e'er** ere   **199 s.p. Gremio** Gra

4.1. 23 s.p. Curtis Gru   **42 their white** the white   **81 sleekly** slickely   **106 s.p. Grumio** Gre   **136 off** of   **168 s.d. Curtis** Curtis a Seruant [after l. 169 in F]

4.2. 4 s.p. Hortensio Luc   **6 s.p. Lucentio** Hor [and at l. 8]   **13 none** me
31 her them   **72 Take . . . alone** [assigned to "Par." in F]   **in** me

4.3. [F has "Actus Quartus. Scena Prima" here]   **63 s.p. Haberdasher** Fel
81 is a is   **88 like a** like   **146 where,** where   **177 account'st** accountedst

4.4. s.d. [booted] [appears at l. 18 in F]   **1 Sir** Sirs   **5 Where . . . Pegasus**
[assigned to Tranio in F]   **68** [F adds a s.d.: "Enter Peter"]   **91 except**
expect

4.5. 18 is in   **35 make a** make the   **37 where** whether   **77 she be** she

5.1. 4. [F has "Exit" here]   **6 master's** mistris   **42 brought** brough
50 master's Mistris   **104 s.d. Exeunt** Exit   **139 No** Mo   **143 than never**
then ueuer
5.2. [F has "Actus Quintus" here]   **2 done** come   **37 thee** the   **45 bitter**
better   **two** too   **52 s.p. Tranio** Tri   **57 ho** oh   **62 two** too   **65 for** sir
132 an fiue   **136 you're** your

Shakespeare's Sources

Most recent critics agree that the play called *The Taming of a Shrew*, published in 1594, is derived from a now-lost earlier version of Shakespeare's play to which the compiler added original material and borrowed or even plagiarized from other literary sources as well. It does not, then, appear to be a source for Shakespeare's play as Geoffrey Bullough has argued in his *Narrative and Dramatic Sources of Shakespeare* (1966). Apart from this question, all critics agree that Shakespeare's play consists of three elements, each with its own source: the romantic love plot of Lucentio and Bianca, the wife-taming plot of Petruchio and Kate, and the framing plot or, induction, of Christopher Sly.

The romantic love plot is derived from George Gascoigne's *Supposes*, a neoclassical comedy performed at Gray's Inn (one of the Inns of Court, where young men studied law in London) in 1566. Gascoigne's play was a rather close translation of Lodovico Ariosto's *I Suppositi* (1509), which in turn was based on two classical plays, Terence's *Eunuchus* and Plautus' *Captivi*. The heroine of Gascoigne's version (as of Ariosto's) is Polynesta, the resourceful daughter of Damon, a widower of Ferrara. Two suitors vie for Polynesta's hand: Dr. Cleander, an aged and miserly lawyer, and Erostrato, a Sicilian gentleman who has purportedly come to Ferrara to study. In fact, however, this "Erostrato" is the servant Dulippo in disguise, having changed places with his master. (These disguisings are the "supposes" of the title.) As a servant in Damon's household, "Dulippo" has secretly become the lover of Polynesta and has made her pregnant. Balia, the nurse, or duenna, is their go-between. Meanwhile, "Erostrato" takes great delight in outwitting Dr. Cleander and his unattractive parasite, Pasiphilo. The counterfeit Erostrato's ruse is to produce a rich father who will guarantee a handsome dowry and thereby outbid Cleander in the contest for Polynesta's hand. The "father" he produces, however, is actually an old Sienese stranger, who is persuaded that he is in danger in Ferrara unless he cloaks his identity. Complications arise when Damon learns of his daughter's affair and throws the

lover, "Dulippo," into a dungeon. The crafty Pasiphilo over-
hears this compromising information and resolves to cause
mischief for all the principals. Moreover, when Erostrato's
real father, Philogano, arrives in Ferrara, he is barred from
his son's house by the counterfeit Philogano and resolves to
get help. His clever servant, Litio, suggests employing the
famous lawyer Cleander. All is happily resolved when the
real Dulippo proves to be the son of Dr. Cleander, and
the real Erostrato is revealed to be rich and socially eligible
for Polynesta's hand in marriage. Cleander is even recon-
ciled to his parasite, Pasiphilo.

Shakespeare, in his play, has almost entirely eliminated
the satire of the law that is in his source. Gremio is aged
and wealthy, but no shyster. The lover is not imprisoned in a
dungeon. The parasite is gone, as also in *The Comedy of Errors*. Bianca does not consummate her affair with Lucentio
as does Polynesta, and hence has no need for a go-between
like Balia. Shakespeare adapts a sophisticated neoclassical
comedy, racy and cosmopolitan, to the moral standards of
his public theater. The witless Hortensio, the tutoring in
Latin, and the music lesson are Shakespeare's invention.

The wife-taming plot of Petruchio and Kate reflects an
ancient comic misogynistic tradition, still extant today in
the Scottish folksong "The Cooper of Fife" or "The Wife
Wrapped in Wether's Skin" (Francis James Child, *The English and Scottish Popular Ballads* [1888–1898], 5:104). Richard Hosley has argued (in *Huntington Library Quarterly* 27,
1964) that Shakespeare's likeliest source was *A Merry Jest
of a Shrewd and Curst Wife Lapped in Morel's Skin, for her
Good Behavior* (printed c. 1550). Excerpts of this ballad follow. In this version, the husband beats his shrewish wife
with birch rods until she bleeds and faints, whereupon he
wraps her in the raw salted skin of an old plow-horse
named Morel. Like Kate, this shrewish wife has a gentle
younger sister who is their father's favorite. This father
warns the man who proposes to marry his older daughter
that she is shrewish, but the suitor goes ahead and subsequently tames his wife with Morel's skin. Thereafter, at a
celebratory dinner, everyone is impressed by the thorough-
ness of the taming.

Shakespeare avoids the misogynistic extremes of this
story, despite the similarity of the narrative. Instead, he

seems to have had in mind the more humanistic spirit of Erasmus's *A Merry Dialogue Declaring the Properties of Shrewd Shrews and Honest Wives* (translated 1557) and Juan Luis Vives's *The Office and Duty of an Husband* (translated 1555). Specific elements of the wife-taming plot have been traced to other possible sources. The scolding of a tailor occurs in Gerard Legh's *Accidence of Armory* (1562); a wife agrees with her husband's assertion of a patent falsehood in Don Juan Manuel's *El Conde Lucanor* (1335); and three husbands wager on the obedience of their wives in *The Book of the Knight of La Tour-Landry* (printed 1484).

The induction story, of the beggar duped into believing himself a rich lord, is an old tale occurring in the *Arabian Nights*. An interesting analogue occurs in P. Heuterus's *De Rebus Burgundicis* (1584), translated into the French of S. Goulart (1606?) and thence into the English of Edward Grimeston (1607). According to Heuterus, in 1440 Philip the Good of Burgundy actually entertained a drunken beggar in his palace "to make trial of the vanity of our life," plying him with fine clothes, bed, a feast, and the performance of "a pleasant comedy."

A Merry Jest
of a Shrewd and Curst Wife
Lapped in Morel's Skin

Listen, friends, and hold you still;
Abide awhile and dwell.
A merry jest tell you I will,
And how that it befell.
As I went walking upon a day
Among my friends to sport,
To an house I took the way
To rest me for my comfort.

A great feast was kept there then,
And many one was thereat,
With wives and maidens and many a good man
That made good game and chat.

Title: **Shrewd** shrewish

It befell then at that tide   13
An honest man was there;
A cursèd dame sat by his side
That often did him dere.   16

His wife she was, I tell you plain,
This dame, ye may me trow.   18
To play the master she would not lain   19
And make her husband bow.
At every word that she did speak
To be peace he was full fain,   22
Or else she would take him on the cheek   23
Or put him to other pain.

When she did wink, he durst not stir   25
Nor play wherever he went
With friend or neighbor to make good cheer,
When she her brows bent.
These folk had two maidens fair and free   29
Which were their daughters dear.
This is true, believe you me:
Of conditions was none their peer.   32

The youngest was meek and gentle, iwis;   33
Her father's condition she had.
The eldest her mother's, withouten miss: 35
Sometimes frantic and sometimes mad.   36
The father had his pleasure in the one alway,
And glad he was her to behold;
The mother in the other, this is no nay,   39
For in all her curstness she made her bold.   40

And at the last she was, in fay,   41
As curst as her mother in word and deed   42
Her mischievous pageants sometime to play,   43
Which caused her father's heart to bleed.

---

13 tide time   **16 dere** vex   **18 trow** believe   **19 lain** i.e., disguise her ambition   **22 be peace** be silent.   **full fain** very willing   **23 take him** give him a
blow   **25 wink** close or avert her eye   **29 free** of good breeding   **32 conditions** quality, nature   **33 iwis** certainly   **35 withouten miss** without doubt
36 frantic ungovernable.   **mad** angry   **39 no nay** certain   **40 in all . . . bold**
i.e., the mother encouraged her shrewishness in every way   **41 at the last**
in sum.   **in fay** in good faith   **42 curst** shrewish   **43 Her . . . play** i.e.,
playing her mischievous tricks

For he was woe and nothing glad,   45
And of her would fain be rid.
He wished to God that some man her had,
But yet to marriage he dust her not bid.

Full many there came the youngest to have,
But her father was loath her to forgo.
None there came the eldest to crave
For fear it should turn them to woe.
The father was loath any man to beguile,
For he was true and just withal.   54
Yet there came one within a while
That her demanded in the hall.

[The meek and gentle younger daughter is quickly wooed
and wedded; the father grieves to lose her, but the mother is
only too glad to get rid of her. When a suitor to the shrewish
elder daughter shows up, much to the father's surprise, the
kind old man warns of the danger: this daughter has been
taught by her mother "to be master of her husband." The
young man persists nonetheless and wins the mother's consent to the match. The mother advises him to pay heed to
his wife's wishes if he wants to enjoy domestic harmony—
especially since the wife will bring with her a considerable
dowry. The young man is not wealthy but is a good craftsman and willing to work hard. The wife-to-be gives him
plain notice of her intention to rule the roost in marriage,
but he has his own plans about that; he knows he is marrying a woman with a "proud heart," but one who will in all
events bring with her "an heap of gold."
    And so the wedding takes place, followed by a wedding
feast with much giving of gifts (including a hundred pounds
to set the bridegroom up in his chosen craft), and dancing.
The wedding night appears to be a success, the new husband playing with his wife "Even as the cat was wont with
the mouse." Their sparring begins on the very next morning, as husband and wife lie abed while the bride's mother
prepares them a caudle, a warm drink of gruel and wine.]

When that the mother departed was,

45 woe woeful.   **nothing** not at all   **54 withal** in addition

They dallied together and had good game.
He hit her awry. She cried, "Alas!
What do ye, man? Hold up, for shame!"   514
"I will, sweet wife," then gan he say,
"Fulfill your mind, both loud and still.   516
But ye be able, I swear in fay,   517
In all sports to abide my will."

And they wrestled so long beforn
That this they had for their great meed: 520
Both shirt and smock was all to-torne,   521
That their uprising had no speed.   522
But yet the mother came again
And said to her daughter, "How dost thou now?"
"Marry, mother, between us twain
Our shirts be torn, I make God a vow.

"By God's dear mother," she sware then,
"This order with us may not continue.   528
I will no more lie by this man,
For he doth me brast both vein and sinew.   530
Nay, nay, dear mother, this world goeth on wheels.   531
By sweet Saint George, ye may me trow:
He lieth kicking with his heels   533
That he is like to bear me a blow."   534

[The newlyweds get past this difficulty and join their friends in the hall for the caudle and more celebration. Even the father's apprehensions are quieted to a degree, and parents and friends leave the happy couple to their new household. The husband sets up his shop "with haberdash ware," i.e., petty merchandise, and bestows great care on his plows and livestock as well. Trouble next erupts when the farm laborers who tend his cattle and sheep come in from the field for their meal only to be greeted by a burst of shrewish temper from their new mistress.]

514 **Hold up** stop 516 **Fulfill** satisfy the desire of 517 **in fay** in good faith 520 **meed** reward 521 **to-torne** torn to bits 522 **their . . . speed** they were in no hurry to get out of bed 528 **order** i.e., condition of matrimony 530 **me brast . . . sinew** i.e., bursts asunder my blood vessels and tendons 531 **goeth on wheels** goes on its own way (i.e., this too will pass) 533 **kicking with his heels** i.e., flat on his back 534 **That . . . bear me** he that is likely to receive from me

With countenance grim and words smart   607
She gave them meat and bade them brast.   608
The poor folk that come from plow and cart
Of her lewd words they were aghast,   610
Saying each to other, "What dame is this?
The devil I trow hath brought us here.   612
Our master shall know it, by heaven's bliss,
That we will not serve him another year."

The goodman was forth in the town abroad   615
About other things, I you say.
When he came homeward, he met with a goad: 617
One of his carters was going away.
To whom he said, "Lob, whither goest thou?"
The carter spied his master then,
And said to him, "I make God a vow,
No longer with thy wife abide I can.

"Master," he said, "by God's blist,   623
Our dame is the devil, thou mayst me believe!
If thou have sought her, thou hast not missed 625
Of one that full often thee shall grieve.   626
By God, a man thou canst not have
To go to cart ne yet to plow,   628
Neither boy nor yet knave,
By God's dear mother, I make God a vow,

"That will bide with thee day or night.
Our dame is not for us, for she doth curse.
When we shall eat or drink with right,   633
She bans and frowns, that we be all the worse. 634
We be not used, wherever we wend,
To be sorely looked on for eating of our meat. 636
The devil I trow is to thee send.   637
God help us a better mistress to get!"

"Come on thy way, Lob, and turn again.
Go home with me and all shall be well.

607 smart stinging **608 brast** stuff themselves until they burst **610 lewd** rude **612 brought us** i.e., brought her to us **615 goodman** yeoman, householder **617 goad** i.e., sting, annoyance **623 blist** bliss **625-626 If . . . grieve** i.e., if you chose her, you picked one that will grieve you very often **628 ne** nor **633 shall** wish to **634 bans** curses **636 sorely looked on** harshly regarded **637 is to thee send** has been sent to you

An ox for my meiny shall be slain   641
And the hide at the market I will sell."
Upon this together home they went.
The goodman was angry in his mind,
But yet to his wife with good intent
He said, "Sweetheart, ye be unkind.

"Entreat our meiny well alway,   647
And give them meat and drink enough,
For they get our living every day,   649
And theirs also, at cart and plough.
Therefore I would that they should have
Meat and drink to their behoof.   652
For, my sweet wife, so God me save,
Ye will do so, if ye me love."

"Give them what thou wilt! I do not care,
By day and night, man, believe thou me.
Whatever they have, or how they fare,
I pray God evil mote they thee.   658
And specially that whoreson that doth complain.
I will quit him once, if ever I live!   660
I will dash the knave upon the brain
That ever after it shall him grieve."

"What, my dear wife? For shame, be still.
This is a pain, such words to hear.
We cannot always have our will,
Though that we were a king's peer.
For, to shame a knave, what can they get?   667
Thou art as lewd, 'fore God, as they.   668
And therefore shalt thou serve them of meat
And drink also, from hence alway.   670

"What, wife? Ye be to blame
To speak to me thus in this wise.
If we should strive, folk would speak shame.
Therefore be still, in mine advice.
I am loath with you to strive,

641 meiny retinue, company 647 Entreat treat 649 get earn 652 behoof
use, benefit 658 mote they thee may they thrive 660 quit repay 667 For
... get i.e., what good does it do to scorn someone who is below you in
social station (?) or, you should be ashamed; what can they get on their
own 668 lewd rude, ill-mannered 670 hence henceforth. alway always

For aught that you shall do or say.
I swear to Christ, wife, by my life,
I had rather take Morel and ride my way

To seek mine adventure till your mood be past.
I say to you, these manners be not good.
Therefore, I pray you that this be the last
Of your furious anger that seemeth so wood.   682
What can it avail you me for to grieve
That loveth you so well as I do, mine heart?
By my troth, wife, you may me believe,
Such toys as these be would make us both smart."   686

"Smart, in the twenty feigning devils' name!
That list me once well for to see.   688
I pray God give thee evil shame.
What shouldest thou be, wert it not for me?   690
A rag on thine arse thou shouldst not have
Except my friends had given it thee.   692
Therefore I tell thee well, thou drunken knave,
Thou art not he that shall rule me."

"O good wife, cease and let this overpass,
For all your great anger and high words eke.   696
I am mine own self even as I was,
And to you will be loving and also meek.
But if ye should do thus as ye do begin,
It may not continue no time, iwis.
I would not let, for kith nor kin,   701
To make you mend all things that is amiss."

"Make me? Marry, out upon thee, drivel!   703
Sayest thou that, wilt thou begin?
I pray God and Our Lady that a foul evil
Lighten upon thee and all thy kin!   706
By God's dear blist, vex me no more,   707
For if thou do thou shalt repent.
I have yet something for thee in store."
And with that a staff in her hand she hent.   710

682 wood furious, mad   **686 toys** antics   **688 That . . . see** I'd really like to
see that   **690 What shouldest thou be** where would you be, what kind of
life would you have   **692 friends** relatives   **696 eke** also   **701 let** hesitate.
kith friends and neighbors   **703 drivel** drudge, imbecile   **706 Lighten**
alight   **707 blist** bliss   **710 hent** seized

At him full soon then she let flee,
And whirled about her as it had been a man.
Her husband then was fain, perdy,   713
To void her stroke and go his way then.   714
"By God's dear mother!" then gan she swear,
"From henceforth I will make thee bow.
For I will trim thee in thy gear,
Or else I would I were called a sow.

"Fie on all wretches that be like thee,
In word or work, both loud and still!
I swear by Him that made man free,
Of me thou shalt not have thy will,
Now nor never, I tell thee plain;
For I will have gold and riches enow
When thou shalt go jagged as a simple swain   725
With whip in hand at cart and plow."

"Of that, my dear wife, I take no scorn,
For many a goodman with mind and heart
Hath gone to plow and cart beforn
My time, iwis, with pain and smart,
Which now be rich and have good will,
Being at home, and make good cheer,
And there they intend to lead their life still
Till our Lord do send for them here.   734

"But now I must ride a little way,
Dear wife. I will come right soon again.
Appoint our dinner, I you pray,   737
For I do take on me great pain.
I do my best, I swear by my life,
To order you like a woman, iwis,
And yet it cannot be withouten strife,
Through your lewd tongue, by heaven's bliss."

"Ride to the devil and to his dame!
I would I should thee never see.
I pray God send thee mickle shame   745
In any place wherever thou be.
Thou wouldest fain the master play,

---

713 **fain, perdy** glad, by God   714 **void** avoid   725 **jagged** i.e., in jagged, tattered clothes   734 **here** i.e., on earth   737 **Appoint** prepare   745 **mickle** much

But thou shalt not, by God I make thee sure!
I swear I will thy petticoat pay, 749
That long with me thou shalt not endure."

[The husband rides away, musing on his misfortune and re-
penting that he ever married but blaming no one but himself. He vows to make his wife regret her behavior by
beating her until she is black and blue and groaning for
woe. Nothing will do, he perceives, except to wrap her in the
skin of Morel, a faithful horse that has long drawn the plow
and the cart but is now old and infirm. Having resolved on
this course of action, he returns home to see what kind of
welcome he will get.]

"Where art thou, wife? Shall I have any meat?
Or am I not so welcome unto thee
That at my commandment I shall aught get?
I pray thee heartily soon tell thou me.
If thou do not serve me, and that anon, 843
I shall thee show mine anger, iwis.
I swear by God and by Saint John
Thy bones will I swaddle, so have I bliss." 846

Forth she came, as breme as a boar, 847
And like a dog she rated him then, 848
Saying thus: "I set no store 849
By thee, thou wretch! Thou art no man.
Get thee hence out of my sight,
For meat nor drink thou gettest none here.
I swear to thee, by Mary bright,
Of me thou gettest here no good cheer."

"Well, wife," he said, "thou dost me compel
To do that thing that I were loath.
If I bereave Morel of his old fell 857
Thou shalt repent it, by the faith now goeth. 858

749 thy petticoat pay flog your waistcoat (with you in it); i.e., I will make
you pay for this

843 anon at once **846 straddle** beat soundly **847 breme** fierce **848 rated**
scolded **849–850 set no store By thee** esteem you of no value **857 fell**
skin **858 by the faith now goeth** by the faith of Christians nowadays;
i.e., that's for sure

For I see well that it will no better be   859
But in it thou must, after the new guise.   860
It had been better, so mote I thee,   861
That thou haddest not begun this enterprise.

"Now will I begin my wife to tame,
That all the world shall it know.
I would be loath her for to shame,
Though she do not care, ye may me trow.   866
Yet will I her honesty regard
And it preserve wherever ye may.   868
But Morel, that is in yonder yard,
His hide therefore he must leese, in fay."   870

And so he commanded anon
To slay old Morel, his great horse,
And flay him then the skin from the bone
To wrap it about his wife's white corse.
Also he commanded of a birchen tree   875
Rods to be made a good great heap,
And sware, by dear God in Trinity
His wife in his cellar should skip and leap.

"The hide must be salted," then he said eke,   879
"Because I would not have it stink.
I hope herewith she will be meek,
For this I trow will make her shrink
And bow at my pleasure when I her bed,
And obey my commandments both loud and still,
Or else I will make her body bleed
And with sharp rods beat her my fill."

Anon with that to her he gan to call.
She bid, "Abide, in the devil's name!
I will not come, whatso befall.
Sit still, with sorrow and mickle shame.
Thou shalt not rule me as pleaseth thee,
I will well thou know, by God's dear mother;   892
But thou shalt be ruled alway by me,

859–860 it will . . . must there is nothing else for it but that you must go
into it   **861 so mote I thee** as I hope to prosper   **866 Though** even
though. **me trow** believe me   **868 wherever ye may** wherever I
may (?)   **870 leese** lose. **in fay** in good faith   **875 birchen** birch
879 eke also   **892 I will** I wish

And I will be master and none other."

"Wilt thou be master, dear wife? In fay,
Then must we wrestle for the best game.
If thou it win, then may I say
That I have done myself great shame.
But first I will make thee sweat, good Joan,   899
Red blood even to the heels a-down,
And lap thee in Morel's skin alone,   901
That the blood shall be seen even from the crown."

"Sayest thou me that, thou wretched knave?
It were better thou haddest me never seen!
I swear to thee, so God me save,
With my nails I will scratch out both thine eyen.   906
And therefore think not to touch me once,
For, by the Mass, if thou begin that,
Thou shalt be handled for the nonce   909
That all thy brains on the ground shall squat."

"Why, then, there is no remedy, I see,
But needs I must do even as I thought.
Seeing it will none otherwise be,
I will thee not spare, by God that me bought!   914
For now I am set thee for to charm   915
And make thee meek, by God's might,
Or else with rods, while thou art warm,
I shall thee scourge with reason and right.

"Now will I my sweet wife trim,
According as she deserveth to me.   920
I swear by God and by Saint Sim
With birchen rods well beat shall she be.
And after that, in Morel's salt skin
I will her lay and full fast bind,
That all her friends and eke her kin
Shall her long seek or they her find."   926

Then he her met, and to her gan say,
"How sayest thou, wife, wilt thou be master yet?"
She sware by God's body, and by that day,
And suddenly with her fist she did him hit,

899 sweat i.e., bleed **901 lap** enwrap **906 eyen** eyes **909 for the nonce** i.e., in such a way **914 bought** redeemed **915 charm** subdue **920 to me** at my hands **926 or** ere

And defied him, drivel, at every word,   931
Saying, "Precious whoreson, what dost thou think?   932
I set not by thee a stinking turd.   933
Thou shalt get of me neither meat nor drink."

"Sayest thou me that, wife?" quoth he then.
With that, in his arms he gan her catch.
Straight to the cellar with her he ran,
And fastened the door with lock and latch
And threw the key down him beside,
Asking her then if she would obey.
Then she said, "Nay, for all thy pride,"
But she was master and would abide alway.   942

"Then," quoth he, "we must make a fray."
And with that her clothes he gan to tear.
"Out upon thee, whoreson!" then she did say,
"Wilt thou rob me of all my gear?
It cost thee naught, thou arrant thief!"   947
And quickly she gat him by the head.
With that she said, "God give thee a mischief,
And them that fed thee first with bread!"   950

They wrestled together thus, they two,
So long that the clothes asunder went,
And to the ground he threw her tho,   953
That clean from the back her smock he rent.
In every hand a rod he gat   955
And laid upon her a right good pace,
Asking of her, "What game was that?"
And she cried out, "Whoreson! Alas! Alas!

"What wilt thou do? Wilt thou kill me?
I have made thee, a man of naught.   960
Thou shalt repent it, by God's pity,
That ever this deed thou hast y-wrought!"   962
"I care not for that, dame," he did say.

---

931 defied him, drivel scorned him as an imbecile (?) **932 Precious whoreson** i.e., worthless rogue **933 I set . . . turd** i.e., I don't give a turd for you
942 But she i.e., but said that she **947 It cost thee naught** i.e., you didn't
pay for it (having had no money when you married me) **950 them . . .
bread** i.e., those who raised you **953 tho** then **955 every hand** both
hands. **gat** got, held **960 I . . . naught** i.e., I and my family made you
what you are from a mere nobody **962 y-wrought** done

"Thou shalt give over, or we depart,   964
The mastership all, or all this day
I will not cease to make thee smart."

Ever he laid on, and ever she did cry,
"Alas! Alas, that ever I was born!
Out on thee, murderer, I thee defy!
Thou hast my white skin and my body all to-torne!   970
Leave off betime, I counsel thee."   971
"Nay, by God, dame, I say not so yet.
I swear to thee, by Mary so free,   973
We begin but now. This is the first fit.   974

"Once again we must dance about,
And then thou shalt rest in Morel's skin."
He gave her then so many a great clout   977
That on the ground the blood was seen.
Within a while he cried, "New rods, new!"
With that she cried full loud, "Alas!"
"Dance yet about, dame; thou came not where it grew."   981
And suddenly with that in a swoon she was.

He spied that, and up he her hent   983
And wrang her hard then by the nose.   984
With her to Morel's skin straight he went
And therein full fast he did her close.   986
Within a while she did revive,
Through the gross salt that did her smart.
She thought she should never have gone on live   989
Out of Morel's skin, so sore is her heart.

When she did spy that therein she lay,   991
Out of her wit she was full nigh,
And to her husband then did she say,
"How canst thou do this villainy?"
"Nay, how sayest thou, thou cursèd wife?
In this foul skin I will thee keep

---

964 or we depart ere we part, before we're done **970 to-torne** torn to pieces
971 betime quickly **973 free** excellent, magnanimous **974 fit** section of a poem or song (i.e., we've just begun) **977 clout** blow **981 thou came . . . grew** i.e., you've just started, you've had only a taste of what I have in store for you **983 hent** seized **984 wrang** wrung, pinched. (Wringing by the nose is a procedure for bringing a person to consciousness.) **986 fast** securely
989 on live alive **991 that therein she lay** what she was lying in

During the time of all thy life,
Therein forever to wail and weep."

With that her mood began to sink,
And said, "Dear husband, for grace I call!
For I shall never sleep or wink   1001
Till I get your love, whatso befall;
And I will never to you offend,
In no manner of wise, of all my life,   1004
Nor to do nothing that may pretend   1005
To displease you with my wits five.

"For father, nor mother, whatsoever they say,
I will not anger you, by God in throne,
But glad will your commandments obey
In presence of people and eke alone."
"Well, on that condition thou shalt have
Grace, and fair bed to rest thy body in.
But if thou rage more, so God me save,
I will wrap thee again in Morel's skin."

Then he took her out in his arms twain
And beheld her so piteously with blood arrayed.
"How thinkest thou, wife, shall we again
Have such business more?" to her he said.
She answered, "Nay, my husband dear.
While I you know and you know me,
Your commandments I will, both far and near,
Fulfill alway in every degree."

"Well, then, I promise thee, by God, even now,
Between thee and me shall never be strife.
If thou to my commandments quickly bow
I will thee cherish all the days of my life."
In bed she was laid, and healed full soon
As fair and clear as she was beforn.
What he her bid was quickly done.
To be diligent, iwis, she took no scorn.   1030

Then was he glad and thought in his mind,
"Now have I done myself great good,
And her also, we shall it find,

1001 **wink** close the eyes   1004 **of** during   1005 **pretend** undertake, presume   1030 **To . . . scorn** she thought it no indignity to be diligent, certainly

Though I have shed part of her blood.
For, as methink she will be meek,
Therefore I will her father and mother
Bid to guest, now the next week,   1037
And of our neighbors many other."

Great pain he made his wife to take
Against the day that they should come.   1040
Of them was none that there did lack,
I dare well say unto my doom.   1042
Yea, father and mother and neighbors all
Did thither come to make good cheer.
Soon they were set in general,   1045
The wife was diligent, as did appear.

Father and mother was welcome then,
And so were they all, in good fay.
The husband sat there like a man;   1049
The wife did serve them all that day.
The goodman commanded what he would have;
The wife was quick at hand.
"What now?" thought the mother. "This arrant knave
Is master, I understand.

"What may this mean," then she gan think,
"That my daughter so diligent is?
Now can I neither eat nor drink
Till I it know, by heaven bliss."
When her daughter came again
To serve at the board as her husband bade,
The mother stared with her eyen twain   1061
Even as one that had been mad.

All the folk that at the board sat
Did her behold then, everychone.   1064
The mother from the board her gat,   1065
Following her daughter, and that anon,
And in the kitchen she her fand,   1067
Saying unto her in this wise:

1037 **Bid to guest** invite as guests   **1040 Against** in anticipation of
1042 unto my doom on pain of divine judgment   **1045 Soon** as soon
as   **1049 like a man** i.e., like the man of the household   **1061 eyen**
eyes   **1064 everychone** everyone   **1065 from the board her gat** got
herself up from the table   **1067 fand** found

"Daughter, thou shalt well understand
I did not teach thee after this guise."

"Ah, good mother, ye say full well.
All things with me is not as ye ween.   1072
If ye had been in Morel's fell
As well as I, it should be seen."   1074
"In Morel's fell! What devil is that?"   1075
"Marry, mother, I will it you show.
But beware that you come not thereat,   1077
Lest you yourself then do beshrew.   1078

"Come down now in this cellar so deep
And Morel's skin there shall you see,
With many a rod that hath made me to weep,
When the blood ran down fast by my knee."
The mother this beheld and cried out, "Alas!"
And ran out of the cellar as she had been wood.   1084
She came to the table where the company was
And said, "Out, whoreson! I will see thy heart blood."   1086

"Peace, good mother! Or, so have I bliss,   1087
Ye must dance else as did my wife,
And in Morel's skin lie, that well salted is,
Which you should repent all the days of your life."
All they that were there held with the young man   1091
And said he did well in every manner degree.
When dinner was done, they departed all then;
The mother no lenger durst there be.   1094

The father abode last and was full glad,
And gave his children his blessing, iwis,
Saying the young man full well done had,
And merrily departed withouten miss.   1098
This young man was glad, ye may be sure,
That he had brought his wife to this.
God give us all grace in rest to endure,
And hereafter to come unto his bliss!

1072 **ween** think   1074 **it should be seen** i.e., you would understand
1075 **What devil** i.e., what in the devil   1077–1078 **come not . . . beshrew**
i.e., be careful you don't get put in Morel's skin, lest you curse yourself then
1084 **as** as if.   **wood** mad   1086 **I will . . . blood** i.e., I'll have your life
1087 **so have I bliss** as I hope to be saved   1091 **held with** sided with
1094 **lenger** longer   1098 **withouten miss** undoubtedly, certainly

Thus was Morel flain out of his skin   1103
To charm a shrew, so have I bliss.   1104
Forgive the young man if he did sin,
But I think he did nothing amiss.
He did all thing even for the best,
As was well provèd then.
God save our wives from Morel's nest!
I pray you say all Amen.

Thus ending the jest of Morel's skin,
Where the curst wife was lappèd in.
Because she was of a shrewd leer,   1113
Thus was she served in this manner.

He that can charm a shrewd wife
    Better than thus,
Let him come to me, and fetch ten pound
    And a golden purse.

This ballad, *A Merry Jest of a Shrewd and Curst Wife Lapped in Morel's Skin*, was printed by Hugh Jackson without date, c. 1550–1560. A single damaged copy is located in the Bodleian Library, Oxford. It has been reprinted by, among others, *The Shakespeare Society (London) Publications*, vol. 4, no. 25, London, 1844.

1103 flain flayed   **1104 charm** subdue.   **so have I bliss** as I hope to be saved   **1113 leer** disposition, countenance

Further Reading

Bean, John C. "Comic Structure and the Humanizing of Kate in *The Taming of the Shrew*." In *The Woman's Part: Feminist Criticism of Shakespeare*, ed. Carolyn Ruth Swift Lenz, Gayle Greene, and Carol Thomas Neely. Urbana, Chicago, and London: Univ. of Illinois Press, 1980. Bean admires the romantic element of the play—the process by which Kate comes to understand herself "through her discovery first of play and then of love"—but finds the taming offensive. He defends Kate's final speech as the expression of a nontyrannical hierarchy in which partners have distinctive but cooperative roles, but he argues that the process that brings Kate to speak it (like "a trained bear") is evidence of a "depersonalizing farce unassimilated from the play's fabliau source."

Berry, Ralph. "The Rules of the Game." *Shakespeare's Comedies: Explorations in Form*. Princeton, N.J.: Princeton Univ. Press, 1972. Throughout the play, Berry argues, different patterns of wooing parallel and contrast with each other. Petruchio and Kate's emerges as the healthiest of the play's relationships, for the "taming" is in reality the process by which a well-matched pair of lovers together work out an agreement "upon the rules of its games."

Charlton, H. B. *"The Taming of the Shrew." Shakespearian Comedy*, 1938. Rpt. London: Methuen; New York: Barnes and Noble, 1966. Charlton examines the structure of Shakespeare's comedy against the background of Renaissance Italian comic models (which are echoed in the Bianca–Lucentio subplot). In the Petruchio–Kate plot, however, Shakespeare moves beyond familiar romantic conventions, focusing instead upon the lovers' "matter-of-fact recognition of the practical and expedient."

Daniell, David. "The Good Marriage of Katherine and Petruchio." *Shakespeare Survey* 37 (1984): 23–31. Daniell discovers in the Kate–Petruchio plot surprising affinities with the language and experience of Shakespeare's early history plays. Daniell uses this insight to explore the play's theatricality—the "special ability of acting to embrace and give form to violence"—which provides the terms in which Kate and Petruchio find the means "of being richly together with all their contradictions—and energies—very much alive and kicking."

Evans, Bertrand. *Shakespeare's Comedies*, pp. 24–32. Oxford: Clarendon Press, 1960. Evans focuses on the contrast between the play's two plots: the minor plot depends upon the dynamics of "false supposes and unperceived realities," while Kate and Petruchio's full awareness of each other's nature, a trait that is unique among Shakespeare's comic lovers, forms the basis of the major plot.

Garber, Marjorie B. "Dream and Structure: *The Taming of the Shrew." Dream in Shakespeare: From Metaphor to Metamorphosis*. New Haven and London: Yale Univ. Press, 1974. For Garber, the induction introduces the play's thematic concern with appearance and reality. Sly's dream "distances later action and insures lightness of tone"; his transformation also prefigures and parallels Kate's, allowing us to see her change as a metamorphosis rather than a taming.

Hibbard, G. R. "*The Taming of the Shrew:* A Social Comedy." In *Shakespearean Essays*, ed. Norman Sanders and Alwin Thaler. Knoxville, Tenn.: Univ. of Tennessee Press, 1964. Hibbard's discussion of the marital customs of Elizabethan England suggests that the play is not only a dramatic exploration of romantic attitudes but also "an incisive piece of social criticism." Kate's frustrations emerge from actual social and economic conditions. Bianca and Lucentio reveal the shallowness of the conventional values of romance, while Kate's and Petruchio's "realistic" approach to life and love gives their marriage an appeal absent from the subplot.

Huston, J. Dennis. "Enter the Hero: The Power of the Play in *The Taming of the Shrew." Shakespeare's Comedies of Play*. New York: Columbia Univ. Press, 1981. Arguing that both the Induction and the marriage in mid-play subvert traditional comic conventions, Huston finds that Shakespeare's handling of literary tradition is analogous to Petruchio's treatment of Kate: Shakespeare animates sterile romantic conventions in the same way as Petruchio summons Kate out of her unthinking and automatic shrewishness "into the human theatre of play."

Kahn, Coppélia. "*The Taming of the Shrew:* Shakespeare's Mirror of Marriage." *Modern Language Studies* 5 (1975): 88–102. Rpt. in "Coming of Age: Marriage and Manhood in *Romeo and Juliet* and *The Taming of the Shrew.*" *Man's Estate: Masculine Identity in Shakespeare.* Berkeley: Univ. of California Press, 1981. For Kahn, Kate's ironic submission liberates Petruchio from his stereotypic male dominance (reversing Huston's assessment; see above). The play satirizes not the shrewish female but the male desire to control women, and Kate's final speech not only "completes the fantasy of male domination but also mocks it as mere fantasy."

Leggatt, Alexander. "*The Taming of the Shrew.*" *Shakespeare's Comedy of Love.* London: Methuen; New York: Barnes and Noble, 1974. Leggatt discovers the relationship between the induction and the play world in their common interest in "sport, playacting, and education." The Lord, Petruchio, and Kate herself have the "power to manipulate convention, to create experience rather than have experience forced upon them."

Nevo, Ruth. "Kate of Kate Hall." *Comic Transformations in Shakespeare.* London and New York: Methuen, 1980. Nevo admires the unconventional Petruchio as "stage manager and chief actor" of the play's psychodrama. His taming of Kate is an "instructive, liberating, and therapeutic" activity, which rescues her from an unenviable family situation in which her only defense is "her insufferability."

Saccio, Peter. "Shrewd and Kindly Farce." *Shakespeare Survey* 37 (1984): 33–40. Defending the farcical quality of the play, Saccio praises the energy, determination, and cleverness of the characters in remedying the static social world of Padua. Kate, he finds, is a participant rather than a victim of the farce, and her growing abilities as a farceur mark the stages of her liberation from a compulsive shrewishness.

Shaw, George Bernard. "*The Taming of the Shrew.*" In *Shaw on Shakespeare,* ed. Edwin Wilson. New York: E. P. Dutton, 1961. Responding to a number of performances of the play, Shaw praises its "realistic" aspects. Petruchio rejects romantic affectation in favor of practical concerns for his own comfort. His taming of Kate is acceptable to an audience, since it is "good-humored and untainted by wanton cruelty." Nonetheless, Shaw is uncomfortable with Kate's final speech of submission: its "lord-of-creation moral," he asserts, is "disgusting to modern sensibility."

Tillyard, E. M. W. "The Fairy-Tale Element in *The Taming of the Shrew*." In *Shakespeare 1564–1964: A Collection of Modern Essays by Various Hands*, ed. Edward A. Bloom. Providence, R.I.: Brown Univ. Press, 1964. Tillyard presents several versions of shrew-taming folktales that may have served Shakespeare as sources, singling out the story of King Thrushbeard as the most likely analogue to the Kate plot and as a model for the induction.

A
MIDSUMMER
NIGHT'S
DREAM

Introduction

A Midsummer Night's Dream (c. 1594–1595) belongs to the period of transition from Shakespeare's experimental, imitative comedy to his mature, romantic, philosophical, festive vein. In its lighthearted presentation of love's tribulations, the play resembles Shakespeare's earlier comedies. The two sets of young lovers (Lysander and Hermia, Demetrius and Helena), scarcely distinguishable one from the other, are conventional figures. In them we find scarcely a hint of the profound self-discovery experienced by Beatrice and Benedick *(Much Ado about Nothing)* or Rosalind and Orlando *(As You Like It)*. At the same time, this play develops the motif of love as an imaginative journey from reality into a fantasy world created by the artist, ending in a return to a reality that has itself been partly transformed by the experience of the journey. (Shakespeare gives us an earlier hint of such an imaginary sylvan landscape in *The Two Gentlemen of Verona*.) This motif, with its contrasting worlds of social order and imaginative escape, remained an enduring vision for Shakespeare to the very last.

In construction, *A Midsummer Night's Dream* is a skillful interweaving of four plots involving four groups of characters: the court party of Theseus, the four young lovers, the fairies, and the "rude mechanicals" or would-be actors. Felix Mendelssohn's incidental music for the play evokes the contrasting textures of the various groups: Theseus' hunting horns and ceremonial wedding marches, the lovers' soaring and throbbing melodies, the fairies' pianissimo staccato, the tradesmen's clownish bassoon. Moreover, each plot is derived from its own set of source materials. The action involving Theseus and Hippolyta, for example, owes several details to Thomas North's translation (1579) of Plutarch's *Lives of the Noble Grecians and Romans*, to Chaucer's "Knight's Tale" and perhaps to his *Legend of Good Women*, and to Ovid's *Metamorphoses* (in the Latin text or in William Golding's popular Elizabethan translation). The lovers' story, meanwhile, is Italianate and Ovidian in tone, and also in the broadest sense follows the conventions of plot in Plautus' and Terence's Roman comedies, although no particular source is known. Shakespeare's rich fairy lore, by contrast, is part folk tradition and part learned. Although he certainly needed no books to tell him about mischievous spirits that could prevent churned milk from turning to butter, for instance, Shakespeare might have borrowed Oberon's name either from the French romance *Huon of Bordeaux* (translated into English by 1540), or from Robert Greene's play *James IV* (c. 1591), or from Edmund Spenser's *The Faerie Queen*, 2.10.75–76 (1590). Similarly, he may have taken Titania's name from the *Metamorphoses*, where it is used as an epithet for both Diana and Circe. Finally, for Bottom the weaver and company, Shakespeare's primary inspiration was doubtless his own theatrical experience, although even here he is indebted to Ovid for the story of Pyramus and Thisbe, and probably to Apuleius' *Golden Ass* (translated by William Adlington, 1566) for Bottom's transformation.

Each of the four main plots in *A Midsummer Night's Dream* contains one or more pairs of lovers whose happiness has been frustrated by misunderstanding or parental opposition. Theseus and Hippolyta, once enemies in battle, become husband and wife; and their court marriage, constituting the overplot of the play, provides a framework for other dramatic actions that similarly oscillate between conflict and harmony. In fact, Theseus' actions are instrumental in setting in motion and finally resolving the tribulations of the other characters. In the beginning of the play, for example, the lovers flee from Theseus' Athenian law; at the end, they are awakened by him from their dream. The king and queen of fairies come to Athens to celebrate Theseus' wedding, but quarrel with each other because Oberon has long been partial to Hippolyta, and Titania partial to Theseus. The Athenian tradesmen go off into the forest to rehearse their performance of "Pyramus and Thisbe" in anticipation of the wedding festivities.

The tragic love story of Pyramus and Thisbe, although it seems absurdly ill-suited for a wedding, simply reinforces by contrast the universal accord reuniting the other couples. This accord is, to be sure, stated in terms of male conquest of the female. Theseus, who originally won the Amazonian Hippolyta with his sword, doing her injuries, finally becomes the devoted husband. Hippolyta, legendary figure of woman's self-assertive longing to dominate the male, emerges as the happily married wife. The reconciliation of Oberon and Titania, meanwhile, reinforces this hierarchy of male over female. Having taught Titania a lesson for trying to keep a changeling boy from him, Oberon relents and eventually frees Titania from her enchantment. Thus, the occasion of Theseus' wedding both initiates and brings to an end the difficulties that have beset the drama's various couples.

Despite Theseus' cheerful preoccupation with marriage, his court embodies at first a stern attitude toward young love. As administrator of the law, Theseus must accede to the remorseless demands of Hermia's father, Egeus. The inflexible Athenian law sides with parentage, age, male dominance, wealth, and position against youth and romantic choice in love. The penalties are harsh: death or perpetual virginity—and virginity is presented in this comedy (despite the nobly chaste examples of Christ, Saint Paul, and Queen Elizabeth) as a fate worse than death. Egeus is a familiar type, the interfering parent found in the Roman comedy of Plautus and Terence (and in Shakespeare's *Romeo and Juliet*). Indeed, the lovers' story is distantly derived from Roman comedy, which conventionally celebrated the triumph of young love over the machinations of age and wealth. Lysander reminds us that "the course of true love never did run smooth," and he sees its enemies as being chiefly external: the conflicting interests of parents or friends; mismating with respect to years and blood; war; death; sickness (1.1.134–142). This description clearly applies to "Pyramus and Thisbe," and it is tested by the action of *A Midsummer Night's Dream* as a whole (as well as by other early Shakespearean plays, such as *Romeo and Juliet*). The archetypal story, whether ending happily or sadly, is an evocation of love's difficulties in the face of social hostility and indifference.

While Shakespeare uses several elements of Roman comedy in setting up the basic conflicts of his drama, he also introduces important modifications from the beginning. For example, he discards one conventional confrontation of classical and neoclassical comedy in which the heroine must choose between an old, wealthy suitor supported by her family and the young but impecunious darling of her heart. Lysander is equal to his rival in social position, income, and attractiveness. Egeus' demand, therefore—that Hermia marry Demetrius rather than Lysander—seems simply arbitrary and unjust. Shakespeare emphasizes in this way the irrationality of Egeus' harsh insistence on being obeyed and Theseus' rather complacent acceptance of the law's inequity. Spurned by an unfeeling social order, Lysander and Hermia are compelled to elope. To be sure, in the end Egeus proves to be no formidable threat; even he must admit the logic of permitting the lovers to couple as they ultimately desire. Thus, the obstacles to love are from the start seen as fundamentally superficial and indeed almost whimsical. Egeus is as heavy a villain as we are likely to find in this jeu d'esprit. Moreover, the very irrationality of his position prepares the way for an ultimate resolution of the conflict. Nevertheless, by the end of the first act the supposedly rational world of conformity and duty, by its customary insensitivity to youthful happiness, has set in motion a temporary escape to a fantasy world where the law cannot reach.

In the forest, all the lovers—including Titania and Bottom—undergo a transforming experience engineered by the mischievous Puck. This experience demonstrates the universal power of love, which can overcome the queen of fairies as readily as the lowliest of men. It also suggests the irrational nature of love and its affinity to enchantment, witchcraft, and even madness. Love is seen as an affliction taken in through the frail senses, particularly the eyes. When it strikes, the victim cannot choose but to embrace the object of his infatuation. By his amusing miscalculations, Puck shuffles the four lovers through various permutations with mathematical predictability. First, two gentlemen compete for one lady, leaving the second lady sadly unrequited in love; then everything is at cross-purposes, with each gentleman pursuing the lady who is in love with the other man; then the two gentlemen compete for the lady they both previously ignored. Finally, of course, Jack shall have his Jill—whom else should he have? The couples are properly united, as they evidently were at some time prior to the commencement of the play, when Demetrius had been in love with Helena, and Lysander and Hermia had courted each other.

We sense that Puck is by no means unhappy about his knavish errors. "Lord, what fools these mortals be!" Along with the other fairies in this play, Puck takes his being and his complex motivation from many denizens of the invisible world. As the agent of all-powerful love, Puck compares himself to Cupid. The love juice he administers comes from Cupid's flower, "love-in-idleness." Like Cupid, Puck acts at the behest of the gods, and yet he wields a power that the chiefest gods themselves cannot resist. Essentially, however, Puck is less a classical love deity than a prankish folk spirit, such as we find in every folklore: gremlin, leprechaun, hobgoblin, and the like. Titania's fairies recognize Puck as one who, for example, can deprive a beer barrel of its yeast so that it spoils rather than ferments. Puck characterizes himself as a practical joker, pulling stools out from under old ladies.

Folk wisdom imagines the inexplicable and unaccountable events in life to be caused by invisible forces who laugh at man's discomfiture and mock him for mere sport. Puck is related to these mysterious forces dwelling in nature who must be placated with gifts and ceremonies. Although Shakespeare restricts Puck to a benign sportive role in dealing with the lovers or with Titania, the actual folk legends about Puck mentioned in this play are frequently disquieting. Puck is known to "mislead night-wanderers, laughing at their harm"; indeed, he demonstrates as much with Demetrius and Lysander, engineering a confrontation that greatly oppresses the lovers even though we perceive the sportful intent. At the play's end, Puck links himself and his fellows with the ghoulish apparitions of death and night: wolves howling at the moon, screech owls, shrouds, gaping graves. Associations of this sort go beyond mere sportiveness to witchcraft and demonology involving spirits rising from the dead. Even Oberon's assurance that the fairies will bless all the marriages of this play, shielding their progeny against mole, harelip, or other birth defects, carries the implication that such misfortunes can be caused by offended spirits. The magic of this play is thus explicitly related to deep irrational powers and forces capable of doing great harm, although of course the spirit of comedy keeps such veiled threats safely at a distance in *A Midsummer Night's Dream*.

Oberon and Titania, in their view of the relationship between gods and men, reflect yet another aspect of the fairies' spiritual ancestry—one more nearly related to the gods and goddesses of the world of Greek mythology. The king and queen of fairies assert that, because they are immortal, their regal quarrels in love must inevitably have dire consequences on earth, either in the love relationship of Theseus and Hippolyta or in the management of the weather. Floods, storms, diseases, and sterility abound, "And this same progeny of evils comes / From our debate, from our dissension; / We are their parents and original" (2.1.115–117). Even though this motif of the gods' quarreling over human affairs is Homeric or Virgilian in conception, the motif in this lighthearted play is more nearly mock-epic than truly epic. The consequences of the gods' anger are simply mirth-provoking, most of all in Titania's love affair with Bottom the weaver.

The story of Bottom and Titania is recognizably a metamorphosis in a playfully classical mode, a love affair between a god and an earthly creature, underscoring man's dual nature. Bottom himself becomes half man and half beast, although he is ludicrously unlike the centaurs, mermaids, and other half-human beings of classical mythology. Whereas the head should be the aspiring part of him and his body the bestial part, Bottom wears an ass's head on his shoulders. His very name suggests the solid nature of his fleshly being (*bottom* is appropriately also a weaving term). He and Titania represent the opposites of flesh and spirit, miraculously yoked for a time in a twofold vision of man's absurd and ethereal nature.

A play bringing together fairies and mortals inevitably raises questions of illusion and reality. These questions reach their greatest intensity in the presentation of "Pyramus and Thisbe." This play within a play focuses our attention on the familiarly Shakespearean metaphor of art as illusion, and of the world itself as a stage on which men and women are merely players. As Theseus observes, apologizing for the ineptness of the tradesmen's performance, "The best in this kind are but shadows" (5.1.210). That is, Shakespeare's own play is of the same order of reality as Bottom's play. Puck too, in his epilogue, invites any spectator offended by Shakespeare's play to dismiss it as a mere dream—as, indeed, the play's very title suggests. Theseus goes even further, linking dream to the essence of imaginative art, although he does so in a clearly critical and rather patronizing way. The artist, he says, is like the madman or the lover in his frenzy of inspiration, giving "to airy nothing / A local habitation and a name" (5.1.16–17). Artistic achievements are too unsubstantial for Theseus; from his point of view they are the products of mere fantasy and irrationality, mere myths or fairy stories or old wives' tales. Behind this critical persona defending the "real" world of his court, however, we can hear Shakespeare's characteristically self-effacing defense of "dreaming."

"Pyramus and Thisbe," like the larger play surrounding it, attempts to body forth "the forms of things unknown." The play within the play gives us personified moonshine, a speaking wall, and an apologetic lion. Of course it is an absurdly bad play, full of lame epithets, bombastic alliteration, and bathos. In part Shakespeare is here satirizing the abuses of a theater he had helped reform. The players' chosen method of portraying imaginative matters is ridiculous, and calls forth deliciously wry comments from the courtly spectators onstage: "Would you desire lime and hair to speak better?" (5.1.164–165). At the same time, those spectators onstage are actors in our play. Their sarcasms render them less sympathetic in our eyes; we see that their kind of sophistication is as restrictive as it is illuminating. Bottom and his friends have conceived moonshine and lion as they did because these simple men are so responsive to the terrifying power of art. A lion might frighten the ladies and get the men hanged. Theirs is a primitive faith, naive but strong, and in this sense it contrasts favorably with the jaded rationality of the court party. Theseus' valuable reminder, that all art is only "illusion," is thus juxtaposed with Bottom's insistence that imaginative art has a reality of its own.

Theseus above all embodies the sophistication of the court in his description of art as a frenzy of seething brains. Genially scoffing at "These antique fables" and "these fairy toys" (5.1.3), he is unmoved by the lovers' account of their dreamlike experience. Limited by his own skepticism, Theseus has never experienced the enchantment of the forest. Even Bottom can claim more than that, for he has been the lover of the queen of fairies; and although his language cannot adequately describe the experience, Bottom will see it made into a ballad called "Bottom's Dream." Shakespeare leaves the status of his fantasy world deliberately complex; Theseus' lofty denial of dreaming is too abrupt. Even if the Athenian forest world can be made only momentarily substantial in the artifact of Shakespeare's play, we as audience respond to its tantalizing vision. We emerge back into our lives wondering if the fairies were "real"; that is, we are puzzled by the relationship of these artistic symbols to the tangible concreteness of our daily existence. Unless our perceptions have been thus enlarged by sharing in the author's dream, we have not surrendered to the imaginative experience.

A Midsummer Night's Dream
in Performance

Two rival staging traditions vie for attention in the performance history of *A Midsummer Night's Dream*. One stresses the musical and magical qualities of the play, the fairy enchantment, the gossamer illusion, the romance. The other, more disenchanting tradition stresses the dark side of the forest, the degrading aspect of erotic love, the conflict between the sexes, and the breaking of theatrical illusion. The first tradition, although it reigned virtually supreme for three centuries and remains important in the twentieth century, has had to contend in recent years with a more radical vision of disillusionment. In today's theater we are able to respond to both and to see in their marked differences a debate about the play's dramatic qualities.

During the seventeenth-century civil wars in England and the closing of its theaters, *A Midsummer Night's Dream* was kept alive in the form of a farcical skit, or droll, called *The Merry Conceited Humours of Bottom the Weaver*, which emphasized the clownish antics of the Athenian tradesmen. The full play itself did not make much of an impression in the Restoration era until Thomas Betterton hit on the idea of a spectacular operatic version with music by Henry Purcell. Under the title of *The Fairy Queen*, it appeared in 1692 and was billed as "an opera represented at the Queen's Theatre." Shakespeare's text was rearranged and cut to make room for elaborate entries at the end of each act in the style of Italian *intermedii*. At the end of Act 2, for example, the woodland scene was transformed into a prospect of grottoes, arches, and walks adorned with flowers in order to provide an elaborate setting for songs, a masque, and a dance by the followers of Night. After Act 3 two great dragons, part of the movable scenery, made themselves into a bridge over a river, forming an arch through which the audience could see swimming in the distance, to symphonic accompaniment, two swans who then transformed themselves into dancing fairies. "Pyramus and Thisbe" was moved to Act 3, just before the transformation of Bottom, to make room for an unusually gorgeous entry near the end of Act 5 that featured Juno in a machine drawn by peacocks with spreading tails, a Chinese garden, six monkeys coming from among the trees, and six moving pedestals, all of which was followed by a grand dance for the finale. The then recent consolidation of England's only two licensed acting companies into one made possible the large cast and resources needed to mount so lavish a display.

David Garrick's *The Fairies*, at the Theatre Royal, Drury Lane, in 1755, continued the musical tradition, its prologue self-consciously attributing the play to "Signor Shakespearelli." It disposed of the Athenian tradesmen entirely, along with their performance of "Pyramus and Thisbe," and dealt with only the fairies and the four young lovers, providing some twenty-eight songs with lyrics by John Dryden, Edmund Waller, John Milton (from his *L'Allegro*), and even Shakespeare. When Garrick tried a more fully operatic version of *A Midsummer Night's Dream* in 1763, this time with thirty-three songs, it lasted exactly one night, though an attempt to salvage some parts of it under the title of *A Fairy Tale* did better. This adaptation included Bottom and his fellows together with their play, but left out the young lovers as well as Theseus and Hippolyta. Frederic Reynolds, in his production at the Theatre Royal, Covent Garden, in 1816, provided music by Thomas Arne and others for its sixteen songs, eliminated the scene with Helena in Act 1, transposed "Pyramus and Thisbe" to the forest as Betterton had done, and concluded with a grand pageant of Theseus' legendary triumphs: his defeat of the Amazons, his finding his way through the labyrinth with Ariadne's help, his killing the Minotaur, his sailing with the Argonauts in search of the Golden Fleece, and still more.

Felix Mendelssohn's well-known musical score for Shakespeare's play, then, follows a long tradition of musical elaboration. Mendelssohn's complete score was first used by Ludwig Tieck in a production at the Neues Palais in Potsdam in 1843 (the overture having been written in 1826 and used first in England by Alfred Bunn in a production at Drury Lane in 1833). It soon became standard fare, since it expressed so well, in nineteenth-century terms, the contrast between the playful fairies, the bumptious tradesmen, the stately Theseus and Hippolyta, and the romantic lovers.

Along with musical elaboration, an increasing tendency in nineteenth-century performances was toward lavishness and verisimilitude in set designs and costumes. The production of Madame Lucia Vestris and Charles Matthews at Covent Garden in 1840, though it restored much of the play that had been cut in earlier musical versions, indulged in numerous songs (fourteen this time, as well as Mendelssohn's overture, "Wedding March," and other incidental music), and spared no expense in creating stage spectacle. During Act 3 the moon sank gradually, its rays disappearing from the tops of the trees until daylight arrived. Act 5 featured staircases, a hall of statues, a gallery along the back of the stage, and Parisian lanterns of various colors for the fairies to carry. The fairies were clad in virgin white, with immaculate silk stockings. Nothing threatening was to be found in this wholesome vision. Madame Vestris herself took the part of Oberon and seems thus to have initiated a tradition of contralto fairy kings.

Samuel Phelps's production at the Sadler's Wells Theatre in 1853, with Phelps himself as Bottom, again gave prominence to the moon, first in the forest and then as it shone upon Theseus' palace in Act 5. Charles Kean, at the Princess's Theatre in 1856, gave Puck's opening speech to a nameless fairy in order that the audience might then see Puck (Ellen Terry, aged eight) rising on a mushroom. Kean's set invoked ancient Athens (admittedly not that of Theseus' era) by showing the Acropolis surrounded by marble temples and the theater of Bacchus. A dummy Puck flew through the air to the accompaniment of Mendelssohn's music, and one evening, when the dummy happened to fall to the stage, Ellen Terry got a laugh by going out in view of the audience to pick it up.

The fairies in Augustin Daly's New York production of 1888 flickered like fireflies through the shadowy mists. Frank Benson at the Globe Theatre in London in 1889 similarly had scampering fairies and glittering lights as well as a fight between a spider and a wasp. In 1900, at Her Majesty's Theatre, Herbert Beerbohm Tree provided a carpet of thyme and wildflowers along with the (by now) usual twinkling lights and floating shapes. In 1911 Tree populated his enchanted forest with live rabbits scurrying across the stage of His Majesty's Theatre. In more recent times, Ty-

rone Guthrie at the Old Vic in London in 1937–1938 con-
cocted a handsome spectacle of dance and moonlit forest,
with Vivien Leigh as Titania, Robert Helpmann as Oberon,
and Ralph Richardson as Bottom. The tradition of innocent
and lavish musical entertainment was fixed on film in
Warner Brothers' 1935 *A Midsummer Night's Dream*, directed by Max Reinhardt with a cast that included Dick
Powell (Lysander), Olivia de Havilland (Hermia), James Cag-
ney (Bottom), and Mickey Rooney (Puck). The romantic
spectacular even included a miniature orchestra of dwarfs
performing in the forest. The Shakespeare Memorial Theatre production of 1949, in Stratford-upon-Avon, directed by
Michael Benthall, continued the romantic tradition with
graceful women in gauze dresses as Titania's fairies.

The other, disillusioning approach to the play dates seemingly from Harley Granville-Barker's interpretation at the
Savoy Theatre in London in 1914 on an apron stage in a
swift-paced continuous performance, with three symbolic
locations (court, forest, town) and a minimum of realistic
effects. The costumes suggested something remote, orien-
tal, exotic. Puck made it plain that he was the theatrical
manager of affairs onstage; he consciously broke the dramatic illusion, reminding spectators that they were in the
theater. From the first, this awareness of the contrivance of
theater was an essential part of this new perspective. Har-
court Williams's production at the Old Vic in 1929 (with
John Gielgud as Oberon) was a Jacobean masque, its fairies
not the gauzy sprites of the Victorians but elemental figures, based on sketches by Inigo Jones, with green faces
and costumes of seaweed. George Devine, at the Shakespeare Memorial Theatre in 1954, gave a strange, birdlike
aspect to his fairies and an ominous tone to the whole production. Peter Hall, in 1959, directed his young lovers to be
foolish and clumsy, devoted to horseplay. Benjamin Brit-
ten's striking opera, performed at the Aldeburgh Festival in
Suffolk in 1960, invoked a forest full of eerie sounds and
disturbing dreamlike effects.

The most influential production in this disillusioning
vein is Peter Brook's with the Royal Shakespeare Company
in 1970, which was subsequently taken on tour. Plainly ac-
knowledging the influence of Bertolt Brecht, Samuel Beck-
ett, Antonin Artaud, and *Shakespeare Our Contemporary*,

by Jan Kott, which argues in an intemperate but insightful way for the darker sexual side of the play, Brook created an intensely self-aware theatrical world within a three-sided brilliantly lit white box. The actors, often on trapezes, were circus performers, athletes, tumblers; Bottom, with his button nose and clumsy shoes, was both ass and circus clown. A fisted arm thrust between his legs as he was carried offstage from his rendezvous with the Fairy Queen suggested a triumphant phallus. The fairies were adult male actors. The production reveled in exposing its stage devices. The actors of Oberon and Titania not only doubled as Theseus and Hippolyta in order to explore a sense in which the fairy king and queen act out the aggressions of their human counterparts, but this doubling was flaunted in the final scene. Oberon and Titania, with a swift change of garments, transformed themselves onstage into Theseus and Hippolyta and were thus able to join the courtly audience of "Pyramus and Thisbe."

Since the time of Brook's pace-setting production, it has not been unusual to see athletic lovers who are unceasingly aggressive toward each other, or fairies who are spaced out on drugs. In 1985, on a bloodred set at the Guthrie Threatre in Minneapolis, Liviu Ciulei produced the play as a dark comedy of sexual strife and patriarchal abuse. The hallmark of modern productions throughout has been the constant use of theatrical illusion as a plaything: Puck and Oberon walk among the mortals, nearly touching them, separated only by the audience's understanding that they are invisible.

Fed by these two acting traditions, Shakespeare's text offers itself for endless speculation and experiment. Certainly the text's own indications for performance encourage the self-conscious methods of presentation that have become so popular in recent productions. Juxtapositions of the seen and unseen run through the play, as when, in Act 2, scene 2, and Act 3, scene 1, Titania sleeps in her bower while first the lovers and then Bottom and company wrestle with love's difficulties or with the problems of rehearsing a play. Possibly her bower was intended for some curtained space backstage in the Elizabethan playhouse, but the full visual contrast is present if she sleeps in view of the audience until she is at length awakened by Bottom's singing. Certainly at the end of Act 4 the four lovers are to remain asleep onstage while Titania first sports with her lover Bottom, then sleeps, and finally is awakened by Oberon; the four lovers are still there when Theseus and his train arrive.

Shakespeare's theater provides ample means, too, of dramatizing the contrasts between court and forest, not (in the original production) through scenery, but by means of costumed actors and their gestures and blocking: Theseus is a figure of noble splendor, richly dressed, accompanied by followers and surrounded by ceremony, while the creatures of the forest visibly come from another world, one of dreams, nighttime, and magic. Whether the fairies are presented benignly, in the romantic tradition of staging, or darkly, through the eyes of disenchantment, the imaginative world they create onstage is one that thrives on tricks of illusion and theatrical self-awareness.

A
MIDSUMMER
NIGHT'S
DREAM

1.1 *Enter Theseus, Hippolyta, [and Philostrate,]
with others.*

THESEUS

Now, fair Hippolyta, our nuptial hour
Draws on apace. Four happy days bring in
Another moon; but, O, methinks, how slow
This old moon wanes! She lingers my desires,   4
Like to a stepdame or a dowager   5
Long withering out a young man's revenue.   6

HIPPOLYTA

Four days will quickly steep themselves in night,
Four nights will quickly dream away the time;
And then the moon, like to a silver bow
New bent in heaven, shall behold the night
Of our solemnities.

THESEUS   Go, Philostrate,
Stir up the Athenian youth to merriments,
Awake the pert and nimble spirit of mirth,
Turn melancholy forth to funerals;
The pale companion is not for our pomp.   15

                                    [*Exit Philostrate.*]

Hippolyta, I wooed thee with my sword   16
And won thy love doing thee injuries;
But I will wed thee in another key,
With pomp, with triumph, and with reveling.   19

    *Enter Egeus and his daughter Hermia, and
    Lysander, and Demetrius.*

EGEUS

Happy be Theseus, our renowned duke!

THESEUS

Thanks, good Egeus. What's the news with thee?

EGEUS

Full of vexation come I, with complaint
Against my child, my daughter Hermia.

1.1. Location: Athens. Theseus' court.
4 lingers postpones, delays the fulfillment of   **5 stepdame** step-
mother.   **dowager** i.e., a widow (whose right of inheritance from her
dead husband is eating into her son's estate)   **6 withering out** causing
to dwindle   **15 companion** fellow.   **pomp** ceremonial magnificence
16 with my sword i.e., in a military engagement against the Amazons,
when Hippolyta was taken captive   **19 triumph** public festivity

Stand forth, Demetrius. My noble lord,
This man hath my consent to marry her.
Stand forth, Lysander. And, my gracious Duke,
This man hath bewitched the bosom of my child.
Thou, thou, Lysander, thou hast given her rhymes
And interchanged love tokens with my child.
Thou hast by moonlight at her window sung
With feigning voice verses of feigning love,   31
And stol'n the impression of her fantasy   32
With bracelets of thy hair, rings, gauds, conceits,   33
Knacks, trifles, nosegays, sweetmeats—messengers   34
Of strong prevailment in unhardened youth.   35
With cunning hast thou filched my daughter's heart,
Turned her obedience, which is due to me,
To stubborn harshness. And, my gracious Duke,
Be it so she will not here before Your Grace   39
Consent to marry with Demetrius,
I beg the ancient privilege of Athens:
As she is mine, I may dispose of her,
Which shall be either to this gentleman
Or to her death, according to our law
Immediately provided in that case.   45

THESEUS
What say you, Hermia? Be advised, fair maid.
To you your father should be as a god—
One that composed your beauties, yea, and one
To whom you are but as a form in wax
By him imprinted, and within his power
To leave the figure or disfigure it.   51
Demetrius is a worthy gentleman.

HERMIA
So is Lysander.

THESEUS   In himself he is;
But in this kind, wanting your father's voice,   54
The other must be held the worthier.

---

31 feigning (1) counterfeiting (2) faining, desirous   **32 And . . . fantasy**
and made her fall in love with you (imprinting your image on her
imagination) by stealthy and dishonest means   **33 gauds** playthings.
conceits fanciful trifles   **34 Knacks** knickknacks   **35 prevailment in**
influence on   **39 Be it so** if   **45 Immediately** directly, with nothing
intervening   **51 leave** i.e., leave unaltered.   **disfigure** obliterate
54 kind respect.   **wanting** lacking.   **voice** approval

HERMIA
I would my father looked but with my eyes.

THESEUS
Rather your eyes must with his judgment look.

HERMIA
I do entreat Your Grace to pardon me.
I know not by what power I am made bold,
Nor how it may concern my modesty   60
In such a presence here to plead my thoughts;
But I beseech Your Grace that I may know
The worst that may befall me in this case
If I refuse to wed Demetrius.

THESEUS
Either to die the death or to abjure
Forever the society of men.
Therefore, fair Hermia, question your desires,
Know of your youth, examine well your blood,   68
Whether, if you yield not to your father's choice,
You can endure the livery of a nun,   70
For aye to be in shady cloister mewed,   71
To live a barren sister all your life,
Chanting faint hymns to the cold fruitless moon.
Thrice blessèd they that master so their blood
To undergo such maiden pilgrimage;
But earthlier happy is the rose distilled   76
Than that which, withering on the virgin thorn,
Grows, lives, and dies in single blessedness.

HERMIA
So will I grow, so live, so die, my lord,
Ere I will yield my virgin patent up   80
Unto his lordship, whose unwishèd yoke
My soul consents not to give sovereignty.

THESEUS
Take time to pause, and by the next new moon—
The sealing day betwixt my love and me
For everlasting bond of fellowship—
Upon that day either prepare to die
For disobedience to your father's will,
Or else to wed Demetrius, as he would,   88

60 concern befit   **68 blood** passions   **70 livery** habit   **71 aye** ever.
mewed shut in. (Said of a hawk, poultry, etc.)   **76 earthlier happy**
happier as respects this world   **80 patent** privilege   **88 Or** either

Or on Diana's altar to protest   89
For aye austerity and single life.

DEMETRIUS
Relent, sweet Hermia, and, Lysander, yield
Thy crazèd title to my certain right.   92

LYSANDER
You have her father's love, Demetrius;
Let me have Hermia's. Do you marry him.

EGEUS
Scornful Lysander! True, he hath my love,
And what is mine my love shall render him.
And she is mine, and all my right of her
I do estate unto Demetrius.   98

LYSANDER
I am, my lord, as well derived as he,   99
As well possessed; my love is more than his;   100
My fortunes every way as fairly ranked,   101
If not with vantage, as Demetrius';   102
And, which is more than all these boasts can be,
I am beloved of beauteous Hermia.
Why should not I then prosecute my right?
Demetrius, I'll avouch it to his head,   106
Made love to Nedar's daughter, Helena,
And won her soul; and she, sweet lady, dotes,
Devoutly dotes, dotes in idolatry,
Upon this spotted and inconstant man.   110

THESEUS
I must confess that I have heard so much,
And with Demetrius thought to have spoke thereof;
But, being overfull of self-affairs,   113
My mind did lose it. But, Demetrius, come,
And come, Egeus, you shall go with me;
I have some private schooling for you both.   116
For you, fair Hermia, look you arm yourself   117
To fit your fancies to your father's will;   118

89 protest vow   **92 crazèd** cracked, unsound   **98 estate unto** settle or
bestow upon   **99 derived** descended, i.e., as well born   **100 possessed**
endowed with wealth   **101 fairly** handsomely   **102 vantage** superiority   **106 head** i.e., face   **110 spotted** i.e., morally stained   **113 self-
affairs** my own concerns   **116 schooling** admonition   **117 look you arm**
take care you prepare   **118 fancies** likings, thoughts of love

Or else the law of Athens yields you up—
Which by no means we may extenuate—   120
To death or to a vow of single life.
Come, my Hippolyta. What cheer, my love?
Demetrius and Egeus, go along.   123
I must employ you in some business
Against our nuptial and confer with you   125
Of something nearly that concerns yourselves.   126

EGEUS
With duty and desire we follow you.
                    Exeunt [all but Lysander and Hermia].

LYSANDER
How now, my love, why is your cheek so pale?
How chance the roses there do fade so fast?

HERMIA
Belike for want of rain, which I could well   130
Beteem them from the tempest of my eyes.   131

LYSANDER
Ay me! For aught that I could ever read,
Could ever hear by tale or history,
The course of true love never did run smooth;
But either it was different in blood—   135

HERMIA
O cross! Too high to be enthralled to low.   136

LYSANDER
Or else misgrafted in respect of years—   137

HERMIA
O spite! Too old to be engaged to young.

LYSANDER
Or else it stood upon the choice of friends—   139

HERMIA
O hell, to choose love by another's eyes!

LYSANDER
Or if there were a sympathy in choice,   141
War, death, or sickness did lay siege to it,
Making it momentany as a sound,   143

120 **extenuate** mitigate   123 **go** i.e., come   125 **Against** in preparation
for   126 **nearly that** that closely   130 **Belike** very likely   131 **Beteem**
grant, afford   135 **blood** hereditary station   136 **cross** vexation
137 **misgrafted** ill grafted, badly matched   139 **friends** relatives
141 **sympathy** agreement   143 **momentany** lasting but a moment

Swift as a shadow, short as any dream,
Brief as the lightning in the collied night,   145
That in a spleen unfolds both heaven and earth,   146
And ere a man hath power to say "Behold!"
The jaws of darkness do devour it up.
So quick bright things come to confusion.   149

HERMIA
If then true lovers have been ever crossed,   150
It stands as an edict in destiny.
Then let us teach our trial patience,   152
Because it is a customary cross,
As due to love as thoughts and dreams and sighs,
Wishes and tears, poor fancy's followers.   155

LYSANDER
A good persuasion. Therefore, hear me, Hermia: 156
I have a widow aunt, a dowager
Of great revenue, and she hath no child.
From Athens is her house remote seven leagues;
And she respects me as her only son.   160
There, gentle Hermia, may I marry thee,
And to that place the sharp Athenian law
Cannot pursue us. If thou lovest me, then,
Steal forth thy father's house tomorrow night;
And in the wood, a league without the town,
Where I did meet thee once with Helena
To do observance to a morn of May,   167
There will I stay for thee.

HERMIA   My good Lysander!
I swear to thee by Cupid's strongest bow,
By his best arrow with the golden head,   170
By the simplicity of Venus' doves,   171
By that which knitteth souls and prospers loves,

---

145 collied blackened (as with coal dust), darkened   **146 in a spleen** in a
swift impulse, in a violent flash.   **unfolds** discloses   **149 quick** quickly;
or, perhaps, living, alive.   **confusion** ruin   **150 ever crossed** always
thwarted   **152 teach . . . patience** i.e., teach ourselves patience in this
trial   **155 fancy's** amorous passion's   **156 persuasion** conviction
160 respects regards   **167 do . . . May** perform the ceremonies of May
Day   **170 best arrow** (Cupid's best gold-pointed arrows were supposed
to induce love, his blunt leaden arrows, aversion.)   **171 simplicity** innocence.   **doves** i.e., those that drew Venus' chariot

And by that fire which burned the Carthage queen   173
When the false Trojan under sail was seen,   174
By all the vows that ever men have broke,
In number more than ever women spoke,
In that same place thou hast appointed me
Tomorrow truly will I meet with thee.

LYSANDER
Keep promise, love. Look, here comes Helena.

Enter Helena.

HERMIA
God speed, fair Helena! Whither away?   180

HELENA
Call you me fair? That "fair" again unsay.
Demetrius loves your fair. O happy fair!   182
Your eyes are lodestars, and your tongue's sweet air   183
More tunable than lark to shepherd's ear   184
When wheat is green, when hawthorn buds appear.
Sickness is catching. O, were favor so!   186
Yours would I catch, fair Hermia, ere I go;
My ear should catch your voice, my eye your eye,
My tongue should catch your tongue's sweet melody.
Were the world mine, Demetrius being bated,   190
The rest I'd give to be to you translated.   191
O, teach me how you look and with what art
You sway the motion of Demetrius' heart.   193

HERMIA
I frown upon him, yet he loves me still.

HELENA
O, that your frowns would teach my smiles such skill!

HERMIA
I give him curses, yet he gives me love.

HELENA
O, that my prayers could such affection move!   197

173, 174 Carthage queen, false Trojan (Dido, Queen of Carthage, immolated herself on a funeral pyre after having been deserted by the Trojan hero Aeneas.) **180 fair** fair-complexioned (generally regarded by the Elizabethans as more beautiful than dark complexion) **182 your fair** your beauty (even though Hermia is dark-complexioned). **happy fair** lucky fair one **183 lodestars** guiding stars. **air** music **184 tunable** tuneful, melodious **186 favor** appearance, looks **190 bated** excepted **191 translated** transformed **193 motion** impulse **197 affection** passion. **move** arouse

HERMIA
The more I hate, the more he follows me.
HELENA
The more I love, the more he hateth me.
HERMIA
His folly, Helena, is no fault of mine.
HELENA
None but your beauty. Would that fault were mine!
HERMIA
Take comfort. He no more shall see my face.
Lysander and myself will fly this place.
Before the time I did Lysander see
Seemed Athens as a paradise to me.
O, then, what graces in my love do dwell
That he hath turned a heaven unto a hell!
LYSANDER
Helen, to you our minds we will unfold.
Tomorrow night, when Phoebe doth behold   209
Her silver visage in the watery glass,   210
Decking with liquid pearl the bladed grass,
A time that lovers' flights doth still conceal,   212
Through Athens' gates have we devised to steal.
HERMIA
And in the wood, where often you and I
Upon faint primrose beds were wont to lie,   215
Emptying our bosoms of their counsel sweet,   216
There my Lysander and myself shall meet;
And thence from Athens turn away our eyes,
To seek new friends and stranger companies.
Farewell, sweet playfellow. Pray thou for us,
And good luck grant thee thy Demetrius!
Keep word, Lysander. We must starve our sight
From lovers' food till morrow deep midnight.
LYSANDER
I will, my Hermia.   *Exit Hermia.*
          Helena, adieu.
As you on him, Demetrius dote on you!
                                        Exit Lysander.

209 Phoebe Diana, the moon   **210 glass** mirror   **212 still** always
215 faint pale   **216 counsel** secret thought

HELENA

How happy some o'er other some can be!   226
Through Athens I am thought as fair as she.
But what of that? Demetrius thinks not so;
He will not know what all but he do know.
And as he errs, doting on Hermia's eyes,
So I, admiring of his qualities.   231
Things base and vile, holding no quantity,   232
Love can transpose to form and dignity.
Love looks not with the eyes, but with the mind,
And therefore is winged Cupid painted blind.
Nor hath Love's mind of any judgment taste;   236
Wings, and no eyes, figure unheedy haste.   237
And therefore is Love said to be a child,
Because in choice he is so oft beguiled.
As waggish boys in game themselves forswear,   240
So the boy Love is perjured everywhere.
For ere Demetrius looked on Hermia's eyne,   242
He hailed down oaths that he was only mine;
And when this hail some heat from Hermia felt,
So he dissolved, and showers of oaths did melt.
I will go tell him of fair Hermia's flight.
Then to the wood will he tomorrow night
Pursue her; and for this intelligence   248
If I have thanks, it is a dear expense.   249
But herein mean I to enrich my pain,
To have his sight thither and back again.   *Exit.*

❖

1.2   *Enter Quince the carpenter, and Snug the
joiner, and Bottom the weaver, and Flute the
bellows mender, and Snout the tinker, and
Starveling the tailor.*

226 o'er . . . can be can be in comparison to some others   **231 admiring
of** wondering at   **232 holding no quantity** i.e., unsubstantial, unshapely
236 Nor . . . taste i.e., nor has Love, which dwells in the fancy or
imagination, any *taste* or least bit of judgment or reason   **237 figure**
are a symbol of   **240 waggish** playful, mischievous.   **game** sport, jest
242 eyne eyes. (Old form of plural.)   **248 intelligence** information   **249 a
dear expense** i.e., a trouble worth taking.   **dear** costly

1.2. Location: Athens.

QUINCE   Is all our company here?

BOTTOM   You were best to call them generally, man by
man, according to the scrip.

QUINCE   Here is the scroll of every man's name which is
thought fit, through all Athens, to play in our interlude
before the Duke and the Duchess on his wedding day
at night.

BOTTOM   First, good Peter Quince, say what the play
treats on, then read the names of the actors, and so
grow to a point.

QUINCE   Marry, our play is "The most lamentable comedy and most cruel death of Pyramus and Thisbe."

BOTTOM   A very good piece of work, I assure you, and
a merry. Now, good Peter Quince, call forth your actors by the scroll. Masters, spread yourselves.

QUINCE   Answer as I call you. Nick Bottom, the weaver.

BOTTOM   Ready. Name what part I am for, and proceed.

QUINCE   You, Nick Bottom, are set down for Pyramus.

BOTTOM   What is Pyramus? A lover or a tyrant?

QUINCE   A lover, that kills himself most gallant for love.

BOTTOM   That will ask some tears in the true performing
of it. If I do it, let the audience look to their eyes. I will
move storms; I will condole in some measure. To the
rest—yet my chief humor is for a tyrant. I could play
Ercles rarely, or a part to tear a cat in, to make all split.

> "The raging rocks
> And shivering shocks
> Shall break the locks
>   Of prison gates;
> And Phibbus' car
> Shall shine from far
> And make and mar
>   The foolish Fates."

This was lofty! Now name the rest of the players. This is

---

2 generally (Bottom's blunder for *individually.*)   **3 scrip** scrap. (Bottom's error for *script*.)   **10 grow to** come to   **11 Marry** (A mild oath,
originally the name of the Virgin Mary.)   **16 Bottom** (As a weaver's
term, a *bottom* was an object around which thread was wound.)
23 condole lament, arouse pity   **24 humor** inclination, whim   **25 Ercles**
Hercules. (The tradition of ranting came from Seneca's *Hercules
Furens.*)   **tear a cat** i.e., rant.   **make all split** i.e., cause a stir, bring the
house down   **30 Phibbus' car** Phoebus', the sun-god's, chariot

Ercles' vein, a tyrant's vein. A lover is more condoling.

QUINCE   Francis Flute, the bellows mender.

FLUTE   Here, Peter Quince.

QUINCE   Flute, you must take Thisbe on you.

FLUTE   What is Thisbe? A wandering knight?

QUINCE   It is the lady that Pyramus must love.

FLUTE   Nay, faith, let not me play a woman. I have a
beard coming.

QUINCE   That's all one. You shall play it in a mask, and   43
you may speak as small as you will.   44

BOTTOM   An I may hide my face, let me play Thisbe too.   45
I'll speak in a monstrous little voice, "Thisne, Thisne!"
"Ah Pyramus, my lover dear! Thy Thisbe dear, and
lady dear!"

QUINCE   No, no, you must play Pyramus, and, Flute,
you Thisbe.

BOTTOM   Well, proceed.

QUINCE   Robin Starveling, the tailor.

STARVELING   Here, Peter Quince.

QUINCE   Robin Starveling, you must play Thisbe's
mother. Tom Snout, the tinker.

SNOUT   Here, Peter Quince.

QUINCE   You, Pyramus' father; myself, Thisbe's father;
Snug, the joiner, you, the lion's part; and I hope here
is a play fitted.

SNUG   Have you the lion's part written? Pray you, if it
be, give it me, for I am slow of study.

QUINCE   You may do it extempore, for it is nothing but
roaring.

BOTTOM   Let me play the lion too. I will roar that I will
do any man's heart good to hear me. I will roar that I
will make the Duke say, "Let him roar again, let him
roar again."

QUINCE   An you should do it too terribly, you would
fright the Duchess and the ladies, that they would
shriek; and that were enough to hang us all.

ALL   That would hang us, every mother's son.

BOTTOM   I grant you, friends, if you should fright the

---

43 That's all one it makes no difference   **44 small** high-pitched   **45 An**
if (also at l. 68)

ladies out of their wits, they would have no more discretion but to hang us; but I will aggravate my voice 74
so that I will roar you as gently as any sucking dove; I 75
will roar you an 'twere any nightingale.

QUINCE   You can play no part but Pyramus; for Pyramus
is a sweet-faced man, a proper man as one shall see in 78
a summer's day, a most lovely gentlemanlike man.
Therefore you must needs play Pyramus.

BOTTOM   Well, I will undertake it. What beard were I
best to play it in?

QUINCE   Why, what you will.

BOTTOM   I will discharge it in either your straw-color 84
beard, your orange-tawny beard, your purple-in-grain 85
beard, or your French-crown-color beard, your perfect 86
yellow.

QUINCE   Some of your French crowns have no hair at all, 88
and then you will play barefaced. But, masters, here
are your parts. [*He distributes parts.*] And I am to entreat you, request you, and desire you to con them by 91
tomorrow night; and meet me in the palace wood, a
mile without the town, by moonlight. There will we
rehearse; for if we meet in the city, we shall be dogged
with company, and our devices known. In the mean- 95
time I will draw a bill of properties, such as our play 96
wants. I pray you, fail me not.

BOTTOM   We will meet, and there we may rehearse most
obscenely and courageously. Take pains, be perfect; 99
adieu.

QUINCE   At the Duke's oak we meet.

BOTTOM   Enough. Hold, or cut bowstrings.   *Exeunt.* 102

❖

74 aggravate (Bottom's blunder for *moderate*.)   **75 roar you** i.e., roar for
you.   **sucking dove** (Bottom conflates *sitting dove* and *sucking lamb*,
two proverbial images of innocence.)   **78 proper** handsome   **84 discharge** perform.   **your** i.e., you know the kind I mean   **85 purple-in-
grain** dyed a very deep red. (From *grain*, the name applied to the dried
insect used to make the dye.)   **86 French-crown-color** i.e., color of a
French crown, a gold coin   **88 crowns** heads bald from syphilis, the
"French disease"   **91 con** learn by heart   **95 devices** plans   **96 bill**
list   **99 obscenely** (An unintentionally funny blunder, whatever Bottom
meant to say.)   **perfect** i.e., letter-perfect in memorizing your parts
102 Hold . . . bowstrings (An archers' expression not definitely explained,
but probably meaning here "keep your promises, or give up the play.")

2.1   *Enter a Fairy at one door, and Robin*
           Goodfellow [Puck] at another.

PUCK
   How now, spirit, whither wander you?
FAIRY
           Over hill, over dale,
               Thorough bush, thorough brier,   3
           Over park, over pale,   4
               Thorough flood, thorough fire,
           I do wander everywhere,
           Swifter than the moon's sphere;   7
           And I serve the Fairy Queen,
           To dew her orbs upon the green.   9
           The cowslips tall her pensioners be.   10
           In their gold coats spots you see:
           Those be rubies, fairy favors;   12
           In those freckles live their savors.   13
       I must go seek some dewdrops here
       And hang a pearl in every cowslip's ear.
       Farewell, thou lob of spirits; I'll be gone.   16
       Our Queen and all her elves come here anon.   17
PUCK
       The King doth keep his revels here tonight.
       Take heed the Queen come not within his sight.
       For Oberon is passing fell and wrath,   20
       Because that she as her attendant hath
       A lovely boy, stolen from an Indian king;
       She never had so sweet a changeling.   23
       And jealous Oberon would have the child
       Knight of his train, to trace the forests wild.   25
       But she perforce withholds the lovèd boy,   26
       Crowns him with flowers, and makes him all her joy.

2.1. Location: A wood near Athens.
3 Thorough through   **4 pale** enclosure   **7 sphere** orbit   **9 orbs** circles,
i.e., fairy rings (circular bands of grass, darker than the surrounding
area, caused by fungi enriching the soil)   **10 pensioners** retainers,
members of the royal bodyguard   **12 favors** love tokens   **13 savors**
sweet smells   **16 lob** country bumpkin   **17 anon** at once   **20 passing
fell** exceedingly angry.   **wrath** wrathful   **23 changeling** child exchanged
for another by the fairies   **25 trace** range through   **26 perforce** forcibly

And now they never meet in grove or green,
By fountain clear, or spangled starlight sheen,   29
But they do square, that all their elves for fear   30
Creep into acorn cups and hide them there.

FAIRY
Either I mistake your shape and making quite,
Or else you are that shrewd and knavish sprite   33
Called Robin Goodfellow. Are not you he
That frights the maidens of the villagery,   35
Skim milk, and sometimes labor in the quern,   36
And bootless make the breathless huswife churn,   37
And sometimes make the drink to bear no barm,   38
Mislead night wanderers, laughing at their harm?
Those that "Hobgoblin" call you, and "Sweet Puck,"
You do their work, and they shall have good luck.
Are you not he?

PUCK   Thou speakest aright;
I am that merry wanderer of the night.
I jest to Oberon and make him smile
When I a fat and bean-fed horse beguile,
Neighing in likeness of a filly foal;
And sometimes lurk I in a gossip's bowl,   47
In very likeness of a roasted crab,   48
And when she drinks, against her lips I bob
And on her withered dewlap pour the ale.   50
The wisest aunt, telling the saddest tale,   51
Sometimes for three-foot stool mistaketh me;
Then slip I from her bùm, down topples she,
And "Tailor" cries, and falls into a cough;   54
And then the whole choir hold their hips and laugh,   55
And waxen in their mirth, and neeze, and swear   56
A merrier hour was never wasted there.
But, room, fairy! Here comes Oberon.   58

FAIRY
And here my mistress. Would that he were gone!

29 **fountain** spring. **starlight sheen** shining starlight   30 **square** quarrel   33 **shrewd** mischievous. **sprite** spirit   35 **villagery** village population   36 **quern** handmill   37 **bootless** in vain. **huswife** housewife   38 **barm** yeast, head on the ale   47 **gossip's** old woman's   48 **crab** crab apple   50 **dewlap** loose skin on neck   51 **aunt** old woman. **saddest** most serious   54 **Tailor** (Possibly because she ends up sitting cross-legged on the floor, looking like a tailor.)   55 **choir** company   56 **waxen** increase. **neeze** sneeze   58 **room** stand aside, make room

Enter [Oberon] the King of Fairies at one door,
with his train; and [Titania] the Queen at
another, with hers.

OBERON
  Ill met by moonlight, proud Titania.

TITANIA
  What, jealous Oberon? Fairies, skip hence.
  I have forsworn his bed and company.

OBERON
  Tarry, rash wanton. Am not I thy lord?   63

TITANIA
  Then I must be thy lady; but I know
  When thou hast stolen away from Fairyland
  And in the shape of Corin sat all day,   66
  Playing on pipes of corn and versing love   67
  To amorous Phillida. Why art thou here   68
  Come from the farthest step of India   69
  But that, forsooth, the bouncing Amazon,
  Your buskined mistress and your warrior love,   71
  To Theseus must be wedded, and you come
  To give their bed joy and prosperity.

OBERON
  How canst thou thus for shame, Titania,
  Glance at my credit with Hippolyta,   75
  Knowing I know thy love to Theseus?
  Didst not thou lead him through the glimmering night
  From Perigenia, whom he ravishèd?   78
  And make him with fair Aegles break his faith,   79
  With Ariadne and Antiopa?   80

63 wanton headstrong creature   **66, 68 Corin, Phillida** (Conventional names of pastoral lovers.)   **67 corn** (Here, oat stalks.)
69 step farthest limit of travel, or, perhaps, *steep*, mountain range
71 buskined wearing half-boots called buskins   **75 Glance . . .
Hippolyta** make insinuations about my favored relationship with
Hippolyta   **78 Perigenia** i.e., Perigouna, one of Theseus' conquests.
(This and the following women are named in Thomas North's translation
of Plutarch's "Life of Theseus.")   **79 Aegles** i.e., Aegle, for whom
Theseus deserted Ariadne according to some accounts   **80 Ariadne**
the daughter of Minos, King of Crete, who helped Theseus to escape
the labyrinth after killing the Minotaur; later she was abandoned
by Theseus.   **Antiopa** Queen of the Amazons and wife of Theseus;
elsewhere identified with Hippolyta, but here thought of as a separate
woman

TITANIA

These are the forgeries of jealousy;
And never, since the middle summer's spring,   82
Met we on hill, in dale, forest, or mead,
By pavèd fountain or by rushy brook,   84
Or in the beachèd margent of the sea,   85
To dance our ringlets to the whistling wind,   86
But with thy brawls thou hast disturbed our sport.
Therefore the winds, piping to us in vain,
As in revenge, have sucked up from the sea
Contagious fogs; which, falling in the land,   90
Hath every pelting river made so proud   91
That they have overborne their continents.   92
The ox hath therefore stretched his yoke in vain,
The plowman lost his sweat, and the green corn   94
Hath rotted ere his youth attained a beard;
The fold stands empty in the drownèd field,   96
And crows are fatted with the murrain flock;   97
The nine-men's-morris is filled up with mud,   98
And the quaint mazes in the wanton green   99
For lack of tread are undistinguishable.
The human mortals want their winter here;   101
No night is now with hymn or carol blessed.
Therefore the moon, the governess of floods,   103
Pale in her anger, washes all the air,
That rheumatic diseases do abound.   105
And thorough this distemperature we see   106
The seasons alter: hoary-headed frosts
Fall in the fresh lap of the crimson rose,
And on old Hiems' thin and icy crown   109

---

82 middle summer's spring beginning of midsummer   **84 pavèd** with pebbled bottom.   **rushy** bordered with rushes   **85 in** on.   **margent** edge, border   **86 ringlets** dances in a ring. (See *orbs* in l. 9.)   **90 Contagious** noxious   **91 pelting** paltry   **92 continents** banks that contain them   **94 corn** grain of any kind   **96 fold** pen for sheep or cattle   **97 murrain** having died of the plague   **98 nine-men's-morris** i.e., portion of the village green marked out in a square for a game played with nine pebbles or pegs   **99 quaint mazes** i.e., intricate paths marked out on the village green to be followed rapidly on foot as a kind of contest.   **wanton** luxuriant   **101 want** lack.   **winter** i.e., regular winter season; or, proper observances of winter, such as the *hymn or carol* in the next line (?)   **103 Therefore** i.e., as a result of our quarrel   **105 rheumatic diseases** colds, flu, and other respiratory infections   **106 distemperature** disturbance in nature   **109 Hiems'** the winter god's

An odorous chaplet of sweet summer buds
Is, as in mockery, set. The spring, the summer,
The childing autumn, angry winter, change   112
Their wonted liveries, and the mazèd world   113
By their increase now knows not which is which.   114
And this same progeny of evils comes
From our debate, from our dissension;   116
We are their parents and original.   117

OBERON
Do you amend it, then; it lies in you.
Why should Titania cross her Oberon?
I do but beg a little changeling boy
To be my henchman.

TITANIA   Set your heart at rest.   121
The fairy land buys not the child of me.
His mother was a vot'ress of my order,
And in the spicèd Indian air by night
Full often hath she gossiped by my side
And sat with me on Neptune's yellow sands,
Marking th' embarkèd traders on the flood,   127
When we have laughed to see the sails conceive
And grow big-bellied with the wanton wind;   129
Which she, with pretty and with swimming gait,   130
Following—her womb then rich with my young squire—
Would imitate, and sail upon the land
To fetch me trifles, and return again
As from a voyage, rich with merchandise.
But she, being mortal, of that boy did die;
And for her sake do I rear up her boy,
And for her sake I will not part with him.

OBERON
How long within this wood intend you stay?

TITANIA
Perchance till after Theseus' wedding day.
If you will patiently dance in our round   140
And see our moonlight revels, go with us;

112 **childing** fruitful, pregnant   113 **wonted liveries** usual apparel.
mazèd bewildered.   114 **their increase** their yield, what they produce
116 **debate** quarrel   117 **original** origin   121 **henchman** attendant,
page   127 **traders** trading vessels. **flood** flood tide   129 **wanton**
sportive   130 **swimming** smooth, gliding   140 **round** circular
dance

If not, shun me, and I will spare your haunts.   142

OBERON
Give me that boy and I will go with thee.

TITANIA
Not for thy fairy kingdom. Fairies, away!
We shall chide downright if I longer stay.
                          Exeunt [Titania with her train].

OBERON
Well, go thy way. Thou shalt not from this grove   146
Till I torment thee for this injury.
My gentle Puck, come hither. Thou rememb'rest
Since once I sat upon a promontory,   149
And heard a mermaid on a dolphin's back
Uttering such dulcet and harmonious breath   151
That the rude sea grew civil at her song,   152
And certain stars shot madly from their spheres
To hear the sea-maid's music.

PUCK   I remember.

OBERON
That very time I saw, but thou couldst not,
Flying between the cold moon and the earth,
Cupid all armed. A certain aim he took   157
At a fair vestal thronèd by the west,   158
And loosed his love shaft smartly from his bow   159
As it should pierce a hundred thousand hearts;   160
But I might see young Cupid's fiery shaft   161
Quenched in the chaste beams of the watery moon,
And the imperial vot'ress passèd on
In maiden meditation, fancy-free.   164
Yet marked I where the bolt of Cupid fell: 165
It fell upon a little western flower,
Before milk-white, now purple with love's wound,
And maidens call it "love-in-idleness."   168
Fetch me that flower; the herb I showed thee once.
The juice of it on sleeping eyelids laid

142 spare shun   **146 from** go from   **149 Since** when   **151 breath** voice,
song   **152 rude** rough   **157 all** fully   **158 vestal** vestal virgin. (Contains
a complimentary allusion to Queen Elizabeth as a votaress of Diana and
probably refers to an actual entertainment in her honor at Elvetham in
1591.)   **159 loosed** released   **160 As** as if   **161 might** could   **164 fancy-
free** free of love's spell   **165 bolt** arrow   **168 love-in-idleness** pansy,
heartsease

Will make or man or woman madly dote   171
Upon the next live creature that it sees.
Fetch me this herb, and be thou here again
Ere the leviathan can swim a league.   174

PUCK
I'll put a girdle round about the earth
In forty minutes.   [*Exit.*]

OBERON   Having once this juice,   176
I'll watch Titania when she is asleep
And drop the liquor of it in her eyes.
The next thing then she waking looks upon,
Be it on lion, bear, or wolf, or bull,
On meddling monkey, or on busy ape,
She shall pursue it with the soul of love.
And ere I take this charm from off her sight,
As I can take it with another herb,
I'll make her render up her page to me.
But who comes here? I am invisible,
And I will overhear their conference.

Enter Demetrius, Helena following him.

DEMETRIUS
I love thee not; therefore pursue me not.
Where is Lysander and fair Hermia?
The one I'll slay; the other slayeth me.
Thou toldst me they were stol'n unto this wood;
And here am I, and wode within this wood,   192
Because I cannot meet my Hermia.
Hence, get thee gone, and follow me no more.

HELENA
You draw me, you hardhearted adamant!   195
But yet you draw not iron, for my heart
Is true as steel. Leave you your power to draw,   197
And I shall have no power to follow you.

DEMETRIUS
Do I entice you? Do I speak you fair?   199

171 or . . . or either . . . or   **174 leviathan** sea monster, whale   **176 forty**
(Used indefinitely.)   **192 wode** mad. (Pronounced "wood" and often
spelled so.)   **195 adamant** lodestone, magnet (with pun on *hardhearted,*
since adamant was also thought to be the hardest of all stones and was
confused with the diamond)   **197 Leave** give up   **199 fair** courteously

Or rather do I not in plainest truth
Tell you I do not nor I cannot love you?

HELENA
And even for that do I love you the more.
I am your spaniel; and, Demetrius,
The more you beat me, I will fawn on you.
Use me but as your spaniel, spurn me, strike me,
Neglect me, lose me; only give me leave,
Unworthy as I am, to follow you.
What worser place can I beg in your love—
And yet a place of high respect with me—
Than to be usèd as you use your dog?

DEMETRIUS
Tempt not too much the hatred of my spirit,
For I am sick when I do look on thee.

HELENA
And I am sick when I look not on you.

DEMETRIUS
You do impeach your modesty too much   214
To leave the city and commit yourself
Into the hands of one that loves you not,
To trust the opportunity of night
And the ill counsel of a desert place   218
With the rich worth of your virginity.

HELENA
Your virtue is my privilege. For that   220
It is not night when I do see your face,
Therefore I think I am not in the night;
Nor doth this wood lack worlds of company,
For you, in my respect, are all the world.   224
Then how can it be said I am alone
When all the world is here to look on me?

DEMETRIUS
I'll run from thee and hide me in the brakes,   227
And leave thee to the mercy of wild beasts.

HELENA
The wildest hath not such a heart as you.
Run when you will, the story shall be changed:

214 impeach call into question   **218 desert** deserted   **220 virtue** goodness or power to attract.   **privilege** safeguard, warrant.   **For that**
because   **224 in my respect** as far as I am concerned   **227 brakes**
thickets

Apollo flies and Daphne holds the chase,   231
The dove pursues the griffin, the mild hind   232
Makes speed to catch the tiger—bootless speed,   233
When cowardice pursues and valor flies!

DEMETRIUS
I will not stay thy questions. Let me go!   235
Or if thou follow me, do not believe
But I shall do thee mischief in the wood.

HELENA
Ay, in the temple, in the town, the field,
You do me mischief. Fie, Demetrius!
Your wrongs do set a scandal on my sex.   240
We cannot fight for love, as men may do;
We should be wooed and were not made to woo.
                                         [Exit Demetrius.]
I'll follow thee and make a heaven of hell,
To die upon the hand I love so well.   *[Exit.]* 244

OBERON
Fare thee well, nymph. Ere he do leave this grove,
Thou shalt fly him and he shall seek thy love.

        Enter Puck.

Hast thou the flower there? Welcome, wanderer.
PUCK
Ay, there it is.   *[He offers the flower.]*
OBERON   I pray thee, give it me.
I know a bank where the wild thyme blows,   249
Where oxlips and the nodding violet grows,   250
Quite overcanopied with luscious woodbine,   251
With sweet muskroses and with eglantine.   252
There sleeps Titania sometimes of the night,
Lulled in these flowers with dances and delight;

---

231 Apollo . . . chase (In the ancient myth, Daphne fled from Apollo and
was saved from rape by being transformed into a laurel tree; here it is
the female who *holds the chase,* or pursues, instead of the male.)
232 griffin a fabulous monster with the head of an eagle and the body
of a lion. **hind** female deer **233 bootless** fruitless **235 stay** wait
for. **questions** talk or argument **240 Your . . . sex** i.e., the wrongs
that you do me cause me to act in a manner that disgraces my sex
244 upon by **249 blows** blooms **250 oxlips** flowers resembling cowslip
and primrose **251 woodbine** honeysuckle **252 muskroses** a kind of
large, sweet-scented rose. **eglantine** sweetbrier, another kind of rose

And there the snake throws her enameled skin,   255
Weed wide enough to wrap a fairy in.   256
And with the juice of this I'll streak her eyes   257
And make her full of hateful fantasies.
Take thou some of it, and seek through this grove.
                    [*He gives some love juice.*]
A sweet Athenian lady is in love
With a disdainful youth. Anoint his eyes,
But do it when the next thing he espies
May be the lady. Thou shalt know the man
By the Athenian garments he hath on.
Effect it with some care, that he may prove
More fond on her than she upon her love;   266
And look thou meet me ere the first cock crow.

PUCK
Fear not, my lord, your servant shall do so.

                                        Exeunt.

                    ❧

2.2   *Enter Titania, Queen of Fairies, with her train.*

TITANIA
Come, now a roundel and a fairy song;   1
Then, for the third part of a minute, hence—
Some to kill cankers in the muskrose buds,   3
Some war with reremice for their leathern wings   4
To make my small elves coats, and some keep back
The clamorous owl, that nightly hoots and wonders
At our quaint spirits. Sing me now asleep.   7
Then to your offices, and let me rest.

        Fairies sing.

FIRST FAIRY
        You spotted snakes with double tongue,   9
            Thorny hedgehogs, be not seen;

255 throws sloughs off, sheds   **256 Weed** garment   **257 streak** anoint,
touch gently   **266 fond on** doting on

2.2. Location: The wood.
1 roundel dance in a ring   **3 cankers** cankerworms (i.e., caterpillars or
grubs)   **4 reremice** bats   **7 quaint** dainty   **9 double** forked

> Newts and blindworms, do no wrong,   11
> Come not near our Fairy Queen.

CHORUS

> Philomel, with melody   13
> Sing in our sweet lullaby;
> Lulla, lulla, lullaby, lulla, lulla, lullaby.
>   Never harm
>   Nor spell nor charm
> Come our lovely lady nigh.
> So good night, with lullaby.

FIRST FAIRY

> Weaving spiders, come not here;
> Hence, you long-legged spinners, hence!
> Beetles black, approach not near;
> Worm nor snail, do no offense.

CHORUS

> Philomel, with melody
> Sing in our sweet lullaby;
> Lulla, lulla, lullaby, lulla, lulla, lullaby.
>   Never harm
>   Nor spell nor charm
> Come our lovely lady nigh.
> So good night, with lullaby.

[Titania sleeps.]

SECOND FAIRY

> Hence, away! Now all is well.
> One aloof stand sentinel.

[Exeunt Fairies.]

*Enter Oberon [and squeezes the flower on
Titania's eyelids].*

OBERON

> What thou seest when thou dost wake,
> Do it for thy true love take;
> Love and languish for his sake.

---

11 Newts water lizards (considered poisonous, as were *blindworms*—
small snakes with tiny eyes—and spiders)   **13 Philomel** the nightingale.
(Philomela, daughter of King Pandion, was transformed into a nightingale, according to Ovid's *Metamorphoses* 6, after she had been raped by
her sister Procne's husband, Tereus.)

Be it ounce, or cat, or bear,   36
Pard, or boar with bristled hair,   37
In thy eye that shall appear
When thou wak'st, it is thy dear.
Wake when some vile thing is near.   [*Exit.*]

Enter Lysander and Hermia.

LYSANDER
Fair love, you faint with wandering in the wood;
    And to speak truth, I have forgot our way.
We'll rest us, Hermia, if you think it good,
    And tarry for the comfort of the day.

HERMIA
Be it so, Lysander. Find you out a bed,
For I upon this bank will rest my head.

LYSANDER
One turf shall serve as pillow for us both;
One heart, one bed, two bosoms, and one troth.   48

HERMIA
Nay, good Lysander, for my sake, my dear,
Lie further off yet; do not lie so near.

LYSANDER
O, take the sense, sweet, of my innocence!   51
Love takes the meaning in love's conference.   52
I mean that my heart unto yours is knit
So that but one heart we can make of it;
Two bosoms interchainèd with an oath—
So then two bosoms and a single troth.
Then by your side no bed-room me deny,
For lying so, Hermia, I do not lie.   58

HERMIA
Lysander riddles very prettily.
Now much beshrew my manners and my pride   60
If Hermia meant to say Lysander lied.
But, gentle friend, for love and courtesy
Lie further off, in human modesty;   63

36 ounce lynx   **37 Pard** leopard   **48 troth** faith, trothplight   **51 take . . . innocence** i.e., interpret my intention as innocent   **52 Love . . . conference** i.e., when lovers confer, love teaches each lover to interpret the other's meaning lovingly   **58 lie** tell a falsehood (with a riddling pun on *lie*, recline)   **60 beshrew** curse. (But mildly meant.)   **63 human** courteous

Such separation as may well be said
Becomes a virtuous bachelor and a maid,
So far be distant; and good night, sweet friend.
Thy love ne'er alter till thy sweet life end!

LYSANDER
Amen, amen, to that fair prayer, say I,
And then end life when I end loyalty!
Here is my bed. Sleep give thee all his rest!

HERMIA
With half that wish the wisher's eyes be pressed!   71
          [*They sleep, separated by a short distance.*]

          Enter Puck.

PUCK
          Through the forest have I gone,
          But Athenian found I none
          On whose eyes I might approve   74
          This flower's force in stirring love.
          Night and silence.—Who is here?
          Weeds of Athens he doth wear.
          This is he, my master said,
          Despisèd the Athenian maid;
          And here the maiden, sleeping sound,
          On the dank and dirty ground.
          Pretty soul, she durst not lie
          Near this lack-love, this kill-courtesy.
          Churl, upon thy eyes I throw
          All the power this charm doth owe.   85
                    [*He applies the love juice.*]
          When thou wak'st, let love forbid
          Sleep his seat on thy eyelid.
          So awake when I am gone,
          For I must now to Oberon.   *Exit.*

          Enter Demetrius and Helena, running.

HELENA
Stay, though thou kill me, sweet Demetrius!

DEMETRIUS
I charge thee, hence, and do not haunt me thus.

---

71 With . . . pressed i.e., may we share your wish, so that your eyes too
are *pressed*, closed, in sleep   **74 approve** test   **85 owe** own

HELENA

O, wilt thou darkling leave me? Do not so.   92

DEMETRIUS

Stay, on thy peril! I alone will go.   *[Exit.]* 93

HELENA

O, I am out of breath in this fond chase!   94
The more my prayer, the lesser is my grace.   95
Happy is Hermia, wheresoe'er she lies,   96
For she hath blessèd and attractive eyes.
How came her eyes so bright? Not with salt tears;
If so, my eyes are oftener washed than hers.
No, no, I am as ugly as a bear;
For beasts that meet me run away for fear.
Therefore no marvel though Demetrius   102
Do, as a monster, fly my presence thus.   103
What wicked and dissembling glass of mine
Made me compare with Hermia's sphery eyne?   105
But who is here? Lysander, on the ground?
Dead, or asleep? I see no blood, no wound.
Lysander, if you live, good sir, awake.

LYSANDER *[Awaking]*

And run through fire I will for thy sweet sake.
Transparent Helena! Nature shows art,   110
That through thy bosom makes me see thy heart.
Where is Demetrius? O, how fit a word
Is that vile name to perish on my sword!

HELENA

Do not say so, Lysander, say not so.
What though he love your Hermia? Lord, what though?
Yet Hermia still loves you. Then be content.

LYSANDER

Content with Hermia? No! I do repent
The tedious minutes I with her have spent.
Not Hermia but Helena I love.
Who will not change a raven for a dove?
The will of man is by his reason swayed,

---

92 darkling in the dark   **93 on thy peril** i.e., on pain of danger to you if
you don't obey me and stay   **94 fond** doting   **95 my grace** the favor I
obtain   **96 lies** dwells   **102–103 no marvel . . . thus** i.e., no wonder that
Demetrius flies from me as from a monster   **105 compare** vie.   **sphery
eyne** eyes as bright as stars in their spheres   **110 Transparent** (1) radiant (2) able to be seen through

And reason says you are the worthier maid.
Things growing are not ripe until their season;
So I, being young, till now ripe not to reason.   124
And touching now the point of human skill,   125
Reason becomes the marshal to my will
And leads me to your eyes, where I o'erlook   127
Love's stories written in love's richest book.

HELENA
Wherefore was I to this keen mockery born?   129
When at your hands did I deserve this scorn?
Is 't not enough, is 't not enough, young man,
That I did never, no, nor never can,
Deserve a sweet look from Demetrius' eye,
But you must flout my insufficiency?
Good troth, you do me wrong, good sooth, you do,   135
In such disdainful manner me to woo.
But fare you well. Perforce I must confess
I thought you lord of more true gentleness.   138
O, that a lady, of one man refused,   139
Should of another therefore be abused!   *Exit.*   140

LYSANDER
She sees not Hermia. Hermia, sleep thou there,
And never mayst thou come Lysander near!
For as a surfeit of the sweetest things
The deepest loathing to the stomach brings,
Or as the heresies that men do leave   145
Are hated most of those they did deceive,   146
So thou, my surfeit and my heresy,
Of all be hated, but the most of me!
And, all my powers, address your love and might   149
To honor Helen and to be her knight!   *Exit.*

HERMIA [*Awaking*]
Help me, Lysander, help me! Do thy best
To pluck this crawling serpent from my breast!
Ay me, for pity! What a dream was here!
Lysander, look how I do quake with fear.

---

124 ripe not (am) not ripened   **125 touching** reaching.   **point** summit.
skill judgment   **127 o'erlook** read   **129 Wherefore** why   **135 Good
troth, good sooth** i.e., indeed, truly   **138 lord of** i.e., possessor of.
gentleness courtesy   **139 of** by   **140 abused** ill treated   **145–146 as . . .
deceive** as renounced heresies are hated most by those persons who
formerly were deceived by them   **149 address** direct, apply

Methought a serpent ate my heart away,
And you sat smiling at his cruel prey.   156
Lysander! What, removed? Lysander! Lord!
What, out of hearing? Gone? No sound, no word?
Alack, where are you? Speak, an if you hear;   159
Speak, of all loves! I swoon almost with fear.   160
No? Then I well perceive you are not nigh.
Either death, or you, I'll find immediately.
                    Exit. [*The sleeping Titania remains.*]

156 prey act of preying   **159 an if** if   **160 of loves** for all love's sake

3.1 *Enter the clowns [Quince, Snug, Bottom, Flute, Snout, and Starveling].*

BOTTOM   Are we all met?

QUINCE   Pat, pat; and here's a marvelous convenient 2
place for our rehearsal. This green plot shall be our
stage, this hawthorn brake our tiring-house, and we 4
will do it in action as we will do it before the Duke.

BOTTOM   Peter Quince?

QUINCE   What sayest thou, bully Bottom? 7

BOTTOM   There are things in this comedy of Pyramus
and Thisbe that will never please. First, Pyramus must
draw a sword to kill himself, which the ladies cannot
abide. How answer you that?

SNOUT   By 'r lakin, a parlous fear. 12

STARVELING   I believe we must leave the killing out,
when all is done. 14

BOTTOM   Not a whit. I have a device to make all well.
Write me a prologue, and let the prologue seem to say 16
we will do no harm with our swords, and that Pyramus
is not killed indeed; and for the more better assurance,
tell them that I, Pyramus, am not Pyramus but Bottom
the weaver. This will put them out of fear.

QUINCE   Well, we will have such a prologue, and it shall
be written in eight and six. 22

BOTTOM   No, make it two more; let it be written in eight
and eight.

SNOUT   Will not the ladies be afeard of the lion?

STARVELING   I fear it, I promise you.

BOTTOM   Masters, you ought to consider with yourselves, to bring in—God shield us!—a lion among la- 28
dies is a most dreadful thing. For there is not a more 29

3.1. Location: The action is continuous.
2 Pat on the dot, punctually   **4 brake** thicket.   **tiring-house** attiring
area, hence backstage   **7 bully** i.e., worthy, jolly, fine fellow   **12 By 'r
lakin** by our ladykin, i.e., the Virgin Mary.   **parlous** alarming   **14 when
all is done** i.e., when all is said and done   **16 Write me** i.e., write at my
suggestion. (*Me* is used colloquially.)   **22 eight and six** alternate lines of
eight and six syllables, a common ballad measure   **28–29 lion among
ladies** (A contemporary pamphlet tells how at the christening in 1594 of
Prince Henry, eldest son of King James VI of Scotland, later James I of
England, a "blackamoor" instead of a lion drew the triumphal chariot,
since the lion's presence might have "brought some fear to the nearest.")

fearful wildfowl than your lion living; and we ought 30
to look to 't.

SNOUT   Therefore another prologue must tell he is not a
lion.

BOTTOM   Nay, you must name his name, and half his
face must be seen through the lion's neck, and he himself must speak through, saying thus, or to the same
defect: "Ladies"—or "Fair ladies—I would wish 37
you"—or "I would request you"—or "I would entreat
you—not to fear, not to tremble; my life for yours. If 39
you think I come hither as a lion, it were pity of my 40
life. No, I am no such thing; I am a man as other men 41
are." And there indeed let him name his name and
tell them plainly he is Snug the joiner.

QUINCE   Well, it shall be so. But there is two hard things:
that is, to bring the moonlight into a chamber; for, you
know, Pyramus and Thisbe meet by moonlight.

SNOUT   Doth the moon shine that night we play our
play?

BOTTOM   A calendar, a calendar! Look in the almanac.
Find out moonshine, find out moonshine.

[They consult an almanac.]

QUINCE   Yes, it doth shine that night.

BOTTOM   Why, then, may you leave a casement of the
great chamber window, where we play, open, and the
moon may shine in at the casement.

QUINCE   Ay; or else one must come in with a bush of 55
thorns and a lantern and say he comes to disfigure, or 56
to present, the person of Moonshine. Then there is 57
another thing: we must have a wall in the great chamber; for Pyramus and Thisbe, says the story, did talk
through the chink of a wall.

SNOUT   You can never bring in a wall. What say you,
Bottom?

BOTTOM   Some man or other must present Wall. And let

30 fearful fear-inspiring   **37 defect** (Bottom's blunder for *effect*.)
39 my life for yours i.e., I pledge my life to make your lives safe
40–41 it were . . . life my life would be endangered   **55–56 bush of
thorns** bundle of thornbush faggots (part of the accoutrements of the
man in the moon, according to the popular notions of the time, along
with his lantern and his dog)   **56 disfigure** (Quince's blunder for *figure*.)   **57 present** represent

him have some plaster, or some loam, or some rough- 64
cast about him, to signify wall; or let him hold his 65
fingers thus, and through that cranny shall Pyramus
and Thisbe whisper.

QUINCE   If that may be, then all is well. Come, sit down,
every mother's son, and rehearse your parts. Pyramus,
you begin. When you have spoken your speech, enter
into that brake, and so everyone according to his cue.

Enter Robin [Puck].

PUCK
What hempen homespuns have we swaggering here 72
So near the cradle of the Fairy Queen? 73
What, a play toward? I'll be an auditor; 74
An actor too perhaps, if I see cause.

QUINCE   Speak, Pyramus. Thisbe, stand forth.

BOTTOM *[As Pyramus]*
"Thisbe, the flowers of odious savors sweet—"

QUINCE   Odors, odors.

BOTTOM   "—Odors savors sweet;
So hath thy breath, my dearest Thisbe dear.
But hark, a voice! Stay thou but here awhile,
And by and by I will to thee appear."   *Exit.*

PUCK
A stranger Pyramus than e'er played here.   *[Exit.]* 83

FLUTE   Must I speak now?

QUINCE   Ay, marry, must you; for you must understand
he goes but to see a noise that he heard, and is to come
again.

FLUTE *[As Thisbe]*
"Most radiant Pyramus, most lily-white of hue,
Of color like the red rose on triumphant brier, 89
Most brisky juvenal and eke most lovely Jew, 90

64–65 roughcast a mixture of lime and gravel used to plaster the outside of buildings   **72 hempen homespuns** i.e., rustics dressed in clothes
woven of coarse, homespun fabric made from hemp   **73 cradle** i.e.,
Titania's bower   **74 toward** about to take place   **83 A stranger . . . here**
(Puck indicates that he has conceived of his plan to present a "stranger"
Pyramus than ever seen before, and so Puck exits to put his plan into
effect.)   **89 triumphant** magnificent   **90 brisky juvenal** lively youth.
eke also.   **Jew** (Probably an absurd repetition of the first syllable of
juvenal, or Flute's error for *jewel*.)

As true as truest horse, that yet would never tire.
I'll meet thee, Pyramus, at Ninny's tomb."

QUINCE "Ninus' tomb," man. Why, you must not 93
speak that yet. That you answer to Pyramus. You
speak all your part at once, cues and all. Pyramus, en- 95
ter. Your cue is past; it is "never tire."

FLUTE
O—"As true as truest horse, that yet would never
tire."   97

[*Enter Puck, and Bottom as Pyramus with the ass
head.*]

BOTTOM
"If I were fair, Thisbe, I were only thine."   98

QUINCE O, monstrous! O, strange! We are haunted.
Pray, masters! Fly, masters! Help!
                    [*Exeunt Quince, Snug, Flute,
                              Snout, and Starveling.*]

PUCK
I'll follow you, I'll lead you about a round,   101
   Through bog, through bush, through brake, through
   brier.
Sometimes a horse I'll be, sometimes a hound,
   A hog, a headless bear, sometimes a fire;   104
And neigh, and bark, and grunt, and roar, and burn,
Like horse, hound, hog, bear, fire, at every turn. *Exit.*

BOTTOM Why do they run away? This is a knavery of
them to make me afeard.

Enter Snout.

SNOUT O Bottom, thou art changed! What do I see on
thee?

BOTTOM What do you see? You see an ass head of your
own, do you?   [*Exit Snout.*]

---

93 Ninus mythical founder of Nineveh (whose wife, Semiramis, was
supposed to have built the walls of Babylon where the story of Pyramus
and Thisbe takes place) **95 part** (An actor's *part* was a script consisting
only of his speeches and their cues.) **97 s.d. with the ass head** (This
stage direction, taken from the Folio, presumably refers to a standard
stage property.) **98 fair** handsome. **were** would be **101 about a
round** roundabout **104 fire** will-o'-the-wisp

Enter Quince.

QUINCE   Bless thee, Bottom, bless thee! Thou art trans-   113
lated.   *Exit.*   114
BOTTOM   I see their knavery. This is to make an ass of
me, to fright me, if they could. But I will not stir from
this place, do what they can. I will walk up and down
here, and will sing, that they shall hear I am not
afraid.   [*Sings.*]

    The ouzel cock so black of hue,   120
      With orange-tawny bill,
    The throstle with his note so true,   122
      The wren with little quill—   123

TITANIA [*Awaking*]
What angel wakes me from my flowery bed?
BOTTOM [*Sings*]
    The finch, the sparrow, and the lark,
      The plainsong cuckoo gray,   126
    Whose note full many a man doth mark,
      And dares not answer nay—   128
For, indeed, who would set his wit to so foolish a
bird? Who would give a bird the lie, though he cry   130
"cuckoo" never so?   131

TITANIA
I pray thee, gentle mortal, sing again.
Mine ear is much enamored of thy note;
So is mine eye enthrallèd to thy shape;
And thy fair virtue's force perforce doth move me   135
On the first view to say, to swear, I love thee.
BOTTOM   Methinks, mistress, you should have little rea-
son for that. And yet, to say the truth, reason and love
keep little company together nowadays. The more the
pity that some honest neighbors will not make them
friends. Nay, I can gleek upon occasion.   141
TITANIA
Thou art as wise as thou art beautiful.

113–114 translated transformed   **120 ouzel cock** male blackbird
122 throstle song thrush   **123 quill** (Literally, a reed pipe; hence, the
bird's piping song.)   **126 plainsong** singing a melody without variations   **128 dares . . . nay** i.e., cannot deny that he is a cuckold   **130 give
. . . lie** call the bird a liar   **131 never so** ever so much   **135 thy . . . force**
the power of your beauty   **141 gleek** scoff, jest

BOTTOM Not so, neither. But if I had wit enough to get
out of this wood, I have enough to serve mine own 144
turn.   145

TITANIA
Out of this wood do not desire to go.
Thou shalt remain here, whether thou wilt or no.
I am a spirit of no common rate.   148
The summer still doth tend upon my state,   149
And I do love thee. Therefore go with me.
I'll give thee fairies to attend on thee,
And they shall fetch thee jewels from the deep,
And sing while thou on pressèd flowers dost sleep.
And I will purge thy mortal grossness so   154
That thou shalt like an airy spirit go.
Peaseblossom, Cobweb, Mote, and Mustardseed!   156

*Enter four Fairies [Peaseblossom, Cobweb, Mote,
and Mustardseed].*

PEASEBLOSSOM Ready.
COBWEB
And I.
MOTE And I.
MUSTARDSEED And I.
ALL   Where shall we go?
TITANIA
Be kind and courteous to this gentleman.
Hop in his walks and gambol in his eyes;   160
Feed him with apricots and dewberries,   161
With purple grapes, green figs, and mulberries;
The honey bags steal from the humble-bees,
And for night tapers crop their waxen thighs
And light them at the fiery glowworms' eyes,
To have my love to bed and to arise;
And pluck the wings from painted butterflies
To fan the moonbeams from his sleeping eyes.
Nod to him, elves, and do him courtesies.

144–145 serve . . . turn answer my purpose **148 rate** rank, value
149 still ever, always. **doth . . . state** waits upon me as a part of my
royal retinue **154 mortal grossness** materiality (i.e., the corporal nature
of a mortal being) **156 Mote** i.e., speck. (The two words *moth* and *mote*
were pronounced alike, and both meanings may be present.) **160 in his
eyes** in his sight (i.e., before him) **161 dewberries** blackberries

PEASEBLOSSOM Hail, mortal!

COBWEB Hail!

MOTE Hail!

MUSTARDSEED Hail!

BOTTOM I cry your worships mercy, heartily. I beseech
your worship's name.

COBWEB Cobweb.

BOTTOM I shall desire you of more acquaintance, good
Master Cobweb. If I cut my finger, I shall make bold   178
with you.—Your name, honest gentleman?   179

PEASEBLOSSOM Peaseblossom.

BOTTOM I pray you, commend me to Mistress Squash,   181
your mother, and to Master Peascod, your father.   182
Good Master Peaseblossom, I shall desire you of more
acquaintance too.—Your name, I beseech you, sir?

MUSTARDSEED Mustardseed.

BOTTOM Good Master Mustardseed, I know your pa-   186
tience well. That same cowardly, giantlike ox-beef   187
hath devoured many a gentleman of your house. I
promise you, your kindred hath made my eyes water   189
ere now. I desire you of more acquaintance, good
Master Mustardseed.

TITANIA

Come, wait upon him; lead him to my bower.

  The moon methinks looks with a watery eye;

And when she weeps, weeps every little flower,   194

  Lamenting some enforcèd chastity.   195

  Tie up my lover's tongue, bring him silently.   196

                                        Exeunt.

❧

3.2 *Enter [Oberon,] King of Fairies.*

OBERON

I wonder if Titania be awaked;

178–179 If . . . you (Cobwebs were used to stanch bleeding.) **181 Squash**
unripe pea pod **182 Peascod** ripe pea pod **186–187 your patience** what
you have endured **189 water** (1) weep for sympathy (2) smart, sting
194 she weeps i.e., she causes dew **195 enforcèd** forced, violated; or, possibly, constrained (since Titania at this moment is hardly concerned about
chastity) **196 Tie . . . tongue** (Presumably Bottom is braying like an ass.)

3.2. Location: The wood.

Then what it was that next came in her eye,
Which she must dote on in extremity.

[*Enter*] *Robin Goodfellow* [*Puck*].

Here comes my messenger. How now, mad spirit?
What night-rule now about this haunted grove?   5
PUCK
My mistress with a monster is in love.
Near to her close and consecrated bower,   7
While she was in her dull and sleeping hour,   8
A crew of patches, rude mechanicals,   9
That work for bread upon Athenian stalls,   10
Were met together to rehearse a play
Intended for great Theseus' nuptial day.
The shallowest thick-skin of that barren sort,   13
Who Pyramus presented in their sport,   14
Forsook his scene and entered in a brake.   15
When I did him at this advantage take,
An ass's noll I fixèd on his head.   17
Anon his Thisbe must be answerèd,
And forth my mimic comes. When they him spy,   19
As wild geese that the creeping fowler eye,   20
Or russet-pated choughs, many in sort,   21
Rising and cawing at the gun's report,
Sever themselves and madly sweep the sky,   23
So, at his sight, away his fellows fly;
And, at our stamp, here o'er and o'er one falls;
He "Murder!" cries and help from Athens calls.
Their sense thus weak, lost with their fears thus strong,
Made senseless things begin to do them wrong,
For briers and thorns at their apparel snatch;
Some, sleeves—some, hats; from yielders all things
  catch.   30

5 **night-rule** diversion for the night.   **haunted** much frequented   7 **close**
secret, private   8 **dull** drowsy   9 **patches** clowns, fools.   **rude mechani-**
cals ignorant artisans   10 **stalls** market booths   13 **barren sort** stupid
company or crew   14 **presented** acted   15 **scene** playing area   17 **noll**
noddle, head   19 **mimic** burlesque actor   20 **fowler** hunter of game
birds   21 **russet-pated choughs** reddish brown or gray-headed jack-
daws.   **in sort** in a flock   23 **Sever** i.e., scatter   30 **from . . . catch** i.e.,
everything preys on those who yield to fear

I led them on in this distracted fear
And left sweet Pyramus translated there,
When in that moment, so it came to pass,
Titania waked and straightway loved an ass.

OBERON
This falls out better than I could devise.
But hast thou yet latched the Athenian's eyes   36
With the love juice, as I did bid thee do?

PUCK
I took him sleeping—that is finished too—
And the Athenian woman by his side,
That, when he waked, of force she must be eyed.   40

Enter Demetrius and Hermia.

OBERON
Stand close. This is the same Athenian.

PUCK
This is the woman, but not this the man.

                                        [*They stand aside.*]

DEMETRIUS
O, why rebuke you him that loves you so?
Lay breath so bitter on your bitter foe.

HERMIA
Now I but chide; but I should use thee worse,
For thou, I fear, hast given me cause to curse.
If thou hast slain Lysander in his sleep,
Being o'er shoes in blood, plunge in the deep,   48
And kill me too.
The sun was not so true unto the day
As he to me. Would he have stolen away
From sleeping Hermia? I'll believe as soon
This whole earth may be bored, and that the moon   53
May through the center creep, and so displease
Her brother's noontide with th' Antipodes.   55
It cannot be but thou hast murdered him;
So should a murderer look, so dead, so grim.   57

36 latched fastened, snared **40 of force** perforce **48 o'er shoes** i.e., so far gone **53 whole** solid **55 Her brother's** i.e., the sun's. **th' Antipodes** the people on the opposite side of the earth (where the moon is imagined bringing night to noontime) **57 dead** deadly, or deathly pale

DEMETRIUS
  So should the murdered look, and so should I,
  Pierced through the heart with your stern cruelty.
  Yet you, the murderer, look as bright, as clear,
  As yonder Venus in her glimmering sphere.

HERMIA
  What's this to my Lysander? Where is he?   62
  Ah, good Demetrius, wilt thou give him me?

DEMETRIUS
  I had rather give his carcass to my hounds.

HERMIA
  Out, dog! Out, cur! Thou driv'st me past the bounds
  Of maiden's patience. Hast thou slain him, then?
  Henceforth be never numbered among men.
  O, once tell true, tell true, even for my sake:
  Durst thou have looked upon him being awake?
  And hast thou killed him sleeping? O brave touch!   70
  Could not a worm, an adder, do so much?   71
  An adder did it; for with doubler tongue
  Than thine, thou serpent, never adder stung.

DEMETRIUS
  You spend your passion on a misprised mood.   74
  I am not guilty of Lysander's blood,
  Nor is he dead, for aught that I can tell.

HERMIA
  I pray thee, tell me then that he is well.

DEMETRIUS
  An if I could, what should I get therefor?

HERMIA
  A privilege never to see me more.
  And from thy hated presence part I so.
  See me no more, whether he be dead or no.   *Exit.*

DEMETRIUS
  There is no following her in this fierce vein.
  Here therefore for a while I will remain.
  So sorrow's heaviness doth heavier grow   84
  For debt that bankrupt sleep doth sorrow owe;   85

---

62 to to do with   **70 brave touch** noble exploit. (Said ironically.)   **71 worm**
serpent   **74 passion** violent feelings.   **misprised mood** anger based on mis-
conception   **84 heavier** (1) harder to bear (2) more drowsy   **85 bankrupt** (Demetrius is saying that his sleepiness adds to the weariness caused by sorrow.)

Which now in some slight measure it will pay,   86
If for his tender here I make some stay.   87

Lie[s] down [and sleeps].

OBERON
What hast thou done? Thou hast mistaken quite
And laid the love juice on some true love's sight.
Of thy misprision must perforce ensue   90
Some true love turned, and not a false turned true.

PUCK
Then fate o'errules, that, one man holding troth,   92
A million fail, confounding oath on oath.   93

OBERON
About the wood go swifter than the wind,
And Helena of Athens look thou find.   95
All fancy-sick she is and pale of cheer   96
With sighs of love, that cost the fresh blood dear.   97
By some illusion see thou bring her here.
I'll charm his eyes against she do appear.   99

PUCK
I go, I go, look how I go,
Swifter than arrow from the Tartar's bow.   101

[Exit.]

OBERON [*Applying love juice to Demetrius' eyes*]
    Flower of this purple dye,
    Hit with Cupid's archery,
    Sink in apple of his eye.
    When his love he doth espy,
    Let her shine as gloriously
    As the Venus of the sky.
    When thou wak'st, if she be by,
    Beg of her for remedy.

Enter Puck.

86-87 Which . . . stay i.e., to a small extent I will be able to
"pay back" and hence find some relief from sorrow, if I pause here
awhile *(make some stay)* while sleep "tenders" or offers itself by
way of paying the debt owed to sorrow   **90 misprision** mistake   **92 troth** faith   **93 confounding . . . oath** i.e., invalidating
one oath with another   **95 look** i.e., be sure   **96 fancy-sick** love-
sick. **cheer** face   **97 sighs . . . blood** (An allusion to the physio-
logical theory that each sigh costs the heart a drop of blood.)
99 against . . . appear in anticipation of her coming   **101 Tartar's
bow** (Tartars were famed for their skill with the bow.)

PUCK

> Captain of our fairy band,
> Helena is here at hand,
> And the youth, mistook by me,
> Pleading for a lover's fee.   113
> Shall we their fond pageant see?   114
> Lord, what fools these mortals be!

OBERON

> Stand aside. The noise they make
> Will cause Demetrius to awake.

PUCK

> Then will two at once woo one;
> That must needs be sport alone.   119
> And those things do best please me
> That befall preposterously.   121

> *[They stand aside.]*

Enter Lysander and Helena.

LYSANDER

> Why should you think that I should woo in scorn?
>   Scorn and derision never come in tears.
> Look when I vow, I weep; and vows so born,   124
>   In their nativity all truth appears.   125
> How can these things in me seem scorn to you,
>   Bearing the badge of faith to prove them true?   127

HELENA

> You do advance your cunning more and more.   128
>   When truth kills truth, O, devilish-holy fray!   129
> These vows are Hermia's. Will you give her o'er?
>   Weigh oath with oath, and you will nothing weigh.
> Your vows to her and me, put in two scales,
> Will even weigh, and both as light as tales.   133

LYSANDER

> I had no judgment when to her I swore.

113 fee privilege, reward   **114 fond pageant** foolish exhibition
119 alone unequaled   **121 preposterously** out of the natural order
124 Look when whenever   **124–125 vows . . . appears** i.e., vows made by
one who is weeping give evidence thereby of their sincerity   **127 badge**
identifying device such as that worn on servants' livery (here, his
tears)   **128 advance** carry forward, display   **129 truth kills truth** i.e.,
one of Lysander's vows must invalidate the other   **133 tales** lies

HELENA
  Nor none, in my mind, now you give her o'er.
LYSANDER
  Demetrius loves her, and he loves not you.
DEMETRIUS [*Awaking*]
  O Helen, goddess, nymph, perfect, divine!
  To what, my love, shall I compare thine eyne?
  Crystal is muddy. O, how ripe in show   139
  Thy lips, those kissing cherries, tempting grow!
  That pure congealèd white, high Taurus' snow,   141
  Fanned with the eastern wind, turns to a crow   142
  When thou hold'st up thy hand. O, let me kiss
  This princess of pure white, this seal of bliss!   144
HELENA
  O spite! O hell! I see you all are bent
  To set against me for your merriment.   146
  If you were civil and knew courtesy,
  You would not do me thus much injury.
  Can you not hate me, as I know you do,
  But you must join in souls to mock me too?
  If you were men, as men you are in show,
  You would not use a gentle lady so—
  To vow, and swear, and superpraise my parts,   153
  When I am sure you hate me with your hearts.
  You both are rivals, and love Hermia;
  And now both rivals, to mock Helena.
  A trim exploit, a manly enterprise,   157
  To conjure tears up in a poor maid's eyes
  With your derision! None of noble sort   159
  Would so offend a virgin and extort   160
  A poor soul's patience, all to make you sport.
LYSANDER
  You are unkind, Demetrius. Be not so;
  For you love Hermia; this you know I know.
  And here, with all good will, with all my heart,
  In Hermia's love I yield you up my part;

139 show appearance   **141 Taurus** a lofty mountain range in Asia
Minor   **142 turns to a crow** i.e., seems black by contrast   **144 seal**
pledge   **146 set against** attack   **153 superpraise** overpraise.   **parts**
qualities   **157 trim** pretty, fine. (Said ironically.)   **159 sort** character,
quality   **160 extort** twist, torture

And yours of Helena to me bequeath,
Whom I do love and will do till my death.

HELENA
Never did mockers waste more idle breath.

DEMETRIUS
Lysander, keep thy Hermia; I will none.   169
If e'er I loved her, all that love is gone.
My heart to her but as guest-wise sojourned,   171
And now to Helen is it home returned,
There to remain.

LYSANDER   Helen, it is not so.

DEMETRIUS
Disparage not the faith thou dost not know,
Lest, to thy peril, thou aby it dear.   175
Look where thy love comes; yonder is thy dear.

Enter Hermia.

HERMIA
Dark night, that from the eye his function takes,   177
The ear more quick of apprehension makes;
Wherein it doth impair the seeing sense,
It pays the hearing double recompense.
Thou art not by mine eye, Lysander, found;
Mine ear, I thank it, brought me to thy sound.
But why unkindly didst thou leave me so?

LYSANDER
Why should he stay whom love doth press to go?

HERMIA
What love could press Lysander from my side?

LYSANDER
Lysander's love, that would not let him bide—
Fair Helena, who more engilds the night   187
Than all yon fiery oes and eyes of light.   188
Why seek'st thou me? Could not this make thee know,
The hate I bear thee made me leave thee so?

HERMIA
You speak not as you think. It cannot be.

HELENA
Lo, she is one of this confederacy!

169 will none i.e., want no part of her **171 to . . . sojourned** only visited
with her **175 aby** pay for **177 his** its **187 engilds** brightens with a
golden light **188 oes** spangles (here, stars)

Now I perceive they have conjoined all three
To fashion this false sport in spite of me.   194
Injurious Hermia, most ungrateful maid!
Have you conspired, have you with these contrived   196
To bait me with this foul derision?   197
Is all the counsel that we two have shared,   198
The sisters' vows, the hours that we have spent,
When we have chid the hasty-footed time
For parting us—O, is all forgot?
All schooldays' friendship, childhood innocence?
We, Hermia, like two artificial gods,   203
Have with our needles created both one flower,
Both on one sampler, sitting on one cushion,
Both warbling of one song, both in one key,
As if our hands, our sides, voices, and minds
Had been incorporate. So we grew together   208
Like to a double cherry, seeming parted
But yet an union in partition,
Two lovely berries molded on one stem;   211
So with two seeming bodies but one heart,
Two of the first, like coats in heraldry,   213
Due but to one and crownèd with one crest.   214
And will you rend our ancient love asunder
To join with men in scorning your poor friend?
It is not friendly, 'tis not maidenly.
Our sex, as well as I, may chide you for it,
Though I alone do feel the injury.

HERMIA
I am amazèd at your passionate words.
I scorn you not. It seems that you scorn me.

HELENA
Have you not set Lysander, as in scorn,
To follow me and praise my eyes and face?
And made your other love, Demetrius,
Who even but now did spurn me with his foot,
To call me goddess, nymph, divine and rare,

194 in spite of me to vex me   **196 contrived** plotted   **197 bait** torment, as one sets on dogs to bait a bear   **198 counsel** confidential talk   **203 artificial** skilled in art or creation   **208 incorporate** of one body   **211 lovely** loving   **213–214 Two . . . crest** i.e., we have two separate bodies, just as a coat of arms in heraldry can be represented twice on a shield but surmounted by a single crest

Precious, celestial? Wherefore speaks he this
To her he hates? And wherefore doth Lysander
Deny your love, so rich within his soul,
And tender me, forsooth, affection,   230
But by your setting on, by your consent?
What though I be not so in grace as you,   232
So hung upon with love, so fortunate,
But miserable most, to love unloved?
This you should pity rather than despise.

HERMIA
I understand not what you mean by this.

HELENA
Ay, do! Persever, counterfeit sad looks,   237
Make mouths upon me when I turn my back,   238
Wink each at other, hold the sweet jest up.   239
This sport, well carried, shall be chronicled.   240
If you have any pity, grace, or manners,
You would not make me such an argument.   242
But fare ye well. 'Tis partly my own fault,
Which death, or absence, soon shall remedy.

LYSANDER
Stay, gentle Helena; hear my excuse,
My love, my life, my soul, fair Helena!

HELENA
O excellent!

HERMIA [*To Lysander*]   Sweet, do not scorn her so.

DEMETRIUS
If she cannot entreat, I can compel.   248

LYSANDER
Thou canst compel no more than she entreat.
Thy threats have no more strength than her weak
     prayers.
Helen, I love thee, by my life, I do!
I swear by that which I will lose for thee,
To prove him false that says I love thee not.

DEMETRIUS
I say I love thee more than he can do.

_____

230 tender offer   **232 grace** favor   **237 sad** grave, serious   **238 mouths**
i.e., mows, faces, grimaces.   **upon** at   **239 hold . . . up** keep up the
joke   **240 carried** managed   **242 argument** subject for a jest   **248 entreat** i.e., succeed by entreaty

LYSANDER
If thou say so, withdraw, and prove it too.
DEMETRIUS
Quick, come!
HERMIA   Lysander, whereto tends all this?
LYSANDER
Away, you Ethiop!
                    [*He tries to break away from Hermia.*]
DEMETRIUS   No, no; he'll   257
Seem to break loose; take on as you would follow,   258
But yet come not. You are a tame man, go!
LYSANDER
Hang off, thou cat, thou burr! Vile thing, let loose,   260
Or I will shake thee from me like a serpent!
HERMIA
Why are you grown so rude? What change is this,
Sweet love?
LYSANDER   Thy love? Out, tawny Tartar, out!
Out, loathèd med'cine! O hated potion, hence!   264
HERMIA
Do you not jest?
HELENA   Yes, sooth, and so do you.   265
LYSANDER
Demetrius, I will keep my word with thee.
DEMETRIUS
I would I had your bond, for I perceive
A weak bond holds you. I'll not trust your word.   268
LYSANDER
What, should I hurt her, strike her, kill her dead?
Although I hate her, I'll not harm her so.
HERMIA
What, can you do me greater harm than hate?
Hate me? Wherefore? O me, what news, my love?   272
Am not I Hermia? Are not you Lysander?
I am as fair now as I was erewhile.   274
Since night you loved me; yet since night you left me.

257 Ethiop (Referring to Hermia's relatively dark hair and complexion;
see also *tawny Tartar* six lines later.)   **258 take on as** act as if   **260 Hang
off** let go   **264 med'cine** i.e., poison   **265 sooth** truly   **268 weak bond**
i.e., Hermia's arm (with a pun on *bond*, oath, in the previous line)
272 what news what is the matter   **274 erewhile** just now

Why, then you left me—O, the gods forbid!—
In earnest, shall I say?

LYSANDER   Ay, by my life!
And never did desire to see thee more.
Therefore be out of hope, of question, of doubt;
Be certain, nothing truer. 'Tis no jest
That I do hate thee and love Helena.

HERMIA [*To Helena*]
O me! You juggler! You cankerblossom!   282
You thief of love! What, have you come by night
And stol'n my love's heart from him?

HELENA   Fine, i' faith!
Have you no modesty, no maiden shame,
No touch of bashfulness? What, will you tear
Impatient answers from my gentle tongue?
Fie, fie! You counterfeit, you puppet, you!   288

HERMIA
"Puppet"? Why, so! Ay, that way goes the game.   289
Now I perceive that she hath made compare
Between our statures; she hath urged her height,
And with her personage, her tall personage,
Her height, forsooth, she hath prevailed with him.
And are you grown so high in his esteem
Because I am so dwarfish and so low?
How low am I, thou painted maypole? Speak!
How low am I? I am not yet so low
But that my nails can reach unto thine eyes.
          [*She flails at Helena but is restrained.*]

HELENA
I pray you, though you mock me, gentlemen,
Let her not hurt me. I was never curst;   300
I have no gift at all in shrewishness;
I am a right maid for my cowardice.   302
Let her not strike me. You perhaps may think,
Because she is something lower than myself,   304
That I can match her.

HERMIA   Lower? Hark, again!

---

282 cankerblossom worm that destroys the flower bud (?)   **288 puppet**
(1) counterfeit (2) dwarfish woman (in reference to Hermia's smaller
stature)   **289 Why, so** i.e., Oh, so that's how it is   **300 curst** shrewish
302 right true   **304 something** somewhat

HELENA
Good Hermia, do not be so bitter with me.
I evermore did love you, Hermia,
Did ever keep your counsels, never wronged you;
Save that, in love unto Demetrius,
I told him of your stealth unto this wood.　　　310
He followed you; for love I followed him.
But he hath chid me hence and threatened me　　　312
To strike me, spurn me, nay, to kill me too.
And now, so you will let me quiet go,　　　314
To Athens will I bear my folly back
And follow you no further. Let me go.
You see how simple and how fond I am.　　　317
HERMIA
Why, get you gone. Who is 't that hinders you?
HELENA
A foolish heart, that I leave here behind.
HERMIA
What, with Lysander?
HELENA　　　　　　　　　　With Demetrius.
LYSANDER
Be not afraid; she shall not harm thee, Helena.
DEMETRIUS
No, sir, she shall not, though you take her part.
HELENA
O, when she is angry, she is keen and shrewd.　　　323
She was a vixen when she went to school,
And though she be but little, she is fierce.
HERMIA
"Little" again? Nothing but "low" and "little"?
Why will you suffer her to flout me thus?
Let me come to her.
LYSANDER　　　　　　　Get you gone, you dwarf!
You minimus, of hindering knotgrass made!　　　329
You bead, you acorn!
DEMETRIUS　　　　　　　You are too officious
In her behalf that scorns your services.
Let her alone. Speak not of Helena;

310 stealth stealing away　**312 chid me hence** driven me away with his scolding　**314 so** if only　**317 fond** foolish　**323 keen** fierce, cruel. **shrewd** shrewish　**329 minimus** diminutive creature.　**knotgrass** a weed, an infusion of which was thought to stunt the growth

Take not her part. For, if thou dost intend   333
Never so little show of love to her,
Thou shalt aby it.

LYSANDER   Now she holds me not;   335
Now follow, if thou dar'st, to try whose right,
Of thine or mine, is most in Helena.   [*Exit.*]

DEMETRIUS
Follow? Nay, I'll go with thee, cheek by jowl.   338
               [*Exit, following Lysander.*]

HERMIA
You, mistress, all this coil is 'long of you.   339
Nay, go not back.

HELENA   I will not trust you, I,   340
Nor longer stay in your curst company.
Your hands than mine are quicker for a fray;
My legs are longer, though, to run away.   [*Exit.*]

HERMIA
I am amazed and know not what to say.   *Exit.*

  [*Oberon and Puck come forward.*]

OBERON
This is thy negligence. Still thou mistak'st,
Or else committ'st thy knaveries willfully.

PUCK
Believe me, king of shadows, I mistook.
Did not you tell me I should know the man
By the Athenian garments he had on?
And so far blameless proves my enterprise
That I have 'nointed an Athenian's eyes;
And so far am I glad it so did sort,   352
As this their jangling I esteem a sport.   353

OBERON
Thou seest these lovers seek a place to fight.
Hie therefore, Robin, overcast the night;   355
The starry welkin cover thou anon   356
With drooping fog as black as Acheron,   357
And lead these testy rivals so astray

333 intend give sign of   **335 aby** pay for   **338 cheek by jowl** i.e., side by
side   **339 coil** turmoil, dissension.   **'long of** on account of   **340 go not
back** i.e., don't retreat. (Hermia is again proposing a fight.)   **352 sort**
turn out   **353 As** that (also at l. 359)   **355 Hie** hasten   **356 welkin** sky
357 Acheron river of Hades (here representing Hades itself)

As one come not within another's way.
Like to Lysander sometimes frame thy tongue,
Then stir Demetrius up with bitter wrong;   361
And sometimes rail thou like Demetrius.
And from each other look thou lead them thus,
Till o'er their brows death-counterfeiting sleep
With leaden legs and batty wings doth creep.   365
Then crush this herb into Lysander's eye,   366
                              [*Giving herb*]
Whose liquor hath this virtuous property,   367
To take from thence all error with his might   368
And make his eyeballs roll with wonted sight.   369
When they next wake, all this derision   370
Shall seem a dream and fruitless vision,
And back to Athens shall the lovers wend
With league whose date till death shall never end.   373
Whiles I in this affair do thee employ,
I'll to my queen and beg her Indian boy;
And then I will her charmèd eye release
From monster's view, and all things shall be peace.

PUCK
My fairy lord, this must be done with haste,
For night's swift dragons cut the clouds full fast,   379
And yonder shines Aurora's harbinger,   380
At whose approach, ghosts, wand'ring here and there,
Troop home to churchyards. Damnèd spirits all,
That in crossways and floods have burial,   383
Already to their wormy beds are gone.
For fear lest day should look their shames upon,
They willfully themselves exile from light
And must for aye consort with black-browed night.   387

OBERON
But we are spirits of another sort.

361 wrong insults **365 batty** batlike **366 this herb** i.e., the antidote
(mentioned in 2.1.184) to love-in-idleness **367 virtuous** efficacious
368 his its **369 wonted** accustomed **370 derision** laughable business
373 date term of existence **379 dragons** (Supposed by Shakespeare to
be yoked to the car of the goddess of night.) **380 Aurora's harbinger**
the morning star, precursor of dawn **383 crossways . . . burial** (Those
who had committed suicide were buried at crossways, with a stake
driven through them; those drowned, i.e., buried in floods or great
waters, would be condemned to wander disconsolate for want of burial
rites.) **387 for aye** forever

I with the Morning's love have oft made sport,   389
And, like a forester, the groves may tread   390
Even till the eastern gate, all fiery red,
Opening on Neptune with fair blessèd beams,
Turns into yellow gold his salt green streams.
But notwithstanding, haste, make no delay.
We may effect this business yet ere day.   [*Exit.*]

PUCK
    Up and down, up and down,
    I will lead them up and down.
    I am feared in field and town.
    Goblin, lead them up and down.
Here comes one.

    Enter Lysander.

LYSANDER
Where art thou, proud Demetrius? Speak thou now.
PUCK [*Mimicking Demetrius*]
Here, villain, drawn and ready. Where art thou?   402
LYSANDER
I will be with thee straight.
PUCK   Follow me, then,   403
    To plainer ground.
    [*Lysander wanders about, following the voice.*]

    Enter Demetrius.

DEMETRIUS   Lysander! Speak again!   404
Thou runaway, thou coward, art thou fled?
Speak! In some bush? Where dost thou hide thy head?
PUCK [*Mimicking Lysander*]
Thou coward, art thou bragging to the stars,
Telling the bushes that thou look'st for wars,
And wilt not come? Come, recreant; come, thou child, 409
I'll whip thee with a rod. He is defiled
That draws a sword on thee.
DEMETRIUS   Yea, art thou there?

389 Morning's love Cephalus, a beautiful youth beloved by Aurora; or perhaps the goddess of the dawn herself   **390 forester** keeper of a royal forest   **402 drawn** with drawn sword   **403 straight** immediately   **404 plainer** more open   **s.d. Lysander wanders about** (It is not clearly necessary that Lysander exit at this point; neither exit nor reentrance is indicated in the early texts.)   **409 recreant** cowardly wretch

PUCK
  Follow my voice. We'll try no manhood here.   412
                                        Exeunt.

      [*Lysander returns.*]

LYSANDER
  He goes before me and still dares me on.
  When I come where he calls, then he is gone.
  The villain is much lighter-heeled than I.
  I followed fast, but faster he did fly,
  That fallen am I in dark uneven way,
  And here will rest me. [*He lies down.*] Come, thou gentle
      day!
  For if but once thou show me thy gray light,
  I'll find Demetrius and revenge this spite. [*He sleeps.*]

      [*Enter*] *Robin* [*Puck*] *and Demetrius.*

PUCK
  Ho, ho, ho! Coward, why com'st thou not?
DEMETRIUS
  Abide me, if thou dar'st; for well I wot   422
  Thou runn'st before me, shifting every place,
  And dar'st not stand nor look me in the face.
  Where art thou now?
PUCK   Come hither. I am here.
DEMETRIUS
  Nay, then, thou mock'st me. Thou shalt buy this dear,   426
  If ever I thy face by daylight see.
  Now, go thy way. Faintness constraineth me
  To measure out my length on this cold bed.
  By day's approach look to be visited.
                          [*He lies down and sleeps.*]

      Enter Helena.

HELENA
  O weary night, O long and tedious night,
    Abate thy hours! Shine comforts from the east,   432
  That I may back to Athens by daylight,
    From these that my poor company detest;

412 try test **422 Abide** confront, face. **wot** know **426 buy** aby, pay
for. **dear** dearly **432 Abate** lessen, shorten

And sleep, that sometimes shuts up sorrow's eye,
Steal me awhile from mine own company.

                    [*She lies down and*] *sleep*[*s*].

PUCK

    Yet but three? Come one more;
    Two of both kinds makes up four.
    Here she comes, curst and sad.   439
    Cupid is a knavish lad,
    Thus to make poor females mad.

    [*Enter Hermia.*]

HERMIA

Never so weary, never so in woe,
  Bedabbled with the dew and torn with briers,
I can no further crawl, no further go;
  My legs can keep no pace with my desires.
Here will I rest me till the break of day.
Heavens shield Lysander, if they mean a fray!

                    [*She lies down and sleeps.*]

PUCK

    On the ground
    Sleep sound.
    I'll apply
    To your eye,
  Gentle lover, remedy.

      [*Squeezing the juice on Lysander's eyes.*]

    When thou wak'st,
    Thou tak'st
    True delight
    In the sight
  Of thy former lady's eye;
  And the country proverb known,
  That every man should take his own,
  In your waking shall be shown:
    Jack shall have Jill;   461
    Naught shall go ill;
  The man shall have his mare again, and all shall be
    well.   [*Exit. The four sleeping lovers remain.*]

439 curst ill-tempered   **461 Jack shall have Jill** (Proverbial for "boy gets girl.")

4.1 *Enter [Titania,] Queen of Fairies, and [Bottom the] clown, and Fairies; and [Oberon,] the King, behind them.*

TITANIA
Come, sit thee down upon this flowery bed,
  While I thy amiable cheeks do coy,   2
And stick muskroses in thy sleek smooth head,
  And kiss thy fair large ears, my gentle joy.
                                                    [They recline.]

BOTTOM Where's Peaseblossom?

PEASEBLOSSOM Ready.

BOTTOM Scratch my head, Peaseblossom. Where's Monsieur Cobweb?

COBWEB Ready.

BOTTOM Monsieur Cobweb, good monsieur, get you your weapons in your hand, and kill me a red-hipped humble-bee on the top of a thistle; and, good monsieur, bring me the honey bag. Do not fret yourself too much in the action, monsieur; and, good monsieur, have a care the honey bag break not; I would be loath to have you overflown with a honey bag, signor. *[Exit Cobweb.]* Where's Monsieur Mustardseed?

MUSTARDSEED Ready.

BOTTOM Give me your neaf, Monsieur Mustardseed.   19
Pray you, leave your courtesy, good monsieur.   20

MUSTARDSEED What's your will?

BOTTOM Nothing, good monsieur, but to help Caval-   22
ery Cobweb to scratch. I must to the barber's, mon-   23
sieur, for methinks I am marvelous hairy about the face; and I am such a tender ass, if my hair do but tickle me, I must scratch.

TITANIA
What, wilt thou hear some music, my sweet love?

4.1. Location: The action is continuous. The four lovers are still asleep onstage.
2 amiable lovely.   **coy** caress   **19 neaf** fist   **20 leave your courtesy** i.e., stop bowing, or put on your hat   **22–23 Cavalery** cavalier. (Form of address for a gentleman.)   **23 Cobweb** (Seemingly an error, since Cobweb has been sent to bring honey while Peaseblossom has been asked to scratch.)

BOTTOM I have a reasonable good ear in music. Let's
have the tongs and the bones.   29

                    [Music: tongs, rural music.]

TITANIA
Or say, sweet love, what thou desirest to eat.

BOTTOM Truly, a peck of provender. I could munch 31
your good dry oats. Methinks I have a great desire to
a bottle of hay. Good hay, sweet hay, hath no fellow. 33

TITANIA
I have a venturous fairy that shall seek
The squirrel's hoard, and fetch thee new nuts.

BOTTOM I had rather have a handful or two of dried
peas. But, I pray you, let none of your people stir me. 37
I have an exposition of sleep come upon me.   38

TITANIA
Sleep thou, and I will wind thee in my arms.
Fairies, begone, and be all ways away.   40

                       [Exeunt Fairies.]

So doth the woodbine the sweet honeysuckle
Gently entwist; the female ivy so
Enrings the barky fingers of the elm.
O, how I love thee! How I dote on thee!

                           [They sleep.]

    Enter Robin Goodfellow [Puck].

OBERON *[Coming forward]*
Welcome, good Robin. Seest thou this sweet sight?
Her dotage now I do begin to pity.
For, meeting her of late behind the wood,
Seeking sweet favors for this hateful fool,   48
I did upbraid her and fall out with her.
For she his hairy temples then had rounded
With coronet of fresh and fragrant flowers;
And that same dew, which sometime on the buds   52

---

29 tongs . . . bones instruments for rustic music. (The tongs were played
like a triangle, whereas the bones were held between the fingers and
used as clappers.) **s.d. Music . . . music** (This stage direction is
added from the Folio.) **31 peck of provender** one-quarter bushel of
grain **33 bottle** bundle. **fellow** equal **37 stir** disturb **38 exposition**
(Bottom's word for *disposition*.) **40 all ways** in all directions **48 favors**
i.e., gifts of flowers **52 sometime** formerly

Was wont to swell like round and orient pearls,   53
Stood now within the pretty flowerets' eyes
Like tears that did their own disgrace bewail.
When I had at my pleasure taunted her,
And she in mild terms begged my patience,
I then did ask of her her changeling child,
Which straight she gave me, and her fairy sent
To bear him to my bower in Fairyland.
And, now I have the boy, I will undo
This hateful imperfection of her eyes.
And, gentle Puck, take this transformèd scalp
From off the head of this Athenian swain,
That he, awaking when the other do,   65
May all to Athens back again repair,   66
And think no more of this night's accidents
But as the fierce vexation of a dream.
But first I will release the Fairy Queen.

> > > > > *[He squeezes a herb on her eyes.]*

     Be as thou wast wont to be;
     See as thou wast wont to see.
     Dian's bud o'er Cupid's flower   72
     Hath such force and blessèd power.
Now, my Titania, wake you, my sweet queen.

TITANIA [*Waking*]
     My Oberon! What visions have I seen!
     Methought I was enamored of an ass.

OBERON
     There lies your love.

TITANIA   How came these things to pass?
     O, how mine eyes do loathe his visage now!

OBERON
     Silence awhile. Robin, take off this head.
     Titania, music call, and strike more dead
     Than common sleep of all these five the sense.   81

---

53 orient pearls i.e., the most beautiful of all pearls, those coming
from the Orient   **65 other** others   **66 repair** return   **72 Dian's bud**
(Perhaps the flower of the *agnus castus* or chaste-tree, supposed to
preserve chastity; or perhaps referring simply to Oberon's herb by
which he can undo the effects of "Cupid's flower," the love-in-
idleness of 2.1.166–168.)   **81 these five** i.e., the four lovers and
Bottom

TITANIA
  Music, ho! Music, such as charmeth sleep!   82
                                    [Music.]

PUCK [*Removing the ass head*]
  Now, when thou wak'st, with thine own fool's eyes peep.

OBERON
  Sound, music! Come, my queen, take hands with me,
  And rock the ground whereon these sleepers be.
                                 [They dance.]

  Now thou and I are new in amity,
  And will tomorrow midnight solemnly   87
  Dance in Duke Theseus' house triumphantly,
  And bless it to all fair prosperity.
  There shall the pairs of faithful lovers be
  Wedded, with Theseus, all in jollity.

PUCK
      Fairy King, attend, and mark:
      I do hear the morning lark.

OBERON
      Then, my queen, in silence sad,   94
      Trip we after night's shade.
      We the globe can compass soon,
      Swifter than the wandering moon.

TITANIA
      Come, my lord, and in our flight
      Tell me how it came this night
      That I sleeping here was found
      With these mortals on the ground.   *Exeunt.*
                           Wind horn [within].

  Enter Theseus and all his train; [Hippolyta,
  Egeus].

THESEUS
  Go, one of you, find out the forester,
  For now our observation is performed;   103
  And since we have the vaward of the day,   104
  My love shall hear the music of my hounds.

---

82 charmeth brings about, as though by a charm **87 solemnly** ceremoniously **94 sad** sober **103 observation** i.e., observance to a morn of May (1.1.167) **104 vaward** vanguard, i.e., earliest part

Uncouple in the western valley, let them go.   106
Dispatch, I say, and find the forester.
                    [*Exit an Attendant.*]
We will, fair queen, up to the mountain's top
And mark the musical confusion
Of hounds and echo in conjunction.

HIPPOLYTA
I was with Hercules and Cadmus once,   111
When in a wood of Crete they bayed the bear   112
With hounds of Sparta. Never did I hear   113
Such gallant chiding; for, besides the groves,   114
The skies, the fountains, every region near
Seemed all one mutual cry. I never heard
So musical a discord, such sweet thunder.

THESEUS
My hounds are bred out of the Spartan kind,   118
So flewed, so sanded; and their heads are hung   119
With ears that sweep away the morning dew;
Crook-kneed, and dewlapped like Thessalian bulls;   121
Slow in pursuit, but matched in mouth like bells,   122
Each under each. A cry more tunable   123
Was never holloed to, nor cheered with horn,   124
In Crete, in Sparta, nor in Thessaly.
Judge when you hear. [*He sees the sleepers.*] But, soft!
    What nymphs are these?

EGEUS
My lord, this is my daughter here asleep,
And this Lysander; this Demetrius is,
This Helena, old Nedar's Helena.
I wonder of their being here together.   130

THESEUS
No doubt they rose up early to observe

106 Uncouple set free for the hunt   **111 Cadmus** mythical founder of
Thebes. (This story about him is unknown.)   **112 bayed** brought to
bay   **113 hounds of Sparta** (A breed famous in antiquity for their
hunting skill.)   **114 chiding** i.e., yelping   **118 kind** strain, breed   **119 So
flewed** similarly having large hanging chaps or fleshy covering of the
jaw.   **sanded** of sandy color   **121 dewlapped** having pendulous folds of
skin under the neck   **122–123 matched . . . each** i.e., harmoniously
matched in their various cries like a set of bells, from treble down to
bass   **123 cry** pack of hounds.   **tunable** well tuned, melodious
124 cheered encouraged   **130 wonder of** wonder at

The rite of May, and hearing our intent,
Came here in grace of our solemnity.   133
But speak, Egeus. Is not this the day
That Hermia should give answer of her choice?

EGEUS   It is, my lord.

THESEUS
Go, bid the huntsmen wake them with their horns.

                              [*Exit an Attendant.*]

Shout within. Wind horns. They all start up.

Good morrow, friends. Saint Valentine is past.   138
Begin these woodbirds but to couple now?

LYSANDER
Pardon, my lord.   [*They kneel.*]

THESEUS   I pray you all, stand up.
I know you two are rival enemies;
How comes this gentle concord in the world,
That hatred is so far from jealousy   143
To sleep by hate and fear no enmity?

LYSANDER
My lord, I shall reply amazedly,
Half sleep, half waking; but as yet, I swear,
I cannot truly say how I came here.
But, as I think—for truly would I speak,
And now I do bethink me, so it is—
I came with Hermia hither. Our intent
Was to be gone from Athens, where we might,   151
Without the peril of the Athenian law—   152

EGEUS
Enough, enough, my lord; you have enough.
I beg the law, the law, upon his head.
They would have stol'n away; they would, Demetrius,
Thereby to have defeated you and me,   156
You of your wife and me of my consent,
Of my consent that she should be your wife.

DEMETRIUS
My lord, fair Helen told me of their stealth,

---

133 in . . . solemnity in honor of our wedding   **138 Saint Valentine**
(Birds were supposed to choose their mates on Saint Valentine's Day.)
143 jealousy suspicion   **151 where** wherever; or, to where   **152 Without**
outside of, beyond   **156 defeated** defrauded

Of this their purpose hither to this wood,   160
And I in fury hither followed them,
Fair Helena in fancy following me.
But, my good lord, I wot not by what power—
But by some power it is—my love to Hermia,
Melted as the snow, seems to me now
As the remembrance of an idle gaud   166
Which in my childhood I did dote upon;
And all the faith, the virtue of my heart,
The object and the pleasure of mine eye,
Is only Helena. To her, my lord,
Was I betrothed ere I saw Hermia,
But like a sickness did I loathe this food;
But, as in health, come to my natural taste,
Now I do wish it, love it, long for it,
And will for evermore be true to it.

THESEUS
Fair lovers, you are fortunately met.
Of this discourse we more will hear anon.
Egeus, I will overbear your will;
For in the temple, by and by, with us
These couples shall eternally be knit.
And, for the morning now is something worn,   181
Our purposed hunting shall be set aside.
Away with us to Athens. Three and three,
We'll hold a feast in great solemnity.
Come, Hippolyta.

      [Exeunt Theseus, Hippolyta, Egeus, and train.]

DEMETRIUS
These things seem small and undistinguishable,
Like far-off mountains turnèd into clouds.

HERMIA
Methinks I see these things with parted eye,   188
When everything seems double.

HELENA   So methinks;
And I have found Demetrius like a jewel,   190
Mine own, and not mine own.

DEMETRIUS   Are you sure   191

160 hither in coming hither   **166 idle gaud** worthless trinket   **181 for**
since.   **something** somewhat   **188 parted** improperly focused
190-191 like . . . mine own i.e., like a jewel that one finds by chance and
therefore possesses but cannot certainly consider one's own property

That we are awake? It seems to me
That yet we sleep, we dream. Do not you think
The Duke was here, and bid us follow him?

HERMIA
Yea, and my father.

HELENA   And Hippolyta.

LYSANDER
And he did bid us follow to the temple.

DEMETRIUS
Why, then, we are awake. Let's follow him,
And by the way let us recount our dreams.   [*Exeunt.*]

BOTTOM [*Awaking*] When my cue comes, call me, and
I will answer. My next is, "Most fair Pyramus." Heigh-
ho! Peter Quince! Flute, the bellows mender! Snout,
the tinker! Starveling! God's my life, stolen hence and   202
left me asleep! I have had a most rare vision. I have
had a dream, past the wit of man to say what dream it
was. Man is but an ass if he go about to expound this   205
dream. Methought I was—there is no man can tell
what. Methought I was—and methought I had—but
man is but a patched fool if he will offer to say what   208
methought I had. The eye of man hath not heard, the   209
ear of man hath not seen, man's hand is not able to
taste, his tongue to conceive, nor his heart to report,   211
what my dream was. I will get Peter Quince to write
a ballad of this dream. It shall be called "Bottom's
Dream," because it hath no bottom; and I will sing it
in the latter end of a play, before the Duke. Peradven-
ture, to make it the more gracious, I shall sing it at her   216
death.   [*Exit.*]

❖

4.2   *Enter Quince, Flute,* [*Snout, and Starveling*].

QUINCE   Have you sent to Bottom's house? Is he come
home yet?

202 **God's** may God save   205 **go about** attempt   208 **patched** wearing
motley, i.e., a dress of various colors.   **offer** venture   209–211 **The eye
. . . report** (Bottom garbles the terms of 1 Corinthians 2:9.)   216 **her**
Thisbe's (?)

4.2. Location: Athens.

STARVELING He cannot be heard of. Out of doubt he is
   transported.   4
FLUTE If he come not, then the play is marred. It goes
   not forward, doth it?
QUINCE It is not possible. You have not a man in all
   Athens able to discharge Pyramus but he.   8
FLUTE No, he hath simply the best wit of any handicraft   9
   man in Athens.
QUINCE Yea, and the best person too, and he is a very   11
   paramour for a sweet voice.
FLUTE You must say "paragon." A paramour is, God
   bless us, a thing of naught.   14

   Enter Snug the joiner.

SNUG Masters, the Duke is coming from the temple,
   and there is two or three lords and ladies more married. If our sport had gone forward, we had all been   17
   made men.   18
FLUTE O sweet bully Bottom! Thus hath he lost six-   19
   pence a day during his life; he could not have scaped 20
   sixpence a day. An the Duke had not given him sixpence a day for playing Pyramus, I'll be hanged. He
   would have deserved it. Sixpence a day in Pyramus, or
   nothing.

   Enter Bottom.

BOTTOM Where are these lads? Where are these hearts?   25
QUINCE Bottom! O most courageous day! O most
   happy hour!
BOTTOM Masters, I am to discourse wonders. But ask   28
   me not what; for if I tell you, I am no true Athenian. I
   will tell you everything, right as it fell out.
QUINCE Let us hear, sweet Bottom.
BOTTOM Not a word of me. All that I will tell you is—   32
   that the Duke hath dined. Get your apparel together,

4 transported carried off by fairies; or, possibly, transformed
8 discharge perform   **9 wit** intellect   **11 person** appearance   **14 a . . .
naught** a shameful thing   **17–18 we . . . men** i.e., we would have had our
fortunes made   **19–20 sixpence a day** i.e., as a royal pension   **25 hearts**
good fellows   **28 am . . . wonders** have wonders to relate   **32 of** out of

good strings to your beards, new ribbons to your 34
pumps; meet presently at the palace; every man look 35
o'er his part; for the short and the long is, our play is
preferred. In any case, let Thisbe have clean linen; and 37
let not him that plays the lion pare his nails, for they
shall hang out for the lion's claws. And, most dear actors, eat no onions nor garlic, for we are to utter sweet
breath; and I do not doubt but to hear them say it is
a sweet comedy. No more words. Away! Go, away!

[*Exeunt.*]

♣

34 strings (to attach the beards)   **35 pumps** light shoes or slippers.
presently immediately   **37 preferred** selected for consideration

5.1   *Enter Theseus, Hippolyta, and Philostrate,*
          [lords, and attendants].

HIPPOLYTA
  'Tis strange, my Theseus, that these lovers speak of.   1
THESEUS
  More strange than true. I never may believe   2
  These antique fables nor these fairy toys.   3
  Lovers and madmen have such seething brains,
  Such shaping fantasies, that apprehend   5
  More than cool reason ever comprehends.   6
  The lunatic, the lover, and the poet
  Are of imagination all compact.   8
  One sees more devils than vast hell can hold;
  That is the madman. The lover, all as frantic,
  Sees Helen's beauty in a brow of Egypt.   11
  The poet's eye, in a fine frenzy rolling,
  Doth glance from heaven to earth, from earth to heaven;
  And as imagination bodies forth
  The forms of things unknown, the poet's pen
  Turns them to shapes and gives to airy nothing
  A local habitation and a name.
  Such tricks hath strong imagination
  That, if it would but apprehend some joy,
  It comprehends some bringer of that joy;   20
  Or in the night, imagining some fear,   21
  How easy is a bush supposed a bear!
HIPPOLYTA
  But all the story of the night told over,
  And all their minds transfigured so together,
  More witnesseth than fancy's images   25
  And grows to something of great constancy;   26
  But, howsoever, strange and admirable.   27

5.1. Location: Athens. The palace of Theseus.
1 that that which   **2 may** can   **3 antique** old-fashioned (punning too on
antic, strange, grotesque).   **fairy toys** trifling stories about fairies
5 fantasies imaginations.   **apprehend** conceive, imagine   **6 comprehends** understands   **8 compact** formed, composed   **11 Helen's** i.e., of
Helen of Troy, pattern of beauty.   **brow of Egypt** i.e., face of a gypsy
20 bringer i.e., source   **21 fear** object of fear   **25 More . . . images** testi-
fies to something more substantial than mere imaginings   **26 constancy**
certainty   **27 howsoever** in any case.   **admirable** a source of wonder

*Enter lovers: Lysander, Demetrius, Hermia, and
Helena.*

THESEUS
   Here come the lovers, full of joy and mirth.
   Joy, gentle friends! Joy and fresh days of love
   Accompany your hearts!

LYSANDER   More than to us
   Wait in your royal walks, your board, your bed!

THESEUS
   Come now, what masques, what dances shall we have   32
   To wear away this long age of three hours
   Between our after-supper and bedtime?
   Where is our usual manager of mirth?
   What revels are in hand? Is there no play
   To ease the anguish of a torturing hour?
   Call Philostrate.

PHILOSTRATE   Here, mighty Theseus.

THESEUS
   Say what abridgment have you for this evening?   39
   What masque? What music? How shall we beguile
   The lazy time, if not with some delight?

PHILOSTRATE [*Giving him a paper*]
   There is a brief how many sports are ripe.   42
   Make choice of which Your Highness will see first.

THESEUS [*Reads*]
   "The battle with the Centaurs, to be sung   44
   By an Athenian eunuch to the harp"?
   We'll none of that. That have I told my love,
   In glory of my kinsman Hercules.   47
   [*Reads.*] "The riot of the tipsy Bacchanals,   48
   Tearing the Thracian singer in their rage"?   49
   That is an old device; and it was played   50

---

32 masques courtly entertainments   **39 abridgment** pastime (to abridge
or shorten the evening)   **42 brief** short written statement, summary
44 battle . . . Centaurs (Probably refers to the battle of the Centaurs and
the Lapithae, when the Centaurs attempted to carry off Hippodamia,
bride of Theseus' friend Pirothous.)   **47 kinsman** (Plutarch's "Life of
Theseus" states that Hercules and Theseus were near kinsmen. Theseus
is referring to a version of the battle of the Centaurs in which Hercules
was said to be present.)   **48–49 The riot . . . rage** (This was the story of
the death of Orpheus, as told in *Metamorphoses* 9.)   **50 device** show,
performance

When I from Thebes came last a conqueror.
[*Reads.*] "The thrice three Muses mourning for the
   death   52
Of Learning, late deceased in beggary"?   53
That is some satire, keen and critical,
Not sorting with a nuptial ceremony.   55
[*Reads.*] "A tedious brief scene of young Pyramus
And his love Thisbe; very tragical mirth"?
Merry and tragical? Tedious and brief?
That is hot ice and wondrous strange snow.   59
How shall we find the concord of this discord?

PHILOSTRATE
A play there is, my lord, some ten words long,
Which is as brief as I have known a play;
But by ten words, my lord, it is too long,
Which makes it tedious. For in all the play
There is not one word apt, one player fitted.
And tragical, my noble lord, it is,
For Pyramus therein doth kill himself.
Which, when I saw rehearsed, I must confess,
Made mine eyes water; but more merry tears
The passion of loud laughter never shed.

THESEUS   What are they that do play it?

PHILOSTRATE
Hard-handed men that work in Athens here,
Which never labored in their minds till now,
And now have toiled their unbreathed memories   74
With this same play, against your nuptial.   75

THESEUS   And we will hear it.

PHILOSTRATE   No, my noble lord,
It is not for you. I have heard it over,
And it is nothing, nothing in the world;
Unless you can find sport in their intents,
Extremely stretched and conned with cruel pain   80
To do you service.

THESEUS   I will hear that play;

52–53 The thrice . . . beggary (Possibly an allusion to Spenser's *Teares of the Muses,* 1591, though "satires" deploring the neglect of learning and the creative arts were commonplace.) **55 sorting with** befitting **59 strange** (Sometimes emended to an adjective that would contrast with *snow,* just as *hot* contrasts with *ice.*) **74 toiled** taxed. **unbreathed** unexercised **75 against** in preparation for **80 stretched** strained. **conned** memorized

For never anything can be amiss
When simpleness and duty tender it.   83
Go bring them in; and take your places, ladies.
          [*Philostrate goes to summon the players.*]

HIPPOLYTA
I love not to see wretchedness o'ercharged,   85
And duty in his service perishing.   86

THESEUS
Why, gentle sweet, you shall see no such thing.

HIPPOLYTA
He says they can do nothing in this kind.   88

THESEUS
The kinder we, to give them thanks for nothing.
Our sport shall be to take what they mistake;
And what poor duty cannot do, noble respect   91
Takes it in might, not merit.   92
Where I have come, great clerks have purposèd   93
To greet me with premeditated welcomes;
Where I have seen them shiver and look pale,
Make periods in the midst of sentences,
Throttle their practiced accent in their fears,   97
And in conclusion dumbly have broke off,
Not paying me a welcome. Trust me, sweet,
Out of this silence yet I picked a welcome;
And in the modesty of fearful duty
I read as much as from the rattling tongue
Of saucy and audacious eloquence.
Love, therefore, and tongue-tied simplicity
In least speak most, to my capacity.   105

          [*Philostrate returns.*]

PHILOSTRATE
So please Your Grace, the Prologue is addressed.   106
THESEUS Let him approach.   [*A flourish of trumpets.*]

---

83 simpleness simplicity   **85 wretchedness o'ercharged** incompetence
overburdened   **86 his service** its attempt to serve   **88 kind** kind of thing
91 respect evaluation, consideration   **92 Takes . . . merit** values it
for the effort made rather than for the excellence achieved   **93 clerks**
learned men   **97 practiced accent** i.e., rehearsed speech; or, usual way of
speaking   **105 least** i.e., saying least.   **to my capacity** in my judgment
and understanding   **106 Prologue** speaker of the prologue.   **addressed**
ready

Enter the Prologue [Quince].

PROLOGUE
If we offend, it is with our good will.
   That you should think, we come not to offend,
But with good will. To show our simple skill,
   That is the true beginning of our end.
Consider then, we come but in despite.
   We do not come, as minding to content you,   113
Our true intent is. All for your delight
   We are not here. That you should here repent you,
The actors are at hand; and, by their show,
You shall know all that you are like to know.

THESEUS   This fellow doth not stand upon points.   118
LYSANDER   He hath rid his prologue like a rough colt;   119
he knows not the stop. A good moral, my lord: it is not   120
enough to speak, but to speak true.

HIPPOLYTA   Indeed he hath played on his prologue like
a child on a recorder; a sound, but not in government.   123

THESEUS   His speech was like a tangled chain: nothing   124
impaired, but all disordered. Who is next?

Enter Pyramus [Bottom] and Thisbe [Flute], and
Wall [Snout], and Moonshine [Starveling], and
Lion [Snug].

PROLOGUE
Gentles, perchance you wonder at this show;
   But wonder on, till truth make all things plain.
This man is Pyramus, if you would know;
   This beauteous lady Thisbe is certain.
This man with lime and roughcast doth present
   Wall, that vile Wall which did these lovers sunder;
And through Wall's chink, poor souls, they are content
   To whisper. At the which let no man wonder.
This man, with lantern, dog, and bush of thorn,
   Presenteth Moonshine; for, if you will know,

113 minding intending   **118 stand upon points** (1) heed niceties or small
points (2) pay attention to punctuation in his reading. (The humor of
Quince's speech is in the blunders of its punctuation.)   **119 rid** ridden.
rough unbroken   **120 stop** (1) the stopping of a colt by reining it in
(2) punctuation mark   **123 recorder** a wind instrument like a flute or fla-
geolet.   **government** control   **124 nothing** not at all

By moonshine did these lovers think no scorn   136
    To meet at Ninus' tomb, there, there to woo.
This grisly beast, which Lion hight by name,   138
The trusty Thisbe coming first by night
Did scare away, or rather did affright;
And as she fled, her mantle she did fall,   141
    Which Lion vile with bloody mouth did stain.
Anon comes Pyramus, sweet youth and tall,   143
    And finds his trusty Thisbe's mantle slain;
Whereat, with blade, with bloody blameful blade,
    He bravely broached his boiling bloody breast.   146
And Thisbe, tarrying in mulberry shade,
    His dagger drew, and died. For all the rest,
Let Lion, Moonshine, Wall, and lovers twain
At large discourse while here they do remain.   150

        Exeunt Lion, Thisbe, and Moonshine.

THESEUS   I wonder if the lion be to speak.
DEMETRIUS   No wonder, my lord. One lion may, when
many asses do.

WALL
In this same interlude it doth befall   154
That I, one Snout by name, present a wall;
And such a wall as I would have you think
That had in it a crannied hole or chink,
Through which the lovers, Pyramus and Thisbe,
Did whisper often, very secretly.
This loam, this roughcast, and this stone doth show
That I am that same wall; the truth is so.
And this the cranny is, right and sinister,   162
Through which the fearful lovers are to whisper.

THESEUS   Would you desire lime and hair to speak
better?
DEMETRIUS   It is the wittiest partition that ever I heard   166
discourse, my lord.

    [*Pyramus comes forward.*]

---

136 think no scorn think it no disgraceful matter   **138 hight** is called
141 fall let fall   **143 tall** courageous   **146 broached** stabbed   **150 At large**
in full, at length   **154 interlude** play   **162 right and sinister** i.e., the right
side of it and the left; or, running from right to left, horizontally   **166 partition** (1) wall (2) section of a learned treatise or oration

THESEUS   Pyramus draws near the wall. Silence!

PYRAMUS
  O grim-looked night! O night with hue so black!   169
    O night, which ever art when day is not!
  O night, O night! Alack, alack, alack,
    I fear my Thisbe's promise is forgot.
  And thou, O wall, O sweet, O lovely wall,
    That stand'st between her father's ground and mine,
  Thou wall, O wall, O sweet and lovely wall,
    Show me thy chink, to blink through with mine eyne!
             [*Wall makes a chink with his fingers.*]
  Thanks, courteous wall. Jove shield thee well for this.
  But what see I? No Thisbe do I see.
  O wicked wall, through whom I see no bliss!
  Cursed be thy stones for thus deceiving me!

THESEUS   The wall, methinks, being sensible, should   181
curse again.

PYRAMUS   No, in truth, sir, he should not. "Deceiving
me" is Thisbe's cue: she is to enter now, and I am to
spy her through the wall. You shall see, it will fall pat   185
as I told you. Yonder she comes.

    Enter Thisbe.

THISBE
  O wall, full often hast thou heard my moans,
    For parting my fair Pyramus and me.
  My cherry lips have often kissed thy stones,
    Thy stones with lime and hair knit up in thee.

PYRAMUS
  I see a voice. Now will I to the chink,
    To spy an I can hear my Thisbe's face.   192
  Thisbe!

THISBE   My love! Thou art my love, I think.

PYRAMUS
  Think what thou wilt, I am thy lover's grace,   194
  And like Limander am I trusty still.   195

THISBE
  And I like Helen, till the Fates me kill.   196

---

169 grim-looked grim-looking   **181 sensible** capable of feeling   **185 pat**
exactly   **192 an** if   **194 lover's grace** i.e., gracious lover   **195, 196 Limander, Helen** (Blunders for *Leander* and *Hero*.)

PYRAMUS
Not Shafalus to Procrus was so true.   197
THISBE
As Shafalus to Procrus, I to you.
PYRAMUS
O, kiss me through the hole of this vile wall!
THISBE
I kiss the wall's hole, not your lips at all.
PYRAMUS
Wilt thou at Ninny's tomb meet me straightway?
THISBE
'Tide life, 'tide death, I come without delay.   202

> *[Exeunt Pyramus and Thisbe.]*

WALL
Thus have I, Wall, my part dischargèd so;
And, being done, thus Wall away doth go.   *[Exit.]*
THESEUS Now is the mural down between the two
neighbors.
DEMETRIUS No remedy, my lord, when walls are so
willful to hear without warning.   208
HIPPOLYTA This is the silliest stuff that ever I heard.
THESEUS The best in this kind are but shadows; and the 210
worst are no worse, if imagination amend them.
HIPPOLYTA It must be your imagination then, and not
theirs.
THESEUS If we imagine no worse of them than they of
themselves, they may pass for excellent men. Here
come two noble beasts in, a man and a lion.

> *Enter Lion and Moonshine.*

LION
You, ladies, you whose gentle hearts do fear
    The smallest monstrous mouse that creeps on floor,
May now perchance both quake and tremble here,
    When lion rough in wildest rage doth roar.
Then know that I, as Snug the joiner, am

---

197 Shafalus, Procrus (Blunders for *Cephalus* and *Procris*, also famous
lovers.)   **202 'Tide** betide, come   **208 willful** willing.   **without warning**
i.e., without warning the parents. (Demetrius makes a joke on the proverb
"Walls have ears.")   **210 in this kind** of this sort.   **shadows** likenesses,
representations

A lion fell, nor else no lion's dam;   222
For, if I should as lion come in strife
Into this place, 'twere pity on my life.

THESEUS   A very gentle beast, and of a good conscience.

DEMETRIUS   The very best at a beast, my lord, that e'er
I saw.

LYSANDER   This lion is a very fox for his valor.   228

THESEUS   True; and a goose for his discretion.   229

DEMETRIUS   Not so, my lord; for his valor cannot carry
his discretion; and the fox carries the goose.

THESEUS   His discretion, I am sure, cannot carry his
valor; for the goose carries not the fox. It is well. Leave
it to his discretion, and let us listen to the moon.

MOON
This lanthorn doth the hornèd moon present—   235

DEMETRIUS   He should have worn the horns on his   236
head.   237

THESEUS   He is no crescent, and his horns are invisible
within the circumference.

MOON
This lanthorn doth the hornèd moon present;
Myself the man i' the moon do seem to be.

THESEUS   This is the greatest error of all the rest. The
man should be put into the lanthorn. How is it else
the man i' the moon?

DEMETRIUS   He dares not come there for the candle, for   245
you see, it is already in snuff.   246

HIPPOLYTA   I am aweary of this moon. Would he would
change!

THESEUS   It appears, by his small light of discretion, that
he is in the wane; but yet, in courtesy, in all reason,
we must stay the time.

---

222 lion fell fierce lion (with a play on the idea of "lion skin")   **228 is . . .
valor** i.e., his valor consists of craftiness and discretion   **229 goose . . .
discretion** i.e., as discreet as a goose, that is, more foolish than discreet
235 lanthorn (This original spelling, *lanthorn*, may suggest a play on the
horn of which lanterns were made, and also on a cuckold's horns; but the
spelling *lanthorn* is not used consistently for comic effect in this play or
elsewhere. At 5.1.134, for example, the word is *lantern* in the original.)
236–237 on his head (as a sign of cuckoldry)   **245 for the** because of the
246 in snuff (1) offended (2) in need of snuffing or trimming

LYSANDER   Proceed, Moon.

MOON   All that I have to say is to tell you that the lanthorn is the moon, I, the man i' the moon, this thornbush my thornbush, and this dog my dog.

DEMETRIUS   Why, all these should be in the lanthorn,
for all these are in the moon. But silence! Here comes
Thisbe.

  Enter Thisbe.

THISBE
  This is old Ninny's tomb. Where is my love?

LION [*Roaring*]   O!

DEMETRIUS   Well roared, Lion.

          [*Thisbe runs off, dropping her mantle.*]

THESEUS   Well run, Thisbe.

HIPPOLYTA   Well shone, Moon. Truly, the moon shines
with a good grace.

          [*The Lion worries Thisbe's mantle.*]

THESEUS   Well moused, Lion.   265

  Enter Pyramus.   [*Exit Lion.*]

DEMETRIUS   And then came Pyramus.

LYSANDER   And so the lion vanished.

PYRAMUS
  Sweet Moon, I thank thee for thy sunny beams;
    I thank thee, Moon, for shining now so bright;.
  For, by thy gracious, golden, glittering gleams,
    I trust to take of truest Thisbe sight.
        But stay, O spite!
        But mark, poor knight,
    What dreadful dole is here?   274
        Eyes, do you see?
        How can it be?
    O dainty duck! O dear!
        Thy mantle good,
        What, stained with blood!
    Approach, ye Furies fell!   280
        O Fates, come, come,   281

265 moused shaken, torn, bitten   **274 dole** grievous event   **280 Furies**
avenging goddesses of Greek myth.   **fell** fierce   **281 Fates** the three
goddesses (Clotho, Lachesis, Atropos) of Greek myth who drew and cut
the thread of human life

    Cut thread and thrum; 282

      Quail, crush, conclude, and quell! 283

THESEUS This passion, and the death of a dear friend, 284
would go near to make a man look sad. 285

HIPPOLYTA Beshrew my heart, but I pity the man.

PYRAMUS

O, wherefore, Nature, didst thou lions frame?

Since lion vile hath here deflowered my dear,

Which is—no, no, which was—the fairest dame

That lived, that loved, that liked, that looked with cheer. 290

      Come, tears, confound,

      Out, sword, and wound

    The pap of Pyramus; 293

      Ay, that left pap,

      Where heart doth hop.   *[He stabs himself.]*

    Thus die I, thus, thus, thus.

      Now am I dead,

      Now am I fled;

    My soul is in the sky.

      Tongue, lose thy light;

      Moon, take thy flight.   *[Exit Moonshine.]*

    Now die, die, die, die, die.   *[Pyramus dies.]*

DEMETRIUS No die, but an ace, for him; for he is 303
but one. 304

LYSANDER Less than an ace, man; for he is dead, he is
nothing.

THESEUS With the help of a surgeon he might yet recover, and yet prove an ass. 308

HIPPOLYTA How chance Moonshine is gone before
Thisbe comes back and finds her lover?

THESEUS She will find him by starlight.

    [Enter Thisbe.]

Here she comes, and her passion ends the play.

---

282 thread and thrum the warp in weaving and the loose end of the
warp **283 Quail** overpower. **quell** kill, destroy **284-285 This . . . sad**
i.e., if one had other reason to grieve, one might be sad, but not from this
absurd portrayal of passion **290 cheer** countenance **293 pap** breast
303 ace the side of the die featuring the single pip, or spot. (The pun is on
die as a singular of *dice*; Bottom's performance is not worth a whole *die*
but rather one single face of it, one small portion.) **304 one** (1) an individual person (2) unique **308 ass** (with a pun on *ace*)

HIPPOLYTA   Methinks she should not use a long one for
such a Pyramus. I hope she will be brief.

DEMETRIUS   A mote will turn the balance, which Pyra-   315
mus, which Thisbe, is the better: he for a man, God   316
warrant us; she for a woman, God bless us.

LYSANDER   She hath spied him already with those sweet
eyes.

DEMETRIUS   And thus she means, videlicet: 320

THISBE

    Asleep, my love?
    What, dead, my dove?
O Pyramus, arise!
    Speak, speak. Quite dumb?
    Dead, dead? A tomb
Must cover thy sweet eyes.
    These lily lips,
    This cherry nose,
These yellow cowslip cheeks,
    Are gone, are gone!
    Lovers, make moan.
His eyes were green as leeks.
    O Sisters Three,   333
    Come, come to me,
With hands as pale as milk;
    Lay them in gore,
    Since you have shore   337
With shears his thread of silk.
    Tongue, not a word.
    Come, trusty sword,
Come, blade, my breast imbrue! [*Stabs herself.*]   341
    And farewell, friends.
    Thus Thisbe ends.
    Adieu, adieu, adieu.   [*She dies.*]

THESEUS   Moonshine and Lion are left to bury the dead.

DEMETRIUS   Ay, and Wall too.

BOTTOM [*Starting up, as Flute does also*]   No, I assure you,
the wall is down that parted their fathers. Will it

---

315 mote small particle   **315–316 which ... which** whether ... or
320 means moans, laments.   **videlicet** to wit   **333 Sisters Three** the
Fates   **337 shore** shorn   **341 imbrue** stain with blood

please you to see the epilogue, or to hear a Bergomask 349
dance between two of our company?   350
                    [*The other players enter.*]
THESEUS   No epilogue, I pray you; for your play needs
no excuse. Never excuse; for when the players are all
dead, there need none to be blamed. Marry, if he that
writ it had played Pyramus and hanged himself in
Thisbe's garter, it would have been a fine tragedy; and
so it is, truly, and very notably discharged. But, come,
your Bergomask. Let your epilogue alone.   [*A dance.*]
The iron tongue of midnight hath told twelve.   358
Lovers, to bed, 'tis almost fairy time.
I fear we shall outsleep the coming morn
As much as we this night have overwatched.   361
This palpable-gross play hath well beguiled   362
The heavy gait of night. Sweet friends, to bed.   363
A fortnight hold we this solemnity,
In nightly revels and new jollity.   *Exeunt.*

       Enter Puck [*carrying a broom*].

PUCK
       Now the hungry lion roars,
           And the wolf behowls the moon;
       Whilst the heavy plowman snores,   368
           All with weary task fordone.   369
       Now the wasted brands do glow,   370
           Whilst the screech owl, screeching loud,
       Puts the wretch that lies in woe
           In remembrance of a shroud.
       Now it is the time of night
           That the graves, all gaping wide,
       Every one lets forth his sprite,   376
           In the church-way paths to glide.
       And we fairies, that do run

349–350 **Bergomask dance** a rustic dance named from Bergamo, a prov-
ince in the state of Venice   358 **iron tongue** i.e., of a bell.   **told** counted,
struck ("tolled")   361 **overwatched** stayed up too late   362 **palpable-gross**
palpably gross, obviously crude   363 **heavy** drowsy, dull   368 **heavy**
tired   369 **fordone** exhausted   370 **wasted brands** burned-out logs
376 **Every . . . sprite** every grave lets forth its ghost

By the triple Hecate's team   379
From the presence of the sun,
    Following darkness like a dream,
Now are frolic. Not a mouse   382
Shall disturb this hallowed house.
I am sent with broom before,
To sweep the dust behind the door.   385

*Enter [Oberon and Titania,] King and Queen of
Fairies, with all their train.*

OBERON

Through the house give glimmering light,
    By the dead and drowsy fire;
Every elf and fairy sprite
    Hop as light as bird from brier;
And this ditty, after me,
Sing, and dance it trippingly.

TITANIA

First, rehearse your song by rote,
To each word a warbling note.
Hand in hand, with fairy grace,
Will we sing, and bless this place.

                              [Song and dance.]

OBERON

Now, until the break of day,
Through this house each fairy stray.
To the best bride-bed will we,
Which by us shall blessèd be;
And the issue there create   400
Ever shall be fortunate.
So shall all the couples three
Ever true in loving be;
And the blots of Nature's hand
Shall not in their issue stand;
Never mole, harelip, nor scar,
Nor mark prodigious, such as are   407
Despisèd in nativity,

379 triple Hecate's (Hecate ruled in three capacities: as Luna or Cynthia
in heaven, as Diana on earth, and as Proserpina in hell.) **382 frolic**
merry **385 behind** from behind. (Robin Goodfellow was a household
spirit who helped good housemaids and punished lazy ones.) **400 create**
created **407 prodigious** monstrous, unnatural

Shall upon their children be.
With this field dew consecrate   410
Every fairy take his gait,   411
And each several chamber bless,   412
Through this palace, with sweet peace;
And the owner of it blest
Ever shall in safety rest.
Trip away; make no stay;
Meet me all by break of day.

             Exeunt [Oberon, Titania, and train].

PUCK [*To the audience*]
If we shadows have offended,
Think but this, and all is mended,
That you have but slumbered here   420
While these visions did appear.
And this weak and idle theme,
No more yielding but a dream,   423
Gentles, do not reprehend.
If you pardon, we will mend.   425
And, as I am an honest Puck,
If we have unearnèd luck
Now to scape the serpent's tongue,   428
We will make amends ere long;
Else the Puck a liar call.
So, good night unto you all.
Give me your hands, if we be friends,   432
And Robin shall restore amends.   [*Exit.*]   433

---

410 consecrate consecrated   **411 take his gait** go his way   **412 several**
separate   **420 That . . . here** i.e., that it is a "midsummer night's
dream"   **423 No . . . but** yielding no more than   **425 mend** improve
428 serpent's tongue i.e., hissing   **432 Give . . . hands** applaud
433 restore amends give satisfaction in return

Date and Text

A Midsummer Night's Dream was entered on the Stationers' Register, the official record book of the London Company of Stationers (booksellers and printers), by Thomas Fisher on October 8, 1600, and printed by him that same year in quarto:

> A Midsommer nights dreame. As it hath beene sundry times pub*lickely acted, by the Right honoura*ble, the Lord Chamberlaine his *seruants. Written by William Shakespeare.* Imprinted at London, for *Thomas Fisher,* and are to be soulde at his shoppe, at the Signe of the White Hart, in *Fleetestreete.* 1600.

This text appears to have been set from Shakespeare's working manuscript. Its inconsistencies in time scheme and other irregularities may reflect some revision, although the inconsistencies are not noticeable in performance. A second quarto appeared in 1619, though falsely dated 1600; it was a reprint of the first quarto, with some minor corrections and many new errors. A copy of this second quarto, evidently with some added stage directions and other minor changes from a theatrical manuscript in the company's possession, served as the basis for the First Folio text of 1623. Essentially, the first quarto remains the authoritative text.

Other than Francis Meres's listing of the play in 1598 in his *Palladis Tamia: Wit's Treasury* (a slender volume on contemporary literature and art; valuable because it lists most of the plays of Shakespeare's that existed at that time), external clues as to date are elusive. The description of unruly weather (2.1.88–114) has been related to the bad summer of 1594, but complaints about the weather are perennial. On the assumption that the play celebrates some noble wedding of the period, scholars have come up with a number of suitable marriages. Chief are those of Sir Thomas Heneage to Mary, Countess of Southampton, in 1594; of William Stanley, Earl of Derby, to Elizabeth Vere, daughter of the Earl of Oxford, in 1595; and of Thomas, son of Lord Berkeley, to Elizabeth, daughter of Lord Carey, in 1596. The Countess of Southampton was the widowed mother of the young Earl of Southampton, to whom Shakespeare had dedicated his *Venus and Adonis* and *The Rape of Lucrece*. No one has ever proved convincingly, however, that the play was written for any occasion other than commercial public performance. The play makes sense for a general audience and does not need to depend on references to a private marriage. Shakespeare was, after all, in the business of writing plays for his fellow actors, who earned their livelihood chiefly by public acting before large paying audiences. In any event the search for a court marriage is a circular argument in terms of dating; suitable court marriages can be found for any year of the decade. In the last analysis, the play has to be dated on the basis of its stylistic affinity to plays like *Romeo and Juliet* and *Richard II*, works of the "lyric" mid 1590s. The "Pyramus and Thisbe" performance in *A Midsummer Night's Dream* would seem to bear an obvious relation to *Romeo and Juliet*, although no one can say for sure which came first.

Textual Notes

These textual notes are not a historical collation, either of the early quartos and the early folios or of more recent editions; they are simply a record of departures in this edition from the copy text. The reading adopted in this edition appears in boldface, followed by the rejected reading from the copy text, i.e., the quarto of 1600. Only major alterations in punctuation are noted. Changes in lineation are not indicated, nor are some minor and obvious typographical errors.

Abbreviations used:
Q the first quarto of 1600
s.d. stage direction
s.p. speech prefix

Copy text: the first quarto of 1600.

1.1. 4 wanes waues   **10 New bent** Now bent   **19 s.d. Lysander** Lysander and Helena   **24 Stand forth, Demetrius** [printed as s.d. in Q]   **26 Stand forth, Lysander** [printed as s.d. in Q]   **74 their** there   **132 Ay** Eigh   **136 low** loue   **187 Yours would** Your words   **191 I'd** ile   **216 sweet** sweld   **219 stranger companies** strange companions

2.1. 1 s.p. [and elsewhere] Puck Robin   **61 s.p. [and elsewhere] Titania** Qu   **61 Fairies** Fairy   **69 step** steppe   **79 Aegles** Eagles   **109 thin** chinne   **158 the west** west   **190 slay** stay.   **slayeth** stayeth   **194 thee** the   **201 not** nor not not   **246 s.d.** [at l. 247 in Q]

2.2. 9 s.p. First Fairy [not in Q; also at l. 20]   **13 s.p. Chorus** [not in Q; also at l. 24]   **45 Be it** Bet it   **49 good** god   **53 is** it

3.1. 27–28 yourselves your selfe   **52 s.p. Bottom** Cet   **72 s.p. Puck** Ro   **77 s.p. Bottom** Pyra [also at ll. 79 and 98]   **78 Odors, odors** Odours, odorous   **83 s.p. Puck** Quin   **84 s.p. Flute** Thys [also at ll. 88 and 97]   **144 own** owe   **157–158 Ready . . . go** [assigned to **Fairies** in Q]   **170 s.p. Peaseblossom** 1. Fai   **171 Hail** [assigned in Q to 1. Fai]   **172 s.p. Mote** 2. Fair   **173 s.p. Mustardseed** 3. Fai   **190 you of** you   **196 s.d. Exeunt** Exit

3.2. s.d. [Q: Enter King of Fairies, and Robin goodfellow]   **19 mimic** Minnick   **38 s.p. [and elsewhere] Puck** Rob   **80 I so** I   **85 sleep** slippe   **213 like** life   **220 passionate words** words   **250 prayers** praise   **260 off** of   **299 gentlemen** gentleman   **344 s.d. Exit** Exeunt   **406 Speak! In** Speake in   **426 shalt** shat   **451 To your** your

4.1. 5 s.p. [and elsewhere] Bottom Clown   **64 off** of   **72 o'er** or   **81 five fine** 82 ho howe   **116 Seemed** Seeme   **127 this is** this   **137 s.d. Wind . . . up** they all start vp. Winde hornes   **171 saw** see   **190 found** fonnd   **198 let us** lets   **205 to expound** expound   **208 a patched** patcht a

4.2. s.d. [Snout, and Starveling] Thisby and the rabble   **3 s.p. Starveling** Flut   **5 s.p. Flute** Thys [and at ll. 9, 13, 19]   **29 no** not

5.1. 34 our Or   **107 s.p. [and elsewhere] Theseus** Duke   **122 his** this   **150 s.d. Exeunt** Exit [and at l. 153 in Q]   **155 Snout** Flute   **190 up in thee**

now againe **205 mural down** Moon vsed **209 s.p. [and elsewhere]** Hippolyta Dutch **270 gleames** beames **309 before** before? **317 warrant** warnd **347 s.p. Bottom** Lyon **366 lion** Lyons **367 behowls** beholds **415–416 And . . . rest** [these lines are transposed in Q]

Shakespeare's Sources

No single source has been discovered that unites the various elements we find in *A Midsummer Night's Dream*, but the four main strands of action can be individually discussed in terms of sources. The four strands are: (1) the marriage of Duke Theseus and Queen Hippolyta, (2) the romantic tribulations and triumphs of the four young lovers, (3) the quarrel of King Oberon and Queen Titania, together with the fairies' manipulations of human affairs, and (4) the "rude mechanicals" and their play of "Pyramus and Thisbe."

For his conception of Theseus, Shakespeare went chiefly to Geoffrey Chaucer's "The Knight's Tale," of which a brief excerpt follows, and to Thomas North's 1579 translation of "The Life of Theseus" in Plutarch's *Lives of the Noble Grecians and Romans*. Chaucer's Theseus is a duke of "wisdom" and "chivalrye," renowned for his conquest of the Amazons and his marriage to Hippolyta. Plutarch provides information concerning Theseus' other conquests (to which Oberon alludes in 2.1.77 ff.), including that of Antiopa. Shakespeare could have learned more about Theseus from Chaucer's *The Legend of Good Women* and from Ovid's *Metamorphoses*. He seems to have blended all or some of these impressions together with his own notion of a noble yet popular Renaissance ruler.

The romantic narrative of the four lovers appears to be original with Shakespeare, although one can find many analogous situations of misunderstanding and rivalry in love. Chaucer's "The Knight's Tale" tells of two friends battling over one woman. Shakespeare's own *The Two Gentlemen of Verona* gives us four lovers, properly matched at first until one of the men shifts his attentions to his friend's ladylove; eventually all is righted when the false lover recovers his senses. Parallel situations arise in Sir Philip Sidney's *Arcadia* (1590) and in Jorge de Montemayor's *Diana* (c. 1559), a source for *The Two Gentlemen*. What Shakespeare adds in *A Midsummer* is the intervention of the fairies in human love affairs.

Shakespeare's knowledge of fairy lore must have been extensive and is hard to trace exactly. Doubtless much of it was from oral traditions about leprechauns, gremlins, and elves, who were thought to cause such mischief as spoiling fermentation or preventing milk from churning into butter; Puck's tricks mentioned in 2.1.34 ff. are derived from such lore. Yet Shakespeare seems to have consulted literary sources as well. In Chaucer's "The Merchant's Tale," Pluto and Proserpina as king and queen of the fairies intervene in the affairs of old January, his young wife May, and her lover Damyan. Fairies appear onstage in John Lyly's *Endymion* (1588), protecting true lovers and tormenting those who are morally tainted. Shakespeare later reflects this tradition in *The Merry Wives of Windsor* (1597–1601). The name Oberon probably comes from the French romance *Huon of Bordeaux* (translated by Lord Berners by about 1540), where Oberon is a dwarfish fairy king from the mysterious East who practices enchantment in a haunted wood. In Edmund Spenser's *The Faerie Queene*, Oberon is the Elfin father of Queen Gloriana (2.10.75–76). Robert Greene's *James IV* (c. 1591) also features Oberon as the fairy king, and a lost play called *Huon of Bordeaux* was performed by Sussex's men, an acting company, at about this same time. The name Titania comes from Ovid's *Metamorphoses*, where it is used as a synonym for both the enchantress Circe and the chaste goddess Diana. The name Titania does not appear in Arthur Golding's translation (1567), suggesting that Shakespeare found it in the original. Puck, or Robin Goodfellow, is essentially the product of oral tradition, although Reginald Scot's *The Discovery of Witchcraft* (1584) discusses Robin in pejorative terms as an incubus or hobgoblin in whom intelligent people no longer believe.

Scot also reports the story of a man who finds an ass's head placed on his shoulders by enchantment. Similar legends of transformation occur in Apuleius' *The Golden Ass* (translated by William Adlington, 1566) and in the well-known story of the ass's ears bestowed by Phoebus Apollo on King Midas for his presumption. Perhaps the most suggestive possible source for Shakespeare's clownish actors, however, is Anthony Munday's play *John a Kent and John a Cumber* (c. 1587–1590). In it a group of rude artisans, led by the intrepid Turnop, stage a ludicrous interlude written by their churchwarden in praise of his millhorse. Turnop's prologue is a medley of lofty comparisons. The entertainment is presented before noble spectators, who are graciously amused. *John a Kent* also features a lot of magic trickery, a boy named Shrimp whose role is comparable to that of Puck, and a multiple love plot.

"Pyramus and Thisbe" itself is based on the *Metamorphoses* (4.55 ff.), as can be seen from the following selection. Other versions Shakespeare may have known include Chaucer's *The Legend of Good Women*, William Griffith's poem *Pyramus and Thisbe* (1562), George Pettie's *A Petite Palace of Pettie His Pleasure* (1576), *A Gorgeous Gallery of Gallant Inventions* (1578), and "A New Sonnet of Pyramus and Thisbe" from Clement Robinson's *A Handful of Pleasant Delights* (1584). Several of these, especially the last three, are bad enough to have given Shakespeare materials to lampoon, though the sweep of his parody goes beyond the particular story of Pyramus and Thisbe. The occasionally stilted phraseology of Golding's translation of *The Metamorphoses* contributed to the fun. According to Kenneth Muir (*Shakespeare's Sources*, 1957), Shakespeare must also have known Thomas Mouffet's *Of the Silkworms and Their Flies* (published 1599, but possibly circulated earlier in manuscript), which contains perhaps the most ridiculous of all versions of the Pyramus and Thisbe story. Shakespeare also appears to be spoofing the inept dramatic style and lame verse of English dramas of the 1560s, 1570s, and 1580s, especially in their treatment of tragic sentiment and high emotion; *Cambises*, *Damon and Pythias*, and *Appius and Virginia* are examples.

The Canterbury Tales
By Geoffrey Chaucer

HERE BEGINNETH THE KNIGHTES TALE

Whilom, as olde stories tellen us,	859
There was a duke that highte Theseus.	860
Of Athens he was lord and governor,	
And in his time swich a conqueror	862
That greater was there none under the sonne.	
Full many a rich country had he wonne;	
What with his wisdom and his chivalrye	
He conquered all the reign of Feminye,	866
That whilom was ycleped Scythia,	867
And weddede the queen Hippolyta	
And brought her home with him in his country	
With muchel glory and great solemnity,	870
And eke her faire suster Emily.	871
And thus with victory and with melody	
Let I this noble duke to Athens ride,	
And all his host in armes him beside.	874
And certes, if it nere too long to hear,	875
I would han told you fully the manner	876
How wonnen was the reign of Feminye	
By Theseus and by his chivalrye,	
And of the greate bataille for the nones	879
Bitwixen Athenes and Amazones,	
And how asseged was Hippolyta,	881
The faire, hardy queen of Scythia,	882
And of the feast that was at hir weddinge,	883
And of the tempest at hir home-cominge;	884
But all that thing I moot as now forbeare.	885
I have, God wot, a large field to eare,	886

859 Whilom once upon a time   **860 highte** was called   **862 swich** such
866 reign of Feminye country of the Amazons   **867 ycleped** called
870 muchel much.   **solemnity** ceremony   **871 eke** also.   **suster** sister
874 him beside beside him   **875 nere too** were not too   **876 would han**
would have   **879 for the nones** in particular   **881 asseged** besieged
882 hardy brave   **883 hir** their (also in l. 884)   **884 tempest** tumult
885 moot must   **886 eare** ear, plow

And weake been the oxen in my plough.
The remnant of the tale is long enough;
I woll nat letten eke none of this route.   889
Let every fellow tell his tale aboute,   890
And let see now who shall the supper winne;   891
And there I left I will again beginne.   892
   This duke, of whom I make mencioun,   893
When he was come almost unto the toun,
In all his weal and in his moste pride,   895
He was war, as he cast his eye aside,   896
Where that there kneeled in the highe waye   897
A company of ladies, tweye and tweye,   898
Each after other, clad in clothes blacke;
But swich a cry and swich a woe they make
That in this world nys creature livinge   901
That hearde swich another waymentinge.   902
And of this cry they nolde nevere stinten   903
Till they the reines of his bridle henten.   904
   "What folk been ye, that at mine home-cominge
Perturben so my feaste with cryinge?"   906
Quod Theseus. "Have ye so great envye   907
Of mine honor, that thus complain and crye?   908
Or who hath you misboden or offended?   909
And telleth me if it may been amended,   910
And why that ye been clothed thus in black?"
   The eldest lady of hem alle spak,   912
When she had swooned with a deadly cheere   913
That it was routhe for to seen and heare,   914
And saide, "Lord, to whom fortune hath given
Victory, and as a conqueror to liven,
Nat grieveth us your glory and your honor,   917
But we beseeken mercy and succor.   918
Have mercy on our woe and our distresse!

---

889 woll nat letten will not hinder.   **route** assembly (the Canterbury pilgrims)   **890 aboute** in succession   **891 let see** let it be seen   **892 there** where   **893 mencioun** mention   **895 weal** splendor   **896 war** aware.   **aside** to one side   **897 highe waye** highway   **898 tweye and tweye** two by two   **901 nys** is not   **902 waymentinge** lamenting   **903 nolde** would not.   **stinten** stint, cease   **904 reines** reins.   **henten** seized, grasped   **906 feaste** feast, festival celebration   **907–908 envye Of** ill will toward   **909 misboden** harmed   **910 telleth** tell.   **been** be   **912 hem** them   **913 deadly cheere** deathlike appearance   **914 routhe** pity   **917 Nat . . . glory** your glory doesn't grieve us   **918 beseeken** beseech, beg

Some drop of pity, through thy gentillesse,   920
Upon us wretched women let thou falle!
For certes, lord, there is none of us alle   922
That she ne hath been a duchess or a queene.   923
Now be we caitives, as it is well seene.   924
Thanked be Fortune and her false wheel
That none estate assureth to be weel.   926
And certes, lord, to abiden your presence,   927
Here in the temple of the goddess Clemence
We han been waiting all this fourteennight;   929
Now help us, lord, sith it is in thy might . . .   930

[The story of rivalry between Palamon and Arcite bears
only a general resemblance to that of the young lovers in
A Midsummer Night's Dream, but when Chaucer and the
Knight return to an account of revels and tournaments in
honor of the wedding of Theseus and Hippolyta, the splendor of the Athenian court is not unlike that in Act 5 of
Shakespeare's play.]

The Canterbury Tales of Chaucer date from 1387–1400. This sparingly modernized selection from "The Knight's Tale" is based on the Ellesmere manuscript, Ellesmere 26 c. 12, now in the Huntington Library, San Marino,
California. Group A, ll. 859–930.

In the following, departures from the original text appear in boldface; the
original readings follow in roman:

868 weddede wedded   **876 han told you** yow haue toold   **897 highe waye** weye

920 gentillesse courtesy, good breeding   **922 certes** certainly   **923 ne hath**
has not   **924 caitives** caitiffs, wretches   **926 none . . . weel** i.e., no human
prosperity can assure itself of long felicity   **927 abiden** await
929 fourteennight fortnight   **930 sith** since

Metamorphoses
By Ovid
Translated by Arthur Golding

BOOK 4

Within the town (of whose huge walls so monstrous
   high and thick
The fame is given Semiramis for making them of
   brick)   68
Dwelt hard together two young folk, in houses joined
   so near   69
That under all one roof well nigh both twain con-
   veyèd were.   70
The name of him was Pyramus, and Thisbe called
   was she.
So fair a man in all the East was none alive as he,
Nor ne'er a woman, maid, nor wife in beauty like to
   her.
This neighborhood bred acquaintance first; this
   neighborhood first did stir   74
The secret sparks; this neighborhood first an en-
   trance in did show
For love to come to that to which it afterward did
   grow.
   And if that right had taken place, they had been
     man and wife;
But still their parents went about to let which, for
   their life,   78
They could not let. For both their hearts with equal
   flame did burn.
No man was privy to their thoughts; and, for to serve
   their turn,
Instead of talk, they usèd signs. The closelier they
   suppressed

68 Semiramis the Queen of Assyria, 810–806 B.C., who was reputed to have
ordered the building of the walls of Babylon   **69 hard together** hard by
70 conveyèd taken, led, placed   **74 neighborhood** friendly relations between
neighbors   **78 still** always.   **let which** hinder that which.   **for their life** even
if their lives depended on it

The fire of love, the fiercer still it ragèd in their
    breast.
  The wall that parted house from house had riven
    therein a cranny,
Which shrunk at making of the wall. This fault, not
    marked of any   84
Of many hundred years before—what doth not love
    espy?—
These lovers first of all found out and made a way
    whereby
To talk together secretly; and through the same did
    go
Their loving whisperings, very light and safely, to and
    fro.
  Now, as at one side Pyramus, and Thisbe on the
    tother,
Stood often drawing one of them the pleasant breath
    from other,
"O thou envious wall!" they said. "Why lett'st thou
    lovers thus?   91
What matter were it if that thou permitted both of us
In arms each other to embrace? Or if thou think that
    this
Were overmuch, yet mightest thou at least make
    room to kiss.
And yet thou shalt not find us churls; we think our-
    selves in debt
For the same piece of courtesy, in vouching safe to let   96
Our sayings to our friendly ears thus freely come and
    go."
Thus having, where they stood in vain, complainèd of
    their woe,
When night drew near they bade adieu, and each
    gave kisses sweet
Unto the parget on their side, the which did never
    meet.   100
  Next morning with her cheerful light had driven
    the stars aside,

84 shrunk i.e., resulted from shrinkage   **91 lett'st thou** do you hinder
96 vouching safe vouchsafing, permitting   **100 parget** roughcast, plaster
usually made of lime and cow-dung. **the which** i.e., which kisses

And Phoebus with his burning beams the dewy grass
   had dried.
These lovers at their wonted place by foreappoint-
   ment met;
Where, after much complaint and moan, they cove-
   nanted to get
Away from such as watchèd them, and in the evening
   late
To steal out of their fathers' house and eke the city
   gate.   106
And to th' intent that in the fields they strayed not
   up and down,   107
They did agree at Ninus' tomb to meet without the
   town   108
And tarry underneath a tree that by the same did
   grow,
Which was a fair high mulberry with fruit as white
   as snow,
Hard by a cool and trickling spring. This bargain
   pleased them both,
And so daylight, which to their thought away but
   slowly go'th,
Did in the ocean fall to rest, and night from thence
   doth rise.
   As soon as darkness once was come, straight
     Thisbe did devise
A shift to wind her out of doors, that none that were
   within   115
Perceivèd her, and muffling her with clothes about
   her chin
That no man might discern her face, to Ninus' tomb
   she came
Unto the tree, and sat her down there underneath the
   same.
   Love made her bold. But see the chance! There
     comes, besmeared with blood
About the chaps, a lioness, all foaming, from the
   wood,

106 eke also   **107 strayed not** would not stray   **108 Ninus** husband of
Semiramis, mythical founder of Nineveh. (Nineveh and Babylon appear to
have been confused.)   **without** outside   **115 shift** device.   **wind her** move by
sinuous course

From slaughter lately made of kine, to stanch her
    bloody thirst   121
With water of the foresaid spring. Whom Thisbe,
    spying first
Afar by moonlight, thereupon with fearful steps gan
    fly,
And in a dark and irksome cave did hide herself
    thereby.
And as she fled away for haste she let her mantle fall,
The which for fear she left behind, not looking back
    at all.
  Now, when the cruel lioness her thirst had
    stanchèd well,
In going to the wood she found the slender weed that
    fell   128
From Thisbe, which with bloody teeth in pieces she
    did tear.
  The night was somewhat further spent ere Pyramus
    came there,
Who, seeing in this subtle sand the print of lion's
    paw,   131
Waxed pale for fear. But when also the bloody cloak
    he saw
All rent and torn, "One night," he said, "shall lovers
    two confound!   133
Of which long life deservèd she of all that live on
    ground.   134
My soul deserves of this mischance the peril for to
    bear.
I, wretch, have been the death of thee, which to this
    place of fear
Did cause thee in the night to come, and came not
    here before.
My wicked limbs and wretched guts with cruel teeth
    therefore
Devour ye, O ye lions all that in this rock do dwell!

---

121 kine cattle. **stanch** slake   **128 weed** garment   **131 subtle** i.e., capable
of preserving an indistinct impression   **133 confound** destroy   **134 Of . . .
ground** one of whom (Thisbe) deserved long life more than any other person
on earth

But cowards use to wish for death." The slender
  weed that fell   140
From Thisbe up he takes and straight doth bear it to
  the tree   141
Which was appointed erst the place of meeting for to
  be.   142
And when he had bewept and kissed the garment
  which he knew,
"Receive thou my blood too!" quoth he, and therewithal he drew
His sword, the which among his guts he thrust, and
  by and by
Did draw it from the bleeding wound, beginning for
  to die,
And cast himself upon his back. The blood did spin
  on high;
As when a conduit pipe is cracked, the water bursting
  out
Doth shoot itself a great way off and pierce the air
  about.
The leaves that were upon the tree, besprinkled with
  his blood,
Were dyèd black. The root also, bestainèd as it stood,
A deep dark purple color straight upon the berries
  cast.
  Anon, scarce ridded of her fear with which she was
  aghast,
For doubt of disappointing him comes Thisbe forth
  in haste   154
And for her lover looks about, rejoicing for to tell
How hardly she had scaped that night the danger
  that befell.   156
And as she knew right well the place and fashion of
  the tree,
As which she saw so late before, even so, when she
  did see   158

---

140 use to make it a practice to. (Cowards only pretend to be ready to die;
brave persons act.)   **141 straight** straightway, at once   **142 erst** at an earlier
time   **154 doubt** fear   **156 hardly** scarcely   **158 As ... before** which she
had seen so recently

The color of the berries turned, she was uncertain
    whether
It were the tree at which they both agreed to meet
        together.
    While in this doubtful stound she stood, she cast
        her eye aside,   161
And there, beweltered in his blood, her lover she
    espied
Lie sprawling with his dying limbs; at which she
    started back
And lookèd pale as any box. A shuddering through
    her strack,   164
Even like the sea which suddenly with whizzing noise
    doth move
When with a little blast of wind it is but touched
    above.
But, when approaching nearer him, she knew it was
    her love,
She beat her breast, she shriekèd out, she tare her
    golden hairs,   168
And, taking him between her arms, did wash his
        wounds with tears.
    She meynt her weeping with his blood, and kissing
        all his face,   170
Which now became as cold as ice, she cried in woeful
    case,
"Alas! What chance, my Pyramus, hath parted thee
    and me?
Make answer, O my Pyramus. It is thy Thisb, even she
Whom thou dost love most heartily, that speaketh
    unto thee.
Give ear, and raise thy heavy head!" He, hearing
    Thisbe's name,
Lift up his dying eyes and, having seen her, closed
    the same.   176
    But when she knew her mantle there and saw his
        scabbard lie

---

161 stound pang, shock; difficult time   **164 pale as any box** i.e., ashen,
pallid, like the color of boxwood.   **strack** struck   **168 tare** tore   **170 meynt**
(past tense of *meng*), mingled   **176 Lift** lifted

Without the sword: "Unhappy man! Thy love hath
   made thee die.
Thy love," she said, "hath made thee slay thyself.
   This hand of mine
Is strong enough to do the like. My love no less than
   thine
Shall give me force to work my wound. I will pursue
   thee dead,   181
And, wretched woman as I am, it shall of me be said
That, like as of thy death I was the only cause and
   blame,   183
So am I thy companion eke and partner in the same.   184
For death, which only could, alas! asunder part us
   twain,   185
Shall never so dissever us but we will meet again.
   "And you the parents of us both, most wretched
      folk alive,
Let this request that I shall make in both our names
   belive   188
Entreat you to permit that we, whom chaste and
   steadfast love
And whom even death hath joined in one, may, as it
   doth behoove,
In one grave be together laid. And thou, unhappy
   tree,
Which shroudest now the corpse of one, and shalt
   anon through me
Shroud two, of this same slaughter hold the sicker
   signs for aye.   193
Black be the color of thy fruit, and mourning-like
   alway,
Such as the murder of us twain may evermore
   bewray."   195
   This said, she took the sword, yet warm with
      slaughter of her love,
And setting it beneath her breast, did to her heart it
   shove.

---

181 work inflict   **183 like as** just as   **184 eke** also   **185 only** alone
188 belive urgently   **193 sicker** sure.   **aye** ever   **195 bewray** reveal

Her prayer with the gods and with their parents took
    effect.
For when the fruit is throughly ripe, the berry is
    bespecked,   199
With color tending to a black. And that which after
    fire   200
Remainèd, rested in one tomb, as Thisbe did desire.

The text is based on *The XV Books of P. Ovidius Naso, Entitled Metamorphosis. Translated out of Latin into English meter by Arthur Golding*. London, 1567. This is the first edition of Golding's translation.

199 throughly thoroughly   **200 fire** i.e., cremation

Further Reading

Barber, C. L. "May Games and Metamorphoses on a Midsummer Night." *Shakespeare's Festive Comedy*. Princeton, N.J.: Princeton Univ. Press, 1959. Barber explores how the social forms of Elizabethan holiday and celebration contribute to the dramatic form of Shakespeare's comedy. *A Midsummer Night's Dream* uses folk customs and aristocratic pageantry to organize its contrasts between reason and feeling, waking and dreaming, enabling the play to acknowledge the creative power of the human imagination while simultaneously recognizing that its creations are often "more strange than true."

Bevington, David. " 'But We Are Spirits of Another Sort': The Dark Side of Love and Magic in *A Midsummer Night's Dream*." *Medieval and Renaissance Studies* 7 (1975): 80–92. Bevington draws attention to the tension in the play "between comic reassurance and the suggestion of something dark and threatening." In pointing to the play's disturbing currents of libidinous sexuality, Bevington recognizes but distances himself from the position of Jan Kott (see below), arguing that the play successfully effects a reconciliation between the dark and affirmative sides of love—reconciliation that finds its symbol in the image of Titania and the ass's head.

Calderwood, James L. "*A Midsummer Night's Dream:* Art's Illusory Sacrifice." *Shakespearean Metadrama*. Minneapolis: Univ. of Minnesota Press, 1971. In Calderwood's metadramatic perspective, *A Midsummer Night's Dream* is the comedy that most fully participates in Shakespeare's ongoing dramatic exploration of the nature, function, and value of art. The characters' experience *in* the play mirrors the audience's experience *of* the play, as each is challenged to discover reality through illusions. Dream thereby becomes an analogue of the drama itself, a drama "in which man sees his dreams."

Dent, R. W. "Imagination in *A Midsummer Night's Dream*." *Shakespeare Quarterly* 15, no. 2 (1964), 115–129. Although Theseus indiscriminately lumps together lunatics, lovers, and poets, Shakespeare, Dent argues, carefully distinguishes between the role of imagination in love and in art. This distinction, demonstrated in Shakespeare's handling of the mechanicals' play, confirms *A Midsummer Night's Dream*'s unity of design, while offering us Shakespeare's own "Defense of Dramatic Poesy."

Evans, Bertrand. "All Shall Be Well: The Way Found." *Shakespeare's Comedies.* Oxford: Clarendon Press, 1960. Evans explores Shakespeare's handling of the different levels of awareness and understanding that characters display in the play. Oberon comes closest to the audience's privileged vantage point, while Bottom, who seems to have a wonderful resistance to understanding, is most distant. *A Midsummer Night's Dream* departs from the usual pattern of Shakespeare's comedies in that the denouement does not raise the characters to a level of awareness equal to that of the audience.

Fender, Stephen. *Shakespeare: "A Midsummer Night's Dream."* London: Edward Arnold, 1968. In a brief (64 pages), engaging book, Fender argues that provocative moral ambiguities emerge from the play's unusual structural complexity. We are constantly made aware of tensions and contradictions in the depiction of characters and settings, even in blind love itself. The play demands of us what Keats called Negative Capability: the ability to accept multiplicity, mystery, and doubt without reaching out for the illusory comforts of certainty and fact.

Garber, Marjorie B. "Spirits of Another Sort: *A Midsummer Night's Dream.*" *Dream in Shakespeare: From Metaphor to Metamorphosis.* New Haven and London: Yale Univ. Press, 1974. The dreams in *A Midsummer Night's Dream*, according to Garber, function both to articulate the central theme of the play—imaginative transformation—and to provide a model for the play's construction. Dreams become emblems of the visionary experience itself, forcing characters as well as the audience out of familiar habits of mind into new modes of perception and understanding.

Girard, René. "Myth and Ritual in Shakespeare: *A Midsummer Night's Dream.*" In *Textual Strategies: Perspectives in Post-Structuralist Criticism*, ed. Josué V. Harari. Ithaca, N.Y.: Cornell Univ. Press, 1979. Girard argues that in the confusions of the forest the lovers lose their identities because of their insistence on loving "through another's eyes." In the destructiveness of this mimetic desire Girard finds not only the theme of this play but also the "basic Shakespearean relationship" of all the comedies and tragedies.

Granville-Barker, Harley. *"A Midsummer Night's Dream."* In *More Prefaces to Shakespeare*, ed. Edward M. Moore. Princeton, N.J.: Princeton Univ. Press, 1974. Granville-Barker, writing as both critic and director, addresses the special problems raised in producing *A Midsummer Night's Dream* in a world accustomed to the realistic conventions of the modern theater. His analysis focuses on how the clowns, fairies, dance, and music could be handled effectively and convincingly, and he urges that the stage business be subordinated to Shakespeare's overriding emphasis on the play's language.

Kermode, Frank. "The Mature Comedies." In *Early Shakespeare*, ed. John Russell Brown and Bernard Harris. Stratford-upon-Avon Studies 3. London: Edward Arnold, 1961. For Kermode, the play, rich in intellectual content and sophisticated in design, is Shakespeare's "best comedy." His essay examines how Shakespeare's thematic preoccupation with blind love draws upon the philosophical treatment of this idea in the works of Macrobius, Apuleius, and Bruno. The result, Kermode argues, is a complex and serious work of art, intellectually and theatrically satisfying in its comic achievement.

Kott, Jan. "Titania and the Ass's Head." *Shakespeare Our Contemporary*, trans. Boleslaw Taborski. New York: Doubleday, 1964. In Kott's dark vision of love and human relations in *A Midsummer Night's Dream*, the night in the forest releases an "erotic madness" of perversity and obsession that is abruptly censured by the coming of day. Love is revealed as undignified and degrading, denying the lovers even their individuality in their compulsive behavior.

Leggatt, Alexander. *"A Midsummer Night's Dream." Shakespeare's Comedy of Love*. London: Methuen, 1974. In a sensitive essay, Leggatt explores Shakespeare's skillful arrangement of characters and perspectives. The play, he argues, achieves its imaginative power through a series of comic contrasts that confirms both the folly and the integrity of each group of characters.

Merchant, W. Moelwyn. *"A Midsummer Night's Dream:* A Visual Recreation."* In *Early Shakespeare,* ed. John Russell Brown and Bernard Harris. Stratford-upon-Avon Studies 3. London: Edward Arnold, 1961. The play, which demanded the full range of the theatrical possibilities of the Elizabethan stage, in the ensuing centuries has received treatments that have tended to oversimplify the play to achieve certain desired theatrical effects. Merchant, surveying this stage history, concludes that directors have generally failed to integrate the undeniable charm of the fairy world with the more unsettling side of the play.

Montrose, Louis Adrian. " 'Shaping Fantasies': Figurations of Gender and Power in Elizabethan Culture." *Representations* 1, no. 2 (1983): 61–94. Montrose is interested in the relationship of Elizabethan drama to the culture that produced it, especially in how Shakespeare's plays reproduce and challenge existing social structures. His discussion of how the world of Queen Elizabeth's England and the world of *A Midsummer Night's Dream* are mutually illuminating focuses on questions of power, patriarchy, and sexual politics, concluding that in a double sense the play is a *"creation* of Elizabethan culture."

Olson, Paul A. *"A Midsummer Night's Dream* and the Meaning of Court Marriage." *ELH* 24 (1957): 95–119. Rpt. in *Shakespeare's Comedies: An Anthology of Modern Criticism,* ed. Laurence Lerner. Baltimore: Penguin, 1967. Olson calls attention to one possible occasion of the play's first performance (the celebration of a courtly marriage) as a sign of its seriousness and sophistication. He surveys Renaissance ideas about love and art to discover the principles that organize the play's elaborate formal contrasts, examining how the language and structure of the play "work together to make luminous a traditional understanding of marriage" that mirrors and reinforces the social order.

Selbourne, David. *The Making of "A Midsummer Night's Dream."* London: Methuen, 1982. Selbourne's account of the development of Peter Brook's Royal Shakespeare

Company production of *A Midsummer Night's Dream* (1970) offers insight into the creative interplay of director, cast, and text that resulted in this remarkable and influential production.

Young, David P. *Something of Great Constancy: The Art of "A Midsummer Night's Dream."* New Haven, Conn.: Yale Univ. Press, 1966. In this book-length study of the carefully constructed and interlocking harmonies of the play, Young examines Shakespeare's fusion of the courtly and popular material of his sources, his integration of stylistic and structural elements, and his manipulation of audience response. For Young, the transforming power of the imagination allows the play's apparently discordant elements to grow into "something of great constancy."

THE MERCHANT OF VENICE

Introduction

Although Shylock is the most prominent character in *The Merchant of Venice*, he takes part in neither the beginning nor the ending of the play. Nor is he the "merchant" of the title, but a moneylender whose usury is portrayed as the very opposite of true commerce. His vengeful struggle to obtain a pound of flesh from Antonio contrasts with the various romantic episodes woven together in this play: Bassanio's choosing of Portia by means of the caskets, Gratiano's wooing of Nerissa, Jessica's elopement with Lorenzo, Launcelot Gobbo's changing of masters, and the episode of the rings. In all these stories, friendship and love triumph over faithlessness and hatred. However much we may come to sympathize with Shylock's misfortunes and question the motives of his enemies, however much we are made uncomfortable by the potential insularity of a Venetian ethic that has no genuine place for non-Christians or cultural outsiders, Shylock remains essentially the villain of a love comedy. His remorseless pursuit of Antonio darkens the mood of the play, and his overthrow signals the providential triumph of love and friendship, even though that triumph is not without its undercurrent of wry melancholy. Before we examine the undoubted ironies of his situation more closely, we need to establish the structural context of this love comedy as a whole.

Like many of Shakespeare's philosophical and festive comedies, *The Merchant of Venice* presents two contrasting worlds, one idealized and the other marked by conflict and anxiety. To an extent, these contrasting worlds can be identified with the locations of Belmont and Venice. Belmont, to which the various happy lovers and their friends eventually retire, is a place of magic and love. As its name implies, it is on a mountain, and it is reached by a journey across water. It is pure, serene, ethereal. As often happens in fairy stories, on this mountain dwells a princess who must be won by means of a riddling contest. We usually see Belmont at night. Music surrounds it, and women preside over it. Even its caskets, houses, and rings are essentially feminine symbols. Venice, on the other hand, is a place of bustle and economic competition, seen most characteristically in the heat of the day. It lies low and flat, at a point where rivers reach the sea. Men preside over its contentious marketplace and its haggling law courts. Actually, the opposition of Venice and Belmont is not quite so clear-cut: Venice contains much compassionate friendship, whereas Belmont is subject to the arbitrary command of Portia's dead father. (Portia somewhat resembles Jessica in being imprisoned by her father's will.) Even though Portia descends to Venice in the angelic role of mercy-giver, she also remains very human: sharp-tongued and even venomous in caricaturing her unwelcome wooers, crafty in her legal maneuvering, saucily prankish in her torturing of Bassanio about the rings. Nevertheless the polarity of two contrasting localities and two groups of characters is vividly real in this play.

The play's opening scene, from which Shylock is excluded, sets forth the interrelated themes of friendship, romantic love, and risk, or "hazard." The merchant of the title, Antonio, is the victim of a mysterious melancholy. He is wealthy enough and surrounded by friends, but something is missing from his life. He assures his solicitous companions that he has no financial worries, for he has been too careful to trust all his cargoes to one sea vessel. Antonio in fact has no idea why he is so sad. The question is haunting: what is the matter? Perhaps the answer is to be found in a paradox: those who strive to prosper in the world's terms are doomed to frustration, not because prosperity will necessarily elude them but because it will not satisfy the spirit. "You have too much respect upon the world," argues the carefree Gratiano. "They lose it that do buy it with much care" (1.1.74–75). Portia and Jessica too are at first afflicted by a melancholy that stems from the incompleteness of living isolated lives, with insufficient opportunities for love and sacrifice. They must learn, as Antonio learns with the help of his dear friend Bassanio, to seek happiness by daring to risk everything for friendship. Antonio's risk is most extreme: only when he has thrown away concern for his life can he discover what there is to live for.

At first, Bassanio's request for assistance seems just as materialistic as the worldliness from which Antonio suffers. Bassanio proposes to marry a rich young lady, Portia, in order to recoup his fortune lost through prodigality, and he needs money from Antonio so that he may woo Portia in proper fashion. She is "richly left," the heiress of a dead father, a golden fleece for whom this new Jason will make a quest. Bassanio's adventure is partly commercial. Yet his pilgrimage for Portia is magnanimous as well. The occasional modern practice of playing Bassanio and Portia as cynical antiheroes of a "black" comedy points up the problematic character of their materialism and calculation, but it inevitably distorts the play. Bassanio has lost his previous fortune through the amiable faults of reckless generosity and a lack of concern for financial prudence. The money he must now borrow, and the fortune he hopes to acquire, are to him no more than a means to carefree happiness. Although Portia's rich dowry is a strong consideration, he describes her also as "fair, and fairer than that word, / Of wondrous virtues" (1.1.162–163). Moreover, he enjoys the element of risk in wooing her. It is like shooting a second arrow in order to recover one that has been lost—double or nothing. This gamble, or "hazard," involves risk for Antonio as well as for Bassanio, and ultimately brings a double reward to them both, spiritual as well as financial. Unless one recognizes these aspects of Bassanio's quest, as well as the clear fairy-tale quality with which Shakespeare deliberately invests this part of the plot, one cannot properly assess Bassanio's role in this romantic comedy.

Bassanio's quest for Portia can in fact never succeed until he disavows the very financial considerations that brought him to Belmont in the first place. This is the paradox of the riddle of the three caskets, an ancient parable stressing the need for choosing by true substance rather than by outward show. To choose "what many men desire," as the Prince of Morocco does, is to pin one's hopes on worldly wealth; to believe that one "deserves" good fortune, as the Prince of Aragon does, is to reveal a fatal pride in one's own merit. Bassanio perceives that in order to win true love he must "give and hazard all he hath." He is not "deceived with ornament" (3.2.74). Just as Antonio must risk all for friendship, and just as Bassanio himself must later be willing to risk losing Portia for the higher cause of true friendship (in the episode of the rings), Bassanio must renounce worldly ambition and beauty before he can be rewarded with success. Paradoxically, only those who learn

to subdue such worldly desires may then legitimately enjoy
the world's pleasures. Only they have acknowledged the hi-
erarchical subservience of the flesh to the spirit. These are
the philosophical truisms of Renaissance Neoplatonism,
depicting love as a chain or ladder from the basest carnality
to the supreme love of God for man. On this ladder, perfect
friendship and spiritual union are more sublimely Godlike
than sexual fulfillment. This idealism may seem a strange
doctrine for Bassanio the fortune hunter, but actually its
conventional wisdom simply confirms his role as romantic
hero. He and Portia are not denied worldly happiness or
erotic pleasure; they are merely asked to give first thought
to their Christian duty in marriage. The essentially Christian paradox of losing the world in order to gain the world
lies at the center of their love relationship. This paradox il-
luminates not only the casket episode but the struggle for
the pound of flesh, the elopement of Jessica, the ring episode, and even the comic foolery of Launcelot Gobbo.

Shylock, in his quest for the pound of flesh, represents
a denial of all the paradoxical Christian truths just described. As a usurer he refuses to lend money interest-free
in the name of friendship. Instead of taking risks, he insists
on his bond. He spurns mercy and demands strict justice.
By calculating all his chances too craftily, he appears to win
at first but must eventually lose all. He has "too much respect upon the world" (1.1.74). His God is the Old Testament God of Moses, the God of wrath, the God of the Ten
Commandments with their forbidding emphasis on "Thou
shalt not." (This oversimplified contrast between Judaism
and Christianity was commonplace in Shakespeare's time.)
Shylock abhors stealing but admires equivocation as a
means of outmaneuvering a competitor; he approvingly
cites Jacob's ruse to deprive Laban of his sheep (1.3.69–88).
Any tactic is permissible so long as it falls within the realm
of legality and contract.

Shylock's ethical outlook, then, justifies both usury and
the old dispensation of the Jewish law. The two are philo-
sophically combined, just as usury and Judaism had become equated in the popular imagination of Renaissance
Europe. Even though lending at interest was becoming increasingly necessary and common, old prejudices against it

still persisted. Angry moralists pointed out that the New
Testament had condemned usury and that Aristotle had described money as barren. To breed money was therefore regarded as unnatural. Usury was considered sinful because
it did not involve the usual risks of commerce; the lender
was assured against loss of his principal by the posting of
collateral and, at the same time, was sure to earn a handsome interest. The usurer seemed to be getting something
for nothing. For these reasons usury was sometimes declared illegal. Its practitioners were viewed as corrupt and
grasping, hated as misers. In some European countries,
Jews were permitted to practice this un-Christian living
(and permitted to do very little else) and then, hypocriti-
cally, were detested for performing un-Christian deeds.
Ironically, the moneylenders of England were Christians,
and few Jews were to be found in any professions. Nominally excluded since Edward I's reign, the Jews had returned in small numbers to London but did not practice
their Judaism openly. They attended Anglican services as
required by law and then worshiped in private, relatively
undisturbed by the authorities. Shylock is not based on observation from London life. He is derived from continental
tradition and reflects a widespread conviction that Jews
and usurers were alike in being non-Christian and sinister.

Shylock is unquestionably sinister. On the Elizabethan
stage the actor portraying him apparently wore a red beard,
as in traditional representations of Judas, and a hooked
nose. He bears an "ancient grudge" against Antonio simply
because Antonio is "a Christian." We recognize in Shylock
the archetype of the supposed Jew who wishes to kill a
Christian and obtain his flesh. In early medieval anti-
Semitic legends of this sort, the flesh thus obtained was
imagined to be eaten ritually during Passover. Because
some Jews had once persecuted Christ, all were unfairly
presumed to be implacable enemies of all Christians. These
anti-Semitic superstitions were likely to erupt into hysteria
at any time, as in 1594 when Dr. Roderigo Lopez, a Portuguese Jewish physician, was accused of having plotted
against the life of Queen Elizabeth and of Don Antonio, pre-
tender to the Portuguese throne. Marlowe's *The Jew of
Malta* was revived for this occasion, enjoying an unusually

successful run of fifteen performances, and scholars have
often wondered if Shakespeare's play was not written under the same impetus. On this score the evidence is incon-
clusive, and the play might have been written any time
between 1594 and 1598 (when it is mentioned by Francis
Meres in his *Palladis Tamia*), but in any case Shakespeare
has made no attempt to avoid the anti-Semitic nature of his
story.

To offset the portrayal of Jewish villainy, however, the
play also dramatizes the possibility of conversion to Christianity, suggesting that Judaism is more a matter of
benighted faith than of ethnic origin. Converted Jews were
not new on the stage: they had appeared in medieval cycle
drama, in the Croxton *Play of the Sacrament* (late fifteenth
century), and more recently in *The Jew of Malta*, in which
Barabas's daughter Abigail falls in love with a Christian
and eventually becomes a nun. Shylock's daughter Jessica
similarly embraces Christianity as Lorenzo's wife and is received into the happy comradeship of Belmont. Shylock is
forced to accept Christianity, presumably for the benefit of
his eternal soul. Earlier in the play, Antonio repeatedly indicates his willingness to befriend Shylock if the latter will
only give up usury, and is even cautiously hopeful when
Shylock offers him an interest-free loan: "The Hebrew will
turn Christian; he grows kind" (1.3.177). To be sure, Antonio's denunciation of Shylock's usurious Judaism has been
vehement and personal; we learn that he has spat on Shylock's gaberdine and kicked him as one would kick a dog.
This violent disapproval offers no opportunity for the toler-
ation of cultural and religious differences that we expect
today from persons of good will, but at least Antonio is prepared to accept Shylock if Shylock will embrace the Christian faith and its ethical responsibilities. Whether the play
itself endorses Antonio's Christian point of view as norma-
tive, or insists on a darker reading by making us uneasy
with intolerance, is a matter of unceasing critical debate.
Quite possibly, the play's power to disturb emanates at
least in part from the dramatic conflict of irreconcilable
sets of values.

To Antonio, then, as well as to other Venetians, true Christianity is both an absolute good from which no deviation is
possible without evil, and a state of faith to which aliens

may turn by abjuring the benighted creeds of their ancestors. By this token, the Prince of Morocco is condemned to failure in his quest for Portia not so much because he is black as because he is an infidel, one who worships "blind fortune" and therefore chooses a worldly rather than a spiritual reward. Although Portia pertly dismisses him with "Let all of his complexion choose me so" (2.7.79), she professes earlier to find him handsome and agrees that he should not be judged by his complexion (2.1.13–22). Unless she is merely being hypocritical, she means by her later remark that black-skinned men are generally infidels, just as Jews are as a group non-Christian. Such pejorative thinking about persons as types is no doubt distressing and suggests at least to a modern audience the cultural limitation of Portia's view, but in any case it shows her to be no less well-disposed toward blacks than toward others who are also alien. She rejects the Prince of Aragon because he too lacks proper faith, though nominally a Christian. All human beings, therefore, may aspire to truly virtuous conduct, and those who choose virtue are equally blessed; but the terms of defining that ideal are essentially Christian. Jews and blacks may rise spiritually only by abandoning their pagan creeds for the new dispensation of charity and forgiveness.

The superiority of Christian teaching to the older Jewish dispensation was of course a widely accepted notion of Shakespeare's time. After all, these were the years when men fought and died to maintain their religious beliefs. Today the notion of a single true church is less widely held, and we have difficulty understanding why anyone would wish to force conversion on Shylock. Modern productions find it tempting to portray Shylock as a victim of bigotry, and to put great stress on his heartrending assertions of his humanity: "Hath not a Jew eyes? . . . If you prick us, do we not bleed?" (3.1.55–61). Shylock does indeed suffer from his enemies, and his sufferings add a tortured complexity to this play—even, one suspects, for an Elizabethan audience. Those who profess Christianity must surely examine their own motives and conduct. Is it right to steal treasure from Shylock's house along with his eloped daughter? Is it considerate of Jessica and Lorenzo to squander Shylock's turquoise ring, the gift of his wife, Leah, on a monkey? Does Shylock's vengeful insistence on law justify the quibbling countermeasures devised by Portia even as she piously declaims about mercy? Do Shylock's misfortunes deserve the mirthful parodies of Solanio ("My daughter! O my ducats!") or the hostile jeering of Gratiano at the conclusion of the trial? Because he stands outside Christian faith, Shylock can provide a perspective whereby we see the hypocrisies of those who profess a higher ethical code. Nevertheless, Shylock's compulsive desire for vengeance according to an Old Testament code of an eye for an eye cannot be justified by the wrongdoings of any particular Christian. Such deeds condemn the doer rather than undermine the Christian standards of true virtue as ideally expressed. Shakespeare humanizes Shylock by portraying him as a believable and sensitive man, and shows much that is to be regretted in Shylock's Christian antagonists, but he also allows Shylock to place himself in the wrong by his refusal to forgive his enemies.

Shylock thus loses everything through his effort to win everything on his own terms. His daughter, Jessica, by her elopement, follows an opposite course. She characterizes her father's home as "hell," and she resents being locked up behind closed windows. Shylock detests music and the sounds of merriment; Jessica's new life in Belmont is immersed in music. He is old, suspicious, miserly; she is young, loving, adventurous. Most important, she seems to be at least part Christian when we first see her. As Launcelot jests half in earnest, "If a Christian did not play the knave and get thee, I am much deceived" (2.3.11–12). Her removal from Shylock's house involves theft, and her running from Venice is, she confesses, an "unthrift love." Paradoxically, however, she sees this recklessness as of more blessed effect than her father's legalistic caution. As she says, "I shall be saved by my husband. He hath made me a Christian" (3.5.17–18).

Launcelot Gobbo's clowning offers a similarly paradoxical comment on the tragedy of Shylock. Launcelot's debate with himself about whether or not to leave Shylock's service is put in terms of a soul struggle between his conscience and the devil (2.2.1–29). Conscience bids him stay, for service is a debt, a bond, an obligation, whereas abandonment of one's indenture is a kind of rebellion or stealing away. Yet Shylock's house is "hell" to Launcelot as to Jessica. Comparing his new master with his old, Launcelot observes to Bassanio, "you have the grace of God, sir, and he hath enough" (142–143). Service with Bassanio involves imprudent risks, since Bassanio is a spendthrift. The miserly Shylock rejoices to see the ever hungry Launcelot, this "huge feeder," wasting the substance of a hated Christian. Once again, however, Shylock will lose everything in his grasping quest for security. Another spiritual renewal occurs when Launcelot encounters his old and nearly blind father (2.2). In a scene echoing the biblical stories of the Prodigal Son and of Jacob and Esau, Launcelot teases the old man with false rumors of Launcelot's own death in order to make their reunion seem all the more unexpected and precious. The illusion of loss gives way to joy: Launcelot is, in language adapted from the liturgy, "your boy that was, your son that is, your child that shall be" (81–82).

In the episode of the rings we encounter a final playful variation on the paradox of winning through losing. Portia and Nerissa cleverly present their new husbands with a cruel choice: disguised as a doctor of laws and his clerk, who have just saved the life of Antonio from Shylock's wrath, the two wives ask nothing more for their services than the rings they see on the fingers of Bassanio and Gratiano. The two husbands, who have vowed never to part with these wedding rings, must therefore choose between love and friendship. The superior claim of friendship is clear, no matter what the cost, and Portia knows well enough that Bassanio's obedience to this Neoplatonic ideal is an essential part of his virtue. Just as he previously renounced beauty and riches before he could deserve Portia, he must now risk losing her for friendship's sake. The testing of the husbands' constancy does border at times on gratuitous harshness and exercise of power, for it deals with the oldest of masculine nightmares, cuckoldry. Wives are not without weapons in the struggle for control in marriage, and Portia and Nerissa enjoy trapping their new husbands in a no-win situation. Still, the threat is easily resolved by the dispelling of farcically mistaken identities. The young men have been tricked into bestowing their rings on their wives for a second time in the name of perfect friendship, thereby confirming a relationship that is both Platonic and fleshly. As Gratiano bawdily points out in the play's last line, the ring is both a spiritual and a sexual symbol of marriage. The resolution of this illusory quarrel also brings to an end the merry battle of the sexes between wives and husbands. Having hinted at the sorts of misunderstandings that afflict even the best of human relationships, and having proved themselves wittily able to torture and deceive their husbands, Portia and Nerissa submit at last to the authority of Bassanio and Gratiano.

All appears to be in harmony in Belmont. The disorders of Venice have been left far behind, however imperfectly they may have been resolved. Jessica and Lorenzo contrast their present happiness with the sufferings of less fortunate lovers of long ago: Troilus and Cressida, Pyramus and Thisbe, Aeneas and Dido, Jason and Medea. The tranquil joy found in Belmont is attuned to the music of the spheres, the singing of the "young-eyed cherubins" (5.1.62), although with a proper Christian humility the lovers also realize that the harmony of immortal souls is infinitely beyond their comprehension. Bound in by the grossness of the flesh, "this muddy vesture of decay" (5.1.64), they can only reach toward the bliss of eternity through music and the perfect friendship of true love. Even in their final joy, accordingly, the lovers find an incompleteness that lends a wistful and slightly melancholy reflective tone to the play's ending; but this Christian sense of the unavoidable incompleteness of all human life is of a very different order from that earlier melancholy of isolation and lack of commitment experienced by Portia, Jessica, Antonio, and others.

The Merchant of Venice
in Performance

"Shylock is a bloody-minded monster," confided Henry Irving in 1879, "but you mustn't play him so, if you wish to succeed; you must get some sympathy with him." The paradox that Irving described is central to the history of *The Merchant of Venice* in performance. Shylock is the play's villain, but he is also a towering presence onstage. Actors who have undertaken the role of Shylock have seldom been content (since the early eighteenth century, at any rate) to see him as simply a villain to be jeered at and cast out; instead, they have been drawn toward a tragic interpretation, sometimes so much so that the rest of the play has suffered.

In the first century and a half of its stage history, *The Merchant of Venice* was not often staged at all, possibly because audiences were not yet ready for a sympathetic Shylock. Shakespeare's acting company, the Lord Chamberlain's men, performed the play "divers times" before 1600 and (now called the King's men) twice at court in February of 1605, and they probably played it in a comic vein of acting (with Richard Burbage as Shylock in a red wig, according to a doubtful tradition), though one would like to think that the original performances also found room for a complex and even troubled response. For a long while thereafter, the play virtually disappeared from the stage. Thomas Betterton took the role not of Shylock but of Bassanio in an adaptation called *The Jew of Venice*, by George Granville, Lord Lansdowne, at the theater in Lincoln's Inn Fields, London, in 1701. Despite its title, this heavily rearranged version reduced the importance of Shylock in order both to ennoble the role of Bassanio and to provide the kind of masquelike spectacle demanded by Restoration audiences. The play opens on a banquet given by Bassanio, at which Antonio proposes a toast to eternal friendship; Bassanio, one to love; Gratiano, to women; and Shylock, sitting apart, to money. The banquet concludes with a long masque of Peleus and Thetis. In an added prison scene, Shylock protests to Antonio that he will have his bond. During the trial scene, Gratiano is given a number of interpolated lines to augment the comedy of his attack on Shylock. Shylock's rage against his daughter's elopement is toned down, and he is not forced to convert to Christianity. The Gobbos have disappeared. Thomas Doggett, the actor who played Shylock, was renowned as a comic actor and may have modeled his performance on disreputable moneylenders of his own day. Granville's version persisted well into the eighteenth century, though sometimes without the masque.

Charles Macklin not only restored Shakespeare's play in 1741 at the Theatre Royal, Drury Lane, reinstating the Gobbos, Morocco, and Aragon, but brought a passionate intensity to the role of Shylock that did much to establish the play as the moneylender's. Tubal also was returned, to heighten the effect of Shylock's scenes of outrage. A contemporary viewer reported that Shylock's calamities made "some tender impression on the audience," even though Shylock was at other times malevolent, cunning, and ferocious. He was, in other words, a complex figure, no longer a low comedy part as in Doggett's interpretation. Later eighteenth-century productions persisted in supplying various distractions—Morocco and Aragon were once again cut from the play, songs were supplied for Portia, Jessica, and Lorenzo by Thomas Arne and others, the casket scene was curtailed, and Kitty Clive amused audiences in her role of Portia by copying the mannerisms of certain well-known lawyers of the day—but the part of Shylock, even if not always conceived in a tragic vein, had proved a triumph for Macklin and was soon coveted by the leading actors of the eighteenth and nineteenth centuries.

George Frederick Cooke played Shylock in London first in 1800 and then, memorably, in 1803–1804, supported by John Philip Kemble, as Antonio, and Sarah Siddons, as Portia. Cooke's Shylock was, according to critic William Hazlitt, "bent with age and ugly with mental deformity, grinning with deadly malice, with the venom of his heart congealed in the expression of his countenance, sullen, morose, gloomy, inflexible." One version of the play, often performed during these years, featured an ending written by the Reverend Richard Valpy, with no fifth act at all but instead a recognition scene between Portia and Bassanio at the end of the trial; the play thus ended with the departure of its central figure, Shylock. Edmund Kean, at Drury Lane in 1814, the first actor to wear a black wig instead of the red wig of the stereotypical stage Jew, depicted Shylock with such scorn and energy that, to William Hazlitt at least, the Christians in the play were made to appear hypocrites by comparison. Romantic sympathies were turning in this direction, in any case; the older comedy of revenge and savagery seemed out of keeping with the play's love comedy and talk of mercy.

Victorian audiences were stirred not only by a sympathetic Shylock but by handsome sets calculated to enhance a mood of poetry, music, and romance. In 1841 at Drury Lane, William Charles Macready provided onstage a number of realistic scenes from Venice, including the cathedral and square of St. Mark's, Shylock's house facing on a canal with a distant view of the campanile, a court of justice reminiscent of the Roman Senate (as it had appeared before in Macready's revival of *Coriolanus*), and, most impressive of all, a moonlit garden in Act 5 that sparkled with soft light and melted away into poetic indistinctness toward the back of the set. Contemporary paintings of Act 5, such as those in John Boydell's Shakespeare gallery of art in Pall Mall, convey the kind of magical effect aimed at by Macready. At the Princess's Theatre in 1858 Charles Kean also began his production in St. Mark's Square, with milling crowds of noblemen and citizens, foreign visitors and flower girls, and the Doge in procession, all before the dialogue had begun. Edwin Booth's production of the play at the Winter Garden Theatre in New York in 1867 had magnificent scenery copied by Henry Hilliard and Charles Witham from famous paintings of well-known Venetian locales. In 1875 Sir Squire and Lady Bancroft, after a trip to Venice with their scene painter to select the sets, produced *The Merchant of Venice* at the Prince of Wales Theatre in Tottenham Court Road; because they could allow only one set to each act in their small theater, the play had to be rearranged considerably. The first tableau was located "under the arches of the Doge's palace," with a lovely view of the Church of Santa Maria della Salute. Merchants, sailors, beggars, and Jews passed and repassed in pantomimic action.

Henry Irving's lavish production at the Lyceum Theatre, London, in 1879 was thus only one, though perhaps the most famous, among a series of splendid visual evocations of Venice and Belmont. Continuing the tradition, begun by Charles Kean, of a usable bridge over the canals in the stage set, Irving employed this location for a memorable staging effect. He placed the elopement of Jessica in a season of carnival celebration: masked crowds walked about, gondolas arrived at waterside, merrymakers raced across the bridge. Shylock's return across the bridge alone to his dark and deserted house introduced a moment of supreme pathos that audiences, and a number of subsequent Shylocks, were quite unable to resist. At the trial scene a crowd of Jews followed the fate of Shylock with avid interest, listening intently to Portia's legal arguments and despairing of the outcome. Irving played Shylock as an aristocrat of his ancient religion, looking down with calm pride on the Europeans and then lashing out in rage and scorn. The nobility added to the pathos. Herbert Beerbohm Tree, in 1908, continued the tradition, and there have been numerous sympathetic Shylocks since.

More recent productions have tended to use sympathy for Shylock as a way of emphasizing the problematic morality of the entire play. George C. Scott, in Joseph Papp's production for the New York Shakespeare Festival in 1962, portrayed Shylock as neither a villain nor a victim but as a desperately defensive, paranoid, and persecuted man. In England, Laurence Olivier, in Jonathan Miller's National Theatre production of 1970 (subsequently televised), expressed through Shylock's long cry of pain as he left the courtroom the anguish of a bereaved and wronged man. The production, set in nineteenth-century Venice, took an unromantic look at the hypocrisy of the Christian community in that city, at its closed and bigoted world of privilege, at its complacent and mercantile ways. The playing of Jewish sacred music during the final scene reminded audiences that the feast of reconciliation at Belmont was achieved by excluding those who did not "belong."

A production at Stratford-upon-Avon in 1953 emphasized the friendship of Antonio and Bassanio in contrast to the solitariness of Michael Redgrave's wily and heavily accented Shylock, and other productions, such as Michael Kahn's at Stratford, Connecticut, in 1967, have gone so far as to see a homoerotic attraction between the Christian friends of this play.

Portia, in modern times, not infrequently becomes something of a calculating vixen, catty in her evaluation of her masculine wooers, insincere in her profession of hospitality to Morocco, ready to cheat by giving unfair hints to Bassanio in the casket scene (as in Theodore Komisarjevsky's production at Stratford-upon-Avon in 1932, in which Portia, singing "Tell me where is fancy bred," heavily stressed the words rhyming with "lead"), and adept at tormenting him in the episode of the rings. Jessica and Lorenzo can be portrayed as thoughtless in their frivolous dissipating of Shylock's wealth and keepsakes. As productions have returned to a full text, the earlier dominance of Shylock has made way for a ceaseless exploration of the play's provocative ambivalence, as, for example, in John Barton's 1978 production at London's Other Place, which sought to make both Shylock and the mercantile world of the Christians psychologically credible. *The Merchant of Venice* has increasingly been seen as one of Shakespeare's problem plays.

Shakespeare's original production had no scenery and so had to rely on costumed actors and on Shakespeare's language to conjure up a sense of place. The contrasts and similarities between Venice and Belmont built into the text must have called for an alternating rhythm of staging effects in the movement back and forth from largely male scenes of business and legal disputation in Venice to scenes of feminine wit, badinage, and the unveiling of caskets in Belmont. Shylock's house was visually invoked in the Elizabethan theater by Jessica's appearance "above" in the gallery, as at Shylock's window; from this vantage she could throw down money to the maskers below in the street before exiting above and then joining them on the main stage for the elopement (2.6). The trial scene (4.1) was visualized presumably by means of robed justices in their seats, by Portia in disguise as a doctor of laws, by Shylock with his bond and his knife, and by an atmosphere of confrontation. The actors established the mood of Belmont in Act 5 chiefly by their talk about the starry night and by their recollection of old tales about the tribulations of love. Twentieth-century theater has attempted, by and large, to find new theatrical ways of suggesting these effects in place of the heavy representational sets of the nineteenth century, recognizing that theater should not mechanically replicate what Shakespeare calls for in the image-laden language of his characters. Above all, staging today seems intent on capturing the dark ambivalences that are so integrally a part of the play's stage history.

THE MERCHANT
OF VENICE

[*Dramatis Personae*

THE DUKE OF VENICE
ANTONIO, *a merchant of Venice*
BASSANIO, *his friend, suitor to Portia*
GRATIANO, *a follower of Bassanio, in love with Nerissa*
SOLANIO,
SALERIO, } *friends to Antonio and Bassanio*
LORENZO, *in love with Jessica*
LEONARDO, *servant to Bassanio*

PORTIA, *a rich heiress of Belmont*
NERISSA, *her waiting-gentlewoman*
BALTHASAR, *servant to Portia*
STEPHANO, *servant to Portia*
THE PRINCE OF MOROCCO, *suitor to Portia*
THE PRINCE OF ARAGON, *suitor to Portia*
A MESSENGER *to Portia*

SHYLOCK, *a rich Jew*
JESSICA, *his daughter*
TUBAL, *a Jew, Shylock's friend*
LAUNCELOT GOBBO, *a clown, servant to Shylock and then to Bassanio*
OLD GOBBO, *Launcelot's father*

Magnificoes of Venice, Officers of the Court of Justice, Jailor, Servants to Portia, and other Attendants

SCENE: *Partly at Venice and partly at Belmont, the seat of Portia*]

1.1 *Enter Antonio, Salerio, and Solanio.*

ANTONIO

In sooth, I know not why I am so sad.
It wearies me, you say it wearies you;
But how I caught it, found it, or came by it,
What stuff 'tis made of, whereof it is born,
I am to learn;   5
And such a want-wit sadness makes of me   6
That I have much ado to know myself.

SALERIO

Your mind is tossing on the ocean,
There where your argosies with portly sail,   9
Like signors and rich burghers on the flood,   10
Or as it were the pageants of the sea,   11
Do overpeer the petty traffickers   12
That curtsy to them, do them reverence   13
As they fly by them with their woven wings.

SOLANIO

Believe me, sir, had I such venture forth,   15
The better part of my affections would
Be with my hopes abroad. I should be still   17
Plucking the grass to know where sits the wind,
Peering in maps for ports and piers and roads;   19
And every object that might make me fear
Misfortune to my ventures, out of doubt
Would make me sad.

SALERIO   My wind cooling my broth
Would blow me to an ague when I thought
What harm a wind too great might do at sea.
I should not see the sandy hourglass run
But I should think of shallows and of flats,   26
And see my wealthy *Andrew* docked in sand,   27

1.1. Location: A street in Venice.
5 am to learn have yet to learn   **6 want-wit** one lacking in good sense
9 argosies large merchant ships. (So named from *Ragusa*, the modern
city of Dubrovnik.)   **portly** majestic   **10 signors** gentlemen
11 pageants mobile stages used in plays or processions   **12 overpeer**
look down upon   **13 curtsy** i.e., bob up and down   **15 venture forth**
investment risked   **17 still** continually   **19 roads** anchorages, open
harbors   **26 But** without it happening that.   **flats** shoals   **27 Andrew**
name of a ship (perhaps after the *St. Andrew,* a Spanish galleon captured at Cadiz in 1596)

Vailing her high-top lower than her ribs   28
To kiss her burial. Should I go to church   29
And see the holy edifice of stone,
And not bethink me straight of dangerous rocks,   31
Which touching but my gentle vessel's side
Would scatter all her spices on the stream,
Enrobe the roaring waters with my silks,
And, in a word, but even now worth this,   35
And now worth nothing? Shall I have the thought
To think on this, and shall I lack the thought
That such a thing bechanced would make me sad?   38
But tell not me; I know Antonio
Is sad to think upon his merchandise.

ANTONIO
Believe me, no. I thank my fortune for it,
My ventures are not in one bottom trusted,   42
Nor to one place; nor is my whole estate
Upon the fortune of this present year.   44
Therefore my merchandise makes me not sad.

SOLANIO
Why, then you are in love.

ANTONIO   Fie, fie!

SOLANIO
Not in love neither? Then let us say you are sad
Because you are not merry; and 'twere as easy
For you to laugh and leap, and say you are merry
Because you are not sad. Now, by two-headed Janus,   50
Nature hath framed strange fellows in her time:
Some that will evermore peep through their eyes
And laugh like parrots at a bagpiper,   53
And other of such vinegar aspect   54
That they'll not show their teeth in way of smile
Though Nestor swear the jest be laughable.   56

---

28 Vailing lowering (usually as a sign of submission).   **high-top** top-
mast   **29 burial** burial place   **31 bethink me straight** be put in mind
immediately   **35 this** i.e., all this concern   **38 bechanced** having happened   **42 bottom** ship's hold   **44 Upon . . . year** i.e., risked upon the
chance of the present   **50 two-headed Janus** a Roman god of all begin-
nings, represented by a figure with two faces   **53 at a bagpiper** i.e.,
even at a bagpiper, whose music was regarded as melancholic
54 vinegar sour, sullen   **56 Nestor** venerable senior officer in the *Iliad*,
noted for gravity

Enter Bassanio, Lorenzo, and Gratiano.

Here comes Bassanio, your most noble kinsman,
Gratiano, and Lorenzo. Fare ye well.
We leave you now with better company.

SALERIO
I would have stayed till I had made you merry,
If worthier friends had not prevented me.   61

ANTONIO
Your worth is very dear in my regard.
I take it your own business calls on you,
And you embrace th' occasion to depart.   64

SALERIO   Good morrow, my good lords.

BASSANIO
Good signors both, when shall we laugh? Say, when?   66
You grow exceeding strange. Must it be so?   67

SALERIO
We'll make our leisures to attend on yours.   68
                              Exeunt Salerio and Solanio.

LORENZO
My lord Bassanio, since you have found Antonio,
We two will leave you, but at dinnertime,
I pray you, have in mind where we must meet.

BASSANIO   I will not fail you.

GRATIANO
You look not well, Signor Antonio.
You have too much respect upon the world;   74
They lose it that do buy it with much care.
Believe me, you are marvelously changed.

ANTONIO
I hold the world but as the world, Gratiano,
A stage where every man must play a part,
And mine a sad one.

GRATIANO   Let me play the fool!
With mirth and laughter let old wrinkles come,
And let my liver rather heat with wine   81

61 prevented forestalled   **64 occasion** opportunity   **66 laugh** i.e., be
merry together   **67 strange** distant.   **Must it be so** must you go; or,
must you show reserve   **68 attend on** wait upon, i.e., suit   **74 respect
. . . world** concern for worldly affairs of business   **81 heat with wine**
(The liver was regarded as the seat of the passions and wine as an
agency for inflaming them.)

Than my heart cool with mortifying groans.   82
Why should a man whose blood is warm within
Sit like his grandsire cut in alabaster?   84
Sleep when he wakes, and creep into the jaundice   85
By being peevish? I tell thee what, Antonio—
I love thee, and 'tis my love that speaks—
There are a sort of men whose visages
Do cream and mantle like a standing pond,   89
And do a willful stillness entertain   90
With purpose to be dressed in an opinion   91
Of wisdom, gravity, profound conceit,   92
As who should say, "I am Sir Oracle,   93
And when I ope my lips let no dog bark!"   94
O my Antonio, I do know of these
That therefore only are reputed wise
For saying nothing, when, I am very sure,
If they should speak, would almost damn those ears
Which, hearing them, would call their brothers fools.   99
I'll tell thee more of this another time.
But fish not with this melancholy bait   101
For this fool gudgeon, this opinion.   102
Come, good Lorenzo. Fare ye well awhile;
I'll end my exhortation after dinner.

LORENZO
Well, we will leave you then till dinnertime.
I must be one of these same dumb wise men,   106
For Gratiano never lets me speak.

GRATIANO
Well, keep me company but two years more,
Thou shalt not know the sound of thine own tongue.

82 mortifying deadly   **84 in alabaster** i.e., in a stone effigy upon a
tomb   **85 jaundice** (Regarded as arising from the effects of too much
choler or yellow bile, one of the four humors, in the blood.)   **89 cream
and mantle** become covered with scum, i.e., acquire a lifeless, stiff
expression.   **standing** stagnant   **90 And . . . entertain** and who maintain
or assume a self-imposed, obstinate silence   **91 opinion** reputation
92 profound conceit deep thought   **93 As . . . say** as if to say   **94 And
. . . bark** i.e., and I am worthy of great respect   **99 fools** (Cf. Matthew
5:22, in which anyone calling another fool is threatened with damnation.)   **101 melancholy bait** i.e., your own melancholy   **102 fool . . .
opinion** i.e., reputation, which is merely gained through others' credu-
lity. (*Gudgeon*, a small fish, was used to mean a gullible person.)
106 dumb mute, speechless

ANTONIO

    Fare you well; I'll grow a talker for this gear.   110

GRATIANO

    Thanks, i' faith, for silence is only commendable
    In a neat's tongue dried and a maid not vendible.   112

               Exeunt [*Gratiano and Lorenzo*].

ANTONIO   Is that anything now?   113

BASSANIO   Gratiano speaks an infinite deal of nothing,
more than any man in all Venice. His reasons are as
two grains of wheat hid in two bushels of chaff; you
shall seek all day ere you find them, and when you
have them they are not worth the search.

ANTONIO

    Well, tell me now what lady is the same   119
    To whom you swore a secret pilgrimage,
    That you today promised to tell me of.

BASSANIO

    'Tis not unknown to you, Antonio,
    How much I have disabled mine estate
    By something showing a more swelling port   124
    Than my faint means would grant continuance.   125
    Nor do I now make moan to be abridged   126
    From such a noble rate; but my chief care   127
    Is to come fairly off from the great debts   128
    Wherein my time, something too prodigal,
    Hath left me gaged. To you, Antonio,   130
    I owe the most, in money and in love,
    And from your love I have a warranty   132
    To unburden all my plots and purposes
    How to get clear of all the debts I owe.

ANTONIO

    I pray you, good Bassanio, let me know it;
    And if it stand, as you yourself still do,
    Within the eye of honor, be assured

---

110 for this gear as a result of this business, i.e., your talk   **112 neat's**
ox's.   **vendible** salable, i.e., in the marriage market   **113 Is . . . now** i.e.,
was all that talk about anything?   **119 the same** i.e., the one   **124 By
. . . port** by showing a somewhat more lavish style of living   **125 grant
continuance** allow to continue   **126–127 make . . . rate** complain at
being cut back from such a high style of living   **128 to . . . off** honorably to extricate myself   **130 gaged** pledged   **132 warranty** authoriza-
tion

My purse, my person, my extremest means,
Lie all unlocked to your occasions.

BASSANIO
In my schooldays, when I had lost one shaft,   140
I shot his fellow of the selfsame flight   141
The selfsame way with more advisèd watch   142
To find the other forth, and by adventuring both   143
I oft found both. I urge this childhood proof
Because what follows is pure innocence.   145
I owe you much, and, like a willful youth,
That which I owe is lost; but if you please
To shoot another arrow that self way   148
Which you did shoot the first, I do not doubt,
As I will watch the aim, or to find both   150
Or bring your latter hazard back again   151
And thankfully rest debtor for the first.

ANTONIO
You know me well, and herein spend but time   153
To wind about my love with circumstance;   154
And out of doubt you do me now more wrong   155
In making question of my uttermost   156
Than if you had made waste of all I have.
Then do but say to me what I should do
That in your knowledge may by me be done,
And I am prest unto it. Therefore speak.   160

BASSANIO
In Belmont is a lady richly left;   161
And she is fair and, fairer than that word,
Of wondrous virtues. Sometime from her eyes   163
I did receive fair speechless messages.
Her name is Portia, nothing undervalued   165
To Cato's daughter, Brutus' Portia.   166

---

140 shaft arrow   **141 his** its.   **selfsame flight** same kind and range
142 advisèd careful   **143 forth** out.   **adventuring** risking   **145 inno-**
cence ingenuousness, sincerity   **148 self** same   **150 or** either   **151 haz-**
ard that which was risked   **153 spend but time** only waste time   **154 To**
... circumstance i.e., in not asking plainly what you want. (*Circum-*
stance here means "circumlocution.")   **155 out of** beyond   **156 In ...**
uttermost in showing any doubt of my intention to do all I can
160 prest ready   **161 richly left** left a large fortune (by her father's
will)   **163 Sometime** once   **165–166 nothing undervalued To** of no less
worth than   **166 Portia** (The same Portia as in Shakespeare's *Julius
Caesar*.)

Nor is the wide world ignorant of her worth,
For the four winds blow in from every coast
Renownèd suitors, and her sunny locks
Hang on her temples like a golden fleece,
Which makes her seat of Belmont Colchis' strand,   171
And many Jasons come in quest of her.
O my Antonio, had I but the means
To hold a rival place with one of them,
I have a mind presages me such thrift   175
That I should questionless be fortunate.

ANTONIO
Thou know'st that all my fortunes are at sea;
Neither have I money nor commodity   178
To raise a present sum. Therefore go forth.
Try what my credit can in Venice do;
That shall be racked, even to the uttermost,   181
To furnish thee to Belmont, to fair Portia.
Go presently inquire, and so will I,   183
Where money is, and I no question make   184
To have it of my trust or for my sake.   *Exeunt.*   185

✦

1.2   *Enter Portia with her waiting-woman, Nerissa.*

PORTIA   By my troth, Nerissa, my little body is aweary
of this great world.
NERISSA   You would be, sweet madam, if your miseries
were in the same abundance as your good fortunes
are; and yet, for aught I see, they are as sick that surfeit   5
with too much as they that starve with nothing. It is
no mean happiness, therefore, to be seated in the   7
mean; superfluity comes sooner by white hairs, but   8
competency lives longer.   9

---

171 Colchis' (Jason adventured for the golden fleece in the land of
Colchis, on the Black Sea.) **strand** shore **175 presages** i.e., which
presages. **thrift** profit and good fortune **178 commodity** merchandise **181 racked** stretched **183 presently** immediately **184 no question make** have no doubt **185 of my trust** on the basis of my credit as
a merchant. **sake** i.e., personal sake

1.2. Location: Belmont. Portia's house.
5 surfeit overindulge **7-8 in the mean** having neither too much nor too
little **8 comes sooner by** acquires sooner **9 competency** modest means

PORTIA   Good sentences, and well pronounced.   10
NERISSA   They would be better if well followed.
PORTIA   If to do were as easy as to know what were
good to do, chapels had been churches and poor
men's cottages princes' palaces. It is a good divine that   14
follows his own instructions. I can easier teach twenty
what were good to be done than to be one of the
twenty to follow mine own teaching. The brain may
devise laws for the blood, but a hot temper leaps o'er   18
a cold decree—such a hare is madness the youth, to
skip o'er the meshes of good counsel the cripple. But   20
this reasoning is not in the fashion to choose me a   21
husband. O, me, the word "choose"! I may neither   22
choose who I would nor refuse who I dislike; so is the
will of a living daughter curbed by the will of a dead   24
father. Is it not hard, Nerissa, that I cannot choose one
nor refuse none?
NERISSA   Your father was ever virtuous, and holy men
at their death have good inspirations; therefore the
lottery that he hath devised in these three chests of
gold, silver, and lead, whereof who chooses his mean-   30
ing chooses you, will no doubt never be chosen by
any rightly but one who you shall rightly love. But
what warmth is there in your affection towards any of
these princely suitors that are already come?
PORTIA   I pray thee, overname them, and as thou nam-   35
est them I will describe them, and according to my
description level at my affection.   37
NERISSA   First, there is the Neapolitan prince.
PORTIA   Ay, that's a colt indeed, for he doth nothing but   39
talk of his horse, and he makes it a great appropriation   40
to his own good parts that he can shoe him him-   41

---

10 sentences maxims.   **pronounced** delivered   **14 divine** clergyman
18 blood (Thought of as a chief agent of the passions, which in turn
were regarded as the enemies of reason.)   **20 meshes** nets (used here for
hunting hares).   **good counsel the cripple** (Wisdom is portrayed as old
and no longer agile.)   **20–22 But . . . husband** but this talk is not the
way to help me choose a husband   **24 will . . . will** volition . . . testament   **30 who** whoever.   **his** i.e., the father's   **35 overname them** name
them over   **37 level** aim, guess   **39 colt** i.e., wanton and foolish young
man (with a punning appropriateness to his interest in horses)
40 appropriation addition   **41 good parts** accomplishments

self. I am much afeard my lady his mother played false
with a smith.

NERISSA Then is there the County Palatine.   44

PORTIA He doth nothing but frown, as who should say,   45
"An you will not have me, choose." He hears merry   46
tales and smiles not. I fear he will prove the weeping   47
philosopher when he grows old, being so full of un-   48
mannerly sadness in his youth. I had rather be married to a death's-head with a bone in his mouth than
to either of these. God defend me from these two!

NERISSA How say you by the French lord, Monsieur   52
Le Bon?

PORTIA God made him, and therefore let him pass for
a man. In truth, I know it is a sin to be a mocker, but
he! Why, he hath a horse better than the Neapolitan's,
a better bad habit of frowning than the Count Palatine; he is every man in no man. If a throstle sing, he   58
falls straight a-capering. He will fence with his own
shadow. If I should marry him, I should marry twenty
husbands. If he would despise me, I would forgive
him, for if he love me to madness, I shall never requite him.

NERISSA What say you, then, to Falconbridge, the
young baron of England?

PORTIA You know I say nothing to him, for he understands not me, nor I him. He hath neither Latin,
French, nor Italian, and you will come into the court
and swear that I have a poor pennyworth in the English. He is a proper man's picture, but alas, who can   70
converse with a dumb show? How oddly he is suited!   71
I think he bought his doublet in Italy, his round hose   72
in France, his bonnet in Germany, and his behavior   73
everywhere.

---

44 County count. **Palatine** one possessing royal privileges **45 who
should say** one might say **46 An** if. **choose** i.e., do as you please
47–48 weeping philosopher i.e., Heraclitus of Ephesus, a melancholic
and retiring philosopher of about 500 B.C., often contrasted with Demo-
critus, the "laughing philosopher" **52 by** about **58 throstle** thrush
70 He . . . picture i.e., he looks handsome **71 dumb show** panto-
mime. **suited** dressed **72 doublet** upper garment corresponding to a
jacket. **round hose** short, puffed-out breeches **73 bonnet** hat

NERISSA What think you of the Scottish lord, his
neighbor?

PORTIA That he hath a neighborly charity in him, for he
borrowed a box of the ear of the Englishman and swore
he would pay him again when he was able. I think the
Frenchman became his surety and sealed under for an- 80
other. 81

NERISSA How like you the young German, the Duke of
Saxony's nephew?

PORTIA Very vilely in the morning, when he is sober,
and most vilely in the afternoon, when he is drunk.
When he is best he is a little worse than a man, and
when he is worst he is little better than a beast. An
the worst fall that ever fell, I hope I shall make shift to 88
go without him.

NERISSA If he should offer to choose, and choose the
right casket, you should refuse to perform your father's
will if you should refuse to accept him.

PORTIA Therefore, for fear of the worst, I pray thee, set
a deep glass of Rhenish wine on the contrary casket, 94
for if the devil be within and that temptation without,
I know he will choose it. I will do anything, Nerissa,
ere I will be married to a sponge.

NERISSA You need not fear, lady, the having any of
these lords. They have acquainted me with their de-
terminations, which is indeed to return to their home
and to trouble you with no more suit, unless you may
be won by some other sort than your father's imposi- 102
tion depending on the caskets. 103

PORTIA If I live to be as old as Sibylla, I will die as chaste 104
as Diana, unless I be obtained by the manner of my
father's will. I am glad this parcel of wooers are so rea- 106
sonable, for there is not one among them but I dote on

80–81 became . . . another guaranteed the Scot's payment (of a box on
the ear) and put himself under obligation to give the Englishman yet
another on his own behalf. (An allusion to the age-old alliance of the
French and the Scots against the English.) **88 fall** befall. **make shift**
manage **94 Rhenish wine** a German white wine from the Rhine Valley. **contrary** i.e., wrong **102 sort** way, manner (with perhaps a suggestion too of "casting" or "drawing of lots") **102–103 imposition**
conditions imposed **104 Sibylla** the Cumaean Sibyl, to whom Apollo
gave as many years as there were grains in her handful of sand
106 parcel assembly, group

his very absence, and I pray God grant them a fair departure.

NERISSA Do you not remember, lady, in your father's time, a Venetian, a scholar and a soldier, that came hither in company of the Marquess of Montferrat?

PORTIA Yes, yes, it was Bassanio, as I think, so was he called.

NERISSA True, madam. He, of all the men that ever my foolish eyes looked upon, was the best deserving a fair lady.

PORTIA I remember him well, and I remember him worthy of thy praise.

Enter a Servingman.

How now, what news?

SERVINGMAN The four strangers seek for you, madam, 121
to take their leave; and there is a forerunner come from 122
a fifth, the Prince of Morocco, who brings word the Prince his master will be here tonight.

PORTIA If I could bid the fifth welcome with so good heart as I can bid the other four farewell, I should be glad of his approach. If he have the condition of a saint 127
and the complexion of a devil, I had rather he should 128
shrive me than wive me.   129

Come, Nerissa. [*To Servingman.*] Sirrah, go before.   130
Whiles we shut the gate upon one wooer, another
   knocks at the door.   *Exeunt.*

❖

1.3 *Enter Bassanio with Shylock the Jew.*

SHYLOCK Three thousand ducats, well.   1
BASSANIO Ay, sir, for three months.
SHYLOCK For three months, well.

121 four (Nerissa actually names six suitors; possibly a sign of revision.) **122 forerunner** herald   **127 condition** disposition, character   **128 complexion of a devil** (Devils were thought to be black; but *complexion* can also mean "temperament," "disposition.")   **129 shrive me** act as my confessor   **130 Sirrah** (Form of address to social inferior.)

1.3. Location: Venice. A public place.
1 ducats gold coins

BASSANIO For the which, as I told you, Antonio shall be
bound.

SHYLOCK Antonio shall become bound, well.

BASSANIO May you stead me? Will you pleasure me? 7
Shall I know your answer?

SHYLOCK Three thousand ducats for three months and
Antonio bound.

BASSANIO Your answer to that.

SHYLOCK Antonio is a good man.   12

BASSANIO Have you heard any imputation to the contrary?

SHYLOCK Ho, no, no, no, no! My meaning in saying he
is a good man is to have you understand me that he is
sufficient. Yet his means are in supposition: he hath an 17
argosy bound to Tripolis, another to the Indies; I understand, moreover, upon the Rialto, he hath a 19
third at Mexico, a fourth for England, and other ventures he hath squandered abroad. But ships are but 21
boards, sailors but men; there be land rats and water
rats, water thieves and land thieves—I mean pirates—
and then there is the peril of waters, winds, and rocks.
The man is, notwithstanding, sufficient. Three thousand ducats; I think I may take his bond.

BASSANIO Be assured you may.   27

SHYLOCK I will be assured I may; and that I may be 28
assured, I will bethink me. May I speak with Antonio?

BASSANIO If it please you to dine with us.

SHYLOCK Yes, to smell pork, to eat of the habitation
which your prophet the Nazarite conjured the devil 32
into. I will buy with you, sell with you, talk with you,
walk with you, and so following, but I will not eat
with you, drink with you, nor pray with you. What
news on the Rialto? Who is he comes here?

---

7 stead supply, assist   **12 good** (Shylock means "solvent," a good credit
risk; Bassanio interprets in the moral sense.)   **17 sufficient** i.e., a good
security.   **in supposition** doubtful, uncertain   **19 Rialto** the merchants'
exchange in Venice and the center of commercial activity   **21 squandered** scattered, spread   **27, 28 assured** (Bassanio means that
Shylock may trust Antonio, whereas Shylock means that he will provide
legal assurances.)   **32 Nazarite** Nazarene. (For the reference to Christ's
casting evil spirits into a herd of swine, see Matthew 8:30–32, Mark
5:1–13, and Luke 8:32–33.)

Enter Antonio.

BASSANIO This is Signor Antonio.

SHYLOCK [*Aside*]
How like a fawning publican he looks!   38
I hate him for he is a Christian,   39
But more for that in low simplicity
He lends out money gratis and brings down
The rate of usance here with us in Venice.   42
If I can catch him once upon the hip,   43
I will feed fat the ancient grudge I bear him.
He hates our sacred nation, and he rails,
Even there where merchants most do congregate,
On me, my bargains, and my well-won thrift,   47
Which he calls interest. Cursèd be my tribe
If I forgive him!

BASSANIO   Shylock, do you hear?

SHYLOCK
I am debating of my present store,   50
And, by the near guess of my memory,
I cannot instantly raise up the gross   52
Of full three thousand ducats. What of that?
Tubal, a wealthy Hebrew of my tribe,
Will furnish me. But soft, how many months   55
Do you desire? [*To Antonio.*] Rest you fair, good signor!
Your worship was the last man in our mouths.   57

ANTONIO
Shylock, albeit I neither lend nor borrow
By taking nor by giving of excess,   59
Yet, to supply the ripe wants of my friend,   60
I'll break a custom. [*To Bassanio.*] Is he yet possessed   61
How much ye would?

SHYLOCK Ay, ay, three thousand ducats.

ANTONIO And for three months.

SHYLOCK
I had forgot—three months, you told me so.

38 publican Roman tax gatherer (a term of opprobrium); or, innkeeper
39 for because **42 usance** usury, interest **43 upon the hip** i.e., at my
mercy. (A figure of speech from wrestling; see Genesis 32:24–29.)
47 thrift thriving **50 store** supply (of money) **52 gross** total **55 soft**
i.e., wait a minute **57 Your . . . mouths** i.e., we were just speaking of
you **59 excess** interest **60 ripe wants** pressing needs **61 possessed**
informed

Well then, your bond. And let me see—but hear you,
Methought you said you neither lend nor borrow
Upon advantage.

ANTONIO   I do never use it.   68

SHYLOCK
When Jacob grazed his uncle Laban's sheep—   69
This Jacob from our holy Abram was,   70
As his wise mother wrought in his behalf,
The third possessor; ay, he was the third—   72

ANTONIO
And what of him? Did he take interest?

SHYLOCK
No, not take interest, not as you would say
Directly interest. Mark what Jacob did.
When Laban and himself were compromised   76
That all the eanlings which were streaked and pied   77
Should fall as Jacob's hire, the ewes, being rank,   78
In end of autumn turnèd to the rams,
And when the work of generation was
Between these woolly breeders in the act,
The skillful shepherd peeled me certain wands,   82
And in the doing of the deed of kind   83
He stuck them up before the fulsome ewes,
Who then conceiving did in eaning time   85
Fall parti-colored lambs, and those were Jacob's.   86
This was a way to thrive, and he was blest;
And thrift is blessing, if men steal it not.

ANTONIO
This was a venture, sir, that Jacob served for,   89
A thing not in his power to bring to pass,
But swayed and fashioned by the hand of heaven.
Was this inserted to make interest good?   92
Or is your gold and silver ewes and rams?

---

68 advantage interest   **69 Jacob** (See Genesis 27, 30:25–43.)   **70 Abram**
Abraham   **72 third** i.e., after Abraham and Isaac.   **possessor** i.e., of the
birthright of which, with the help of Rebecca, he was able to cheat
Esau, his elder brother   **76 compromised** agreed   **77 eanlings** young
lambs or kids.   **pied** spotted   **78 hire** wages, share.   **rank** in heat
82 me (*Me* is used colloquially.)   **83 deed of kind** i.e., copulation
85 eaning lambing   **86 Fall** give birth to   **89 venture . . . for** uncertain
commercial venture on which Jacob risked his wages   **92 inserted . . .**
good brought in to justify the practice of usury

SHYLOCK
  I cannot tell; I make it breed as fast.
  But note me, signor—
ANTONIO   Mark you this, Bassanio,
  The devil can cite Scripture for his purpose.   96
  An evil soul producing holy witness
  Is like a villain with a smiling cheek,
  A goodly apple rotten at the heart.
  O, what a goodly outside falsehood hath!
SHYLOCK
  Three thousand ducats. 'Tis a good round sum.
  Three months from twelve, then let me see, the rate—
ANTONIO
  Well, Shylock, shall we be beholding to you?   103
SHYLOCK
  Signor Antonio, many a time and oft
  In the Rialto you have rated me   105
  About my moneys and my usances.
  Still have I borne it with a patient shrug,
  For sufferance is the badge of all our tribe.   108
  You call me misbeliever, cutthroat dog,
  And spit upon my Jewish gaberdine,   110
  And all for use of that which is mine own.
  Well then, it now appears you need my help.
  Go to, then. You come to me and you say,   113
  "Shylock, we would have moneys"—you say so,
  You, that did void your rheum upon my beard   115
  And foot me as you spurn a stranger cur   116
  Over your threshold! Moneys is your suit.
  What should I say to you? Should I not say,
  "Hath a dog money? Is it possible
  A cur can lend three thousand ducats?" Or
  Shall I bend low and in a bondman's key,   121
  With bated breath and whispering humbleness,   122
  Say this:
  "Fair sir, you spit on me on Wednesday last,
  You spurned me such a day, another time

96 devil . . . Scripture (See Matthew 4:6.)   **103 beholding** beholden,
indebted   **105 rated** berated, rebuked   **108 sufferance** endurance
110 gaberdine loose upper garment like a cape or mantle   **113 Go to**
(An exclamation of impatience or annoyance.)   **115 rheum** spittle
116 spurn kick   **121 bondman's** serf's   **122 bated** subdued, reduced

You called me dog, and for these courtesies
I'll lend you thus much moneys"?

ANTONIO
I am as like to call thee so again,   128
To spit on thee again, to spurn thee too.
If thou wilt lend this money, lend it not
As to thy friends, for when did friendship take
A breed for barren metal of his friend?   132
But lend it rather to thine enemy,
Who, if he break, thou mayst with better face   134
Exact the penalty.

SHYLOCK   Why, look you how you storm!
I would be friends with you and have your love,
Forget the shames that you have stained me with,
Supply your present wants, and take no doit   138
Of usance for my moneys, and you'll not hear me.
This is kind I offer.

BASSANIO This were kindness.   141

SHYLOCK   This kindness will I show.
Go with me to a notary. Seal me there
Your single bond; and, in a merry sport,   144
If you repay me not on such a day,
In such a place, such sum or sums as are
Expressed in the condition, let the forfeit
Be nominated for an equal pound   148
Of your fair flesh, to be cut off and taken
In what part of your body pleaseth me.

ANTONIO
Content, in faith. I'll seal to such a bond
And say there is much kindness in the Jew.

BASSANIO
You shall not seal to such a bond for me!
I'll rather dwell in my necessity.   154

ANTONIO
Why, fear not, man, I will not forfeit it.

---

128 like likely   **132 breed . . . metal** offspring from money, which
cannot naturally breed. (One of the oldest arguments against usury was
that it was thereby "unnatural.")   **134 Who** from whom. **break** fail to
pay on time   **138 doit** a Dutch coin of very small value   **141 were**
would be (if seriously offered)   **144 single bond** bond signed alone
without other security   **148 nominated** named, specified. **equal**
exact   **154 dwell** remain

Within these two months—that's a month before
This bond expires—I do expect return
Of thrice three times the value of this bond.

SHYLOCK
O father Abram, what these Christians are,
Whose own hard dealings teaches them suspect
The thoughts of others! Pray you, tell me this:
If he should break his day, what should I gain
By the exaction of the forfeiture?
A pound of man's flesh taken from a man
Is not so estimable, profitable neither,   165
As flesh of muttons, beefs, or goats. I say
To buy his favor I extend this friendship.
If he will take it, so; if not, adieu.
And for my love, I pray you, wrong me not.   169

ANTONIO
Yes, Shylock, I will seal unto this bond.

SHYLOCK
Then meet me forthwith at the notary's;
Give him direction for this merry bond,
And I will go and purse the ducats straight,
See to my house, left in the fearful guard   174
Of an unthrifty knave, and presently
I'll be with you.   *Exit.*

ANTONIO   Hie thee, gentle Jew.
The Hebrew will turn Christian; he grows kind.

BASSANIO
I like not fair terms and a villain's mind.

ANTONIO
Come on. In this there can be no dismay;
My ships come home a month before the day.
                                            Exeunt.

❖

---

165 estimable valuable   **169 wrong me not** do not think evil of me
174 fearful to be mistrusted

2.1   [*Flourish of cornets.*] *Enter* [*the Prince of*]
*Morocco, a tawny Moor all in white, and three
or four followers accordingly, with Portia,
Nerissa, and their train.*

MOROCCO
  Mislike me not for my complexion,
  The shadowed livery of the burnished sun,   2
  To whom I am a neighbor and near bred.   3
  Bring me the fairest creature northward born,
  Where Phoebus' fire scarce thaws the icicles,   5
  And let us make incision for your love
  To prove whose blood is reddest, his or mine.   7
  I tell thee, lady, this aspect of mine   8
  Hath feared the valiant. By my love I swear,   9
  The best-regarded virgins of our clime
  Have loved it too. I would not change this hue,
  Except to steal your thoughts, my gentle queen.

PORTIA
  In terms of choice I am not solely led
  By nice direction of a maiden's eyes;   14
  Besides, the lottery of my destiny
  Bars me the right of voluntary choosing.
  But if my father had not scanted me,   17
  And hedged me by his wit to yield myself   18
  His wife who wins me by that means I told you,
  Yourself, renownèd Prince, then stood as fair
  As any comer I have looked on yet
  For my affection.
MOROCCO   Even for that I thank you.
  Therefore, I pray you, lead me to the caskets
  To try my fortune. By this scimitar
  That slew the Sophy and a Persian prince,   25
  That won three fields of Sultan Solyman,   26

2.1. Location: Belmont. Portia's house.
s.d. accordingly similarly (i.e., dressed in white and dark-skinned like
Morocco) **2 shadowed livery** i.e., dark complexion, worn as though it
were a costume of the sun's servants **3 near bred** closely related
5 Phoebus' i.e., the sun's **7 reddest** (Red blood was regarded as a sign
of courage.) **8 aspect** visage **9 feared** frightened **14 nice direction**
careful guidance **17 scanted** limited **18 wit** wisdom **25 Sophy** Shah
of Persia **26 fields** battles. **Solyman** a Turkish sultan ruling 1520–1566

I would o'erstare the sternest eyes that look,   27
Outbrave the heart most daring on the earth,
Pluck the young sucking cubs from the she-bear,
Yea, mock the lion when 'a roars for prey,   30
To win thee, lady. But alas the while!
If Hercules and Lichas play at dice   32
Which is the better man, the greater throw
May turn by fortune from the weaker hand.
So is Alcides beaten by his page,
And so may I, blind Fortune leading me,
Miss that which one unworthier may attain,
And die with grieving.

PORTIA   You must take your chance,
And either not attempt to choose at all
Or swear before you choose, if you choose wrong
Never to speak to lady afterward
In way of marriage. Therefore be advised.

MOROCCO
Nor will not. Come, bring me unto my chance.   43

PORTIA
First, forward to the temple. After dinner   44
Your hazard shall be made.

MOROCCO   Good fortune then!
To make me blest or cursed'st among men.

                              [*Cornets, and*] *exeunt.*

❖

2.2   *Enter* [*Launcelot*] *the Clown, alone.*

LAUNCELOT   Certainly my conscience will serve me to 1
run from this Jew my master. The fiend is at mine
elbow and tempts me, saying to me, "Gobbo, Launcelot
Gobbo, good Launcelot," or "Good Gobbo," or "Good
Launcelot Gobbo, use your legs, take the start, run
away." My conscience says, "No, take heed, honest
Launcelot, take heed, honest Gobbo," or, as aforesaid,

27 o'erstare outstare   30 'a he   32 Lichas a page of Hercules (Alcides)
43 Nor will not i.e., nor indeed will I violate the oath   44 to the
temple i.e., in order to take the oaths

2.2. Location: Venice. A street.
1 serve permit

"honest Launcelot Gobbo, do not run; scorn running
with thy heels." Well, the most courageous fiend bids 9
me pack. "Fia!" says the fiend; "Away!" says the fiend. 10
"For the heavens, rouse up a brave mind," says the 11
fiend, "and run." Well, my conscience, hanging about 12
the neck of my heart, says very wisely to me, "My hon- 13
est friend Launcelot, being an honest man's son," or
rather an honest woman's son—for indeed my father
did something smack, something grow to, he had a 16
kind of taste—well, my conscience says, "Launcelot, 17
budge not." "Budge," says the fiend. "Budge not," says
my conscience. "Conscience," say I, "you counsel
well." "Fiend," say I, "you counsel well." To be ruled by
my conscience, I should stay with the Jew my master,
who, God bless the mark, is a kind of devil; and to run 22
away from the Jew, I should be ruled by the fiend, who,
saving your reverence, is the devil himself. Certainly
the Jew is the very devil incarnation; and, in my con- 25
science, my conscience is but a kind of hard conscience,
to offer to counsel me to stay with the Jew. The fiend
gives the more friendly counsel. I will run, fiend; my
heels are at your commandment; I will run.

Enter Old Gobbo, with a basket.

GOBBO   Master young man, you, I pray you, which is 30
the way to master Jew's?
LAUNCELOT   [*Aside*]   O   heavens,   this   is   my   true-
begotten father, who, being more than sand-blind, 33
high-gravel-blind, knows me not. I will try confusions 34
with him.
GOBBO   Master young gentleman, I pray you, which is
the way to master Jew's?

9 with thy heels i.e., emphatically (with a pun on the literal sense)
10 pack begone.   **Fia** i.e., via, away   **11 For the heavens** i.e., in heaven's
name   **12–13 hanging . . . heart** i.e., timidly   **16–17 something . . . taste**
i.e., had a tendency to lechery   **22 God . . . mark** (An expression by way
of apology for introducing something potentially offensive, as also in
saving your reverence.)   **25 incarnation** (Launcelot means "incarnate.")
30 you (Gobbo uses the formal *you* but switches to the familiar
thou, l. 88, when he accepts Launcelot as his son.)   **33 sand-blind** dim-
sighted   **34 high-gravel-blind** blinder than sand-blind. (A term seemingly
invented by Launcelot.)   **try confusions** (Launcelot's blunder for *try
conclusions,* i.e., experiment, though his error is comically apt.)

LAUNCELOT Turn up on your right hand at the next
turning, but at the next turning of all on your left;
marry, at the very next turning, turn of no hand, but 40
turn down indirectly to the Jew's house.

GOBBO By God's sonties, 'twill be a hard way to hit. 42
Can you tell me whether one Launcelot, that dwells
with him, dwell with him or no?

LAUNCELOT Talk you of young Master Launcelot?
[*Aside.*] Mark me now; now will I raise the waters.— 46
Talk you of young Master Launcelot?

GOBBO No master, sir, but a poor man's son. His father, 48
though I say 't, is an honest exceeding poor man and,
God be thanked, well to live. 50

LAUNCELOT Well, let his father be what 'a will, we talk 51
of young Master Launcelot.

GOBBO Your worship's friend, and Launcelot, sir. 53

LAUNCELOT But I pray you, ergo, old man, ergo, I be- 54
seech you, talk you of young Master Launcelot?

GOBBO Of Launcelot, an 't please your mastership.

LAUNCELOT Ergo, Master Launcelot. Talk not of Master
Launcelot, Father, for the young gentleman, according 58
to Fates and Destinies and such odd sayings, the Sis- 59
ters Three and such branches of learning, is indeed 60
deceased, or, as you would say in plain terms, gone to
heaven.

GOBBO Marry, God forbid! The boy was the very staff
of my age, my very prop.

LAUNCELOT Do I look like a cudgel or a hovel post, a 65
staff, or a prop? Do you know me, Father?

GOBBO Alack the day, I know you not, young gentleman. But I pray you, tell me, is my boy, God rest his
soul, alive or dead?

LAUNCELOT Do you not know me, Father?

GOBBO Alack, sir, I am sand-blind. I know you not.

40 marry i.e., by the Virgin Mary, indeed. (A mild interjection.)
42 sonties saints **46 raise the waters** start tears **48 master** (The title
was applied to gentlefolk only.) **50 well to live** enjoying a good livelihood. (Perhaps Old Gobbo intends the phrase to mean "in good health,
since he protests that he is poor.) **51 'a** he **53 Your . . . Launcelot**
(Again, Old Gobbo denies that Launcelot is entitled to be called "Master.") **54 ergo** therefore (if it means anything) **58 Father** (1) old man
(2) Father **59-60 the Sisters Three** the three Fates **65 hovel post** support for a hovel or open shed

LAUNCELOT Nay, indeed, if you had your eyes you
might fail of the knowing me; it is a wise father that 73
knows his own child. Well, old man, I will tell you 74
news of your son. [*He kneels.*] Give me your blessing;
truth will come to light; murder cannot be hid long; a
man's son may, but in the end truth will out.

GOBBO Pray you, sir, stand up. I am sure you are not
Launcelot, my boy.

LAUNCELOT Pray you, let's have no more fooling about
it, but give me your blessing. I am Launcelot, your 81
boy that was, your son that is, your child that shall be. 82

GOBBO I cannot think you are my son.

LAUNCELOT I know not what I shall think of that; but I
am Launcelot, the Jew's man, and I am sure Margery
your wife is my mother.

GOBBO Her name is Margery, indeed. I'll be sworn, if
thou be Launcelot, thou art mine own flesh and blood.
Lord worshiped might he be, what a beard hast thou 89
got! Thou hast got more hair on thy chin than Dobbin
my fill horse has on his tail. 91

LAUNCELOT [*Rising*] It should seem, then, that Dobbin's tail grows backward. I am sure he had more hair 93
of his tail than I have of my face when I last saw him. 94

GOBBO Lord, how art thou changed! How dost thou and
thy master agree? I have brought him a present. How
'gree you now?

LAUNCELOT Well, well; but for mine own part, as I
have set up my rest to run away, so I will not rest till 99
I have run some ground. My master's a very Jew. Give 100
him a present? Give him a halter! I am famished in his 101
service; you may tell every finger I have with my ribs. 102
Father, I am glad you are come. Give me your present 103

73–74 it is . . . child (Reverses the proverb "It is a wise child that knows
his own father.") **81–82 your . . . shall be** (Echoes the *Gloria* from the
Book of Common Prayer: "As it was in the beginning, is now, and ever
shall be.") **89 beard** (Stage tradition has Old Gobbo mistake Launcelot's long hair for a beard.) **91 fill horse** cart horse **93 grows backward** (1) grows inward, shorter (2) grows at the wrong end **94 of** in, on
99 set up my rest determined, risked all. (A metaphor from the card
game *primero*, in which a final wager is made.) **100 very** veritable
101 halter hangman's noose **102 tell** count. **tell . . . ribs** (Comically
reverses the usual saying of counting one's ribs with one's fingers.)
103 Give me give. (*Me* is used colloquially.)

to one Master Bassanio, who indeed gives rare new
liveries. If I serve not him, I will run as far as God has 105
any ground. O rare fortune, here comes the man! To
him, Father, for I am a Jew if I serve the Jew any longer.

> *Enter Bassanio, with [Leonardo and] a follower*
> *or two.*

BASSANIO   You may do so, but let it be so hasted that 108
supper be ready at the farthest by five of the clock. See 109
these letters delivered, put the liveries to making, and
desire Gratiano to come anon to my lodging.

> *[Exit a Servant.]*

LAUNCELOT   To him, Father.

GOBBO [*Advancing*]   God bless your worship!

BASSANIO   Gramercy. Wouldst thou aught with me?   114

GOBBO   Here's my son, sir, a poor boy—

LAUNCELOT   Not a poor boy, sir, but the rich Jew's man,
that would, sir, as my father shall specify—

GOBBO   He hath a great infection, sir, as one would say, 118
to serve—

LAUNCELOT   Indeed, the short and the long is, I serve
the Jew, and have a desire, as my father shall specify—

GOBBO   His master and he, saving your worship's reverence, are scarce cater-cousins—   123

LAUNCELOT   To be brief, the very truth is that the Jew,
having done me wrong, doth cause me, as my father,
being, I hope, an old man, shall frutify unto you—   126

GOBBO   I have here a dish of doves that I would bestow
upon your worship, and my suit is—

LAUNCELOT   In very brief, the suit is impertinent to my- 129
self, as your worship shall know by this honest old
man, and, though I say it, though old man, yet poor
man, my father.

BASSANIO   One speak for both. What would you?

LAUNCELOT   Serve you, sir.

GOBBO   That is the very defect of the matter, sir.   135

---

105 liveries uniforms or costumes for servants   **108 hasted** hastened,
hurried   **109 farthest** latest   **114 Gramercy** many thanks.   **aught**
anything   **118 infection** (Blunder for *affection* or *inclination*.)
123 cater-cousins good friends   **126 frutify** (Launcelot may be trying to
say "fructify," but he means "certify" or "notify.")   **129 impertinent**
(Blunder for *pertinent*.)   **135 defect** (Blunder for *effect*, i.e., "purport.")

BASSANIO

I know thee well; thou hast obtained thy suit.
Shylock thy master spoke with me this day,
And hath preferred thee, if it be preferment   138
To leave a rich Jew's service to become
The follower of so poor a gentleman.

LAUNCELOT The old proverb is very well parted be- 141
tween my master Shylock and you, sir: you have the
grace of God, sir, and he hath enough.

BASSANIO

Thou speak'st it well. Go, father, with thy son.
Take leave of thy old master, and inquire
My lodging out. [*To a Servant.*] Give him a livery
More guarded than his fellows'. See it done.   147

LAUNCELOT Father, in. I cannot get a service, no! I have
ne'er a tongue in my head, well! [*Looks at his palm.*] If
any man in Italy have a fairer table which doth offer to 150
swear upon a book, I shall have good fortune. Go to,
here's a simple line of life. Here's a small trifle of
wives! Alas, fifteen wives is nothing. Eleven widows
and nine maids is a simple coming-in for one man. 154
And then to scape drowning thrice, and to be in peril
of my life with the edge of a feather bed! Here are 156
simple scapes. Well, if Fortune be a woman, she's a 157
good wench for this gear. Father, come, I'll take my 158
leave of the Jew in the twinkling.

                    Exit Clown [*with Old Gobbo*].

BASSANIO

I pray thee, good Leonardo, think on this:
                    [*Giving him a list*]
These things being bought and orderly bestowed,
Return in haste, for I do feast tonight   162
My best-esteemed acquaintance. Hie thee, go.

LEONARDO

My best endeavors shall be done herein.
                    [*He starts to leave.*]

---

138 preferred recommended   **141 proverb** i.e., "He who has the grace
of God has enough"   **147 guarded** trimmed with braided ornament
150 table palm of the hand. (Launcelot now reads the lines of his
palm.)   **154 simple coming-in** modest income (with sexual suggestion)
156 feather bed (suggesting marriage bed or love bed; Launcelot sees
sexual adventure in his palm reading)   **157 Fortune . . . woman** (Fortune
was personified as a goddess.)   **158 gear** matter   **162 feast** give a feast for

Enter Gratiano.

GRATIANO
  Where's your master?
LEONARDO   Yonder, sir, he walks.
                                        Exit Leonardo.
GRATIANO   Signor Bassanio!
BASSANIO   Gratiano!
GRATIANO
  I have a suit to you.
BASSANIO   You have obtained it.
GRATIANO   You must not deny me. I must go with you
  to Belmont.
BASSANIO
  Why, then you must. But hear thee, Gratiano;
  Thou art too wild, too rude and bold of voice—
  Parts that become thee happily enough,   173
  And in such eyes as ours appear not faults,
  But where thou art not known, why, there they show
  Something too liberal. Pray thee, take pain   176
  To allay with some cold drops of modesty   177
  Thy skipping spirit, lest through thy wild behavior
  I be misconstered in the place I go to   179
  And lose my hopes.
GRATIANO   Signor Bassanio, hear me:
  If I do not put on a sober habit,
  Talk with respect and swear but now and then,
  Wear prayer books in my pocket, look demurely,
  Nay more, while grace is saying, hood mine eyes   184
  Thus with my hat, and sigh and say "amen,"
  Use all the observance of civility,
  Like one well studied in a sad ostent   187
  To please his grandam, never trust me more.
BASSANIO   Well, we shall see your bearing.
GRATIANO
  Nay, but I bar tonight. You shall not gauge me
  By what we do tonight.
BASSANIO   No, that were pity.
  I would entreat you rather to put on

173 Parts qualities   **176 liberal** free of manner (often with sexual conno-
tation)   **177 allay** temper, moderate   **179 misconstered** misconstrued
184 saying being said   **187 sad ostent** grave appearance

Your boldest suit of mirth, for we have friends
That purpose merriment. But fare you well;
I have some business.

GRATIANO
And I must to Lorenzo and the rest,
But we will visit you at suppertime.   *Exeunt.*

❖

2.3   *Enter Jessica and [Launcelot] the Clown.*

JESSICA
I am sorry thou wilt leave my father so.
Our house is hell, and thou, a merry devil,
Didst rob it of some taste of tediousness.
But fare thee well; there is a ducat for thee.
                              [*Giving money.*]
And, Launcelot, soon at supper shalt thou see
Lorenzo, who is thy new master's guest.
Give him this letter; do it secretly.   [*Giving a letter.*]
And so farewell; I would not have my father
See me in talk with thee.
LAUNCELOT   Adieu! Tears exhibit my tongue. Most 10
     beautiful pagan, most sweet Jew! If a Christian did not
     play the knave and get thee, I am much deceived. But, 12
     adieu! These foolish drops do something drown my
     manly spirit. Adieu!
JESSICA   Farewell, good Launcelot.   [*Exit Launcelot.*]
Alack, what heinous sin is it in me
To be ashamed to be my father's child!
But though I am a daughter to his blood,
I am not to his manners. O Lorenzo,
If thou keep promise, I shall end this strife,
Become a Christian and thy loving wife.   *Exit.*

❖

2.3. **Location: Venice. Shylock's house.**
10 exhibit (Blunder for *inhibit*, "restrain.")   **12 get** beget

2.4   *Enter Gratiano, Lorenzo, Salerio, and Solanio.*

LORENZO
Nay, we will slink away in suppertime,   1
Disguise us at my lodging, and return
All in an hour.
GRATIANO
We have not made good preparation.
SALERIO
We have not spoke us yet of torchbearers.   5
SOLANIO
'Tis vile, unless it may be quaintly ordered,   6
And better in my mind not undertook.
LORENZO
'Tis now but four o'clock. We have two hours
To furnish us.

       Enter Launcelot [with a letter].

              Friend Launcelot, what's the news?
LAUNCELOT An it shall please you to break up this, it 10
shall seem to signify.   *[Giving the letter.]*
LORENZO
I know the hand. In faith, 'tis a fair hand,
And whiter than the paper it writ on
Is the fair hand that writ.
GRATIANO   Love news, in faith.
LAUNCELOT By your leave, sir.   *[He starts to leave.]*
LORENZO Whither goest thou?
LAUNCELOT Marry, sir, to bid my old master the Jew to
sup tonight with my new master the Christian.
LORENZO
Hold here, take this. *[He gives money.]* Tell gentle Jessica
I will not fail her; speak it privately.
                          Exit Clown [Launcelot].
Go, gentlemen,
Will you prepare you for this masque tonight?
I am provided of a torchbearer.

2.4. Location: Venice. A street.
1 in during   **5 spoke . . . of** yet bespoken, ordered   **6 quaintly ordered**
skillfully and tastefully managed   **10 An** if. **break up** i.e., open the
seal. (Literally, a term from carving.)

SALERIO
  Ay, marry, I'll be gone about it straight.
SOLANIO
  And so will I.
LORENZO   Meet me and Gratiano
  At Gratiano's lodging some hour hence.
SALERIO 'Tis good we do so.   *Exit [with Solanio].*
GRATIANO
  Was not that letter from fair Jessica?
LORENZO
  I must needs tell thee all. She hath directed
  How I shall take her from her father's house,
  What gold and jewels she is furnished with,
  What page's suit she hath in readiness.
  If e'er the Jew her father come to heaven,
  It will be for his gentle daughter's sake;   34
  And never dare Misfortune cross her foot,   35
  Unless she do it under this excuse,   36
  That she is issue to a faithless Jew.   37
  Come, go with me; peruse this as thou goest.
          [He gives Gratiano the letter.]
  Fair Jessica shall be my torchbearer.   *Exeunt.*

❖

2.5   *Enter [Shylock the] Jew and [Launcelot,] his
      man that was, the Clown.*

SHYLOCK
  Well, thou shalt see, thy eyes shall be thy judge,
  The difference of old Shylock and Bassanio.—   2
  What, Jessica!—Thou shalt not gormandize,   3
  As thou hast done with me—What, Jessica!—
  And sleep and snore, and rend apparel out—   5
  Why, Jessica, I say!
LAUNCELOT Why, Jessica!

---

34 gentle (with pun on *gentile*?) **35 foot** footpath **36 she**
i.e., Misfortune **37 she is issue** i.e., Jessica is child. **faithless**
pagan

2.5. Location: Venice. Before Shylock's house.
2 of between **3 gormandize** eat gluttonously **5 rend apparel out** i.e.,
wear out your clothes

SHYLOCK
  Who bids thee call? I do not bid thee call.
LAUNCELOT   Your worship was wont to tell me I could
  do nothing without bidding.

    Enter Jessica.

JESSICA   Call you? What is your will?
SHYLOCK
  I am bid forth to supper, Jessica.
  There are my keys. But wherefore should I go?
  I am not bid for love—they flatter me—
  But yet I'll go in hate, to feed upon
  The prodigal Christian. Jessica, my girl,
  Look to my house. I am right loath to go.   17
  There is some ill a-brewing towards my rest,
  For I did dream of moneybags tonight.   19
LAUNCELOT   I beseech you, sir, go. My young master
  doth expect your reproach.   21
SHYLOCK   So do I his.
LAUNCELOT   And they have conspired together. I will
  not say you shall see a masque, but if you do, then it
  was not for nothing that my nose fell a-bleeding on
  Black Monday last at six o'clock i' the morning, falling   26
  out that year on Ash Wednesday was four year in th'
  afternoon.
SHYLOCK
  What, are there masques? Hear you me, Jessica:
  Lock up my doors, and when you hear the drum
  And the vile squealing of the wry-necked fife,   31
  Clamber not you up to the casements then,
  Nor thrust your head into the public street
  To gaze on Christian fools with varnished faces,   34
  But stop my house's ears, I mean my casements.
  Let not the sound of shallow foppery enter
  My sober house. By Jacob's staff I swear   37

17 right loath reluctant   **19 tonight** last night   **21 reproach** (Launcelot's blunder for *approach*. Shylock takes it in grim humor.)   **26 Black
Monday** Easter Monday. (So called, according to Stow, because of a cold
and stormy Easter Monday when Edward III was besieging Paris. Launcelot's talk of omens is perhaps intentional gibberish, a parody of Shylock's fears.)   **31 wry-necked** i.e., played with the musician's head awry;
or, on an instrument with the head twisted awry   **34 varnished faces** i.e.,
painted masks   **37 Jacob's staff** (See Genesis 32:10 and Hebrews 11:21.)

I have no mind of feasting forth tonight.
But I will go. Go you before me, sirrah;
Say I will come.

LAUNCELOT I will go before, sir. [*To Jessica.*] Mistress,
look out at window, for all this;
    There will come a Christian by,
    Will be worth a Jewess' eye.   [*Exit.*]

SHYLOCK
What says that fool of Hagar's offspring, ha?   45

JESSICA
His words were "Farewell, mistress," nothing else.

SHYLOCK
The patch is kind enough, but a huge feeder,   47
Snail-slow in profit, and he sleeps by day   48
More than the wildcat. Drones hive not with me;
Therefore I part with him, and part with him
To one that I would have him help to waste
His borrowed purse. Well, Jessica, go in.
Perhaps I will return immediately.
Do as I bid you; shut doors after you.
Fast bind, fast find—   55
A proverb never stale in thrifty mind.   *Exit.*

JESSICA
Farewell, and if my fortune be not crossed,
I have a father, you a daughter, lost.   *Exit.*

✦

2.6   *Enter the maskers, Gratiano and Salerio.*

GRATIANO
This is the penthouse under which Lorenzo   1
Desired us to make stand.

SALERIO   His hour is almost past.

GRATIANO
And it is marvel he outdwells his hour,   4

45 Hagar's offspring (Hagar, a gentile and Abraham's servant, gave
birth to Ishmael; both mother and son were cast out after the birth of
Isaac.) **47 patch** fool **48 profit** profitable labor **55 Fast . . . find** i.e.,
something firmly secured or bound will always be easily located

2.6. Location: Before Shylock's house, as in scene 5.
1 penthouse projecting roof from a house **4 it . . . hour** i.e., it is surprising that he is late

For lovers ever run before the clock.

SALERIO

O, ten times faster Venus' pigeons fly   6
To seal love's bonds new-made than they are wont
To keep oblègèd faith unforfeited!   8

GRATIANO

That ever holds. Who riseth from a feast
With that keen appetite that he sits down?
Where is the horse that doth untread again   11
His tedious measures with the unbated fire
That he did pace them first? All things that are,
Are with more spirit chasèd than enjoyed.
How like a younger or a prodigal   15
The scarfèd bark puts from her native bay,   16
Hugged and embracèd by the strumpet wind!   17
How like the prodigal doth she return,
With overweathered ribs and ragged sails,   19
Lean, rent, and beggared by the strumpet wind!   20

     Enter Lorenzo, [masked].

SALERIO

Here comes Lorenzo. More of this hereafter.

LORENZO

Sweet friends, your patience for my long abode;   22
Not I, but my affairs, have made you wait.
When you shall please to play the thieves for wives,
I'll watch as long for you then. Approach;
Here dwells my father Jew. Ho! Who's within?   26

     [Enter] Jessica, above [in boy's clothes].

JESSICA

Who are you? Tell me for more certainty,
Albeit I'll swear that I do know your tongue.

LORENZO   Lorenzo, and thy love.

---

6 **Venus' pigeons** the doves that drew Venus' chariot   8 **oblègèd** bound
by marriage or engagement.   **unforfeited** unbroken   11 **untread** re-
trace   15 **younger** i.e., younger son, as in the parable of the Prodigal
Son (Luke 15). (Often emended to *younker*, youth.)   16 **scarfèd** decorated
with flags or streamers   17 **strumpet** i.e., inconsistent, variable. (Refers
metaphorically to the harlots with whom the Prodigal Son wasted his
fortune.)   19 **overweathered** weatherbeaten   20 **rent** torn   22 **your patience** i.e., I beg your patience.   **abode** delay   26 **father** i.e., father-in-law

JESSICA
Lorenzo, certain, and my love indeed,
For who love I so much? And now who knows
But you, Lorenzo, whether I am yours?

LORENZO
Heaven and thy thoughts are witness that thou art.

JESSICA [*Throwing down a casket*]
Here, catch this casket; it is worth the pains.
I am glad 'tis night, you do not look on me,
For I am much ashamed of my exchange.   36
But love is blind, and lovers cannot see
The pretty follies that themselves commit,   38
For if they could, Cupid himself would blush
To see me thus transformèd to a boy.

LORENZO
Descend, for you must be my torchbearer.

JESSICA
What, must I hold a candle to my shames?   42
They in themselves, good sooth, are too too light.   43
Why, 'tis an office of discovery, love,   44
And I should be obscured.

LORENZO   So are you, sweet,
Even in the lovely garnish of a boy.   46
But come at once,
For the close night doth play the runaway,   48
And we are stayed for at Bassanio's feast.   49

JESSICA
I will make fast the doors, and gild myself   50
With some more ducats, and be with you straight.
                                        [*Exit above.*]

GRATIANO
Now, by my hood, a gentle and no Jew.   52

LORENZO
Beshrew me but I love her heartily,   53
For she is wise, if I can judge of her,

36 exchange change of clothes   **38 pretty** ingenious, artful   **42 hold a
candle** stand by and witness (with a play on the idea of acting as torchbearer)   **43 light** immodest (with pun on literal meaning)   **44 'tis . . .
discovery** i.e., torchbearing is intended to shed light on matters
46 garnish outfit, trimmings   **48 close** dark.   **doth . . . runaway** i.e., is
quickly passing   **49 stayed** waited   **50 gild** adorn. (Literally, cover with
gold.)   **52 gentle** (with pun on *gentile*, as at 2.4.34)   **53 Beshrew** i.e., a
mischief on. (A mild oath.)

And fair she is, if that mine eyes be true,
And true she is, as she hath proved herself;
And therefore, like herself—wise, fair, and true—
Shall she be placèd in my constant soul.

    Enter Jessica [below].

What, art thou come? On, gentlemen, away!
Our masking mates by this time for us stay.
                Exit [with Jessica and Salerio;
                Gratiano is about to follow them].

    Enter Antonio.

ANTONIO Who's there?
GRATIANO Signor Antonio?
ANTONIO
Fie, fie, Gratiano! Where are all the rest?
'Tis nine o'clock; our friends all stay for you.
No masque tonight. The wind is come about;
Bassanio presently will go aboard.
I have sent twenty out to seek for you.
GRATIANO
I am glad on 't. I desire no more delight
Than to be under sail and gone tonight.   *Exeunt.*

                    ✤

2.7   *[Flourish of cornets.] Enter Portia, with [the*
        Prince of] Morocco, and both their trains.

PORTIA
Go draw aside the curtains and discover   1
The several caskets to this noble prince.
                [The curtains are drawn.]
Now make your choice.
MOROCCO
The first, of gold, who this inscription bears,
"Who chooseth me shall gain what many men desire";
The second, silver, which this promise carries,
"Who chooseth me shall get as much as he deserves";
This third, dull lead, with warning all as blunt,

2.7. Location: Belmont. Portia's house.
1 discover reveal

"Who chooseth me must give and hazard all he hath."
How shall I know if I do choose the right?

PORTIA
The one of them contains my picture, Prince.
If you choose that, then I am yours withal.

MOROCCO
Some god direct my judgment! Let me see.
I will survey th' inscriptions back again.
What says this leaden casket?
"Who chooseth me must give and hazard all he hath."
Must give—for what? For lead? Hazard for lead?
This casket threatens. Men that hazard all
Do it in hope of fair advantages.
A golden mind stoops not to shows of dross;   20
I'll then nor give nor hazard aught for lead.   21
What says the silver with her virgin hue?
"Who chooseth me shall get as much as he deserves."
As much as he deserves! Pause there, Morocco,
And weigh thy value with an even hand.
If thou be'st rated by thy estimation,   26
Thou dost deserve enough; and yet enough
May not extend so far as to the lady;
And yet to be afeard of my deserving
Were but a weak disabling of myself.   30
As much as I deserve? Why, that's the lady.
I do in birth deserve her, and in fortunes,
In graces, and in qualities of breeding;
But more than these, in love I do deserve.
What if I strayed no farther, but chose here?
Let's see once more this saying graved in gold:
"Who chooseth me shall gain what many men desire."
Why, that's the lady; all the world desires her.
From the four corners of the earth they come
To kiss this shrine, this mortal breathing saint.
The Hyrcanian deserts and the vasty wilds   41
Of wide Arabia are as throughfares now

---

20 dross worthless matter. (Literally, the impurities cast off in the
melting down of metals.) **21 nor give** neither give **26 estimation**
valuation **30 disabling** underrating **41 Hyrcanian** (Hyrcania was the
country south of the Caspian Sea celebrated for its wildness.)

For princes to come view fair Portia.
The watery kingdom, whose ambitious head
Spits in the face of heaven, is no bar
To stop the foreign spirits, but they come,
As o'er a brook, to see fair Portia.
One of these three contains her heavenly picture.
Is 't like that lead contains her? 'Twere damnation
To think so base a thought; it were too gross
To rib her cerecloth in the obscure grave.   51
Or shall I think in silver she's immured,   52
Being ten times undervalued to tried gold?   53
O, sinful thought! Never so rich a gem
Was set in worse than gold. They have in England
A coin that bears the figure of an angel   56
Stamped in gold, but that's insculped upon;   57
But here an angel in a golden bed
Lies all within. Deliver me the key.
Here do I choose, and thrive I as I may!

PORTIA
There, take it, Prince; and if my form lie there,
Then I am yours.   [*He unlocks the golden casket.*]

MOROCCO   O hell! What have we here?
A carrion Death, within whose empty eye   63
There is a written scroll! I'll read the writing.
[*Reads.*] "All that glisters is not gold;
          Often have you heard that told.
          Many a man his life hath sold
          But my outside to behold.
          Gilded tombs do worms infold.
          Had you been as wise as bold,
          Young in limbs, in judgment old,
          Your answer had not been enscrolled.   72
          Fare you well; your suit is cold."
Cold, indeed, and labor lost.
Then, farewell, heat, and welcome, frost!

51 **rib** i.e., enclose. **cerecloth** wax cloth used in wrapping for burial
52 **immured** enclosed, confined 53 **Being . . . to** which has only one
tenth of the value of 56 **coin** i.e., the gold coin known as the *angel,*
which bore the device of the archangel Michael treading on the
dragon 57 **insculped upon** merely engraved upon the surface
63 **carrion Death** death's-head 72 **enscrolled** i.e., written on this scroll

Portia, adieu. I have too grieved a heart
To take a tedious leave. Thus losers part.
         Exit [*with his train. Flourish of cornets*].

PORTIA
A gentle riddance. Draw the curtains, go.
Let all of his complexion choose me so.   79
        [*The curtains are closed, and*] *Exeunt*.

❖

2.8   *Enter Salerio and Solanio.*

SALERIO
Why, man, I saw Bassanio under sail.
With him is Gratiano gone along,
And in their ship I am sure Lorenzo is not.
SOLANIO
The villain Jew with outcries raised the Duke,
Who went with him to search Bassanio's ship.
SALERIO
He came too late; the ship was under sail.
But there the Duke was given to understand
That in a gondola were seen together
Lorenzo and his amorous Jessica.
Besides, Antonio certified the Duke
They were not with Bassanio in his ship.
SOLANIO
I never heard a passion so confused,
So strange, outrageous, and so variable
As the dog Jew did utter in the streets:
"My daughter! O, my ducats! O, my daughter!
Fled with a Christian! O, my Christian ducats!
Justice! The law! My ducats, and my daughter!
A sealèd bag, two sealèd bags of ducats,
Of double ducats, stol'n from me by my daughter!
And jewels, two stones, two rich and precious stones,
Stol'n by my daughter! Justice! Find the girl!
She hath the stones upon her, and the ducats."

79 complexion temperament (not merely skin color)
2.8. Location: Venice. A street.

SALERIO
    Why, all the boys in Venice follow him,
    Crying, his stones, his daughter, and his ducats.
SOLANIO
    Let good Antonio look he keep his day,   25
    Or he shall pay for this.
SALERIO   Marry, well remembered.
    I reasoned with a Frenchman yesterday,   27
    Who told me, in the narrow seas that part   28
    The French and English, there miscarried
    A vessel of our country richly fraught.   30
    I thought upon Antonio when he told me,
    And wished in silence that it were not his.
SOLANIO
    You were best to tell Antonio what you hear.
    Yet do not suddenly, for it may grieve him.
SALERIO
    A kinder gentleman treads not the earth.
    I saw Bassanio and Antonio part.
    Bassanio told him he would make some speed
    Of his return; he answered, "Do not so.
    Slubber not business for my sake, Bassanio,   39
    But stay the very riping of the time;   40
    And for the Jew's bond which he hath of me,   41
    Let it not enter in your mind of love.
    Be merry, and employ your chiefest thoughts
    To courtship and such fair ostents of love   44
    As shall conveniently become you there."
    And even there, his eye being big with tears,   46
    Turning his face, he put his hand behind him,
    And with affection wondrous sensible   48
    He wrung Bassanio's hand; and so they parted.
SOLANIO
    I think he only loves the world for him.
    I pray thee, let us go and find him out

25 look . . . day see to it that he repays his loan on time   27 reasoned
talked   28 narrow seas English Channel   30 fraught freighted
39 Slubber do hastily and badly   40 But . . . time i.e., pursue your
business at Belmont until it is brought to completion   41 for as for
44 ostents expressions, shows   46 there thereupon, then   48 sensible
strongly evident

And quicken his embracèd heaviness   52
With some delight or other.
SALERIO   Do we so.   *Exeunt.*

✣

2.9   *Enter Nerissa and a Servitor.*

NERISSA
    Quick, quick, I pray thee, draw the curtain straight.   1
                          [*The curtains are drawn.*]
    The Prince of Aragon hath ta'en his oath,
    And comes to his election presently.   3

        [*Flourish of cornets.*] *Enter* [*the Prince of*]
        Aragon, his train, and Portia.

PORTIA
    Behold, there stand the caskets, noble Prince.
    If you choose that wherein I am contained,
    Straight shall our nuptial rites be solemnized;
    But if you fail, without more speech, my lord,
    You must be gone from hence immediately.
ARAGON
    I am enjoined by oath to observe three things:
    First, never to unfold to anyone
    Which casket 'twas I chose; next, if I fail
    Of the right casket, never in my life
    To woo a maid in way of marriage;
    Lastly,
    If I do fail in fortune of my choice,
    Immediately to leave you and be gone.
PORTIA
    To these injunctions everyone doth swear
    That comes to hazard for my worthless self.
ARAGON
    And so have I addressed me. Fortune now   19
    To my heart's hope! Gold, silver, and base lead.

52 quicken . . . heaviness lighten the sorrow he has embraced

2.9. Location: Belmont. Portia's house.
s.d. Servitor servant   **1 straight** at once   **3 election** choice.   **presently**
immediately   **19 addressed me** prepared myself (by this swearing)

"Who chooseth me must give and hazard all he hath."
You shall look fairer ere I give or hazard.
What says the golden chest? Ha, let me see:
"Who chooseth me shall gain what many men desire."
What many men desire! That "many" may be meant　25
By the fool multitude that choose by show,
Not learning more than the fond eye doth teach,　27
Which pries not to th' interior, but like the martlet　28
Builds in the weather on the outward wall,　29
Even in the force and road of casualty.　30
I will not choose what many men desire,
Because I will not jump with common spirits　32
And rank me with the barbarous multitudes.
Why then, to thee, thou silver treasure-house!
Tell me once more what title thou dost bear:
"Who chooseth me shall get as much as he deserves."
And well said too; for who shall go about
To cozen fortune and be honorable　38
Without the stamp of merit? Let none presume　39
To wear an undeservèd dignity.
O, that estates, degrees, and offices　41
Were not derived corruptly, and that clear honor
Were purchased by the merit of the wearer!
How many then should cover that stand bare?　44
How many be commanded that command?　45
How much low peasantry would then be gleaned　46
From the true seed of honor, and how much honor　47
Picked from the chaff and ruin of the times
To be new-varnished? Well, but to my choice:　49
"Who chooseth me shall get as much as he deserves."
I will assume desert. Give me a key for this,
And instantly unlock my fortunes here.
　　　　　　　　　　　[*He opens the silver casket.*]

---

25 meant interpreted　**27 fond** foolish　**28 martlet** swift　**29 in** exposed
to　**30 force . . . casualty** power and path of mischance　**32 jump**
agree　**38 cozen** cheat　**39 stamp** seal of approval　**41 estates, degrees**
status, social rank　**44 cover . . . bare** i.e., wear hats (of authority) who
now stand bareheaded　**45 How . . . command** how many then should
be servants that are now masters　**46 gleaned** culled out　**47 the true
seed of honor** i.e., persons of noble descent　**49 new-varnished** i.e.,
having the luster of their true nobility restored to them

PORTIA

Too long a pause for that which you find there.

ARAGON

What's here? The portrait of a blinking idiot,
Presenting me a schedule! I will read it.   55
How much unlike art thou to Portia!
How much unlike my hopes and my deservings!
"Who chooseth me shall have as much as he deserves."
Did I deserve no more than a fool's head?
Is that my prize? Are my deserts no better?

PORTIA

To offend and judge are distinct offices   61
And of opposèd natures.

ARAGON   What is here?   62
[*Reads.*] "The fire seven times tried this;   63
          Seven times tried that judgment is
          That did never choose amiss.
          Some there be that shadows kiss;
          Such have but a shadow's bliss.
          There be fools alive, iwis,   68
          Silvered o'er, and so was this.   69
          Take what wife you will to bed,
          I will ever be your head.   71
          So begone; you are sped."   72

Still more fool I shall appear   73
By the time I linger here.   74
With one fool's head I came to woo,
But I go away with two.
Sweet, adieu. I'll keep my oath,
Patiently to bear my wroth.   78

[*Exeunt Aragon and train.*]

PORTIA

Thus hath the candle singed the moth.

55 schedule written paper   **61–62 To offend . . . natures** i.e., you have
no right, having submitted your case to judgment, to attempt to judge
your own case   **63 tried** tested, purified (?)   **this** i.e., the wise sayings on
the scroll (that have often been proved right by hard experience)
68 iwis certainly   **69 Silvered o'er** i.e., with silver hair and so apparently wise   **71 I . . . head** i.e., you will always have a fool's head
72 sped done for   **73–74 Still . . . here** i.e., I shall seem all the greater
fool for wasting any more time here   **78 wroth** sorrow, unhappy lot. (A
variant of *ruth*.)

O, these deliberate fools! When they do choose,   80
They have the wisdom by their wit to lose.

NERISSA
The ancient saying is no heresy:
Hanging and wiving goes by destiny.

PORTIA   Come, draw the curtain, Nerissa.

                          [*The curtains are closed.*]

        Enter Messenger.

MESSENGER
Where is my lady?

PORTIA   Here. What would my lord?   85

MESSENGER
Madam, there is alighted at your gate
A young Venetian, one that comes before
To signify th' approaching of his lord,
From whom he bringeth sensible regreets,   89
To wit, besides commends and courteous breath,   90
Gifts of rich value. Yet I have not seen   91
So likely an ambassador of love.   92
A day in April never came so sweet
To show how costly summer was at hand   94
As this fore-spurrer comes before his lord.   95

PORTIA
No more, I pray thee. I am half afeard
Thou wilt say anon he is some kin to thee,
Thou spend'st such high-day wit in praising him.   98
Come, come, Nerissa, for I long to see
Quick Cupid's post that comes so mannerly.   100

NERISSA
Bassanio, Lord Love, if thy will it be!   *Exeunt.*

                    ♣

---

80 deliberate reasoning, calculating   **85 my lord** (A jesting response to "my lady.")   **89 sensible regreets** tangible gifts, greetings   **90 commends** greetings.   **breath** speech   **91 Yet** heretofore   **92 likely** promising   **94 costly** lavish, rich   **95 fore-spurrer** herald, harbinger   **98 high-day** holiday (i.e., extravagant)   **100 post** messenger

3.1   [*Enter*] *Solanio and Salerio.*

SOLANIO   Now, what news on the Rialto?

SALERIO   Why, yet it lives there unchecked that Antonio ²
hath a ship of rich lading wrecked on the narrow ³
seas—the Goodwins, I think they call the place, a very ⁴
dangerous flat, and fatal, where the carcasses of many ⁵
a tall ship lie buried, as they say, if my gossip Report ⁶
be an honest woman of her word.

SOLANIO   I would she were as lying a gossip in that as
ever knapped ginger or made her neighbors believe ⁹
she wept for the death of a third husband. But it is
true, without any slips of prolixity or crossing the ¹¹
plain highway of talk, that the good Antonio, the hon- ¹²
est Antonio—O, that I had a title good enough to keep
his name company!—

SALERIO   Come, the full stop.   ¹⁵

SOLANIO   Ha, what sayest thou? Why, the end is, he
hath lost a ship.

SALERIO   I would it might prove the end of his losses.

SOLANIO   Let me say "amen" betimes, lest the devil ¹⁹
cross my prayer, for here he comes in the likeness of ²⁰
a Jew.

  Enter Shylock.

How now, Shylock, what news among the merchants?

SHYLOCK   You knew, none so well, none so well as you,
of my daughter's flight.

SALERIO   That's certain. I for my part knew the tailor
that made the wings she flew withal.   ²⁶

SOLANIO   And Shylock for his own part knew the bird

3.1. Location: Venice. A street.
2 unchecked undenied   **3–4 the narrow seas** the English Channel, as at
2.8.28.   **4 Goodwins** Goodwin Sands, off the Kentish coast near the
Thames estuary   **5 flat** shoal, sandbank   **6 gossip Report** i.e., Dame
Rumor   **9 knapped** nibbled   **11 slips of prolixity** lapses into long-
windedness; or, longwinded lies   **11–12 crossing . . . talk** deviating
from honest plain speech   **15 Come . . . stop** finish your story   **19 betimes** while there is yet time   **20 cross** thwart   **26 wings** i.e., the
boy's clothes in which she fled. Jessica's flight is compared to a bird's
(cf. ll. 27–28), but *wings* is also a tailor's word to describe an ornamental flap near the shoulder of a garment.

was fledge, and then it is the complexion of them all 28
to leave the dam.   29

SHYLOCK   She is damned for it.

SALERIO   That's certain, if the devil may be her judge.

SHYLOCK   My own flesh and blood to rebel!

SOLANIO   Out upon it, old carrion! Rebels it at these 33
years?   34

SHYLOCK   I say, my daughter is my flesh and my blood.

SALERIO   There is more difference between thy flesh and
hers than between jet and ivory, more between your 37
bloods than there is between red wine and Rhenish. 38
But tell us, do you hear whether Antonio have had
any loss at sea or no?

SHYLOCK   There I have another bad match! A bankrupt, 41
a prodigal, who dare scarce show his head on the
Rialto; a beggar, that was used to come so smug upon
the mart! Let him look to his bond. He was wont to
call me usurer. Let him look to his bond. He was wont
to lend money for a Christian courtesy. Let him look to
his bond.

SALERIO   Why, I am sure, if he forfeit, thou wilt not take
his flesh. What's that good for?

SHYLOCK   To bait fish withal. If it will feed nothing else, 50
it will feed my revenge. He hath disgraced me, and
hindered me half a million, laughed at my losses,
mocked at my gains, scorned my nation, thwarted my
bargains, cooled my friends, heated mine enemies;
and what's his reason? I am a Jew. Hath not a Jew
eyes? Hath not a Jew hands, organs, dimensions,
senses, affections, passions? Fed with the same food,
hurt with the same weapons, subject to the same diseases, healed by the same means, warmed and cooled
by the same winter and summer, as a Christian is? If
you prick us, do we not bleed? If you tickle us, do we
not laugh? If you poison us, do we not die? And if you
wrong us, shall we not revenge? If we are like you in

---

28 **fledge** ready to fly.   **complexion** natural disposition   **29 dam**
mother   **33–34 Rebels . . . years** (Solanio pretends to interpret Shylock's
cry about the rebellion of his own flesh and blood as referring to his
own carnal desires.)   **37 jet** a hard form of coal capable of taking a
brilliant polish   **38 Rhenish** i.e., a German white wine from the Rhine
valley   **41 match** bargain   **50 To bait** to lure, to act as bait for

the rest, we will resemble you in that. If a Jew wrong
a Christian, what is his humility? Revenge. If a Chris-   65
tian wrong a Jew, what should his sufferance be by   66
Christian example? Why, revenge. The villainy you
teach me I will execute, and it shall go hard but I will
better the instruction.

Enter a Man from Antonio.

MAN   Gentlemen, my master Antonio is at his house
and desires to speak with you both.

SALERIO   We have been up and down to seek him.

Enter Tubal.

SOLANIO   Here comes another of the tribe. A third cannot be matched, unless the devil himself turn Jew.   74

Exeunt gentlemen [Solanio, Salerio, with Man].

SHYLOCK   How now, Tubal, what news from Genoa?
Hast thou found my daughter?

TUBAL   I often came where I did hear of her, but cannot
find her.

SHYLOCK   Why, there, there, there, there! A diamond
gone, cost me two thousand ducats in Frankfort! The
curse never fell upon our nation till now; I never felt it
till now. Two thousand ducats in that, and other precious, precious jewels. I would my daughter
were dead at my foot, and the jewels in her ear! Would she
were hearsed at my foot, and the ducats in her coffin!   85
No news of them? Why, so—and I know not what's
spent in the search. Why, thou loss upon loss! The
thief gone with so much, and so much to find the
thief, and no satisfaction, no revenge! Nor no ill luck
stirring but what lights o' my shoulders, no sighs but
o' my breathing, no tears but o' my shedding.

TUBAL   Yes, other men have ill luck too. Antonio, as I
heard in Genoa—

SHYLOCK   What, what, what? Ill luck, ill luck?

TUBAL   —hath an argosy cast away, coming from Tripolis.

SHYLOCK   I thank God, I thank God. Is it true, is it true?

TUBAL   I spoke with some of the sailors that escaped the
wreck.

65-66 his ... his the Christian's ... the Jew's   **74 matched** i.e., found to
match them   **85 hearsed** coffined

SHYLOCK I thank thee, good Tubal. Good news, good
news! Ha, ha! Heard in Genoa?

TUBAL Your daughter spent in Genoa, as I heard, one
night fourscore ducats.

SHYLOCK Thou stick'st a dagger in me. I shall never see
my gold again. Fourscore ducats at a sitting, fourscore
ducats!

TUBAL There came divers of Antonio's creditors in my
company to Venice that swear he cannot choose but
break.   108

SHYLOCK I am very glad of it. I'll plague him, I'll torture
him. I am glad of it.

TUBAL One of them showed me a ring that he had of
your daughter for a monkey.

SHYLOCK Out upon her! Thou torturest me, Tubal. It
was my turquoise; I had it of Leah when I was a bach-   114
elor. I would not have given it for a wilderness of
monkeys.

TUBAL But Antonio is certainly undone.

SHYLOCK Nay, that's true, that's very true. Go, Tubal,
fee me an officer; bespeak him a fortnight before. I will 119
have the heart of him if he forfeit, for were he out of
Venice I can make what merchandise I will. Go,   121
Tubal, and meet me at our synagogue; go, good Tubal;
at our synagogue, Tubal.   *Exeunt.*

❧

3.2   *Enter Bassanio, Portia, Gratiano, [Nerissa,] and
all their trains.*

PORTIA
I pray you, tarry. Pause a day or two
Before you hazard, for in choosing wrong   2
I lose your company. Therefore forbear awhile.
There's something tells me, but it is not love,
I would not lose you; and you know yourself,

108 break go bankrupt **114 Leah** Shylock's wife **119 fee** hire. **officer**
bailiff. **bespeak** engage **121 make . . . I will** drive whatever bargains I
please

3.2. Location: Belmont. Portia's house.
2 in choosing in your choosing

Hate counsels not in such a quality.   6
But lest you should not understand me well—
And yet a maiden hath no tongue but thought—
I would detain you here some month or two
Before you venture for me. I could teach you
How to choose right, but then I am forsworn.
So will I never be. So may you miss me.   12
But if you do, you'll make me wish a sin,
That I had been forsworn. Beshrew your eyes,
They have o'erlooked me and divided me!   15
One half of me is yours, the other half yours—
Mine own, I would say; but if mine, then yours,
And so all yours. O, these naughty times   18
Puts bars between the owners and their rights!   19
And so, though yours, not yours. Prove it so,   20
Let Fortune go to hell for it, not I.
I speak too long, but 'tis to peise the time,   22
To eke it and to draw it out in length,   23
To stay you from election.

BASSANIO   Let me choose,
For as I am, I live upon the rack.

PORTIA
Upon the rack, Bassanio? Then confess   26
What treason there is mingled with your love.   27

BASSANIO
None but that ugly treason of mistrust,   28
Which makes me fear th' enjoying of my love.   29
There may as well be amity and life
'Tween snow and fire, as treason and my love.

PORTIA
Ay, but I fear you speak upon the rack,
Where men enforcèd do speak anything.

BASSANIO
Promise me life, and I'll confess the truth.

---

6 quality way, manner   **12 So . . . So** that . . . therefore.   **miss**
i.e., fail to win   **15 o'erlooked** bewitched   **18 naughty** worthless, wicked   **19 bars** barriers   **20 Prove it so** if it prove so
22 peise retard (by hanging on of weights)   **23 eke** eke out, augment   **26–27 confess What treason** (The rack was used to force
traitors to confess.)   **28 mistrust** misapprehension   **29 fear** fearful
about

PORTIA
  Well then, confess and live.
BASSANIO   "Confess and love"
  Had been the very sum of my confession.
  O happy torment, when my torturer
  Doth teach me answers for deliverance!
  But let me to my fortune and the caskets.   39
PORTIA
  Away, then! I am locked in one of them.
  If you do love me, you will find me out.
  Nerissa and the rest, stand all aloof.   42
  Let music sound while he doth make his choice;
  Then, if he lose, he makes a swanlike end,   44
  Fading in music. That the comparison
  May stand more proper, my eye shall be the stream
  And watery deathbed for him. He may win;
  And what is music then? Then music is
  Even as the flourish when true subjects bow   49
  To a new-crownèd monarch. Such it is
  As are those dulcet sounds in break of day
  That creep into the dreaming bridegroom's ear
  And summon him to marriage. Now he goes,
  With no less presence, but with much more love,
  Than young Alcides, when he did redeem   55
  The virgin tribute paid by howling Troy   56
  To the sea monster. I stand for sacrifice;   57
  The rest aloof are the Dardanian wives,   58
  With blearèd visages, come forth to view   59
  The issue of th' exploit. Go, Hercules!   60
  Live thou, I live. With much, much more dismay   61
  I view the fight than thou that mak'st the fray.

39 fortune . . . caskets (Presumably the curtains are drawn at about
this point, as in the previous "casket" scenes, revealing the three
caskets.)   **42 aloof** apart, at a distance   **44 swanlike** (Swans were
believed to sing when they came to die.)   **49 flourish** sounding of
trumpets   **55 Alcides** (Hercules rescued Hesione, daughter of the Trojan king Laomedon, from a monster to which, by command of Neptune,
she was about to be sacrificed. Hercules was rewarded, however, not
with the lady's love, but with a famous pair of horses.)   **56 howling**
lamenting   **57 stand for sacrifice** represent the sacrificial victim
58 Dardanian Trojan   **59 blearèd** weeping   **60 issue** outcome   **61 Live
thou** if you live

*A song, [sung by one of Portia's train,] the whilst
Bassanio comments on the caskets to himself.*

[Song.]

Tell me where is fancy bred,   63
Or in the heart or in the head?   64
How begot, how nourishèd?
  Reply, reply.
It is engenderèd in the eyes,   67
With gazing fed, and fancy dies
In the cradle where it lies.   69
   Let us all ring fancy's knell.
   I'll begin it—Ding, dong, bell.
ALL   Ding, dong, bell.

BASSANIO
So may the outward shows be least themselves;   73
The world is still deceived with ornament.   74
In law, what plea so tainted and corrupt
But, being seasoned with a gracious voice,
Obscures the show of evil? In religion,
What damnèd error but some sober brow
Will bless it and approve it with a text,   79
Hiding the grossness with fair ornament?
There is no vice so simple but assumes   81
Some mark of virtue on his outward parts.   82
How many cowards, whose hearts are all as false
As stairs of sand, wear yet upon their chins   84
The beards of Hercules and frowning Mars,
Who, inward searched, have livers white as milk!   86
And these assume but valor's excrement   87
To render them redoubted. Look on beauty,   88
And you shall see 'tis purchased by the weight,
Which therein works a miracle in nature,

---

63 fancy love   **64 Or** either   **67 eyes** (Love entered the heart especially
through the eyes.)   **69 In the cradle** i.e., in its infancy, in the eyes
73 be least themselves least represent the inner reality   **74 still** ever
79 approve confirm   **81 simple** unadulterated   **82 his** its   **84 stairs**
steps   **86 livers** (The liver was thought to be the seat of courage; for it
to be deserted by the blood would be the condition of cowardice.)
87 excrement outgrowth, such as a beard (as in this case) or finger-
nails   **88 redoubted** feared

Making them lightest that wear most of it.   91
So are those crispèd snaky golden locks,   92
Which maketh such wanton gambols with the wind
Upon supposèd fairness, often known   94
To be the dowry of a second head,   95
The skull that bred them in the sepulcher.   96
Thus ornament is but the guilèd shore   97
To a most dangerous sea, the beauteous scarf
Veiling an Indian beauty; in a word,   99
The seeming truth which cunning times put on
To entrap the wisest. Therefore, thou gaudy gold,
Hard food for Midas, I will none of thee;   102
Nor none of thee, thou pale and common drudge   103
'Tween man and man. But thou, thou meager lead,   104
Which rather threaten'st than dost promise aught,
Thy paleness moves me more than eloquence;
And here choose I. Joy be the consequence!

PORTIA [*Aside*]
How all the other passions fleet to air,
As doubtful thoughts, and rash-embraced despair,   109
And shuddering fear, and green-eyed jealousy!
O love, be moderate, allay thy ecstasy,
In measure rain thy joy, scant this excess!   112
I feel too much thy blessing. Make it less,
For fear I surfeit.

BASSANIO [*Opening the leaden casket*]
                    What find I here?
Fair Portia's counterfeit! What demigod   115
Hath come so near creation? Move these eyes?
Or whether, riding on the balls of mine,
Seem they in motion? Here are severed lips,
Parted with sugar breath; so sweet a bar   119
Should sunder such sweet friends. Here in her hairs   120

---

91 lightest most lascivious (with pun on the sense of "least heavy")
92 crispèd curly   **94 Upon supposèd fairness** i.e., on a woman supposed
beautiful and fairhaired   **95–96 To . . . sepulcher** i.e., to be a wig of hair
taken from a woman now dead   **97 guilèd** treacherous   **99 Indian** i.e.,
swarthy, not fair   **102 Midas** the Phrygian king whose touch turned
everything to gold, including his food   **103–104 pale . . . man** i.e., silver,
used in commerce   **109 As** such as   **112 rain** rain down, or perhaps
rein.   **scant** lessen   **115 counterfeit** portrait.   **demigod** i.e., the painter
as creator   **119 so sweet a bar** i.e., Portia's breath   **120 sweet friends**
i.e., her lips

The painter plays the spider, and hath woven
A golden mesh t' entrap the hearts of men
Faster than gnats in cobwebs. But her eyes—   123
How could he see to do them? Having made one,
Methinks it should have power to steal both his
And leave itself unfurnished. Yet look how far   126
The substance of my praise doth wrong this shadow   127
In underprizing it, so far this shadow
Doth limp behind the substance. Here's the scroll,   129
The continent and summary of my fortune.   130
    [*Reads.*] "You that choose not by the view,
        Chance as fair, and choose as true!   132
        Since this fortune falls to you,
        Be content and seek no new.
        If you be well pleased with this,
        And hold your fortune for your bliss,
        Turn you where your lady is
        And claim her with a loving kiss."
A gentle scroll. Fair lady, by your leave,
I come by note, to give and to receive.   140
Like one of two contending in a prize,   141
That thinks he hath done well in people's eyes,
Hearing applause and universal shout,
Giddy in spirit, still gazing in a doubt
Whether those peals of praise be his or no,   145
So, thrice-fair lady, stand I even so,
As doubtful whether what I see be true,
Until confirmed, signed, ratified by you.

PORTIA
You see me, Lord Bassanio, where I stand,
Such as I am. Though for myself alone
I would not be ambitious in my wish
To wish myself much better, yet for you
I would be trebled twenty times myself,
A thousand times more fair, ten thousand times more
   rich,
That only to stand high in your account   155

123 **Faster** more tightly   126 **unfurnished** i.e., without a companion.
look how far however far   127 **shadow** painting   129 **the substance** the
subject, i.e., Portia   130 **continent** container   132 **Chance as fair** hazard
as fortunately   140 **by note** as indicated (i.e., as directed by the scroll)
141 **prize** competition   145 **his** for him   155 **account** estimation

I might in virtues, beauties, livings, friends,   156
Exceed account. But the full sum of me   157
Is sum of something, which, to term in gross,   158
Is an unlessoned girl, unschooled, unpracticèd;
Happy in this, she is not yet so old
But she may learn; happier than this,
She is not bred so dull but she can learn;
Happiest of all is that her gentle spirit
Commits itself to yours to be directed,
As from her lord, her governor, her king.
Myself and what is mine to you and yours
Is now converted. But now I was the lord   167
Of this fair mansion, master of my servants,
Queen o'er myself; and even now, but now,
This house, these servants, and this same myself
Are yours, my lord's. I give them with this ring,
Which when you part from, lose, or give away,
Let it presage the ruin of your love
And be my vantage to exclaim on you.   174

                    [*She puts a ring on his finger.*]

BASSANIO
Madam, you have bereft me of all words.
Only my blood speaks to you in my veins,
And there is such confusion in my powers   177
As, after some oration fairly spoke
By a belovèd prince, there doth appear
Among the buzzing pleasèd multitude,
Where every something being blent together   181
Turns to a wild of nothing save of joy   182
Expressed and not expressed. But when this ring   183
Parts from this finger, then parts life from hence.
O, then be bold to say Bassanio's dead!

NERISSA
My lord and lady, it is now our time,
That have stood by and seen our wishes prosper,   187
To cry, good joy. Good joy, my lord and lady!

---

156 livings possessions   **157 account** calculation   **158 something** i.e., at
least something.   **term in gross** relate in full   **167 But now** a moment
ago   **174 exclaim on** reproach   **177 powers** faculties   **181–183 Where
. . . expressed** i.e., in which every individual utterance, being blended
and confused, turns into a hubbub of joy that speaks and yet in no
understood tongue   **187 That** we who

GRATIANO
  My lord Bassanio and my gentle lady,
  I wish you all the joy that you can wish—
  For I am sure you can wish none from me.   191
  And when your honors mean to solemnize
  The bargain of your faith, I do beseech you,
  Even at that time I may be married too.

BASSANIO
  With all my heart, so thou canst get a wife.   195

GRATIANO
  I thank your lordship, you have got me one.
  My eyes, my lord, can look as swift as yours.
  You saw the mistress, I beheld the maid;   198
  You loved, I loved; for intermission   199
  No more pertains to me, my lord, than you.
  Your fortune stood upon the caskets there,
  And so did mine too, as the matter falls;
  For wooing here until I sweat again,   203
  And swearing till my very roof was dry   204
  With oaths of love, at last, if promise last,   205
  I got a promise of this fair one here
  To have her love, provided that your fortune
  Achieved her mistress.

PORTIA   Is this true, Nerissa?

NERISSA
  Madam, it is, so you stand pleased withal.   209

BASSANIO
  And do you, Gratiano, mean good faith?

GRATIANO   Yes, faith, my lord.

BASSANIO
  Our feast shall be much honored in your marriage.

GRATIANO   We'll play with them the first boy for a thou-   213
  sand ducats.

NERISSA   What, and stake down?   215

---

191 For . . . me i.e., I'm sure I can't wish you any more joy than you
could wish for yourselves   **195 so** provided   **198 maid** (Nerissa is a
lady-in-waiting, not a house servant.)   **199 intermission** delay (in loving)   **203 sweat again** sweated repeatedly   **204 roof** roof of my mouth
205 if promise last i.e., if Nerissa's promise should last, hold out
209 so provided   **213 play** wager   **215 stake down** cash placed in
advance. (But Gratiano, in his reply, turns the phrase into a bawdy joke;
stake down to him suggests a nonerect phallus.)

GRATIANO   No, we shall ne'er win at that sport, and
stake down.
But who comes here? Lorenzo and his infidel?
What, and my old Venetian friend Salerio?

*Enter Lorenzo, Jessica, and Salerio, a messenger
from Venice.*

BASSANIO
Lorenzo and Salerio, welcome hither,
If that the youth of my new interest here   221
Have power to bid you welcome.—By your leave,
I bid my very friends and countrymen,   223
Sweet Portia, welcome.
PORTIA   So do I, my lord.
They are entirely welcome.
LORENZO
I thank your honor. For my part, my lord,
My purpose was not to have seen you here,
But meeting with Salerio by the way,
He did intreat me, past all saying nay,
To come with him along.
SALERIO   I did, my lord,
And I have reason for it. Signor Antonio
Commends him to you.   [*He gives Bassanio a letter.*]
BASSANIO   Ere I ope his letter,   232
I pray you tell me how my good friend doth.
SALERIO
Not sick, my lord, unless it be in mind,
Nor well, unless in mind. His letter there
Will show you his estate. [*Bassanio*] *open*[*s*] *the letter.* 236
GRATIANO
Nerissa, cheer yond stranger, bid her welcome.   237
Your hand, Salerio. What's the news from Venice?
How doth that royal merchant, good Antonio?   239
I know he will be glad of our success;
We are the Jasons, we have won the fleece.   241

---

221 youth . . . interest i.e., newness of my household authority
223 very true   **232 Commends him** desires to be remembered   **236 estate** condition   **237 stranger** i.e., Jessica   **239 royal merchant** i.e., chief
among merchants   **241 Jasons . . . fleece** (Cf. 1.1.170–172.)

SALERIO
I would you had won the fleece that he hath lost.

PORTIA
There are some shrewd contents in yond same paper   243
That steals the color from Bassanio's cheek—
Some dear friend dead, else nothing in the world
Could turn so much the constitution
Of any constant man. What, worse and worse?   247
With leave, Bassanio; I am half yourself,
And I must freely have the half of anything
That this same paper brings you.

BASSANIO   O sweet Portia,
Here are a few of the unpleasant'st words
That ever blotted paper! Gentle lady,
When I did first impart my love to you,
I freely told you all the wealth I had
Ran in my veins, I was a gentleman;
And then I told you true. And yet, dear lady,
Rating myself at nothing, you shall see
How much I was a braggart. When I told you
My state was nothing, I should then have told you   259
That I was worse than nothing; for indeed
I have engaged myself to a dear friend,
Engaged my friend to his mere enemy,   262
To feed my means. Here is a letter, lady,
The paper as the body of my friend,
And every word in it a gaping wound
Issuing lifeblood. But is it true, Salerio?
Hath all his ventures failed? What, not one hit?   267
From Tripolis, from Mexico, and England,
From Lisbon, Barbary, and India,
And not one vessel scape the dreadful touch
Of merchant-marring rocks?

SALERIO   Not one, my lord.   271
Besides, it should appear that if he had
The present money to discharge the Jew,   273
He would not take it. Never did I know   274
A creature that did bear the shape of man

---

243 shrewd cursed, grievous **247 constant** settled, not swayed by
passion **259 state** estate **262 mere** absolute **267 hit** success
271 merchant merchant ship **273 present** available. **discharge** pay
off **274 He** i.e., Shylock

So keen and greedy to confound a man.   276
He plies the Duke at morning and at night,
And doth impeach the freedom of the state   278
If they deny him justice. Twenty merchants,
The Duke himself, and the magnificoes   280
Of greatest port have all persuaded with him,   281
But none can drive him from the envious plea
Of forfeiture, of justice, and his bond.

JESSICA
When I was with him I have heard him swear
To Tubal and to Chus, his countrymen,
That he would rather have Antonio's flesh
Than twenty times the value of the sum
That he did owe him; and I know, my lord,
If law, authority, and power deny not,
It will go hard with poor Antonio.

PORTIA
Is it your dear friend that is thus in trouble?

BASSANIO
The dearest friend to me, the kindest man,
The best-conditioned and unwearied spirit   293
In doing courtesies, and one in whom
The ancient Roman honor more appears
Than any that draws breath in Italy.

PORTIA   What sum owes he the Jew?

BASSANIO
For me, three thousand ducats.

PORTIA   What, no more?
Pay him six thousand, and deface the bond;   299
Double six thousand, and then treble that,
Before a friend of this description
Shall lose a hair through Bassanio's fault.
First go with me to church and call me wife,
And then away to Venice to your friend;
For never shall you lie by Portia's side
With an unquiet soul. You shall have gold
To pay the petty debt twenty times over.
When it is paid, bring your true friend along.

---

276 keen cruel. **confound** destroy **278 impeach . . . state** i.e., call in question the ability of Venice to defend legally the freedom of commerce of its citizens **280 magnificoes** chief men of Venice **281 port** dignity. **persuaded** argued **293 best-conditioned** best natured **299 deface** erase

My maid Nerissa and myself meantime
Will live as maids and widows. Come, away!
For you shall hence upon your wedding day.
Bid your friends welcome, show a merry cheer;   312
Since you are dear bought, I will love you dear.
But let me hear the letter of your friend.

BASSANIO [*Reads*] "Sweet Bassanio, my ships have all
miscarried, my creditors grow cruel, my estate is very
low, my bond to the Jew is forfeit; and since in paying
it, it is impossible I should live, all debts are cleared
between you and I, if I might but see you at my death.
Notwithstanding, use your pleasure; if your love do
not persuade you to come, let not my letter."

PORTIA
O love, dispatch all business, and begone!

BASSANIO
Since I have your good leave to go away,
I will make haste; but till I come again,
No bed shall e'er be guilty of my stay,
Nor rest be interposer twixt us twain.   *Exeunt.*

❖

3.3   *Enter [Shylock] the Jew and Solanio and
Antonio and the Jailer.*

SHYLOCK
Jailer, look to him. Tell not me of mercy.
This is the fool that lent out money gratis.
Jailer, look to him.

ANTONIO   Hear me yet, good Shylock.

SHYLOCK
I'll have my bond. Speak not against my bond!
I have sworn an oath that I will have my bond.
Thou calledst me dog before thou hadst a cause,
But since I am a dog, beware my fangs.
The Duke shall grant me justice. I do wonder,
Thou naughty jailer, that thou art so fond   9

312 **cheer** countenance

3.3. Location: Venice. A street.
9 **naughty** worthless.   **fond** foolish

To come abroad with him at his request.   10
ANTONIO   I pray thee, hear me speak.
SHYLOCK
  I'll have my bond. I will not hear thee speak.
  I'll have my bond, and therefore speak no more.
  I'll not be made a soft and dull-eyed fool,
  To shake the head, relent, and sigh, and yield
  To Christian intercessors. Follow not;
  I'll have no speaking. I will have my bond.   *Exit Jew.*
SOLANIO
  It is the most impenetrable cur
  That ever kept with men.
ANTONIO   Let him alone.   19
  I'll follow him no more with bootless prayers.   20
  He seeks my life. His reason well I know:
  I oft delivered from his forfeitures
  Many that have at times made moan to me;
  Therefore he hates me.
SOLANIO   I am sure the Duke
  Will never grant this forfeiture to hold.
ANTONIO
  The Duke cannot deny the course of law;
  For the commodity that strangers have   27
  With us in Venice, if it be denied,
  Will much impeach the justice of the state,
  Since that the trade and profit of the city   30
  Consisteth of all nations. Therefore go.
  These griefs and losses have so bated me   32
  That I shall hardly spare a pound of flesh
  Tomorrow to my bloody creditor.
  Well, jailer, on. Pray God Bassanio come
  To see me pay his debt, and then I care not.   *Exeunt.*

❖

3.4   *Enter Portia, Nerissa, Lorenzo, Jessica, and*
       [Balthasar,] a man of Portia's.

10 abroad outside   **19 kept** associated, dwelt   **20 bootless** unavailing
27 commodity facilities or privileges for trading.   **strangers** noncitizens, including Jews   **30 Since that** since   **32 bated** reduced

3.4. Location: Belmont. Portia's house.

LORENZO
  Madam, although I speak it in your presence,
  You have a noble and a true conceit   2
  Of godlike amity, which appears most strongly
  In bearing thus the absence of your lord.
  But if you knew to whom you show this honor,
  How true a gentleman you send relief,
  How dear a lover of my lord your husband,
  I know you would be prouder of the work
  Than customary bounty can enforce you.   9

PORTIA
  I never did repent for doing good,
  Nor shall not now; for in companions
  That do converse and waste the time together,   12
  Whose souls do bear an equal yoke of love,
  There must be needs a like proportion   14
  Of lineaments, of manners, and of spirit;   15
  Which makes me think that this Antonio,
  Being the bosom lover of my lord,
  Must needs be like my lord. If it be so,
  How little is the cost I have bestowed
  In purchasing the semblance of my soul   20
  From out the state of hellish cruelty!
  This comes too near the praising of myself;
  Therefore no more of it. Hear other things:
  Lorenzo, I commit into your hands
  The husbandry and manage of my house   25
  Until my lord's return. For mine own part,
  I have toward heaven breathed a secret vow
  To live in prayer and contemplation,
  Only attended by Nerissa here,
  Until her husband and my lord's return.
  There is a monastery two miles off,
  And there we will abide. I do desire you
  Not to deny this imposition,   33
  The which my love and some necessity
  Now lays upon you.

2 conceit understanding   **9 Than . . . you** than ordinary benevolence can make you   **12 waste** spend   **14 must be needs** must be   **15 lineaments** physical features   **20 the semblance of my soul** i.e., Antonio, so like my Bassanio   **25 husbandry and manage** care of the household   **33 deny this imposition** refuse this charge imposed

LORENZO   Madam, with all my heart.
  I shall obey you in all fair commands.
PORTIA
  My people do already know my mind,
  And will acknowledge you and Jessica
  In place of Lord Bassanio and myself.
  So fare you well till we shall meet again.
LORENZO
  Fair thoughts and happy hours attend on you!
JESSICA
  I wish your ladyship all heart's content.
PORTIA
  I thank you for your wish and am well pleased
  To wish it back on you. Fare you well, Jessica.
                          Exeunt [*Jessica and Lorenzo*].
  Now, Balthasar,
  As I have ever found thee honest-true,
  So let me find thee still. Take this same letter,
                          [*Giving a letter*]
  And use thou all th' endeavor of a man
  In speed to Padua. See thou render this
  Into my cousin's hands, Doctor Bellario;
  And look what notes and garments he doth give thee,   51
  Bring them, I pray thee, with imagined speed   52
  Unto the traject, to the common ferry   53
  Which trades to Venice. Waste no time in words,.   54
  But get thee gone. I shall be there before thee.
BALTHASAR
  Madam, I go with all convenient speed.   [*Exit.*] 56
PORTIA
  Come on, Nerissa, I have work in hand
  That you yet know not of. We'll see our husbands
  Before they think of us.
NERISSA   Shall they see us?
PORTIA
  They shall, Nerissa, but in such a habit   60
  That they shall think we are accomplishèd   61

---

51 look what whatever **52 imagined** imaginable **53 traject** ferry.
(Italian *traghetto*.) **54 trades** plies back and forth **56 convenient** due,
proper **60 habit** apparel, garb **61 accomplishèd** supplied

With that we lack. I'll hold thee any wager,   62
When we are both accoutred like young men,
I'll prove the prettier fellow of the two,
And wear my dagger with the braver grace,
And speak between the change of man and boy
With a reed voice, and turn two mincing steps
Into a manly stride, and speak of frays
Like a fine bragging youth, and tell quaint lies,   69
How honorable ladies sought my love,
Which I denying, they fell sick and died—
I could not do withal! Then I'll repent,   72
And wish, for all that, that I had not killed them;
And twenty of these puny lies I'll tell,   74
That men shall swear I have discontinued school   75
Above a twelvemonth. I have within my mind   76
A thousand raw tricks of these bragging Jacks,   77
Which I will practice.

NERISSA   Why, shall we turn to men?   78

PORTIA   Fie, what a question's that,
If thou wert near a lewd interpreter!
But come, I'll tell thee all my whole device
When I am in my coach, which stays for us
At the park gate; and therefore haste away,
For we must measure twenty miles today.   *Exeunt.*

❖

3.5   *Enter [Launcelot the] Clown and Jessica.*

LAUNCELOT   Yes truly, for look you, the sins of the father are to be laid upon the children; therefore, I promise you, I fear you. I was always plain with you, and   3
so now I speak my agitation of the matter. Therefore   4
be o' good cheer, for truly I think you are damned.

---

62 that that which (with a bawdy suggestion)   **69 quaint** elaborate,
clever   **72 do withal** help it   **74 puny** childish   **75–76 I . . . twelvemonth** i.e., that I am no mere schoolboy   **76 Above** more than
77 Jacks fellows   **78 turn to** turn into. (But Portia sees the occasion
for a bawdy quibble on the idea of "turning toward, lying next to.")

3.5. Location: Belmont. Outside Portia's house.
3 fear you fear for you   **4 agitation** consideration

There is but one hope in it that can do you any good,
and that is but a kind of bastard hope neither.   7

JESSICA   And what hope is that, I pray thee?

LAUNCELOT   Marry, you may partly hope that your father got you not, that you are not the Jew's daughter.   10

JESSICA   That were a kind of bastard hope indeed! So
the sins of my mother should be visited upon me.

LAUNCELOT   Truly then I fear you are damned both by
father and mother. Thus when I shun Scylla, your fa-   14
ther, I fall into Charybdis, your mother. Well, you are   15
gone both ways.   16

JESSICA   I shall be saved by my husband. He hath made   17
me a Christian.

LAUNCELOT   Truly, the more to blame he! We were
Christians enough before, e'en as many as could well   20
live one by another. This making of Christians will   21
raise the price of hogs. If we grow all to be pork eaters,
we shall not shortly have a rasher on the coals for   23
money.   24

   Enter Lorenzo.

JESSICA   I'll tell my husband, Launcelot, what you say.
Here he comes.

LORENZO   I shall grow jealous of you shortly, Launcelot,
if you thus get my wife into corners.

JESSICA   Nay, you need not fear us, Lorenzo. Launcelot
and I are out. He tells me flatly there's no mercy for me   30
in heaven because I am a Jew's daughter; and he says
you are no good member of the commonwealth, for in
converting Jews to Christians you raise the price of
pork.

LORENZO   I shall answer that better to the commonwealth than you can the getting up of the Negro's
belly. The Moor is with child by you, Launcelot.

---

7 neither i.e., to be sure   **10 got** begot   **14, 15 Scylla, Charybdis** twin
dangers of the *Odyssey*, 12.255, a monster and a whirlpool guarding the
straits presumably between Italy and Sicily   **16 gone** done for   **17 I . . .
husband** (Cf. 1 Corinthians 7:14: "the unbelieving wife is sanctified by
the husband.")   **20 enough** i.e., there were enough of us   **21 one by
another** together   **23 rasher** i.e., of bacon   **23–24 for money** even for
ready money, at any price   **30 are out** have fallen out

LAUNCELOT   It is much that the Moor should be more   38
   than reason; but if she be less than an honest woman,   39
   she is indeed more than I took her for.

LORENZO   How every fool can play upon the word! I
   think the best grace of wit will shortly turn into si-   42
   lence, and discourse grow commendable in none only
   but parrots. Go in, sirrah, bid them prepare for
   dinner.

LAUNCELOT   That is done, sir. They have all stomachs.   46

LORENZO   Goodly Lord, what a wit-snapper are you!
   Then bid them prepare dinner.

LAUNCELOT   That is done too, sir, only "cover" is the   49
   word.

LORENZO   Will you cover then, sir?   51

LAUNCELOT   Not so, sir, neither. I know my duty.

LORENZO   Yet more quarreling with occasion! Wilt thou   53
   show the whole wealth of thy wit in an instant? I pray
   thee, understand a plain man in his plain meaning: go
   to thy fellows, bid them cover the table, serve in the
   meat, and we will come in to dinner.   57

LAUNCELOT   For the table, sir, it shall be served in; for   58
   the meat, sir, it shall be covered; for your coming in to   59
   dinner, sir, why, let it be as humors and conceits shall   60
   govern.   *Exit Clown.*

LORENZO
   O dear discretion, how his words are suited!   62
   The fool hath planted in his memory
   An army of good words; and I do know
   A many fools, that stand in better place,   65
   Garnished like him, that for a tricksy word   66
   Defy the matter. How cheer'st thou, Jessica?   67

38–39 more than reason larger than is reasonable (with wordplay on
Moor, more, continued in l. 40)   **39 honest** chaste   **42 best grace** highest quality   **46 stomachs** appetites   **49, 51 cover** spread the table for
the meal. (But in his next speech Launcelot uses the word to mean "put
on one's hat.")   **53 Yet . . . occasion** i.e., still quibbling at every opportunity   **57 meat** food   **58 table** (Here Launcelot quibblingly uses the word
to mean the food itself.)   **59 covered** (Here used in the sense of providing a cover for each separate dish.)   **60 humors and conceits** whims and
fancies   **62 discretion** discrimination.   **suited** suited to the occasion
65 A many many.   **better place** higher social station   **66 Garnished** i.e.,
furnished with words.   **tricksy** playful   **66–67 that . . . matter** who for
the sake of ingenious wordplay do violence to common sense   **67 How
cheer'st thou** i.e., what cheer

And now, good sweet, say thy opinion,
How dost thou like the Lord Bassanio's wife?

JESSICA
Past all expressing. It is very meet   70
The Lord Bassanio live an upright life,
For, having such a blessing in his lady,
He finds the joys of heaven here on earth;
And if on earth he do not merit it,
In reason he should never come to heaven.   75
Why, if two gods should play some heavenly match
And on the wager lay two earthly women,   77
And Portia one, there must be something else   78
Pawned with the other, for the poor rude world   79
Hath not her fellow.

LORENZO   Even such a husband
Hast thou of me as she is for a wife.

JESSICA
Nay, but ask my opinion too of that!

LORENZO
I will anon. First let us go to dinner.

JESSICA
Nay, let me praise you while I have a stomach.   84

LORENZO
No, pray thee, let it serve for table talk;
Then, howsoe'er thou speak'st, 'mong other things
I shall digest it.

JESSICA   Well, I'll set you forth.   *Exeunt.* 87

❖

70 **meet** fitting   75 **In reason** it stands to reason. (Jessica jokes that for
Bassanio to receive unmerited bliss on earth—unmerited because no
person can earn bliss through his or her own deserving—is to run the
risk of eternal damnation.)   77 **lay** stake   78 **else** more   79 **Pawned**
staked, wagered   84 **stomach** (1) appetite (2) inclination   87 **digest**
(1) ponder, analyze (2) "swallow," put up with (with a play also on the
gastronomic sense).   **set you forth** (1) serve you up, as at a feast (2) set
forth your praises

4.1   *Enter the Duke, the Magnificoes, Antonio,*
          Bassanio, [Salerio,] and Gratiano [with others.
          The judges take their places.]

DUKE   What, is Antonio here?
ANTONIO   Ready, so please Your Grace.
DUKE
  I am sorry for thee. Thou art come to answer   3
  A stony adversary, an inhuman wretch
  Uncapable of pity, void and empty
  From any dram of mercy.
ANTONIO   I have heard   6
  Your Grace hath ta'en great pains to qualify   7
  His rigorous course; but since he stands obdurate
  And that no lawful means can carry me
  Out of his envy's reach, I do oppose   10
  My patience to his fury and am armed
  To suffer with a quietness of spirit
  The very tyranny and rage of his.   13
DUKE
  Go one, and call the Jew into the court.
SALERIO
  He is ready at the door; he comes, my lord.

    Enter Shylock.

DUKE
  Make room, and let him stand before our face.   16
  Shylock, the world thinks, and I think so too,
  That thou but leadest this fashion of thy malice   18
  To the last hour of act, and then 'tis thought   19
  Thou'lt show thy mercy and remorse more strange   20
  Than is thy strange apparent cruelty;   21
  And where thou now exacts the penalty,
  Which is a pound of this poor merchant's flesh,

**4.1. Location: Venice. A court of justice. Benches, etc., are provided for
the justices.**
3 answer defend yourself against. (A legal term.)   **6 dram** 60 grains
apothecaries' weight, a tiny quantity   **7 qualify** moderate   **10 envy's**
malice's   **13 tyranny** cruelty   **16 our** (The royal plural.)   **18 thou . . .
fashion** you only maintain this pretense or form   **19 act** action, performance   **20 remorse** pity.   **strange** remarkable   **21 apparent** conspicu-
ous, overt

Thou wilt not only loose the forfeiture,   24
But, touched with human gentleness and love,
Forgive a moiety of the principal,   26
Glancing an eye of pity on his losses
That have of late so huddled on his back—
Enough to press a royal merchant down
And pluck commiseration of his state
From brassy bosoms and rough hearts of flint,   31
From stubborn Turks and Tartars never trained
To offices of tender courtesy.
We all expect a gentle answer, Jew.

SHYLOCK
I have possessed Your Grace of what I purpose,   35
And by our holy Sabbath have I sworn
To have the due and forfeit of my bond.
If you deny it, let the danger light   38
Upon your charter and your city's freedom!   39
You'll ask me why I rather choose to have
A weight of carrion flesh than to receive
Three thousand ducats. I'll not answer that,
But say it is my humor. Is it answered?   43
What if my house be troubled with a rat
And I be pleased to give ten thousand ducats
To have it baned? What, are you answered yet?   46
Some men there are love not a gaping pig,   47
Some that are mad if they behold a cat,
And others, when the bagpipe sings i' the nose,
Cannot contain their urine; for affection,   50
Mistress of passion, sways it to the mood
Of what it likes or loathes. Now, for your answer:
As there is no firm reason to be rendered
Why he cannot abide a gaping pig,   54
Why he a harmless necessary cat,   55
Why he a woolen bagpipe, but of force   56
Must yield to such inevitable shame

---

24 loose release, waive   **26 moiety** part, portion   **31 brassy** unfeeling,
i.e., hard like brass   **35 possessed** informed   **38 danger** injury
39 Upon . . . freedom (See 3.2.278.)   **43 humor** whim   **46 baned** killed,
especially by poison or ratsbane   **47 love** who love.   **gaping pig** pig
roasted whole with its mouth open   **50 affection** feeling, inclination
54, 55, 56 he, he, he one person, another, yet another   **56 woolen** i.e.,
with flannel-covered bag

As to offend, himself being offended;
So can I give no reason, nor I will not,
More than a lodged hate and a certain loathing   60
I bear Antonio, that I follow thus
A losing suit against him. Are you answered?   62

BASSANIO
This is no answer, thou unfeeling man,
To excuse the current of thy cruelty.   64

SHYLOCK
I am not bound to please thee with my answers.

BASSANIO
Do all men kill the things they do not love?

SHYLOCK
Hates any man the thing he would not kill?

BASSANIO
Every offense is not a hate at first.

SHYLOCK
What, wouldst thou have a serpent sting thee twice?

ANTONIO
I pray you, think you question with the Jew.   70
You may as well go stand upon the beach
And bid the main flood bate his usual height;   72
You may as well use question with the wolf   73
Why he hath made the ewe bleat for the lamb;
You may as well forbid the mountain pines
To wag their high tops and to make no noise
When they are fretten with the gusts of heaven;   77
You may as well do anything most hard
As seek to soften that—than which what's harder?—
His Jewish heart. Therefore I do beseech you
Make no more offers, use no farther means,
But with all brief and plain conveniency   82
Let me have judgment, and the Jew his will.

BASSANIO
For thy three thousand ducats here is six.

SHYLOCK
If every ducat in six thousand ducats

60 lodged settled, steadfast. **certain** unwavering, fixed **62 losing**
unprofitable **64 current** flow, tendency **70 think** bear in mind.
question argue **72 main flood** sea at high tide. **bate** abate **73 use
question with** interrogate **77 fretten** fretted, i.e., disturbed, ruffled
82 conveniency propriety

Were in six parts, and every part a ducat,
I would not draw them. I would have my bond.   87

DUKE
How shalt thou hope for mercy, rendering none?

SHYLOCK
What judgment shall I dread, doing no wrong?
You have among you many a purchased slave,
Which, like your asses and your dogs and mules,
You use in abject and in slavish parts,   92
Because you bought them. Shall I say to you,
"Let them be free, marry them to your heirs!
Why sweat they under burdens? Let their beds
Be made as soft as yours, and let their palates
Be seasoned with such viands"? You will answer,   97
"The slaves are ours." So do I answer you:
The pound of flesh which I demand of him
Is dearly bought, is mine, and I will have it.
If you deny me, fie upon your law!
There is no force in the decrees of Venice.
I stand for judgment. Answer: shall I have it?

DUKE
Upon my power I may dismiss this court,   104
Unless Bellario, a learnèd doctor,
Whom I have sent for to determine this,
Come here today.

SALERIO   My lord, here stays without   107
A messenger with letters from the doctor,
New come from Padua.

DUKE
Bring us the letters. Call the messenger.

BASSANIO
Good cheer, Antonio! What, man, courage yet!
The Jew shall have my flesh, blood, bones, and all,
Ere thou shalt lose for me one drop of blood.

ANTONIO
I am a tainted wether of the flock,   114
Meetest for death. The weakest kind of fruit   115
Drops earliest to the ground, and so let me.

---

87 draw receive   **92 parts** duties, capacities   **97 viands** food   **104 Upon** in accordance with   **107 stays without** waits outside   **114 tainted wether** old and diseased ram   **115 Meetest** fittest

You cannot better be employed, Bassanio,
Than to live still and write mine epitaph.

   Enter Nerissa [dressed like a lawyer's clerk].

DUKE
Came you from Padua, from Bellario?
NERISSA
From both, my lord. Bellario greets Your Grace.
       [She presents a letter. Shylock whets his knife
                       on his shoe.]

BASSANIO
Why dost thou whet thy knife so earnestly?
SHYLOCK
To cut the forfeiture from that bankrupt there.
GRATIANO
Not on thy sole, but on thy soul, harsh Jew,
Thou mak'st thy knife keen; but no metal can,
No, not the hangman's ax, bear half the keenness   125
Of thy sharp envy. Can no prayers pierce thee?   126
SHYLOCK
No, none that thou hast wit enough to make.
GRATIANO
O, be thou damned, inexecrable dog!   128
And for thy life let justice be accused.   129
Thou almost mak'st me waver in my faith
To hold opinion with Pythagoras,   131
That souls of animals infuse themselves
Into the trunks of men. Thy currish spirit
Governed a wolf who, hanged for human slaughter,   134
Even from the gallows did his fell soul fleet,   135
And, whilst thou layest in thy unhallowed dam,   136
Infused itself in thee; for thy desires
Are wolvish, bloody, starved, and ravenous.

---

125 hangman's executioner's.   **keenness** (1) sharpness (2) savagery
126 envy malice   **128 inexecrable** that cannot be overly execrated or
detested   **129 for thy life** i.e., because you are allowed to live
131 Pythagoras ancient Greek philosopher who argued for the transmigration of souls   **134 hanged for human slaughter** (A possible allusion
to the ancient practice of trying and punishing animals for various
crimes.)   **135 fell** fierce, cruel.   **fleet** flit, i.e., pass from the body
136 dam mother (usually used of animals)

SHYLOCK

  Till thou canst rail the seal from off my bond,   139

  Thou but offend'st thy lungs to speak so loud.   140

  Repair thy wit, good youth, or it will fall

  To cureless ruin. I stand here for law.   142

DUKE

  This letter from Bellario doth commend

  A young and learnèd doctor to our court.

  Where is he?

NERISSA   He attendeth here hard by

  To know your answer, whether you'll admit him.

DUKE

  With all my heart. Some three or four of you

  Go give him courteous conduct to this place.

                         [*Exeunt some.*]

  Meantime the court shall hear Bellario's letter.

  [*Reads.*] "Your Grace shall understand that at the 150
receipt of your letter I am very sick; but in the instant
that your messenger came, in loving visitation was
with me a young doctor of Rome. His name is Balthasar. I acquainted him with the cause in controversy
between the Jew and Antonio the merchant. We
turned o'er many books together. He is furnished with
my opinion, which, bettered with his own learning,
the greatness whereof I cannot enough commend,
comes with him, at my importunity, to fill up Your 159
Grace's request in my stead. I beseech you, let his lack
of years be no impediment to let him lack a reverend 161
estimation, for I never knew so young a body with so
old a head. I leave him to your gracious acceptance,
whose trial shall better publish his commendation." 164

    Enter Portia for Balthasar [*dressed like a doctor
    of laws, escorted*].

  You hear the learned Bellario, what he writes;

---

139 rail revile, use abusive language **140 offend'st** injurest **142 cureless** incurable **150 [Reads.]** (In many modern editions, the reading of
the letter is assigned to a clerk, but the original text gives no such indication.) **159 comes with him** i.e., my opinion is brought by him. **importunity** insistence **161 to let him lack** such as would deprive him of **164 trial**
testing, performance. **publish** make known **s.d., for** i.e., disguised as

And here, I take it, is the doctor come.
Give me your hand. Come you from old Bellario?

PORTIA
I did, my lord.

DUKE   You are welcome. Take your place.
                                [*Portia takes her place.*]
Are you acquainted with the difference   169
That holds this present question in the court?

PORTIA
I am informèd throughly of the cause.   171
Which is the merchant here, and which the Jew?

DUKE
Antonio and old Shylock, both stand forth.

PORTIA
Is your name Shylock?

SHYLOCK   Shylock is my name.

PORTIA
Of a strange nature is the suit you follow,
Yet in such rule that the Venetian law   176
Cannot impugn you as you do proceed.—   177
You stand within his danger, do you not?   178

ANTONIO
Ay, so he says.

PORTIA   Do you confess the bond?

ANTONIO
I do.

PORTIA Then must the Jew be merciful.

SHYLOCK
On what compulsion must I? Tell me that.

PORTIA
The quality of mercy is not strained.   182
It droppeth as the gentle rain from heaven
Upon the place beneath. It is twice blest: 184
It blesseth him that gives and him that takes.
'Tis mightiest in the mightiest; it becomes
The thronèd monarch better than his crown.
His scepter shows the force of temporal power,

169 difference argument **171 throughly** thoroughly. **cause** case
176 rule order **177 impugn** find fault with **178 danger** power to do
harm **182 strained** forced, constrained **184 is twice blest** grants a
double blessing

The attribute to awe and majesty,   189
Wherein doth sit the dread and fear of kings.
But mercy is above this sceptered sway;
It is enthronèd in the hearts of kings;
It is an attribute to God himself;
And earthly power doth then show likest God's
When mercy seasons justice. Therefore, Jew,
Though justice be thy plea, consider this,
That in the course of justice none of us
Should see salvation. We do pray for mercy,
And that same prayer doth teach us all to render
The deeds of mercy. I have spoke thus much
To mitigate the justice of thy plea,   201
Which if thou follow, this strict court of Venice
Must needs give sentence 'gainst the merchant there.

SHYLOCK
My deeds upon my head! I crave the law,   204
The penalty and forfeit of my bond.

PORTIA
Is he not able to discharge the money?

BASSANIO
Yes, here I tender it for him in the court,
Yea, twice the sum. If that will not suffice,
I will be bound to pay it ten times o'er,
On forfeit of my hands, my head, my heart.
If this will not suffice, it must appear
That malice bears down truth. And I beseech you,   212
Wrest once the law to your authority.   213
To do a great right, do a little wrong,
And curb this cruel devil of his will.

PORTIA
It must not be. There is no power in Venice
Can alter a decree establishèd.
'Twill be recorded for a precedent,
And many an error by the same example
Will rush into the state. It cannot be.

189 attribute to symbol of   **201 To . . . plea** i.e., to moderate your plea
for strict justice   **204 My . . . head** i.e., I am prepared to be judged,
as well as live, by a code of strict justice   **212 bears down truth** over-
whelms righteousness   **213 Wrest once** for once, forcibly subject

SHYLOCK
A Daniel come to judgment! Yea, a Daniel!   221
O wise young judge, how I do honor thee!
PORTIA
I pray you, let me look upon the bond.
SHYLOCK [*Giving the bond*]
Here 'tis, most reverend doctor, here it is.
PORTIA
Shylock, there's thrice thy money offered thee.
SHYLOCK
An oath, an oath, I have an oath in heaven!
Shall I lay perjury upon my soul?
No, not for Venice.
PORTIA   Why, this bond is forfeit,
And lawfully by this the Jew may claim
A pound of flesh, to be by him cut off
Nearest the merchant's heart. Be merciful.
Take thrice thy money; bid me tear the bond.
SHYLOCK
When it is paid according to the tenor.   233
It doth appear you are a worthy judge;
You know the law, your exposition
Hath been most sound. I charge you by the law,
Whereof you are a well-deserving pillar,
Proceed to judgment. By my soul I swear
There is no power in the tongue of man
To alter me. I stay here on my bond.   240
ANTONIO
Most heartily I do beseech the court
To give the judgment.
PORTIA   Why then, thus it is:
You must prepare your bosom for his knife.
SHYLOCK
O noble judge! O excellent young man!
PORTIA
For the intent and purpose of the law
Hath full relation to the penalty   246
Which here appeareth due upon the bond.

221 Daniel (In the apocryphal Book of Susannah, Daniel is the young
judge who rescues Susannah from her false accusers.)   **233 tenor**
conditions   **240 stay here on** remain committed to, insist upon
246 Hath . . . to is fully in accord with

SHYLOCK
  'Tis very true. O wise and upright judge!
  How much more elder art thou than thy looks!
PORTIA
  Therefore lay bare your bosom.
SHYLOCK   Ay, his breast;
  So says the bond, doth it not, noble judge?
  "Nearest his heart," those are the very words.
PORTIA
  It is so. Are there balance here   253
  To weigh the flesh?
SHYLOCK   I have them ready.
PORTIA
  Have by some surgeon, Shylock, on your charge,   255
  To stop his wounds, lest he do bleed to death.
SHYLOCK
  Is it so nominated in the bond?
PORTIA
  It is not so expressed, but what of that?
  'Twere good you do so much for charity.
SHYLOCK
  I cannot find it; 'tis not in the bond.
PORTIA
  You, merchant, have you anything to say?
ANTONIO
  But little. I am armed and well prepared.   262
  Give me your hand, Bassanio; fare you well!
  Grieve not that I am fall'n to this for you,
  For herein Fortune shows herself more kind
  Than is her custom. It is still her use   266
  To let the wretched man outlive his wealth,
  To view with hollow eye and wrinkled brow
  An age of poverty; from which lingering penance
  Of such misery doth she cut me off.
  Commend me to your honorable wife.
  Tell her the process of Antonio's end.   272
  Say how I loved you, speak me fair in death;   273
  And, when the tale is told, bid her be judge
  Whether Bassanio had not once a love.   275

253 balance scales   **255 on your charge** at your personal expense   **262 armed**
ready   **266 still her use** i.e., commonly Fortune's practice   **272 process**
story   **273 speak me fair** speak well of me   **275 a love** a friend's love

Repent but you that you shall lose your friend,   276
And he repents not that he pays your debt.
For if the Jew do cut but deep enough,
I'll pay it instantly with all my heart.

BASSANIO
Antonio, I am married to a wife
Which is as dear to me as life itself;
But life itself, my wife, and all the world
Are not with me esteemed above thy life.
I would lose all, ay, sacrifice them all
Here to this devil, to deliver you.

PORTIA
Your wife would give you little thanks for that,
If she were by to hear you make the offer.   287

GRATIANO
I have a wife who I protest I love;
I would she were in heaven, so she could
Entreat some power to change this currish Jew.

NERISSA
'Tis well you offer it behind her back;
The wish would make else an unquiet house.

SHYLOCK
These be the Christian husbands. I have a daughter;
Would any of the stock of Barabbas   294
Had been her husband rather than a Christian!—
We trifle time. I pray thee, pursue sentence.   296

PORTIA
A pound of that same merchant's flesh is thine.
The court awards it, and the law doth give it.

SHYLOCK   Most rightful judge!

PORTIA
And you must cut this flesh from off his breast.
The law allows it, and the court awards it.

SHYLOCK
Most learnèd judge! A sentence! Come, prepare.

PORTIA
Tarry a little; there is something else.

276 Repent but you grieve only   **287 by** nearby   **294 Barabbas** a thief
whom Pontius Pilate set free instead of Christ in response to the people's demand (see Mark 15); also, the villainous protagonist of
Marlowe's *The Jew of Malta*   **296 trifle** waste.   **pursue** proceed with

This bond doth give thee here no jot of blood;
The words expressly are "a pound of flesh."
Take then thy bond, take thou thy pound of flesh;
But in the cutting it if thou dost shed
One drop of Christian blood, thy lands and goods
Are by the laws of Venice confiscate
Unto the state of Venice.

GRATIANO
O upright judge! Mark, Jew. O learnèd judge!

SHYLOCK
Is that the law?

PORTIA   Thyself shalt see the act;
For, as thou urgest justice, be assured
Thou shalt have justice, more than thou desir'st.

GRATIANO
O learnèd judge! Mark, Jew, a learnèd judge!

SHYLOCK
I take this offer, then. Pay the bond thrice
And let the Christian go.

BASSANIO   Here is the money.

PORTIA   Soft!   318
The Jew shall have all justice. Soft, no haste.   319
He shall have nothing but the penalty.

GRATIANO
O Jew! An upright judge, a learnèd judge!

PORTIA
Therefore prepare thee to cut off the flesh.
Shed thou no blood, nor cut thou less nor more
But just a pound of flesh. If thou tak'st more
Or less than a just pound, be it but so much
As makes it light or heavy in the substance   326
Or the division of the twentieth part   327
Of one poor scruple, nay, if the scale do turn   328
But in the estimation of a hair,
Thou diest, and all thy goods are confiscate.

GRATIANO
A second Daniel, a Daniel, Jew!
Now, infidel, I have you on the hip.   332

318 Soft i.e., not so fast   **319 all** nothing but   **326 substance** mass or gross weight   **327 division** fraction   **328 scruple** 20 grains apothecaries' weight, a small quantity   **332 on the hip** i.e., at a disadvantage (a phrase from wrestling)

PORTIA
  Why doth the Jew pause? Take thy forfeiture.
SHYLOCK
  Give me my principal, and let me go.
BASSANIO
  I have it ready for thee; here it is.
PORTIA
  He hath refused it in the open court.
  He shall have merely justice and his bond.
GRATIANO
  A Daniel, still say I, a second Daniel!
  I thank thee, Jew, for teaching me that word.
SHYLOCK
  Shall I not have barely my principal?
PORTIA
  Thou shalt have nothing but the forfeiture,
  To be so taken at thy peril, Jew.
SHYLOCK
  Why, then the devil give him good of it!
  I'll stay no longer question.   [*He starts to go.*]
PORTIA   Tarry, Jew!   344
  The law hath yet another hold on you.
  It is enacted in the laws of Venice,
  If it be proved against an alien
  That by direct or indirect attempts
  He seek the life of any citizen,
  The party 'gainst the which he doth contrive
  Shall seize one half his goods; the other half
  Comes to the privy coffer of the state,   352
  And the offender's life lies in the mercy   353
  Of the Duke only, 'gainst all other voice.
  In which predicament, I say, thou stand'st;
  For it appears, by manifest proceeding,
  That indirectly and directly too
  Thou hast contrived against the very life
  Of the defendant; and thou hast incurred
  The danger formerly by me rehearsed.   360
  Down therefore, and beg mercy of the Duke.

344 I'll . . . question I'll stay no further pursuing of the case   **352 privy coffer** private treasury   **353 lies in** lies at   **360 danger . . . rehearsed** penalty already cited by me

GRATIANO

  Beg that thou mayst have leave to hang thyself!
  And yet, thy wealth being forfeit to the state,
  Thou hast not left the value of a cord;
  Therefore thou must be hanged at the state's charge.   365

DUKE

  That thou shalt see the difference of our spirit,
  I pardon thee thy life before thou ask it.
  For half thy wealth, it is Antonio's;   368
  The other half comes to the general state,
  Which humbleness may drive unto a fine.   370

PORTIA

  Ay, for the state, not for Antonio.   371

SHYLOCK

  Nay, take my life and all! Pardon not that!
  You take my house when you do take the prop
  That doth sustain my house. You take my life
  When you do take the means whereby I live.

PORTIA

  What mercy can you render him, Antonio?

GRATIANO

  A halter gratis! Nothing else, for God's sake.   377

ANTONIO

  So please my lord the Duke and all the court
  To quit the fine for one half of his goods,   379
  I am content, so he will let me have   380
  The other half in use, to render it,   381
  Upon his death, unto the gentleman
  That lately stole his daughter.
  Two things provided more: that for this favor
  He presently become a Christian;   385
  The other, that he do record a gift
  Here in the court of all he dies possessed   387
  Unto his son Lorenzo and his daughter.

---

365 charge expense   **368 For** as for   **370 Which . . . fine** i.e., which
penitence on your part may persuade me to reduce to a fine   **371 Ay
. . . Antonio** i.e., yes, the state's half may be reduced to a fine, but not
Antonio's half   **377 halter** hangman's noose   **379 quit** remit, relinquish,
or perhaps settle for. (That is, Antonio may ask the court to forgive even
the fine imposed in lieu of a heavier penalty.)   **380 so** provided that
381 in use in trust, or possibly, to be used as a source of income   **385 presently** at once   **387 of . . . possessed** i.e., what remains of the portion not
placed under Antonio's trust (which will also go to Lorenzo and Jessica)

DUKE
　He shall do this, or else I do recant
　The pardon that I late pronouncèd here.
PORTIA
　Art thou contented, Jew? What dost thou say?
SHYLOCK
　I am content.
PORTIA　　　　　　Clerk, draw a deed of gift.
SHYLOCK
　I pray you, give me leave to go from hence;
　I am not well. Send the deed after me,
　And I will sign it.
DUKE　　　　　　Get thee gone, but do it.
GRATIANO
　In christening shalt thou have two godfathers.
　Had I been judge, thou shouldst have had ten more,　397
　To bring thee to the gallows, not to the font.
　　　　　　　　　　　　　　　Exit [Shylock].
DUKE
　Sir, I entreat you home with me to dinner.
PORTIA
　I humbly do desire Your Grace of pardon.
　I must away this night toward Padua,
　And it is meet I presently set forth.
DUKE
　I am sorry that your leisure serves you not.
　Antonio, gratify this gentleman,　　　　　　404
　For in my mind you are much bound to him.
　　　　　　　　　　Exeunt Duke and his train.
BASSANIO
　Most worthy gentleman, I and my friend
　Have by your wisdom been this day acquitted
　Of grievous penalties, in lieu whereof,　　　408
　Three thousand ducats due unto the Jew
　We freely cope your courteous pains withal.　410
　　　　　　　　　　　　　[He offers money.]
ANTONIO
　And stand indebted over and above
　In love and service to you evermore.

397 ten more i.e., to make up a jury of twelve. (Jurors were colloquially termed *godfathers.*)　**404 gratify** reward　**408 in lieu whereof** in return for which　**410 cope** requite

PORTIA

He is well paid that is well satisfied,
And I, delivering you, am satisfied
And therein do account myself well paid.
My mind was never yet more mercenary.
I pray you, know me when we meet again.
I wish you well, and so I take my leave.

                              [*She starts to leave.*]

BASSANIO

Dear sir, of force I must attempt you further.   419
Take some remembrance of us as a tribute,
Not as fee. Grant me two things, I pray you:
Not to deny me, and to pardon me.

PORTIA

You press me far, and therefore I will yield.
Give me your gloves; I'll wear them for your sake.   424
And, for your love, I'll take this ring from you.
Do not draw back your hand; I'll take no more,
And you in love shall not deny me this.

BASSANIO

This ring, good sir? Alas, it is a trifle!
I will not shame myself to give you this.

PORTIA

I will have nothing else but only this;
And now methinks I have a mind to it.

BASSANIO

There's more depends on this than on the value.
The dearest ring in Venice will I give you,   433
And find it out by proclamation.
Only for this, I pray you, pardon me.

PORTIA

I see, sir, you are liberal in offers.   436
You taught me first to beg, and now, methinks,
You teach me how a beggar should be answered.

BASSANIO

Good sir, this ring was given me by my wife,
And when she put it on, she made me vow
That I should neither sell nor give nor lose it.

---

419 attempt urge   **424 gloves** (Perhaps Bassanio removes his gloves,
thereby revealing the ring that "Balthasar" asks of him.)   **433 dearest**
most expensive   **436 liberal** generous

PORTIA
  That 'scuse serves many men to save their gifts.
  An if your wife be not a madwoman,
  And know how well I have deserved this ring,
  She would not hold out enemy forever   445
  For giving it to me. Well, peace be with you!
                      Exeunt [Portia and Nerissa].

ANTONIO
  My lord Bassanio, let him have the ring.
  Let his deservings and my love withal
  Be valued 'gainst your wife's commandement.   449

BASSANIO
  Go, Gratiano, run and overtake him;
  Give him the ring, and bring him, if thou canst,
  Unto Antonio's house. Away, make haste!
                  Exit Gratiano [with the ring].
  Come, you and I will thither presently,
  And in the morning early will we both
  Fly toward Belmont. Come, Antonio.   *Exeunt.*

❖

4.2   *Enter [Portia and] Nerissa [still disguised].*

PORTIA [*Giving a deed to Nerissa*]
  Inquire the Jew's house out; give him this deed   1
  And let him sign it. We'll away tonight
  And be a day before our husbands home.
  This deed will be well welcome to Lorenzo.

    Enter Gratiano.

GRATIANO   Fair sir, you are well o'erta'en.
  My lord Bassanio upon more advice   6
  Hath sent you here this ring and doth entreat
  Your company at dinner.   [*He gives a ring.*]
PORTIA   That cannot be.
  His ring I do accept most thankfully,

---

445 would . . . out i.e., would not remain   **449 commandement** (Pronounced in four syllables.)

4.2. Location: Venice. A street.
1 deed i.e., the deed of gift   **6 advice** consideration

And so, I pray you, tell him. Furthermore,
I pray you, show my youth old Shylock's house.

GRATIANO
  That will I do.

NERISSA   Sir, I would speak with you.
  [*Aside to Portia.*] I'll see if I can get my husband's ring,
  Which I did make him swear to keep forever.

PORTIA [*Aside to Nerissa*]
  Thou mayst, I warrant. We shall have old swearing   15
  That they did give the rings away to men;
  But we'll outface them, and outswear them too.—   17
  Away, make haste! Thou know'st where I will tarry.

NERISSA
  Come, good sir, will you show me to this house?
                    [*Exeunt, Nerissa and Gratiano together,
                              Portia another way.*]

❖

15 old plenty of   **17 outface** boldly contradict

5.1 *Enter Lorenzo and Jessica.*

LORENZO
  The moon shines bright. In such a night as this,
  When the sweet wind did gently kiss the trees
  And they did make no noise, in such a night
  Troilus methinks mounted the Trojan walls   4
  And sighed his soul toward the Grecian tents
  Where Cressid lay that night.
JESSICA   In such a night
  Did Thisbe fearfully o'ertrip the dew,   7
  And saw the lion's shadow ere himself,
  And ran dismayed away.
LORENZO   In such a night
  Stood Dido with a willow in her hand   10
  Upon the wild sea banks, and waft her love   11
  To come again to Carthage.
JESSICA   In such a night
  Medea gathered the enchanted herbs   13
  That did renew old Aeson.
LORENZO   In such a night
  Did Jessica steal from the wealthy Jew   15
  And with an unthrift love did run from Venice 16
  As far as Belmont.
JESSICA   In such a night
  Did young Lorenzo swear he loved her well,
  Stealing her soul with many vows of faith,
  And ne'er a true one.
LORENZO   In such a night
  Did pretty Jessica, like a little shrew,
  Slander her love, and he forgave it her.

5.1. Location: Belmont. Outside Portia's house.
4 Troilus Trojan prince deserted by his beloved, Cressida, after she had
been transferred to the Greek camp **7 Thisbe** beloved of Pyramus who,
arranging to meet him by night, was frightened by a lion. (See *A Midsummer Night's Dream*, Act 5.) **10 Dido** Queen of Carthage, deserted by
Aeneas. **willow** (A symbol of forsaken love.) **11 waft** wafted, beck-
oned **13 Medea** famous sorceress of Colchis who, after falling in love
with Jason and helping him to gain the Golden Fleece, used her magic
to restore youth to Aeson, Jason's father **15 steal** (1) escape (2) rob
16 unthrift prodigal

JESSICA
I would out-night you, did nobody come;   23
But hark, I hear the footing of a man.   24

    Enter [Stephano,] a messenger.

LORENZO
Who comes so fast in silence of the night?
STEPHANO   A friend.
LORENZO
A friend? What friend? Your name, I pray you, friend?
STEPHANO
Stephano is my name, and I bring word
My mistress will before the break of day
Be here at Belmont. She doth stray about
By holy crosses, where she kneels and prays   31
For happy wedlock hours.
LORENZO   Who comes with her?
STEPHANO
None but a holy hermit and her maid.
I pray you, is my master yet returned?
LORENZO
He is not, nor we have not heard from him.
But go we in, I pray thee, Jessica,
And ceremoniously let us prepare
Some welcome for the mistress of the house.

    Enter [Launcelot, the] Clown.

LAUNCELOT   Sola, sola! Wo ha, ho! Sola, sola!   39
LORENZO   Who calls?
LAUNCELOT   Sola! Did you see Master Lorenzo? Master
Lorenzo, sola, sola!
LORENZO   Leave holloing, man! Here.
LAUNCELOT   Sola! Where, where?
LORENZO   Here.
LAUNCELOT   Tell him there's a post come from my mas-
ter, with his horn full of good news: my master will be
here ere morning.   [*Exit.*]
LORENZO
Sweet soul, let's in, and there expect their coming.   49

23 **out-night** i.e., outdo in the verbal games we've been playing   24 **footing** footsteps   31 **holy crosses** wayside shrines   39 **Sola** (Imitation of a
posthorn.)   49 **expect** await

And yet no matter. Why should we go in?
My friend Stephano, signify, I pray you,   51
Within the house, your mistress is at hand,
And bring your music forth into the air.
                              [*Exit Stephano.*]
How sweet the moonlight sleeps upon this bank!
Here will we sit and let the sounds of music
Creep in our ears. Soft stillness and the night
Become the touches of sweet harmony.   57
Sit, Jessica. [*They sit.*] Look how the floor of heaven
Is thick inlaid with patens of bright gold.   59
There's not the smallest orb which thou behold'st
But in his motion like an angel sings,
Still choiring to the young-eyed cherubins;   62
Such harmony is in immortal souls,
But whilst this muddy vesture of decay   64
Doth grossly close it in, we cannot hear it.   65

     [*Enter Musicians.*]

Come, ho, and wake Diana with a hymn!   66
With sweetest touches pierce your mistress' ear
And draw her home with music.   *Play music.*

JESSICA
I am never merry when I hear sweet music.

LORENZO
The reason is, your spirits are attentive.   70
For do but note a wild and wanton herd
Or race of youthful and unhandled colts   72
Fetching mad bounds, bellowing and neighing loud,
Which is the hot condition of their blood;
If they but hear perchance a trumpet sound,
Or any air of music touch their ears,
You shall perceive them make a mutual stand,   77
Their savage eyes turned to a modest gaze

51 signify make known   **57 Become** suit.   **touches** notes (produced by
the fingering of an instrument)   **59 patens** thin, circular plates of
metal   **62 choiring** singing.   **young-eyed** eternally clear-sighted
64 muddy . . . decay i.e., mortal flesh   **65 close it in** i.e., enclose the
soul.   **hear it** i.e., hear the music of the spheres   **66 Diana** (Here,
goddess of the moon; cf. 1.2.105.)   **70 spirits are attentive** (The spirits
would be in motion within the body in merriment, whereas in sadness
they would be drawn to the heart and, as it were, busy listening.)
72 race herd   **77 mutual** common or simultaneous

By the sweet power of music. Therefore the poet   79
Did feign that Orpheus drew trees, stones, and floods, 80
Since naught so stockish, hard, and full of rage   81
But music for the time doth change his nature.
The man that hath no music in himself,
Nor is not moved with concord of sweet sounds,
Is fit for treasons, stratagems, and spoils;   85
The motions of his spirit are dull as night
And his affections dark as Erebus.   87
Let no such man be trusted. Mark the music.

Enter Portia and Nerissa.

PORTIA
That light we see is burning in my hall.
How far that little candle throws his beams!
So shines a good deed in a naughty world.   91
NERISSA
When the moon shone, we did not see the candle.
PORTIA
So doth the greater glory dim the less.
A substitute shines brightly as a king
Until a king be by, and then his state   95
Empties itself, as doth an inland brook
Into the main of waters. Music! Hark!   97
NERISSA
It is your music, madam, of the house.
PORTIA
Nothing is good, I see, without respect.   99
Methinks it sounds much sweeter than by day.
NERISSA
Silence bestows that virtue on it, madam.
PORTIA
The crow doth sing as sweetly as the lark
When neither is attended; and I think   103
The nightingale, if she should sing by day,
When every goose is cackling, would be thought

79 **poet** possibly Ovid, with whom the story of Orpheus was a favorite
theme   80 **Orpheus** legendary musician.   **drew** attracted, charmed
81 **stockish** unfeeling   85 **spoils** acts of pillage   87 **Erebus** a place of
primeval darkness on the way to Hades   91 **naughty** wicked   95 **his**
i.e., the substitute's   97 **main of waters** sea   99 **respect** comparison,
context   103 **neither is attended** i.e., either is alone

No better a musician than the wren.
How many things by season seasoned are   107
To their right praise and true perfection!
Peace, ho! The moon sleeps with Endymion   109
And would not be awaked.   [*The music ceases.*]

LORENZO   That is the voice,
Or I am much deceived, of Portia.

PORTIA
He knows me as the blind man knows the cuckoo,
By the bad voice.

LORENZO   Dear lady, welcome home.

PORTIA
We have been praying for our husbands' welfare,
Which speed, we hope, the better for our words.
Are they returned?

LORENZO   Madam, they are not yet;
But there is come a messenger before,
To signify their coming.

PORTIA   Go in, Nerissa.
Give order to my servants that they take
No note at all of our being absent hence;
Nor you, Lorenzo; Jessica, nor you. [*A tucket sounds.*]   121

LORENZO
Your husband is at hand. I hear his trumpet.
We are no telltales, madam, fear you not.

PORTIA
This night methinks is but the daylight sick;
It looks a little paler. 'Tis a day
Such as the day is when the sun is hid.

*Enter Bassanio, Antonio, Gratiano, and their
followers.*

BASSANIO
We should hold day with the Antipodes,   127
If you would walk in absence of the sun.   128

107 season favorable occasion   **109 Endymion** a shepherd loved by the
moon goddess, who caused him to sleep a perennial sleep in a cave on
Mount Latmos where she could visit him   **121 s.d. tucket** flourish on a
trumpet   **127–128 We . . . sun** i.e., if you, Portia, like a second sun,
would always walk about during the sun's absence, we should never
have night, but would enjoy daylight even when the Antipodes, those
who dwell on the opposite side of the globe, enjoy daylight

PORTIA

Let me give light, but let me not be light;   129

For a light wife doth make a heavy husband,   130

And never be Bassanio so for me.

But God sort all! You are welcome home, my lord.   132

BASSANIO

I thank you, madam. Give welcome to my friend.

This is the man, this is Antonio,

To whom I am so infinitely bound.

PORTIA

You should in all sense be much bound to him,   136

For, as I hear, he was much bound for you. .

ANTONIO

No more than I am well acquitted of.   138

PORTIA

Sir, you are very welcome to our house.

It must appear in other ways than words;

Therefore I scant this breathing courtesy.   141

GRATIANO [*To Nerissa*]

By yonder moon I swear you do me wrong!

In faith, I gave it to the judge's clerk.

Would he were gelt that had it, for my part,   144

Since you do take it, love, so much at heart.

PORTIA

A quarrel, ho, already? What's the matter?

GRATIANO

About a hoop of gold, a paltry ring

That she did give me, whose posy was   148

For all the world like cutler's poetry

Upon a knife, "Love me, and leave me not."

NERISSA

What talk you of the posy or the value?

You swore to me, when I did give it you,

That you would wear it till your hour of death

And that it should lie with you in your grave.

Though not for me, yet for your vehement oaths,

You should have been respective and have kept it.   156

---

129 be light be wanton, unchaste   **130 heavy** sad   **132 sort** decide, dispose   **136 in all sense** in every way, with every reason   **138 acquitted of** repaid for   **141 scant . . . courtesy** make brief this empty (i.e., merely verbal) courtesy   **144 gelt** gelded.   **for my part** as far as I'm concerned   **148 posy** a motto on a ring   **156 respective** mindful

Gave it a judge's clerk! No, God's my judge,
The clerk will ne'er wear hair on 's face that had it.

GRATIANO
He will, an if he live to be a man.   159

NERISSA
Ay, if a woman live to be a man.

GRATIANO
Now, by this hand, I gave it to a youth,
A kind of boy, a little scrubbèd boy,   162
No higher than thyself, the judge's clerk,
A prating boy, that begged it as a fee.   164
I could not for my heart deny it him.

PORTIA
You were to blame—I must be plain with you—
To part so slightly with your wife's first gift,
A thing stuck on with oaths upon your finger,
And so riveted with faith unto your flesh.
I gave my love a ring and made him swear
Never to part with it; and here he stands.
I dare be sworn for him he would not leave it,
Nor pluck it from his finger, for the wealth
That the world masters. Now, in faith, Gratiano,   174
You give your wife too unkind a cause of grief.
An 'twere to me, I should be mad at it.   176

BASSANIO [Aside]
Why, I were best to cut my left hand off
And swear I lost the ring defending it.

GRATIANO
My lord Bassanio gave his ring away
Unto the judge that begged it and indeed
Deserved it too; and then the boy, his clerk,
That took some pains in writing, he begged mine;
And neither man nor master would take aught   183
But the two rings.

PORTIA   What ring gave you, my lord?
Not that, I hope, which you received of me.

BASSANIO
If I could add a lie unto a fault,
I would deny it; but you see my finger

159 **an if** if   162 **scrubbèd** stunted   164 **prating** chattering
174 **masters** owns   176 **An** if.   **mad** beside myself   183 **aught** anything

Hath not the ring upon it. It is gone.

PORTIA
Even so void is your false heart of truth.
By heaven, I will ne'er come in your bed
Until I see the ring!

NERISSA   Nor I in yours
Till I again see mine.

BASSANIO   Sweet Portia,
If you did know to whom I gave the ring,
If you did know for whom I gave the ring,
And would conceive for what I gave the ring,
And how unwillingly I left the ring,
When naught would be accepted but the ring,
You would abate the strength of your displeasure.

PORTIA
If you had known the virtue of the ring,   199
Or half her worthiness that gave the ring,
Or your own honor to contain the ring,   201
You would not then have parted with the ring.
What man is there so much unreasonable,
If you had pleased to have defended it
With any terms of zeal, wanted the modesty   205
To urge the thing held as a ceremony?   206
Nerissa teaches me what to believe:
I'll die for 't but some woman had the ring.

BASSANIO
No, by my honor, madam! By my soul,
No woman had it, but a civil doctor,   210
Which did refuse three thousand ducats of me
And begged the ring, the which I did deny him
And suffered him to go displeased away—
Even he that had held up the very life
Of my dear friend. What should I say, sweet lady?
I was enforced to send it after him.
I was beset with shame and courtesy.
My honor would not let ingratitude
So much besmear it. Pardon me, good lady!
For by these blessèd candles of the night,   220

199 **virtue** power   201 **contain** retain   205 **wanted the modesty** who
would have been so lacking in consideration as   206 **urge** insist upon
receiving.   **ceremony** something sacred   210 **civil doctor** i.e., doctor of
civil law   220 **blessèd . . . night** i.e., stars

Had you been there, I think you would have begged
The ring of me to give the worthy doctor.

PORTIA

Let not that doctor e'er come near my house.
Since he hath got the jewel that I loved,
And that which you did swear to keep for me,
I will become as liberal as you: 226
I'll not deny him anything I have,
No, not my body nor my husband's bed.
Know him I shall, I am well sure of it.
Lie not a night from home. Watch me like Argus;   230
If you do not, if I be left alone,
Now, by mine honor, which is yet mine own,
I'll have that doctor for my bedfellow.

NERISSA

And I his clerk; therefore be well advised
How you do leave me to mine own protection.

GRATIANO

Well, do you so. Let not me take him, then!   236
For if I do, I'll mar the young clerk's pen.   237

ANTONIO

I am th' unhappy subject of these quarrels.

PORTIA

Sir, grieve not you; you are welcome notwithstanding.

BASSANIO

Portia, forgive me this enforcèd wrong,
And in the hearing of these many friends
I swear to thee, even by thine own fair eyes
Wherein I see myself—

PORTIA   Mark you but that!
In both my eyes he doubly sees himself;
In each eye, one. Swear by your double self,   245
And there's an oath of credit.

BASSANIO   Nay, but hear me.   246
Pardon this fault, and by my soul I swear
I never more will break an oath with thee.

ANTONIO

I once did lend my body for his wealth,   249

226 liberal generous (sexually as well as otherwise) **230 from** away
from. **Argus** mythological monster with a hundred eyes **236 take**
apprehend **237 pen** (with sexual double meaning) **245 double** i.e.,
deceitful **246 of credit** worthy to be believed **249 wealth** welfare

Which, but for him that had your husband's ring,
Had quite miscarried. I dare be bound again,
My soul upon the forfeit, that your lord
Will never more break faith advisedly.   253

PORTIA
Then you shall be his surety. Give him this,   254
And bid him keep it better than the other.
                    [*She gives the ring to Antonio, who
                              gives it to Bassanio.*]

ANTONIO
Here, Lord Bassanio. Swear to keep this ring.

BASSANIO
By heaven, it is the same I gave the doctor!

PORTIA
I had it of him. Pardon me, Bassanio,
For by this ring the doctor lay with me.

NERISSA
And pardon me, my gentle Gratiano,
For that same scrubbèd boy, the doctor's clerk,
In lieu of this last night did lie with me.   262
                    [*Presenting her ring.*]

GRATIANO
Why, this is like the mending of highways
In summer, where the ways are fair enough.   264
What, are we cuckolds ere we have deserved it?   265

PORTIA
Speak not so grossly. You are all amazed.   266
Here is a letter; read it at your leisure.[*She gives a letter.*]
It comes from Padua, from Bellario.
There you shall find that Portia was the doctor,
Nerissa there her clerk. Lorenzo here
Shall witness I set forth as soon as you,
And even but now returned; I have not yet
Entered my house. Antonio, you are welcome,
And I have better news in store for you
Than you expect. Unseal this letter soon.
                    [*She gives him a letter.*]
There you shall find three of your argosies

253 advisedly intentionally **254 surety** guarantor **262 In lieu of** in
return for **264 In . . . enough** i.e., before repair is necessary
265 cuckolds husbands whose wives are unfaithful **266 grossly** stu-
pidly, licentiously. **amazed** bewildered

Are richly come to harbor suddenly.
You shall not know by what strange accident
I chancèd on this letter.

ANTONIO   I am dumb.

BASSANIO
Were you the doctor and I knew you not?

GRATIANO
Were you the clerk that is to make me cuckold?

NERISSA
Ay, but the clerk that never means to do it,
Unless he live until he be a man.

BASSANIO
Sweet doctor, you shall be my bedfellow.
When I am absent, then lie with my wife.

ANTONIO
Sweet lady, you have given me life and living;
For here I read for certain that my ships
Are safely come to road.

PORTIA   How now, Lorenzo?   288
My clerk hath some good comforts too for you.

NERISSA
Ay, and I'll give them him without a fee.
                         [*She gives a deed.*]
There do I give to you and Jessica,
From the rich Jew, a special deed of gift,
After his death, of all he dies possessed of.

LORENZO
Fair ladies, you drop manna in the way   294
Of starvèd people.

PORTIA   It is almost morning,
And yet I am sure you are not satisfied
Of these events at full. Let us go in;
And charge us there upon inter'gatories,   298
And we will answer all things faithfully.

GRATIANO
Let it be so. The first inter'gatory
That my Nerissa shall be sworn on is,

288 road anchorage **294 manna** the food miraculously supplied to the
Israelites in the wilderness (Exodus 16) **298 charge . . . inter'gatories**
require ourselves to answer all things under oath

Whether till the next night she had rather stay   302
Or go to bed now, being two hours to day.
But were the day come, I should wish it dark
Till I were couching with the doctor's clerk.
Well, while I live I'll fear no other thing
So sore as keeping safe Nerissa's ring.   *Exeunt.* 307

302 stay wait   307 ring (with sexual suggestion)

Date and Text

The Stationers' Register, the official record book of the London Company of Stationers (booksellers and printers), for July 22, 1598, contains an entry on behalf of the printer James Roberts for "a booke of the Marchaunt of Venyce, or otherwise called the Jewe of Venyce, Prouided, that yt bee not prynted by the said James Robertes or anye other whatsoeuer without lycence first had from the Right honorable the lord Chamberlen." Roberts evidently enjoyed a close connection with the Chamberlain's men (Shakespeare's acting company) and seemingly was granted the special favor of registering the play at this time even though the company did not wish to see the play published until later. In 1600, at any rate, Roberts transferred his rights as publisher to Thomas Heyes and printed the volume for him with the following title:

> The most excellent Historie of the *Merchant of Venice*. VVith the extreame crueltie of *Shylocke* the Iewe towards the sayd Merchant, in cutting a iust pound of his flesh: and the obtayning of *Portia* by the choyse of three chests. *As it hath beene diuers times acted by the Lord Chamberlaine his Seruants.* Written by William Shakespeare. AT LONDON, Printed by *I. R.* [James Roberts] for Thomas Heyes, and are to be sold in Paules Church-yard, at the signe of the Greene Dragon. 1600.

The text of this 1600 quarto is generally a good one, based seemingly on the author's papers. It served as copy for the second quarto of 1619 (printed by William Jaggard for Thomas Pavier, and fraudulently dated 1600) and for the First Folio of 1623. The Folio stage directions may represent some authoritative consultation of a theatrical document.

Francis Meres mentions the play in 1598 in his *Palladis Tamia: Wit's Treasury* (a slender volume on contemporary literature and art; valuable because it lists most of Shakespeare's plays that existed at that time). Establishing an earlier limit for dating has proven not so easy. Many scholars have urged a connection with the Roderigo Lopez affair of 1594 (see the Introduction to the play). The supposed allusion to Lopez in the lines about "a wolf, who, hanged for human slaughter" (4.1.134) may simply indicate, however, that wolves were actually hanged for attacking men in Shakespeare's day (as dogs were for killing sheep). Besides, the Lopez case remained so notorious throughout the 1590s that even a proven allusion to it in *The Merchant* would not limit the play to 1594 or 1595. Christopher Marlowe's play *The Jew of Malta* was revived in 1594 to exploit anti-Lopez sentiment but was also revived in 1596. There may, on the other hand, be an allusion in 1.1.27 to the *St. Andrew,* a Spanish ship captured at Cadiz in 1596. Any date between 1594 and early 1598 is possible, though the latter half of this period is more likely.

Textual Notes

These textual notes are not a historical collation, either of the early quartos and the early folios or of more recent editions; they are simply a record of departures in this edition from the copy text. The reading adopted in this edition appears in boldface, followed by the rejected reading from the copy text, i.e., the quarto of 1600. Only major alterations in punctuation are noted. Changes in lineation are not indicated, nor are some minor and obvious typographical errors.

Abbreviations used:
Q quarto
s.d. stage direction
s.p. speech prefix

Copy text: the first quarto of 1600 [Q1].

1.1. s.d. [and elsewhere] Salerio, and Solanio Salaryno, and Salanio
19 Peering Piring **27 docked** docks **85 jaundice** Iaundies **112 tongue** togue **113 Is** It is **128 off** of **151 back** bake

1.2. 44 Palatine Palentine [and at ll. 57–58] **53 Bon** Boune **58 throstle** Trassell **119 s.d. Enter a Servingman** [after l. 120 in Q1]

1.3. 28 s.p. [and elsewhere] Shylock Jew **76 compromised** compremyzd **110 spit** spet [also at ll. 124 and 129]

2.1. s.d. Morocco Morochus **25 Sophy ... prince,** Sophy, and a Persian Prince **31 thee** the **35 page** rage

2.2. 1 s.p. [and elsewhere] Launcelot Clowne **3 [and elsewhere in this scene] Gobbo** Iobbe **42 By** Be **76 murder** muder **94 last** lost **165 s.d. Exit Leonardo** [after l. 164 in Q1] **168 a suit** sute

2.3. 11 did doe

2.4. 39 s.d. Exeunt Exit

2.6. 26 Who's whose [also at l. 61] **35 night, you** night you **59 gentlemen** gentleman

2.7. 18 threatens. Men threatens men **45 Spits** Spets **69 tombs** timber

2.8. 8 gondola Gondylo **39 Slubber** slumber

2.9. 64 judgment iudement

3.1. 21 s.d. Enter Shylock [after l. 22 in Q1] **70 s.p. Man** [not in Q1] **74 s.d.** [Q1 repeats the s.d. "Enter Tuball"] **100 Heard** heere **114 turquoise** Turkies

3.2. 61 live. With liue with **67 eyes** eye **81 vice** voyce **84 stairs** stayers **199 loved; for intermission** lou'd for intermission, **204 roof** rough **315 s.p. Bassanio** [not in Q1]

3.3 s.d. Solanio Salerio **24 s.p. Solanio** Sal

3.4. 49 Padua Mantua **50 cousin's** cosin **53 traject** Tranect **80 near**
nere **81 my** my my

3.5. 20 e'en in **26 comes** come **74 merit it** meane it, it **81 a wife** wife
87 s.d. Exeunt Exit

4.1. 30 his state this states **31 flint** flints **35 s.p. [and elsewhere in this
scene] Shylock** Jew **50 urine; for affection,** vrine for affection. **51 Mistress**
Maisters **73 You may as well** well **74 Why he hath made the** the . bleat
bleake **75 pines** of Pines **100 is** as **113 lose** loose **136 whilst** whilest
228 No, not Not not **270 off** of **322 off** of **396 s.p. Gratiano** Shy **405 s.d.
Exeunt** Exit

5.1. 26 s.p. Stephano Messen [also at ll. 28 and 33] **41 Lorenzo** Lorenzo,
& **49 Sweet soul** [assigned in Q1 to Launcelot] **51 Stephano** Stephen
87 Erebus Terebus **109 ho** how **152 give it** giue **233 my** mine

Shakespeare's Sources

Shakespeare's probable chief source for *The Merchant of Venice* was the first story of the fourth day of *Il Pecorone* (The Dunce), by Ser Giovanni Fiorentino. This collection of tales dates from the late fourteenth century but was first published in 1558 at Milan and was not published in English translation in Shakespeare's time. If Shakespeare was unable to read it in Italian, he may conceivably have consulted a translation in some now-lost manuscript; such translations did sometimes circulate. Behind Ser Giovanni's story lies an old tradition of a bond given for human flesh, as found in Persia, India, and the Twelve Tables of Roman Law. This legend first appears in English in the thirteenth-century *Cursor Mundi* (a long verse history of the world from creation to doomsday), with a Jew as the creditor. A thirteenth-century version of the *Gesta Romanorum* (a popular collection of stories in Latin) adds a romantic love plot; the evil moneylender in this story is not Jewish. The hero pawns his own flesh to a merchant in order to win a lady. He succeeds on his third attempt, having learned to avoid a magic spell that had previously put him to sleep and cost him a large number of florins. When he goes to pay his forfeit, the lady follows him disguised as a knight and foils the evil merchant by pointing out a quibbling distinction between flesh and blood.

Il Pecorone, presented here in a new and complete translation, provided Shakespeare with a number of essential elements, although not all that he included in his play. Ser Giovanni's story tells of Giannetto, the adventurous youngest son of a Florentine merchant, who goes to live with his father's dearest friend, Ansaldo, in Venice. This worthy merchant gives him money to seek his fortune at sea. Unbeknownst to Ansaldo, Giannetto twice risks everything to woo the lady of Belmont: if he can succeed in sleeping with her, he will win her and her country, but if he fails, he loses all his wealth. Twice Giannetto is given a sleeping medicine in his wine and has to forfeit everything. Returning destitute to Venice twice, he is reunited each time with Ansaldo and given the means to seek his fortune again. For the third such voyage, however, Ansaldo is driven to borrow ten thousand florins from a Jew, using the forfeiture of a pound of flesh as a guarantee. This time, one of the lady's maids warns Giannetto not to drink his wine, and he finally possesses the lady as his wife. Sometime later, remembering that the day of Ansaldo's forfeiture has arrived, Giannetto explains the predicament to his wife and is sent by her to Venice with a hundred thousand florins, but he arrives after the forfeiture has fallen due. The lady, however, following after him in the disguise of a doctor of laws, decrees that the Jew may have no blood and must take no more or no less than one pound of flesh. The Jew is jeered at and receives no money. The "doctor of laws" refuses any payment other than the ring Giannetto was given by his lady. Yielding it up unwillingly, he returns to Belmont, where his lady vexes him about the ring but finally relents and tells him all. Shakespeare could thus have found in one source the wooing, the borrowing from a Jewish moneylender, the pound of flesh, the trial, and the business of the rings. The story provides no casket episode, courtship of Nerissa by Gratiano, elopement of Jessica, or clowning of Launcelot Gobbo. The Jew's motive is not prompted by the way he has been treated.

Shakespeare may also have known "The Ballad of Gernutus," a popular English work that seems to be older than the play. It has no love plot but dwells on the unnatural cruelty of a Jewish Venetian usurer who takes a bond of flesh for "a merry jest." Anthony Munday's prose *Zelauto* (1580), though its villain is a Christian rather than a Jewish moneylender, also features a bond of this sort, taken purportedly as a mere sport but with hidden malice. Truculento, the villain, takes the bond of two young men, Rodolfo and his friend Strabino, as surety for a loan. If they forfeit the loan, the young men are to lose their lands and their right eyes as well. The villain has a daughter, Brisana, whom he permits to marry Rodolfo since Truculento expects to marry Rodolfo's sister Cornelia himself. When Cornelia instead marries Strabino, Truculento angrily takes the young men to court to demand his bond. The two brides disguise themselves as scholars and go to court, where they appeal for mercy and then foil Truculento by means of the legal quibble about blood.

Another possible source for the courtroom scene is *The Orator*, translated into English in 1596 from the French of Alexandre Sylvain. An oration, entitled "Of a Jew, who would for his debt have a pound of the flesh of a Christian," uses many specious arguments also employed by Shylock, and is forthrightly confuted in "The Christian's Answer."

Shylock's relationship to his daughter finds obvious earlier parallels in *Zelauto* and in Christopher Marlowe's play *The Jew of Malta* (c. 1589), in which Barabas's daughter Abigail loves a Christian and ultimately renounces her faith. The actual elopement, however, is closer to the fourteenth story in Masuccio of Salerno's fifteenth-century *Il Novellino* (not published in English translation in Shakespeare's day).

The casket-choosing episode, not found in *Il Pecorone*, was a widespread legend, occurring for example in the story of *Barlaam and Josophat* (ninth-century Greek, translated into Latin by the thirteenth century), in Vincent of Beauvais's *Speculum Historiale*, in the *Legenda Aurea*, in Giovanni Boccaccio's *Decameron* (Day 10, Story 1), in John Gower's *Confessio Amantis*, and—closest to Shakespeare—in the *Gesta Romanorum* (translated into English in 1577 by Richard Robinson and "bettered" by him in 1595). In this last account, the choice is between a gold, silver, and lead casket, each with its own inscription. The first two inscriptions are like Shakespeare's; the third reads, "They that choose me, shall find [in] me that God hath disposed." The chooser, however, is a maiden, and she is not preceded by other contestants.

An old play called *The Jew* is referred to by Stephen Gosson in 1579 as containing "the greediness of worldly choosers, and bloody minds of usurers." Scholars have speculated that this was a source play for Shakespeare, but actually we have too little to go on to make a reliable judgment. Gosson was surely not referring to Robert Wilson's *The Three Ladies of London* (c. 1581) in any case, even though it is sometimes suggested as an analogue to *The Merchant of Venice*, for its Jewish figure named Gerontus (compare Gernutus in the ballad) is an exemplary person. Besides, the probable date of this play is later than Gosson's remark.

Il Pecorone

By Ser Giovanni Fiorentino
Translated by David Bevington and Kate Bevington

FOURTH DAY, FIRST STORY: GIANNETTO
AND THE LADY OF BELMONT

There once was in Florence, in the house of the Scali, a merchant named Bindo, who had been to Tana and to Alexandria many times, and on all the usual long voyages that are made for the sake of merchandise. This Bindo was very rich, and he had three strapping sons. As he was approaching death, he summoned the eldest and the middle son and, in their presence, made his last will and testament, designating the two of them heirs of all he had in the world, and making no mention of his youngest son.

When he had made his will, his youngest son, named Giannetto, hearing of this, went to him in his bed and said, "Father, I am much amazed at what you have done, not to have remembered me in your will."

"Giannetto," his father answered, "there is no creature in the world whom I hold dearer than you. And for that reason I do not want you to stay here after my death, but wish instead that you go to Venice when I am dead, to your godfather, Signor Ansaldo, who has no son of his own and who has many times written me to send you to him. I can tell you that he is the richest merchant today in all Christendom. So I want you, when I am dead, to go to him and take this letter; if you behave wisely, you will become a rich man."

"Father," the young man said, "I am ready to do what you command me."

Then the father gave him his blessing, and a few days later he died. All the sons lamented bitterly and gave to the body the ceremonies that were its due.

A few days later the two brothers summoned Giannetto and said, "Brother, it is true that our father made his will and left us his heirs, and did not mention you; nonetheless, you are our brother, and whatever we have is also yours as long as it lasts."

"Brothers," answered Giannetto, "I thank you for your

offer, but, as for me, I intend to seek my fortune elsewhere. My mind is made up on this, so let the inheritance be yours by right of law and with our father's blessing."

The brothers, seeing that his mind was made up, gave him a horse and money for expenses. Giannetto took leave of them and went to Venice, and, arriving at the counting-house of Signor Ansaldo, presented him with the letter his father had given him before his death. Signor Ansaldo, as he read the letter, realized that this was the son of his dearest friend, Bindo; and when he had finished the letter, he at once embraced the young man, saying, "Welcome, my son, whom I have so much desired to see." And immediately he asked about Bindo, to which Giannetto replied that he was dead. With many tears Signor Ansaldo embraced and kissed Giannetto, and said, "I am very grieved at the death of Bindo, for it was he who helped me earn a great part of what I have; but the happiness that I have in seeing you is so great that it takes away some of my sorrow." And he had him conducted to his house, and told his clerks and attendants and servants and grooms and whoever else belonged to the household that Giannetto was to be obeyed and served more than his own self. He consigned to him the keys to all his ready money and said, "My son, whatever there is is yours; spend it on clothes today as you please; keep a table for the important people of the city, and become known. For I leave this thought with you: The more you win others' good will, the more I will love you."

And so Giannetto began to enter into Venetian society, to dine out and give dinner parties, to make gifts, to keep liveried servants, to buy fine horses, and to take part in jousts and tournaments, for he was expert and well versed in such matters and magnanimous and gracious in all things, knowing well how to show respect and courtesy as was fitting; and always he honored Signor Ansaldo more than if he had been a hundred times his father. So sensible was his behavior toward persons of all conditions that virtually everyone in Venice liked him, seeing him to be so wise and pleasing in manner and courteous beyond measure. Women and men alike were quite taken with him, and Signor Ansaldo had eyes for no one but him, so pleasing were his behavior and his manners. Scarcely a party went by to which Giannetto was not invited, so well was he liked by one and all.

Now, it happened that two dear friends of his planned to make a voyage to Alexandria with their two ships and their merchandise, as they did each year. They spoke of this to Giannetto and asked if he wished to enjoy himself by going with them to see the world, especially Damascus and the region where it lies.

"In good faith," answered Giannetto, "I would very much like to go, if my father Signor Ansaldo gives me his permission."

"We'll see to it that he does," they said, "and that he will be content."

And so right away they went to Signor Ansaldo and said, "We want to ask you please to give your permission for Giannetto to go next spring with us to Alexandria, and to furnish him with some kind of ship so that he can see a little of the world."

"I am content," said Signor Ansaldo, "if he wants to."

"Sir," said they, "he does."

So Signor Ansaldo at once had him furnished with a splendid ship and arranged for it to be loaded with a great deal of merchandise and decked out with flags and provided with whatever arms were needed. And when all was ready, Signor Ansaldo ordered the captain and those others who served on board that they were to do what Giannetto commanded them and that his safety was in their hands. "For," said Signor Ansaldo, "I am not sending him out for any profits that I want him to make, but rather for him to enjoy himself and see something of the world."

When Giannetto was about to leave, all Venice gathered to see, for not in a long while had so magnificent and well equipped a vessel sailed from Venice. Everyone was sorry at his departure. He took leave of Signor Ansaldo and of all his friends, then put out to sea, hoisted sail, and set his course for Alexandria in the name of God and good fortune.

As the three friends in their three ships were sailing along day after day, early one morning, before it was broad daylight, Giannetto looked out and saw a most splendid harbor in a gulf of the sea, and asked the captain what it was called.

"Sir," the captain answered, "that harbor belongs to a widowed lady, one who has meant trouble for a lot of gentlemen."

"How?" said Giannetto.

"Sir," said the other, "the truth is that she is a beautiful woman, and enchanting too, and she has established this law: Whatever man arrives there must sleep with her, and if he succeeds in enjoying her, he is to take her as his wife and be lord of the whole country, but if he does not succeed in enjoying her, he loses everything that he has in the world."

Giannetto thought about that for a bit, and then said, "Devise any means you can to bring me into that harbor."

"Sir," the captain said, "take care what you say, for many gentlemen have gone there only to lose all their goods and their lives in the bargain."

"Don't interfere," said Giannetto. "Do what I tell you."

And so it was done. Quickly they changed the ship's course and brought her to berth in that harbor, without his friends in the other ships seeing a thing. Now, when morning came, the news spread that this splendid ship had arrived in the harbor; everybody gathered to see it, and the news was brought to the lady, who sent for Giannetto. He went to her at once, and greeted her with great respect. She took him by the hand and asked who he was and where he was from, and if he knew the custom of the country.

Giannetto replied that he did, and that he had come for no other reason.

"You are a hundred times welcome," she said.

She paid him great honor all that day, and had many barons, counts, and knights who were her subjects invited to attend on him. The manners of this young man delighted all the barons, so well educated was he, so pleasing of person, and so well spoken, and nearly everybody was taken with him. All that day there was dancing and singing and festivity at the court as an expression of affection for him, and everyone would have been well content to have him as lord.

Now, as evening approached, the lady took him by the hand and led him into her room, and said, "It seems to me that it's time to go to bed."

"My lady," said Giannetto, "I am at your service."

Immediately two damsels came into the room, one with wine and the other with sweetmeats.

"You must be thirsty," said the lady. "Have something to drink."

Giannetto took some of the sweetmeats and drank some

wine, which had been drugged to make him sleep, though he didn't know this, and so he drank half a glass, since it seemed good to him. Immediately he undressed and went to lie down. And as soon as he reached the bed, he fell sound asleep. The lady lay down at his side, but he was out for the rest of the night, until nine o'clock. The lady, as soon as it was day, arose and gave orders to unload the ship, and found it full of rich and worthy merchandise. When it was nine o'clock, the lady's maidservants went to the bed, roused Giannetto, and told him to begone with God's blessing, for he had lost his ship and all that was in it. He was ashamed and realized he had done badly. The lady gave him money for expenses and a horse, which he mounted, and, sad and gloomy, he made his way toward Venice. Arriving there, he was too ashamed to want to go home to Signor Ansaldo, and so by night he went to the house of a friend.

This friend marveled at him and said, "Giannetto, what happened?"

"My ship struck a rock one night," he answered, "and split apart and scattered every which way. I lashed myself to a timber that cast me ashore, and so I have come home on dry land, and here I am."

He remained several days hidden in the house of his friend.

One day this friend paid a visit to Signor Ansaldo and found him very melancholy. "What's wrong," he said, "that you are so downhearted?"

"I'm greatly afraid," said Signor Ansaldo, "that my son is dead, or that the sea has brought him misfortune. I can find no peace of mind or happiness until I see him again, so great is the love I bear him."

"Sir," said the young man, "I can tell you news of him, which is that he was shipwrecked and lost everything, but saved himself."

"Praised be God!" said Signor Ansaldo. "If he is saved, I am happy. As to what he lost, I don't care at all." And immediately he got up and went off to see Giannetto. And when he saw him, immediately he ran to embrace him, and said, "My son, there is no need for you to be ashamed as far as I am concerned. Shipwrecks happen all the time. So, my son, don't be downcast. As long as no harm has come to you, I am happy." And he led him home, comforting him all the while. The news spread through all Venice, and everyone felt sorry for the loss that Giannetto had suffered.

Now, it happened that a short time later the two friends of Giannetto came back from Alexandria, very wealthy. And when they arrived, they inquired after Giannetto and were told the whole business. At once they ran to greet him, saying, "How did you get separated, or where did you go, that we were unable to get any news of you? We doubled back on our track all day long, but could never see you or find out where you had gone. And we were so sorry about this that all our journey we could not succeed in cheering ourselves up, thinking you were dead."

"A wind came up in a gulf of the sea," Giannetto answered, "and drove my ship against a rock close to the shore. I hardly was able to save myself, and everything was scattered."

Such was the excuse that Giannetto gave in order not to reveal his error. Together they made a great feast, thanking God that he had been saved, saying, "Next spring, God willing, we will make enough profit to recover what you have lost this time, but now let's give ourselves a good time without any gloominess." And so they devoted themselves to pleasure and enjoyment, as they used to do.

But Giannetto did nothing but think about how he might return to that lady, dreaming of this and saying to himself, "Certainly I must have her for my wife, or I will die," and for the most part he could not be merry.

Signor Ansaldo said to him many times, "My son, don't give yourself up to melancholy. We have goods enough to live very well."

"My lord," answered Giannetto, "I can never be content unless I make that journey again."

Seeing that his mind was made up, Signor Ansaldo, when it was time, fitted out another ship for him with much more merchandise and of better value than before. And he began so early that, when the time finally came, the ship was well furnished and adorned. He gave for it the greater part of all that he had in the world. The friends, when they had fitted out their ships with what they needed, put out to sea, hoisted sail, and set forth on their voyage.

They sailed along for several days, and Giannetto constantly kept a lookout, to see once more the harbor of that lady, which was called the Harbor of the Lady of Belmont. Arriving one night at the mouth of the harbor, which was in a gulf of the sea, Giannetto recognized it at once, had the sails and the rudder brought about, and berthed within the harbor.

The lady, when she arose in the morning, looked down to the harbor and saw the flags of that ship flying. At once she recognized it, and summoned a maidservant and said, "Do you recognize those flags?"

"My lady," said the maidservant, "it seems to me they are the insignia of the young man who arrived here a year ago and who brought such an abundance of riches with his merchandise."

"Certainly what you say is true," said the lady, "and truly this is no ordinary matter; truly he must be in love with me, for I never saw anyone come back a second time."

"I never saw a more courteous and graceful man than he," said the maidservant.

The lady sent many damsels and squires for him, who greeted him with great festivity; and he treated all of them with cheerfulness and joy. And so he came into the presence of the lady. When she saw him, she embraced him with joy and delight, and he embraced her with reverential courtesy. They passed all that day in revelry and pleasure, for the lady sent invitations to many barons and ladies, who came to her court to celebrate in Giannetto's honor. Almost all the barons were full of regret and gladly would have had him for their lord, because of his amiability and liberality, and almost all the ladies were in love with him, seeing with what skill he led the dancing and that he held his countenance always cheerful, so that everyone believed him to be the son of some great nobleman.

When it came time for sleep, the lady took Giannetto by the hand and said, "Let us go and lie down." They went to her room and sat down, and behold, two damsels came with wine and sweetmeats, and the couple drank and ate, and then they went to bed. And as soon as Giannetto was in bed, he fell sound asleep. The lady undressed and lay down beside him, and—to be brief—he was out for the whole night. And when morning came, the lady arose and immediately ordered the unloading of the ship. When it was nine o'clock,

Giannetto came to his senses and looked about for the lady but could not find her. He lifted up his head and saw that it was broad daylight, and so got up and began to feel ashamed. He was given a horse and money for expenses and quickly departed, sad and gloomy, and he did not rest until he was at Venice. By night he went to the house of his friend, who, on seeing him, was the most astonished person in the world, saying, "What happened?"

"Things are bad with me," said Giannetto. "Accursed be the fortune that ever brought me to this country!"

"Certainly you have reason to curse your fortune," said his friend, "for you have ruined Signor Ansaldo, who was the greatest and richest merchant in Christendom, and the shame of that is worse than the loss."

For several days Giannetto remained hidden in his friend's house, not knowing what to do or to say. He almost decided to go back to Florence without saying a word to Signor Ansaldo, but in the end he made up his mind to go to him, and so he did.

When Signor Ansaldo saw him, he got up and ran and embraced him, saying, "Welcome, my dear son." And Giannetto, weeping, embraced him. Signor Ansaldo said, "Do you know what? Do not give yourself the slightest grief. Since I have you once again, I am happy. There is still enough remaining for us to be able to live simply."

The news of what had happened went all over Venice, and everyone talked of Signor Ansaldo, wishing him well and grieving for what he had suffered. And it was necessary for him to sell many of his possessions to pay his creditors who had provided him with the lost merchandise.

Now, it happened that Giannetto's two friends returned, rich from their journey, and arrived in Venice, where they were told that Giannetto had come back having been shipwrecked and having lost everything. They marveled at this, saying, "This is the most amazing thing ever seen." And they went to Signor Ansaldo and Giannetto in a jovial mood, saying, "Signors, don't be downcast, for we intend to go this coming year and make a profit on your behalf. After all, we are partly responsible for your loss, since we are the ones who induced Giannetto to come with us in the first place. Don't worry. As long as we have any goods ourselves, treat them as your own."

Signor Ansaldo thanked them and said that he still had enough to get by on.

Now, it happened that Giannetto, thinking day and night on what had taken place, could not bring himself to be cheerful. Signor Ansaldo asked him what was the matter.

"I shall never be content," he said, "until I have gotten back what I lost."

"My son," said Signor Ansaldo, "I don't want you to go away any more, for it is better that we live here simply, with what little we have, than that you again undertake such a risky journey."

"I am firmly resolved to do what I've said," said Giannetto, "for I would consider myself in a shameful state if I left things as they are."

Signor Ansaldo, seeing that his mind was made up, made arrangements to sell everything he had in the world and fit out another ship for him. And he did this, so that he had nothing left, and fitted out a magnificent ship with merchandise. Because he still needed ten thousand florins, he went to a Jew at Mestre and borrowed the money on these terms and conditions: If he had not repaid him by St. John's Day in the following June, the said Jew should have the right to take a pound of his flesh from whatever part of the body he pleased. Signor Ansaldo was content with this, and so the Jew had a deed drawn up for the purpose, authenticated by witnesses and with those forms and ceremonies pertaining in such a case; and then he counted out ten thousand gold florins. With this money Signor Ansaldo supplied what was still lacking for the ship; and if the other two were fine, this one was much richer and better equipped. And so the friends did the same for their two ships, having it in mind that whatever profit they made would be for Giannetto. When it came time for departure, Signor Ansaldo said to Giannetto, "My son, you are going away, and you know how things stand with me. One favor I ask of you: If you come to grief, please come see me, so that I can see you again before I die, and I will depart content." Giannetto promised him this, and Signor Ansaldo gave him his blessing. And so the three took their leave and set off on their voyage.

The two friends kept a constant eye on Giannetto's ship. Giannetto meanwhile was always watching to see how he might drop into the harbor of Belmont. And so he made a deal with one of the sailors that one night the man would pilot the ship into the harbor of that lady. When the morning light grew clear, his friends in the other two ships looked about them, but nowhere did they see Giannetto's ship. They said to each other, "Bad luck again, for sure!" And they decided to keep on their way, wondering greatly all the while.

Now, it happened that when the ship came into the harbor, the whole city drew near to see, realizing that Giannetto had returned. They marveled greatly at this, saying, "Certainly this must be the son of some very important man, seeing how he comes here each year with so much merchandise and so beautiful a ship. Would to God he were our lord!" And so he was waited on by all the dignitaries, barons, and knights of that city.

Word was brought to the lady that Giannetto had come. She placed herself at a window and saw the handsome ship and recognized the flags. Whereupon she made the sign of the cross, saying, "Certainly this is the same man who brought such riches into this country," and she sent for him. Giannetto came to her, and with many embraces they greeted each other and offered their respects. And the whole day was spent amid joy and festivity. For love of Giannetto a splendid joust was held, and many barons and knights jousted that day. Giannetto wanted to joust also, and that day he performed many miraculous feats himself, so skillful was he in arms and horsemanship. So much did his conduct please all the barons that everyone wanted him to be their lord.

Now, when evening came and it was time for bed, the lady took Giannetto by the hand and said, "Let us go and rest."

And as he was about to leave the room, one of the maid-servants, feeling sorry for Giannetto, whispered in his ear in a soft voice, "Pretend to drink, but don't drink tonight." Giannetto understood her words, and went into the bed-chamber.

"You must be thirsty," said the lady, "and I want you to drink before you go to sleep."

And right away two damsels came in, looking like angels, with wine and sweetmeats according to the usual custom, and offered him drink.

"Who could refuse drink," said Giannetto, "seeing two such beautiful damsels?"

The lady laughed at that. And Giannetto took the cup and pretended to drink, but instead poured the wine into his bosom. The lady, believing him to have drunk, said to herself, "You will have to bring another ship, since you've just lost this one." Giannetto went to bed, feeling wide awake and in good spirits, and it seemed to him to take a thousand years for the lady to come to bed, and he said to himself, "For certain I've caught her this time; turnabout is fair play." To make the lady come to bed sooner, he began to snore and to feign sleep. "Everything is going fine," said the lady, and she quickly undressed and lay down by Giannetto. He lost no time: as soon as the lady was under the sheets, he turned toward her and embraced her and said, "Now I have what I have so much desired." And with these words he gave her the blissful peace that comes with holy matrimony, and all night long she did not leave his arms, so content was she. And next morning she arose before daylight and sent for all the barons and knights and other worthy citizens and said to them: "Giannetto is your lord; therefore make ready to celebrate." With that, a shout went up through all the land, "Long live our lord!" while bells and trumpets sounded. And she sent for many barons and counts from the surrounding countryside to come and see their lord. Then began a huge and splendid celebration. When Giannetto came out of the bedchamber, he was knighted and placed on the throne, and the scepter was put in his hand, and he was named lord with great ceremony and splendor. And as soon as all the barons and lords and ladies had come to court, he married the lady with such festivity and joy as can scarcely be told or imagined. All the lords and barons of the country came to the city to celebrate with jousts, trials of arms, dances, singing, the playing of instruments, and all that belongs to such a celebration. Signor Giannetto, like the generous and noble youth that he was, commenced to make gifts of silken materials and other rich things that he had brought with him. And he showed himself to be a strong ruler, one to be respected and feared, one who maintained right and justice on behalf of all sorts and conditions of men. And so he continued in joy and happiness, and took no thought or remembrance of poor Signor Ansaldo, who had pledged himself for ten thousand florins to the Jew.

One day it happened that Signor Giannetto was at a window with his lady and saw pass through the square a company of men with torches in their hands who were going to make an offering.

"What does that mean?" asked Signor Giannetto.

His lady answered, "That is a company of craftsmen, who are going to make an offering at the Church of St. John, whose festival is today."

At this Signor Giannetto remembered Signor Ansaldo. He left the window, sighing deeply, his countenance changed, and paced up and down the room several times thinking the matter over. His wife asked him what was the matter.

"Nothing," he answered.

His wife began to question him, saying, "Something certainly is the matter with you, but you don't want to tell me." And she kept asking so insistently that Signor Giannetto told her the whole story, how Signor Ansaldo had pledged himself for ten thousand florins, how the time for repayment had expired this very day, and how Signor Ansaldo would have to lose a pound of his flesh. His lady said to him, "Quick, to horse, and take whatever company seems best to you and a hundred thousand florins, and don't rest until you are at Venice; and if he isn't dead yet, bring him back here."

And so he at once ordered a trumpet to be sounded, and mounted on horseback, with more than a hundred companions, and carrying enough money with him, he took his leave and journeyed without delay toward Venice.

Now, it happened that with the arrival of the due date, the Jew had Signor Ansaldo arrested and made clear his intention of taking a pound of flesh. Signor Ansaldo begged him please to delay his death several days, so that if his Giannetto were to come, he would be able to see him.

"I am content to do what you wish as far as the delay is concerned," said the Jew, "but even if he were to come a hundred times, I intend to take a pound of flesh as specified in the bond."

Signor Ansaldo answered that he was satisfied with this. All Venice buzzed with this matter, and everyone was sorry for Signor Ansaldo, and many merchants got together with a view to paying the money, but the Jew would not agree to that, wishing instead to carry out the homicide so that he might say that he had put to death the greatest merchant in Christendom.

Now, it happened that when Signor Giannetto had set forth eagerly on his way, his lady had quickly followed after him, clad as a doctor of laws and taking two servants with her. Arriving in Venice, Signor Giannetto went to the house of the Jew, joyfully embraced Signor Ansaldo, and then said to the Jew that he was ready to pay him his money and as much more as he cared to demand. The Jew answered that he didn't want the money, since he had not received it on the date it was due, but that he wanted to take a pound of Signor Ansaldo's flesh. Over this matter there arose a great debate, and everyone blamed the Jew, but since Venice was a city that respected the rule of law and the Jew had his legal rights fully set forth and in the proper form, no one could find arguments to deny him; all they could do was plead with him. And so all the merchants of Venice came there to entreat the Jew, but he grew harder than ever. Signor Giannetto was willing to give him twenty thousand, and he refused that. He advanced his offer to thirty thousand, then forty, then fifty, and finally a hundred thousand florins.

The Jew said to him, "Do you want to know something? If you were to give me more than this whole city is worth, it would not satisfy me. I would rather have what the bond says is mine."

And that is where things stood in this dispute when, behold, the lady arrived in Venice, dressed like a doctor of laws, and alighted at an inn. The innkeeper asked one of the servants, "Who is this gentleman?"

The servant answered, "This gentleman is a doctor of laws coming from his studies at Bologna and returning home."

The innkeeper, hearing this, treated him with great respect. And while he was at the dinner table the doctor of laws said to the innkeeper, "How is this city of yours governed?"

"Sir," the innkeeper answered, "we make too much of justice here."

"How can that be?" said the doctor of laws.

"Sir," said the innkeeper, "I will tell you. Once there came here from Florence a young man called Giannetto, and he came here to his godfather, called Signor Ansaldo. He was so gracious and pleasing in his behavior that all the women, and the men too, were quite taken with him. Never before has there come to this city anyone so engaging as he. Now, this godfather of his fitted out for him, on three different occasions, three ships, all of the greatest value, and every time disaster struck. Signor Ansaldo didn't have enough money for the last ship, and so he borrowed ten thousand florins of a certain Jew on the condition that if he didn't repay what was due by St. John's Day in the following June, the said Jew would be authorized to take a pound of flesh from whatever part of him he pleased. Now this fortunate young man has come back and has offered to give, in place of those ten thousand florins, a hundred thousand, but the wicked Jew won't accept them. And all the good people of this place have been to him to plead with him, but to no avail."

"This is an easy question to settle," answered the doctor of laws.

"If you will only take the trouble to settle it," said the host, "so that this good man won't have to die, you will win the thanks and love of the worthiest young man that ever was born and of all the citizens of this land."

And so this doctor of laws had it proclaimed throughout the city that whoever had any legal question to settle should come to him. This was told to Signor Giannetto, that a doctor of laws had come from Bologna who was ready to settle any legal dispute.

Said Signor Giannetto to the Jew, "Let us go to this doctor of laws who I hear has arrived."

"All right, let us go," said the Jew.

When they came into the presence of the doctor of laws and offered him the respect that was his due, the doctor of laws at once recognized Signor Giannetto, but Signor Giannetto did not recognize him, because he had disguised his face with certain herbs. Signor Giannetto and the Jew stated their cases, each in turn and in proper order, before the doctor of laws.

The doctor of laws took the Jew's bond and read it, and

then said to the Jew, "I would rather you took the hundred thousand florins and freed this good man, who will always be obliged to you."

"Nothing doing," said the Jew.

"It's your best course," said the doctor of laws.

The Jew said he absolutely refused.

"Now, come forward then," said the doctor of laws, "and take a pound of flesh from wherever you choose."

With that the Jew called for Signor Ansaldo. And when he had arrived, the doctor of laws said to the Jew, "Do your business." And so the Jew had him stripped naked and took in his hand a razor that he had prepared for the purpose and approached him from behind to seize him.

Signor Giannetto turned to the doctor of laws and said, "Sir, this is not what I asked you to do."

"Don't interfere," said the doctor of laws. "Let me handle this." And seeing that the Jew was about to start, the doctor of laws said, "Take care what you do. For if you take more or less than one pound, I will have your head struck off. And let me tell you, moreover, that if you shed a single drop of blood, I will have you put to death. Your bond makes no mention of the shedding of blood, but says only that you are to take a pound of flesh, neither more nor less. Now, if you are wise, you will think carefully what is the best way to do this." And then he at once had the executioner sent for and had him bring his block and ax, and said, "When I see a drop of blood flow, I will have your head struck off."

The Jew began to be afraid, and Signor Giannetto began to take heart. And after much argument, the Jew said, "Master Doctor, you are wiser than I am in these matters; let me be given those hundred thousand florins and I am content."

"I agree to your taking a pound of flesh," said the doctor of laws, "as your bond specifies; otherwise, I will not give you a penny. You should have taken it when I was willing to give it to you."

The Jew came down to ninety thousand, then eighty, but the doctor of laws held firm.

"Give him what he wants," said Signor Giannetto to the doctor of laws, "as long as he releases Signor Ansaldo."

"Let me handle this, I tell you," said the doctor of laws.

"Give me fifty thousand," said the Jew.

"I wouldn't give you the most miserable coin you've ever had," said the doctor of laws.

"Give me at least my ten thousand," said the Jew, "and a curse be on the air you breathe and the place where you live!"

"Didn't you hear what I said?" said the doctor of laws. "I won't give you a thing. If you want to take your forfeit from him, take it. If not, I will declare a nonperformance and void your bond."

Everyone present rejoiced greatly at this, and they all jeered at the Jew, saying, "He who thought to lay a trap has fallen into it himself." And so, seeing that he could not have his will, the Jew took his bond and tore it to pieces in a fury. Then Signor Ansaldo was freed and, with great rejoicing, was led home, and Signor Giannetto took those hundred thousand florins and went to the doctor of laws, finding him in his chambers making ready to depart.

Signor Giannetto went to him and said, "Sir, you have done me the greatest possible service, and for that reason I would like you to take home this money; you have well earned it."

"My dear Signor Giannetto," said the doctor of laws, "I thank you very much, but I have no need of it; take it yourself so that your lady won't be saying that you have spent it recklessly."

"By my faith," answered Signor Giannetto, "she is so generous and kind and good that even if I were to spend four times this, she would not mind; she asked if I wanted to bring much more than this."

"Are you happy with her?" said the doctor of laws.

"There is no creature in the world whom I love so dearly," answered Signor Giannetto, "for she is wise and beautiful, so much so that nature could do nothing more. And if you would do me the great favor of coming home to see her, you would marvel at the honorable reception she would give you, and you would see if she is all that I tell you."

"See to it, when you see her," said the doctor of laws, "that you greet her on my behalf."

"I shall do so," said Signor Giannetto, "but I wish you would take this money."

While he was saying this, the doctor of laws saw on his finger a ring, and so he said, "I would like that ring. I don't want any money."

"It shall be as you wish," said Signor Giannetto, "but I give it most unwillingly, since my wife gave it to me and said that I should wear it always for love of her; and if she sees me without it, she will think that I have given it to some woman and so be angry with me and believe that I am unfaithful; and the truth is that I love her more than I love myself."

"I am certain," answered the doctor of laws, "that she must love you well enough to believe you when you tell her that you have given it to me. But perhaps you want to give it to some former mistress of yours?"

"Such is the love and faith that I bear her," answered Signor Giannetto, "that there is no woman in the whole wide world for whom I would exchange her, so utterly beautiful is she in every way."

And thereupon he took the ring from his finger and gave it to the doctor of laws. Then they embraced and respectfully saluted each other and took their leave.

"Do me one favor," said the doctor of laws.

"You have only to ask," answered Signor Giannetto.

"Do not remain here," said the doctor of laws. "Go home quickly to see your wife."

"It seems to me a hundred thousand years," answered Signor Giannetto, "until I see her again."

And so they took their leave. The doctor of laws put out to sea, and with God's grace went on his journey. For his part Signor Giannetto gave banquets and made presents of horses and money to his friends, and thus made merry and kept open house, and then took his leave of all the Venetians, taking Signor Ansaldo with him; and many of his old friends went with them. And almost all the men and women of Venice were tearful at his departure, so graciously had he borne himself toward one and all the whole time that he had been in Venice. And so he left and returned to Belmont.

Now, it happened that his lady arrived some time before him and pretended she had been to the baths. She dressed herself as a woman, made festive preparations, had the streets hung in silk, and ordered many companies of soldiers to array themselves. When Signor Giannetto and

Signor Ansaldo arrived, all the barons and the court went to greet them, shouting, "Long live our lord! Long live our lord!" And when they arrived at the city, the lady ran to embrace Signor Ansaldo but pretended to be a little angry with Signor Giannetto, even though she loved him better than herself. A great celebration was made, with jousting, feats of arms, and dancing and singing by all the barons and ladies and damsels who were there. But Signor Giannetto, seeing that his wife did not receive him with her accustomed kindness, went to their room and called her, and said, "What's wrong?" and tried to embrace her.

"There's no need here for these embraces," said the lady, "for I know only too well that you have been meeting your former mistresses."

Signor Giannetto started to deny this.

"Where is the ring I gave you?" said his lady.

"What I thought would happen has indeed happened," said Signor Giannetto. "I said you would think badly of me. But I swear by the faith I bear to God and to you that I gave that ring to the doctor of laws who brought me victory in the case."

"And I swear by the faith I bear to God and to you," said his lady, "that you gave it to a woman. I know it, and aren't you ashamed to swear as you have sworn?"

"May God wipe me from the face of the earth," said Signor Giannetto, "if I am not speaking true, and if I did not say to that doctor of laws as I have told you, when he asked for the ring."

"You should have stayed in Venice," said his lady, "and sent Signor Ansaldo here while you enjoyed yourself with your mistresses, who, I hear, were all in tears when you left."

Then Signor Giannetto began to weep and to give himself over to grief, saying, "You are swearing what isn't true and couldn't possibly be true."

When his lady saw him weeping, it seemed to her like a knife wound to the heart, and at once she ran and embraced him, laughing heartily; and she showed him the ring and told him everything—what he had said to the doctor of laws, how she herself was that doctor of laws. Signor Giannetto was greatly astonished at this and, seeing that it was all true, was immensely amused. He went out of the room and told the story to some of his barons and friends. And this adventure increased and multiplied the love between the couple. Then Signor Giannetto summoned the maidservant who had warned him that evening not to drink, and gave her in marriage to Signor Ansaldo. And so they lived ever after in happiness and pleasure, and enjoyed good things and good fortune.

———————————

Il Pecorone by Ser Giovanni Fiorentino was first published in Milan in 1558. This new translation is based on the critical edition prepared under the supervision of Enzo Esposito, Longo Editore, Ravenna, 1974, which was based in turn on manuscript sources as well as the early printed texts.

Further Reading

Auden, W. H. "Brothers and Others." *"The Dyer's Hand" and Other Essays*. New York: Random House, 1948. In a casual but seminal essay on the play, Auden calls *The Merchant of Venice* one of Shakespeare's "Unpleasant Plays." The presence of Antonio and Shylock disrupts the unambiguous fairy-tale world of romantic comedy, reminding us that the utopian qualities of Belmont are illusory: "in the real world, no hatred is totally without justification, no love totally innocent."

Barber, C. L. "The Merchants and the Jew of Venice: Wealth's Communion and an Intruder." *Shakespeare's Festive Comedy*. Princeton, N.J.: Princeton Univ. Press, 1959. Barber acknowledges that while *"on reflection"* Shakespeare's handling of the use of wealth and his depiction of Shylock are disturbing, in the theater the play's insistent festive design works to affirm "its concern for the grace of community." As a threat to the social harmony that the comedy celebrates, Shylock, "who embodies the evil side of the power of money," must be removed.

Barnet, Sylvan, ed. *Twentieth Century Interpretations of "The Merchant of Venice."* Englewood Cliffs, N.J.: Prentice-Hall, 1970. To help modern students see the play as Elizabethans would have, Barnet provides a useful collection of interpretive and historical essays, including studies by Auden, Barber, Granville-Barker, Kermode, and Moody that are discussed here.

Brown, John Russell. "The Realization of Shylock: A Theatrical Criticism." In *Early Shakespeare*, ed. John Russell Brown and Bernard Harris. Stratford-upon-Avon Studies 3. London: Edward Arnold, 1961. Brown argues that Shylock dominates the stage and that the meaning of the character can fully be discovered only in performance. He examines the "opportunities given to the actor by Shakespeare" and the acting traditions established by Charles Macklin, Edmund Kean, Henry Irving, and Sir John Gielgud.

Burckhardt, Sigurd. "*The Merchant of Venice:* The Gentle Bond." *ELH* 29 (1962): 239–262. Rpt. in *Shakespearean Meanings.* Princeton, N.J.: Princeton Univ. Press, 1968. Burckhardt identifies "the bond" as the play's controlling metaphor and explores the way attention to it reveals the play's exacting structure. The comic design of the play, Burckhardt argues, emerges when "the vicious circle of the bond's law" is "transformed into the ring of love."

Cohen, D. M. "The Jew and Shylock." *Shakespeare Quarterly* 31 (1980): 53–63. In spite of its many defenders, the play, for Cohen, remains profoundly anti-Semitic. Shylock's humanity is effaced and his Jewishness used to alienate him from the world of the play and the audience. "It is as though," Cohen writes, "*The Merchant of Venice* is an anti-Semitic play written by an author who is not an anti-Semite—but an author who has been willing to use the cruel stereotypes of that ideology for mercenary and artistic purposes."

Danson, Lawrence. *The Harmonies of "The Merchant of Venice."* New Haven, Conn.: Yale Univ. Press, 1978. As his title reveals, Danson is concerned with the play's "harmonies" rather than the discordant notes heard by many modern critics. He sensitively explores a series of dramatic oppositions that are posed but finally resolved by the play: law/freedom, justice/mercy, feuding/marriage, Jew/Christian, Venice/Belmont.

Evans, Bertrand. *Shakespeare's Comedies.* Esp. pp. 46–67. Oxford: Clarendon Press, 1960. The comic design of *The Merchant of Venice*, Evans finds, is determined by the manipulation of discrepancies of awareness between characters and the audience of the play. Only when these discrepancies dissolve in the trial scene, with the revelation of Portia's remarkable control of events, can we be confident that "the world of *The Merchant of Venice* is one in which goodness and mirth prevail," and only then can we experience any sympathy for Shylock.

Girard, René. " 'To Entrap the Wisest': A Reading of *The Merchant of Venice.*" In *Literature and Society: Selected Papers from the English Institute, 1978,* ed. Edward W. Said. Baltimore and London: The Johns Hopkins Univ. Press, 1980. Girard explores the disturbing symmetries that the play establishes between Jew and Christian.

Their mutual hatred, according to Girard, turns Shylock and Antonio into "doubles of each other," creating a moral burden for an audience confronted with action that simultaneously produces and undermines the scapegoating of Shylock.

Granville-Barker, Harley. *"The Merchant of Venice."* In *Prefaces to Shakespeare*, vol. 4, 1946. Rpt. Princeton, N.J.: Princeton Univ. Press, 1966. With his characteristic sensitivity to the demands of performance, Granville-Barker examines the play's form and temper. For him, *"The Merchant of Venice* is the simplest of plays, so long as we do not bedevil it with sophistries": the "unlikelihood" of its fairy-tale plot is "redeemed by veracity of character."

Kermode, Frank. "The Mature Comedies." In *Early Shakespeare*, ed. John Russell Brown and Bernard Harris. Stratford-upon-Avon Studies 3. London: Edward Arnold, 1961. In his account of Shakespeare's mature comic vision, Kermode finds *The Merchant of Venice* designed around a contrast between "gentleness" and "its opposite, for which Shylock stands." The comedy, Kermode says, confirms Christian values and patterns: it begins with "usury and corrupt love" and moves purposefully toward "harmony and perfect love."

Leggatt, Alexander. *"The Merchant of Venice." Shakespeare's Comedy of Love*. New York: Barnes and Noble, 1974. Leggatt explores the tension the play generates between its formalized and conventional plot and its characters' "human reality, naturalistically conceived." The formal design moves toward harmony and happiness but can have, Leggatt argues, "only a limited success in bringing order out of an intractable world."

Moody, A. D. *Shakespeare: "The Merchant of Venice."* London: Edward Arnold, 1964. In this short book (64 pages), Moody argues that the play presents a deeply ironic portrait of the Christian community. It reveals the essential "likeness" of Shylock and his accusers and "does not celebrate the Christian virtues so much as expose their absence."

Nevo, Ruth. "Jessica's Monkey; or, the Goodwins." *Comic Transformations in Shakespeare*. London and New York: Methuen, 1980. Nevo explores "the rupture of comic form" in the play, which never fully credits either the idealizations of Belmont or the scapegoating of Venice. The play, Nevo finds, takes its power precisely from this refusal to resolve the dichotomies it poses.

Palmer, D. J. *"The Merchant of Venice,* or the Importance of Being Earnest."* In *Shakespearian Comedy,* ed. Malcolm Bradbury and D. J. Palmer. Stratford-upon-Avon Studies 14. London: Edward Arnold, 1972. Palmer recognizes the powerful discords of the play and its prevailing seriousness. Antonio's sadness at the opening of the play, Palmer finds, "sets in motion the forces of division and disharmony which will take the play to the brink of tragedy before it is retrieved as a comedy."

Rabkin, Norman. "Meaning and *The Merchant of Venice."* *Shakespeare and the Problem of Meaning.* Chicago: Univ. of Chicago Press, 1981. As part of an argument about the limitation of "meaning as the principle of unity in a work," Rabkin explores the tensions, contradictions, and ambivalent signals that the play generates. The structure of the play, Rabkin finds, demands from an audience a constant reassessment of what it has seen, presenting it with elements "provocative of inconsistent responses."

Stoll, E. E. "Shylock." *Journal of English and Germanic Philology* 10 (1911): 236–279. Rpt. in *Shakespeare Studies: Historical and Comparative in Method.* New York: Macmillan, 1927. Stoll denies that Shylock is presented sympathetically; rather, he is a conventional, comic stage villain who exists to be foiled. From an analysis of the literary and cultural traditions underlying the character, Stoll concludes that our "notions of justice and social responsibility" distort the play's "intention."

TWELFTH NIGHT
or
WHAT YOU WILL

Introduction

Twelfth Night is possibly the latest of the three festive comedies, including *Much Ado about Nothing* and *As You Like It*, with which Shakespeare climaxed his distinctively philosophical and joyous vein of comic writing. Performed on February 2, 1602, at the Middle Temple (one of the Inns of Court, where young men studied law) and written possibly as early as 1599, *Twelfth Night* is usually dated 1600 or 1601. This play is indeed the most festive of the lot. Its keynote is Saturnalian release and the carnival pursuit of love and mirth. Along with such familiar motifs (found, for example, in *As You Like It* and *The Merchant of Venice*) as the plucky heroine disguised as a man, *Twelfth Night* also returns to the more farcical routines of mistaken identity found in Shakespeare's early comedy. As a witness of the 1602 performance, John Manningham, observed, the play is "much like the *Comedy of Errors*, or *Menaechmi* in Plautus, but most like and near to that in Italian called *Inganni*." Manningham might have added Shakespeare's *The Two Gentlemen of Verona* as another early instance, since it too employs the device of the heroine, Julia, disguised in the service of her unresponsive lover, Proteus.

The carnival atmosphere is appropriate to the season designated in the play's title: the twelfth night of Christmas, January 6, the Feast of Epiphany. (The prologue to *Gl'Ingannati*, perhaps the Italian play referred to by Manningham, speaks of "La Notte di Beffania," Epiphany night.) Although Epiphany has of course a primary Christian significance as the Feast of the Magi, it was also in Renaissance times the last day of the Christmas revels. Over a twelve-day period, from Christmas until January 6, noble households sponsored numerous performances of plays, masques, banquets, and every kind of festivity. (Leslie Hotson argues, in fact, that *Twelfth Night* was first performed on twelfth night in early 1601, in the presence of Queen Elizabeth.) Students left schools for vacations, celebrating release from study with plays and revels of their own. The stern rigors of a rule-bound society gave way temporarily to playful inversions of authority. The reign of the Boy Bishop and the Feast of Fools, for example, gave choristers and minor church functionaries the cherished opportunity to boss the hierarchy around, mock the liturgy with outrageous lampooning, and generally let off steam. Although such customs occasionally got out of hand, the idea was to channel potentially destructive insubordination into playacting and thereby promote harmony. Behind these Elizabethan midwinter customs lies the Roman Saturnalia, with its pagan spirit of gift-giving, sensual indulgence, and satirical hostility to those who would curb merriment.

Shakespeare's choice of sources for *Twelfth Night* underscores his commitment to mirth. Renaissance literature offered numerous instances of mistaken identity among twins and of the disguised heroine serving as page to her beloved. Among those in English were the anonymous play *Sir Clyomon and Sir Clamydes* (c. 1570–1583), Sidney's *Arcadia* (1590), and the prose romance *Parismus* by Emmanuel Forde (1598), featuring both a shipwreck and two characters with the names of Olivia and Violetta. Of particular significance, but largely for negative reasons, is Barnabe Riche's tale of "Apollonius and Silla" in *Riche His Farewell to Military Profession* (1581), which was based on François de Belleforest's 1571 French version of Matteo Bandello's *Novelle* (1554). Here we find most of the requisite plot elements: the shipwreck; Silla's disguise as a page in Duke Apollonius's court; her office as ambassador of love from Apollonius to the Lady Julina, who thereupon falls in love with Silla; the arrival of Silla's twin brother, Silvio; and his consequent success in winning Julina's affection. To Riche, however, this tale is merely a long warning against the enervating power of infatuation. Silvio gets Julina with child and disappears forthwith, making his belated reappearance almost too late to save the wrongly accused Silla. Riche's moralizing puts the blame on the gross and drunken appetite of carnal love. The total mismatching of affection with which the story begins, and the sudden realignments of desire based on mere outward resemblances, are seen as proofs of love's unreasonableness. Shakespeare of course retains and capitalizes on the irrational quality of love, as in *A Midsummer Night's Dream*, but in doing so he minimizes the harm done (Olivia is not made pregnant) and repudiates any negative moral judgments. The added subplot, with its rebuking of Malvolio's censoriousness, may have been conceived as a further answer to Riche, Fenton, and their sober school.

Shakespeare's festive spirit owes much, as Manningham observed, to Plautus and the neoclassical Italian comic writers. At least three Italian comedies called *Gl'Inganni* ("The Frauds") employ the motif of mistaken identity, and one of them, by Curzio Gonzaga (1592), supplies Viola's assumed name of "Cesare," or Cesario. Another play with the same title appeared in 1562. More useful is *Gl'Ingannati* ("The Deceived"), performed in 1531, translated into French in 1543. Besides a plot line generally similar to that of *Twelfth Night*, and the reference to "La Notte di Beffania" (Epiphany), this play offers the suggestive name *Malevolti*, "evil-faced," and *Fabio* (which resembles "Fabian"). It also contains possible hints for Malvolio, Toby, and company, although the plot of the counterfeit letter is original with Shakespeare. Essentially, Shakespeare superimposes his own subplot on an Italianate novella plot, as he did in *The Taming of the Shrew* and *Much Ado about Nothing*. And it is in the Malvolio story that Shakespeare most pointedly defends merriment. Feste, the professional fool, an original stage type for Shakespeare in *Twelfth Night* and in *As You Like It*, also reinforces the theme of seizing the moment of mirth.

This great lesson, of savoring life's pleasures while one is still young, is something that Orsino and Olivia have not yet learned when the play commences. Although suited to each other in rank, wealth, and attractiveness, they are unable to overcome their own willful posturing in the elaborate charade of courtship. Like Silvius in *As You Like It*, Orsino is the conventional wooer trapped in the courtly artifice of love's rules. He opens the play on a cloying note of self-pity. He is fascinated with his own degradation as a rejected suitor, and bores his listeners with his changeable moods and fondness for poetical "conceits." He sees himself as a hart pursued by his desires "like fell and cruel hounds," reminding us that enervating lovesickness has in fact robbed him of his manly occupation, hunting. He sends ornately contrived messages to Olivia but has not seen her in so long that his passion has become unreal and fantastical, feeding on itself.

Olivia plays the opposite role of chaste, denying woman-hood. She explains her retirement from the world as mourning for a dead brother (whose name we never learn) but this withdrawal from life is another unreal vision. Olivia's practice of mourning, whereby she will "water once a day her chamber round / With eye-offending brine" (1.1.28–29), is a lifeless ritual. As others view the matter, she is senselessly wasting her beauty and affection on the dead. "What a plague means my niece to take the death of her brother thus?" Sir Toby expostulates (1.3.1–2). Viola, though she too has seemingly lost a brother, is an important foil in this regard, for she continues to hope for her broth-er's safety, trusts his soul is in heaven if he is dead, and refuses to give up her commitment to life in any case. We suspect that Olivia takes a willful pleasure in self-denial not unlike Orsino's self-congratulatory suffering. She ap-pears to derive satisfaction from the power she holds over Orsino, a power of refusal. And she must know that she looks stunning in black.

Olivia's household reflects in part her mood of self-denial. She keeps Malvolio as steward because he too dresses somberly, insists on quiet as befits a house in mourning, and maintains order. Yet Olivia also retains a fool, Feste, who is Malvolio's opposite in every way. Hard-pressed to defend his mirthful function in a household so given over to melancholy, Feste must find some way of per-suading his mistress that her very gravity is itself the es-sence of folly. This is a paradox, because sobriety and order appeal to the conventional wisdom of the world. Malvolio, sensing that his devotion to propriety is being challenged by the fool's prating, chides Olivia for taking "delight in such a barren rascal" (1.5.80–81).

Feste must argue for an inversion of appearance and real-ity whereby many of the world's ordinary pursuits can be seen to be ridiculous. As he observes, in his habitually ellip-tical manner of speech, "*cucullus non facit monachum* [the cowl doesn't make the monk]; that's as much to say as I wear not motley in my brain" (1.5.52–54). Feste wins his case by making Olivia laugh at her own illogic in grieving for a brother whose soul she assumes to be in heaven. By extension, Olivia has indeed been a fool for allowing herself to be deprived of happiness in love by her brother's death ("there is no true cuckold but calamity"), and for failing to consider the brevity of youth ("beauty's a flower"). Yet, paradoxically, only one who professes to be a fool can point this out, enabled by his detachment and innocence to perceive simple but profound truths denied to supposedly rational persons. This vision of the fool as naturally wise, and of society as self-indulgently insane, fascinated Renaissance writers, from Erasmus in *In Praise of Folly* and Cervantes in *Don Quixote* to Shakespeare in *King Lear*.

Viola, although not dressed in motley, aligns herself with Feste's rejection of self-denial. Refreshingly, even comically, she challenges the staid artifice of Orsino's and Olivia's lives. She is an ocean traveler, like many of Shakespeare's later heroines (Marina in *Pericles*, Perdita in *The Winter's Tale*), arriving on Illyria's shore plucky and determined. On her first embassy to Olivia from Orsino, she exposes with disarming candor the willfully ritualistic quality of Olivia's existence. Viola discards the flowery set speech she had prepared and memorized at Orsino's behest; despite her charmingly conceited assertion that the speech has been "excellently well penned," she senses that its elegant but empty rhetoric is all too familiar to the disdainful Olivia. Instead, Viola departs from her text to urge seizing the moment of happiness. "You do usurp yourself," she lectures Olivia, "for what is yours to bestow is not yours to reserve" (1.5.183–184). Beauty is a gift of nature, and failure to use it is a sin against nature. Or, again, "Lady, you are the cruel'st she alive / If you will lead these graces [Olivia's beauty] to the grave / And leave the world no copy" (236–238). An essential argument in favor of love, as in Shakespeare's sonnets, is the necessity of marriage and childbearing in order to perpetuate beauty. This approach is new to Olivia, and catches her wholly by surprise. In part she reacts, like Phoebe in *As You Like It*, with perverse logic, rejecting a too-willing wooer for one who is hard to get. Yet Olivia is also attracted by a new note of sincerity, prompting her to reenter life and accept maturely both the risks and rewards of romantic involvement. Her longing for Cesario is of course sexually misdirected, but the appearance of Viola's identical twin, Sebastian, soon puts all to rights.

The motifs of Olivia's attraction for another woman (both

actors would have been boys), and of Orsino's deep fondness for Cesario that matures into sexual love, delicately evoke homosexual suggestions as in *As You Like It*. Once again, however, we must approach the notion circumspectly, remembering that these elements are also found in Shakespeare's sources and reflect a convention wholly different from a modern psychological analysis of sexual aberration. Like Rosalind, Viola uses her male attire to win Orsino's pure affection, in a friendship devoid of sexual interest since both seemingly are men. Viola as Cesario can teach Orsino about the conventions of love in relaxed and frank conversations that would not be possible if she were known to be a woman. She teaches him to avoid the beguiling but misleading myths of Petrarchan love (named after the Italian sonneteer Francis Petrarch, whose poems embody the idealization of courtly love), and so prepares him for the realities of marriage. Comparing men and women in love, she confides, "We men may say more, swear more, but indeed / Our shows are more than will; for still we prove / Much in our vows, but little in our love" (2.4.116–118). Once she and Orsino have achieved an instinctive rapport all the more remarkable for their talking so often at cross-purposes, Viola's unmasking can make possible a physical communion as well. The friendship of Sebastian and Antonio, sorely tested by the mix-ups of the mistaken identity plot, presents further insight into the debate of love and friendship.

The belowstairs characters of the subplot, Sir Toby and the rest, share with Feste and Viola a commitment to joy. As Sir Toby proclaims in his first speech, "care's an enemy to life" (1.3.2–3). Even the simpleton Sir Andrew, although gulled by Sir Toby into spending his money on a hopeless pursuit of Olivia, seems none the worse for his treatment; he loves to drink in Sir Toby's company and can afford to pay for his entertainment. Sir Toby gives us some of the richly inventive humor of Falstaff, another lovable fat roguish knight. In this subplot, however, the confrontations between merriment and sobriety are more harshly drawn than in the main plot. Whereas the gracious Olivia is won away from her folly, the obdurate Malvolio can only be exposed to ridicule. He is chiefly to blame for the polarization of attitudes, for he insists on rebuking the mirth of others. His name (*Mal-volio*, the "ill-wisher") implies a self-satisfied determination to impose his rigid moral code on others. As Sir Toby taunts him, "Dost thou think, because thou art virtuous, there shall be no more cakes and ale?" (2.3.114–115). Malvolio's inflexible hostility provokes a desire for comic vengeance. The method is satiric: the clever manipulators, Maria and Toby, invent a scheme to entrap Malvolio in his own self-deceit. The punishment fits the crime, for he has long dreamed of himself as Count Malvolio, rich, powerful, in a position to demolish Toby and the rest. Without Malvolio's infatuated predisposition to believe that Olivia could actually love him and write such a letter as he finds, Maria's scheme would have no hope of success. He tortures the text to make it yield a suitable meaning, much in the style of Puritan theologizing.

Indeed, Malvolio does in some ways resemble a Puritan, as Maria observes (2.3.139–147), even though she qualifies the assertion by saying that he is not a religious fanatic but a "time-pleaser." She directs her observation not at a religious group but at all who would be killjoys; if the Puritans are like that, she intimates, so much the worse for them. This uncharacteristic lack of charity gives a sharp tone to the vengeance practiced on Malvolio, evoking from Olivia a protestation that "He hath been most notoriously abused" (5.1.379). The belated attempt to make a reconciliation with him seems, however, doomed to failure, in light of his grim resolve to "be revenged on the whole pack of you." At the height of his discomfiture he has been tricked into doing the two things he hates most: smiling affably, and wearing sportive attire. The appearance of merriment is so grossly unsuited to him that he is declared mad and put into safe-keeping. The apostle of sobriety in this play thus comes before us as a declared madman, while the fool Feste offers him sage comment in the guise of a priest. Wisdom and folly have changed places. The upside-down character of the play is epitomized in Malvolio's plaintive remark to Feste (no longer posing as the priest): "I am as well in my wits, Fool, as thou art" (4.2.88). Malvolio's comeuppance is richly deserved, but the severity of vengeance and counter-vengeance suggests that the triumph of festival will not last long. This brevity is, of course, inherent in the nature of such holiday release from responsibility. As Feste sings, "What's to come is still unsure. / In delay there lies no plenty."

Twelfth Night
in Performance

Although *Twelfth Night* has almost always been popular on-stage, many theatrical producers in past years have treated the play as though its stage popularity had to be achieved in defiance of the text rather than through it. Not until recently have they trusted the play to conjure up its own sense of magic and imagination; too often they have relied, counterproductively, on excessively detailed realism instead of theatrical evocation. This literalized and revisionistic approach dominated much of the play's stage history during the Restoration and the eighteenth and nineteenth centuries, despite evidence that *Twelfth Night* (presumably as Shakespeare wrote it) was very popular in his own day and for some time after. Following his death the play was staged at court in 1618 and 1622, and, along with *Much Ado about Nothing*, it was identified by the poet Leonard Digges in 1640 as still among Shakespeare's most popular dramas. Digges suggested one important reason for this popularity when he commented that crowds were filling the theater "To hear *Malvolio*, that cross-gartered gull." Digges's observation also points to a distortion that would occur in subsequent productions of *Twelfth Night:* the play would become a vehicle for lead actors and actresses in a few key roles at the expense of the play as a whole. Revision of this sort was common in the Restoration and eighteenth century, whereas scenic overemphasis came to be a predictable feature of much nineteenth-century production.

The diarist Samuel Pepys saw a version of *Twelfth Night* on three occasions in the 1660s and thought it "a silly play." What Pepys objected to can perhaps be surmised from Charles Burnaby's adaptation in 1703, called *Love Betrayed, or the Agreeable Disappointment*, in which Burnaby undertook to "improve" the play with the kind of symmetry and neoclassical unity that he evidently felt it lacked. In this version, produced at the theater in Lincoln's Inn Fields, London, Malvolio, having been merged with the character of Sir Andrew, is tricked into fighting an abortive comic duel with the disguised Viola, whom he believes to be his rival for the love of Olivia. Maria becomes two characters, one an old servant in love with Sir Toby and the other a confidante of Olivia. Sebastian is provided with a wise-cracking servant. The characters are all renamed, and only some fifty-eight lines of Shakespeare's text (including "If music be the food of love, play on") remain intact. The major effect of Burnaby's revision is to reduce the number of subplots and to bring to the foreground the opposition of Malvolio and Viola. Malvolio is no longer the focus of a separate comic plot but at the center of the play, where, audiences evidently felt, he belonged.

Something more like Shakespeare's original of *Twelfth Night* did return in 1741, to the Theatre Royal, Drury Lane, evidently at the actor Charles Macklin's instigation (and with Macklin as Malvolio), and enjoyed during the next century a number of popular runs. John Henderson and John Philip Kemble, among others, took the part of Malvolio, while Hannah Pritchard, Peg Woffington, Dorothea Jordan (paired with her brother, George Bland, as Sebastian), Sarah Siddons, and Helen Faucit played Viola. Feste's concluding song, customarily absent throughout the eighteenth century, was finally restored in 1799. Nevertheless, adaptation continued to be a major factor in eighteenth- and nineteenth-century productions of the play. Songs were frequently added. Frederic Reynolds produced an operatic version in 1820 at the Theatre Royal, Covent Garden, with an overture compiled from various composers including Thomas Morley, Thomas Ravenscroft, and Mozart. "Full many a glorious morning" was introduced from the sonnets, "Even as the sun" from *Venus and Adonis*, "Orpheus with his lute" from *Henry VIII*, and "Come unto these yellow sands" from *The Tempest*, all set off by elegant scenery in what was supposed to be the style of the architect and set designer Inigo Jones.

Even when Shakespeare's text was treated with more respect, the emphasis on lead actors and actresses remained an unavoidable feature of nineteenth-century production. At the Haymarket Theatre in London in 1846, Charlotte and Susan Cushman, famous for their epicene Romeo and Juliet, starred as Viola and Olivia and made their pairing the center of the theatrical experience. When Samuel Phelps produced the play at the Sadler's Wells Theatre in 1848 and again in 1857, he gave prominence to his own portrayal of Malvolio as a grave and self-important Spanish grandee. In 1849, at the Theatre Royal, Marrylebone, Cora Mowatt and Fanny Vining (who, like the Cushmans, had done an epicene *Romeo and Juliet*) emulated their predecessors by pairing themselves in the roles of Olivia and Viola.

Twelfth Night does not call for the spectacular effects of battle sieges and royal pageantry that gave such impressive scope to the epic productions of the history plays by Charles Kean and others (as, for example, in Kean's *King John*), but theater managers who were insistent on visual opulence soon found a way to dress *Twelfth Night* in the splendor they wished to emphasize. Kean opened at the Princess's Theatre in 1850 with *Twelfth Night* and performed it some forty times, bestowing upon the play every realistic scenic device known to nineteenth-century theater. Henry Irving chose for his 1884 production, at the Lyceum Theatre, London, a Venetian setting in the age of Queen Elizabeth. Orsino's palace and Olivia's scarcely less palatial villa were sumptuously Palladian in decor, while the art of landscape gardening, as a contemporary observer marveled, appeared "to have reached a very high pitch of excellence." Olivia's house featured an adjoining cloister. No less impressive were the depictions of the seacoast, the courtyard and terrace of Olivia's house, the road near Olivia's house, and the dungeon for Malvolio. Ellen Terry played a spritely Viola opposite Irving's sentimental Malvolio, and although the performance was not a success, it was not for lack of handsome scene design.

In 1894, not to be outdone, producer Augustin Daly, at his Daly's Theatre in London, began with an exciting storm scene worthy of *The Tempest*. Unexpectedly, Daly showed his audiences the landing of Sebastian and Antonio rather than that of Viola and the Captain, which allowed the production's star, Ada Rehan (Viola), to enter more impressively in the next scene. The rearrangement also made possible the employment of an elaborate set for the Duke's palace. So elaborate was this set that, in order to keep it in use for a continuous stretch of dramatic action, Daly ran together Act 1, scene 1 (showing Orsino's love melancholy), with Act 1, scene 4 (in which Viola as Cesario is dispatched to Olivia), before making the cumbersome shift to Olivia's house. Once there, Daly devised another long composite scene, in which Toby and Andrew carouse (1.3), Olivia receives Viola-Cesario (1.5), and Malvolio returns the ring to Viola-Cesario (2.2). Music was prominent throughout the production. During its first scene, for instance, on the seacoast after the storm happy villagers sang "Come unto these yellow sands" from *The Tempest;* other songs were introduced into the scenes at Olivia's house. Moonlight beamed onto the set as Orsino's minstrels sang "Who is Olivia?" (taken from "Who is Sylvia?" in *The Two Gentlemen of Verona*) set to music by Franz Schubert. Rehan, the scenery, and the music made the play a great success; it ran for 119 performances.

Herbert Beerbohm Tree's *Twelfth Night,* at Her Majesty's Theatre in 1901, achieved a kind of pinnacle in the verisimilar staging of *Twelfth Night.* His set for Olivia's house featured a terrace that extended to the extreme back of the stage and a garden complete with real grass, fountains, pathways, and descending steps. It was, according to an eyewitness report, literally an Italian garden, going beyond anything hitherto seen in beauty and realistic illusion. As in Daly's production, the set was so nearly immovable that scenes had to be rearranged extensively, even to the point of staging in Olivia's garden some dramatic material that properly belonged at Orsino's court or elsewhere. Tree also focused, in traditional nineteenth-century fashion, on the leading characters, playing Malvolio himself to the Viola of Lily Brayton.

Nonetheless, a major new direction was at hand. Already, in 1895, *Twelfth Night* had become the first of the revivals by actor-manager William Poel and the Elizabethan Stage Society, who staged it once at Burlington Hall, Savile Row, and again at St. George's Hall. Featuring Elizabethan costumes, a stage bare of scenery, and a single ten-minute intermission, the production tried to approximate the conditions of Shakespeare's own theater. Two years later, in a production in the Hall of the Middle Temple (one of the Inns of Court, where young men studied law in London), Poel sought to produce the play as it might have been done at Shakespeare's Blackfriars Theatre. A table and chair were the only props on the raised platform stage, which was surrounded by halberdiers (guards); costumes were based on the dress of the Elizabethan court, and the songs were, wherever possible, given their original settings and played on sixteenth-century instruments.

In the spirit of Poel's reforms, the twentieth century has generally turned against the excesses of nineteenth-century verisimilar staging. The anti-illusionism implicit in Poel's attempts to restore Elizabethan staging practices was successfully translated into a more modern idiom in a swift-moving ensemble production directed by Harley Granville-Barker at London's Savoy Theatre in 1912, and then in a performance on an apron stage (i.e., a stage thrust out in front of the proscenium) directed by Barry Jackson at the Birmingham Repertory Theatre in 1913, which was revived in 1916 with an uncut text. Since then the play has had its share of new settings and adaptations, including a rock musical version called *Your Own Thing* (1968), but on the whole, of all Shakespeare's comedies *Twelfth Night* seems the least in need of being made "relevant." Allowed to speak for itself, the play has had memorable theatrical triumphs. Tyrone Guthrie's London production at the Old Vic in 1937 successfully doubled Jessica Tandy as Viola and Sebastian and had Laurence Olivier as Toby and Alec Guinness as Andrew Aguecheek. In 1954 the play again graced the Old Vic, directed by Denis Carey, with Claire Bloom as an energetic, almost ferocious Viola and Richard Burton as Toby. A year later, John Gielgud directed Vivien Leigh as Viola and Olivier as Malvolio at Stratford-upon-Avon. John Barton's 1969 Stratford-upon-Avon production was movingly autumnal, dominated by Emrys James's melancholy Feste.

Elizabethan costuming, which was used in Barton's production, seems admirably suited to the play's winsome blend of satire and foolery about love; onstage the play seems quintessentially of Shakespeare's age and yet timeless. It can fully employ the talents of repertory companies expert in ensemble work and willing to distribute the acting honors beyond the roles of Viola, Toby, and Feste. It is a favorite of amateurs, and acts well out-of-doors. It has become a staple of summer festivals at Stratford, in Canada, at Ashland, in Oregon, and many others, where a sturdy and rollicking performance can be counted on to pack the house. New interpretation is usually a matter not of a wholly new or of an anachronistic setting but of nuance, as in the 1969 Barton production when Malvolio, played by Donald Sinden, coming onstage in Act 3, scene 4, stopped to correct the sundial by consulting his pocket watch; the gratuitous officiousness of the gesture was comically eloquent.

Apron, or thrust, stages and quick-paced productions of recent years enable actors to stage *Twelfth Night* much as it must have been performed in Shakespeare's Globe Theatre. The scene of eavesdropping on Malvolio (2.5), for instance, requires only that the actors playing Sir Toby and his belowstairs companions hide themselves where their antics can be visible to spectators during the reading of the letter; on Shakespeare's stage, the pillars would have been especially convenient for such a purpose. When they performed the play at Middle Temple Hall, in February of 1602, as John Manningham's diary tells us, the actors would have had the magnificent screen with its two arched doorways and other architectural features in which to hide from Malvolio or, later, for use as a makeshift prison in which to incarcerate him. The comic duel of Sir Andrew and Viola-Cesario requires only that the contenders approach one another from opposite entrances, with Sir Toby and Fabian moving back and forth between the two unwilling contenders to frighten them or propose terms.

When, in Act 2, scene 2, Malvolio hastens after Viola-Cesario and encounters him in a street, no stage business is required other than that they enter *at several* (i.e., separate) *doors*. They need not (and indeed are instructed that they should not) enter one after the other by the same door to signify that they are coming from Olivia's house, for doors are not used in this illusionistic way on the Shakespearean stage. The previous scene, in any case, has been located in an entirely different part of Illyria, so that Shakespeare makes no attempt to provide a visual continuity between the end of Act 1, scene 5, when Cesario-Viola leaves Olivia's house with Malvolio in pursuit, and their meeting in Act 2, scene 2. Instead, Elizabethan theatrical convention asks the audience to understand that actors entering by separate doors are encountering one another. Realistically identified doorways, or, in the scene of eavesdropping, real shrubbery, not only slow down changes of scene but miss the point by literalizing Illyria. The world in which *Twelfth Night* is located is, or should be, one of theatrical imagination. Illyria is above all a place of the artist's creation, his play world, his theater. *Twelfth Night* frequently calls attention to its self-reflexive quality, as when Fabian says of Malvolio's comic discomfiture, "If this were played upon a stage now, I could condemn it as an improbable fiction" (3.4.129–130). Shakespeare's play revels in this paradox of illusion, making improbable fiction wholly convincing and defying the more ordinary conventions by which dramatic art is made to appear "real."

TWELFTH NIGHT
or
WHAT YOU WILL

[*Dramatis Personae*

ORSINO, *Duke (or Count) of Illyria*
VALENTINE, *gentleman attending on Orsino*
CURIO, *gentleman attending on Orsino*

VIOLA, *a shipwrecked lady, later disguised as Cesario*
SEBASTIAN, *twin brother of Viola*
ANTONIO, *a sea captain, friend to Sebastian*
CAPTAIN *of the shipwrecked vessel*

OLIVIA, *a rich countess of Illyria*
MARIA, *gentlewoman in Olivia's household*
SIR TOBY BELCH, *Olivia's uncle*
SIR ANDREW AGUECHEEK, *a companion of Sir Toby*
MALVOLIO, *steward of Olivia's household*
FABIAN, *a member of Olivia's household*
FESTE, *a clown, also called* FOOL, *Olivia's jester*

A PRIEST
FIRST OFFICER
SECOND OFFICER

Lords, Sailors, Musicians, and other Attendants

SCENE: *A city in Illyria, and the seacoast near it*]

1.1 *Enter Orsino Duke of Illyria, Curio, and other
lords [with musicians].*

ORSINO
  If music be the food of love, play on;
  Give me excess of it, that surfeiting,
  The appetite may sicken and so die.
  That strain again! It had a dying fall;   4
  O, it came o'er my ear like the sweet sound
  That breathes upon a bank of violets,
  Stealing and giving odor. Enough, no more.
  'Tis not so sweet now as it was before.
  O spirit of love, how quick and fresh art thou,   9
  That, notwithstanding thy capacity
  Receiveth as the sea, naught enters there,
  Of what validity and pitch soe'er,   12
  But falls into abatement and low price   13
  Even in a minute. So full of shapes is fancy   14
  That it alone is high fantastical.   15
CURIO
  Will you go hunt, my lord?
ORSINO   What, Curio?
CURIO   The hart.
ORSINO
  Why, so I do, the noblest that I have.   17
  O, when mine eyes did see Olivia first,
  Methought she purged the air of pestilence.
  That instant was I turned into a hart,
  And my desires, like fell and cruel hounds,   21
  E'er since pursue me.

      Enter Valentine.

                        How now, what news from her?   22

1.1. Location: Orsino's court.
s.d. **Illyria** country on the east coast of the Adriatic Sea   **4 fall** cadence   **9 quick and fresh** keen and hungry   **12 validity** value.   **pitch**
superiority. (Literally, the highest point of a falcon's flight.)   **13 abatement** depreciation   **14 shapes** imagined forms.   **fancy** love   **15 it . . .
fantastical** it surpasses everything else in imaginative power   **17 the
noblest . . . have** i.e., my noblest part, my heart (punning on *hart*)
21 fell fierce   **22 pursue me** (Alludes to the story in Ovid of Actaeon,
who, having seen Diana bathing, was transformed into a stag and killed
by his own hounds.)

VALENTINE
So please my lord, I might not be admitted,
But from her handmaid do return this answer:
The element itself, till seven years' heat,   25
Shall not behold her face at ample view;
But like a cloistress she will veilèd walk,   27
And water once a day her chamber round
With eye-offending brine—all this to season   29
A brother's dead love, which she would keep fresh   30
And lasting in her sad remembrance.

ORSINO
O, she that hath a heart of that fine frame   32
To pay this debt of love but to a brother,
How will she love, when the rich golden shaft   34
Hath killed the flock of all affections else   35
That live in her; when liver, brain, and heart,   36
These sovereign thrones, are all supplied, and filled   37
Her sweet perfections, with one self king!   38
Away before me to sweet beds of flowers.
Love thoughts lie rich when canopied with bowers.

Exeunt.

✦

1.2   *Enter Viola, a Captain, and sailors.*

VIOLA   What country, friends, is this?
CAPTAIN   This is Illyria, lady.
VIOLA
And what should I do in Illyria?
My brother he is in Elysium.   4

---

25 element sky.   **seven years' heat** seven summers   **27 cloistress** nun
secluded in a religious community   **29 season** keep fresh (playing on
the idea of the salt in her tears)   **30 brother's dead** dead brother's
32 frame construction   **34 golden shaft** i.e., of Cupid   **35 affections else**
other feelings   **36 liver, brain, and heart** (In medieval and Elizabethan
psychology these organs were the seats of the passions, of thought, and
of feeling.)   **37 supplied** filled   **37–38 and . . . perfections** and her sweet
perfections filled   **38 self king** single lord (the object of her entire
affection)

1.2. Location: The seacoast.
4 Elysium classical abode of the blessed dead

Perchance he is not drowned. What think you, sailors? 5
CAPTAIN
It is perchance that you yourself were saved.   6
VIOLA
O, my poor brother! And so perchance may he be.
CAPTAIN
True, madam, and to comfort you with chance,   8
Assure yourself, after our ship did split,
When you and those poor number saved with you
Hung on our driving boat, I saw your brother,   11
Most provident in peril, bind himself,
Courage and hope both teaching him the practice,
To a strong mast that lived upon the sea;   14
Where, like Arion on the dolphin's back,   15
I saw him hold acquaintance with the waves
So long as I could see.
VIOLA   For saying so, there's gold. [*She gives money.*]
Mine own escape unfoldeth to my hope,   19
Whereto thy speech serves for authority,   20
The like of him. Know'st thou this country?   21
CAPTAIN
Ay, madam, well, for I was bred and born
Not three hours' travel from this very place.
VIOLA   Who governs here?
CAPTAIN
A noble duke, in nature as in name.
VIOLA   What is his name?
CAPTAIN   Orsino.
VIOLA
Orsino! I have heard my father name him.
He was a bachelor then.
CAPTAIN
And so is now, or was so very late;
For but a month ago I went from hence,

5–6 Perchance . . . perchance perhaps . . . by mere chance **8 chance**
i.e., what one may hope that chance will bring about **11 driving** drift-
ing, driven by the seas **14 lived** i.e., kept afloat **15 Arion** a Greek poet
who so charmed the dolphins with his lyre that they saved him when he
leaped into the sea to escape murderous sailors **19–21 unfoldeth . . .
him** i.e., offers a hopeful example that he may have escaped similarly, to
which hope your speech provides support

And then 'twas fresh in murmur—as, you know,   32
What great ones do the less will prattle of—   33
That he did seek the love of fair Olivia.

VIOLA   What's she?

CAPTAIN
A virtuous maid, the daughter of a count
That died some twelvemonth since, then leaving her
In the protection of his son, her brother,
Who shortly also died; for whose dear love,
They say, she hath abjured the sight
And company of men.

VIOLA   O, that I served that lady,
And might not be delivered to the world   42
Till I had made mine own occasion mellow,   43
What my estate is!

CAPTAIN   That were hard to compass,   44
Because she will admit no kind of suit,
No, not the Duke's.

VIOLA
There is a fair behavior in thee, Captain,
And though that nature with a beauteous wall
Doth oft close in pollution, yet of thee
I will believe thou hast a mind that suits
With this thy fair and outward character.   51
I prithee, and I'll pay thee bounteously,
Conceal me what I am, and be my aid
For such disguise as haply shall become   54
The form of my intent. I'll serve this duke.   55
Thou shalt present me as an eunuch to him.   56
It may be worth thy pains, for I can sing
And speak to him in many sorts of music
That will allow me very worth his service.   59
What else may hap, to time I will commit;
Only shape thou thy silence to my wit.   61

---

32 murmur rumor   **33 less** i.e., social inferiors   **42 delivered** revealed,
made known   **43 mellow** ready or convenient (to be made known)
44 estate position in society.   **compass** bring about, encompass
51 character face or features as indicating moral qualities   **54 become** suit   **55 form of my intent** nature of my purpose (with suggestion
of outward appearance in *form*)   **56 eunuch** castrato, high-voiced
singer   **59 allow me** cause me to be acknowledged   **61 wit** plan,
invention

CAPTAIN
   Be you his eunuch, and your mute I'll be;
   When my tongue blabs, then let mine eyes not see.
VIOLA   I thank thee. Lead me on.   *Exeunt.*

❖

1.3   *Enter Sir Toby [Belch] and Maria.*

SIR TOBY   What a plague means my niece to take the
   death of her brother thus? I am sure care's an enemy
   to life.
MARIA   By my troth, Sir Toby, you must come in earlier
   o' nights. Your cousin, my lady, takes great exceptions 5
   to your ill hours.
SIR TOBY   Why, let her except before excepted.   7
MARIA   Ay, but you must confine yourself within the
   modest limits of order.   9
SIR TOBY   Confine? I'll confine myself no finer than I am. 10
   These clothes are good enough to drink in, and so be
   these boots too. An they be not, let them hang them- 12
   selves in their own straps.
MARIA   That quaffing and drinking will undo you. I
   heard my lady talk of it yesterday, and of a foolish
   knight that you brought in one night here to be her
   wooer.
SIR TOBY   Who, Sir Andrew Aguecheek?
MARIA   Ay, he.
SIR TOBY   He's as tall a man as any's in Illyria.   20
MARIA   What's that to the purpose?
SIR TOBY   Why, he has three thousand ducats a year.
MARIA   Ay, but he'll have but a year in all these ducats. 23
   He's a very fool and a prodigal.
SIR TOBY   Fie, that you'll say so! He plays o' the viol-de- 25
   gamboys, and speaks three or four languages word for 26

1.3. Location: Olivia's house.
5 cousin i.e., kinswoman   **7 except before excepted** (Plays on the legal
phrase *exceptis excipiendis,* "with the exceptions before named." Sir
Toby means that enough exceptions to his behavior have already been
taken.)   **9 modest** moderate   **10 confine myself** dress myself (playing
on Maria's use of *confine,* limit).   **finer** (1) better (2) tighter   **12 An** if
20 tall brave   **23 he'll . . . ducats** i.e., he'll spend all his money within a
year   **25–26 viol-de-gamboys** viola da gamba, leg-viol, bass viol

word without book, and hath all the good gifts of 27
nature.

MARIA He hath indeed, almost natural, for, besides that 29
he's a fool, he's a great quarreler, and but that he hath
the gift of a coward to allay the gust he hath in quar- 31
reling, 'tis thought among the prudent he would
quickly have the gift of a grave.

SIR TOBY By this hand, they are scoundrels and sub- 34
stractors that say so of him. Who are they?   35

MARIA They that add, moreover, he's drunk nightly in
your company.

SIR TOBY With drinking healths to my niece. I'll drink
to her as long as there is a passage in my throat and
drink in Illyria. He's a coward and a coistrel that will 40
not drink to my niece till his brains turn o' the toe like
a parish top. What, wench? *Castiliano vulgo!* For here 42
comes Sir Andrew Agueface.   43

Enter Sir Andrew [Aguecheek].

SIR ANDREW Sir Toby Belch! How now, Sir Toby Belch?

SIR TOBY Sweet Sir Andrew!

SIR ANDREW Bless you, fair shrew.

MARIA And you too, sir.

SIR TOBY Accost, Sir Andrew, accost.   48

SIR ANDREW What's that?

SIR TOBY My niece's chambermaid.   50

SIR ANDREW Good Mistress Accost, I desire better acquaintance.

MARIA My name is Mary, sir.

SIR ANDREW Good Mistress Mary Accost—

---

27 without book by heart   **29 natural** (with a play on the sense "born
idiot")   **31 allay the gust** moderate the taste   **34–35 substractors** i.e.,
detractors   **40 coistrel** horse-groom, base fellow   **42 parish top** a large
top provided by the parish to be spun by whipping, apparently for
exercise in cold weather.   **Castiliano vulgo** (Of uncertain meaning.
Castilians were noted for their decorum, and possibly Sir Toby is urging
Maria to behave politely to Sir Andrew.)   **43 Agueface** (Like *Aguecheek*,
this name betokens the thin, pale countenance of one suffering from an
ague.)   **48 Accost** go alongside (a nautical term), i.e., greet her, address
her   **50 chambermaid** lady in waiting (a gentlewoman, not one who
would do menial tasks)

SIR TOBY   You mistake, knight. "Accost" is front her, board her, woo her, assail her.   56

SIR ANDREW   By my troth, I would not undertake her in this company. Is that the meaning of "accost"?

MARIA   Fare you well, gentlemen.   [*Going.*]

SIR TOBY   An thou let part so, Sir Andrew, would thou 60 mightst never draw sword again.

SIR ANDREW   An you part so, mistress, I would I might never draw sword again. Fair lady, do you think you have fools in hand?   64

MARIA   Sir, I have not you by the hand.

SIR ANDREW   Marry, but you shall have, and here's my 66 hand.

MARIA   Now, sir, thought is free. I pray you, bring your 68 hand to the buttery-bar, and let it drink.   69

SIR ANDREW   Wherefore, sweetheart? What's your metaphor?

MARIA   It's dry, sir.   72

SIR ANDREW   Why, I think so. I am not such an ass but I can keep my hand dry. But what's your jest?

MARIA   A dry jest, sir.   75

SIR ANDREW   Are you full of them?

MARIA   Ay, sir, I have them at my fingers' ends. Marry, now I let go your hand, I am barren.   *Exit Maria.* 78

SIR TOBY   O knight, thou lack'st a cup of canary! When 79 did I see thee so put down?

SIR ANDREW   Never in your life, I think, unless you see canary put me down. Methinks sometimes I have no more wit than a Christian or an ordinary man has. But I am a great eater of beef, and I believe that does harm to my wit.

SIR TOBY   No question.

---

56 board greet, approach (as though preparing to board in a naval encounter)   **60 An . . . part** if you let her leave   **64 have . . . hand** i.e., have to deal with fools. (But Maria puns on the literal sense.)   **66 Marry** i.e., indeed. (Originally, "By the Virgin Mary.")   **68 thought is free** i.e., I may think what I like. (Proverbial; replying to *do you think . . . in hand,* above.)   **69 buttery-bar** ledge on top of the half-door to the buttery or wine cellar   **72 dry** thirsty; also dried up, a sign of age and debility   **75 dry** (1) ironic (2) dull, barren (referring to Sir Andrew)   **78 barren** i.e., barren of jests and of Andrew's hand   **79 canary** a sweet wine from the Canary Islands

SIR ANDREW   An I thought that, I'd forswear it. I'll ride
  home tomorrow, Sir Toby.

SIR TOBY   *Pourquoi*, my dear knight?   89

SIR ANDREW   What is *"pourquoi"*? Do or not do? I
  would I had bestowed that time in the tongues that I   91
  have in fencing, dancing, and bearbaiting. O, had I
  but followed the arts!   93

SIR TOBY   Then hadst thou had an excellent head of hair.

SIR ANDREW   Why, would that have mended my hair?   95

SIR TOBY   Past question, for thou seest it will not curl by
  nature.

SIR ANDREW   But it becomes me well enough, does 't
  not?

SIR TOBY   Excellent. It hangs like flax on a distaff, and I 100
  hope to see a huswife take thee between her legs and
  spin it off.   102

SIR ANDREW   Faith, I'll home tomorrow, Sir Toby. Your
  niece will not be seen, or if she be, it's four to one
  she'll none of me. The Count himself here hard by   105
  woos her.

SIR TOBY   She'll none o' the Count. She'll not match
  above her degree, neither in estate, years, nor wit; I   108
  have heard her swear 't. Tut, there's life in 't, man.   109

SIR ANDREW   I'll stay a month longer. I am a fellow o' the
  strangest mind i' the world; I delight in masques and
  revels sometimes altogether.

SIR TOBY   Art thou good at these kickshawses, knight?   113

SIR ANDREW   As any man in Illyria, whatsoever he be,
  under the degree of my betters, and yet I will not com-   115
  pare with an old man.   116

SIR TOBY   What is thy excellence in a galliard, knight?   117

---

89 Pourquoi why   **91 tongues** languages. (Perhaps also suggests *tongs*,
curling irons.)   **93 the arts** the liberal arts, learning. (But Sir Toby plays
on the phrase as meaning "artifice," the antithesis of *nature*.)   **95 mended**
improved   **100 distaff** a staff for holding the flax, tow, or wool in
spinning   **102 spin it off** i.e., cause you to lose hair as a result of vene-
real disease, gotten from the *huswife* (suggesting *hussy*, "whore")
105 Count i.e., Duke Orsino, sometimes referred to as Count.   **hard**
near   **108 degree** social position.   **estate** fortune, social position
109 there's life in 't i.e., while there's life there's hope   **113 kickshawses** delicacies, fancy trifles. (From the French, *quelque chose*.)
115 under . . . betters excepting those who are above me   **116 old
man** experienced person (?)   **117 galliard** lively dance in triple time

SIR ANDREW Faith, I can cut a caper. 118

SIR TOBY And I can cut the mutton to 't.

SIR ANDREW And I think I have the back-trick simply as 120
strong as any man in Illyria.

SIR TOBY Wherefore are these things hid? Wherefore have
these gifts a curtain before 'em? Are they like to 123
take dust, like Mistress Mall's picture? Why dost thou 124
not go to church in a galliard and come home in a
coranto? My very walk should be a jig; I would not so 126
much as make water but in a sink-a-pace. What dost 127
thou mean? Is it a world to hide virtues in? I did think, 128
by the excellent constitution of thy leg, it was formed
under the star of a galliard. 130

SIR ANDREW Ay, 'tis strong, and it does indifferent well 131
in a dun-colored stock. Shall we set about some re- 132
vels?

SIR TOBY What shall we do else? Were we not born under Taurus? 135

SIR ANDREW Taurus? That's sides and heart.

SIR TOBY No, sir, it is legs and thighs. Let me see thee
caper. Ha, higher! Ha, ha, excellent!

[*Sir Andrew capers.*] *Exeunt.*

✤

1.4 *Enter Valentine, and Viola in man's attire.*

VALENTINE If the Duke continue these favors towards
you, Cesario, you are like to be much advanced. He
hath known you but three days, and already you are
no stranger.

---

118 cut a caper make a lively leap. (But Sir Toby puns on the *caper* used
to make a sauce served with mutton. *Mutton* in turn suggests "whore.")
120 back-trick backward step in the galliard   **123–124 like to take**
likely to collect   **124 Mistress Mall's picture** i.e., perhaps the portrait
of some woman protected from light and dust, as many pictures were,
by curtains   **126 coranto** lively running dance   **127 sink-a-pace** dance
like the galliard. (French *cinquepace*.)   **128 virtues** talents   **130 under
. . . galliard** i.e., under a star favorable to dancing   **131 indifferent**
moderately   **132 stock** stocking   **135 Taurus** zodiacal sign. (Sir Andrew
is mistaken, since Leo governed sides and hearts in medical astrology.
Taurus governed legs and thighs, or, more commonly, neck and throat.)

1.4. Location: Orsino's court.

VIOLA You either fear his humor or my negligence, that ⁵
you call in question the continuance of his love. Is he
inconstant, sir, in his favors?

VALENTINE No, believe me.

Enter Duke [Orsino], Curio, and attendants.

VIOLA I thank you. Here comes the Count.

ORSINO Who saw Cesario, ho?

VIOLA On your attendance, my lord, here.

ORSINO

  Stand you awhile aloof. [*The others stand aside.*]
    Cesario,
  Thou know'st no less but all. I have unclasped
  To thee the book even of my secret soul.
  Therefore, good youth, address thy gait unto her;   15
  Be not denied access, stand at her doors,
  And tell them, there thy fixèd foot shall grow   17
  Till thou have audience.

VIOLA   Sure, my noble lord,
  If she be so abandoned to her sorrow
  As it is spoke, she never will admit me.

ORSINO

  Be clamorous and leap all civil bounds   21
  Rather than make unprofited return.

VIOLA

  Say I do speak with her, my lord, what then?

ORSINO

  O, then unfold the passion of my love;
  Surprise her with discourse of my dear faith.   25
  It shall become thee well to act my woes;   26
  She will attend it better in thy youth
  Than in a nuncio's of more grave aspect.   28

VIOLA

  I think not so, my lord.

ORSINO   Dear lad, believe it;
  For they shall yet belie thy happy years
  That say thou art a man. Diana's lip

---

5 humor changeableness   **15 address thy gait** go   **17 them** i.e., Olivia's
servants   **21 civil bounds** bounds of civility   **25 Surprise** take by storm.
(A military term.)   **26 become** suit   **28 nuncio's** messenger's

Is not more smooth and rubious; thy small pipe   32
Is as the maiden's organ, shrill and sound,   33
And all is semblative a woman's part.   34
I know thy constellation is right apt   35
For this affair.—Some four or five attend him;
All, if you will, for I myself am best
When least in company.—Prosper well in this,
And thou shalt live as freely as thy lord,
To call his fortunes thine.

VIOLA   I'll do my best
To woo your lady. [*Aside*.] Yet a barful strife!   41
Whoe'er I woo, myself would be his wife.   *Exeunt*.

❖

1.5 *Enter Maria and Clown* [*Feste*].

MARIA Nay, either tell me where thou hast been, or I
will not open my lips so wide as a bristle may enter in
way of thy excuse. My lady will hang thee for thy absence.

FESTE Let her hang me. He that is well hanged in this
world needs to fear no colors.   6

MARIA Make that good.   7

FESTE He shall see none to fear.

MARIA A good lenten answer. I can tell thee where that 9
saying was born, of "I fear no colors."

FESTE Where, good Mistress Mary?

MARIA In the wars, and that may you be bold to say in   12
your foolery.

FESTE Well, God give them wisdom that have it; and
those that are fools, let them use their talents.   15

---

32 rubious ruby red. **pipe** voice, throat **33 shrill and sound** high and
clear, uncracked **34 semblative** resembling, like **35 constellation** i.e.,
nature as determined by your horoscope **41 barful strife** endeavor full
of impediments

1.5. Location: Olivia's house.
6 fear no colors i.e., fear no foe, fear nothing (with pun on *colors*,
worldly deceptions, and *collars*, halters or nooses) **7 Make that good**
explain that **9 lenten** meager, scanty (like lenten fare) **12 In the wars**
(where *colors* would mean "military standards") **15 talents** abilities
(also alluding to the parable of the talents, Matthew 25:14–29)

MARIA   Yet you will be hanged for being so long absent;
or to be turned away, is not that as good as a hanging   17
to you?

FESTE   Many a good hanging prevents a bad marriage;
and for turning away, let summer bear it out.   20

MARIA   You are resolute, then?

FESTE   Not so, neither, but I am resolved on two
points.   23

MARIA   That if one break, the other will hold; or if both
break, your gaskins fall.   25

FESTE   Apt, in good faith, very apt. Well, go thy way;
if Sir Toby would leave drinking, thou wert as witty a   27
piece of Eve's flesh as any in Illyria.   28

MARIA   Peace, you rogue, no more o' that. Here comes
my lady. Make your excuse wisely, you were best.   30

                                              [*Exit.*]

Enter Lady Olivia with Malvolio [and attendants].

FESTE   Wit, an 't be thy will, put me into good fooling!   31
Those wits that think they have thee do very oft prove
fools, and I that am sure I lack thee may pass for a wise
man. For what says Quinapalus? "Better a witty fool   34
than a foolish wit."—God bless thee, lady!

OLIVIA   Take the fool away.

FESTE   Do you not hear, fellows? Take away the lady.

OLIVIA   Go to, you're a dry fool. I'll no more of you. Be- 38
sides, you grow dishonest.   39

FESTE   Two faults, madonna, that drink and good   40
counsel will amend. For give the dry fool drink, then
is the fool not dry. Bid the dishonest man mend himself; if he mend, he is no longer dishonest; if he cannot, let the botcher mend him. Anything that's   44

17 turned away dismissed (possibly also meaning "turned off,"
"hanged") **20 for** as for. **let . . . out** i.e., let mild weather make dis-
missal endurable **23 points** (Maria plays on the meaning "laces used to
hold up hose or breeches.") **25 gaskins** wide breeches **27–28 thou . . .
Illyria** (Feste may be observing ironically that Maria is as likely to prove
witty as Sir Toby is to give up drinking; or he may hint at a match
between the two.) **30 you were best** it would be best for you **31 an 't**
if it **34 Quinapalus** (Feste's invented authority.) **38 dry** dull **39 dishonest** unreliable; wicked **40 madonna** my lady **44 botcher** mender of
old clothes and shoes

mended is but patched; virtue that transgresses is but
patched with sin, and sin that amends is but patched
with virtue. If that this simple syllogism will serve, so;
if it will not, what remedy? As there is no true cuckold 48
but calamity, so beauty's a flower. The lady bade take 49
away the fool; therefore I say again, take her away.

OLIVIA   Sir, I bade them take away you.

FESTE   Misprision in the highest degree! Lady, *cucul-* 52
lus non facit monachum; that's as much to say as I 53
wear not motley in my brain. Good madonna, give me 54
leave to prove you a fool.

OLIVIA   Can you do it?

FESTE   Dexterously, good madonna.

OLIVIA   Make your proof.

FESTE   I must catechize you for it, madonna. Good my 59
mouse of virtue, answer me.   60

OLIVIA   Well, sir, for want of other idleness, I'll bide 61
your proof.

FESTE   Good madonna, why mourn'st thou?

OLIVIA   Good Fool, for my brother's death.

FESTE   I think his soul is in hell, madonna.

OLIVIA   I know his soul is in heaven, Fool.

FESTE   The more fool, madonna, to mourn for your
brother's soul, being in heaven. Take away the fool,
gentlemen.

OLIVIA   What think you of this fool, Malvolio? Doth he
not mend?   71

MALVOLIO   Yes, and shall do till the pangs of death
shake him. Infirmity, that decays the wise, doth ever
make the better fool.

FESTE   God send you, sir, a speedy infirmity, for the
better increasing your folly! Sir Toby will be sworn
that I am no fox, but he will not pass his word for twopence that you are no fool.

48–49 As . . . flower i.e., Olivia has wedded calamity but will not be
faithful to it, for the natural course is to seize the moment of youth and
beauty before we lose it   **52 Misprision** mistake, misunderstanding (a
legal term meaning a wrongful action or misdemeanor)   **52–53 cucullus
. . . monachum** the cowl does not make the monk   **54 motley** the many-
colored garment of jesters   **59–60 Good . . . virtue** my good virtuous
mouse. (A term of endearment.)   **61 idleness** pastime.   **bide** endure
71 mend i.e., improve, grow more amusing. (But Malvolio uses the word
to mean "grow more like a fool.")

OLIVIA How say you to that, Malvolio?

MALVOLIO I marvel your ladyship takes delight in such
a barren rascal. I saw him put down the other day with 81
an ordinary fool that has no more brain than a stone.
Look you now, he's out of his guard already. Unless 83
you laugh and minister occasion to him, he is gagged. 84
I protest I take these wise men that crow so at these set 85
kind of fools no better than the fools' zanies. 86

OLIVIA O, you are sick of self-love, Malvolio, and taste
with a distempered appetite. To be generous, guiltless,
and of free disposition is to take those things for bird- 89
bolts that you deem cannon bullets. There is no slan- 90
der in an allowed fool, though he do nothing but rail; 91
nor no railing in a known discreet man, though he do
nothing but reprove.

FESTE Now Mercury endue thee with leasing, for 94
thou speak'st well of fools!

Enter Maria.

MARIA Madam, there is at the gate a young gentleman
much desires to speak with you.

OLIVIA From the Count Orsino, is it?

MARIA I know not, madam. 'Tis a fair young man, and
well attended.

OLIVIA Who of my people hold him in delay?

MARIA Sir Toby, madam, your kinsman.

OLIVIA Fetch him off, I pray you. He speaks nothing
but madman. Fie on him! [*Exit Maria.*] Go you, Mal- 104
volio. If it be a suit from the Count, I am sick, or not at
home; what you will, to dismiss it. (*Exit Malvolio.*)
Now you see, sir, how your fooling grows old, and 107
people dislike it.

FESTE Thou hast spoke for us, madonna, as if thy eldest son should be a fool; whose skull Jove cram with
brains, for—here he comes—

81 **with** by   83 **out of his guard** defenseless, unprovided with a witty
answer   84 **minister occasion** provide opportunity (for his fooling)
85 **protest** avow, declare.   **crow** laugh stridently.   **set** artificial, stereo-
typed   86 **zanies** assistants, aping attendants   89 **free** magnanimous
89–90 **bird-bolts** blunt arrows for shooting small birds   91 **allowed**
licensed (to speak freely)   94 **Now . . . leasing** i.e., may Mercury, the god
of deception, make you a skillful liar   104 **madman** i.e., the words of
madness   107 **old** stale

Enter Sir Toby.

one of thy kin has a most weak *pia mater*.   112

OLIVIA By mine honor, half drunk. What is he at the
gate, cousin?

SIR TOBY A gentleman.

OLIVIA A gentleman? What gentleman?

SIR TOBY 'Tis a gentleman here—[*He belches.*] A plague o'
these pickle-herring! How now, sot?   118

FESTE Good Sir Toby.

OLIVIA Cousin, cousin, how have you come so early by
this lethargy?

SIR TOBY Lechery? I defy lechery. There's one at the
gate.

OLIVIA Ay, marry, what is he?

SIR TOBY Let him be the devil, an he will, I care not.
Give me faith, say I. Well, it's all one.   *Exit.* 126

OLIVIA What's a drunken man like, Fool?

FESTE Like a drowned man, a fool, and a madman.
One draft above heat makes him a fool, the second   129
mads him, and a third drowns him.

OLIVIA Go thou and seek the crowner, and let him sit 131
o' my coz; for he's in the third degree of drink, he's 132
drowned. Go, look after him.

FESTE He is but mad yet, madonna; and the fool shall
look to the madman.   [*Exit.*]

Enter Malvolio.

MALVOLIO Madam, yond young fellow swears he will
speak with you. I told him you were sick; he takes on
him to understand so much, and therefore comes to
speak with you. I told him you were asleep; he seems
to have a foreknowledge of that too, and therefore
comes to speak with you. What is to be said to him,
lady? He's fortified against any denial.

OLIVIA Tell him he shall not speak with me.

MALVOLIO He's been told so; and he says he'll stand at

---

112 **pia mater** i.e., brain (actually the soft membrane enclosing the
brain) 118 **sot** (1) fool (2) drunkard 126 **Give me faith** i.e., to resist the
devil. **it's all one** it doesn't matter 129 **draft** drinking portion. **above
heat** above the point needed to make him normally warm 131 **crowner**
coroner 131–132 **sit o' my coz** hold an inquest on my kinsman (Sir Toby)

your door like a sheriff's post, and be the supporter to 145
a bench, but he'll speak with you.

OLIVIA   What kind o' man is he?

MALVOLIO   Why, of mankind.

OLIVIA   What manner of man?

MALVOLIO   Of very ill manner. He'll speak with you,
will you or no.

OLIVIA   Of what personage and years is he?

MALVOLIO   Not yet old enough for a man, nor young
enough for a boy; as a squash is before 'tis a peascod, 154
or a codling when 'tis almost an apple. 'Tis with him 155
in standing water, between boy and man. He is very 156
well-favored and he speaks very shrewishly. One 157
would think his mother's milk were scarce out
of him.

OLIVIA   Let him approach. Call in my gentlewoman.

MALVOLIO   Gentlewoman, my lady calls.   *Exit.*

    Enter Maria.

OLIVIA

Give me my veil. Come, throw it o'er my face.
We'll once more hear Orsino's embassy.

                        [Olivia veils.]

    Enter Viola.

VIOLA   The honorable lady of the house, which is she?

OLIVIA   Speak to me; I shall answer for her. Your will?

VIOLA   Most radiant, exquisite, and unmatchable
beauty—I pray you, tell me if this be the lady of the
house, for I never saw her. I would be loath to cast
away my speech; for besides that it is excellently well
penned, I have taken great pains to con it. Good beau- 170
ties, let me sustain no scorn; I am very comptible, even 171
to the least sinister usage.   172

OLIVIA   Whence came you, sir?

VIOLA   I can say little more than I have studied, and that

---

145 sheriff's post post before the sheriff's door on which proclamations
and notices were fixed   **154 squash** unripe pea pod.   **peascod** pea pod
155 codling unripe apple   **156 in standing water** at the turn of the
tide   **157 well-favored** good-looking.   **shrewishly** sharply   **170 con**
learn by heart   **171 comptible** susceptible, sensitive   **172 least sinister**
slightest discourteous

question's out of my part. Good gentle one, give me
modest assurance if you be the lady of the house, that 176
I may proceed in my speech.

OLIVIA   Are you a comedian?   178

VIOLA   No, my profound heart; and yet, by the very 179
fangs of malice, I swear I am not that I play. Are you
the lady of the house?

OLIVIA   If I do not usurp myself, I am.   182

VIOLA   Most certain, if you are she, you do usurp your- 183
self; for what is yours to bestow is not yours to reserve. 184
But this is from my commission. I will on with my 185
speech in your praise, and then show you the heart of
my message.

OLIVIA   Come to what is important in 't. I forgive you 188
the praise.

VIOLA   Alas, I took great pains to study it, and 'tis poetical.

OLIVIA   It is the more like to be feigned. I pray you, keep
it in. I heard you were saucy at my gates, and allowed
your approach rather to wonder at you than to hear
you. If you be not mad, begone; if you have reason, 195
be brief. 'Tis not that time of moon with me to make 196
one in so skipping a dialogue.   197

MARIA   Will you hoist sail, sir? Here lies your way.

VIOLA   No, good swabber, I am to hull here a little 199
longer.—Some mollification for your giant, sweet lady. 200
Tell me your mind; I am a messenger.

OLIVIA   Sure you have some hideous matter to deliver,
when the courtesy of it is so fearful. Speak your office. 203

VIOLA   It alone concerns your ear. I bring no overture of

---

176 modest reasonable   **178 comedian** actor   **179 profound** very wise.
figuratively deep   **182 do . . . myself** am not an impostor   **183–184 usurp
yourself** i.e., betray yourself, by withholding yourself from Orsino
185 from outside of   **188 forgive you** excuse you from repeating   **195 If
. . . mad** i.e., if you don't have madness to excuse your saucy behavior (?)
Possibly an error for *If . . . but mad* (?)   **reason** sanity   **196 moon** (The
moon was thought to affect lunatics according to its changing phases.)
196–197 make one take part   **199 swabber** one in charge of washing
the decks. (A nautical retort to *hoist sail.*)   **hull** lie with sails furled
200 Some . . . for i.e., please mollify, pacify.   **giant** i.e., the diminutive
Maria who, like many giants in medieval romances, is guarding the
lady   **203 courtesy** i.e., introduction.   **office** commission

war, no taxation of homage. I hold the olive in my 205
hand; my words are as full of peace as matter.

OLIVIA Yet you began rudely. What are you? What
would you?

VIOLA The rudeness that hath appeared in me have I
learned from my entertainment. What I am, and what 210
I would, are as secret as maidenhead—to your ears,
divinity; to any other's, profanation.

OLIVIA Give us the place alone; we will hear this divinity. [*Exeunt Maria and attendants.*] Now, sir, what is
your text?

VIOLA Most sweet lady—

OLIVIA A comfortable doctrine, and much may be said 217
of it. Where lies your text?

VIOLA In Orsino's bosom.

OLIVIA In his bosom? In what chapter of his bosom?

VIOLA To answer by the method, in the first of his 221
heart.

OLIVIA O, I have read it; it is heresy. Have you no more
to say?

VIOLA Good madam, let me see your face.

OLIVIA Have you any commission from your lord to ne-
gotiate with my face? You are now out of your text.
But we will draw the curtain and show you the picture. [*Unveiling.*] Look you, sir, such a one I was this 229
present. Is 't not well done?   230

VIOLA Excellently done, if God did all.

OLIVIA 'Tis in grain, sir; 'twill endure wind and 232
weather.

VIOLA

'Tis beauty truly blent, whose red and white   234
Nature's own sweet and cunning hand laid on.   235
Lady, you are the cruel'st she alive
If you will lead these graces to the grave
And leave the world no copy.   238

205 taxation demand for the payment   **210 entertainment** reception
217 comfortable comforting   **221 To . . . method** i.e., to continue the
metaphor (of delivering a sermon, begun with *divinity* and *what is your
text* and continued in *doctrine, heresy,* etc.)   **229–230 this present** at this
present time. (Since it was customary to hang curtains in front of pictures,
Olivia in unveiling speaks as if she were displaying a picture of herself.)
232 in grain fast dyed   **234 blent** blended   **235 cunning** skillful   **238 copy**
i.e., a child. (But Olivia uses the word to mean "transcript.")

OLIVIA   O, sir, I will not be so hardhearted. I will give
out divers schedules of my beauty. It shall be inven- 240
toried, and every particle and utensil labeled to my will: 241
as, item, two lips, indifferent red; item, two gray eyes, 242
with lids to them; item, one neck, one chin, and so
forth. Were you sent hither to praise me?   244

VIOLA
I see you what you are, you are too proud;
But, if you were the devil, you are fair.   246
My lord and master loves you. O, such love
Could be but recompensed, though you were crowned 248
The nonpareil of beauty!

OLIVIA   How does he love me?

VIOLA
With adorations, fertile tears,   250
With groans that thunder love, with sighs of fire.

OLIVIA
Your lord does know my mind; I cannot love him.
Yet I suppose him virtuous, know him noble,
Of great estate, of fresh and stainless youth;
In voices well divulged, free, learned, and valiant, 255
And in dimension and the shape of nature
A gracious person. But yet I cannot love him.   257
He might have took his answer long ago.

VIOLA
If I did love you in my master's flame,   259
With such a suffering, such a deadly life,   260
In your denial I would find no sense;
I would not understand it.

OLIVIA   Why, what would you?

VIOLA
Make me a willow cabin at your gate,   263
And call upon my soul within the house;   264
Write loyal cantons of contemnèd love,   265

240 schedules inventories **241 utensil** article, item. **labeled** added as
a codicil **242 indifferent** somewhat **244 praise** appraise **246 if** even
if **248 but . . . though** no more than evenly repaid even though
250 fertile copious **255 In . . . divulged** well reported in public opinion. **free** generous **257 gracious** graceful, attractive **259 flame**
passion **260 deadly** deathlike **263 willow cabin** shelter, hut. (Willow
was a symbol of unrequited love.) **264 my soul** i.e., Olivia **265 cantons**
songs. **contemnèd** rejected

And sing them loud even in the dead of night;
Hallow your name to the reverberate hills, 267
And make the babbling gossip of the air 268
Cry out "Olivia!" O, you should not rest
Between the elements of air and earth
But you should pity me!

OLIVIA   You might do much.
What is your parentage?

VIOLA
Above my fortunes, yet my state is well: 273
I am a gentleman.

OLIVIA   Get you to your lord.
I cannot love him. Let him send no more—
Unless, perchance, you come to me again
To tell me how he takes it. Fare you well.
I thank you for your pains. Spend this for me.
                              [*She offers a purse.*]

VIOLA
I am no fee'd post, lady; keep your purse. 279
My master, not myself, lacks recompense.
Love make his heart of flint that you shall love, 281
And let your fervor, like my master's, be
Placed in contempt! Farewell, fair cruelty.   *Exit.*

OLIVIA "What is your parentage?"
"Above my fortunes, yet my state is well:
I am a gentleman." I'll be sworn thou art!
Thy tongue, thy face, thy limbs, actions, and spirit
Do give thee fivefold blazon. Not too fast! Soft, soft! 288
Unless the master were the man. How now?
Even so quickly may one catch the plague?
Methinks I feel this youth's perfections
With an invisible and subtle stealth
To creep in at mine eyes. Well, let it be.
What ho, Malvolio!

    Enter Malvolio.

MALVOLIO   Here, madam, at your service.

---

267 Hallow (1) halloo (2) bless **268 babbling . . . air** echo **273 state**
social standing **279 fee'd post** messenger to be tipped **281 Love . . .**
love may Love make the heart of the man you love as hard as flint
288 blazon heraldic description

OLIVIA
 Run after that same peevish messenger,
 The County's man. He left this ring behind him,   296
                              [*Giving a ring*]
 Would I or not. Tell him I'll none of it.   297
 Desire him not to flatter with his lord,   298
 Nor hold him up with hopes; I am not for him.
 If that the youth will come this way tomorrow,
 I'll give him reasons for 't. Hie thee, Malvolio.
MALVOLIO   Madam, I will.   *Exit*.
OLIVIA
 I do I know not what, and fear to find
 Mine eye too great a flatterer for my mind.   304
 Fate, show thy force. Ourselves we do not owe;   305
 What is decreed must be, and be this so.   [*Exit*.]

❧

296 County's Count's, i.e., Duke's   **297 Would I or not** whethèr I
wanted it or not   **298 flatter with** encourage   **304 Mine . . . mind** i.e.,
that my eyes (through which love enters the soul) have betrayed my
reason   **305 owe** own, control

2.1 *Enter Antonio and Sebastian.*

ANTONIO Will you stay no longer? Nor will you not that 1
I go with you?

SEBASTIAN By your patience, no. My stars shine darkly 3
over me. The malignancy of my fate might perhaps 4
distemper yours; therefore I shall crave of you your 5
leave, that I may bear my evils alone. It were a bad
recompense for your love to lay any of them on you.

ANTONIO Let me yet know of you whither you are
bound.

SEBASTIAN No, sooth, sir; my determinate voyage is 10
mere extravagancy. But I perceive in you so excellent 11
a touch of modesty that you will not extort from me
what I am willing to keep in; therefore it charges me 13
in manners the rather to express myself. You must 14
know of me then, Antonio, my name is Sebastian,
which I called Roderigo. My father was that Sebastian
of Messaline whom I know you have heard of. He left 17
behind him myself and a sister, both born in an hour. 18
If the heavens had been pleased, would we had so
ended! But you, sir, altered that, for some hour before 20
you took me from the breach of the sea was my sister 21
drowned.

ANTONIO Alas the day!

SEBASTIAN A lady, sir, though it was said she much resembled me, was yet of many accounted beautiful. But
though I could not with such estimable wonder over- 26
far believe that, yet thus far I will boldly publish her: 27
she bore a mind that envy could not but call fair. She
is drowned already, sir, with salt water, though I seem
to drown her remembrance again with more.

2.1. Location: Somewhere in Illyria.
1 Nor will you not do you not wish **3 patience** leave **4 malignancy**
malevolence (of the stars; also in a medical sense) **5 distemper** disor-
der, disturb **10 sooth** truly. **determinate** intended, determined upon
11 extravagancy aimless wandering **13 am willing . . . in** wish to keep
secret **13–14 it . . . manners** it is incumbent upon me in all courtesy
14 express reveal **17 Messaline** probably Messina, or, more likely,
Massila (the modern Marseilles). In Plautus' *Menaechmi*, Massilians and
Illyrians are mentioned together. **18 in an hour** in the same hour
20 some hour about an hour **21 breach of the sea** surf **26 estimable**
wonder admiring judgment **27 publish** proclaim

ANTONIO Pardon me, sir, your bad entertainment.   31
SEBASTIAN O good Antonio, forgive me your trouble.   32
ANTONIO If you will not murder me for my love, let me 33
be your servant.
SEBASTIAN If you will not undo what you have done,
that is, kill him whom you have recovered, desire it 36
not. Fare ye well at once. My bosom is full of kindness, 37
and I am yet so near the manners of my mother that 38
upon the least occasion more mine eyes will tell tales
of me. I am bound to the Count Orsino's court. Fare-
well.   *Exit.*

ANTONIO
The gentleness of all the gods go with thee!
I have many enemies in Orsino's court,
Else would I very shortly see thee there.
But come what may, I do adore thee so
That danger shall seem sport, and I will go.   *Exit.*

❖

2.2   *Enter Viola and Malvolio, at several doors.*

MALVOLIO Were not you even now with the Countess
Olivia?
VIOLA Even now, sir. On a moderate pace I have since
arrived but hither.
MALVOLIO She returns this ring to you, sir. You might
have saved me my pains, to have taken it away yourself. She adds, moreover, that you should put your
lord into a desperate assurance she will none of him. 8
And one thing more, that you be never so hardy to 9
come again in his affairs, unless it be to report your
lord's taking of this. Receive it so.
VIOLA She took the ring of me. I'll none of it.   12

31 entertainment reception, hospitality **32 your trouble** the trouble
I put you to **33 murder me for** i.e., be the cause of my death in
return for **36 recovered** rescued, restored **37 kindness** tenderness,
natural emotion (of grief) **38 manners of my mother** womanish
qualities

2.2. Location: Outside Olivia's house.
s.d. several different **8 desperate** without hope **9 hardy** bold **12 She**
. . . it (Viola tells a quick and friendly lie to shield Olivia.)

MALVOLIO Come, sir, you peevishly threw it to her, and
her will is it should be so returned. [*He throws down
the ring.*] If it be worth stooping for, there it lies, in 15
your eye; if not, be it his that finds it.   *Exit.* 16
VIOLA [*Picking up the ring*]
I left no ring with her. What means this lady?
Fortune forbid my outside have not charmed her!
She made good view of me, indeed so much   19
That sure methought her eyes had lost her tongue,   20
For she did speak in starts distractedly.
She loves me, sure! The cunning of her passion
Invites me in this churlish messenger.   23
None of my lord's ring? Why, he sent her none.
I am the man. If it be so—as 'tis—
Poor lady, she were better love a dream.
Disguise, I see, thou art a wickedness
Wherein the pregnant enemy does much.   28
How easy is it for the proper false   29
In women's waxen hearts to set their forms!   30
Alas, our frailty is the cause, not we,
For such as we are made of, such we be.   32
How will this fadge? My master loves her dearly,   33
And I, poor monster, fond as much on him;   34
And she, mistaken, seems to dote on me.
What will become of this? As I am man,
My state is desperate for my master's love;
As I am woman—now, alas the day!—
What thriftless sighs shall poor Olivia breathe!   39
O Time, thou must untangle this, not I;
It is too hard a knot for me t' untie.   [*Exit.*]

❧

15–16 **in your eye** in plain sight   19 **made good view of** took a careful
look at   20 **lost** caused her to lose; or, ruined   23 **Invites** tries to
attract   28 **pregnant** quick, resourceful. **enemy** i.e., Satan   29 **proper
false** men who are handsome and deceitful   30 **waxen** i.e., malleable,
impressionable.   **set their forms** stamp their images (as of a seal)
32 **such as . . . of** i.e., feminine frailty   33 **fadge** turn out   34 **monster**
i.e., being both man and woman.   **fond** dote   39 **thriftless** unprofitable

2.3　　*Enter Sir Toby and Sir Andrew.*

SIR TOBY　Approach, Sir Andrew. Not to be abed after
　midnight is to be up betimes; and *diluculo surgere,* 2
　thou know'st—
SIR ANDREW　Nay, by my troth, I know not, but I know
　to be up late is to be up late.
SIR TOBY　A false conclusion. I hate it as an unfilled can. 6
　To be up after midnight and to go to bed then, is early;
　so that to go to bed after midnight is to go to bed
　betimes. Does not our lives consist of the four ele- 9
　ments?　　　　　　　　　　　　　　　　　　　　　10
SIR ANDREW　Faith, so they say, but I think it rather con-
　sists of eating and drinking.
SIR TOBY　Thou'rt a scholar; let us therefore eat and
　drink. Marian, I say, a stoup of wine!　　　　　14

　　　Enter Clown [Feste].

SIR ANDREW　Here comes the Fool, i' faith.
FESTE　How now, my hearts! Did you never see the
　picture of "we three"?　　　　　　　　　　　　17
SIR TOBY　Welcome, ass. Now let's have a catch.　　18
SIR ANDREW　By my troth, the Fool has an excellent
　breast. I had rather than forty shillings I had such a 20
　leg, and so sweet a breath to sing, as the Fool has. In
　sooth, thou wast in very gracious fooling last night,
　when thou spok'st of Pigrogromitus, of the Vapians 23
　passing the equinoctial of Queubus. 'Twas very good, 24
　i' faith. I sent thee sixpence for thy leman. Hadst it? 25
FESTE　I did impeticos thy gratillity; for Malvolio's 26
　nose is no whipstock. My lady has a white hand, and 27

2.3. Location: Olivia's house.
2 betimes early.　diluculo surgere [saluberrimum est] to rise early is most
healthful. (A sentence from Lilly's *Latin Grammar*.)　6 can tankard
9–10 four elements i.e., fire, air, water, and earth, the elements that were
thought to make up all matter　14 stoup drinking vessel　17 picture of
"we three" picture of two fools or asses inscribed "we three," the spectator being the third　18 catch round　20 breast voice　23–24 Pigrogromitus
. . . Queubus (Feste's mock erudition.)　25 leman sweetheart　26 impeticos
thy gratillity (Suggests "impetticoat, or pocket up, thy gratuity.")
27 whipstock whip handle. (Possibly suggests that Malvolio is not very
formidable as overseer in Olivia's household; or, just nonsense.)　has a
white hand i.e., is ladylike. (But Feste's speech may be mere nonsense.)

the Myrmidons are no bottle-ale houses.   28

SIR ANDREW   Excellent! Why, this is the best fooling,
when all is done. Now, a song.

SIR TOBY   Come on, there is sixpence for you. [*He gives
money.*] Let's have a song.

SIR ANDREW   There's a testril of me too. [*He gives money.*]   33
If one knight give a—

FESTE   Would you have a love song, or a song of good   35
life?   36

SIR TOBY   A love song, a love song.

SIR ANDREW   Ay, ay, I care not for good life.

FESTE (*Sings*)
> O mistress mine, where are you roaming?
> O, stay and hear, your true love's coming,
>   That can sing both high and low.
> Trip no further, pretty sweeting;
> Journeys end in lovers meeting,
>   Every wise man's son doth know.

SIR ANDREW   Excellent good, i' faith.

SIR TOBY   Good, good.

FESTE [*Sings*]
> What is love? 'tis not hereafter;
> Present mirth hath present laughter;
>   What's to come is still unsure.
> In delay there lies no plenty,
> Then come kiss me, sweet and twenty;   51
>   Youth's a stuff will not endure.

SIR ANDREW   A mellifluous voice, as I am true knight.

SIR TOBY   A contagious breath.

SIR ANDREW   Very sweet and contagious, i' faith.

SIR TOBY   To hear by the nose, it is dulcet in contagion.   56
But shall we make the welkin dance indeed? Shall we   57

---

28 Myrmidons followers of Achilles.   **bottle-ale houses** (Used contemptuously of taverns because they sold low-class drink.)   **33 testril** i.e.,
tester, a coin worth sixpence   **35–36 good life** virtuous living. (Or perhaps Feste means simply "life's pleasures," but is misunderstood by
Sir Andrew to mean "virtuous living.")   **51 sweet and twenty** i.e., sweet
and twenty times sweet   **56 To . . . nose** i.e., to describe hearing in
olfactory terms.   **dulcet in contagion** (Sir Toby may be mocking Sir
Andrew's unfortunate choice of words.)   **57 make . . . dance** i.e., drink
till the sky seems to turn around

    rouse the night owl in a catch that will draw three 58
souls out of one weaver? Shall we do that? 59

SIR ANDREW An you love me, let's do 't. I am dog at a 60
catch. 61

FESTE By 'r Lady, sir, and some dogs will catch well.

SIR ANDREW Most certain. Let our catch be "Thou
knave."

FESTE "Hold thy peace, thou knave," knight? I shall
be constrained in 't to call thee knave, knight.

SIR ANDREW 'Tis not the first time I have constrained
one to call me knave. Begin, Fool. It begins, "Hold thy
peace."

FESTE I shall never begin if I hold my peace.

SIR ANDREW Good, i' faith. Come, begin.   *Catch sung.*

    Enter Maria.

MARIA What a caterwauling do you keep here! If my
lady have not called up her steward Malvolio and bid
him turn you out of doors, never trust me.

SIR TOBY My lady's a Cataian, we are politicians, Mal- 75
volio's a Peg-a-Ramsey, and [*Sings*] "Three merry 76
men be we." Am not I consanguineous? Am I not of 77
her blood? Tillyvally! Lady! [*Sings.*] "There dwelt a 78
man in Babylon, lady, lady." 79

FESTE Beshrew me, the knight's in admirable fooling.

SIR ANDREW Ay, he does well enough if he be disposed,
and so do I too. He does it with a better grace, but I
do it more natural. 83

SIR TOBY [*Sings*] "O' the twelfth day of December"— 84

58–59 draw three souls (Refers to the threefold nature of the soul, vegetal, sensible, and intellectual; or to the three singers of the three-part catch; or, just a comic exaggeration.) **59 weaver** (Weavers were often associated with psalm-singing.) **60 dog at** very clever at. (But Feste uses the word literally.) **61 catch** round. (But Feste uses it to mean "seize.") **75 Cataian** Cathayan, i.e., Chinese, a trickster; or, just nonsense. **politicians** schemers, intriguers **76 Peg-a-Ramsey** character in a popular song. (Used here contemptuously.) **76–77 Three . . . we** (A snatch of an old song.) **77 consanguineous** i.e., a blood relative of Olivia **78 Tillyvally** i.e., nonsense, fiddle-faddle **78–79 There . . . lady** (The first line of a ballad, "The Constancy of Susanna," together with the refrain, "Lady, lady.") **83 natural** naturally (but unconsciously suggesting idiocy) **84 O'. . . December** (Possibly part of a ballad about the Battle of Musselburgh Field, or Toby's error for the "twelfth day of Christmas," i.e., Twelfth Night.)

MARIA   For the love o' God, peace!

Enter Malvolio.

MALVOLIO   My masters, are you mad? Or what are you?
Have you no wit, manners, nor honesty but to gabble
like tinkers at this time of night? Do ye make an alehouse of my lady's house that ye squeak out your coz- 89
iers' catches without any mitigation or remorse of 90
voice? Is there no respect of place, persons, nor time in
you?

SIR TOBY   We did keep time, sir, in our catches. Sneck 93
up! 94

MALVOLIO   Sir Toby, I must be round with you. My 95
lady bade me tell you that though she harbors you as
her kinsman, she's nothing allied to your disorders. If
you can separate yourself and your misdemeanors,
you are welcome to the house; if not, an it would
please you to take leave of her, she is very willing to
bid you farewell.

SIR TOBY [*Sings*]
"Farewell, dear heart, since I must needs be gone." 102

MARIA   Nay, good Sir Toby.

FESTE [*Sings*]
"His eyes do show his days are almost done."

MALVOLIO   Is 't even so?

SIR TOBY [*Sings*]
"But I will never die."

FESTE
Sir Toby, there you lie.

MALVOLIO   This is much credit to you.

SIR TOBY [*Sings*]
"Shall I bid him go?"

FESTE [*Sings*]
"What an if you do?"

SIR TOBY [*Sings*]
"Shall I bid him go, and spare not?"

FESTE [*Sings*]
"O, no, no, no, no, you dare not."

89–90 coziers' cobblers'   **90 mitigation or remorse** i.e., considerate
lowering   **93–94 Sneck up** go hang   **95 round** blunt   **102 Farewell . . . gone** (From the ballad "Corydon's Farewell to Phyllis.")

SIR TOBY Out o' tune, sir? Ye lie. Art any more than a steward? Dost thou think, because thou art virtuous, there shall be no more cakes and ale?

FESTE Yes, by Saint Anne, and ginger shall be hot i' 116 the mouth too.

SIR TOBY Thou'rt i' the right. Go, sir, rub your chain 118 with crumbs. A stoup of wine, Maria! 119

MALVOLIO Mistress Mary, if you prized my lady's favor at anything more than contempt, you would not give 121 means for this uncivil rule. She shall know of it, by 122 this hand. *Exit.*

MARIA Go shake your ears. 124

SIR ANDREW 'Twere as good a deed as to drink when a man's a-hungry, to challenge him the field, and then 126 to break promise with him and make a fool of him.

SIR TOBY Do 't, knight. I'll write thee a challenge, or I'll deliver thy indignation to him by word of mouth.

MARIA Sweet Sir Toby, be patient for tonight. Since the youth of the Count's was today with my lady, she is much out of quiet. For Monsieur Malvolio, let me alone with him. If I do not gull him into a nayword 133 and make him a common recreation, do not think I 134 have wit enough to lie straight in my bed. I know I can do it.

SIR TOBY Possess us, possess us, tell us something of 137 him.

MARIA Marry, sir, sometimes he is a kind of puritan. 139

SIR ANDREW O, if I thought that, I'd beat him like a dog.

SIR TOBY What, for being a puritan? Thy exquisite reason, dear knight?

116 **Saint Anne** mother of the Virgin Mary. (Her cult was derided in the Reformation.) **ginger** (Commonly used to spice ale.) 118–119 **Go . . . crumbs** i.e., scour or polish your steward's chain; attend to your own business and remember your station 121–122 **give means** i.e., supply drink 122 **rule** conduct 124 **your ears** i.e., your ass's ears 126 **the field** i.e., to a duel 133 **gull** trick. **nayword** byword 134 **recreation** sport 137 **Possess** inform 139 **puritan** (Maria's point is that Malvolio is sometimes a *kind* of puritan, insofar as he is precise about moral conduct and censorious of others for immoral conduct, but that he is nothing consistently except a time-server. He is not then simply a satirical type of the Puritan sect. The extent of the resemblance is left unstated.)

SIR ANDREW I have no exquisite reason for 't, but I have
reason good enough.

MARIA The devil a puritan that he is, or anything constantly, but a time-pleaser; an affectioned ass, that cons 147
state without book and utters it by great swaths; the 148
best persuaded of himself, so crammed, as he thinks, 149
with excellencies, that it is his grounds of faith that all 150
that look on him love him; and on that vice in him
will my revenge find notable cause to work.

SIR TOBY What wilt thou do?

MARIA I will drop in his way some obscure epistles of
love; wherein, by the color of his beard, the shape of
his leg, the manner of his gait, the expressure of his 156
eye, forehead, and complexion, he shall find himself 157
most feelingly personated. I can write very like my 158
lady your niece; on a forgotten matter we can hardly
make distinction of our hands.

SIR TOBY Excellent! I smell a device.

SIR ANDREW I have 't in my nose too.

SIR TOBY He shall think, by the letters that thou wilt
drop, that they come from my niece, and that she's in
love with him.

MARIA My purpose is indeed a horse of that color.

SIR ANDREW And your horse now would make him an
ass.

MARIA Ass, I doubt not. 169

SIR ANDREW O, 'twill be admirable!

MARIA Sport royal, I warrant you. I know my physic 171
will work with him. I will plant you two, and let the
Fool make a third, where he shall find the letter. Observe
his construction of it. For this night, to bed, and
dream on the event. Farewell.   *Exit.* 175

SIR TOBY Good night, Penthesilea. 176

---

147 time-pleaser time-server, sycophant. **afffectioned** affected
147–148 cons . . . book learns by heart the phrases and mannerisms of
the great **149 best persuaded** having the best opinion **150 grounds of
faith** creed, belief **156 expressure** expression **157 complexion** countenance **158 personated** represented **169 Ass, I** (with a pun on
"as I") **171 physic** medicine **175 event** outcome **176 Penthesilea**
Queen of the Amazons. (Another ironical allusion to Maria's diminutive
stature.)

SIR ANDREW Before me, she's a good wench.   17

SIR TOBY She's a beagle true-bred and one that adores
me. What o' that?

SIR ANDREW I was adored once too.

SIR TOBY Let's to bed, knight. Thou hadst need send for
more money.

SIR ANDREW If I cannot recover your niece, I am a foul   183
way out.   184

SIR TOBY Send for money, knight. If thou hast her not
i' the end, call me cut.   186

SIR ANDREW If I do not, never trust me, take it how you
will.

SIR TOBY Come, come, I'll go burn some sack. 'Tis too   189
late to go to bed now. Come, knight; come, knight.

                                   Exeunt.

❖

2.4   *Enter Duke [Orsino], Viola, Curio,*
        and others.

ORSINO
Give me some music. Now, good morrow, friends.
Now, good Cesario, but that piece of song,   2
That old and antique song we heard last night;   3
Methought it did relieve my passion much,
More than light airs and recollected terms   5
Of these most brisk and giddy-pacèd times.
Come, but one verse.

CURIO He is not here, so please your lordship, that
should sing it.

ORSINO Who was it?

CURIO Feste the jester, my lord, a fool that the Lady
Olivia's father took much delight in. He is about the
house.

177 Before me i.e., on my soul **183 recover** win **183–184 foul way out**
i.e., miserably out of pocket. (Literally, out of my way and in the mire.)
186 cut a horse with a docked tail; also, a gelding, or the female genital
organ **189 burn some sack** warm some Spanish wine

2.4. Location: Orsino's court.
2 but i.e., I ask only **3 antique** old, quaint, fantastic **5 recollected
terms** studied and artificial expressions (?)

ORSINO
     Seek him out, and play the tune the while.
                              [*Exit Curio.*] *Music plays.*
—   Come hither, boy. If ever thou shalt love,
     In the sweet pangs of it remember me;
     For such as I am, all true lovers are,
     Unstaid and skittish in all motions else   18
     Save in the constant image of the creature
     That is beloved. How dost thou like this tune?

VIOLA
     It gives a very echo to the seat   21
     Where Love is throned.

ORSINO   Thou dost speak masterly.
     My life upon 't, young though thou art, thine eye
     Hath stayed upon some favor that it loves.   24
     Hath it not, boy?

VIOLA   A little, by your favor.   25

ORSINO
     What kind of woman is 't?

VIOLA   Of your complexion.

ORSINO
     She is not worth thee, then. What years, i' faith?

VIOLA   About your years, my lord.

ORSINO
     Too old, by heaven. Let still the woman take   29
     An elder than herself; so wears she to him,   30
     So sways she level in her husband's heart.   31
     For, boy, however we do praise ourselves,
     Our fancies are more giddy and unfirm,
     More longing, wavering, sooner lost and worn,
     Than women's are.

VIOLA   I think it well, my lord.

ORSINO
     Then let thy love be younger than thyself,
     Or thy affection cannot hold the bent;   37
     For women are as roses, whose fair flower
     Being once displayed, doth fall that very hour.

18 motions else other thoughts and emotions **21 the seat** i.e., the heart
24 stayed . . . favor rested upon some face **25 by your favor** (1) if you
please (2) like you in feature **29 still** always **30 wears she** she adapts
herself **31 sways she level** she keeps steady, constant **37 hold the bent**
hold steady (like the tension of a bow)

VIOLA
And so they are. Alas, that they are so,
To die, even when they to perfection grow! 41

Enter Curio and Clown [Feste].

ORSINO
O fellow, come, the song we had last night.
Mark it, Cesario, it is old and plain;
The spinsters and the knitters in the sun, 44
And the free maids that weave their thread with bones, 45
Do use to chant it. It is silly sooth, 46
And dallies with the innocence of love,
Like the old age. 48
FESTE Are you ready, sir?
ORSINO Ay, prithee, sing.   *Music.*

The Song.

FESTE
Come away, come away, death,
   And in sad cypress let me be laid. 52
Fly away, fly away, breath;
   I am slain by a fair cruel maid.
My shroud of white, stuck all with yew, 55
   O, prepare it!
My part of death, no one so true 57
   Did share it. 58

Not a flower, not a flower sweet
   On my black coffin let there be strown; 60
Not a friend, not a friend greet
   My poor corpse, where my bones shall be thrown.
A thousand thousand sighs to save,
      Lay me, O, where
Sad true lover never find my grave,
      To weep there!

---

41 even when just as   **44 spinsters** spinners   **45 free** carefree, innocent.
bones bobbins on which bone-lace was made   **46 Do use** are accustomed.
silly sooth simple truth   **48 Like . . . age** as in the good old times   **52 cypress** i.e., a coffin of cypress wood, or bier strewn with sprigs of cypress
55 yew i.e., yew sprigs. (Emblematic of mourning, like cypress.)   **57–58 My
. . . it** i.e., no one died for love so true to love as I   **60 strown** strewn

ORSINO   There's for thy pains.   [*Offering money.*]

FESTE   No pains, sir. I take pleasure in singing, sir.

ORSINO   I'll pay thy pleasure then.

FESTE   Truly, sir, and pleasure will be paid, one time   70
or another.   71

ORSINO   Give me now leave to leave thee.   72

FESTE   Now, the melancholy god protect thee, and the   73
tailor make thy doublet of changeable taffeta, for thy   74
mind is a very opal. I would have men of such constancy put to sea, that their business might be every-   76
thing and their intent everywhere, for that's it that   77
always makes a good voyage of nothing. Farewell.   78

                                              Exit.

ORSINO
Let all the rest give place.

              [*Curio and attendants withdraw.*]
                        Once more, Cesario,   79
Get thee to yond same sovereign cruelty.
Tell her my love, more noble than the world,
Prizes not quantity of dirty lands;
The parts that fortune hath bestowed upon her,   83
Tell her, I hold as giddily as fortune;   84
But 'tis that miracle and queen of gems   85
That nature pranks her in attracts my soul.   86

VIOLA   But if she cannot love you, sir?

ORSINO
I cannot be so answered.

VIOLA   Sooth, but you must.
Say that some lady, as perhaps there is,

70–71 pleasure . . . another i.e., sooner or later one must pay for
indulgence   72 leave to leave permission to take leave of, dismiss
73 the melancholy god i.e., Saturn, whose planet was thought to control the melancholy temperament   74 doublet close-fitting jacket.
changeable taffeta a silk so woven of various-colored threads
that its color shifts with changing perspective   76–77 that . . .
everywhere i.e., so that in the changeableness of the sea their in-
constancy could always be exercised   77–78 for . . . nothing i.e., because such inconstant men would (1) make a good voyage come to
nothing but (2) think a voyage that led anywhere a good one   79 give
place withdraw   83 parts attributes such as wealth or rank   84 I . . .
fortune i.e., I esteem as carelessly as does fortune, that fickle goddess
85 miracle . . . gems i.e., her beauty   86 pranks adorns. attracts i.e.,
that attracts

Hath for your love as great a pang of heart
As you have for Olivia. You cannot love her;
You tell her so. Must she not then be answered?

ORSINO   There is no woman's sides
Can bide the beating of so strong a passion   94
As love doth give my heart; no woman's heart
So big, to hold so much; they lack retention.   96
Alas, their love may be called appetite,
No motion of the liver, but the palate,   98
That suffer surfeit, cloyment, and revolt;   99
But mine is all as hungry as the sea,
And can digest as much. Make no compare
Between that love a woman can bear me
And that I owe Olivia.

VIOLA   Ay, but I know—   103

ORSINO   What dost thou know?

VIOLA
Too well what love women to men may owe.
In faith, they are as true of heart as we.
My father had a daughter loved a man
As it might be perhaps, were I a woman,
I should your lordship.

ORSINO   And what's her history?

VIOLA
A blank, my lord. She never told her love,
But let concealment, like a worm i' the bud,
Feed on her damask cheek. She pined in thought,   112
And with a green and yellow melancholy
She sat like Patience on a monument,   114
Smiling at grief. Was not this love indeed?
We men may say more, swear more, but indeed
Our shows are more than will; for still we prove   117
Much in our vows, but little in our love.

ORSINO
But died thy sister of her love, my boy?

___

94 bide withstand   **96 retention** constancy, power of retaining
98 motion impulse.   **liver . . . palate** (Real love is a passion of the liver, whereas fancy, light love, is born in the eye and nourished in the palate.)   **99 cloyment** satiety.   **revolt** sickness, revulsion   **103 owe** have for   **112 damask** pink and white like the damask rose   **114 on a monument** carved in statuary on a tomb   **117 more than will** greater than our feelings.   **still** always

VIOLA
I am all the daughters of my father's house,
And all the brothers too—and yet I know not.
Sir, shall I to this lady?
ORSINO   Ay, that's the theme.
To her in haste; give her this jewel. [*He gives a jewel.*] Say
My love can give no place, bide no denay.   *Exeunt.* 124

✢

2.5   *Enter Sir Toby, Sir Andrew, and Fabian.*

SIR TOBY   Come thy ways, Signor Fabian.
FABIAN   Nay, I'll come. If I lose a scruple of this sport, 2
let me be boiled to death with melancholy.   3
SIR TOBY   Wouldst thou not be glad to have the nig-
gardly rascally sheep-biter come by some notable 5
shame?
FABIAN   I would exult, man. You know he brought me
out o' favor with my lady about a bearbaiting here.
SIR TOBY   To anger him we'll have the bear again, and
we will fool him black and blue. Shall we not, Sir 10
Andrew?
SIR ANDREW   An we do not, it is pity of our lives.   12

        Enter Maria.

SIR TOBY   Here comes the little villain.—How now, my 13
metal of India?   14
MARIA   Get ye all three into the boxtree. Malvolio's
coming down this walk. He has been yonder i' the sun
practicing behavior to his own shadow this half hour.
Observe him, for the love of mockery, for I know this
letter will make a contemplative idiot of him. Close, in 19
the name of jesting! [*The others hide.*] Lie thou there

---

124 can . . . denay cannot yield or endure denial

2.5. Location: Olivia's garden.
2 scruple bit   **3 boiled** (with a pun on *biled;* black bile was the "humor"
of melancholy)   **5 sheep-biter** a dog that bites sheep, i.e., a nuisance
10 fool . . . blue mock him until he is figuratively black and blue
12 pity of our lives a pity we should live   **13 villain** (Here a term of
endearment.)   **14 metal** gold, i.e., priceless one   **19 contemplative** i.e.,
from his musings.   **Close** i.e., keep close, stay hidden

[*Throwing down a letter*]; for here comes the trout that
must be caught with tickling.   *Exit.* 22

    Enter Malvolio.

MALVOLIO 'Tis but fortune, all is fortune. Maria once
told me she did affect me; and I have heard herself 24
come thus near, that should she fancy, it should be 25
one of my complexion. Besides, she uses me with a
more exalted respect than anyone else that follows 27
her. What should I think on 't?

SIR TOBY Here's an overweening rogue!

FABIAN O, peace! Contemplation makes a rare turkey-
cock of him. How he jets under his advanced plumes! 31

SIR ANDREW 'Slight, I could so beat the rogue! 32

SIR TOBY Peace, I say.

MALVOLIO To be Count Malvolio.

SIR TOBY Ah, rogue!

SIR ANDREW Pistol him, pistol him.

SIR TOBY Peace, peace!

MALVOLIO There is example for 't. The lady of the Stra- 38
chy married the yeoman of the wardrobe. 39

SIR ANDREW Fie on him, Jezebel! 40

FABIAN O, peace! Now he's deeply in. Look how imagination blows him. 42

MALVOLIO Having been three months married to her,
sitting in my state— 44

SIR TOBY O, for a stone-bow, to hit him in the eye! 45

MALVOLIO Calling my officers about me, in my
branched velvet gown; having come from a daybed, 47
where I have left Olivia sleeping—

SIR TOBY Fire and brimstone!

FABIAN O, peace, peace!

MALVOLIO And then to have the humor of state; and 51

---

22 tickling (1) stroking gently about the gills—an actual method of
fishing (2) flattery **24 she** i.e., Olivia. **affect** have fondness for
25 fancy fall in love **27 follows** serves **31 jets** struts. **advanced**
raised **32 'Slight** by His (God's) light **38 example** precedent
38–39 lady of the Strachy (Apparently a lady who had married below
her station; no certain identification.) **40 Jezebel** the proud queen of
Ahab, King of Israel **42 blows** puffs up **44 state** chair of state
45 stone-bow crossbow that shoots stones **47 branched** adorned with a
figured pattern suggesting branched leaves or flowers. **daybed** sofa,
couch **51 have . . . state** adopt the imperious manner of authority

after a demure travel of regard, telling them I know my 52
place as I would they should do theirs, to ask for my
kinsman Toby—   54

SIR TOBY Bolts and shackles!

FABIAN O, peace, peace, peace! Now, now.

MALVOLIO Seven of my people, with an obedient start,
make out for him. I frown the while, and perchance
wind up my watch, or play with my—some rich 59
jewel. Toby approaches; curtsies there to me—

SIR TOBY Shall this fellow live?

FABIAN Though our silence be drawn from us with 62
cars, yet peace.   63

MALVOLIO I extend my hand to him thus, quenching
my familiar smile with an austere regard of control— 65

SIR TOBY And does not Toby take you a blow o' the lips 66
then?

MALVOLIO Saying, "Cousin Toby, my fortunes having
cast me on your niece give me this prerogative of
speech—"

SIR TOBY What, what?

MALVOLIO "You must amend your drunkenness."

SIR TOBY· Out, scab!   73

FABIAN Nay, patience, or we break the sinews of our
plot.

MALVOLIO "Besides, you waste the treasure of your
time with a foolish knight—"

SIR ANDREW That's me, I warrant you.

MALVOLIO "One Sir Andrew—"

SIR ANDREW I knew 'twas I, for many do call me fool.

MALVOLIO What employment have we here?   81
                              [Taking up the letter.]

FABIAN Now is the woodcock near the gin.   82

SIR TOBY O, peace, and the spirit of humors intimate 83
reading aloud to him!

---

52 demure . . . regard grave survey of the company. **telling** indicating
to **54 Toby** (Malvolio omits the title *Sir*.) **59 play with my** (Malvolio
perhaps means his steward's chain, but checks himself in time; as
"Count Malvolio" he would not be wearing it. A bawdy meaning is also
suggested.) **62–63 with cars** with chariots, i.e., by force **65 familiar**
friendly. **regard of control** look of authority **66 take** deliver **73 scab**
scurvy fellow **81 employment** business **82 woodcock** (A bird proverbial for its stupidity.) **gin** snare **83 humors** whim, caprice

MALVOLIO By my life, this is my lady's hand. These be
her very c's, her u's, and her t's; and thus makes she 86
her great P's. It is in contempt of question her hand.   87
SIR ANDREW Her c's, her u's, and her t's. Why that?
MALVOLIO [*Reads*] "To the unknown beloved, this, and
my good wishes."—Her very phrases! By your leave, 90
wax. Soft! And the impressure her Lucrece, with 91
which she uses to seal. 'Tis my lady. To whom should 92
this be?   [*He opens the letter.*]
FABIAN This wins him, liver and all.   94
MALVOLIO [*Reads*]

> "Jove knows I love,
>   But who?
> Lips, do not move;
>   No man must know."

"No man must know." What follows? The numbers 99
altered! "No man must know." If this should be thee,
Malvolio?
SIR TOBY Marry, hang thee, brock!   102
MALVOLIO [*Reads*]

> "I may command where I adore,
>   But silence, like a Lucrece knife,
> With bloodless stroke my heart doth gore;
>   M.O.A.I. doth sway my life."

FABIAN A fustian riddle!   107
SIR TOBY Excellent wench, say I.
MALVOLIO "M.O.A.I. doth sway my life." Nay, but
first, let me see, let me see, let me see.
FABIAN What dish o' poison has she dressed him!   111
SIR TOBY And with what wing the staniel checks 112
at it!   113
MALVOLIO "I may command where I adore." Why, she
may command me; I serve her, she is my lady. Why,

---

86 c's . . . t's i.e., *cut*, slang for the female pudenda   **87 great** (1) upper-
case (2) copious.   **in contempt of** beyond   **90–91 By . . . wax** (Addressed
to the seal on the letter.)   **91 Soft** softly, not so fast.   **impressure** device
imprinted on the seal.   **Lucrece** Lucretia, chaste matron who, ravished
by Tarquin, committed suicide   **92 uses** is accustomed   **94 liver** i.e., the
seat of passion   **99 numbers** meter   **102 brock** badger. (Used contemptuously.)   **107 fustian** bombastic, ridiculously pompous   **111 dressed**
prepared for   **112 staniel** kestrel, a sparrow hawk. (The word is used
contemptuously because of the uselessness of the staniel for fal-
conry.)   **112–113 checks at it** turns to fly at it

this is evident to any formal capacity. There is no ob-   116
struction in this. And the end—what should that al-
phabetical position portend? If I could make that resemble something in me! Softly! M.O.A.I.—

SIR TOBY O, ay, make up that. He is now at a cold scent.   120

FABIAN Sowter will cry upon 't for all this, though it be   121
as rank as a fox.   122

MALVOLIO M—Malvolio! M! Why, that begins my
name!

FABIAN Did not I say he would work it out? The cur is
excellent at faults.   126

MALVOLIO M—But then there is no consonancy in the   127
sequel that suffers under probation: A should follow,   128
but O does.

FABIAN And O shall end, I hope.   130

SIR TOBY Ay, or I'll cudgel him, and make him cry O!

MALVOLIO And then I comes behind.

FABIAN Ay, an you had any eye behind you, you might
see more detraction at your heels than fortunes before   134
you.

MALVOLIO M.O.A.I. This simulation is not as the for-   136
mer. And yet, to crush this a little, it would bow to
me, for every one of these letters are in my name. Soft!
Here follows prose.

[*Reads.*] "If this fall into thy hand, revolve. In my stars   140
I am above thee, but be not afraid of greatness. Some
are born great, some achieve greatness, and some have
greatness thrust upon 'em. Thy Fates open their
hands; let thy blood and spirit embrace them; and, to
inure thyself to what thou art like to be, cast thy hum-   145

116 formal capacity normal mind   **120 O, ay** (playing on *O.I.* of
M.O.A.I.)   **make up** work out   **121 Sowter** cobbler. (Here, the name for
a hound.)   **cry upon 't** bay aloud (as though picking up the scent)
122 rank as a fox (i.e., Malvolio is so crude a hunter that he will leave
the trail of a hare and follow the rank scent of a fox.)   **126 at faults** i.e.,
at maneuvering his way past breaks in the line of scent   **127–128 consonancy in the sequel** pattern in the following letters. (In fact, the
letters M.O.A.I. represent the first, last, second, and next to last letters
of Malvolio's name.)   **128 suffers under probation** stands up under
examination   **130 O shall end** (1) O ends Malvolio's name (2) a noose
shall end his life (3) omega ends the Greek alphabet (4) his cry of pain
will end the joke   **134 detraction** defamation   **136 simulation** disguised
meaning   **140 revolve** consider.   **stars** fortune   **145 inure** accustom.
cast cast off

ble slough and appear fresh. Be opposite with a kins-   146
man, surly with servants. Let thy tongue tang argu-   147
ments of state; put thyself into the trick of singularity.   148
She thus advises thee that sighs for thee. Remember
who commended thy yellow stockings, and wished to
see thee ever cross-gartered. I say, remember. Go to,   151
thou art made, if thou desir'st to be so. If not, let me
see thee a steward still, the fellow of servants, and not
worthy to touch Fortune's fingers. Farewell. She that
would alter services with thee,   155
                    The Fortunate-Unhappy."
Daylight and champaign discovers not more! This is   157
open. I will be proud, I will read politic authors, I will   158
baffle Sir Toby, I will wash off gross acquaintance, I   159
will be point-devise the very man. I do not now fool   160
myself, to let imagination jade me; for every reason   161
excites to this, that my lady loves me. She did commend my yellow stockings of late, she did praise my
leg being cross-gartered; and in this she manifests herself to my love, and with a kind of injunction drives
me to these habits of her liking. I thank my stars, I am   166
happy. I will be strange, stout, in yellow stockings,   167
and cross-gartered, even with the swiftness of putting
on. Jove and my stars be praised! Here is yet a post-
script. [*Reads.*] "Thou canst not choose but know who I
am. If thou entertain'st my love, let it appear in thy
smiling; thy smiles become thee well. Therefore in my
presence still smile, dear my sweet, I prithee." Jove, I
thank thee. I will smile; I will do everything that
thou wilt have me.   *Exit.*
FABIAN   I will not give my part of this sport for a pension of thousands to be paid from the Sophy.   177
SIR TOBY   I could marry this wench for this device.

---

146 slough skin of a snake; hence, former demeanor of humbleness.
opposite contradictory   **147 tang** sound loud with   **148 state** politics,
statecraft.   **trick of singularity** eccentricity of manner   **151 cross-gartered**
wearing garters above and below the knee so as to cross behind it
155 alter services i.e., exchange place of mistress and servant   **157 cham-**
paign open country   **158 politic** dealing with state affairs   **159 baffle**
deride, degrade (a technical chivalric term used to describe the disgrace
of a perjured knight).   **gross** base   **160 point-devise** correct to the letter
161 jade trick   **166 these habits** this attire   **167 happy** fortunate.   **strange**
aloof.   **stout** haughty   **177 Sophy** Shah of Persia

SIR ANDREW   So could I too.

SIR TOBY   And ask no other dowry with her but such another jest.

Enter Maria.

SIR ANDREW   Nor I neither.

FABIAN   Here comes my noble gull-catcher.

SIR TOBY   Wilt thou set thy foot o' my neck?

SIR ANDREW   Or o' mine either?

SIR TOBY   Shall I play my freedom at tray-trip, and be-   186
come thy bondslave?

SIR ANDREW   I' faith, or I either?

SIR TOBY   Why, thou hast put him in such a dream that
when the image of it leaves him he must run mad.

MARIA   Nay, but say true, does it work upon him?

SIR TOBY   Like aqua vitae with a midwife.   192

MARIA   If you will then see the fruits of the sport, mark
his first approach before my lady. He will come to her
in yellow stockings, and 'tis a color she abhors, and
cross-gartered, a fashion she detests; and he will smile
upon her, which will now be so unsuitable to her disposition, being addicted to a melancholy as she is, that
it cannot but turn him into a notable contempt. If you   199
will see it, follow me.

SIR TOBY   To the gates of Tartar, thou most excellent   201
devil of wit!

SIR ANDREW   I'll make one too.   *Exeunt.*

❖

186 play gamble.   **tray-trip** a game of dice, success in which depended
on throwing a three *(tray)*   **192 aqua vitae** brandy or other distilled
liquors   **199 notable contempt** notorious object of contempt
201 Tartar Tartarus, the infernal regions

3.1 *Enter Viola, and Clown [Feste, playing his pipe and tabor].*

VIOLA Save thee, friend, and thy music. Dost thou live ¹
by thy tabor? ²

FESTE No, sir, I live by the church.

VIOLA Art thou a churchman?

FESTE No such matter, sir. I do live by the church; for
I do live at my house, and my house doth stand by the
church.

VIOLA So thou mayst say the king lies by a beggar, if ⁸
a beggar dwell near him; or, the church stands by thy ⁹
tabor, if thy tabor stand by the church. ¹⁰

FESTE You have said, sir. To see this age! A sentence ¹¹
is but a cheveril glove to a good wit. How quickly the ¹²
wrong side may be turned outward!

VIOLA Nay, that's certain. They that dally nicely with ¹⁴
words may quickly make them wanton. ¹⁵

FESTE I would therefore my sister had had no name,
sir.

VIOLA Why, man?

FESTE Why, sir, her name's a word, and to dally with
that word might make my sister wanton. But indeed, ²⁰
words are very rascals since bonds disgraced them. ²¹

VIOLA Thy reason, man?

FESTE Troth, sir, I can yield you none without words,
and words are grown so false I am loath to prove reason with them.

VIOLA I warrant thou art a merry fellow and car'st for
nothing.

FESTE Not so, sir, I do care for something; but in my
conscience, sir, I do not care for you. If that be to care
for nothing, sir, I would it would make you invisible. ³⁰

VIOLA Art not thou the Lady Olivia's fool?

3.1. Location: Olivia's garden.
1 Save God save   **1–2 live by** earn your living with. (But Feste uses the
phrase to mean "dwell near.")   **2 tabor** small drum   **8 lies by** dwells
near   **9–10 stands by . . . stand by** (1) is maintained by (2) is placed
near   **11 sentence** maxim, judgment, opinion   **12 cheveril** kidskin
14 dally nicely play subtly   **15 wanton** i.e., unmanageable   **20 wanton**
unchaste   **21 since . . . them** i.e., since sworn statements have been
needed to make them good   **30 invisible** i.e., nothing; absent

FESTE No indeed, sir, the Lady Olivia has no folly.
  She will keep no fool, sir, till she be married, and fools
  are as like husbands as pilchers are to herrings; the 34
  husband's the bigger. I am indeed not her fool, but
  her corrupter of words.

VIOLA I saw thee late at the Count Orsino's.   37

FESTE Foolery, sir, does walk about the orb like the 38
  sun; it shines everywhere. I would be sorry, sir, but 39
  the fool should be as oft with your master as with my
  mistress. I think I saw your wisdom there.   41

VIOLA Nay, an thou pass upon me, I'll no more with thee. 42
  Hold, there's expenses for thee.   [She gives a coin.]

FESTE Now Jove, in his next commodity of hair, send 44
  thee a beard!

VIOLA By my troth, I'll tell thee, I am almost sick for
  one—[Aside] though I would not have it grow on my
  chin.—Is thy lady within?

FESTE Would not a pair of these have bred, sir?

VIOLA Yes, being kept together and put to use.   50

FESTE I would play Lord Pandarus of Phrygia, sir, to 51
  bring a Cressida to this Troilus.

VIOLA I understand you, sir. 'Tis well begged.
                              [She gives another coin.]

FESTE The matter, I hope, is not great, sir, begging 54
  but a beggar; Cressida was a beggar. My lady is 55
  within, sir. I will conster to them whence you come. 56
  Who you are and what you would are out of my
  welkin—I might say "element," but the word is 58
  overworn.   Exit.

VIOLA
  This fellow is wise enough to play the fool,
  And to do that well craves a kind of wit.

34 **pilchers** pilchards, fish resembling herring   37 **late** recently   38 **orb**
earth   39 **but** unless   41 **your wisdom** i.e., you   42 **pass upon me** fence
(verbally) with me, joke at my expense   44 **commodity** supply   50 **put
to use** put out at interest   51 **Pandarus** the go-between in the love story
of Troilus and Cressida; uncle to Cressida   54–55 **begging . . . Cressida**
(A reference to Henryson's *Testament of Cresseid* in which Cressida
became a leper and a beggar. Feste desires another coin to be the mate
of the one he has, as Cressida, the beggar, was mate to Troilus.)
56 **conster** construe, explain   58 **welkin** sky. **element** (The word can be
synonymous with *welkin*, but the common phrase *out of my element*
means "beyond my scope.")

He must observe their mood on whom he jests,
The quality of persons, and the time,   63
And, like the haggard, check at every feather   64
That comes before his eye. This is a practice   65
As full of labor as a wise man's art;
For folly that he wisely shows is fit,   67
But wise men, folly-fall'n, quite taint their wit.   68

Enter Sir Toby and [Sir] Andrew.

SIR TOBY   Save you, gentleman.
VIOLA   And you, sir.
SIR ANDREW   *Dieu vous garde, monsieur.*   71
VIOLA   *Et vous aussi; votre serviteur.*   72
SIR ANDREW   I hope, sir, you are, and I am yours.
SIR TOBY   Will you encounter the house? My niece is   74
   desirous you should enter, if your trade be to her.   75
VIOLA   I am bound to your niece, sir; I mean she is the   76
   list of my voyage.   77
SIR TOBY   Taste your legs, sir, put them to motion.   78
VIOLA   My legs do better understand me, sir, than I un-   79
   derstand what you mean by bidding me taste my legs.
SIR TOBY   I mean, to go, sir, to enter.
VIOLA   I will answer you with gait and entrance.—But   82
   we are prevented.   83

Enter Olivia and Gentlewoman [Maria].

Most excellent accomplished lady, the heavens rain
odors on you!
SIR ANDREW   That youth's a rare courtier. "Rain odors,"
well.

---

63 quality character   **64 haggard** untrained adult hawk, hence unmanageable   **64–65 check . . . eye** strike at every bird it sees, i.e., dart
adroitly from subject to subject   **65 practice** exercise of skill   **67 folly
. . . fit** the folly he displays is a proper skill   **68 folly-fall'n** having fallen
into folly.   **taint** impair   **71 Dieu . . . monsieur** God keep you, sir
72 Et . . . serviteur and you, too; (I am) your servant. (Sir Andrew is
not quite up to a reply in French.)   **74 encounter** (High-sounding word
to express "enter.")   **75 trade** course, path. (Viola picks up the commercial meaning of the word in her reply.)   **76 I am bound** I am on a
journey. (Continues Sir Toby's metaphor in *trade*.)   **77 list** limit, destina-
tion   **78 Taste** try   **79 understand** stand under, support   **82 gait and
entrance** going and entering   **83 prevented** anticipated

VIOLA My matter hath no voice, lady, but to your own 88
    most pregnant and vouchsafed ear.   89
SIR ANDREW "Odors," "pregnant," and "vouchsafed."
    I'll get 'em all three all ready.   91
OLIVIA Let the garden door be shut, and leave me to
    my hearing. [*Exeunt Sir Toby, Sir Andrew, and Maria.*]
    Give me your hand, sir.
VIOLA
    My duty, madam, and most humble service.
OLIVIA What is your name?
VIOLA
    Cesario is your servant's name, fair princess.
OLIVIA
    My servant, sir? 'Twas never merry world
    Since lowly feigning was called compliment.   99
    You're servant to the Count Orsino, youth.
VIOLA
    And he is yours, and his must needs be yours;
    Your servant's servant is your servant, madam.
OLIVIA
    For him, I think not on him. For his thoughts, 103
    Would they were blanks, rather than filled with me! 104
VIOLA
    Madam, I come to whet your gentle thoughts
    On his behalf.
OLIVIA   O, by your leave, I pray you.
    I bade you never speak again of him.
    But, would you undertake another suit,
    I had rather hear you to solicit that
    Than music from the spheres.
VIOLA   Dear lady—   110
OLIVIA
    Give me leave, beseech you. I did send,
    After the last enchantment you did here,

---

88 hath no voice cannot be uttered **89 pregnant** receptive. **vouchsafed**
proffered, i.e., attentive **91 all ready** i.e., for future use **99 lowly
feigning** affected humility. **was called** began to be called **103 For** as
for **104 blanks** blank spaces or empty sheets of paper **110 music
from the spheres** (The heavenly bodies were thought to be fixed in
hollow concentric spheres that revolved one about the other, producing
a harmony too exquisite to be heard by human ears.)

A ring in chase of you; so did I abuse
Myself, my servant, and, I fear me, you.
Under your hard construction must I sit,   115
To force that on you in a shameful cunning   116
Which you knew none of yours. What might you think?
Have you not set mine honor at the stake   118
And baited it with all th' unmuzzled thoughts   119
That tyrannous heart can think? To one of your
  receiving   120
Enough is shown; a cypress, not a bosom,   121
Hides my heart. So, let me hear you speak.

VIOLA
I pity you.

OLIVIA   That's a degree to love.

VIOLA
No, not a grece; for 'tis a vulgar proof   124
That very oft we pity enemies.

OLIVIA
Why then methinks 'tis time to smile again.   126
O world, how apt the poor are to be proud!   127
If one should be a prey, how much the better
To fall before the lion than the wolf!   *Clock strikes.* 129
The clock upbraids me with the waste of time.
Be not afraid, good youth, I will not have you;
And yet, when wit and youth is come to harvest,
Your wife is like to reap a proper man.   133
There lies your way, due west.

VIOLA   Then westward ho!   134
Grace and good disposition attend your ladyship.
You'll nothing, madam, to my lord by me?

OLIVIA Stay.
I prithee, tell me what thou think'st of me.

115 hard construction harsh interpretation   **116 To force** for forcing
118 stake (The figure is from bearbaiting.)   **119 baited** harassed (as
dogs *bait* a bear)   **120 tyrannous** cruel.   **receiving** capacity, intelligence   **121 cypress** a thin, gauzelike, black material   **124 grece** step.
(Synonymous with *degree* in the preceding line.)   **vulgar proof** common
experience   **126 smile** i.e., cast off love's melancholy   **127 the poor** i.e.,
the unfortunate and rejected (like Olivia).   **proud** i.e., of their distress
129 To fall . . . wolf i.e., to fall before a noble adversary   **133 proper**
handsome, worthy   **134 westward ho** (The cry of Thames watermen to
attract westward-bound passengers from London to Westminster.)

VIOLA
That you do think you are not what you are.   139
OLIVIA
If I think so, I think the same of you.   140
VIOLA
Then think you right. I am not what I am.
OLIVIA
I would you were as I would have you be!
VIOLA
Would it be better, madam, than I am?
I wish it might, for now I am your fool.   144
OLIVIA
O, what a deal of scorn looks beautiful
In the contempt and anger of his lip!
A murderous guilt shows not itself more soon
Than love that would seem hid; love's night is noon.   148
Cesario, by the roses of the spring,
By maidhood, honor, truth, and everything,
I love thee so that, maugre all thy pride,   151
Nor wit nor reason can my passion hide.   152
Do not extort thy reasons from this clause,   153
For that I woo, thou therefore hast no cause;   154
But rather reason thus with reason fetter,   155
Love sought is good, but given unsought is better.
VIOLA
By innocence I swear, and by my youth,
I have one heart, one bosom, and one truth,
And that no woman has, nor never none
Shall mistress be of it save I alone.
And so adieu, good madam. Nevermore
Will I my master's tears to you deplore.   162

139 That . . . are i.e., that you think you are in love with a man, and you
are mistaken   **140 If . . . you** (Olivia may interpret Viola's cryptic
statement as suggesting that Olivia "does not know herself," i.e., is
distracted with passion; she may also hint at her suspicion that "Cesario" is higher born than he admits.)   **144 fool** butt   **148 love's . . . noon**
i.e., love, despite its attempt to be secret, reveals itself as plain as day
151 maugre in spite of   **152 Nor** neither   **153–154 Do . . . cause** i.e., do
not rationalize your indifference along these lines, that because I am the
wooer you have no cause to reciprocate   **155 But . . . fetter** but instead
take possession of your reasoning with the following reason   **162 deplore**
beweep

OLIVIA

  Yet come again; for thou perhaps mayst move
  That heart, which now abhors, to like his love.
                       Exeunt [*separately*].

❖

3.2   *Enter Sir Toby, Sir Andrew, and Fabian.*

SIR ANDREW   No, faith, I'll not stay a jot longer.

SIR TOBY   Thy reason, dear venom, give thy reason.   2

FABIAN   You must needs yield your reason, Sir Andrew.

SIR ANDREW   Marry, I saw your niece do more favors to
  the Count's servingman than ever she bestowed upon
  me. I saw 't i' the orchard.   6

SIR TOBY   Did she see thee the while, old boy? Tell me
  that.

SIR ANDREW   As plain as I see you now.

FABIAN   This was a great argument of love in her toward   10
  you.

SIR ANDREW   'Slight, will you make an ass o' me?   12

FABIAN   I will prove it legitimate, sir, upon the oaths of   13
  judgment and reason.

SIR TOBY   And they have been grand-jurymen since before Noah was a sailor.

FABIAN   She did show favor to the youth in your sight
  only to exasperate you, to awake your dormouse valor,   18
  to put fire in your heart and brimstone in your liver.
  You should then have accosted her, and with some
  excellent jests, fire-new from the mint, you should
  have banged the youth into dumbness. This was   22
  looked for at your hand, and this was balked. The dou-   23
  ble gilt of this opportunity you let time wash off, and   24
  you are now sailed into the north of my lady's opinion,   25

3.2. Location: Olivia's house.
2 venom i.e., person filled with venom   **6 orchard** garden   **10 argu-**
ment proof   **12 'Slight** by his (God's) light   **13 oaths** i.e., testimony
under oath   **18 dormouse** i.e., sleepy   **22 banged** struck   **23 balked**
missed, neglected   **23–24 double gilt** thick layer of gold, i.e., rare
worth   **25 north** i.e., out of the warmth and sunshine of her favor

where you will hang like an icicle on a Dutchman's 26
beard, unless you do redeem it by some laudable at- 27
tempt either of valor or policy. 28

SIR ANDREW An 't be any way, it must be with valor,
for policy I hate. I had as lief be a Brownist as a poli- 30
tician. 31

SIR TOBY Why, then, build me thy fortunes upon the 32
basis of valor. Challenge me the Count's youth to fight
with him; hurt him in eleven places. My niece shall
take note of it; and assure thyself, there is no love-bro- 35
ker in the world can more prevail in man's commen- 36
dation with woman than report of valor.

FABIAN There is no way but this, Sir Andrew.

SIR ANDREW Will either of you bear me a challenge to
him?

SIR TOBY Go, write it in a martial hand. Be curst and 41
brief; it is no matter how witty, so it be eloquent and
full of invention. Taunt him with the license of ink. If 43
thou "thou"-est him some thrice, it shall not be amiss; 44
and as many lies as will lie in thy sheet of paper, al- 45
though the sheet were big enough for the bed of Ware 46
in England, set 'em down. Go, about it. Let there be
gall enough in thy ink, though thou write with a 48
goose pen, no matter. About it. 49

SIR ANDREW Where shall I find you?

SIR TOBY We'll call thee at the cubiculo. Go. 51

Exit Sir Andrew.

FABIAN This is a dear manikin to you, Sir Toby. 52

SIR TOBY I have been dear to him, lad, some two thou- 53
sand strong, or so.

26–27 icicle . . . beard (Alludes to the arctic voyage of William Barentz
in 1596–1597.) **28 policy** stratagem **30 Brownist** (Early name of the
Congregationalists, from the name of the founder, Robert Browne.)
30–31 politician intriguer **32 build me** i.e., build **35–36 love-broker**
agent between lovers **41 curst** fierce **43 with . . . ink** i.e., with the
freedom that may be risked in writing but not in conversation
44 "thou"-est ("Thou" was used only between friends or to inferiors.)
45 lies charges of lying **46 bed of Ware** (A famous bedstead capable of
holding twelve persons, about eleven feet square, said to have been at
the Stag Inn in Ware, Hertfordshire.) **48 gall** (1) bitterness, rancor (2) a
growth found on certain oaks, used as an ingredient of ink **49 goose
pen** (1) goose quill (2) foolish style **51 call thee** call for you. **cubiculo**
little chamber **52 manikin** puppet **53 dear** expensive (playing on *dear*,
fond, in the previous speech)

FABIAN We shall have a rare letter from him; but you'll not deliver 't?

SIR TOBY Never trust me, then; and by all means stir on the youth to an answer. I think oxen and wainropes 58 cannot hale them together. For Andrew, if he were 59 opened and you find so much blood in his liver as will 60 clog the foot of a flea, I'll eat the rest of th' anatomy. 61

FABIAN And his opposite, the youth, bears in his vis- 62 age no great presage of cruelty.

Enter Maria.

SIR TOBY Look where the youngest wren of nine 64 comes.

MARIA If you desire the spleen, and will laugh your- 66 selves into stitches, follow me. Yond gull Malvolio is turned heathen, a very renegado; for there is no Chris- 68 tian that means to be saved by believing rightly can ever believe such impossible passages of grossness. 70 He's in yellow stockings.

SIR TOBY And cross-gartered?

MARIA Most villainously; like a pedant that keeps a 73 school i' the church. I have dogged him like his mur- derer. He does obey every point of the letter that I dropped to betray him. He does smile his face into more lines than is in the new map with the augmen- 77 tation of the Indies. You have not seen such a thing as 'tis. I can hardly forbear hurling things at him. I know my lady will strike him. If she do, he'll smile and take 't for a great favor.

SIR TOBY Come, bring us, bring us where he is.

Exeunt omnes.

❖

58 **wainropes** wagon ropes 59 **hale** haul 60 **liver** (Seat of the passions.) 61 **anatomy** cadaver 62 **opposite** adversary 64 **youngest** . . .
nine i.e., the last hatched and smallest of a nest of wrens 66 **the spleen**
a laughing fit. (The spleen was thought to be the seat of immoderate
laughter.) 68 **renegado** renegade, deserter of his religion 70 **passages
of grossness** improbable statements (i.e., in the letter) 73 **villainously**
i.e., abominably. **pedant** schoolmaster 77 **new map** (Probably a
reference to a map made by Emmeric Mollineux in 1599 for the pur-
chasers of Hakluyt's *Voyages*, showing more of the East Indies, including Japan, than had ever been mapped before.)

3.3   *Enter Sebastian and Antonio.*

SEBASTIAN
  I would not by my will have troubled you,
  But since you make your pleasure of your pains,
  I will no further chide you.

ANTONIO
  I could not stay behind you. My desire,
  More sharp than filèd steel, did spur me forth;
  And not all love to see you, though so much   6
  As might have drawn one to a longer voyage,
  But jealousy what might befall your travel,   8
  Being skilless in these parts, which to a stranger,   9
  Unguided and unfriended, often prove
  Rough and unhospitable. My willing love,
  The rather by these arguments of fear,   12
  Set forth in your pursuit.

SEBASTIAN   My kind Antonio,
  I can no other answer make but thanks,
  And thanks; and ever oft good turns   15
  Are shuffled off with such uncurrent pay.   16
  But were my worth, as is my conscience, firm,   17
  You should find better dealing. What's to do?   18
  Shall we go see the relics of this town?   19

ANTONIO
  Tomorrow, sir. Best first go see your lodging.

SEBASTIAN
  I am not weary, and 'tis long to night.
  I pray you, let us satisfy our eyes
  With the memorials and the things of fame
  That do renown this city.

ANTONIO   Would you'd pardon me.   24
  I do not without danger walk these streets.
  Once in a sea fight 'gainst the Count his galleys   26

3.3. Location: A street.
6 not all not only, not altogether   **8 jealousy** anxiety   **9 skilless in**
unacquainted with   **12 The rather** the more quickly   **15 And . . . turns**
(This probably corrupt line is usually made to read, "And thanks and
ever thanks; and oft good turns.")   **16 uncurrent** worthless (such as
mere thanks)   **17 worth** wealth.   **conscience** i.e., moral inclination to
assist   **18 dealing** treatment   **19 relics** antiquities   **24 renown** make
famous   **26 Count his** Count's, i.e., Duke's

I did some service, of such note indeed
That were I ta'en here it would scarce be answered.   28
SEBASTIAN
Belike you slew great number of his people?   29
ANTONIO
Th' offense is not of such a bloody nature,
Albeit the quality of the time and quarrel
Might well have given us bloody argument.   32
It might have since been answered in repaying   33
What we took from them, which for traffic's sake   34
Most of our city did. Only myself stood out,
For which, if I be lapsèd in this place,   36
I shall pay dear.
SEBASTIAN   Do not then walk too open.
ANTONIO
It doth not fit me. Hold, sir, here's my purse.
                          [*He gives his purse.*]
In the south suburbs, at the Elephant,   39
Is best to lodge. I will bespeak our diet,   40
Whiles you beguile the time and feed your knowledge
With viewing of the town. There shall you have me.
SEBASTIAN   Why I your purse?
ANTONIO
Haply your eye shall light upon some toy   44
You have desire to purchase; and your store   45
I think is not for idle markets, sir.   46
SEBASTIAN
I'll be your purse-bearer and leave you
For an hour.
ANTONIO   To th' Elephant.
SEBASTIAN   I do remember.
                          Exeunt [*separately*].

❖

28 it . . . answered i.e., I'd be hard put to offer a defense   29 Belike
probably, perhaps   32 bloody argument cause for bloodshed   33 answered compensated   34 traffic's trade's   36 lapsèd i.e., caught
39 Elephant (The name of an inn.)   40 bespeak our diet order our
food   44 toy trifle   45 store store of money   46 idle markets unneces-
sary purchases, luxuries

3.4 *Enter Olivia and Maria.*

OLIVIA [*Aside*]
I have sent after him; he says he'll come.   1
How shall I feast him? What bestow of him?   2
For youth is bought more oft than begged or borrowed.
I speak too loud.—
Where's Malvolio? He is sad and civil,   5
And suits well for a servant with my fortunes.
Where is Malvolio?

MARIA He's coming, madam, but in very strange manner. He is, sure, possessed, madam.   9

OLIVIA Why, what's the matter? Does he rave?

MARIA No, madam, he does nothing but smile. Your
ladyship were best to have some guard about you if
he come, for sure the man is tainted in 's wits.

OLIVIA
Go call him hither. [*Maria summons Malvolio.*] I am as
mad as he,
If sad and merry madness equal be.

Enter Malvolio.

How now, Malvolio?

MALVOLIO Sweet lady, ho, ho!

OLIVIA Smil'st thou? I sent for thee upon a sad occasion.

MALVOLIO Sad, lady? I could be sad. This does make
some obstruction in the blood, this cross-gartering,
but what of that? If it please the eye of one, it is with
me as the very true sonnet is, "Please one and please   23
all."   24

OLIVIA Why, how dost thou, man? What is the matter
with thee?

MALVOLIO Not black in my mind, though yellow in my   27
legs. It did come to his hands, and commands shall be   28
executed. I think we do know the sweet Roman hand.   29

3.4. Location: Olivia's garden.
1 he . . . come i.e., suppose he says he'll come   **2 of** on   **5 sad and civil**
sober and decorous   **9 possessed** i.e., possessed with an evil spirit
23 sonnet song, ballad   **23–24 Please . . . all** (The refrain of a ballad.)
27 black i.e., melancholic   **28 It** i.e., the letter   **29 Roman hand** fash-
ionable Italian style of handwriting

OLIVIA Wilt thou go to bed, Malvolio?

MALVOLIO To bed? Ay, sweetheart, and I'll come to 31
thee. 32

OLIVIA God comfort thee! Why dost thou smile so and
kiss thy hand so oft?

MARIA How do you, Malvolio?

MALVOLIO At your request? Yes, nightingales answer 36
daws. 37

MARIA Why appear you with this ridiculous boldness
before my lady?

MALVOLIO "Be not afraid of greatness." 'Twas well writ.

OLIVIA What mean'st thou by that, Malvolio?

MALVOLIO "Some are born great—"

OLIVIA Ha?

MALVOLIO "Some achieve greatness—"

OLIVIA What sayst thou?

MALVOLIO "And some have greatness thrust upon
them."

OLIVIA Heaven restore thee!

MALVOLIO "Remember who commended thy yellow
stockings—"

OLIVIA Thy yellow stockings?

MALVOLIO "And wished to see thee cross-gartered."

OLIVIA Cross-gartered?

MALVOLIO "Go to, thou art made, if thou desir'st to
be so—"

OLIVIA Am I made?

MALVOLIO "If not, let me see thee a servant still."

OLIVIA Why, this is very midsummer madness. 58

Enter Servant.

SERVANT Madam, the young gentleman of the Count
Orsino's is returned. I could hardly entreat him back.
He attends your ladyship's pleasure.

OLIVIA I'll come to him. [*Exit Servant.*] Good Maria, let
this fellow be looked to. Where's my cousin Toby? Let
some of my people have a special care of him. I would

31–32 Ay . . . thee (Malvolio quotes from a popular song of the day.)
36–37 nightingales answer daws i.e., (to Maria), do you suppose a fine
fellow like me would answer a lowly creature (a *daw,* a crow) like you
58 midsummer madness (A proverbial phrase; the midsummer moon
was supposed to cause madness.)

not have him miscarry for the half of my dowry.   65
          Exeunt [Olivia and Maria, different ways.]
MALVOLIO   O ho, do you come near me now? No worse   66
man than Sir Toby to look to me! This concurs directly
with the letter. She sends him on purpose that I may
appear stubborn to him, for she incites me to that in
the letter. "Cast thy humble slough," says she; "be opposite with a kinsman, surly with servants; let thy
tongue tang with arguments of state; put thyself into
the trick of singularity." And consequently sets down   73
the manner how: as, a sad face, a reverend carriage, a   74
slow tongue, in the habit of some sir of note, and so   75
forth. I have limed her, but it is Jove's doing, and Jove   76
make me thankful! And when she went away now,
"Let this fellow be looked to." "Fellow!" Not "Malvo-   78
lio," nor after my degree, but "fellow." Why, every-   79
thing adheres together, that no dram of a scruple, no   80
scruple of a scruple, no obstacle, no incredulous or un-   81
safe circumstance—What can be said? Nothing that   82
can be can come between me and the full prospect of
my hopes. Well, Jove, not I, is the doer of this, and he
is to be thanked.

          Enter [Sir] Toby, Fabian, and Maria.

SIR TOBY   Which way is he, in the name of sanctity? If
all the devils of hell be drawn in little, and Legion him-   87
self possessed him, yet I'll speak to him.
FABIAN   Here he is, here he is.—How is 't with you, sir?
How is 't with you, man?
MALVOLIO   Go off. I discard you. Let me enjoy my pri-   91
vate. Go off.   92
MARIA   Lo, how hollow the fiend speaks within him!

---

65 miscarry come to harm   **66 come near** understand   **73 consequently**
thereafter   **74 sad** serious   **75 habit . . . note** attire suited to a gentleman of distinction   **76 limed** caught like a bird with birdlime (a sticky
substance spread on branches)   **78 Fellow** (Malvolio takes the original
meaning, "companion.")   **79 after my degree** according to my position   **80 dram** (Literally, one-eighth of a fluid ounce.)   **scruple** (Literally, one-third of a dram.)   **81 incredulous** incredible   **81–82 unsafe**
uncertain, unreliable   **87 drawn in little** gathered into a small space,
i.e., in Malvolio's heart.   **Legion** (Cf. "My name is Legion, for we are
many," Mark 5:9.)   **91–92 private** privacy

Did not I tell you? Sir Toby, my lady prays you to have
a care of him.

MALVOLIO Aha, does she so?

SIR TOBY Go to, go to! Peace, peace, we must deal
gently with him. Let me alone.—How do you, Mal- 98
volio? How is 't with you? What, man, defy the devil!
Consider, he's an enemy to mankind.

MALVOLIO Do you know what you say?

MARIA La you, an you speak ill of the devil, how he 102
takes it at heart! Pray God he be not bewitched!

FABIAN Carry his water to the wisewoman. 104

MARIA Marry, and it shall be done tomorrow morning,
if I live. My lady would not lose him for more than
I'll say.

MALVOLIO How now, mistress?

MARIA O Lord!

SIR TOBY Prithee, hold thy peace; this is not the way.
Do you not see you move him? Let me alone with
him.

FABIAN No way but gentleness, gently, gently. The
fiend is rough, and will not be roughly used.

SIR TOBY Why, how now, my bawcock? How dost 115
thou, chuck? 116

MALVOLIO Sir!

SIR TOBY Ay, biddy, come with me. What, man, 'tis not 118
for gravity to play at cherry-pit with Satan. Hang him, 119
foul collier! 120

MARIA Get him to say his prayers, good Sir Toby, get
him to pray.

MALVOLIO My prayers, minx?

MARIA No, I warrant you, he will not hear of godliness.

MALVOLIO Go hang yourselves all! You are idle shallow things; I am not of your element. You shall know 126
more hereafter.   *Exit.* 127

SIR TOBY Is 't possible?

---

98 Let me alone leave him to me **102 La you** look you **104 water**
urine (for medical analysis) **115 bawcock** fine fellow. (From French
beau-coq.) **116 chuck** (A form of "chick," term of endearment.)
118 biddy chicken **119 for gravity** suitable for a man of your dignity.
cherry-pit a children's game consisting of throwing cherry stones into a
hole **120 collier** i.e., Satan. (Literally, a coal vendor.) **126–127 know
more** i.e., hear about this

FABIAN   If this were played upon a stage now, I could condemn it as an improbable fiction.

SIR TOBY   His very genius hath taken the infection of the 131 device, man.

MARIA   Nay, pursue him now, lest the device take air 133 and taint. 134

FABIAN   Why, we shall make him mad indeed.

MARIA   The house will be the quieter.

SIR TOBY   Come, we'll have him in a dark room and bound. My niece is already in the belief that he's mad. We may carry it thus, for our pleasure and his penance, till our very pastime, tired out of breath, prompt us to have mercy on him; at which time we will bring the device to the bar and crown thee for a finder of 142 madmen. But see, but see!

Enter Sir Andrew [with a letter].

FABIAN   More matter for a May morning. 144

SIR ANDREW   Here's the challenge. Read it. I warrant there's vinegar and pepper in 't.

FABIAN   Is 't so saucy? 147

SIR ANDREW   Ay, is 't, I warrant him. Do but read.

SIR TOBY   Give me. [*Reads.*] "Youth, whatsoever thou art, thou art but a scurvy fellow."

FABIAN   Good, and valiant.

SIR TOBY [*Reads*] "Wonder not, nor admire not in thy 152 mind, why I do call thee so, for I will show thee no reason for 't."

FABIAN   A good note, that keeps you from the blow of 155 the law.

SIR TOBY [*Reads*] "Thou com'st to the Lady Olivia, and in my sight she uses thee kindly. But thou liest in thy throat; that is not the matter I challenge thee for."

FABIAN   Very brief, and to exceeding good sense—less.

SIR TOBY [*Reads*] "I will waylay thee going home, where if it be thy chance to kill me—"

FABIAN   Good.

131 genius i.e., soul, spirit   **133–134 take . . . taint** become exposed to air (i.e., become known) and thus spoil   **142 bar** i.e., bar of judgment
144 matter . . . morning sport for Mayday   **147 saucy** (1) spicy
(2) insolent   **152 admire** marvel   **155 note** observation, remark

SIR TOBY [*Reads*] "Thou kill'st me like a rogue and a villain."

FABIAN Still you keep o' the windy side of the law. 166 Good.

SIR TOBY [*Reads*] "Fare thee well, and God have mercy upon one of our souls! He may have mercy upon mine, but my hope is better, and so look to thyself. Thy friend, as thou usest him, and thy sworn enemy,
Andrew Aguecheek."
If this letter move him not, his legs cannot. I'll give 't him.

MARIA You may have very fit occasion for 't. He is now in some commerce with my lady, and will by and by 176 depart.

SIR TOBY Go, Sir Andrew. Scout me for him at the cor- 178 ner of the orchard like a bum-baily. So soon as ever 179 thou seest him, draw, and as thou draw'st, swear hor- rible; for it comes to pass oft that a terrible oath, with a swaggering accent sharply twanged off, gives man- hood more approbation than ever proof itself would 183 have earned him. Away!

SIR ANDREW Nay, let me alone for swearing. *Exit.* 185

SIR TOBY Now will not I deliver his letter; for the behav- ior of the young gentleman gives him out to be of good capacity and breeding; his employment between his lord and my niece confirms no less. Therefore this letter, being so excellently ignorant, will breed no ter- ror in the youth. He will find it comes from a clodpoll. 191 But, sir, I will deliver his challenge by word of mouth, set upon Aguecheek a notable report of valor, and drive the gentleman, as I know his youth will aptly receive it, into a most hideous opinion of his rage, skill, fury, and impetuosity. This will so fright them both that they will kill one another by the look, like cockatrices. 198

---

166 windy windward, i.e., safe, where the law may get no scent of you
176 commerce conference **178 Scout me** keep watch **179 bum-baily** minor
sheriff's officer employed in making arrests **183 approbation** reputation
(for courage). **proof** performance **185 let . . . swearing** don't worry about
my ability in swearing **191 clodpoll** blockhead **198 cockatrices** basilisks,
fabulous serpents reputed to be able to kill by a mere look

Enter Olivia and Viola.

FABIAN   Here he comes with your niece. Give them way   199
till he take leave, and presently after him.   200
SIR TOBY   I will meditate the while upon some horrid   201
message for a challenge.
                    [*Exeunt Sir Toby, Fabian, and Maria.*]

OLIVIA
I have said too much unto a heart of stone
And laid mine honor too unchary on 't.   204
There's something in me that reproves my fault,
But such a headstrong potent fault it is
That it but mocks reproof.

VIOLA
With the same havior that your passion bears
Goes on my master's griefs.

OLIVIA [*Giving a locket*]
Here, wear this jewel for me. 'Tis my picture.   210
Refuse it not; it hath no tongue to vex you.
And I beseech you come again tomorrow.
What shall you ask of me that I'll deny,
That honor, saved, may upon asking give?   214

VIOLA
Nothing but this: your true love for my master.

OLIVIA
How with mine honor may I give him that
Which I have given to you?

VIOLA   I will acquit you.   217

OLIVIA
Well, come again tomorrow. Fare thee well.
A fiend like thee might bear my soul to hell.   [*Exit.*]   219

Enter [Sir] Toby and Fabian.

SIR TOBY   Gentleman, God save thee.
VIOLA   And you, sir.
SIR TOBY   That defense thou hast, betake thee to 't. Of
what nature the wrongs are thou hast done him, I

---

199 Give them way stay out of their way   **200 presently** immediately
201 horrid terrifying (literally, "bristling")   **204 laid** hazarded.   **unchary on 't** recklessly on it   **210 jewel** (Any piece of jewelry; here, seemingly, a locket.)   **214 That . . . give** i.e., that can be granted without compromising any honor   **217 acquit you** release you of your promise
219 like resembling

know not; but thy intercepter, full of despite, bloody 224
as the hunter, attends thee at the orchard end. Dis- 225
mount thy tuck, be yare in thy preparation, for thy 226
assailant is quick, skillful, and deadly.

VIOLA   You mistake sir. I am sure no man hath any
quarrel to me. My remembrance is very free and clear
from any image of offense done to any man.

SIR TOBY   You'll find it otherwise, I assure you. Therefore, if you hold your life at any price, betake you to
your guard; for your opposite hath in him what youth,
strength, skill, and wrath can furnish man withal.

VIOLA   I pray you, sir, what is he?

SIR TOBY   He is knight, dubbed with unhatched rapier 236
and on carpet consideration, but he is a devil in 237
private brawl. Souls and bodies hath he divorced
three, and his incensement at this moment is so implacable that satisfaction can be none but by pangs of
death and sepulcher. Hob, nob, is his word; give 't or 241
take 't.

VIOLA   I will return again into the house and desire
some conduct of the lady. I am no fighter. I have heard 244
of some kind of men that put quarrels purposely on
others, to taste their valor. Belike this is a man of that 246
quirk. 247

SIR TOBY   Sir, no. His indignation derives itself out of a
very competent injury; therefore, get you on and give 249
him his desire. Back you shall not to the house, unless
you undertake that with me which with as much 251
safety you might answer him. Therefore, on, or strip
your sword stark naked; for meddle you must, that's 253
certain, or forswear to wear iron about you. 254

VIOLA   This is as uncivil as strange. I beseech you, do
me this courteous office, as to know of the knight what

---

224 intercepter i.e., he who lies in wait.   **despite** defiance   **224–225 bloody
as the hunter** bloodthirsty as a hunting dog   **225–226 Dismount thy
tuck** draw your rapier   **226 yare** ready, nimble   **236 unhatched** un-
hacked, unused in battle   **237 carpet consideration** (A carpet knight was
one whose title was obtained not in battle but through connections at
court.)   **241 Hob, nob** have or have not, i.e., give it or take it.   **word**
motto   **244 conduct** escort   **246 taste** test   **247 quirk** peculiar humor
249 competent sufficient   **251 that** i.e., to give satisfaction in a duel
253 meddle engage (in conflict)   **254 forswear . . . iron** give up your
right to wear a sword

my offense to him is. It is something of my negligence,
nothing of my purpose.

SIR TOBY I will do so. Signor Fabian, stay you by this
gentleman till my return.   *Exit Toby.*

VIOLA Pray you, sir, do you know of this matter?

FABIAN I know the knight is incensed against you, even
to a mortal arbitrament, but nothing of the circum- 263
stance more.

VIOLA I beseech you, what manner of man is he?

FABIAN Nothing of that wonderful promise, to read 266
him by his form, as you are like to find him in the 267
proof of his valor. He is, indeed, sir, the most skillful,
bloody, and fatal opposite that you could possibly
have found in any part of Illyria. Will you walk towards him? I will make your peace with him if I can.

VIOLA I shall be much bound to you for 't. I am one that
had rather go with Sir Priest than Sir Knight. I care not 273
who knows so much of my mettle.   *Exeunt.*

        Enter [Sir] Toby and [Sir] Andrew.

SIR TOBY Why, man, he's a very devil; I have not seen
such a firago. I had a pass with him, rapier, scabbard, 276
and all, and he gives me the stuck in with such a mor- 277
tal motion that it is inevitable; and on the answer, he 278
pays you as surely as your feet hits the ground they
step on. They say he has been fencer to the Sophy.

SIR ANDREW Pox on 't, I'll not meddle with him.

SIR TOBY Ay, but he will not now be pacified. Fabian
can scarce hold him yonder.

SIR ANDREW Plague on 't, an I thought he had been valiant and so cunning in fence, I'd have seen him
damned ere I'd have challenged him. Let him let the
matter slip, and I'll give him my horse, gray Capilet. 287

SIR TOBY I'll make the motion. Stand here, make a good 288
show on 't. This shall end without the perdition of 289
souls. [*Aside, as he crosses to meet Fabian.*] Marry, I'll 290
ride your horse as well as I ride you.

---

263 mortal arbitrament trial to the death **266–267 read . . . form** judge
him by his appearance **273 Sir Priest** (*Sir* was a courtesy title for priests.)
276 firago virago. **pass** bout **277 stuck in** stoccado, a thrust in fencing **278 answer** return hit **287 Capilet** i.e., "little horse." (From "ca-
pel," a nag.) **288 motion** offer **289–290 perdition of souls** loss of lives

Enter Fabian and Viola.

[*To Fabian.*] I have his horse to take up the quarrel. I 292
have persuaded him the youth's a devil.

FABIAN   He is as horribly conceited of him, and pants 294
and looks pale as if a bear were at his heels.

SIR TOBY [*To Viola*]   There's no remedy, sir, he will fight
with you for 's oath's sake. Marry, he hath better be-
thought him of his quarrel, and he finds that now
scarce to be worth talking of. Therefore draw, for the
supportance of his vow; he protests he will not hurt 300
you.

VIOLA [*Aside*]   Pray God defend me! A little thing
would make me tell them how much I lack of a man.

FABIAN   Give ground, if you see him furious.

SIR TOBY [*Crossing to Sir Andrew*]   Come, Sir Andrew,
there's no remedy. The gentleman will, for his
honor's sake, have one bout with you. He cannot by
the *duello* avoid it. But he has promised me, as he is 308
a gentleman and a soldier, he will not hurt you. Come
on, to 't.

SIR ANDREW   Pray God he keep his oath!

VIOLA   I do assure you, 'tis against my will.

                         [*They draw.*]

     Enter Antonio.

ANTONIO
     Put up your sword. If this young gentleman
     Have done offense, I take the fault on me;
     If you offend him, I for him defy you.

SIR TOBY   You, sir? Why, what are you?

ANTONIO
     One, sir, that for his love dares yet do more
     Than you have heard him brag to you he will.

SIR TOBY
     Nay, if you be an undertaker, I am for you.   319

                         [*They draw.*]

     Enter Officers.

---

292 take up settle, make up   **294 He . . . him** i.e., Cesario has as
horrible a conception of Sir Andrew   **300 supportance** upholding
308 duello duelling code   **319 undertaker** one who takes upon himself a
task or business; here, a challenger.   **for you** i.e., ready for you

FABIAN O good Sir Toby, hold! Here come the officers.

SIR TOBY [*To Antonio*] I'll be with you anon.

VIOLA [*To Sir Andrew*] Pray, sir, put your sword up, if you please.

SIR ANDREW Marry, will I, sir; and for that I promised you, I'll be as good as my word. He will bear you eas- 325 ily, and reins well.

FIRST OFFICER This is the man; do thy office.

SECOND OFFICER
Antonio, I arrest thee at the suit
Of Count Orsino.

ANTONIO   You do mistake me, sir.

FIRST OFFICER
No, sir, no jot. I know your favor well,   330
Though now you have no sea-cap on your head.—
Take him away. He knows I know him well.

ANTONIO
I must obey. [*To Viola.*] This comes with seeking you.
But there's no remedy, I shall answer it.   334
What will you do, now my necessity
Makes me to ask you for my purse? It grieves me
Much more for what I cannot do for you
Than what befalls myself. You stand amazed,
But be of comfort.

SECOND OFFICER   Come, sir, away.

ANTONIO
I must entreat of you some of that money.

VIOLA What money, sir?
For the fair kindness you have showed me here,
And part being prompted by your present trouble,   343
Out of my lean and low ability
I'll lend you something. My having is not much;   345
I'll make division of my present with you.   346
Hold, there's half my coffer.   [*She offers money.*] 347

ANTONIO Will you deny me now?
Is 't possible that my deserts to you   349
Can lack persuasion? Do not tempt my misery,   350
Lest that it make me so unsound a man   351

325 He i.e., the horse **330 favor** face **334 answer it** suffer for it **343 part** partly **345 having** wealth **346 present** present store **347 coffer** purse. (Literally, strong box.) **349–350 deserts . . . persuasion** claims on you can fail to persuade you to help me **351 unsound** weak

As to upbraid you with those kindnesses
That I have done for you.
VIOLA   I know of none,
Nor know I you by voice or any feature.
I hate ingratitude more in a man
Than lying, vainness, babbling drunkenness,
Or any taint of vice whose strong corruption
Inhabits our frail blood.
ANTONIO   O heavens themselves!
SECOND OFFICER   Come, sir, I pray you, go.
ANTONIO
Let me speak a little. This youth that you see here
I snatched one half out of the jaws of death,
Relieved him with such sanctity of love,
And to his image, which methought did promise   364
Most venerable worth, did I devotion.   365
FIRST OFFICER
What's that to us? The time goes by. Away!
ANTONIO
But, O, how vile an idol proves this god!
Thou hast, Sebastian, done good feature shame.   368
In nature there's no blemish but the mind;
None can be called deformed but the unkind.   370
Virtue is beauty, but the beauteous evil   371
Are empty trunks o'erflourished by the devil.   372
FIRST OFFICER
The man grows mad. Away with him! Come, come, sir.
ANTONIO   Lead me on.   *Exit [with Officers].*
VIOLA [*To herself*]
Methinks his words do from such passion fly
That he believes himself; so do not I.   376
Prove true, imagination, O, prove true,
That I, dear brother, be now ta'en for you!
SIR TOBY   Come hither, knight; come hither, Fabian.

---

364 image what he appeared to be (playing on the idea of a religious
icon to be venerated)   **365 venerable worth** worthiness of being venerated   **368 Thou . . . shame** i.e., you have shamed physical beauty by
showing that it does not always reflect inner beauty   **370 unkind**
unnatural   **371 beauteous evil** those who are outwardly beautiful but
evil within   **372 trunks** (1) chests (2) bodies.   **o'erflourished** (1) covered with ornamental carvings (2) made outwardly beautiful   **376 so
. . . I** i.e., I do not believe myself (in the hope that has arisen in me)

We'll whisper o'er a couplet or two of most sage saws.   380
                    [They gather apart from Viola.]

VIOLA
He named Sebastian. I my brother know   381
Yet living in my glass; even such and so   382
In favor was my brother, and he went
Still in this fashion, color, ornament,
For him I imitate. O, if it prove,   385
Tempests are kind, and salt waves fresh in love!
                                 [Exit.]

SIR TOBY   A very dishonest, paltry boy, and more a cow-   387
ard than a hare. His dishonesty appears in leaving his   388
friend here in necessity and denying him; and for his   389
cowardship, ask Fabian.

FABIAN   A coward, a most devout coward, religious in it.

SIR ANDREW   'Slid, I'll after him again and beat him.   392

SIR TOBY   Do, cuff him soundly, but never draw thy
sword.

SIR ANDREW   An I do not—   *[Exit.]*

FABIAN   Come, let's see the event.   396

SIR TOBY   I dare lay any money 'twill be nothing yet.   397
                                 Exeunt.

❖

---

380 saws sayings   **381–382 I . . . glass** i.e., I know my brother is virtually alive every time I look in a mirror, because we looked so much
alike   **385 prove** prove true   **387 dishonest** dishonorable   **388 dishonesty** dishonor   **389 denying** refusing to acknowledge   **392 'Slid** i.e., by
his (God's) eyelid   **396 event** outcome   **397 yet** nevertheless, after all

4.1 *Enter Sebastian and Clown [Feste].*

FESTE Will you make me believe that I am not sent for
you?

SEBASTIAN Go to, go to, thou art a foolish fellow. Let
me be clear of thee.

FESTE Well held out, i' faith! No, I do not know you, 5
nor I am not sent to you by my lady to bid you come
speak with her, nor your name is not Master Cesario,
nor this is not my nose neither. Nothing that is so is so.

SEBASTIAN I prithee, vent thy folly somewhere else. 9
Thou know'st not me.

FESTE Vent my folly! He has heard that word of some
great man, and now applies it to a fool. Vent my folly!
I am afraid this great lubber, the world, will prove a 13
cockney. I prithee now, ungird thy strangeness and 14
tell me what I shall vent to my lady. Shall I vent to her
that thou art coming?

SEBASTIAN I prithee, foolish Greek, depart from me. 17
There's money for thee. [*He gives money.*] If you tarry
longer, I shall give worse payment.

FESTE By my troth, thou hast an open hand. These 20
wise men that give fools money get themselves a good
report—after fourteen years' purchase. 22

Enter [Sir] Andrew, [Sir] Toby, and Fabian.

SIR ANDREW Now, sir, have I met you again? There's
for you!   [*He strikes Sebastian.*]

SEBASTIAN Why, there's for thee, and there, and there!
          [*He beats Sir Andrew with the hilt of his dagger.*]
Are all the people mad?

SIR TOBY Hold, sir, or I'll throw your dagger o'er the
house.

FESTE This will I tell my lady straight. I would not be 29
in some of your coats for twopence.   [*Exit.*]

4.1. Location: Before Olivia's house.
5 held out kept up   **9 vent** give vent to   **13 lubber** lout   **14 cockney**
effeminate or foppish fellow.   **ungird thy strangeness** put off your
affectation of being a stranger   **17 Greek** i.e., buffoon. (From "merry
Greek.")   **20 open** generous   **22 after . . . purchase** i.e., at great cost.
(Land was ordinarily valued at the price of twelve years' rental; the Fool
adds two years to this figure.)   **29 straight** at once

SIR TOBY   Come on, sir, hold!   [*He grips Sebastian.*]

SIR ANDREW   Nay, let him alone. I'll go another way to
work with him; I'll have an action of battery against   33
him, if there be any law in Illyria. Though I struck him
first, yet it's no matter for that.

SEBASTIAN   Let go thy hand!

SIR TOBY   Come, sir, I will not let you go. Come, my
young soldier, put up your iron. You are well fleshed;   38
come on.

SEBASTIAN
I will be free from thee. [*He breaks free and draws his
    sword.*] What wouldst thou now?
If thou dar'st tempt me further, draw thy sword.

SIR TOBY   What, what? Nay, then I must have an ounce
or two of this malapert blood from you.   [*He draws.*]   43

        Enter Olivia.

OLIVIA
Hold, Toby! On thy life I charge thee, hold!

SIR TOBY   Madam—

OLIVIA
Will it be ever thus? Ungracious wretch,
Fit for the mountains and the barbarous caves,
Where manners ne'er were preached! Out of my sight!
Be not offended, dear Cesario.
Rudesby, begone!
        [*Exeunt Sir Toby, Sir Andrew, and Fabian.*]
                        I prithee, gentle friend,   50
Let thy fair wisdom, not thy passion, sway
In this uncivil and unjust extent   52
Against thy peace. Go with me to my house,
And hear thou there how many fruitless pranks
This ruffian hath botched up, that thou thereby   55
Mayst smile at this. Thou shalt not choose but go.
Do not deny. Beshrew his soul for me!   57
He started one poor heart of mine, in thee.   58

---

33 action of battery lawsuit for beating (me)   **38 fleshed** initiated into
battle   **43 malapert** saucy, impudent   **50 Rudesby** ruffian   **52 extent**
attack   **55 botched up** clumsily contrived   **57 Beshrew** curse   **58 He
. . . thee** i.e., he alarmed half of my heart, which lies in your bosom.
(The word *started* also suggests a play on *heart, hart*.)

SEBASTIAN [*Aside*]
  What relish is in this? How runs the stream?
  Or I am mad, or else this is a dream.   60
  Let fancy still my sense in Lethe steep;   61
  If it be thus to dream, still let me sleep!
OLIVIA
  Nay, come, I prithee. Would thou'dst be ruled by me!
SEBASTIAN
  Madam, I will.
OLIVIA   O, say so, and so be!   *Exeunt.*

                          ❦

4.2   *Enter Maria [with garments] and Clown
           [Feste].*

MARIA   Nay, I prithee, put on this gown and this beard;
  make him believe thou art Sir Topas the curate. Do it   2
  quickly. I'll call Sir Toby the whilst.   [*Exit.*]   3
FESTE   Well, I'll put it on, and I will dissemble myself   4
  in 't, and I would I were the first that ever dissembled
  in such a gown. [*He disguises himself in gown and
  beard.*] I am not tall enough to become the function   7
  well, nor lean enough to be thought a good student;   8
  but to be said an honest man and a good housekeeper   9
  goes as fairly as to say a careful man and a great
  scholar. The competitors enter.   11

       Enter [Sir] Toby [and Maria].

SIR TOBY   Jove bless thee, Master Parson.

60 Or either   **61 fancy** imagination.   **still** ever.   **Lethe** the river of
forgetfulness in the underworld; i.e., forgetfulness

4.2. Location: Olivia's house.
2 Sir (Honorific title for priests.)   **Topas** (A name perhaps derived from
Chaucer's comic knight in the "Rime of Sir Thopas" or from a similar
character in Lyly's *Endymion*. Topaz, a semiprecious stone, was believed to be a cure for lunacy.)   **3 the whilst** in the meantime   **4 dissemble** disguise (with a play on "feign")   **7 become** grace, adorn.
function profession   **8 student** scholar (in divinity)   **9 said** called,
known as.   **housekeeper** household manager, hospitable person
11 competitors associates, partners

FESTE   *Bonos dies,* Sir Toby. For, as the old hermit of 13
Prague, that never saw pen and ink, very wittily said 14
to a niece of King Gorboduc, "That that is, is"; so I, 15
being Master Parson, am Master Parson; for what is
"that" but "that," and "is" but "is"?

SIR TOBY   To him, Sir Topas.

FESTE   What, ho, I say! Peace in this prison!

[*He approaches the door
behind which Malvolio is confined.*]

SIR TOBY   The knave counterfeits well; a good knave.

MALVOLIO   (*Within*) Who calls there?

FESTE   Sir Topas the curate, who comes to visit Malvolio the lunatic.

MALVOLIO   Sir Topas, Sir Topas, good Sir Topas, go to
my lady—

FESTE   Out, hyperbolical fiend! How vexest thou this 26
man! Talkest thou nothing but of ladies?

SIR TOBY   Well said, Master Parson.

MALVOLIO   Sir Topas, never was man thus wronged.
Good Sir Topas, do not think I am mad. They have
laid me here in hideous darkness.

FESTE   Fie, thou dishonest Satan! I call thee by the
most modest terms, for I am one of those gentle ones
that will use the devil himself with courtesy. Sayst
thou that house is dark?   35

MALVOLIO   As hell, Sir Topas.

FESTE   Why, it hath bay windows transparent as bar- 37
ricadoes, and the clerestories toward the south north 38
are as lustrous as ebony; and yet complainest thou of
obstruction?

MALVOLIO   I am not mad, Sir Topas. I say to you this
house is dark.

FESTE   Madman, thou errest. I say there is no darkness but ignorance, in which thou art more puzzled
than the Egyptians in their fog.   45

---

13 Bonos dies good day   **13–14 hermit of Prague** (Probably another invented authority.)   **15 King Gorboduc** a legendary king of ancient Britain,
protagonist in the English tragedy *Gorboduc* (1562)   **26 hyperbolical**
vehement, boisterous.   **fiend** i.e., the devil supposedly possessing Malvolio   **35 house** i.e., room   **37–38 barricadoes** barricades   **38 clerestories**
windows in an upper wall   **45 Egyptians . . . fog** (Alluding to the darkness
brought upon Egypt by Moses; see Exodus 10:21–23.)

MALVOLIO I say this house is as dark as ignorance,
  though ignorance were as dark as hell; and I say there
  was never man thus abused. I am no more mad than
  you are. Make the trial of it in any constant question. 49

FESTE What is the opinion of Pythagoras concerning 50
  wildfowl? 51

MALVOLIO That the soul of our grandam might haply 52
  inhabit a bird.

FESTE What think'st thou of his opinion?

MALVOLIO I think nobly of the soul, and no way approve his opinion.

FESTE Fare thee well. Remain thou still in darkness.
  Thou shalt hold th' opinion of Pythagoras ere I will
  allow of thy wits, and fear to kill a woodcock lest thou 59
  dispossess the soul of thy grandam. Fare thee well.
                    [*He moves away from Malvolio's prison.*]

MALVOLIO Sir Topas, Sir Topas!

SIR TOBY My most exquisite Sir Topas!

FESTE Nay, I am for all waters. 63

MARIA Thou mightst have done this without thy beard
  and gown. He sees thee not.

SIR TOBY To him in thine own voice, and bring me
  word how thou find'st him. I would we were well rid
  of this knavery. If he may be conveniently delivered, I 68
  would he were, for I am now so far in offense with
  my niece that I cannot pursue with any safety this
  sport to the upshot.—Come by and by to my chamber. 71
                    Exit [*with Maria*].

FESTE [*Singing as he approaches Malvolio's prison*]
        "Hey, Robin, jolly Robin, 72
        Tell me how thy lady does." 73

MALVOLIO Fool!

FESTE "My lady is unkind, pardie." 75

MALVOLIO Fool!

---

49 constant question set problem **50–51 Pythagoras . . . wildfowl** (An
opening for the discussion of transmigration of souls, a doctrine held by
Pythagoras.) **52 haply** perhaps **59 allow of thy wits** i.e., certify your
sanity. **woodcock** (A proverbially stupid bird, easily caught.) **63 for all
waters** i.e., ready for anything **68 delivered** i.e., delivered from prison
71 upshot conclusion **72–73 Hey, Robin . . . does** (Another fragment of
an old song, a version of which is attributed to Sir Thomas Wyatt.)
75 pardie i.e., by God, certainly

FESTE "Alas, why is she so?"

MALVOLIO Fool, I say!

FESTE "She loves another—" Who calls, ha?

MALVOLIO Good Fool, as ever thou wilt deserve well at my hand, help me to a candle, and pen, ink, and paper. As I am a gentleman, I will live to be thankful to thee for 't.

FESTE Master Malvolio?

MALVOLIO Ay, good Fool.

FESTE Alas, sir, how fell you beside your five wits? 86

MALVOLIO Fool, there was never man so notoriously abused. I am as well in my wits, Fool, as thou art.

FESTE But as well? Then you are mad indeed, if you be no better in your wits than a fool.

MALVOLIO They have here propertied me, keep me in 91 darkness, send ministers to me—asses!—and do all they can to face me out of my wits. 93

FESTE Advise you what you say. The minister is here. 94 [He speaks as Sir Topas.] Malvolio, Malvolio, thy wits the heavens restore! Endeavor thyself to sleep, and leave thy vain bibble-babble.

MALVOLIO Sir Topas!

FESTE [In Sir Topas's voice] Maintain no words with him, good fellow. [In his own voice.] Who, I, sir? Not I, sir. God b' wi' you, good Sir Topas. [In Sir Topas's voice.] 101 Marry, amen. [In his own voice.] I will, sir, I will.

MALVOLIO Fool! Fool! Fool, I say!

FESTE Alas, sir, be patient. What say you, sir? I am shent for speaking to you. 105

MALVOLIO Good Fool, help me to some light and some paper. I tell thee I am as well in my wits as any man in Illyria.

FESTE Welladay that you were, sir! 109

MALVOLIO By this hand, I am. Good Fool, some ink,

---

86 beside out of. **five wits** (The intellectual faculties, usually listed as common wit, imagination, fantasy, judgment, and memory.) **91 propertied me** i.e., treated me as property and thrown me into the lumber-room **93 face . . . wits** brazenly represent me as having lost my wits **94 Advise you** take care **101 God b' wi' you** God be with you. (Feste uses two voices in this passage to carry on a dialogue between himself and "Sir Topas.") **105 shent** scolded, rebuked **109 Welladay** alas, would that

paper, and light; and convey what I will set down to
my lady. It shall advantage thee more than ever the
bearing of letter did.

FESTE I will help you to 't. But tell me true, are you
not mad indeed, or do you but counterfeit?

MALVOLIO Believe me, I am not. I tell thee true.

FESTE Nay, I'll ne'er believe a madman till I see his
brains. I will fetch you light and paper and ink.

MALVOLIO Fool, I'll requite it in the highest degree. I
prithee, begone.

FESTE [*Sings*]

    I am gone, sir,
    And anon, sir,
  I'll be with you again,
    In a trice,
    Like to the old Vice,   125
  Your need to sustain;

    Who, with dagger of lath,   127
    In his rage and his wrath,
  Cries "Aha!" to the devil;
    Like a mad lad,
    "Pare thy nails, dad?
  Adieu, goodman devil!"   *Exit.* 132

❖

4.3   *Enter Sebastian [with a pearl].*

SEBASTIAN
  This is the air; that is the glorious sun;
  This pearl she gave me, I do feel 't and see 't;
  And though 'tis wonder that enwraps me thus,
  Yet 'tis not madness. Where's Antonio, then?
  I could not find him at the Elephant;
  Yet there he was, and there I found this credit,   6
  That he did range the town to seek me out.

125 Vice comic tempter of the morality plays **127 dagger of lath** comic
weapon of the Vice **132 goodman** title for a person of substance but
not of gentle birth

4.3. Location: Olivia's garden.
6 was was previously. **credit** report

His counsel now might do me golden service;
For though my soul disputes well with my sense   9
That this may be some error, but no madness,
Yet doth this accident and flood of fortune
So far exceed all instance, all discourse,   12
That I am ready to distrust mine eyes
And wrangle with my reason that persuades me
To any other trust but that I am mad,   15
Or else the lady's mad. Yet if 'twere so,
She could not sway her house, command her followers,   17
Take and give back affairs and their dispatch,   18
With such a smooth, discreet, and stable bearing
As I perceive she does. There's something in 't
That is deceivable. But here the lady comes.   21

Enter Olivia and Priest.

OLIVIA
Blame not this haste of mine. If you mean well,
Now go with me and with this holy man
Into the chantry by. There, before him,   24
And underneath that consecrated roof,
Plight me the full assurance of your faith,
That my most jealous and too doubtful soul   27
May live at peace. He shall conceal it
Whiles you are willing it shall come to note,   29
What time we will our celebration keep   30
According to my birth. What do you say?   31

SEBASTIAN
I'll follow this good man, and go with you,
And having sworn truth, ever will be true.

OLIVIA
Then lead the way, good Father, and heavens so shine
That they may fairly note this act of mine!   *Exeunt.* 35

❖

9 my soul . . . sense i.e., both my rational faculties and my physical
senses come to the conclusion   12 instance precedent.   discourse
reasoning   15 trust belief   17 sway rule   18 Take . . . dispatch undertake matters of business and see to their execution   21 deceivable
deceptive   24 chantry by privately endowed chapel nearby   27 jealous
anxious, mistrustful.   doubtful full of doubts   29 Whiles until.   come
to note become known   30 What time at which time.   our celebration
i.e., the actual marriage; what they are about to perform is a binding
betrothal   31 birth social position   35 fairly note look upon with favor

5.1 *Enter Clown [Feste] and Fabian.*

FABIAN   Now, as thou lov'st me, let me see his letter.

FESTE   Good Master Fabian, grant me another request.

FABIAN   Anything.

FESTE   Do not desire to see this letter.

FABIAN   This is to give a dog and in recompense desire 5
my dog again. 6

Enter Duke [Orsino], Viola, Curio, and lords.

ORSINO   Belong you to the Lady Olivia, friends?

FESTE   Ay, sir, we are some of her trappings. 8

ORSINO   I know thee well. How dost thou, my good fellow?

FESTE   Truly, sir, the better for my foes and the worse 10
for my friends.

ORSINO   Just the contrary; the better for thy friends.

FESTE   No, sir, the worse.

ORSINO   How can that be?

FESTE   Marry, sir, they praise me, and make an ass of
me. Now my foes tell me plainly I am an ass; so that
by my foes, sir, I profit in the knowledge of myself,
and by my friends I am abused; so that, conclusions to 18
be as kisses, if your four negatives make your two af- 19
firmatives, why then the worse for my friends and the 20
better for my foes.

ORSINO   Why, this is excellent.

FESTE   By my troth, sir, no; though it please you to be
one of my friends. 24

ORSINO   Thou shalt not be the worse for me. There's gold.
                                            [He gives a coin.]

FESTE   But that it would be double-dealing, sir, I 26
would you could make it another.

5.1. Location: Before Olivia's house.
5–6 This . . . again (Apparently a reference to a well-known reply of Dr.
Bulleyn when Queen Elizabeth asked for his dog and promised a gift of
his choosing in return.) **8 trappings** ornaments, decorations **10 for**
because of **18 abused** flatteringly deceived **18–20 conclusions . . .**
affirmatives i.e., as when a young lady, asked for a kiss, says "no, no"
really meaning "yes, yes"; or, as the four lips of two contrary lovers
come together to make one passionate kiss **24 friends** i.e., those who,
according to Feste's syllogism, flatter him **26 But** except for the fact.
double-dealing (1) giving twice (2) deceit, duplicity

ORSINO   O, you give me ill counsel.

FESTE   Put your grace in your pocket, sir, for this once, 29
and let your flesh and blood obey it.

ORSINO   Well, I will be so much a sinner to be a double-
dealer. There's another.   [*He gives another coin.*]

FESTE   *Primo, secundo, tertio* is a good play, and the 33
old saying is, the third pays for all. The triplex, sir, is 34
a good tripping measure; or the bells of Saint Bennet, 35
sir, may put you in mind—one, two, three.

ORSINO   You can fool no more money out of me at this
throw. If you will let your lady know I am here to 38
speak with her, and bring her along with you, it may
awake my bounty further.

FESTE   Marry, sir, lullaby to your bounty till I come
again. I go, sir, but I would not have you to think that
my desire of having is the sin of covetousness; but as
you say, sir, let your bounty take a nap, I will awake
it anon.   *Exit.*

        Enter Antonio and Officers.

VIOLA
Here comes the man, sir, that did rescue me.

ORSINO
That face of his I do remember well,
Yet when I saw it last it was besmeared
As black as Vulcan in the smoke of war.   49
A baubling vessel was he captain of,   50
For shallow draft and bulk unprizable,   51
With which such scatheful grapple did he make   52
With the most noble bottom of our fleet   53
That very envy and the tongue of loss   54

29 Put . . . pocket (1) pocket up your virtue, your grace before God
(2) reach in your pocket or purse and show your customary grace or
munificence   **33 play** (Perhaps a children's game or game of dice.)
34 triplex triple time in music   **35 Saint Bennet** church of St. Bene-
dict   **38 throw** (1) time (2) throw of the dice   **49 Vulcan** Roman god of
fire and smith to the other gods; his face was blackened by the fire
50 baubling insignificant, trifling   **51 For** because of.   **draft** depth of
water a ship draws.   **unprizable** of value too slight to be estimated, not
worth taking as a "prize"   **52 scatheful** destructive   **53 bottom** ship
54 very envy i.e., even those who had most reason to hate him, his
enemies.   **loss** i.e., the losers

Cried fame and honor on him. What's the matter?

FIRST OFFICER
Orsino, this is that Antonio
That took the *Phoenix* and her freight from Candy, 57
And this is he that did the *Tiger* board
When your young nephew Titus lost his leg.
Here in the streets, desperate of shame and state, 60
In private brabble did we apprehend him. 61

VIOLA
He did me kindness, sir, drew on my side,
But in conclusion put strange speech upon me. 63
I know not what 'twas but distraction. 64

ORSINO
Notable pirate, thou saltwater thief,
What foolish boldness brought thee to their mercies
Whom thou in terms so bloody and so dear 67
Hast made thine enemies?

ANTONIO   Orsino, noble sir,
Be pleased that I shake off these names you give me. 69
Antonio never yet was thief or pirate,
Though I confess, on base and ground enough, 71
Orsino's enemy. A witchcraft drew me hither.
That most ingrateful boy there by your side
From the rude sea's enraged and foamy mouth
Did I redeem; a wrack past hope he was. 75
His life I gave him, and did thereto add
My love, without retention or restraint, 77
All his in dedication. For his sake
Did I expose myself—pure for his love— 79
Into the danger of this adverse town, 80
Drew to defend him when he was beset;
Where being apprehended, his false cunning,
Not meaning to partake with me in danger,
Taught him to face me out of his acquaintance 84

---

57 from Candy on her return from Candia, or Crete   **60 desperate . . .
state** recklessly disregarding disgrace and his status as a wanted man
61 brabble brawl   **63 put . . . me** spoke to me strangely   **64 but distraction** unless (it was) madness   **67 dear** costly, grievous   **69 Be pleased
that** allow me to   **71 base and ground** solid grounds   **75 wrack** goods
from a wrecked vessel   **77 retention** reservation   **79 pure** entirely,
purely   **80 Into** unto.   **adverse** hostile   **84 face . . . acquaintance**
brazenly deny he knew me

And grew a twenty years' removèd thing   85
While one would wink; denied me mine own purse,   86
Which I had recommended to his use   87
Not half an hour before.

VIOLA   How can this be?

ORSINO   When came he to this town?

ANTONIO
Today, my lord; and for three months before,
No interim, not a minute's vacancy,
Both day and night did we keep company.

Enter Olivia and attendants.

ORSINO
Here comes the Countess; now heaven walks on earth.
But for thee, fellow—fellow, thy words are madness.
Three months this youth hath tended upon me;
But more of that anon. Take him aside.

OLIVIA
What would my lord—but that he may not have—   98
Wherein Olivia may seem serviceable?
Cesario, you do not keep promise with me.

VIOLA   Madam?

ORSINO   Gracious Olivia—

OLIVIA
What do you say, Cesario? Good my lord—

VIOLA
My lord would speak; my duty hushes me.

OLIVIA
If it be aught to the old tune, my lord,
It is as fat and fulsome to mine ear   106
As howling after music.

ORSINO   Still so cruel?

OLIVIA   Still so constant, lord.

ORSINO
What, to perverseness? You uncivil lady,
To whose ingrate and unauspicious altars

85–86 grew . . . wink in the twinkling of an eye acted as though we had
been estranged for twenty years   **87 recommended** consigned   **98 but
that** except that which.   **he . . . have** i.e., my love   **106 fat and fulsome**
gross and offensive

My soul the faithfull'st offerings have breathed out
That e'er devotion tendered! What shall I do?

OLIVIA
Even what it please my lord that shall become him.

ORSINO
Why should I not, had I the heart to do it,
Like to th' Egyptian thief at point of death,   116
Kill what I love?—a savage jealousy
That sometimes savors nobly. But hear me this: 118
Since you to nonregardance cast my faith,   119
And that I partly know the instrument
That screws me from my true place in your favor,   121
Live you the marble-breasted tyrant still.
But this your minion, whom I know you love,   123
And whom, by heaven I swear, I tender dearly,   124
Him will I tear out of that cruel eye
Where he sits crownèd in his master's spite.—   126
Come, boy, with me. My thoughts are ripe in mischief.
I'll sacrifice the lamb that I do love,
To spite a raven's heart within a dove.   [*Going.*]

VIOLA
And I, most jocund, apt, and willingly,
To do you rest, a thousand deaths would die.   131

                                                [*Going.*]

OLIVIA
Where goes Cesario?

VIOLA   After him I love
More than I love these eyes, more than my life,
More by all mores than e'er I shall love wife.   134
If I do feign, you witnesses above
Punish my life for tainting of my love!

OLIVIA
Ay me, detested! How am I beguiled!

---

116 Egyptian thief (An allusion to the story of Theagenes and Chariclea
in the *Ethiopica*, a Greek romance by Heliodorus. The robber chief,
Thyamis of Memphis, having captured Chariclea and fallen in love with
her, is attacked by a larger band of robbers; threatened with death, he
attempts to slay her first.) **118 savors nobly** is not without nobility
119 nonregardance neglect **121 screws** pries, forces **123 minion**
darling, favorite **124 tender** regard **126 in . . . spite** in defiance of his
master **131 do you rest** give you ease **134 by all mores** by all such
comparisons

VIOLA
Who does beguile you? Who does do you wrong?

OLIVIA
Hast thou forgot thyself? Is it so long?
Call forth the holy father.   [*Exit an Attendant.*]

ORSINO [*To Viola*]   Come, away!

OLIVIA
Whither, my lord? Cesario, husband, stay.

ORSINO
Husband?

OLIVIA   Ay, husband. Can he that deny?

ORSINO
Her husband, sirrah?

VIOLA   No, my lord, not I.

OLIVIA
Alas, it is the baseness of thy fear
That makes thee strangle thy propriety.   145
Fear not, Cesario, take thy fortunes up;
Be that thou know'st thou art, and then thou art   147
As great as that thou fear'st.

    Enter Priest.

                       O, welcome, Father!   148
Father, I charge thee by thy reverence
Here to unfold, though lately we intended
To keep in darkness what occasion now
Reveals before 'tis ripe, what thou dost know
Hath newly passed between this youth and me.

PRIEST
A contract of eternal bond of love,
Confirmed by mutual joinder of your hands,   155
Attested by the holy close of lips,   156
Strengthened by interchangement of your rings,
And all the ceremony of this compact
Sealed in my function, by my testimony;   159
Since when, my watch hath told me, toward my grave
I have traveled but two hours.

ORSINO
O thou dissembling cub! What wilt thou be

---

145 strangle thy propriety deny what you are   **147 that** that which
148 that thou fear'st him you fear, i.e., Orsino   **155 joinder** joining
156 close meeting   **159 Sealed** ratified

When time hath sowed a grizzle on thy case?   163
Or will not else thy craft so quickly grow
That thine own trip shall be thine overthrow?   165
Farewell, and take her, but direct thy feet
Where thou and I henceforth may never meet.

VIOLA
My lord, I do protest—

OLIVIA   O, do not swear!
Hold little faith, though thou hast too much fear.   169

      Enter Sir Andrew.

SIR ANDREW   For the love of God, a surgeon! Send one
  presently to Sir Toby.

OLIVIA   What's the matter?

SIR ANDREW   He's broke my head across and has given   173
  Sir Toby a bloody coxcomb too. For the love of God, 174
  your help! I had rather than forty pound I were at
  home.

OLIVIA   Who has done this, Sir Andrew?

SIR ANDREW   The Count's gentleman, one Cesario. We
  took him for a coward, but he's the very devil incar- 179
  dinate.   180

ORSINO   My gentleman, Cesario?

SIR ANDREW   'Od's lifelings, here he is!—You broke my 182
  head for nothing, and that that I did, I was set on to
  do 't by Sir Toby.

VIOLA
Why do you speak to me? I never hurt you.
You drew your sword upon me without cause,
But I bespake you fair, and hurt you not.   187

SIR ANDREW   If a bloody coxcomb be a hurt, you have
  hurt me. I think you set nothing by a bloody cox- 189
  comb.

      Enter [Sir] Toby and Clown [Feste].

Here comes Sir Toby halting; you shall hear more. But 191

---

163 a grizzle gray hair. **case** sheath, skin   **165 trip** wrestling trick (i.e.,
you'll get overclever, and trip yourself up) **169 little** i.e., a little
173 broke broken the skin, cut   **174 coxcomb** fool's cap resembling the
crest of a cock; here, head   **179–180 incardinate** (for *incarnate*)
182 'Od's lifelings by God's little lives **187 fair** courteously **189 set
nothing by** regard as insignificant **191 halting** limping

if he had not been in drink, he would have tickled you
othergates than he did.   193

ORSINO How now, gentleman? How is 't with you?

SIR TOBY That's all one. He's hurt me, and there's th'
end on 't.—Sot, didst see Dick surgeon, sot?   196

FESTE O, he's drunk, Sir Toby, an hour agone; his
eyes were set at eight i' the morning.   198

SIR TOBY Then he's a rogue, and a passy measures   199
pavane. I hate a drunken rogue.   200

OLIVIA Away with him! Who hath made this havoc
with them?

SIR ANDREW I'll help you, Sir Toby, because we'll be   203
dressed together.   204

SIR TOBY Will you help? An ass-head and a coxcomb
and a knave, a thin-faced knave, a gull!

OLIVIA
Get him to bed, and let his hurt be looked to.
                    [*Exeunt Feste, Fabian, Sir Toby, and Sir
                                               Andrew.*]

        Enter Sebastian.

SEBASTIAN
I am sorry, madam, I have hurt your kinsman;
But, had it been the brother of my blood,
I must have done no less with wit and safety.—   210
You throw a strange regard upon me, and by that   211
I do perceive it hath offended you.
Pardon me, sweet one, even for the vows
We made each other but so late ago.

ORSINO
One face, one voice, one habit, and two persons,   215
A natural perspective, that is and is not!   216

SEBASTIAN
Antonio, O my dear Antonio!

193 othergates otherwise 196 Sot (1) fool (2) drunkard 198 set fixed
or extinguished, closed 199–200 passy measures pavane a slow-moving
eight-bar grave and stately dance (suggesting Sir Toby's impatience to
have his wounds dressed) 203–204 be dressed i.e., have our wounds
surgically dressed 210 with wit and safety with intelligent concern for
my own safety 211 strange regard look such as one directs at a stranger
215 habit dress 216 natural perspective an optical device or illusion
created by nature

How have the hours racked and tortured me
Since I have lost thee!

ANTONIO   Sebastian are you?

SEBASTIAN   Fear'st thou that, Antonio?   221

ANTONIO
How have you made division of yourself?
An apple cleft in two is not more twin
Than these two creatures. Which is Sebastian?

OLIVIA   Most wonderful!

SEBASTIAN [*Seeing Viola*]
Do I stand there? I never had a brother;
Nor can there be that deity in my nature
Of here and everywhere. I had a sister,   228
Whom the blind waves and surges have devoured.   229
Of charity, what kin are you to me?   230
What countryman? What name? What parentage?

VIOLA
Of Messaline; Sebastian was my father.
Such a Sebastian was my brother too;
So went he suited to his watery tomb.   234
If spirits can assume both form and suit,
You come to fright us.

SEBASTIAN   A spirit I am indeed,
But am in that dimension grossly clad   237
Which from the womb I did participate.   238
Were you a woman, as the rest goes even,   239
I should my tears let fall upon your cheek,
And say "Thrice welcome, drownèd Viola!"

VIOLA
My father had a mole upon his brow.

SEBASTIAN   And so had mine.

VIOLA
And died that day when Viola from her birth
Had numbered thirteen years.

SEBASTIAN
O, that record is lively in my soul!   246

---

221 Fear'st thou that do you doubt that   **228 here and everywhere**
omnipresence   **229 blind** heedless, indiscriminating   **230 Of charity**
(tell me) in kindness   **234 suited** dressed; clad in human form
237 in . . . clad clothed in that fleshly shape   **238 participate** possess
239 as . . . even since everything else agrees   **246 record** recollection

He finishèd indeed his mortal act
That day that made my sister thirteen years.

VIOLA
If nothing lets to make us happy both   249
But this my masculine usurped attire,
Do not embrace me till each circumstance
Of place, time, fortune, do cohere and jump   252
That I am Viola—which to confirm,
I'll bring you to a captain in this town,
Where lie my maiden weeds; by whose gentle help   255
I was preserved to serve this noble count.
All the occurrence of my fortune since
Hath been between this lady and this lord.

SEBASTIAN [*To Olivia*]
So comes it, lady, you have been mistook.
But nature to her bias drew in that.   260
You would have been contracted to a maid;
Nor are you therein, by my life, deceived.
You are betrothed both to a maid and man.   263

ORSINO
Be not amazed; right noble is his blood.
If this be so, as yet the glass seems true,   265
I shall have share in this most happy wrack.   266
[*To Viola.*] Boy, thou hast said to me a thousand times
Thou never shouldst love woman like to me.

VIOLA
And all those sayings will I over swear,   269
And all those swearings keep as true in soul
As doth that orbèd continent the fire   271
That severs day from night.

ORSINO   Give me thy hand,
And let me see thee in thy woman's weeds.

VIOLA
The captain that did bring me first on shore
Hath my maid's garments. He upon some action   275

---

249 lets hinders   **252 jump** coincide, fit exactly   **255 weeds** clothes
260 nature . . . that nature followed her bent in that   **263 a maid** i.e., a
virgin man   **265 glass** i.e., the *natural perspective* of l. 216   **266 wrack**
goods from a wrecked vessel   **269 over swear** swear again   **271 As . . .
fire** i.e., as the sphere of the sun keeps the fire   **275 action** legal charge

Is now in durance, at Malvolio's suit,   276
A gentleman and follower of my lady's.

OLIVIA

He shall enlarge him. Fetch Malvolio hither.   278
And yet, alas, now I remember me,
They say, poor gentleman, he's much distract.

Enter Clown [Feste] with a letter, and Fabian.

A most extracting frenzy of mine own   281
From my remembrance clearly banished his.
How does he, sirrah?

FESTE   Truly, madam, he holds Belzebub at the stave's 284
end as well as a man in his case may do. He's here 285
writ a letter to you; I should have given 't you today
morning. But as a madman's epistles are no gospels, 287
so it skills not much when they are delivered.   288

OLIVIA   Open 't, and read it.

FESTE   Look then to be well edified, when the fool de- 290
livers the madman. [*Reads loudly.*] "By the Lord, 291
madam—"

OLIVIA   How now, art thou mad?

FESTE   No, madam, I do but read madness. An your
ladyship will have it as it ought to be, you must allow
vox.   296

OLIVIA   Prithee, read i' thy right wits.

FESTE   So I do, madonna; but to read his right wits is
to read thus. Therefore perpend, my princess, and 299
give ear.

OLIVIA [*To Fabian*]   Read it you, sirrah.

FABIAN [*Reads*]   "By the Lord, madam, you wrong me,
and the world shall know it. Though you have put me
into darkness and given your drunken cousin rule
over me, yet have I the benefit of my senses as well as

---

276 durance captivity   **278 enlarge** release   **281 extracting** i.e., that
obsessed me and drew all thoughts except of Cesario from my mind
284–285 holds . . . end i.e., keeps the devil at a safe distance   **287 a
madman's . . . gospels** i.e., there is no truth in a madman's letters. (An
allusion to readings in the church service of selected passages from the
epistles and the gospels.)   **288 skills** matters   **290–291 delivers** speaks
the words of   **296 vox** voice, i.e., an appropriately loud voice   **299 perpend** consider, attend

your ladyship. I have your own letter that induced me
to the semblance I put on, with the which I doubt not   307
but to do myself much right or you much shame.
Think of me as you please. I leave my duty a little
unthought of and speak out of my injury.

                       The madly used Malvolio."

OLIVIA   Did he write this?

FESTE   Ay, madam.

ORSINO   This savors not much of distraction.

OLIVIA
See him delivered, Fabian; bring him hither.   315

                              [Exit Fabian.]

My lord, so please you, these things further thought on,   316
To think me as well a sister as a wife,   317
One day shall crown th' alliance on 't, so please you,   318
Here at my house and at my proper cost.   319

ORSINO
Madam, I am most apt t' embrace your offer.
[To Viola.] Your master quits you; and for your service
   done him,   321
So much against the mettle of your sex,   322
So far beneath your soft and tender breeding,
And since you called me master for so long,
Here is my hand. You shall from this time be
Your master's mistress.

OLIVIA   A sister! You are she.

    Enter [Fabian, with] Malvolio.

ORSINO
Is this the madman?

OLIVIA   Ay, my lord, this same.
How now, Malvolio?

MALVOLIO   Madam, you have done me wrong,
Notorious wrong.

OLIVIA   Have I, Malvolio? No.

---

307 the which i.e., the letter   **315 delivered** released   **316 so . . . on** if
you are pleased on further consideration   **317 To . . . wife** to regard
me as favorably as a sister-in-law as you had hoped to regard me as a
wife   **318 crown . . . on 't** i.e., serve as occasion for two marriages
confirming our new relationship   **319 proper** own   **321 quits** releases
322 mettle natural disposition

MALVOLIO
  Lady, you have. Pray you, peruse that letter.
                                    [*He gives letter.*]
  You must not now deny it is your hand.
  Write from it, if you can, in hand or phrase,   332
  Or say 'tis not your seal, not your invention.   333
  You can say none of this. Well, grant it then,
  And tell me, in the modesty of honor,   335
  Why you have given me such clear lights of favor,
  Bade me come smiling and cross-gartered to you,
  To put on yellow stockings, and to frown
  Upon Sir Toby and the lighter people?   339
  And, acting this in an obedient hope,
  Why have you suffered me to be imprisoned,
  Kept in a dark house, visited by the priest,
  And made the most notorious geck and gull   343
  That e'er invention played on? Tell me why?   344
OLIVIA
  Alas, Malvolio, this is not my writing,
  Though, I confess, much like the character;   346
  But out of question 'tis Maria's hand.   347
  And now I do bethink me, it was she
  First told me thou wast mad; then cam'st in smiling,   349
  And in such forms which here were presupposed   350
  Upon thee in the letter. Prithee, be content.
  This practice hath most shrewdly passed upon thee;   352
  But when we know the grounds and authors of it,
  Thou shalt be both the plaintiff and the judge
  Of thine own cause.
FABIAN   Good madam, hear me speak,
  And let no quarrel nor no brawl to come
  Taint the condition of this present hour,
  Which I have wondered at. In hope it shall not,
  Most freely I confess, myself and Toby
  Set this device against Malvolio here,

332 from it differently   **333 invention** composition   **335 modesty of
honor** sense of propriety belonging to honorable persons   **339 lighter**
lesser   **343 geck** dupe   **344 invention** contrivance   **346 character**
handwriting   **347 out of** beyond   **349 cam'st** you came   **350 presupposed** specified beforehand   **352 shrewdly** cruelly, grievously.   **passed
upon** imposed on

Upon some stubborn and uncourteous parts   361
We had conceived against him. Maria writ   362
The letter at Sir Toby's great importance,   363
In recompense whereof he hath married her.
How with a sportful malice it was followed   365
May rather pluck on laughter than revenge,   366
If that the injuries be justly weighed
That have on both sides passed.

OLIVIA
Alas, poor fool, how have they baffled thee!   369

FESTE Why, "some are born great, some achieve
greatness, and some have greatness thrown upon
them." I was one, sir, in this interlude, one Sir Topas,   372
sir, but that's all one. "By the Lord, Fool, I am not
mad." But do you remember? "Madam, why laugh
you at such a barren rascal? An you smile not, he's
gagged." And thus the whirligig of time brings in his   376
revenges.

MALVOLIO I'll be revenged on the whole pack of you!
                                                        [*Exit.*]

OLIVIA
He hath been most notoriously abused.

ORSINO
Pursue him, and entreat him to a peace.
He hath not told us of the captain yet.
When that is known, and golden time convents,   382
A solemn combination shall be made
Of our dear souls. Meantime, sweet sister,
We will not part from hence. Cesario, come—
For so you shall be, while you are a man;
But when in other habits you are seen,
Orsino's mistress and his fancy's queen.
                              Exeunt [*all, except Feste*].

FESTE (*Sings*)
          When that I was and a little tiny boy,
              With hey, ho, the wind and the rain,

361 Upon on account of.   **parts** qualities, deeds   **362 conceived against
him** seen and resented in him   **363 importance** importunity   **365 followed** carried out   **366 pluck on** induce   **369 baffled** disgraced,
quelled   **372 interlude** little play   **376 whirligig** spinning top   **382 convents** (1) summons, calls together (2) suits

A foolish thing was but a toy,
  For the rain it raineth every day.

But when I came to man's estate,
  With hey, ho, the wind and the rain,
'Gainst knaves and thieves men shut their gate,
  For the rain it raineth every day.

But when I came, alas, to wive,
  With hey, ho, the wind and the rain,
By swaggering could I never thrive,
  For the rain it raineth every day.

But when I came unto my beds,
  With hey, ho, the wind and the rain,
With tosspots still had drunken heads,   403
  For the rain it raineth every day.

A great while ago the world begun,
  With hey, ho, the wind and the rain,
But that's all one, our play is done,
  And we'll strive to please you every day.

                                            [*Exit.*]

403 tosspots drunkards

Date and Text

Twelfth Night was registered with the London Company of Stationers (booksellers and printers) in 1623 and first published in the First Folio that year in a good text set up from what may have been a scribal transcript of Shakespeare's foul papers, or draft manuscript. There was a brief delay in printing *Twelfth Night* in the First Folio, possibly because a transcript was being prepared. The play was first mentioned, however, on Candlemas Day, February 2, 1602, in the following entry from the *Diary* of a Middle Temple (one of the Inns of Court, where law was studied) law student or barrister named John Manningham:

> At our feast wee had a play called "Twelue Night, or What you Will," much like the Commedy of Errores, or Menechmi in Plautus, but most like and neere to that in Italian called *Inganni*. A good practise in it to make the Steward beleeve his Lady widdowe was in love with him, by counterfeyting a letter as from his Lady in generall termes, telling him what shee liked best in him, and prescribing his gesture in smiling, his apparaile, & c., and then when he came to practise making him beleeue they tooke him to be mad.

This entry was once suspected to be a forgery perpetrated by John Payne Collier, who published the *Diary* in 1831, but its authenticity is now generally accepted. The date accords with several possible allusions in the play itself. When Fabian jokes about "a pension of thousands to be paid from the Sophy" (2.5.176–177), he seems to be recalling Sir Anthony Shirley's reception by the Shah of Persia (the Sophy) in 1599–1600. An account of this visit was entered in the Stationers' Register in November of 1601. Viola's description of Feste as "wise enough to play the fool" (3.1.60) may recall a poem beginning "True it is, he plays the fool indeed" published in 1600–1601 by Robert Armin (who had played the role of Feste). Maria's comparison of Malvolio's smiling face to "the new map with the augmentation of the Indies" (3.2.77–78) refers to new maps of about 1600 in which America (the Indies) was increased in size. Leslie Hotson (*The First Night of Twelfth Night*, 1954) has argued for a first performance at court on Twelfth Night in January of 1601, when Queen Elizabeth entertained Don Virginio Orsino, Duke of Bracciano, but this hypothesis has not gained general acceptance partly because the role of Orsino in the play would scarcely flatter such a noble visitor and partly because there is no proof that any of Shakespeare's plays were originally commissioned for private performance. Nevertheless, a date between 1600 and early 1602 seems most likely. Francis Meres does not mention the play in 1598 in his *Palladis Tamia: Wit's Treasury* (a slender volume on contemporary literature and art; valuable because it lists most of Shakespeare's plays that existed at that time).

Textual Notes

These textual notes are not a historical collation, either of the early folios or of more recent editions; they are simply a record of departures in this edition from the copy text. The reading adopted in this edition appears in boldface, followed by the rejected reading from the copy text, i.e., the First Folio. Only a few major alterations in punctuation are noted. Changes in lineation are not indicated, nor are some minor and obvious typographical errors.

Abbreviations used:
F the First Folio
s.d. stage direction
s.p. speech prefix

Copy Text: the First Folio.

1.1. 1 s.p. [and throughout] Orsino Duke   **11 sea, naught** sea. Nought

1.2. 15 Arion Orion

1.3. 51 s.p. Sir Andrew Ma   **54 Mary Accost** Mary, accost   **96 curl by** coole my   **98 me** we   **132 dun** dam'd.   **set** sit   **136 That's** That

1.5. 5 s.p. [and throughout] Feste Clown   **163 s.d. Viola** Uiolenta   **296 County's** Countes   **306 s.d.** [F adds "Finis, Actus primus"]

2.2. 31 our O   **32 of** if

2.3. 25 leman Lemon

2.4. 51 s.p. Feste [not in F]   **53 Fly . . . fly** Fye . . . fie   **55 yew** Ew   **88 I** It

2.5. 112 staniel stallion   **118 portend?** portend,   **142 born** become.   **achieve** atcheeues   **173 dear** deero   **203 s.d.** [F adds "Finis Actus secundus"]

3.1. 8 king Kings   **68 wise men** wisemens   **91 all ready** already

3.2. 7 thee the the   **64 nine** mine

3.4. 15 s.d. [at l. 14 in F]   **25 s.p. Olivia** Mal   **65 s.d. Exeunt** Exit   **72 tang** langer   **175 You** Yon   **222 thee** the   **249 competent** computent   **312 s.d.** [at l. 311 in F]   **397 s.d. Exeunt** Exit

4.2. 6 in in in   **38 clerestories** cleere stores   **71 sport to** sport

4.3. 1 s.p. Sebastian [not in F]   **35 s.d.** [F adds "Finis Actus Quartus"]

5.1. 190 s.d. [at l. 187 in F]   **200 pavane** panyn   **205 help? An** helpe an   **389 tiny** tine   **406 With hey** hey

Shakespeare's Sources

John Manningham's description of a performance of
Twelfth Night on February 2, 1602, at the Middle Temple
(one of the Inns of Court, where young men studied law in
London), compares the play to Plautus' *The Menaechmi*
and to an Italian play called *Inganni*. The comment offers
a helpful hint on sources. *The Menaechmi* had been the
chief source for Shakespeare's earlier play *The Comedy of
Errors,* and that farce of mistaken identity clearly resembles *Twelfth Night* in the hilarious mixups resulting from
the confusion of two look-alike twins. Shakespeare clearly
profited from his earlier experimenting with this sort of
comedy. *Twelfth Night* is not necessarily directly indebted
to *The Menaechmi,* however, for Renaissance Italian comedy offered many imitations of Plautus from which Shakespeare could have taken his *Twelfth Night* plot. These
include *Gl'Inganni* (1562) by Nicolò Secchi, another
Gl'Inganni (1592) by Curzio Gonzaga, and most important
an anonymous *Gl'Ingannati* (published 1537). This last play
was translated into French by Charles Estienne as *Les
Abusés* (1543) and adapted into Spanish by Lope de Rueda
in *Los Engaños* (1567). A Latin version, *Laelia,* based on the
French, was performed at Cambridge in the 1590s but never
printed. Obviously, *Gl'Ingannati* was widely known, and
Manningham was probably referring to it in his diary. To
trace Shakespeare's own reading in this matter is difficult,
owing to the large number of versions available to him, but
we can note the suggestive points of comparison in each.

Both *Inganni* plays feature a brother and a sister mistaken for one another. In the later play (by Gonzaga), the
sister uses the disguise name of "Cesare." In Secchi's *Inganni* the disguised sister is in love with her master, who is
told that a woman the exact age of his supposed page is secretly in love with him. Another play by Secchi, *L'Interesse*
(1581), has a comic duel involving a disguised heroine. Of
the Italian plays considered here, however, *Gl'Ingannati* is
closest to Shakespeare's play. A short prefatory entertainment included with it in most editions features the name
Malevolti. In the play itself, the heroine, Lelia, disguises

herself as a page in the service of Flaminio, whom she secretly loves, and is sent on embassies to Flaminio's disdainful mistress Isabella. This lady falls in love with "Fabio,"
as Lelia calls herself. Lelia's father, Virginio, learning of
her disguise and resolving to marry her to old Gherardo
(Isabella's father), seeks out Lelia but instead mistakenly
arrests her long-lost twin brother, Fabrizio, who has just
arrived in Modena. Fabrizio is locked up as a mad person in
Isabella's room, whereupon Isabella takes the opportunity
to betroth herself to the person she mistakes for "Fabio." A
recognition scene clears up everything and leads to the
marriages of Fabrizio to Isabella and Flaminio to Lelia.
This story lacks the subplot of Malvolio, Sir Toby, et al. Nor
is there a shipwreck.

Matteo Bandello based one of the stories in his *Novelle*
(1554) on *Gl'Ingannati*, and this prose version was then
translated into French by François de Belleforest in his *His-
toires Tragiques* (1579 edition). Shakespeare may well have
read both, for he consulted these collections of stories in
writing *Much Ado about Nothing*. His most direct source,
however, seems to have been the story of "Apollonius and
Silla," by Barnabe Riche (an English soldier and fiction
writer), in *Riche His Farewell to Military Profession* (1581),
which was derived from Belleforest. A full modernized text
of Riche's story appears in the following pages. Riche involves his characters in more serious moral predicaments
than Shakespeare allows in his festive comedy. The plot situation is much the same: Silla (the equivalent of Shakespeare's Viola) is washed ashore near Constantinople,
where, disguised as "Silvio," she takes service with a duke,
Apollonius (Shakespeare's Orsino), and goes on embassies
to the wealthy widow Julina (Shakespeare's Olivia), who
proceeds at once to fall in love with "Silvio." When Silla's
twin brother, the real Silvio, arrives, he is mistaken by Julina for his twin and is invited to a rendezvous, like Shakespeare's Sebastian. The differences at this point are
marked, however, for Silvio becomes Julina's lover and
leaves her pregnant when he departs the next day on his
quest for Silla. Apollonius is understandably furious to
learn of "Silvio's" apparent success with Julina and throws
his page into prison. Julina is no less distressed when she
learns that the supposed father of her child is in actuality a

woman. Only Silla's revelation of her identity and Silvio's eventual return to marry Julina resolves these complications. Shakespeare eschews the pregnancy, the desertion, the imprisonment, and all of Riche's stern moralizings about the bestiality of lust that accompany this lurid tale. Moreover he adds the plot of Malvolio, for which Riche provides little suggestion. Shakespeare changes the location to Illyria, with its hint of delirium and illusion, and provides an English flavor in the comic scenes that intensifies the festive character of the play.

Shakespeare's reading may also have included the anonymous play *Sir Clyomon and Sir Clamydes* (c. 1570–1583), Sir Philip Sidney's *Arcadia* (1590), and Emmanuel Forde's prose romance *Parismus* (1598) in which one "Violetta" borrows the disguise of a page. Scholars have suggested that the Malvolio plot may reflect an incident at Queen Elizabeth's court in which the Comptroller of the Household, Sir William Knollys, interrupted a noisy late-night party dressed in only his nightshirt and a pair of spectacles, with a copy of the Italian pornographic writer Aretino's work in his hand. A similar confrontation between revelry and sobriety occurred in 1598: Ambrose Willoughby quieted a disturbance after the Queen had gone to bed, and was afterward thanked by her for doing his duty. Such incidents were no doubt common, however, and there is no compelling reason to suppose Shakespeare was sketching from current court gossip.

Riche His Farewell to Military Profession
Barnabe Riche

APOLLONIUS AND SILLA

Apollonius, Duke, having spent a year's service in the wars against the Turk, returning homeward with his company by sea, was driven by force of weather to the isle of Cyprus, where he was well received by Pontus, governor of the same isle; with whom Silla, daughter to Pontus, fell so strangely in love that after Apollonius was departed to Constantinople, Silla, with one man, followed. And coming to Constantinople she served Apollonius in the habit of a man; and after many pretty accidents falling out she was known to Apollonius, who, in requital of her love, married her.

There is no child that is born into this wretched world but, before it doth suck the mother's milk, it taketh first a sip* of the cup of error, which maketh us, when we come to riper years, not only to enter into actions of injury but many times to stray from that[1] is right and reason. But in[2] all other things wherein we show ourselves to be most drunken with this poisoned cup, it is in our actions of love. For the lover is so estranged from that[3] is right and wandereth so wide from the bounds of reason that he is not able to deem[4] white from black, good from bad, virtue from vice; but, only led[5] by the appetite of his own affections, and grounding them on the foolishness of his own fancies, will so settle his liking on such a one as either by desert or unworthiness will merit rather to be loathed than loved.

If a question might be asked, what is the ground indeed of reasonable love whereby the knot is knit of true and perfect friendship, I think those that be wise would answer: desert.[6] That is, where the party beloved doth requite us with the like. For otherwise, if the bare show of beauty or the comeliness of personage might be sufficient to confirm us in our love, those that be accustomed to go to fairs and

1 **that** that which   2 **But in** i.e., but more than in   3 **that** that which
4 **deem** distinguish   5 **only led** led only   6 **desert** deserving of recompense, offering something in return

markets might sometimes fall into love with twenty in a day. Desert must then be, of force,[7] the ground of reasonable love; for to love them that hate us, to follow them that fly from us, to fawn on them that frown on us, to curry favor with them that disdain us, to be glad to please them that care not how they offend us—who will not confess this to be an erroneous love, neither grounded upon wit nor reason? Wherefore, right courteous gentlewomen, if it please you with patience to peruse this history following, you shall see Dame Error so play her part with a leash[8] of lovers, a male and two females, as shall work a wonder to your wise judgment in noting the effect of their amorous devices and conclusions of their actions: the first neglecting the love of a noble dame, young, beautiful, and fair, who only for his good will[9] played the part of a servingman, contented to abide any manner of pain only to behold him. He again setting his love of[10] a dame that, despising him, being a noble duke, gave herself to a servingman, as she had thought. But it otherwise fell out, as the substance of this tale shall better describe. And because I have been something[11] tedious in my first discourse, offending your patient ears with the hearing of a circumstance[12] overlong, from henceforth that which I mind[13] to write shall be done with such celerity as the matter that I pretend to pen[14] may in any wise permit me. And thus followeth the history.

During the time that the famous city of Constantinople remained in the hands of the Christians, amongst many other noblemen that kept their abiding in that flourishing city there was one whose name was Apollonius, a worthy duke, who, being but a very young man and even then new come to his possessions, which were very great, levied a mighty band of men at his own proper charges,[15] with whom he served against the Turk during the space of one whole year; in which time, although it were very short, this young duke so behaved himself, as well by prowess and valiance showed with his own hands as otherwise by his wisdom and liberality used towards his soldiers, that all the

7 **of force** of necessity   8 **leash** set of three. (Said of hounds, hawks, etc.)
9 **for his good will** to obtain his affection   10 **setting his love of** fixing his love on   11 **something** somewhat   12 **a circumstance** an incident
13 **mind** intend   14 **pretend to pen** set forth, profess to write   15 **his own proper charges** his own expense

world was filled with the fame of this noble duke. When he had thus spent one year's service, he caused his trumpet to sound a retreat, and gathering his company together and embarking themselves, he set sail, holding his course towards Constantinople. But being upon the sea, by the extremity of a tempest which suddenly fell, his fleet was dissevered, some one way and some another; but he himself recovered[16] the isle of Cyprus, where he was worthily received by Pontus, duke and governor of the same isle, with whom he lodged while his ships were new repairing.

This Pontus, that was lord and governor of this famous isle, was an ancient[17] duke, and had two children, a son and a daughter. His son was named Silvio, of whom hereafter we shall have further occasion to speak; but at this instant he was in the parts of Africa, serving in the wars.

The daughter her[18] name was Silla, whose beauty was so peerless that she had the sovereignty amongst all other dames as well for her beauty as for the nobleness of her birth. This Silla, having heard of the worthiness of Apollonius, this young duke, who besides his beauty and good graces had a certain natural allurement, that, being now in his company in her father's court, she was so strangely attached with the love of Apollonius that there was nothing might content her but his presence and sweet sight. And although she saw no manner of hope to attain to that she most desired—knowing Apollonius to be but a guest and ready to take the benefit of the next wind and to depart into a strange country, whereby she was bereaved of all possibility ever to see him again, and therefore strived with herself to leave her fondness,[19] but all in vain—it would not be, but like the fowl which is once limed,[20] the more she striveth the faster she tieth herself. So Silla was now constrained, perforce[21] her will, to yield to love. Wherefore from time to time she used so great familiarity with him as her honor might well permit, and fed him with such amorous baits as the modesty of a maid could reasonably afford; which when she perceived did take but small effect, feeling herself so much outraged[22] with the extremity of her passion, by the

16 **recovered** reached   17 **ancient** of ancient family   18 **daughter her** daughter's   19 **fondness** doting   20 **limed** caught with sticky lime placed on a branch   21 **perforce** contrary to   22 **so much outraged** driven to such an intemperate passion

only countenance that she bestowed upon Apollonius it might have been well perceived that the very eyes pleaded unto him for pity and remorse. But Apollonius, coming but lately from out the field from the chasing of his enemies, and his fury not yet thoroughly dissolved nor purged from his stomach, gave no regard to those amorous enticements which, by reason of his youth, he had not been acquainted withal.[23] But his mind ran more to hear his pilots bring news of a merry[24] wind to serve his turn to Constantinople, which in the end came very prosperously; and giving Duke Pontus hearty thanks for his great entertainment, taking his leave of himself and the lady Silla, his daughter, departed with his company, and with a happy[25] gale arrived at his desired port.

Gentlewomen, according to my promise, I will here, for brevity's sake, omit to make repetition of the long and dolorous discourse recorded by Silla for this sudden departure of her Apollonius, knowing you to be as tenderly hearted as Silla herself, whereby you may the better conjecture the fury of her fever. But Silla, the further that she saw herself bereaved of all hope ever any more to see her beloved Apollonius, so much the more contagious were her passions, and made the greater speed to execute that[26] she had premeditated in her mind, which was this. Amongst many servants that did attend upon her, there was one whose name was Pedro, who had a long time waited upon her in her chamber, whereby she was well assured of his fidelity and trust; to that Pedro therefore she bewrayed[27] first the fervency of her love borne to Apollonius, conjuring him in the name of the Goddess of Love herself and binding him by the duty that a servant ought to have that tendereth[28] his mistress's safety and good liking, and desiring him, with tears trickling down her cheeks, that he would give his consent to aid and assist her in that[29] she had determined, which was for that[30] she was fully resolved to go to Constantinople, where she might again take the view of her beloved Apollonius; that he,[31] according to the trust she had reposed in him, would not refuse to give his consent secretly to con-

23 **withal** with   24 **merry** pleasant, favorable   25 **happy** prosperous
26 **that** what   27 **bewrayed** revealed   28 **tendereth** has a tender regard for, holds dearly   29 **that** what   30 **for that** that   31 **he** i.e., Pedro

vey her from out her father's court according as she should
give him direction; and also to make himself partaker of her
journey and to wait upon her till she had seen the end of her
determination.

Pedro, perceiving with what vehemency his lady and mistress had made request unto him, albeit he saw many perils
and doubts depending in her pretense,[32] notwithstanding
gave his consent to be at her disposition, promising her to
further her with his best advice and to be ready to obey
whatsoever she would please to command him. The match
being thus agreed upon and all things prepared in a readiness for their departure, it happened there was a galley of
Constantinople ready to depart, which Pedro, understanding, came to the captain, desiring him to have passage for
himself and for a poor maid that was his sister which were
bound to Constantinople upon certain urgent affairs. To
which request the captain granted, willing him to prepare[33]
aboard with all speed because the wind served him presently[34] to depart.

Pedro now coming to his mistress and telling her how he
had handled the matter with the captain, she, liking very
well of the device, disguising herself into very simple attire,
stole away from out her father's court and came with
Pedro—whom now she calleth brother—aboard the galley,
where, all things being in readiness and the wind serving
very well, they launched forth with their oars and set sail.
When they were at the sea, the captain of the galley, taking
the view of Silla, perceiving her singular beauty, he was
better pleased in beholding of her face than in taking the
height either of the sun or stars;* and thinking her by the
homeliness of her apparel to be but some simple maiden,
calling her into his cabin, he began to break[35] with her, after
the sea fashion, desiring her to use his own cabin for her
better ease, and during the time that she remained at the
sea she should not want a bed; and then, whispering softly
in her ear, he said that for want of a bedfellow he himself
would supply that room. Silla, not being acquainted with
any such talk, blushed for shame but made him no answer
at all. My captain, feeling such a bickering within himself

32 depending in her pretense arising from her profession of purpose
33 prepare i.e., get ready, come   **34 presently** immediately   **35 break**
converse, declare his intention

the like whereof he had never endured upon the sea, was like[36] to be taken prisoner aboard his own ship and forced to yield himself a captive without any cannon shot; wherefore, to salve all sores and thinking it the readiest way to speed,[37] he began to break with Silla in the way of marriage, telling her how happy a voyage she had made to fall into the liking of such a one as himself was, who was able to keep and maintain her like a gentlewoman, and for her sake would likewise take her brother into his fellowship, whom he would by some means prefer[38] in such sort that both of them should have good cause to think themselves thrice happy—she to light of[39] such a husband, and he to light of such a brother. But Silla, nothing pleased with these preferments, desired him to cease his talk for that she did think herself indeed to be too unworthy such a one as he was; neither was she minded yet to marry, and therefore desired him to fix his fancy upon some that were better worthy than herself was and that could better like of his courtesy than she could do. The captain, seeing himself thus refused, being in a great chafe he said as followeth:

"Then, seeing you make so little account of my courtesy, proffered to one that is so far unworthy of it, from henceforth I will use the office of my authority. You shall know that I am the captain of this ship and have power to command and dispose of things at my pleasure; and seeing you have so scornfully rejected me to be your loyal husband, I will now take you by force and use you at my will, and so long as it shall please me will keep you for mine own store. There shall be no man able to defend you nor yet to persuade me from that[40] I have determined."

Silla, with these words being struck into a great fear, did think it now too late to rue her rash attempt, determined[41] rather to die with her own hands than to suffer herself to be abused in such sort. Therefore she most humbly desired the captain so much as he could to save her credit,[42] and saying that she must needs be at his will and disposition, that for that present he would depart and suffer[43] her till night, when in the dark he might take his pleasure without any

---

36 was like was about   **37 speed** succeed   **38 prefer** give advancement to   **39 light of** happen upon   **40 that** what   **41 determined** i.e., and determined   **42 credit** reputation   **43 suffer** excuse, indulge

manner of suspicion to the residue of his company. The captain, thinking now the goal to be more than half won, was contented so far to satisfy her request and departed out, leaving her alone in his cabin.

Silla, being alone by herself, drew out her knife, ready to strike herself to the heart, and, falling upon her knees, desired God to receive her soul as an acceptable sacrifice for her follies which she had so willfully committed, craving pardon for her sins and so forth, continuing a long and pitiful reconciliation to God, in the midst whereof there suddenly fell a wonderful storm, the terror whereof was such that there was no man but did think the seas would presently have swallowed them. The billows so suddenly arose with the rage of the wind that they were all glad to fall to[44] heaving out of water, for otherwise their feeble galley had never been able to have brooked[45] the seas. This storm continued all that day and the next night; and they, being driven to put room[46]* before the wind to keep the galley ahead the billow, were driven upon the main shore, where the galley brake all to pieces. There was every man providing to save his own life. Some gat upon hatches, boards, and casks, and were driven with the waves to and fro; but the greatest number were drowned, amongst the which Pedro was one. But Silla herself being in the cabin, as you have heard, took hold of a chest that was the captain's, the which, by the only providence of God, brought her safe to the shore. The which when she had recovered,[47] not knowing what was become of Pedro her man, she deemed that both he and all the rest had been drowned, for that she saw nobody upon the shore but herself. Wherefore, when she had awhile made great lamentations, complaining her mishaps, she began in the end to comfort herself with the hope that she had to see her Apollonius, and found such means that she brake open the chest that brought her to land, wherein she found good store of coin and sundry suits of apparel that were the captain's. And now, to prevent a number of injuries that might be proffered to a woman that was left in her case, she determined to leave her own apparel and to sort herself into some of those suits, that, being taken for a man, she might pass

44 fall to turn to   **45 brooked** endured   **46 room** sea room (? The original text reads "romer.")   **47 recovered** reached

through the country in the better safety. And as she changed her apparel she thought it likewise convenient to change her name, wherefore, not readily happening of any other, she called herself Silvio, by the name of her own brother, whom you have heard spoken of before.

In this manner she traveled to Constantinople, where she inquired out the palace of the Duke Apollonius; and thinking herself now to be both fit and able to play the servingman, she presented herself to the Duke, craving his service. The Duke, very willing to give succor unto strangers, perceiving him to be a proper smug[48] young man, gave him entertainment. Silla thought herself now more than satisfied for all the casualties that had happened unto her in her journey that she might at her pleasure take but the view of the Duke Apollonius, and above the rest of his servants was very diligent and attendant upon him, the which the Duke perceiving began likewise to grow into good liking with the diligence of his man, and therefore made him one of his chamber. Who but Silvio then was most near about him in helping of him to make him ready in a morning, in the setting of his ruffs, in the keeping of his chamber? Silvio pleased his master so well that above all the rest of his servants about him he had the greatest credit, and the Duke put him most in trust.

At this very instant there was remaining in the city a noble dame, a widow whose husband was but lately deceased, one of the noblest men that were in the parts of Grecia, who left his lady and wife large possessions and great livings. This lady's name was called Julina, who, besides the abundance of her wealth and the greatness of her revenues, had likewise the sovereignty of all the dames of Constantinople for her beauty. To this Lady Julina, Apollonius became an earnest suitor; and, according to the manner of wooers, besides fair words, sorrowful sighs, and piteous countenances, there must be sending of loving letters, chains, bracelets, brooches, rings, tablets, gems, jewels, and presents—I know not what. So my Duke, who in the time that he remained in the isle of Cyprus had no skill at all in the art of love although it were more than half proffered unto him, was now become a scholar in love's school and had already

48 **smug** spruce, trim

learned his first lesson: that is, to speak pitifully, to look ruthfully, to promise largely, to serve diligently, and to please carefully. Now he was learning his second lesson: that is, to reward liberally, to give bountifully, to present willingly, and to write lovingly. Thus Apollonius was so busied in his new study that I warrant you there was no man that could challenge him for playing the truant, he followed his profession with so good a will. And who must be the messenger to carry the tokens and love letters to the Lady Julina but Silvio, his man. In him the Duke reposed his only confidence to go between him and his lady.

Now, gentlewomen, do you think there could have been a greater torment devised wherewith to afflict the heart of Silla than herself to be made the instrument to work her own mishap, and to play the attorney in a cause that made so much against herself? But Silla, altogether desirous to please her master, cared nothing at all to offend herself, followed[49] his business with so good a will as if it had been in her own preferment.

Julina, now having many times taken the gaze of this young youth, Silvio, perceiving him to be of such excellent perfect grace, was so entangled with the often sight of this sweet temptation that she fell into as great a liking with the man as the master was with herself. And on a time Silvio being sent from his master with a message to the Lady Julina, as he began very earnestly to solicit in his master's behalf, Julina, interrupting him in his tale, said, "Silvio, it is enough that you have said for your master. From henceforth either speak for yourself or say nothing at all." Silla, abashed to hear these words, began in her mind to accuse the blindness of love, that Julina, neglecting the good will of so noble a duke, would prefer her love unto such a one as nature itself had denied to recompense her liking.

And now, for a time leaving matters depending[50] as you have heard, it fell out that the right Silvio indeed—whom you have heard spoken of before, the brother of Silla—was come to his father's court into the isle of Cyprus; where, understanding that his sister was departed in manner as you have heard, conjectured that the very occasion did pro-

---

49 followed i.e., and followed   **50 depending** pending, awaiting outcome

ceed of some liking had between Pedro her man that was missing with her and herself. But Silvio, who loved his sister as dearly as his own life, and the rather for that—as she was his natural sister, both by father and mother—so the one of them was so like the other in countenance and favor that there was no man able to discern the one from the other by their faces saving by their apparel, the one being a man, the other a woman.

Silvio therefore vowed to his father not only to seek out his sister Silla but also to revenge the villainy which he conceived in Pedro for the carrying away of his sister. And thus departing, having traveled through many cities and towns without hearing any manner of news of those he went to seek for, at the last he arrived at Constantinople, where, as he was walking in an evening for his own recreation on a pleasant green yard without[51] the walls of the city, he fortuned to meet with the Lady Julina, who likewise had been abroad to take the air. And as she suddenly cast her eyes upon Silvio, thinking him to be her old acquaintance—by reason they were so like one another, as you have heard before—said[52] unto him, "Sir Silvio, if your haste be not the greater, I pray you, let me have a little talk with you, seeing I have so luckily met you in this place."

Silvio, wondering to hear himself so rightly named, being but a stranger not of above two days' continuance in the city, very courteously came towards her, desirous to hear what she would say.

Julina, commanding her train something[53] to stand back, said as followeth: "Seeing my good will and friendly love hath been the only cause to make me so prodigal to offer that[54] I see is so lightly rejected, it maketh me to think that men be of this condition rather to desire those things which they cannot come by than to esteem or value of that which both largely and liberally is offered unto them. But if the liberality of my proffer hath made to seem less the value of the thing that I meant to present, it is but in your own conceit,[55] considering how many noble men there hath been here before, and be yet at this present, which hath both served, sued, and most humbly entreated to attain to that

51 without outside of   **52 said** i.e., she said   **53 something** somewhat
54 that what   **55 conceit** conception

which to you of myself I have freely offered and, I perceive, is despised or at the least very lightly regarded."

Silvio, wondering at these words but more amazed that she could so rightly call him by his name, could not tell what to make of her speeches, assuring himself that she was deceived and did mistake him, did[56] think notwithstanding it had been a point of great simplicity[57] if he should forsake that which fortune had so favorably proffered unto him, perceiving by her train that she was some lady of great honor; and, viewing the perfection of her beauty and the excellency of her grace and countenance, did think it unpossible that she should be despised, and therefore answered thus:

"Madam, if before this time I have seemed to forget myself in neglecting your courtesy which so liberally you have meant[58] unto me, please it you to pardon what is past, and from this day forwards Silvio remaineth ready prest[59] to make such reasonable amends as his ability may any ways permit or as it shall please you to command."

Julina, the gladdest woman that might be to hear these joyful news, said, "Then, my Silvio, see you fail not tomorrow at night to sup with me at my own house, where I will discourse farther with you what amends you shall make me." To which request Silvio gave his glad consent, and thus they departed, very well pleased. And as Julina did think the time very long till she had reaped the fruit of her desire, so Silvio he[60] wished for harvest before corn could grow, thinking the time as long till he saw how matters would fall out. But, not knowing what lady she might be, he presently, before Julina was out of sight, demanded of one that was walking by what she was and how she was called, who satisfied Silvio in every point, and also in what part of the town her house did stand, whereby he might inquire it out.

Silvio, thus departing to his lodging, passed the night with very unquiet sleeps, and the next morning his mind ran so much of[61] his supper that he never cared neither for his breakfast nor dinner; and the day, to his seeming,

---

56 did i.e., he did   **57 simplicity** simplemindedness   **58 meant** intended to convey   **59 ready prest** ready and willing   **60 Silvio he** Silvio   **61 of** on

passed away so slowly that he had thought the stately steeds had been tired that draw the chariot of the sun, or else some other Joshua[62] had commanded them again to stand, and wished that Phaëthon[63] had been there with a whip.

Julina, on the other side, she had thought the clock setter had played the knave, the day came no faster forwards. But six o'clock being once strucken recovered comfort to both parties; and Silvio, hastening himself to the palace of Julina, where by her he was friendly welcomed and a sumptuous supper being made ready furnished with sundry sorts of delicate dishes, they sat them down, passing the suppertime with amorous looks, loving countenances, and secret glances conveyed from the one to the other, which did better satisfy them than the feeding of their dainty dishes.

Suppertime being thus spent, Julina did think it very unfitly[64] if she should turn Silvio to go seek his lodging in an evening, desired him therefore that he would take a bed in her house for that night; and, bringing him up into a fair chamber that was very richly furnished, she found such means that when all the rest of her household servants were abed and quiet, she came herself to bear Silvio company, where, concluding upon conditions that were in question between them, they passed the night with such joy and contentation[65] as might in that convenient time be wished for. But only[66] that Julina, feeding too much of some one dish above the rest, received a surfeit whereof she could not be cured in forty weeks after—a natural inclination in all women which are subject to longing and want[67] the reason to use a moderation in their diet. But, the morning approaching, Julina took her leave and conveyed herself into her own chamber; and when it was fair daylight, Silvio,* making himself ready, departed likewise about his affairs in the town, debating with himself how things had happened, being well assured that Julina had mistaken him; and therefore, for fear of further evils, determined to come no more there, but took his journey towards other places in

62 **Joshua** (For Joshua's commanding the sun to stand still, see Joshua 10:12–13.)   63 **Phaëthon** son of the sun-god, destroyed by Jupiter in his rash attempt to steer the sun-god's chariot   64 **unfitly** unsuitable, inappropriate   65 **contentation** contentment   66 **But only** except   67 **want** lack

the parts of Grecia to see if he could learn any tidings of his sister Silla.

The Duke Apollonius, having made a long suit and never a whit the nearer of his purpose, came to Julina to crave her direct answer, either to accept of him and such conditions as he proffered unto her or else to give him his last farewell.

Julina, as you have heard, had taken an earnest-penny[68] of another, whom she* had thought had been Silvio, the Duke's man, was[69] at a controversy in herself what she might do. One while[70] she thought, seeing her occasion served so fit, to crave the Duke's good will for the marrying of his man; then again, she could not tell what displeasure the Duke would conceive, in that she should seem to prefer his man before himself, did[71] think it therefore best to conceal the matter till she might speak with Silvio, to use his opinion how these matters should be handled; and hereupon resolving herself, desiring the Duke to pardon her speeches, said as followeth:

"Sir Duke, for that from this time forwards I am no longer of myself, having given my full power and authority over to another whose wife I now remain by faithful vow and promise, and albeit I know the world will wonder when they shall understand the fondness[72] of my choice, yet I trust you yourself will nothing dislike with me, sith[73] I have meant no other thing than the satisfying of mine own contentation and liking."

The Duke, hearing these words, answered: "Madam, I must then content myself, although against my will, having the law in your own hands to like of whom you list and to make choice where it pleaseth you."

Julina, giving the Duke great thanks that would content himself with such patience, desired him likewise to give his free consent and good will to the party whom she had chosen to be her husband.

"Nay, surely, madam," quoth the Duke, "I will never give my consent that any other man shall enjoy you than myself. I have made too great account of you than so lightly to pass you away with my good will. But seeing it lieth not in me to

68 earnest-penny small sum paid in earnest to secure a bargain **69 was** i.e., and she was **70 One while** on the one hand **71 did** i.e., and did **72 fondness** foolishness **73 nothing dislike with me, sith** take no dislike to me, since

let[74] you, having, as you say, made your own choice, so from henceforwards I leave you to your own liking, always willing you well, and thus will take my leave."

The Duke departed towards his own house, very sorrowful that Julina had thus served him. But in the mean space[75] that the Duke had remained in the house of Julina, some of his servants fell into talk and conference with the servants of Julina, where, debating between them of the likelihood of the marriage between the Duke and the lady, one of the servants of Julina said that he never saw his lady and mistress use so good countenance to the Duke himself as she had done to Silvio his man, and began to report with what familiarity and courtesy she had received him, feasted him, and lodged him, and that in his opinion Silvio was like to speed[76] before the Duke or any other that were suitors.

This tale was quickly brought to the Duke himself, who, making better inquiry in the matter, found it to be true that was reported; and, better considering of the words which Julina had used towards himself, was very well assured that it could be no other than his own man that had thrust his nose so far out of joint. Wherefore, without any further respect,[77] caused[78] him to be thrust into a dungeon, where he was kept prisoner in a very pitiful plight.

Poor Silvio, having got intelligence by some of his fellows what was the cause that the Duke his master did bear such displeasure unto him, devised all the means he could, as well by mediation* by his fellows as otherwise by petitions and supplications to the Duke, that he would suspend his judgment till perfect proof were had in the matter, and then, if any manner of thing did fall out against him whereby the Duke had cause to take any grief, he would confess himself worthy not only of imprisonment but also of most vile and shameful death. With these petitions he daily plied the Duke, but all in vain, for the Duke thought he had made so good proof that he was thoroughly confirmed in his opinion against his man.

But the Lady Julina, wondering what made Silvio that he was so slack in his visitation and why he absented himself so long from her presence, began to think that all was not

74 **let** hinder   75 **space** time   76 **like to speed** likely to succeed
77 **respect** consideration   78 **caused** i.e., he caused

well. But in the end, perceiving no decoction[79] of her former surfeit—received as you have heard—and finding in herself an unwonted swelling in her belly, assuring herself to be with child, fearing to become quite bankrupt of her honor, did think it more than time to seek out a father, and made such secret search and diligent inquiry that she learned the truth how Silvio was kept in prison by the Duke his master. And minding[80] to find a present remedy, as well for the love she bare[81] to Silvio as for the maintenance of her credit and estimation, she speedily hasted to the palace of the Duke, to whom she said as followeth:

"Sir Duke, it may be that you will think my coming to your house in this sort doth something[82] pass the limits of modesty, the which, I protest before God, proceedeth of this desire that the world should know how justly I seek means to maintain my honor. But to the end I seem not tedious with prolixity of words, nor to use other than direct circumstances, know, sir, that the love I bear to my only beloved Silvio, whom I do esteem more than all the jewels in the world, whose personage I regard more than my own life, is the only cause of my attempted journey, beseeching you that all the whole displeasure which I understand you have conceived against him may be imputed unto my charge, and that it would please you lovingly to deal with him whom of myself I have chosen rather for the satisfaction of mine honest liking than for the vain preeminences or honorable dignities looked after[83] by ambitious minds."

The Duke, having heard this discourse, caused Silvio presently[84] to be sent for and to be brought before him, to whom he said: "Had it not been sufficient for thee, when I had reposed[85] myself in thy fidelity and the trustiness of thy service, that thou shouldst so traitorously deal with me, but since that time hast not spared still to abuse me with so many forgeries and perjured protestations, not only hateful unto me, whose simplicity thou thinkest to be such that by the plot of thy pleasant tongue thou wouldst make me believe a manifest untruth, but most abominable be thy doings in the presence and sight of God, that hast[86] not spared to blaspheme his holy name by calling him to be a witness

79 decoction diminishing   **80 minding** intending   **81 bare** bore
82 something somewhat   **83 looked after** sought after   **84 presently** immediately   **85 reposed** entrusted   **86 that hast** (you) who have

to maintain thy leasings,[87] and so detestably wouldst forswear thyself in a matter that is so openly known."

Poor Silvio, whose innocency was such that he might lawfully swear, seeing Julina to be there in place, answered thus:

"Most noble Duke, well understanding your conceived grief, most humbly I beseech you patiently to hear my excuse, not minding[88] thereby to aggravate or heap up your wrath and displeasure, protesting before God that there is nothing in the world which I regard so much or do esteem so dear as your good grace and favor, but desirous that Your Grace should know my innocency, and to clear myself of such impositions[89] wherewith I know I am wrongfully accused; which, as I understand, should be in the practicing[90] of the Lady Julina, who standeth here in place, whose acquittance for my better discharge[91] now I most humbly crave, protesting before the almighty God that neither in thought, word, nor deed I have not otherwise used myself than according to the bond and duty of a servant that is both willing and desirous to further his master's suits; which if I have otherwise said than that is true, you, Madam Julina, who can very well decide the depths of all this doubt, I most humbly beseech you to certify a truth if I have in anything missaid or have otherwise spoken than is right and just."

Julina, having heard this discourse which Silvio had made, perceiving that he stood in great awe of the Duke's displeasure, answered thus: "Think not, my Silvio, that my coming hither is to accuse you of any misdemeanor towards your master, so I do not deny but[92] in all such embassages wherein towards me you have been employed you have used the office of a faithful and trusty messenger. Neither am I ashamed to confess that the first day that mine eyes did behold the singular behavior, the notable courtesy, and other innummerable gifts wherewith my Silvio is endowed, but that beyond all measure my heart was so inflamed that impossible it was for me to quench the fervent love or extinguish the least part of my conceived torment before I had bewrayed[93] the same unto him and of my own motion craved

87 leasings lies **88 minding** intending **89 impositions** accusations
90 practicing devising **91 discharge** clearing of blame **92 so . . . but**
and so I do not deny but that **93 bewrayed** revealed

his promised faith and loyalty of marriage. And now is the time to manifest the same unto the world which hath been done before God and between ourselves, knowing that it is not needful to keep secret that which is neither evil done nor hurtful to any person. Therefore, as I said before, Silvio is my husband by plighted faith, whom I hope to obtain without offense or displeasure of anyone, trusting that there is no man that will so far forget himself as to restrain that which God hath left at liberty for every wight,[94] or that will seek by cruelty to force ladies to marry otherwise than according to their own liking. Fear not then, my Silvio, to keep your faith and promise which you have made unto me; and as for the rest, I doubt not things will so fall out as you shall have no manner of cause to complain."

Silvio, amazed to hear these words, for that Julina by her speech seemed to confirm that which he most of all desired to be quit of,[95] said: "Who would have thought that a lady of so great honor and reputation would herself be the ambassador of a thing so prejudicial and uncomely for her estate! What plighted promises be these which be spoken of? Altogether ignorant unto me, which, if it be otherwise than I have said, you, sacred goddess, consume me straight with flashing flames of fire! But what words might I use to give credit to the truth and innocency of my cause? Ah, Madam Julina! I desire no other testimony than your own honesty and virtue, thinking that you will not so much blemish the brightness of your honor, knowing that a woman is or should be the image of courtesy, continency, and shamefastness—from the which, so soon as she stoopeth and leaveth the office of her duty and modesty, besides the degradation of her honor, she thrusteth herself into the pit of perpetual infamy. And as I cannot think you would so far forget yourself by the refusal of a noble duke to dim the light of your renown and glory, which hitherto you have maintained amongst the best and noblest ladies, by such a one as I know myself to be, too far unworthy your degree and calling, so most humbly I beseech you to confess a truth whereto tendeth those vows and promises you speak of—which speeches be so obscure unto me as I know not for my life how I might understand them."

94 wight person   **95 quit of** acquitted of

Julina, something nipped with[96] these speeches, said: "And what is the matter, that now you make so little account of your Julina? That, being my husband indeed, have the face to deny me to whom thou art contracted by so many solemn oaths? What? Art thou ashamed to have me to thy wife? How much oughtst thou rather to be ashamed to break thy promised faith and to have[97] despised the holy and dreadful name of God? But that time[98] constraineth me to lay open[99] that which shame rather willeth I should dissemble and keep secret. Behold me then here, Silvio, whom thou has gotten with child; who, if thou be of such honesty as I trust for all this[100] I shall find, then the thing is done without prejudice or any hurt to my conscience, considering that by the professed faith[101] thou didst account me for thy wife and I received thee for my spouse and loyal husband, swearing by the almighty God that no other than you have made the conquest and triumph of my chastity, whereof I crave no other witness than yourself and mine own conscience."

I pray you, gentlewomen, was not this a foul oversight of Julina, that would so precisely swear so great an oath that she was gotten with child by one that was altogether unfurnished with implements for such a turn? For God's love take heed, and let this be an example to you when you be with child how you swear who is the father before you have had good proof and knowledge of the party; for men be so subtle and full of sleight that, God knoweth, a woman may quickly be deceived.

But now to return to our Silvio, who, hearing an oath sworn so divinely that he had gotten a woman with child, was like to believe[102] that it had been true in very deed; but, remembering his own impediment, thought it impossible that he should commit such an act and therefore, half in a chafe,[103] he said:

"What law is able to restrain the foolish indiscretion of a woman that yieldeth herself to her own desires? What shame is able to bridle or withdraw her from her mind and

96 **something nipped with** somewhat taken aback by   97 **have** cause to be·   98 **that time** i.e., the time of my pregnancy   99 **lay open** reveal   100 **for all this** despite all this (denial)   101 **the professed faith** the faith we all profess   102 **like to believe** near to believing   103 **in a chafe** angry

madness, or with what snaffle is it possible to hold her back from the execution of her filthiness? But what abomination is this, that a lady of such a house should so forget the greatness of her estate, the alliance whereof she is descended, the nobility of her deceased husband, and maketh no conscience to shame and slander herself with such a one as I am, being so far unfit and unseemly for her degree! But how horrible is it to hear the name of God so defaced that we make no more account, but for the maintenance of our mischiefs we fear no whit at all to forswear his holy name, as though he were not in all his dealings most righteous, true, and just, and will not only lay open our leasings[104] to the world but will likewise punish the same with most sharp and bitter scourges."

Julina, not able to endure him to proceed any farther in his sermon, was already surprised with a vehement grief, began bitterly to cry out, uttering these speeches following:

"Alas! Is it possible that the sovereign justice of God can abide a mischief so great and cursed? Why may I not now suffer death rather than the infamy which I see to wander before mine eyes? Oh, happy, and more than right happy, had I been if inconstant Fortune had not devised this treason wherein I am surprised and caught! Am I thus become to be entangled with snares and in the hands of him who, enjoying the spoils of my honor, will openly deprive me of my fame by making me a common fable to all posterity in time to come? Ah, traitor and discourteous wretch! Is this the recompense of the honest and firm amity which I have borne thee? Wherein have I deserved this discourtesy? By loving thee more than thou art able to deserve? Is it I, arrant thief, is it I upon whom thou thinkest to work thy mischiefs? Dost thou think me no better worth but that thou mayst prodigally waste my honor at thy pleasure? Didst thou dare to adventure upon me, having my conscience wounded with so deadly a treason? Ah, unhappy and above all other most unhappy, that have so charily[105] preserved mine honor and now am made a prey to satisfy a young man's lust that hath coveted nothing but the spoil of my chastity and good name!"

104 leasings lies   **105 charily** carefully, frugally

Herewithal her tears so gushed down her cheeks that she was not able to open her mouth to use any farther speech.

The Duke, who stood by all this while and heard this whole discourse, was wonderfully moved with compassion towards Julina, knowing that from her infancy she had ever so honorably used herself that there was no man able to detect her of[106] any misdemeanor otherwise than beseemed a lady of her estate. Wherefore, being fully resolved that Silvio, his man, had committed this villainy against her, in a great fury, drawing his rapier, he said unto Silvio:

"How canst thou, arrant thief, show thyself so cruel and careless to such as do thee honor? Hast thou so little regard of such a noble lady as humbleth herself to such a villain as thou art, who, without any respect either of her renown or noble estate, canst be content to seek the wrack and utter ruin of her honor? But frame[107] thyself to make such satisfaction as she requireth—although I know, unworthy wretch, that thou art not able to make her the least part of amends—or I swear by God that thou shalt not escape the death which I will minister to thee with my own hands. And therefore advise thee well what thou dost."

Silvio, having heard this sharp sentence, fell down on his knees before the Duke, craving for mercy, desiring that he might be suffered to speak with the Lady Julina apart, promising to satisfy her according to her own contentation.[108]

"Well," quoth the Duke, "I take thy word; and therewithal I advise thee that thou perform thy promise, or otherwise I protest, before God, I will make thee such an example to the world that all traitors shall tremble for fear how they do seek the dishonoring of ladies."

But now Julina had conceived so great grief against Silvio that there was much ado to persuade her to talk with him. But remembering her own case, desirous to hear what excuse he could make, in the end she agreed, and, being brought into a place severally[109] by themselves, Silvio began with a piteous voice to say as followeth:

"I know not, madam, of whom I might make complaint, whether of you or of myself, or rather of Fortune, which

106 of in   **107 frame** prepare   **108 to her own contentation** to her heart's content   **109 severally** separately

hath conducted and brought us both into so great adversity. I see that you receive great wrong, and I am condemned against all right; you in peril to abide the bruit[110] of spiteful tongues, and I in danger to lose the thing that I most desire. And although I could allege many reasons to prove my sayings true, yet I refer myself to the experience and bounty of your mind." And herewithal loosing his garments down to his stomach, and showed Julina his breasts and pretty teats surmounting far the whiteness of snow itself, saying: "Lo, madam! Behold here the party whom you have challenged to be the father of your child. See, I am a woman, the daughter of a noble duke, who, only for the love of him whom you so lightly have shaken off, have forsaken my father, abandoned my country, and, in manner as you see, am become a servingman, satisfying myself but with the only[111] sight of my Apollonius. And now, madam, if my passion were not vehement and my torments without comparison, I would wish that my feigned griefs might be laughed to scorn and my dissembled pains to be rewarded with flouts. But my love being pure, my travail[112] continual, and my griefs endless, I trust, madam, you will not only excuse me of crime but also pity my distress, the which, I protest, I would still have kept secret if my fortune would so have permitted."

Julina did now think herself to be in a worse case than ever she was before, for now she knew not whom to challenge to be the father of her child; wherefore, when she had told the Duke the very certainty of the discourse which Silvio had made unto her, she departed to her own house with such grief and sorrow that she purposed never to come out of her own doors again alive to be a wonder and mocking stock to the world.

But the Duke, more amazed to hear this strange discourse of Silvio, came unto him, whom, when he had viewed with better consideration, perceived indeed that it was Silla, the daughter of Duke Pontus, and embracing her in his arms he said:

"Oh, the branch of all virtue and the flower of courtesy itself! Pardon me, I beseech you, of all such discourtesies as I have ignorantly committed towards you, desiring you that

110 bruit clamor   **111 but with the only** only with the   **112 travail** hardship without farther memory of ancient griefs you will accept of me, who is more joyful and better contented with your presence than if the whole world were at my commandment. Where hath there ever been found such liberality in a lover which, having been trained up and nourished amongst the delicacies and banquets of the court, accompanied with trains of many fair and noble ladies, living in pleasure and in the midst of delights, would so prodigally adventure yourself, neither fearing mishaps nor misliking to take such pains as I know you have not been accustomed unto? O liberality never heard of before! O fact that can never be sufficiently rewarded! O true love most pure and unfeigned!" Herewithal sending for the most artificial workmen,[113] he provided for her sundry suits of sumptuous apparel, and the marriage day appointed, which was celebrated with great triumph through the whole city of Constantinople, everyone praising the nobleness of the Duke. But so many as did behold the excellent beauty of Silla gave her the praise above all the rest of the ladies in the troop.

The matter seemed so wonderful and strange that the bruit[114] was spread throughout all the parts of Grecia, insomuch that it came to the hearing of Silvio, who, as you have heard, remained in those parts to inquire of his sister. He, being the gladdest man in the world, hasted to Constantinople where, coming to his sister, he was joyfully received and most lovingly welcomed and entertained of the Duke his brother-in-law. After he had remained there two or three days, the Duke revealed unto Silvio the whole discourse how it happened between his sister and the Lady Julina, and how his sister was challenged for getting a woman with child. Silvio, blushing with these words, was stricken with great remorse to make Julina amends, understanding her to be a noble lady and was left defamed to the world through his default.[115] He therefore bewrayed[116] the whole circumstance to the Duke, whereof the Duke, being very joyful, immediately repaired[117] with Silvio to the house of Julina, whom they found in her chamber in great lamentation and mourning. To whom the Duke said: "Take courage, madam,

---

113 artificial workmen craftsmen skilled in their art **114 bruit** rumor
115 default fault **116 bewrayed** revealed **117 repaired** went

for behold here a gentleman that will not stick[118] both to father your child and to take you for his wife; no inferior person, but the son and heir of a noble duke, worthy of your estate and dignity."

Julina, seeing Silvio in place, did know very well that he was the father of her child and was so ravished with joy that she knew not whether she were awake or in some dream. Silvio, embracing her in his arms, craving forgiveness of all that was past, concluded[119] with her the marriage day, which was presently accomplished with great joy and contentation to all parties. And thus, Silvio having attained a noble wife, and Silla, his sister, her desired husband, they passed the residue of their days with such delight as those that have accomplished the perfection of their felicities.

The text is based on Barnabe Riche, *Riche His Farewell to Military Profession*, London, 1581.

In the following, departures from the original text appear in boldface; the original readings follow in roman:

p. 524 *sip soope   **p. 528 *stars** Starre   **p. 530 *room** romer   **p. 535 *Silvio** Silvano
p. 536 *she he   **p. 537 *mediation** meditation

118 stick hesitate   **119 concluded** settled

Further Reading

Auden, W. H. "Music in Shakespeare." *"The Dyer's Hand" and Other Essays*. New York: Random House, 1948. Auden finds dark tones disturbing the comedy of *Twelfth Night*. Viola and Antonio are characters whose desires are too strong to be contained by the play's comic conventions. The songs, Auden argues, express the play's complex comic feeling: by themselves they are beautiful, but located within the psychological matrix of the play they are cruel, selfish, and self-indulgent.

Barber, C. L. "Testing Courtesy and Humanity in *Twelfth Night*." *Shakespeare's Festive Comedy*. Princeton, N.J.: Princeton Univ. Press, 1959. Focusing on the relation of the dramatic form to the social forms of Elizabethan holidays, Barber examines the Saturnalian patterns in Shakespearean comedy. In *Twelfth Night*, the reversal of sexual and social roles permits both characters and audiences to move, in Barber's phrase, "through release to clarification," as characters (with the telling exception of the puritanical Malvolio), caught up in delusions and misapprehensions, ultimately discover freedom, love, and self-knowledge through the festive action.

Barton, Anne. "*As You Like It* and *Twelfth Night*: Shakespeare's Sense of an Ending." In *Shakespearian Comedy*, ed. Malcolm Bradbury and D. J. Palmer. Stratford-upon-Avon Studies 14. London: Edward Arnold, 1972. Except for Malvolio, Barton argues, all characters and the audience participate in the play's festivity, but she finds the play's harmonies to be elusive and fragile: the improbable romantic world of escape, disguise, and irrational love is announced as a triumph of art, and Feste's final song gently leads us out of the golden world of fiction back to our imperfect world of fact.

Brown, John Russell. "Directions for *Twelfth Night*, or What You Will." *Tulane Drama Review* 5, no. 4 (1961): 77–88. Rpt. in *Shakespeare's Plays in Performance*. New York: St. Martin's Press, 1967. Brown surveys *Twelfth Night* on the stage in the 1950s to reveal the multiplicity of dramatic interpretations that it permits and to suggest the possibility of a production fully responsive to the play's range and complexity. He offers his own solution to the visual problems that *Twelfth Night* poses as an example of one way in which a director might use available theatrical resources to respond to the demands made by the unity and the imaginative power of the text.

Hartwig, Joan. "*Twelfth Night* and Parodic Subplot." *Shakespeare's Analogical Scene*. Lincoln, Neb.: Univ. of Nebraska Press, 1983. Finding the play to be concerned with the conflict between individual will and a design beyond human control, Hartwig considers the relation of the play's two plots. Only Malvolio's fate is determined by acts of human will, and the lack of forgiveness at his exit points to the central difference between the plots: the subplot is motivated by revenge, a human act that fragments and destroys; the main plot is directed by love, the concern of some benevolent higher agency, which creates and directs the play's harmonies.

Hollander, John. "*Twelfth Night* and the Morality of Indulgence." *Sewanee Review* 67 (1959): 220–238. Rpt. in *Discussions of Shakespeare's Romantic Comedy*, ed. Herbert Weil, Jr. Boston: D. C. Heath, 1966; and in *Essays in Shakespearean Criticism*, ed. James L. Calderwood and Harold E. Toliver. Englewood Cliffs, N.J.: Prentice-Hall, 1970. Arguing that in its use of a fully dramatized metaphor (of feasting and satiety) the play rejects the comic model provided by Ben Jonson (the characteristically static comedy of humors), Hollander sees *Twelfth Night* as a comedy of emotional and moral purgation in which excessive appetite is corrected through its indulgence. Except in the case of Malvolio, indulgence succeeds in releasing the fully human self from the limitations of comic stereotype.

Howard, Jean E. "The Orchestration of *Twelfth Night:* The Rhythm of Restraint and Release." *Shakespeare's Art of Orchestration: Stage Technique and Audience Response*. Urbana and Chicago: Univ. of Illinois Press, 1984. Howard considers how Shakespeare orchestrates an audience's experience of the play. The inadequacy of the characters' emotional postures is revealed through their inhibiting effects on the play's action and language. The audience's desire for the generosity and joy that has been frustrated is finally satisfied by the recognitions of the ending.

Jenkins, Harold. "Shakespeare's *Twelfth Night.*" *Rice Institute Pamphlets* 45 (1959): 19–42. Rpt. in *Shakespeare, the Comedies: A Collection of Critical Essays*, ed. Kenneth Muir. Englewood Cliffs, N.J.: Prentice-Hall, 1965. Identifying *Twelfth Night*'s most important source as Shakespeare's own *The Comedy of Errors* and *The Two Gentlemen of Verona*, Jenkins examines the play's deepening of the emotional patterns of the earlier plays. The genuineness of Viola's feeling serves not only to measure the emotions of others but also to release both Orsino and Olivia from their self-indulgence, a movement that finds an ironic echo in the subplot as Malvolio remains locked in his self-love.

Kermode, Frank. "The Mature Comedies." In *Early Shakespeare*, ed. John Russell Brown and Bernard Harris. Stratford-upon-Avon Studies 3. London: Edward Arnold, 1961. In an essay seeking to characterize the achievement of the mature comedies, Kermode considers *Twelfth Night* in relation to two aspects of the Twelfth Night celebrations: its licensing of misrule and the confounding of identity and authority. The play's comic confusions and misapprehensions reflect the festive pattern, moving from a superficial comedy of errors to a complex and sophisticated comedy of identity.

King, Walter N., ed. *Twentieth Century Interpretations of "Twelfth Night."* Englewood Cliffs, N.J.: Prentice-Hall, 1968. King's introductory essay to this collection of criticism considers the collision of perspectives in *Twelfth Night*, and his selection of essays is designed to demonstrate the variety of critical approaches that it permits. King includes studies by Sylvan Barnet, H. B. Charlton, Alan Downer, and Leslie Hotson, as well as essays, considered here, by Barber, Hollander, Leech, Salingar, and Summers.

Leech, Clifford. "*Twelfth Night*, or What Delights You." "*Twelfth Night" and Shakespearian Comedy*. Toronto: Univ. of Toronto Press, 1965. *Twelfth Night*, according to Leech, tempers its harmonies with the awareness of the contrivance needed to produce them. The play is never harsh, Leech finds, but the precariousness of the comic triumph is evident—in our discomfort at Malvolio's humiliation, in the poignancy of Antonio's relationship with Sebastian, in the complicated sexual awareness produced by boy actors playing women disguised as men, and in the refusal of the ending fully to credit the imminent marriages.

Leggatt, Alexander. *"Twelfth Night." Shakespeare's Comedy of Love*. London: Methuen, 1974. Leggatt examines *Twelfth Night*'s emphasis upon individuals isolated by nature or circumstance. The play dramatizes the difficulties of forming relationships, and significantly, Leggatt finds, it ends not with a dance or procession of lovers but with the solitary figure of Feste. The love plot is resolved happily, but its resolution depends upon formal organization rather than upon psychological growth, revealing the tension between conventional and realistic art.

Lewalski, Barbara K. "Thematic Patterns in *Twelfth Night*." *Shakespeare Studies* 1 (1965): 168–181. Lewalski considers the religious dimension of *Twelfth Night*, exploring the significance of the play's title (Twelfth Night celebrates the journey of the Magi to Bethlehem and is observed on the twelfth and final day of the Christmas season, January 6). The play, Lewalski argues, is not an allegory of Christ's action in the world but a secular analogue of it: Sebastian and Viola bring peace and love to a disordered world, though Feste's final song reminds us that the real world is less easily perfected than the comic universe of the play.

Nevo, Ruth. "Nature's Bias." *Comic Transformations in Shakespeare*. London and New York: Methuen, 1980. Nevo regards *Twelfth Night* as Shakespeare's most brilliant realization of the possibilities of a dramatic form that is at once comic and corrective. The play enacts and exorcises characters' fantasies and obsessions. Nevo explores the gentle masculinity of Sebastian in this process, whose presence permits the joyful recognitions and remedies of the end.

Palmer, D. J. *Shakespeare, "Twelfth Night": A Casebook*. London: Macmillan, 1972. Palmer's introduction to this collection of critical commentary discusses the subtle play of lyrical and dissonant notes in *Twelfth Night* and usefully surveys the play's occasion, date, and sources as well as the history of criticism that it has provoked. The selections that he offers partially trace this history, from seventeenth-century comments on the play to the work of twentieth-century critics such as Barber, Bradley, Charlton, and Hotson.

Salingar, Leo G. "The Design of *Twelfth Night*." *Shakespeare Quarterly* 9 (1958): 117–139. Rpt. in *Discussions of Shakespeare's Romantic Comedy*, ed. Herbert Weil, Jr. Boston: D. C. Heath, 1966. Salingar examines Shakespeare's transformation of classical and Renaissance romance materials into a comedy of misrule exploring the psychology of love. The narrative and emotional improbabilities of the sources are used to reveal love's folly as well as its life-affirming power. *Twelfth Night* presents and interrogates this paradoxical conception of love, as self-deception gives way to mistaken identities sorted out by the action of a fate responsive to human desire.

Summers, Joseph H. "The Masks of *Twelfth Night*." *University Review of Kansas City* 22 (1955): 25–32. Rpt. in *Discussions of Shakespeare's Romantic Comedy*, ed. Herbert Weil, Jr. Boston: D. C. Heath, 1966; and in *Shakespeare: Modern Essays in Criticism*, ed. Leonard F. Dean. Rev. ed., London, Oxford, and New York: Oxford Univ. Press, 1967. *Twelfth Night*, according to Summers, in its elaborate dance of maskers enacts their pursuit of self-knowledge and happiness. Everyone wears a mask, and, in general, we laugh *with* those who are aware of and in control of the roles they play, and we laugh *at* those who are not. The clown, Feste—the one professional in the business of masking—is able to unmask the pretensions of others, even revealing the mask of the play itself to be only a fiction of an idealized world.

Welsford, Enid. *The Fool: His Social and Literary History*. Esp. pp. 251–252. London: Faber and Faber, 1935. In her study of the literary and social history of the Fool, Welsford considers Feste as a lord of misrule presiding over the festivities of *Twelfth Night*. His wit gives unity to the play's action, focusing its values. Appropriately he is given the play's final word, dissolving the fiction into a song that points to harsher realities than the comedy would admit.

Memorable Lines

The Taming of the Shrew

I'll not budge an inch . . .   (SLY   Ind.1.13)

Dost thou love pictures? We will fetch thee straight
Adonis painted by a running brook,
And Cytherea all in sedges hid,
Which seem to move and wanton with her breath.
                              (SERVANT   Ind.2.49–52)

Come, madam wife, sit by my side and let the world slip; we
shall ne'er be younger.   (SLY   Ind.2.138–139)

No profit grows where is no pleasure ta'en.
In brief, sir, study what you most affect.
                              (TRANIO   1.1.39–40)

To seek their fortunes further than at home,
Where small experience grows.   (PETRUCHIO   1.2.50–51)

I come to wive it wealthily in Padua;
If wealthily, then happily in Padua.   (PETRUCHIO   1.2.74–75)

Katharine the curst!
A title for a maid of all titles the worst.
                              (GRUMIO   1.2.128–129)

And do as adversaries do in law,
Strive mightily, but eat and drink as friends.
                              (TRANIO   1.2.276–277)

I am as peremptory as she proud-minded;
And where two raging fires meet together,
They do consume the thing that feeds their fury.
                              (PETRUCHIO   2.1.131–133)

BAPTISTA
   Why, then thou canst not break her to the lute?

HORTENSIO
  Why, no, for she hath broke the lute to me.   (2.1.147–148)

KATHARINA
  They call me Katharine that do talk of me.
PETRUCHIO
  You lie, in faith, for you are called plain Kate.
                                            (2.1.184–185)

And, will you, nill you, I will marry you.
                                  (PETRUCHIO   2.1.268)

Kiss me, Kate, we will be married o' Sunday.
                                  (PETRUCHIO   2.1.322)

Old fashions please me best.   (BIANCA   3.1.79)

. . . a little pot and soon hot.   (GRUMIO   4.1.5)

This is a way to kill a wife with kindness.
                                  (PETRUCHIO   4.1.196)

He that knows better how to tame a shrew,
Now let him speak; 'tis charity to show.
                                  (PETRUCHIO   4.1.198–199)

Our purses shall be proud, our garments poor,
For 'tis the mind that makes the body rich.
                                  (PETRUCHIO   4.3.167–168)

Why, so this gallant will command the sun.
                                  (HORTENSIO   4.3.192)

He that is giddy thinks the world turns round.
                                  (WIDOW   5.2.20)

Fie, fie! Unknit that threatening unkind brow.
                                  (KATHARINA   5.2.140)

A woman moved is like a fountain troubled,
Muddy, ill-seeming, thick, bereft of beauty.
                                  (KATHARINA   5.2.146–147)

Memorable Lines

A Midsummer Night's Dream

The course of true love never did run smooth.
(LYSANDER 1.1.134)

So quick bright things come to confusion.
(LYSANDER 1.1.149)

Love looks not with the eyes, but with the mind,
And therefore is winged Cupid painted blind.
(HELENA 1.1.234–235)

. . ."The most lamentable comedy and most cruel death of
Pyramus and Thisbe." (QUINCE 1.2.11–12)

Over hill, over dale,
  Thorough bush, thorough brier,
Over park, over pale,
  Thorough flood, thorough fire . . . (FAIRY 2.1.2–5)

Ill met by moonlight, proud Titania. (OBERON 2.1.60)

I'll put a girdle round about the earth
In forty minutes. (PUCK 2.1.175–176)

I know a bank where the wild thyme blows,
Where oxlips and the nodding violet grows,
Quite overcanopied with luscious woodbine,
With sweet muskroses and with eglantine.
(OBERON 2.1.249–252)

You spotted snakes with double tongue,
  Thorny hedgehogs, be not seen;
Newts and blindworms, do no wrong,
  Come not near our Fairy Queen. (FAIRY 2.2.9–12)

Lord, what fools these mortals be! (PUCK 3.2.115)

And though she be but little, she is fierce.   (HELENA   3.2.325)

My Oberon! What visions have I seen!
Methought I was enamored of an ass.   (TITANIA   4.1.75–76)

The lunatic, the lover, and the poet
Are of imagination all compact.
One sees more devils than vast hell can hold;
That is the madman. The lover, all as frantic,
Sees Helen's beauty in a brow of Egypt.
The poet's eye, in a fine frenzy rolling,
Doth glance from heaven to earth, from earth to heaven;
And as imagination bodies forth
The forms of things unknown, the poet's pen
Turns them to shapes and gives to airy nothing
A local habitation and a name.   (THESEUS   5.1.7–17)

. . . the true beginning of our end.   (PROLOGUE   5.1.111)

The iron tongue of midnight hath told twelve.
Lovers, to bed, 'tis almost fairy time.
                                        (THESEUS   5.1.358–359)

If we shadows have offended,
Think but this, and all is mended,
That you have but slumbered here
While these visions did appear.   (PUCK   5.1.419–422)

Memorable Lines

The Merchant of Venice

Your mind is tossing on the ocean.   (SALERIO   1.1.8)

You have too much respect upon the world;
They lose it that do buy it with much care.
                                        (GRATIANO   1.1.74–75)

I hold the world but as the world, Gratiano,
A stage where every man must play a part,
And mine a sad one.   (ANTONIO   1.1.77–79)

Let me play the fool!   (GRATIANO   1.1.79)

   "I am Sir Oracle,
And when I ope my lips let no dog bark!"
                                        (GRATIANO   1.1.93–94)

They are as sick that surfeit with too much as they that
starve with nothing.   (NERISSA   1.2.5–6)

God made him, and therefore let him pass for a man.
                                        (PORTIA   1.2.54–55)

When he is best he is a little worse than a man, and when he
is worst he is little better than a beast.   (PORTIA   1.2.86–87)

I will buy with you, sell with you, talk with you, walk with
you, and so following, but I will not eat with you, drink with
you, nor pray with you.   (SHYLOCK   1.3.33–35)

What news on the Rialto?   (SHYLOCK   1.3.35–36)

The devil can cite Scripture for his purpose.
                                        (ANTONIO   1.3.96)

It is a wise father that knows his own child.
                                        (LAUNCELOT   2.2.73–74)

But love is blind, and lovers cannot see
The pretty follies that themselves commit.

(JESSICA   2.6.37–38)

"Who chooseth me must give and hazard all he hath."

(*Inscription*   2.7.9)

"My daughter! O, my ducats! O, my daughter!"

(SALERIO parodying Shylock   2.8.15)

I am a Jew. Hath not a Jew eyes? Hath not a Jew hands, organs, dimensions, senses, affections, passions?

(SHYLOCK   3.1.55–57)

If you prick us, do we not bleed? If you tickle us, do we not laugh? If you poison us, do we not die? And if you wrong us, shall we not revenge?   (SHYLOCK   3.1.60–63)

Tell me where is fancy bred,
Or in the heart or in the head?
How begot, how nourishèd?
  Reply, reply.

(*Song*   3.2.63–66)

The world is still deceived with ornament.

(BASSANIO   3.2.74)

"I never knew so young a body with so old a head."

(*Letter*   4.1.162–163)

The quality of mercy is not strained.
It droppeth as the gentle rain from heaven
Upon the place beneath. It is twice blessed:
It blesseth him that gives and him that takes.

(PORTIA   4.1.182–185)

And earthly power doth then show likest God's
When mercy seasons justice.   (PORTIA   4.1.194–195)

He is well paid that is well satisfied.   (PORTIA   4.1.413)

The moon shines bright. In such a night as this . . .

(LORENZO   5.1.1)

How sweet the moonlight sleeps upon this bank!
(LORENZO   5.1.54)

   Look how the floor of heaven
Is thick inlaid with patens of bright gold.
(LORENZO   5.1.58–59)

There's not the smallest orb which thou behold'st
But in his motion like an angel sings,
Still choiring to the young-eyed cherubins.
(LORENZO   5.1.60–62)

The man that hath no music in himself,
Nor is not moved with concord of sweet sounds,
Is fit for treasons, stratagems, and spoils.
(LORENZO   5.1.83–85)

How far that little candle throws his beams!
So shines a good deed in a naughty world.
(PORTIA   5.1.90–91)

The crow doth sing as sweetly as the lark
When neither is attended.   (PORTIA   5.1.102–103)

Memorable Lines

Twelfth Night

If music be the food of love, play on.   (ORSINO 1.1.1)

And what should I do in Illyria?   (VIOLA 1.2.3)

Care's an enemy to life.   (SIR TOBY 1.3.2–3)

I am a great eater of beef, and I believe that does harm to my wit.   (SIR ANDREW 1.3.84–85)

God give them wisdom that have it; and those that are fools, let them use their talents.   (FESTE 1.5.14–15)

As there is no true cockold but calamity, so beauty's a flower.   (FESTE 1.5.48–49)

I wear not motley in my brain.   (FESTE 1.5.53–54)

You do usurp yourself; for what is yours to bestow is not yours to reserve.   (VIOLA 1.5.183–184)

Lady, you are the cruel'st she alive
If you will lead these graces to the grave
And leave the world no copy.   (VIOLA 1.5.236–238)

[Song] O mistress mine, where are you roaming?   (FESTE 2.3.39)

[Song] What is love? 'tis not hereafter;
Present mirth hath present laughter;
   What's to come is still unsure.
In delay there lies no plenty,
Then come kiss me, sweet and twenty;
   Youth's a stuff will not endure.   (FESTE 2.3.47–52)

Dost thou think, because thou art virtuous, there shall be no more cakes and ale?   (SIR TOBY 2.3.114–115)

We men may say more, swear more, but indeed
Our shows are more than will; for still we prove
Much in our vows, but little in our love.

(VIOLA   2.4.116–118)

I am all the daughters of my father's house,
And all the brothers too.   (VIOLA   2.4.120–121)

'Tis but fortune, all is fortune.   (MALVOLIO   2.5.23)

Be not afraid of greatness. Some are born great, some
achieve greatness, and some have greatness thrust upon 'em.

(*Letter*   2.5.141–143)

Remember who commended thy yellow stockings, and
wished to see thee ever cross-gartered.

(*Letter*   2.5.149–151)

This fellow is wise enough to play the fool,
And to do that well craves a kind of wit.   (VIOLA   3.1.60–61)

Then westward ho!   (VIOLA   3.1.134)

This is very midsummer madness.   (OLIVIA   3.4.58)

Thus the whirligig of time brings in his revenges.

(FESTE   5.1.376–377)

I'll be revenged on the whole pack of you!

(MALVOLIO   5.1.378)

He hath been most notoriously abused.   (OLIVIA   5.1.379)

[*Song*]   When that I was and a little tiny boy,
     With hey, ho, the wind and the rain,
A foolish thing was but a toy,
     For the rain it raineth every day.   (FESTE   5.1.389–392)

Contributors

DAVID BEVINGTON, Phyllis Fay Horton Professor of Humanities at the University of Chicago, is editor of *The Complete Works of Shakespeare* (Scott, Foresman, 1980) and of *Medieval Drama* (Houghton Mifflin, 1975). His latest critical study is *Action Is Eloquence: Shakespeare's Language of Gesture* (Harvard University Press, 1984).

DAVID SCOTT KASTAN, Professor of English and Comparative Literature at Columbia University, is the author of *Shakespeare and the Shapes of Time* (University Press of New England, 1982).

JAMES HAMMERSMITH, Associate Professor of English at Auburn University, has published essays on various facets of Renaissance drama, including literary criticism, textual criticism, and printing history.

ROBERT KEAN TURNER, Professor of English at the University of Wisconsin–Milwaukee, is a general editor of the New Variorum Shakespeare (Modern Language Association of America) and a contributing editor to *The Dramatic Works in the Beaumont and Fletcher Canon* (Cambridge University Press, 1966–).

JAMES SHAPIRO, who coedited the bibliographies with David Scott Kastan, is Assistant Professor of English at Columbia University.

❖

JOSEPH PAPP, one of the most important forces in theater today, is the founder and producer of the New York Shakespeare Festival, America's largest and most prolific theatrical institution. Since 1954 Mr. Papp has produced or directed all but one of Shakespeare's plays—in Central Park, in schools, off and on Broadway, and at the Festival's permanent home, The Public Theater. He has also produced such award-winning plays and musical works as *Hair, A Chorus Line, Plenty,* and *The Mystery of Edwin Drood,* among many others.

THE BANTAM SHAKESPEARE COLLECTION

The Complete Works in 28 Volumes

Edited with Introductions by David Bevington

Forewords by Joseph Papp
